21st Conferencia Iberoamericana en Software Engineering (CIbSE 2018)

Bogota, Columbia
23-27 April 2018

Editors:

Rubby Casallas
Mario Sanchez
Kelly Garces

ISBN: 978-1-5108-6937-0

Printed from e-media with permission by:

Curran Associates, Inc.
57 Morehouse Lane
Red Hook, NY 12571

proceedings.com

Some format issues inherent in the e-media version may also appear in this print version.

Printed by Curran Associates, Inc. (2018)

For permission requests, please contact CIbSE - IberoAmerican Conference on Software Engineering at the address below.

CIbSE - IberoAmerican Conference on Software Engineering
c/o Luca Cernuzzi
Universidad Católica "Nuestra Seóra de la Asunción",
Campus Universitario, Asunción
Barrio Santa Ana, C.C.1683, C.P. 1364
Asunción - Paraguay

Phone: +595 21 334650
Fax: +595 21 310587

lcernuzz@uca.edu.py

Additional copies of this publication are available from:

Curran Associates, Inc.
57 Morehouse Lane
Red Hook, NY 12571 USA
Phone: 845-758-0400
Fax: 845-758-2633
Email: curran@proceedings.com
Web: www.proceedings.com

Rubby Casallas

Kelly Garcés

Mario Sánchez

Avances en Ingeniería de Software a nivel Iberoamericano

CIbSE 2018

Bogotá, Colombia
April 23 – 27, 2018

Avances en Ingeniería de Software a nivel Iberoamericano

Rubby Casallas
Universidad de los Andes
Bogotá, Colombia

Kelly Garcés
Universidad de los Andes
Bogotá, Colombia

Mario Sánchez Puccini
Universidad de los Andes
Bogotá, Colombia

Preface

The 21st Ibero-American Conference on Software Engineering (CIbSE 2018) brought a vibrant community of software engineering researchers, educators, students and industrial practitioners together in Bogotá, Colombia, from April 23 to 27, 2018. The hosting institution was the *Universidad de los Andes.*

CIbSE is the leading research forum on software engineering in Ibero-America. The main objective of this conference is to promote high-quality scientific research in Ibero-American countries, thus supporting the researchers in this community in publishing and discussing their work. In addition, the conference fosters collaboration and cross-fertilization among software academics, students, and industry. In line with this spirit, a varied program was prepared, including keynote speeches by influential researchers of the software engineering community, scientific tracks with high-quality research paper presentations, a doctoral symposium to discuss work in progress, insightful industry presentations, and a fruitful debate on how to engage and retain talent in software engineering.

This year, we received 133 submissions (121 to the main scientific tracks and 12 to the doctoral symposium) from authors of 18 different countries. All submissions were reviewed by at least three members of the program committee, and an open electronic discussion was held post-review period to assure sufficient quality for the accepted contributions.

The SET (Software Engineering and Tools) scientific track received 71 submissions (51 technical papers, 15 emerging ideas papers and 5 tool papers), out of which 24 (33.8%) were accepted and included in the final program (20 technical papers, 3 emerging ideas, and 1 tool paper). The WER (Requirements Engineering) scientific track received 18 submissions (17 technical papers and 1 emerging ideas paper), out of which 7 (38.8%) were accepted and included in the final program (6 technical papers and 1 emerging ideas paper). The ESELAW (Experimental Software Engineering) scientific track received 32 submissions (27 technical papers and 5 emerging ideas paper), out of which 12 (37.5%) were accepted and included in the final program (11 technical papers and 1 emerging ideas paper). The papers are all included in the proceedings and will be made available by Curran Associates and indexed by Scopus. After a thorough review process, three papers were selected as the Best Papers of each track. We invited the authors of these papers to submit an extended version of their work in a special issue of an international journal.

Finally, the Doctoral Symposium received 12 submissions out of which 7 were accepted to enable the PhD candidates to discuss their work in progress and to receive feedback from an international board of advisors.

The carefully selected keynote speakers were among the main conference highlights. Schahram Dustdar (Vienna University of Technology – Austria, keynote for the SET track) addressed challenges for IoT systems engineering in his enlightening talk "From the Edge to the Cloud - Research and Engineering challenges for IoT systems". Daniel Méndez (Technical University of Munich – Germany, keynote of the WER track) discussed how to strengthen the practical relevance of research outcomes in his talk entitled "In Quest of Requirements Engineering Research that Industry needs". Fabio da Silva (UFPE - Brazil, keynote for the ESELAW track) provided an insightful speech on "Designing and Conducting Case Studies in Software Companies: Challenges and Stories from the Field".

Additionally, this year CIbSE strengthened its initiative to disseminate software engineering knowledge, promoting the Ibero-American School on Software Engineering (EIbAIS), a natural evolution of the CIbSE tutorials and short courses, including the following prospective topics:

- "Articulation of Agile and Experience Design (UX) tools to define digital projects centered on the user" by *Alejandro Posada Leal, Ana Martínez Villate, Juliana Iregui & Rafael Buitrago Osorio (Scotiabank Colpatria, Colombia)*;
- "Deriving Requirements using e3value and e3fraud techniques" by *Roel Wieringa (University of Twente, The Netherlands)*;
- "Design of serious games for software engineering education" by *Carlos Zapata (Universidad Nacional de Colombia, Colombia) & Hernán Astudillo (Universidad Técnica Federico Santa María, Chile)*;
- "IoT Systems Engineering" by *Schahram Dustdar (Vienna University of Technology, Austria)*;
- "Qualitative Studies in Software Engineering" by *Fabio Q.B. da Silva (Federal University of Pernambuco, Brasil)*; and
- "Survey Research in Software Engineering" by *Daniel Méndez (Technical University of Munich, Germany).*

We are thankful for having had the opportunity to organize the program of CIbSE 2018 in Bogotá. The Program Committee track chairs, members and additional reviewers provided excellent support in reviewing the papers. We are also grateful to all speakers, authors, and session chairs for their time and effort that helped to make CIbSE 2018 a success. We thank the CIbSE steering committee members for the guidance and support in the organization process.

Special thanks to the General Conference Chairs from *Universidad de los Andes*, Rubby Casallas and Kelly Garcés, and all the people of the organization team for making CIbSE 2018 a pleasant academic and social experience that will remain in the memories of the participants for years to come.

April, 2018

Marcela Genero
Marcos Kalinowski
General Program Chairs

Organization

CIbSE 2018 has been organized by:

ORGANIZING COMMITTEE

General Conference Chairs:	Rubby Casallas and Kelly Garcés
General Program Chairs:	Marcela Genero and Marcos Kalinowski
SET Program Chairs:	Francisco Pino and Jesús García Molina
WER Program Chairs:	Isabel Sofia Brito and Giovanni Giachetti
ESELAW Program Chairs:	Beatriz Marín and Tayana Conte
Doctoral Symposium Chairs:	Oscar Dieste and Gleison Santos
Ibero-American School Chair:	Guilherme Travassos
Tools Papers Chairs:	Mario Linares and Andrea Delgado
Industry Presentations Chairs:	Nicolas Cardozo and César Pardo
Proceedings Chair:	Mario Sánchez
Publicity Chairs:	Laura Moreno and Martin Solari

PROGRAM COMMITTEES

SET- Software Engineering Track

Ademar Aguiar, Universidade do Porto, Portugal
David Ameller, Universitat Politècnica de Catalunya, España
Hugo Arboleda, Universidad ICESI, Colombia
Hernán Astudillo, Universidad Técnica Federico Santa María, Chile
María Cecilia Bastarrica, Universidad de Chile, Chile
David Benavides, Universidad de Sevilla, España
Nelly Bencomo, Aston University, United Kingdom
Veronica AndreaBollati, Universidad Tecnológica Nacional, Argentina
Regina Braga, Universidade Federal de Juiz de Fora, Brazil
Rosana Braga, University of São Paulo, Brazil
Fernando Brito e Abreu, Instituto Universitário de Lisboa, Portugal

Antonio Brogi, Università di Pisa, Italia
Agustina Buccella, Universidad Nacional del Comahue, Argentina
Sandra-Lorena Buitrón, Universidad del Cauca, Colombia
Nelio Cacho, Universidade Federal do Rio Grande do Norte, Brazil
Juan Pablo Carvallo, Universidad del Azuay, Ecuador
Alejandro Catala, University of Twente, Netherlands
Luca Cernuzzi, Universidad Católica, Paraguay
Carlos Cetina, Universidad San Jorge, España
Fabio Costa, Universidade Federal de Goias, Brazil
Dolors Costal, Universitat Politècnica de Catalunya, España
Jacome Cunha, Universidade Nova de Lisboa, Portugal
Breno de França, Universidade de Campinas, Brazil
Juan De Lara, Universidad Autónoma de Madrid, España
Andrea Delgado, Universidad de la República, Uruguay
Adler Diniz De Souza, Universidade Federal do Rio de Janeiro, Brazil
Kleinner Farias, University of Vale do Rio dos Sinos, Brazil
Eduardo Figueiredo, Universidade Federal de Minas Gerais, Brazil
Brenda Leticia Flores, Universidad Autónoma de Baja California, Mexico
Nestor Garay-Vitoria, Universidad del País Vasco, España
Kelly Garces Pernett, Universidad de los Andes, Colombia
Alejandra Garrido, Universidad Nacional de la Plata, Argentina
Roxana Giandini, Universidad Nacional de la Plata, Argentina
Daniela Godoy, Universidad Nacional del Centro de la Provincia de Buenos Aires, Argentina
Julio Ariel Hurtado, Universidad del Cauca, Colombia
Emilio Insfran, Universitat Politecnica de Valencia, España
Miguel Katrib, Universidad de la Habana, Cuba
Ivan Machado, Universidade Federal da Bahia, Brazil
Silverio Martinez-Fernandez, Universitat Politècnica de Catalunya, España
Miguel Monteiro, Universidade Nova de Lisboa, Portugal
Miguel Morales-Trujillo, Universidad Nacional Autónoma de México, México
Lourdes Moreno, Universidad Carlos III de Madrid, España
Elena Navarro, Universidad de Castilla-La Mancha, España
Toacy Oliveira, Universidade Federal do Rio de Janeiro, Brazil
Luis Olsina, Universidad Nacional de La Pampa, Argentina
Jose Ignacio Panach, Universitat de Valencia, España
Cesar Pardo, Universidad del Cauca, Colombia
Oscar Pastor, Universitat Politécnica de Valencia, España
Vicente Pelechano, Universitat Politécnica de Valencia, España

ESELAW – Experimental Software Engineering Track

WER – Requirements Engineering Track

Fernanda Alencar, Universidade Federal de Pernambuco, Brasil
Leandro Antonelli, LIFIA - Universidad Nacional de La Plata, Argentina
Nathalie Aquino, Universidad Católica Nuestra Señora de la Asunción, Paraguay
Joao Araujo, Universidade Nova de Lisboa, Portugal
Clara Ayora, Treelogic, España
Jorge Barreiros, Universidade NOVA de Lisboa, Portugal
Judith Barrios Albornoz, Universidad de los Andes, Colombia
Dan Berry, University of Waterloo, Canada
Luiz Marcio Cysneiros, York University, Canada
José Luis de La Vara, Universidad Carlos III de Madrid, España
Amador Durán Toro, Universidad de Sevilla, España
Gonzalo Génova, Universidad Carlos III de Madrid, España
Renata Guizzardi, Universidade Federal do Espirito Santo, Brasil
Graciela Dora Susana Hadad, Universidad Nacional del Oeste, Argentina
Anaisa Hernández González, Universidad Tecnológica de La Habana, Cuba
Gladys Kaplan, Universidad Nacional de La Matanza, Argentina
Uirá Kulesza, Universidade Federal do Rio Grande do Norte, Brasil
Maria Lencastre, Universidade de Pernambuco, Brasil
Lidia Lopez, Universitat Politècnica de Catalunya (UPC), España
Marcia Lucena, Universidade Federal do Rio Grande do Norte, Brasil
Alicia Martinez, Centro Nacional de Investigación y Desarrollo Tecnológico, México
Luiz Eduardo Galvão Martins, Universidad Federal de São Paulo, Brasil
Alejandro Maté, Universidad de Alicante, España
Roberto Avila Paldes, Centro Universitário de Brasília, Brasil
Cristina Palomares, Universitat Politècnica de Catalunya, España
María Pinto Albuquerque, Instituto ISCTE-IUL – Universidade de Lisboa, Portugal
Carme Quer,Universitat Politècnica de Catalunya, España
Marcela Ridao, INTIA - Universidad Nacional del Centro de la Provincia de Buenos Aires, Argentina
Luis Rojas, Universidad Andrés Bello, Chile
Alejandra Ruiz, Tecnalia, España
Juan Sanchez,Universitat Politècnica de València, España
Lyrene Silva, Universidade Federal do Rio Grande do Norte, Brasil

Table of Contents

WER - Requirements Engineering

Doctoral Symposium

A Taste of the Software Industry Perception of Technical Debt and its Management in Brazil

Victor Machado da Silva[1], Helvio Jeronimo Junior[1], and Guilherme Horta Travassos[1]

[1] Universidade Federal do Rio de Janeiro/UFRJ - COPPE, Rio de Janeiro, Brasil
{victorms, jeronimohjr, ght}@cos.ufrj.br

Abstract. Technical debt (TD) is receiving more and more attention in software engineering. Although it was initially used as a communication tool for technical and non-technical stakeholders, nowadays this concept supports the improvement of software's internal quality. Despite the increasing number of studies regarding TD and its management, only a few are concerned with the industry. Therefore, this primary study aims to characterize TD and its management under the perspective of Brazilian software organizations using their practitioners as proxies. A survey was performed with 58 practitioners, representing about 12 organizations and 30 software projects. The analysis of 37 valid questionnaires indicates that TD is still unknown to a considerable fraction of the participants, and only a small group of organizations adopt TD management activities in their projects. The survey package is available and can be used to support further investigations on TD management in Brazilian and other software organizations.

Keywords: Technical debt; survey; experimental software engineering.

1 Introduction

In the face of an increasingly dynamic and competitive market, software development organizations need to support continuous and fast delivery of value to the customer in both short and long terms [1]. Therefore, many software organizations introduce agility practices into their development processes to handle the everyday requirements changes and the continuous delivery demand [2]. This working environment brings challenges to practitioners regarding the decision-making, which sets up a trade-off that can lead to "Technical Debt" creation in software projects (TD, see details in section 2).

The TD metaphor interest and use have grown over the years [3]. Many studies have been discussing different knowledge areas of TD and supporting solutions to software engineers, to achieve better results in their projects.

Using an *ad-hoc* literature review, we observed some studies discussing the concept of TD and technologies to support the Technical Debt Management (TDM). As mentioned in [3] and [4], only a few studies deal directly with the question of how software organizations perceive and apply the TD metaphor in their working environment. The investigations covering TD aspects and its management under the software organizations' perception focus on a single aspect or use limited population samples. Also, the software development process is influenced by the country's culture, language, and beliefs [5], and it can influence how TD is perceived and managed.

Particularly in Brazil, there is a more latent gap regarding how the Brazilian software organizations (BSOs) perceive TD and how their practitioners handle it in their software projects. Authors in [6] reported that TDM is a topic of interest in departments of the Brazilian federal administration. However, there is scarce information whether TD is adequately managed in BSOs.

This context motivated us to investigate how BSOs (represented in this study by their practitioners) are adopting and managing TD. In addition, it is our interest to observe whether the BSOs'practitioners perception of TD and its management match the findings of other TD investigations. Our study intends to raise the level of knowledge on TD and its management in BSOs. Therefore, a survey was designed and conducted with software practitioners engaged in Brazilian software organizations. This paper presents the primary results of this survey, intending to provide the following initial contributions:

- To get an initial perception of TD metaphor and its management in BSOs, using their engaged professionals as proxies;
- To make available a survey package with empirically evaluated instruments to support the gathering and aggregation of information regarding the TD perception and TDM activities, which can be tailored to other localities.

The remainder of this paper is structured as follows: Section 2 provides some background on TD; Section 3 presents the survey design; Section 4 explains the survey results and discussion about them; Section 5 presents the threats to validity, and Section 6 presents the final considerations.

2 Background

Ward Cunningham [7] first coined the term "Technical Debt" when discussing with stakeholders the consequences of releasing a poorly written piece of code to accelerate the development process. Although the code attends the core system requirements in the current release, in case of future changes, the consequences might spread over other software areas, affecting its evolvability.

Since then, the use of the TD metaphor spread to allow better communication with non-technical stakeholders (e.g., corporate managers, clients, among others). Moreover, it has been used as a quality improvement instrument, bringing to the software development context terms such as "*principal*" (used to refer to the required effort to eliminate the TD source) and "*interest*" (the additional effort needed on software maintenance due to the presence of TD) [4].

Nowadays, TD has a deeper meaning than its initial definition. It can be applied to all software development phases as presented by Li et al. [3] and Alves et al. [4]. Different TD types can be incurred in the software development process, and each one of them may have different influences. However, it does not mean that TD can be generalized to all the software issues currently faced in the projects.

The current definition of TD was proposed at the *Dagstuhl* Seminar [8]: "a *collection of design or implementation constructs that are expedient in the short term, but set up a technical context that can make future changes more costly or impossible.*" TD is also acknowledged for being restricted to internal software quality issues, like maintainability or evolvability. Thus, some glaring issues, such as known defects and unimplemented features should not be considered TD [3].

Depending on the perspective, the presence of TD can influence positively or negatively a software project and the quality of its software products. Strategical, controlled decisions that opt to postpone some tasks to obtain short-term gains such as shortening time-to-delivery can be decisive for a product's success [9]. However, TD can cause damage to the project, since it might be incurred unintentionally throughout the software development cycle. TD items of this nature can be incurred due to many factors, such as a lack of knowledge of team members on writing the source code without following a specific programming style.

Concerning investigations on TD, some secondary studies gathered consolidated observations about it ([10] [11]) and its management ([3] [4] [12] [13] [14]). Although they present a TD concept overview and state of the art regarding the activities and technologies that may be used to support its management, there is a need to observe the perception of TD and its management under the industry point of view.

In this context, some investigations are covering TD aspects and its management under the industry point-of-view. These investigations can be grouped into two categories. The first category refers to works ([15] [16] [17]) investigating the software practitioners' perception regarding the TD concept, its impact, and in which context it occurs. The second category refers to works ([9] [18] [19] [20] [21]) investigating the software practitioners' perception regarding activities, strategies, and technologies that can support TDM. Also, it is worth to highlight that [15] [16] [17] [18] [19] [20] are surveys conducted in different countries. However, to our knowledge, no survey covers the perspective of TD in BSOs using their practitioners as proxies. This research gap motivated us to develop further the study presented in this paper.

3 Survey Design

3.1 Research Objectives and Questions

This study's objectives were stated according to GQM [22]: ***analyze*** the TD and its management; ***with the purpose of*** characterizing; ***with respect to*** the level of knowledge and the adopted strategies, activities and technologies; ***from the point of view of*** software practitioners; ***in the context of*** Brazilian software organizations.

The research questions are explained as follows:

- **RQ1: Is there a consensus on the perception of TD among software practitioners in BSOs?** The purpose of this question is to determine whether the perception of

TD is homogeneous among professionals in BSOs. If so, it can support the observation of the existence of a universal perspective on TD between the industry and academia (a positive side effect of this survey).

- **RQ2: Do the practitioners in the BSOs perceive TD in their software projects?** Before characterizing the TDM activities, it is essential to confirm that the software organizations (through their practitioners) perceive, i.e., observe the presence of TD in their projects.
  - **RQ2.1: Do BSOs manage their TD?** If TD is perceived, it is essential to know whether BSOs manage the TD in their software projects.
    - **RQ2.1.1: What TDM activities are most relevant to software projects?** The goal of this question is to identify, among professionals, which TDM activities, among those proposed by Li et al. [3], are more relevant, or at least more considered during the software projects.
    - **RQ2.1.2: Which technologies and strategies are adopted for each TDM activity?** For all eight TDM activities proposed by Li et al. [3], which strategies and technologies are used to their support.

Even though this survey had been designed to identify the most common technologies used by the practitioners in their BSOs to support TDM activities, it is not possible to make any judgment regarding their efficiency and effectiveness. Furthermore, this survey did not look for the benefits of applying such technologies in BSOs.

3.2 Procedures and Data Collection

The survey was designed according to the guidelines presented in [23]. We performed an *ad-hoc* literature review to gather specific information about the perception of TD and TDM. Regarding the perception of TD, we collected a set of statements related to the concept of TD. Concerning TDM, we organized the activities as proposed by Li et al. [3], as such activities cover the ones mentioned in different studies. Moreover, we accepted them as consistent since no disagreements were observed during pilot trials.

For each activity, we identified a set of specific strategies and technologies used to conduct the activity, as well as a list of possible roles for each activity. From this information, a questionnaire was designed, and specific questions for each activity were included. For instance, on TD identification, a set of questions involving the TD classification was included (as per [4]).

Regarding the questionnaire structure, it is divided into fourteen sections, described as follows: three are associated with the participant characterization, the organization, and the software project; one regarding the TD perception; one on TDM in general; and eight sections concerned with specific TDM activities. The last section is provided to gather information regarding other TDM activities that eventually are not on the list proposed by Li et al. [3] and yet are used in the participant's software organization. The questionnaire sections are detailed in Table 1.

The questionnaire is composed mostly of closed-ended questions. A small number of open-ended questions was necessary to get further information from the participant. It also contains partially closed-ended questions to deal with issues related to tools and strategies for each TDM activity when the given options do not cover the entire possibility of the participant´s answers.

Table 1. Questionnaire Sections

Sections	Topic	Description
1	Participant characterization	Obtain personal information regarding the participant, such as professional experience and academic degrees.
2	Organization characterization	Gather information about the organization the participant works for or has worked before.
3	Project characterization	Obtain information about the project that will be considered by the participant in the survey.
4	TD perception	Collect information on the participant's knowledge regarding TD, including what can be considered TD. Also, determine if the organization or the project he works at has strategies for TDM.
5	TDM (general)	Ask the participant which TDM activities are adopted in the working project. Obtain information about the responsibilities and importance associated with each activity from the participant's point of view.
6-13	TDM (activities)	Gather information on several aspects regarding each of the TDM activities proposed in [3].
14	TDM (other)	Provide space for the participant to describe other activities that are executed in the organization.

Table 2 presents an extract of our questionnaire translated into English, with some questions on TD identification. Each section starts with a brief explanation of its content and specific instructions. The *LimeSurvey* platform available at the Experimental Software Engineering (ESE) Group at COPPE/UFRJ supported the questionnaire implementation and survey execution.

The questionnaire was configured to ensure the participant's anonymity. A welcome message describes the survey structure and explains its importance for BSOs. The participants are asked to answer the questions based on their current (or most recent) software project and organization. Each set of questions related to a specific TDM activity was conditioned to be provided to the participants only if they have some experience with that activity to avoid the problem of lengthy survey questionnaires. For example, if a participant is experienced only with TD identification and TD communication, only these two sets of questions should be answered. Also, other conditional breakpoints in the questionnaire were set to end the survey whether the participant is not familiar with the TD concept and whether the organization or the project do not apply any TDM activity.

3.3 Pilot Execution

A pilot trial has to be conducted using the same artifacts and procedures designed for the final survey, including the survey questionnaire and the execution method, but with a small number of participants from the target population [23].

Table 2. Survey - TD Identification Section

Question	Answer options
Is there a formal strategy to identify TD?	( ) Yes, we have a formal procedure to identify the TD. ( ) No, the TD identification is executed only informally.
Are all the stakeholders required to apply the TD identification strategy?"	( ) Yes, the strategy is mandatory for all stakeholders. ( ) No, the strategy is considered only a suggestion.
At what point in the project is the TD identified?	( ) There is no defined period; we identify the TD whenever we perceive some issue. ( ) We always identify the TD at the end of each iteration/sprint. ( ) The TD identification is continuous, i.e., occurs throughout the development process.
Mark below all tools or techniques that are used to identify TD.	[ ] Manual coding inspection [ ] Dependency analysis [ ] Checklist [ ] *SonarQube/SQALE* [ ] *CheckStyle* [ ] *FindBugs* [ ] *CodeVizard* [ ] *CLIO* [ ] Other (cite which)

Seven practitioners were invited to the pilot trials. Five of them work on software projects and come from the ESE Group at COPPE/UFRJ, which conducts this research. The other two participants also work on software projects but are from outside the research group. All of them have some prior experience with TD and/or TDM, mostly in the industry.

An invitation containing the main instructions and questionnaire link was sent by e-mail. They were asked to answer the questionnaire and return their feedback regarding, but not restricted to: (*i*) total response time; (*ii*) question chaining, i.e., whether the questions have a logical connection between them; (*iii*) proper understanding of questions and answer options; (*iv*) answers completeness; (*v*) lack of ambiguity in questions and answers; and (*vi*) clarity of the instructions.

Feedback from pilot participants. All pilot participants answered the pilot survey within a week. The average answering time was 15.2 minutes. The relevant comments were associated with: (*i*) usability issues, due to *LimeSurvey*'s default configurations; (*ii*) clarity of questions and answer options; (*iii*) suggestions to further detail the differences of TD activities to avoid misunderstandings; and (*iv*) suggestions to define the mandatory questions to avoid incomplete responses that could invalidate the questionnaire. These were later discussed internally, and modifications were applied to the final questionnaire. Overall, we did not observe negative comments or doubts about either the answer options or the questions descriptions, suggesting that the questionnaire was consistent to be used in the study.

Final revisions and survey release. After the pilot trial, the final survey was released. The sampling technique was by convenience, using professional social networks databases, contacts in BSOs from the researchers involved in the study and participation in Brazilian workshops and conferences during the survey execution time. The target audience is any practitioner engaged in BSOs. A lab package is available at https://doi.org/10.6084/m9.figshare.5923969. This package file contains the survey plan and the questionnaire (.pdf format) in English and Portuguese.

4 Survey Results

The survey was conducted between June and December 2017. In total, 58 participants answered the survey, with 33 complete answers. Four participants did not complete the survey but reached the questionnaire's section 4 (TD perception), so they were included in this initial analysis. The remaining 21 incomplete responses were not included in the analysis. Fig. 1 summarizes the survey responses.

Fig. 1. Summary of the survey responses

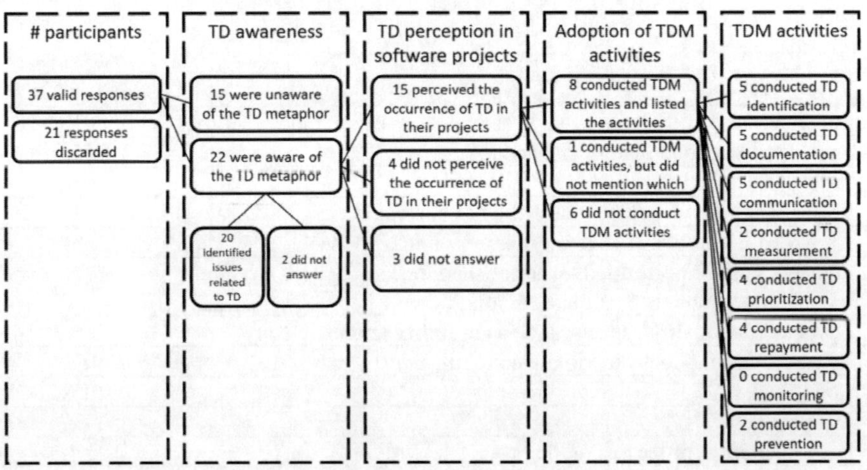

4.1 Participants' Characterization

The respondents have an average work experience of 14.7 years in software projects. Only four respondents reported having an incomplete undergraduate degree, while the remaining 33 respondents hold at least an undergraduate degree. 23 participants reported holding a specialization degree, master or doctorate degree.

Regarding the BSOs in which the respondents work, most of them (20) are from the Information Technology sector, followed by Government (7), Consulting, Telecommunications, Financing (2 participants each), Education, Media, Oil & Gas and Software Engineering (1 participant each). Referring to the project development, most of them

(32) adopt agile or incremental lifecycle models. Two projects adopt the spiral model, while three adopt the waterfall model. Due to the questionnaire anonymity, it is not possible to precise the number of organizations represented in the survey. However, it is possible to roughly estimate it, based on the information provided by the participants in the characterization sections. Therefore, we could estimate around 12 organizations and 30 projects included in the survey.

4.2 TD Awareness and TD Perception

Regarding the perception of TD, from 37 valid answers, we found that 15 respondents (41%) claimed not to be aware of the TD metaphor. The 22 remaining participants (59%) were asked to select the options that best matched the TD definition. Two of them did not answer this question. As it can be observed in Table 3, seven issues out of 12 were marked by 50% or more of the 20 participants: low internal quality, poorly written code, that violates code rules; "shortcuts" taken during design; the presence of known defects that were not eliminated; architectural problems; planned but unfinished or unplanned tasks; and issues associated with low external quality.

Table 3. TD perception by the participants

Issue	% of participants
Low internal quality aspects, such as maintainability and reusability	80%
Poorly written code that violates code rules	75%
"Shortcuts" taken during design	70%
Presence of known defects that were not corrected	70%
Architectural problems (like modularity violation)	55%
Planned, but not performed, or unfinished, tasks (e.g., requirements specification, models, test plans, among others)	50%
Low external quality aspects, such as usability and efficiency	50%
Trivial code that does not violate code rules	40%
Code smells	40%
Defects	35%
Lack of support processes to the project activities	25%
Required, but unimplemented, features	15%

Regarding the TD perception, from the 22 participants that were aware of the TD meaning, 15 informed that some issues associated with the TD concept were perceived in their projects, whereas four did not perceive the TD occurrence, and three participants did not answer this particular question.

From the 15 participants that informed that perceived the TD occurrence in their projects, nine answered that their organizations or the project managers adopt TDM activities in their projects.

4.3 Technical Debt Management

From the eight TDM activities proposed by Li et al. [3], as shown in Fig. 1, only TD monitoring was not marked by the participants when asked about which TDM activities were conducted in their projects. TD identification, TD documentation, and TD communication are conducted in projects for five participants each, while four participants each marked TD prioritization and TD repayment. TD measurement and TD prevention are conducted in projects according to two participants.

TDM responsibilities. There was no consensus among participants on which roles should be responsible for each TDM activity. Moreover, some distinction was observed between the participants' responses and the TDM framework presented in [9]. For instance, the TDM framework presented in [9] states that software architects and the team leader are the responsible roles for the activity of TD measurement. However, in our survey, no respondent selected software architects as responsible for this activity. Regarding the relevant TDM activities to eight respondents, 50% considered TD prevention as the most relevant activity to their projects, whereas TD measurement and TD monitoring were marked as least relevant by 38%.

TD identification and documentation. For both activities, two out of five participants answered that there is a mandatory strategy to conduct the TD identification and documentation activities, while two participants answered that there is a formal strategy, albeit not mandatory. Two participants claimed to adopt only simple strategies. Three out of five answers suggested that TD identification was conducted continuously throughout the project. Regarding TD identification, one participant affirmed that the TD was classified as Design Debt or Documentation Debt in the project, while one participant claimed to use the artifact that initially incurred the TD to classify it. All five participants that answered the TD documentation section claimed the TD was documented using a general backlog, without specific details.

TD communication. From the five participants that answered the TD communication section, four affirmed that the TD was discussed during project meetings, but with the participation of only a few of the necessary stakeholders. One participant said that the TD was only discussed informally.

TD measurement and prioritization. Out of the two participants that answered the TD measurement section, one affirmed that the activity was conducted informally, through the analysis of metrics and indicators based on specific information regarding the TD item. The other participant indicated that there is a mandatory strategy to measure TD, based on pure information, like person-hours to repay the TD item or the item LOC. Regarding the TD prioritization, three of four participants answered that the TD items were prioritized according to "guesses" or simplified estimative based on previous experiences, while the other participant used the TD item criticality to prioritize it.

All four participants affirmed that they tend to prioritize the TD items that most impact the client [24], and three participants answered that they prioritize the TD items that could cause most impact the project.

TD repayment and prevention. From the four participants that answered the TD repayment section, two of them answered that the TD repayment is planned according to the current project necessities, while one of the participants answered that the TD repayment is planned continuously, with specific periods during the development process destined to this activity. One participant answered that the TD is only repaid when it is not possible to avoid it anymore. Finally, both respondents answering the TD prevention section mentioned that it is an activity conducted only by each member of the team individually.

Technologies and Strategies for TDM. Table 4 presents a list of practices, techniques, and tools used in each TDM activity. The numbers in parentheses represent the number of participants answering that specific section (column "TDM activity") and the number of participants that affirmed using that tool or technique (column "Tools and techniques"). We can observe that different technologies support TDM and there is no consensus about which one to use.

4.4 Revisiting the Findings

RQ1: Consensus on the perception of TD. We did not observe consensus in the overall TD perception. Each participant was asked to select which of the 12 issues suggested on TD should be associated with the TD concept, as presented in Table 3. Out of those options, only two issues were evaluated by 75% or more of the 20 respondents. From the issues associated with the TD concept by 50% or more of participant's, only one ("*issues associated with low external quality*") is not considered TD [3].

Only one issue associated with the TD concept was marked by less than 50% of the 20 answers, which is "*Code smells*" (42%). Therefore, although we could not find consensus between the industry and academia, we consider that there is some agreement among participants of what should be considered TD since 16 out of 20 participants identified that TD should be related to internal quality issues. However, 50% of the participants believe that TD should also be associated with external quality issues, which is worrisome and contradicts the definition asserted at the *Dagstuhl* Seminar [8]. It could indicate that there is a misconception of what should be considered TD, associating its definition with any issue occurring during the software development.

We could observe some alignments in the views on TD between the participants and academia since most of the issues associated by more than half of the participants are also in agreement with the definition indicated in the technical literature. We believe that despite the reasonable TD definition understanding by some software practitioners, it is vital to disseminate better the distinction between issues related to internal quality (TD) and those related to external quality (defects).

Table 4. TDM activities - technologies and strategies

TDM activity	Technologies and strategies
TD identification (5)	Manual code inspection (4), dependency analysis (1), checklist (2), *SonarQube*[1]/*SQALE*[2] (3), *CheckStyle* (1), *FindBugs*[3] (1)
TD documentation /representation (5)	TD backlog (3), specific artifacts for TD documentation (1), *JIRA*[4] (1), others - *Trello* (1)
TD communication (5)	Discussion forums (3), specific meetings about TD (1), others - *GitLab* (1), others - *Trello*[5] (1)
TD measurement (2)	Manual measurement (1), *SonarQube* (2), *JIRA* (1)
TD prioritization (4)	Cost/benefit analysis (1), classification of issues (3)
TD repayment (4)	Refactoring (3), redesign (1), code rewriting (4), meetings/workshops/training (1)
TD monitoring (0)	N/A
TD prevention (2)	Guidelines (2), coding standards (2), code revisions (1), retrospective meetings (1), Definition of Done (2)

RQ2: BSOs' practitioners perception of TD. Only 42% of 37 participants claimed to perceive TD in their software projects, which could be considered low, given the importance of the topic. Moreover, only 25% of the 37 participants adopt TDM activities, possibly indicating the existence of a severe gap in the overall product quality perspective. However, we did not assess the adoption of other internal quality assurance methods to replace the low perception of the TD presence in the organizations.

RQ2.1.1: Most relevant TDM activities. The results of our survey show that there was no consensus on which TDM activities are more relevant to surveyed software projects. However, half of the participants that answered this question mentioned that TD prevention is relevant to a project. It is a possible research gap for future works since most of the studies regarding TDM focus on TD identification, measurement, and prioritization. Regarding the main TDM activities conducted by the participants, our results are mostly in line with Yli-Huumo et al. [9] in which indicates that TD communication is most commonly adopted by the development teams, followed by TD identification, documentation, prioritization, repayment, and prevention. The rarely managed TD activities described in [9] are TD measurement and TD monitoring, as also observed in our study. Despite the number of participants indicating the importance of TD prevention, only two reported performing TD prevention activities.

RQ2.1.2: Technologies and strategies. As presented in section 4.3, a list of tools and technologies used to manage TD activities (see **Table 4**) can be used in further studies looking for evidence on their effectiveness and efficiency in managing the TD.

---

[1] https://www.sonarqube.org
[2] http://www.sqale.org/
[3] http://findbugs.sourceforge.net/
[4] https://br.atlassian.com/software/jira
[5] https://trello.com/

5 Threats to Validity

The main threat to validity is the results generalization. Since the target sampling is non-probabilistic, it is not possible to determine *a priori* the population size and the expected total number of participants. Then, the results confidence level might be low, making hard to generalize the results to the entire population (BSOs). Despite that, the inevitable conclusions can suggest the TD research with initial indications of the level of knowledge of BSOs regarding the TD concept and TDM activities. A potential internal threat comes from the participants that might have misunderstood some terms and concepts of the questionnaire based on different experiences. There is also a construct threat of a biased survey, from the researchers' perspectives and the collected information from the technical literature such as the TDM activities organized in [3]. To reduce the level of this menace, we conducted three revision cycles during the survey development with two researchers. Furthermore, two pilot trials were executed, followed by a final revision by all the pilot survey participants aiming to ensure the modifications were aligned with their perspectives.

6 Concluding Remarks

This paper presented background about the TD definition and the results of a survey conducted with practitioners in BSOs. The results provide initial observations regarding how BSOs (represented by their software practitioners) perceive and manage TD in their projects. Regarding the TD perception, our results indicate no unanimity concerning on how Brazilian software practitioners perceive TD. Regarding TDM, it was observed that only a few BSOs report the TD management in their software projects, indicating that TDM seems to be still incipient in BSOs. Four out of eight practitioners reporting TDM activities claimed that TD prevention is the most critical activity in their projects, despite only two participants indicated to perform it.

We believe that the results of this study provide the following contributions to both industry and academia:

- To the BSOs (industry) - the initial results indicate that software practitioners and their organizations need to understand better the concept of TD. It is necessary to achieve better results in their projects since the perception of TD and its management in this scenario is apparently still incipient. The findings also present a list of technologies that can be used to support TDM activities, as long as the software engineers evaluate their usage based on the organizations' needs at the time. Moreover, findings indicate that the TDM activities usually involve distinct roles throughout the projects. In general, we consider that the BSOs need to systematize some actions (e.g., training) to enable their teams to perceive and manage existing TD.
- To the researchers - our results indicate that there is a need for more investigations aiming to disseminate the TD knowledge to practitioners on BSOs, as well as provide strategies and software technologies to support the TDM on these organizations. Besides, we believe the sharing of this study package can contribute to support the

development of investigations on TD and its management more connected to the software organization needs in Brazil and other regions.

Overall, we could observe that the results of this TD research are coherent and complementary to the findings of other investigations (such as [9, 15-21]) concerning the perception and management of TD by software practitioners in the organizations. As future research, we intend to discuss this matter further. Also, we intend to gather the obtained information from this survey to systematize actions and technologies for supporting BSOs to perceive and manage the TD in their projects.

Acknowledgements

The authors thank CAPES and CNPq for supporting this research and all the professionals that took part in this study. Prof. Travassos is a CNPq researcher and an ISERN member.

References

1. Barry, B.: Making a Difference in the Software Century. Computer 41(3), 32-38 (2008).
2. de França, B. B., Jeronimo Junior, H., Travassos, G.: Characterizing DevOps by Hearing Multiple Voices. In: Proc. of the 30th SBES, Brazil, pp.53-62 (2016).
3. Li, Z., Avgeriou, P., Liang, P.: A systematic mapping study on technical debt and its management. J SYST SOFTWARE 101, 193-220 (2015).
4. Alves, N., Mendes, T., Mendonça, M., Spínola, R., Shull, F., Seaman, C.: Identification and management of technical debt: A systematic mapping study. INFORM SOFTWARE TECH 70, 100-121 (2016).
5. Rafael, P., Audy, J. L., Damian, Oliveira, T.: Distributed Software Development: Practices and challenges in different business strategies of offshoring and onshoring. In: 2nd ICGSE, Germany, pp.262-274 (2007).
6. de Assunção, T., Rodrigues, I., Venson, E., Figueredo, R., de Sousa, T.: Technical Debt Management in the Brazilian Federal Administration. In: 6th WBMA, Brazil (2015).
7. Cunningham, W.: The WyCash portfolio management system. In: Addendum to OOPSLA, Canada, vol. 4 (2), pp.29-30 (1992).
8. Avgeriou, P., Kruchten, P., Ozkaya, I., Seaman, C.: Managing Technical Debt in Software Engineering. Dagstuhl Reports 16162, Germany (2016).
9. Yli-Huumo, J., Maglyas, A., Smolander, K.: How do software development teams manage technical debt? – An empirical study. J SYST SOFTWARE 120, 195-218 (2016).
10. Tom, E., Aurum, A., Vidgen, R.: An exploration of technical debt. J SYST SOFTWARE 86(6), 1498-1516 (2013).

11. Villar, A., Matalonga, S.: Definiciones y tendencia de deuda técnica: Un mapeo sistemático de la literatura. In: 16th CIbSE, Uruguay, pp.33-46 (2013).

12. Fernández-Sánchez, C., Garbajosa, J., Yagüe, A., Perez, J.: Identification and analysis of the elements required to manage technical debt by means of a systematic mapping study. J SYST SOFTWARE 124, 22-38 (2017).

13. Besker, T., Martini, A., Bosch, J.: A Systematic Literature Review and a Unified Model of ATD. In: 42th SEAA, Cyprus, pp.189-197 (2016).

14. Behutiye, W., Rodríguez, P., Oivo, M., Tosun, A.: Analyzing the concept of technical debt in the context of agile software development: A systematic literature review. INFORM SOFTWARE TECH 82, 139-158 (2017).

15. Klinger, T., Tarr, P., Wagstrom, P., Williams, C.: An enterprise perspective on technical debt. In: 2nd IWMTD, USA, pp.35-38 (2011).

16. Spínola, R., Vetrò, A., Zazworka, N., Seaman, C., Shull, F.: Investigating technical debt folklore: Shedding some light on technical debt opinion. In: 4th IWMTD, USA, pp.1-7 (2013).

17. Lim, E., Taksande, N., Seaman, C.: A Balancing Act: What Software Practitioners Have to Say about Technical Debt. IEEE Software 29(6), 22-27 (2012).

18. Ernst, N., Bellomo, S., Ozkaya, I., Nord, R., Gorton, I.: Measure it? Manage it? Ignore it? Software practitioners and technical debt. In: 10th FSE, Italy, pp.50-60 (2015).

19. Holvitie, J., Leppänen, V., Hyrynsalmi, S.: Technical Debt and the Effect of Agile Software Development Practices on It - An Industry Practitioner Survey. In: 6th IWMTD, Canada, pp.35-42 (2014).

20. Vassallo, C., Zampetti, F., Romano, D., Beller, M., Panichella, A., Di Penta, M., Zaidman, A.: Continuous delivery practices in a large financial organization. In: 2016 ICSME, USA, pp.519-528 (2016).

21. Martini, A., Besker, T., Bosch, J.: The introduction of technical debt tracking in large companies. In: 23rd APSEC, New Zealand, pp.161-168 (2016).

22. Basili, V., Caldiera, G., Rombach, D.: Goal question metric (GQM) approach. In: Encyclopedia of software engineering (2002).

23. Linåker, J., Sulaman, S., Maiani de Mello, R., Höst, M.: Guidelines for conducting surveys in software engineering. Technical Report TR 5366801, Lund University (2015).

24. Ribeiro, L., Spínola, R.: Um Survey sobre a Pertinência e Relevância de Critérios de Decisão para Apoiar o Gerenciamento de Itens de Dívida Técnica. In: 15º SBQS, Brazil, vol. 15, pp.256-270 (2016).

A tertiary study on model-based testing areas, tools and challenges: Preliminary results

Leonardo Villalobos-Arias, Christian Quesada-López, Alexandra Martinez, Marcelo Jenkins

University of Costa Rica, San Pedro, Costa Rica
{leonardo.villalobos, cristian.quesadalopez, alexandra.martinez, marcelo.jenkins}@ucr.ac.cr

Abstract. Context: Model-based testing (MBT) is one of the most studied approaches by secondary studies in the area of software testing. A tertiary study that aggregates knowledge from secondary studies on MBT can be useful to both academia and industry. **Objective**: The goal of this study is to identify and characterize secondary studies in model-based testing, in terms of the areas, tools and challenges they have investigated. **Method**: We conducted a tertiary study in MBT. Our systematic mapping of secondary studies included 12 literature surveys and 10 systematic reviews over the period 1996–2016.**Results**: We found that the two most studied areas of MBT are UML models and Transition-based notations. We also found that only 5 studies compared and classified MBT tools. The main challenges and limitations found were related to the need for more empirical evidence that supports the selection of MBT approaches and tools. **Conclusions**: Not many systematic reviews on MBT were found, consequently some areas still lack secondary studies: test execution aspects, language types, model dynamics, and some model paradigms and generation methods.
We thus encourage the MBT community to perform further systematic reviews and mapping studies, following known protocols and reporting procedures, in order to increase the quality and quantity of empirical studies in MBT.

Keywords: Model-based testing, software testing, mapping study, software engineering, tertiary study

1 Introduction

Software testing is an essential part of software engineering [1], but it has several limitations. Traditional testing techniques are based on the design of a test suite, which is later translated into a series of test cases. These test cases are then manually executed by testers on the software under test (SUT) [1, 2]. Model-based testing (MBT) attempts to solve this by automating parts of the software testing process, mainly the test design step and the test case execution. MBT has been proven to find at least as many errors as manual testing [3]. Investing in MBT has been shown to reduce the overall cost, time and effort of the testing process [2]. Also, MBT may improve testing quality by ensuring that certain criteria (e.g., code coverage) is always met [2]. Finally, MBT tools can aid with requirements traceability and evolution, which can be hard in the traditional testing process [2].

Despite the benefits of MBT, it has some limitations. Particularly, it requires a different set of skills than manual testing [2] since the model designer must be capable of abstracting and designing the model from the requirements (i.e., knowing which aspects should be model and which should not). This also implies training costs and a learning curve before starting to use MBT [2]. Besides, a considerable amount of effort has to be invested in building the model, since the quality of generated tests depends on the quality of the model.

Some tertiary studies have been recently conducted in software engineering [4, 5, 6], but only one [4] focuses on software testing. Garousi et al. [4] identified 15 secondary studies related to MBT, positioning it as the testing method with more secondary studies. However, we did not find any tertiary study specific to MBT. A tertiary study that aggregates and synthesizes knowledge from secondary studies on MBT can be useful to both academia and industry.

To address the lack of tertiary studies in MBT, our research goal was to identify and characterize secondary studies in model-based testing, in terms of the areas, tools, challenges, problems and limitations they have investigated. We conducted a tertiary study based on the guidelines described in [7, 8] and recommendations stated in [9, 10, 11]. The studies were characterized in terms of the specific areas and research questions, model types, test selection criteria, test generation and test execution techniques, testing tools, as well as challenges and limitations. We established three specific research questions to guide our analysis:

RQ1: What model-based testing specific areas have been investigated in secondary studies? Answering this question will enable us to determine the specific MBT areas addressed by secondary studies, including model representations, criteria for test case selection, and techniques for both test case generation and test case execution.

RQ2: How have model-based testing tools been characterized in the literature? This question will allow us to identify the characteristics of model based testing tools as well existing tool classifications.

RQ3: What are the challenges, open problems and limitations reported in the literature of model-based testing? This question will allow us to identify common challenges and limitations of the current research on MBT, as well as potential areas of future research.

The remainder of our paper is structured as follows. We discuss the background in Section 2. Section 3 presents the methodology. Section 4 answers our research questions. And section 5 offers our conclusions and future work.

2 Background

Software testing consists of verifying if a program matches its expected behavior [1]. It can be performed at different levels: unit, integration, and system. Software testing approaches can also be categorized as white-box or black-box, depending on whether they use information about the internal structure of the SUT [1]. Model-based testing is the automation of the design of black-box tests [2]. It is based on a model of the SUT that represents aspects that will be tested. From this model, test cases can be generated in an automated way, usually with the help of a tool. Model-based testing is usually performed at the unit level and covers the functional behavior of the SUT [2].

Utting and Legeard's book on model-based testing [2] is essentially a body of knowledge in MBT, containing existing approaches, process stages, tools and examples. It offers valuable insight for those new to the area. The process of model-based testing has five stages [12]: (1) building the model of the SUT from the requirements, (2) choosing the test selection criteria, (3) transforming these criteria (and the model) into test case specifications, (4) generating test cases, and (5) executing the test cases. The model should be built for testing purposes (i.e., simpler than the model used for development) [2]. A MBT tool may provide support for activities in any of these stages.

In [12], Utting et al. attempt to sort out the MBT body of knowledge by defining a taxonomy of MBT approaches. This taxonomy has six dimensions: (1) model scope, which encompasses aspects of the SUT that are being represented by the model, (2) model characteristics, like non-determinism, (3) model paradigm, which groups modeling notations into families, (4) test selection criteria, which covers the criteria that is used to generate the test cases, (5) test generation technology, which comprises techniques that generate test cases from the model, and (6) test execution, which includes the different ways of generating and/or executing the test cases. Authors suggest that other taxonomies may be defined to express different aspects of MBT's approaches or tools.

The International Software Testing Qualifications Board's Foundation Level Certified Model-Based Tester Syllabus [13] is a guide for certification on MBT. It explains multiple aspects of model-based testing in a concise way, and it focuses on the practical part of MBT. This guide also covers an important topic on how to evaluate and deploy an MBT approach.

Anand et al. [14] performed an orchestrated survey on existing test case generation techniques. In their paper they include five generation techniques. In their model-based testing section, they cover some of the previous work in MBT. They explain the finite-state machine and labeled transition system approaches. They also showcase some commercial tools.

We have found few tertiary studies related to model-based testing. However, we haven't stumbled upon a tertiary study in which MBT is the main emphasis, rather it has been only one area of knowledge from multiple that each study covers. Our study will perform a deeper, more accurate mapping of model-based testing than the existing tertiary studies. We believe it will useful for those new to research in model based testing as a guide for other studies.

3 Methodology

A tertiary study using the same methodology stated in [7, 8] was conducted. In our design, recommendations stated in [9, 10, 11, 15] were also incorporated.

3.1 Search process and study selection

We initially conducted an exploratory search to identify the terms (or keywords) relevant for our mapping. Then we selected this search string:

```
(''model driven * test*'' OR ''model based * test*'' OR ''model-based
    test*'') AND (''review'' OR ''survey'' OR ''systematic mapping'' OR
    ''mapping study'' ) AND (''Software'' OR ''system under test'' OR ''
    SUT'') AND (''tool'' OR ''test* automat*'' OR ''automat* test*'')
```

This search string was used to conduct a search on the Scopus (subareas: "COMP" and "ENG") and Web of Science online academic engine, up to April 2017. The search terms could appear anywhere in the title, abstract or keywords.

Inclusion and exclusion criteria. Articles that met the following criteria were included: (I1) Language: English, (I2) Type of study: Secondary study (survey, map or review) and (I3) Approach: Model based testing. Articles that met the following criteria were excluded: (E1) Papers not available in full text, (E2) Publications not related to the software engineering domain and (E3) Non peer reviewed publications. When a secondary study was published in more than one journal/conference, both versions of the study were compared for the purpose of data extraction.

Selection process. Our search string produced an initial set of 47 potentially relevant studies. The inclusion and exclusion criteria were applied to the title, keywords and abstract of extracted articles. Any paper that was clearly irrelevant became excluded. To complete the inclusion and exclusion process, the following steps were performed: (1) each paper was evaluated by 5 members of the research group, (2) each member independently screened the paper for inclusion and exclusion criteria, and decided whether or not to include the paper, offering a justification, (3) the team met and compared their results. Any disagreement about the inclusion of a paper was discussed until a final consensus was reached, and the decision was documented. We tried not to reject potentially relevant papers. After applying the exclusion criteria, 13 studies were selected. To expand the scope of our search, backward snowballing was applied to the selected secondary studies as well as to three relevant tertiary studies [4, 5, 6]. As a result, 9 more papers were included, for a total of 22 papers. Our automated search did not find the snowball papers because they did not math our search string: some targeted specific models such as UML and FSMs, some used a different name for MBT (e.g., formal testing approach) and others focused on a specific aspect of MBT (e.g., test case generation). From these, 12 were literature surveys and 10 were systematic reviews. Figure 1 shows the number and type of secondary studies over time. The complete list of secondary papers along with their origin (automated search or snowballing), type (literature surveys or systematic reviews), quality assessment and extraction form, is available at `https://goo.gl/gX2WKe`.

3.2 Quality assessment

The quality of all secondary studies was evaluated according to the DARE assessment based upon four questions [6, 15]: (Q1) Are the study's inclusion and exclusion

Table 1: Quality assessment of secondary studies.

Ref.	Type	Year	Guid.	Q1	Q2	Q3	Q4	Total	Ref.	Type	Year	Guid.	Q1	Q2	Q3	Q4	Total
S01	LS	1996		0	0	0	0.5	0.5	S12	SR	2010	[8, 9]	1	1	0.5	1	3.5
S02	LS	2005		0	0	0	1	1	S13	LS	2012		0	0	0	1	1
S03	LS	2006		0	0	0	1	1	S14	SR	2012		1	0.5	0	1	1.5
S04	SR	2007	[8, 9]	1	1	0	1	3	S15	LS	2013		0	0	0	1	1
S05	SR	2008	[8, 9]	1	1	0	1	3	S16	SR	2014	[8]	1	1	1	1	4
S06	SR	2008	[8, 9]	1	1	0	1	3	S17	LS	2015		1	1	0	1	3
S07	LS	2009		0	0	0	0	0	S18	SR	2015	[7, 8, 9]	1	0.5	1	1	3.5
S08	LS	2009		0	0	0	0.5	0.5	S19	SR	2015	[8]	1	1	0	1	3
S09	LS	2010		0	0	0	0	0	S20	SR	2015	[5]	1	1	1	1	4
S10	LS	2010		0	0	0	1	1	S21	LS	2016		0	0	0	0	0
S11	LS	2010		0	0	0	0	0	S22	SR	2016	[8, 5]	0.5	1	0.5	1	3

criteria explicitly and clearly defined? Y (yes): the inclusion criteria are explicitly and clearly defined; P (partially): the inclusion criteria are implicit; N (no): the inclusion criteria are not defined and cannot be easily inferred. (Q2) Is the literature search likely to have covered relevant studies? Y: the authors have either searched a digital library and included additional search strategies or identified and referenced all journals addressing the topic of interest; P: the authors have searched searched a digital library with no extra search strategies; N: the authors have searched an extremely restricted set of journals or conferences. (Q3) Did the reviewers assess the quality/validity of the included studies? Y: the authors have explicitly defined quality criteria and extracted them from each primary study; P: the research question involves quality issues that are addressed by the study; N: no explicit quality assessment of individual papers has been attempted, or quality data has been extracted but not used. (Q4) Were the basic data/studies adequately described? Y: information is presented about each paper so that data summaries can clearly be traced to relevant papers; P: only summary information is presented about individual papers, it is not possible to link individual studies to each category; N: the results of the individual studies are not specified, the individual primary studies are not cited. The score assignment was Y = 1, P = 0.5, N = 0, and the overall score was computed by summing the scores of individual questions. A high quality score corresponds to a detailed report of the secondary study. Our quality assessment is presented in Table 1. We observe from this table that all but one of the systematic reviews (SR) exhibited high quality scores (3 or more, out 4). On the other hand, only one literature surveys (LS) had a high quality score (3), the rest had low scores (1 or less, out of 4), as expected. Studies with low quality scores were not excluded from the analysis.

3.3 Data extraction and analysis

The extraction process was performed in four steps, described next. First, each paper was randomly assigned to a pair of researchers (from the research team of six in-

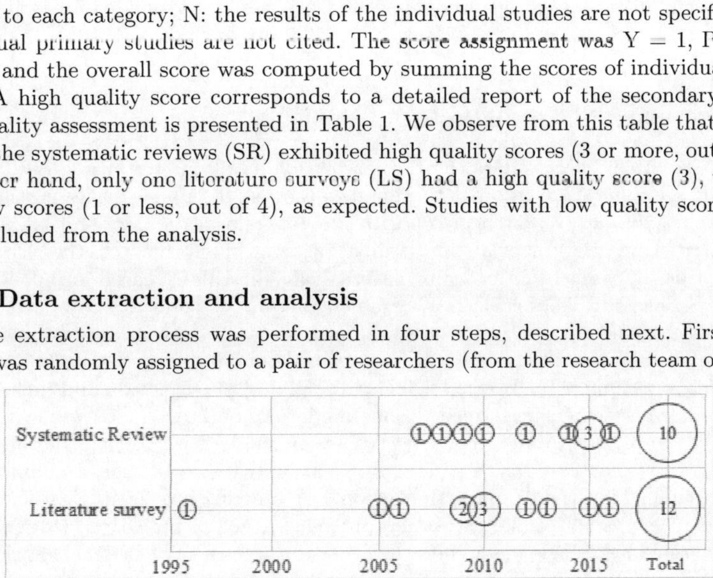

Fig. 1: Number and type of secondary studies in time.

Table 2: Extracted data items.

Category	Data Items
Id	Reference, forum (conference or journal), year, title, authors, google scholar hits
Study	Type of study and guidelines used
Areas	Model types, test selection criteria, test generation and execution techniques, taxonomies and classifications used
Tools	Tools classification (model representation, test case generation, test case execution and analysis techniques), system under test (SUT) domain(s)
Challenges	Challenges, open problems and limitations

cluding the authors of this paper). Then, each member of a pair independently screened the paper for extraction. After that, the pair met and compared their results, discussing any disagreement until a consensus was reached and the decision was documented. Finally, for each research question, one author of this paper validated the data extraction and complemented any information when necessary. We analyzed each study and extracted any relevant data to answer our research questions. In Table 2, we list the data items extracted from each study. A spreadsheet was created to aid in the organization and categorization of data. For RQ1, our initial hierarchy was the union of the categories in our reference taxonomies [12, 16] ([16] is also S17 in Table 1). Then, we kept adding categories (areas) that emerged from the studies. Since we wanted to create a tree rather than a flat structure (for better understanding and categorization of data), we had to group subareas sharing one or more characteristics into an upper-level node (area). We tried to respect the category names originally given by the authors, but sometimes we had to choose (whenever two different names were given to the same area), and in one case, we had to create the label. When in doubt about the classification of an approach, we followed our reference taxonomies. For RQ2, MBT tools mentioned in secondary studies were identified. We extracted information reported about each tool and attempted to group them in categories. For RQ3, reported challenges and limitations were identified. We perform grounded analysis to allow the categories to emerge from the data.

3.4 Threats to validity

We briefly discuss here the threats to validity of our tertiary study. *Search terms and digital libraries:* In order to minimize the risk of missing relevant studies, we first did an exploratory search in order to identify relevant papers and keywords for our search string. Several trials and validations were performed on the search string by multiple researchers, in order to have a stable and final search string. We only used the Scopus and Web of Science search engine, but to counter we applied snowballing, as recommended by [11]. The snowballing process was a backward process based only in titles. Some studies could still be missing from our analysis. *Selection of studies:* In order to minimize the researcher bias in applying the exclusion and inclusion criteria, multiple researchers performed various validations of the excluded and included studies. Since we included only secondary studies in model-base testing, our findings apply only in this context. *Data extraction and categorization:* In order to minimize possible inaccuracies in the data extraction as well as researcher bias in the classification, various researchers validated the extraction process. Although the categorization was mainly performed by a single researcher, the other researchers gave feedback on the categories, as a way to validate them. Moreover, most of our categories for RQ1 and RQ2 were based on previous MBT studies.

4 Results and discussion

In this section we present the results of our mapping study, based on 22 secondary studies, and address our specific research questions.

4.1 RQ1: Model-based testing research areas

This research question helped us identify MBT areas that have been investigated by secondary studies. Particularly, we aimed to discover which model representations, test case selection criteria, test case generation methods and test case execution techniques have been most (and least) studied. For this, we built a hierarchy of MBT areas and subareas based upon two existing taxonomies: one proposed by Utting et al. [12] (aimed for MBT approaches) and other proposed by Marinescu et al. [16] (aimed for MBT tools). Areas (or categories) were added, merged or renamed as papers were read and analyzed. When the hierarchy was finalized, we reviewed again all the studies in order to complete the list of supporting studies per area. The final hierarchy of MBT areas is shown in Figure 2. References inside internal nodes are studies that actually use or propose the category represented by the node. The reference list per leaf node corresponds to studies that support that specific category. A study was considered to 'support' a category or area if it mentions the category (not necessarily if it was a mainstream topic).

We found that the two most studied areas in MBT are UML (16 secondary studies) and Transition-based notations (12 secondary studies), both falling into the Model paradigm area. Within UML, behavioral models (including state machine, sequence and activity diagrams) are the most common, with 15 secondary studies in total. Among Transition-based notations, Finite state machines is the most common, with 10 secondary studies. The third and fourth most studied areas in MBT are Test levels, particularly Unit testing (10 studies) and Integration testing (9 studies).

With respect to test case selection criteria, the most studied is Structural model coverage, with 6 studies. Regarding test case generation methods, Random and Search-based are the most studied algorithms, with 4 studies each. Among the most studied test artifacts found were Functional behavior (or properties), with 6 studies, and extra-functional behavior (or non-functional aspects), with 5 studies. On the other hand, among the most studied test types were Functional testing and Regression testing, with 5 studies each. Also, we found that the most studied test execution subarea is Technology (online/offline), with 4 studies. In regard to the type of SUT that MBT targets, the most studied SUT domains are Real-time systems, Reactive systems, Embedded systems, and Web applications (each with 4 studies), whereas the most studied software paradigm is Object-oriented (with 4 studies also).

During the construction of our hierarchy, we also found some inconsistencies among the classifications given by different authors. For example, some studies [S12] classified FSM and LTS as state-based models, whereas Utting et al. [12] and Marinescu et al. [S17] classified them as transition-based models in their taxonomies. Another example is regression testing, which Dias et al. [S04] classified as a test level but we consider it a test type (based on [17]). On the other hand, [S21] placed search-based algorithms for test case generation (also known as meta-heuristic search) in a category outside of MBT, while other authors [S13, S15, S21][12] categorized it as a test generation method in MBT.

4.2 RQ2: Model-based testing tools

This research question led us to identify classifications that have been used in secondary studies for MBT tools. In what follows, we present the results with respect

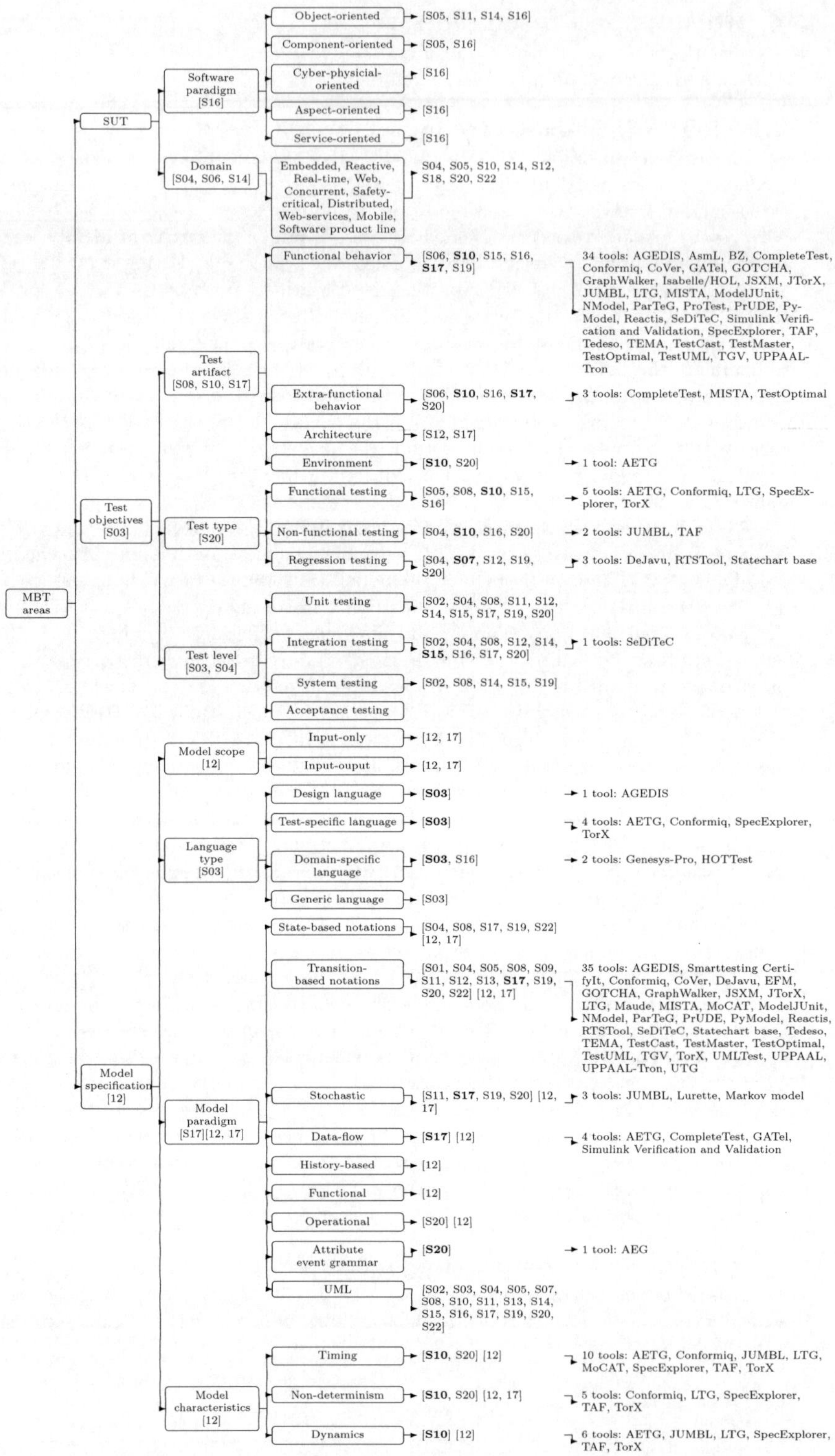

Fig. 2: MBT areas investigated by secondary studies.

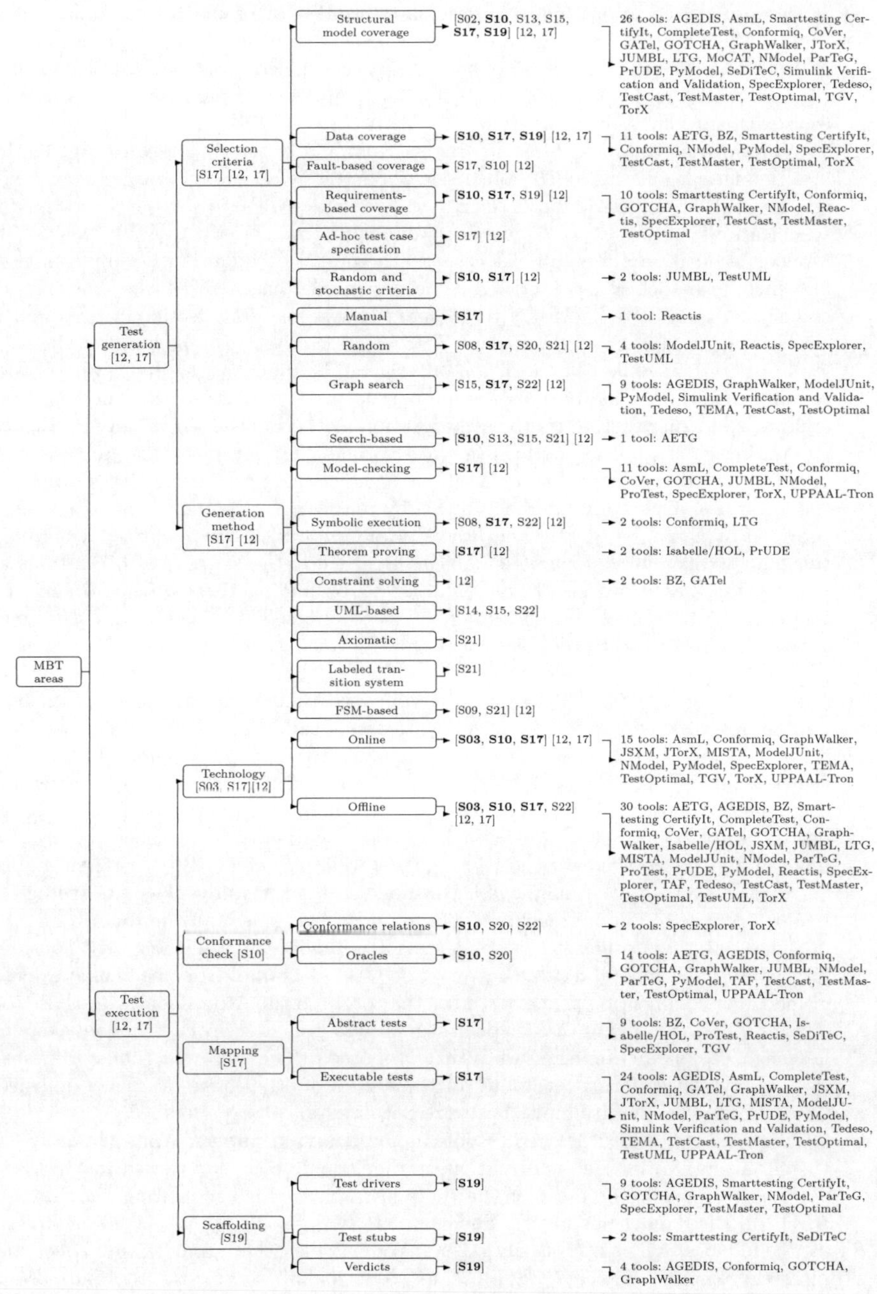

Fig. 2: (Continued) MBT areas investigated by secondary studies

to the tool classifications found in secondary studies. We found 11 secondary studies that mentioned MBT tools. Of these, only 5 gathered multiple tools and classified them in some dimensions. The other 6 papers simply mentioned tools. Several studies hinted the existence of tools, but offered no name for them. For the purpose of our study, only tools with a name were considered.

Studies that classified tools used some common criteria that can be generalized into: model specification [S03, S10, S19, S20], test selection criteria [S10, S17, S19], test generation criteria [S10, S17], and test execution related [S10, S17, S19]. Model specification was the most common criterion used to classify tools, with 4 studies. Model specification refers in most cases to the model paradigm in Figure 2, but some also include model scope, language type and model characteristics. The next most common criteria used to classify tools were support for test selection criteria and test execution criteria, each with 3 studies. Test selection criteria can be found in the second level of Figure 2, while test execution criteria can be found in the first level. The least common criteria to classify tools was support for test generation criterion, with only 2 studies. Test generation refers to the generation method in the second level of Figure 2.

Marinescu et al. [S17] perform a state-of-the-art survey in tool-supported model-based testing by presenting and classifying some of the most mature tools available in the literature. The study approaches this by proposing a taxonomy based on the one provided by Utting et al. [12] and others. Many tools were characterized according to this new taxonomy. Shafique and Labiche [S19] study the support of MBT tools that rely on state-based models. They attempt this by finding these tools and comparing them according to many criteria, mainly test coverage. This is one of the studies that perform a more in-depth tool classification. The tools were characterized by their support of three general criteria: test, test scaffolding, and support for related activities criteria. These criteria are further sub-divided into more specific classes, like model-flow, script-flow, and data-flow coverage criteria. Saifan and Dingel [S10] perform a survey on how MBT has been used to test quality attributes of software. In their work, they extend the taxonomy of Utting et al. [12] by adding three additional criteria and characterize tools based on this categories. Siavashi and Truscan [S20] perform a study on the use of environment models in MBT. They gather a list of tools that use these models, and group them by model language. Mahdian et al. [S07] perform a survey on regression testing that employs UML models. In their study, they cite studies that research on regression approaches, types of UML diagrams, and the tool proposed.

The studies that did not perform a classification of MBT tools were also considered for this study. In general terms, they mention tools as examples of a particular approach or model, or comment on primary studies that propose and experiment with those tools. The information found in these type of studies was: tool description, the tool's model or language, tool's functioning, studies that proposed or employed the tool, and its usage in industry. The information found in these kind of studies was very heterogeneous, but it allowed to identify tools that were not cited in other papers.

We found a total of 99 MBT tools in the analyzed papers. Approximately 39 of these tools had little or no information, so they could not be associated to MBT areas. The table is sparse for most of the tools and some areas, indicating that no study covers all the dimensions found. The complete list of tools and their characterization can be found at `https://goo.gl/gX2WKe`. We classified these tools with respect to the hierarchy of areas depicted Figure 2, in order to find areas with tool support. For each low-level area ('leaves' of the hierarchy tree), we list the tools that support that area, and highlight (with boldface) the secondary studies from which the tools were extracted.

4.3 RQ3: Challenges, limitations and open problems

This research question directed us to identify the challenges, open problems and limitations that have been reported in the secondary studies. Next we describe the main challenges and limitations with respect to the factors of influence and empirical evidence for MBT approaches and tools.

We found that more empirical evidence is needed to support the selection of MBT approaches and tools. There is only a few evidence about experiences in the industry [S06], and case studies on practice using different approaches are needed [S03]. Moreover, evidence are usually published biased towards success stories [S03]. More research is needed in evaluating and analyzing the applicability of different models in MBT [S20] and the landscape of MBT approaches and tools should be compared [S07, S19]. It is necessary to evaluate not just small modules, but full systems to find the better suited approach for an specific context [S04] Evidence showing MTB approaches capabilities compared to conventional testing techniques is also required [S04]. Further, more evidence in checking a system against non-functional aspects should be investigated [S16, S20]. MBT approaches have to be evaluated on non-functional characteristics such as safety, security, usability, S10, S16, S17, S20]. In addition, research on the comparison and evaluation on how various criteria relate to each other in terms of the coverage and fault detection is required [S02]. There is no conclusive evidence about how one model outstands others when more than one model is appropriate for a specific context [S11]. Therefore, decisions need to be made based on what model (or set of models) are most suitable [S20].

In practice, evidence in determining whether MBT approaches are useful to different domains and contexts is necessary to support the selection process. Different factors such as type and level of testing, models, types of software projects, tool characteristics should be studied to objectively measure the performance, effectiveness, complexity, costs, effort, flexibility, feasibility, advantages and benefits [S03, S04, S05, S06, S13, S20]. Many MBT approaches have not been empirically evaluated or not transferred to the industrial environments [S04]. The understanding about the similarities and differences among approaches could lead to determining appropriate MBT techniques and tools in specific operating contexts in practice. For [S11], a real work that remains is fitting specific models to specific application domains because many models have implicit drawbacks. Also, the number of techniques proposed for test case generation is very large and a deeper insight on the techniques proposed is needed [S16]. In some cases, the generated test cases may get irreverent due to the disparity between a model and its corresponding code [S11]. A key step in any MBT methodology is the validation of the model, this is an essential step in resolving specification ambiguities and synchronizing the understanding of the requirements [S03].

It is still a challenge to expand modeling notations in complex systems and development environments [S20]. Models should consider concurrent sub states and events [S13]. Models state identification and verification are still a challenge in dealing with the state explosion problem [S01]. A prominent problem for state models is state space explosion, as it propagates to almost all MBT tasks such as model maintenance, checking and review, test case generation and achieving coverage criteria [S11]. Some approaches use genetic algorithms for test case generation [S13]. These techniques could provide feasible test sequences [S13] but also suffer on providing balanced transition coverage and unfeasible transition and looping problems [S13]. Many studies ignore concurrent and integration testing resulting in less efficient test cases generation [S14]. In some cases the test adaptation is manually implemented and need multiple test adaptations [S20]. Ensuring adequate traceability or coverage of test scenarios is needed [S14]. In terms of test case generation assessment, most of the studies are based on coverage criteria [S13, S16, S19]. Complexity levels depend on modeling language and algorithms necessary to perform each step in the MTB process [S04]. Models for nontrivial software functionality can grow beyond management even with tool support [S11]. Finding the right level of abstraction for the test model is one of the challenges in MBT [S20].

The choice of a model also depends on aspects of the system under test and skills of user [S10, S11]. One of the disadvantages of the languages for modelling is that they are usually complex to learn and use [S03]. Requirements to use a MBT approach include knowledge about the modeling language, testing coverage criteria, generated output format and supporting tools. These make the adoption of MBT difficult or unfeasible [S04]. Moreover, practitioners require different skills and expertise in modeling notations, test criteria, test metrics, and tools [S04, S11]. Most testers would probably prefer visual languages for understanding a model [S03]. There is a necessity of increasing automation using simple and known notations. MBT approach must be obtainable with low effort, time, and skill to perform the its steps [S04, S11]. For practitioners, the leap from traditional scripted testing to MBT seems as hard as moving from manual to automatic test [S03]. Creating models and keeping them updated demands require significant time and effort [S03, S06]. Practitioners also perceived that they perform system design twice, once for development and once for testing [S03]. It is necessary to be clear that MBT is an activity that requires investment, planning and knowledge [S11].

Some of the main risks associated to MTB are related to the quality assurance of the artifacts used for test generation, the testing schedule planning, the selection of MBT approaches, the behavior or structural model construction, the selection criteria for test cases, tracking and change managing, manual tasks in the MBT process, test generation and execution process controlling [S05]. To increase the practical application of MBT, tools have to support modeling and test generation steps. It is necessary to integrate automated and manual steps because the complex no automated steps makes any approach unfeasible. Thus, increasing the automation levels of the steps in a MBT approach and reducing requirements to use these approaches determines the feasibility of using MBT. The construction of models is not a trivial task due to the lack of a systematic methodology and of supporting tools for its automation [S20]. The MBT testing tools should be integrated with the software development processes [S04, S11, S14, S20].

There exist many MBT tools which vary significantly in their specific designs, testing target, tool support, and evaluation strategies [S08]. MBT tools generate many test cases and not having full automation support for managing could make the use of MBT infeasible [S19]. Practitioners faced problems related with the learning and understanding of the features of MBT tools [S19, S20]. Many of them can generate executable test cases but still some just generate abstract tests [S17]. In many cases, there are no tools available for modeling and generating tests in a particular domain and custom made tools are needed [S03]. In other cases, MBT tools are not available to the public [S18, S21]. Furthermore, most of open source tools have incomplete or outdated documentation [S19].

5 Conclusions and future work

In this paper, we have reported the results of a tertiary study that performs a systematic mapping of secondary studies in MBT, published between 1996 and 2016. From an initial set of 47 secondary studies, we ended up analyzing 22 papers (10 systematic reviews and 12 literature surveys), after applying the exclusion and inclusion criteria. The complete data extraction form is available online. We created a hierarchy of MBT areas, partially based on taxonomies from previous studies. We also categorized the MBT tools into this hierarchy. Finally, we grouped and classified the main challenges and limitations found in secondary studies.

Our main findings regarding the areas of MBT that have been investigated are the following: (1) the two most studied areas in MBT are model paradigms, particularly UML and Transition-based notations, (2) the most studied test case selection criteria is Structural model coverage, (3) the most studied test case generation methods are Random and Search-based algorithms, and (4) the most studied test execution area is Technology: online/offline.

With respect to the characterization of MBT tools, we found 99 MBT tools which were classified according to model specification, test selection criteria, test generation criteria, and test execution. We found that there are many MBT areas not supported by tools. These include testing of non-functional characteristics, modeling of architecture and environment, multiple modeling paradigms (history-based, functional, and operational), several coverage criteria (data-flow, data, and fault-based), specific test generation techniques (axiomatic and UML-, LTS-, and FSM-based), and test scaffolding support. Very few studies categorize tools by test level, model scope, modeling language, and model characteristics. Also, no studies reported the SUT domain or paradigm targeted by the tool.

The main challenges and limitations stated by secondary studies were: (1) more empirical evidence is needed to support the selection of MTB approaches and tools, (2) an understanding of the similarities and differences among MBT approaches could lead to choose the appropriate technique and tool in specific operating contexts, and (3) both functional and non-functional testing should be considered in MBT studies.

Since there are few secondary studies on MBT, we consider important to develop studies encompassing the following areas: test execution aspects such as scaffolding and mapping of test cases, languages types (e.g., design, test-specific and generic languages), model dynamics (e.g., discrete, continuous, hybrid), model paradigms like history-based and functional, generation methods like constraint solving, axiomatic and LTS, as well as different software paradigms.

A recommendation for the MBT researchers is to use a systematic approach when performing secondary studies, and follow standard reporting procedures. Systematic reviews scored high in our quality assessment, and tended to offer information in a more structured and useful way. We also encourage the use of existing taxonomies for MBT (including the one presented in this work) when performing primary or secondary studies. Classifying tools and approaches under known classification schemes makes information easier to extract for others, and more comparable across papers. MBT is gaining popularity as a research area, and we believe that the adoption of a systematic methodology is important in order to increase the quality of the studies.

In the future, we plan on expanding this tertiary study to cover recently published secondary studies in MBT (2017-2018) and analize additionally aspects of these studies. A recent search yielded a number of interesting and relevant systematic studies that we could be interested in reviewing.

6 Acknowledgements

This work was supported by University of Costa Rica (UCR)'s project No. 834-B7-749. We thank the SE Research Group at UCR for the valuable feedback and help.

References

1. Bourque, P., Fairley, R.E., et al.: Guide to the software engineering body of knowledge (SWEBOK (R)): Version 3.0. IEEE Computer Society Press (2014)
2. Utting, M., Legeard, B.: Practical model-based testing: a tools approach. Morgan Kaufmann (2010)
3. Pretschner, A., Prenninger, W., Wagner, S., Kühnel, C., Baumgartner, M., Sostawa, B., Zölch, R., Stauner, T.: One evaluation of model-based testing and its automation. In: Proceedings of the 27th international conference on Software engineering, ACM (2005) 392–401
4. Garousi, V., Mäntylä, M.V.: A systematic literature review of literature reviews in software testing. Information and Software Technology **80** (2016) 195–216
5. Kitchenham, B., Brereton, O.P., Budgen, D., Turner, M., Bailey, J., Linkman, S.: Systematic literature reviews in software engineering–a systematic literature review. Information and software technology **51** (2009) 7–15
6. Kitchenham, B., Pretorius, R., Budgen, D., Brereton, O.P., Turner, M., Niazi, M., Linkman, S.: Systematic literature reviews in software engineering–a tertiary study. Information and Software Technology **52** (2010) 792–805
7. Petersen, K., Vakkalanka, S., Kuzniarz, L.: Guidelines for conducting systematic mapping studies in software engineering: An update. Information and Software Technology **64** (2015) 1–18
8. Kitchenham, B., Charters, S.: Guidelines for performing systematic literature reviews in software engineering. In: Technical report, Ver. 2.3 EBSE Technical Report. EBSE. School of Computer Science and Mathematics, Keele University (2007)
9. Biolchini, J., Mian, P.G., Natali, A.C.C., Travassos, G.H.: Systematic review in software engineering. System Engineering and Computer Science Department COPPE/UFRJ, Technical Report ES (**679**)
10. Wohlin, C.: Guidelines for snowballing in systematic literature studies and a replication in software engineering. In: Proceedings of the 18th international conference on evaluation and assessment in software engineering, ACM (2014) 38
11. Mourao, E., Kalinowski, M., Mendes, E., Wohlin, C.: Investigating the use of a hybrid search strategy for systematic reviews. (In: Proceedings of the 11th international symposium on empirical software engineering and measurement)
12. Utting, M., Pretschner, A., Legeard, B.: A taxonomy of model-based testing approaches. Software Testing, Verification and Reliability **22** (2012) 297–312
13. ISTQB®: Foundation level certified model-based tester. (2015)
14. Anand, S., Burke, E.K., Chen, T.Y., Clark, J., Cohen, M.B., Grieskamp, W., Harman, M., Harrold, M.J., Mcminn, P., Bertolino, A., Li, J., Zhu, H.: An orchestrated survey of methodologies for automated software test case generation. Journal of Systems and Software **86** (2013) 1978–2001
15. Budgen, D., Brereton, P., Drummond, S., Williams, N.: Reporting systematic reviews: Some lessons from a tertiary study. Information and Software Technology (2017) 62–74
16. Marinescu, R., Seceleanu, C., Le Guen, H., Pettersson, P.: Chapter three-a research overview of tool-supported model-based testing of requirements-based designs. Advances in Computers **98** (2015) 89–140
17. Utting, M., Legeard, B., Bouquet, F., Fourneret, E., Peureux, F., Vernotte, A.: Chapter two - recent advances in model-based testing. Volume 101 of Advances in Computers. Elsevier (2016) 53 – 120

An Empirical Study on the Knowledge Management Practice in Software Testing

Claudia P. C. Maciel[1], Érica Ferreira de Souza[1], Nandamudi L. Vijaykumar[2], Ricardo de Almeida Falbo[3], Giovani Volnei Meinerz[1], and Katia Romero Felizardo[1]

Department of Computer, Federal Technological University of Paraná - UTFPR[1]
Cornélio Procópio/PR - Brazil
claudiamaciel@alunos.utfpr.edu.br,{ericasouza,giovanimeinerz, katiascannavino}@utfpr.edu.br
Lab. of Comp. and Applied Math., National Institute for Space Research - INPE[2]
São José dos Campos/SP - Brazil
vijay.nl@inpe.br
Depart. of Computer Science, Federal University of Espírito Santo - UFES[3]
Vitória/ES, Brazil
falbo@inf.ufes.br

Abstract. Context: Software testing is a knowledge intensive process, and therefore can benefit from the use of experience gained from past projects. In this context, principles of Knowledge Management (KM) can be applied to promote knowledge capture and sharing as well as the emergence of new knowledge. In spite of this, there are only few studies that present practitioners' perspective about KM initiatives in software testing. **Objective:** The main goal of this study is to identify the perception of professionals in software testing on the use of KM initiatives in software engineering companies, such as KM adoption, potential benefits or hindrances. **Method:** A survey was conducted in software development companies. In addition, the survey results were compared with another survey conducted previously in the same context, however, with different objectives and target audience. 39 software companies participated in this research. **Results:** Testing planning activity and the test case reuse are the aspects that have received more attention by companies. A strategic planning and reuse of existing test cases have a potential to significantly reduce software development costs and time. **Conclusion:** Applying KM in software companies can bring several benefits in terms of quality of results, reduction costs, time and effort. However, it is still a challenge to be faced and tackled.

1 Introduction

A major Software Engineering challenge is the creation of systematic strategies to integrate the knowledge of the actors involved in a project. Software organizations seek solutions that give an emphasis on different knowledge types when planning initiatives to manage them [1]. According to Levy and Hazzan

[2], a systematic routine to capture knowledge is important in an organization, making the knowledge transparent for all those involved, since without it an organization cannot benefit from its accumulated knowledge. However, although the importance of working with generated knowledge has been widely recognized in several areas, few organizations are able to manage such a generated knowledge. Knowledge Management (KM) principles are mechanisms that can solve, at least partially, such problems [3].

KM is concerned with how to capture, store and reuse dispersed knowledge in an environment [4]. Due to the importance of the developing products and services in companies, KM has become a promising area for conducting research and analysis to show evidence on its benefits [5]. Software Engineering, for instance, has concentrated efforts on how to efficiently conduct KM, since it facilitates the knowledge flow and use in all phases of the entire software development process. Software processes generate a significant amount of information, and KM entails formally managing this information to facilitate access and reuse, as well as transfer best practices in the organization to build competitive advantage and cost reduction through the appropriation from knowledge [3].

One important subarea of Software Engineering is software testing. Software testing activities are strategic elements for conducting development of projects and ensuring product quality. However, with technological advancement and the emergence of increasingly critical applications, testing activity has become a complex task that can generate a lot of important information to be manipulated [3]. Software testing is a knowledge intensive process. Past experiences and knowledge gained can be reused, for example, in test case design, or in the recognition of faults [6].

Software testing can produce an important intellectual capital and thus new projects can benefit from the experience acquired with past projects. Given the great importance of knowledge for software testing and the potential benefits in managing this knowledge, several studies have recommended the application of KM in software testing [3]. However, there are only few studies that present practitioners' perspective from the area.

This paper aims to provide the perception of software testing professionals about the practical application of KM in software testing, such as KM adoption, potential benefits or hindrances in some testing process activities. We intend to provide an insight on the actual benefit of applying KM in software testing activities, in the professionals' vision, that may serve as a practical help for companies that want to conduct initiatives of such type, specially, novice companies.

In order to achieve the objective of this study, we adapted and reapplied the survey conducted by Souza et al. [7]. In [7], the goal was to identify the best scenario to apply KM in software testing. In that survey, the authors made available an online questionnaire within research groups and social networks, which was answered by participants with different profiles, among them, professionals, graduate students, professors and researchers with some experience in software testing. 86 participants answered the survey. The main difference in relation to Souza et al. [7] and our survey is the objectives and target audience.

In the survey presented in this paper, we analyze only answers from software testing professionals working in Brazilian software development companies. We conducted a survey with 39 Brazilian software development companies that systematically conduct software testing activities in their projects. From the 39 companies, 75 employees answered the survey. In addition, the results of this study were compared with the results from Souza et al. [7].

The remainder of this paper is organized as follows. Section 2 presents the main concepts related to the background of this paper. Section 3 presents the research planning, the main results and discussions. Section 4 presents related works. Finally, Section 5 presents the final considerations, as well as the potential threats to the study validity.

2 Background

Software testing consists of dynamic verification activities that analyze the behavior of a program in relation to its expected behavior. Testing activities can be supported by a well-defined process [8]. In general, a testing process consists of following activities: Test Planning, Test Case Design, Test Execution, and Test Results Analysis [8]. In the planning, the test environment for the project, planning and scheduling testing activities are defined. All test planning should be documented in a Test Plan. The test case design activity is intended to design, document, and implement test cases. During the execution activity, the test cases are run and the results are analyzed to determine whether the test cases can provide a verdict of passed or failed. In addition to the process, software testing involves, testing levels, artifacts, techniques, procedures, resources and tools that seek to control and organize tests to achieve high quality software.

Since testing activities have attracted significant attention from both industry and academia, different improvement models have been used to guide testing. However, during software testing, a large amount of information is processed and generated, and such models alone are not sufficient to improve the organizational testing process. It is still necessary to provide automated support for tasks of acquisition, processing, analysis and dissemination of test knowledge for reuse [3]. In this context, Knowledge Management (KM) can be used to manage knowledge of software testing [3, 7].

KM became more present within organizations in the 1980s, coming from the need to gain knowledge from the vast amount of information to develop new products, processes, and more flexible organizational arrangements, providing a sustainable competitive advantage [9]. Having control and ease of access to knowledge has now become a competitive and economic differential for organizations. According to Markkula [10], knowledge is information combined with experience, interpretation and reflection. It is a form of information ready to be applied in decision making.

Knowledge can be classified into two types: tacit and explicit [11]. Tacit knowledge is the subjective and experience-based knowledge, that cannot be documented, and typically remains only in people's mind. This type of knowledge depends on personal experience and involves intangible factors such as beliefs, perspectives, values and intuition. Explicit knowledge, in turn, represents the objective and rational knowledge that can be documented, and thus it can be accessed by multiple people. The conversion of tacit to explicit knowledge offers greater value to the organization as it leads to the creation of new knowledge [4].

The major challenge to manage knowledge is that most of the knowledge in Software Engineering is tacit and hard to dedicate efforts to make it explicit. When tacit knowledge is transformed into explicit, the organization begins to enable the dissemination of strategic knowledge [4]. In the context of software testing, KM can be used to capture knowledge and experience generated during the testing process. However, generally, this knowledge has been stored in documents or in people's minds. Unfortunately, paper has limited accessibility and it is difficult to be updated. On the other hand, tacit knowledge can easily be lost when experienced individuals leave the organization. This is the reason that knowledge in tests should be collected systematically through systems or applications, stored in an organizational and shared repository throughout the organization. This fact encouraged the development of this research in trying to understand and to make evident the perception of experts in the software testing area on the application of KM initiatives in Brazilian software development companies.

3 Survey on Knowledge Management Practice in Software Testing

In order to analyze the professionals' perspective with respect to the application of KM initiatives in software testing, we conducted a survey with 39 Brazilian software development companies. A survey is an empirical research strategy for the collection of information from heterogeneous sources. It has been used to provide a general picture of technology usage in the software industry [12]. According to Kitchenham and Pfleeger [13], a survey is conducted to identify the opinion of a specific population, for example, about a new method, process, tool or technique that has been used for a while. A survey can be conducted following a process with the following phases [13]: (i) definition of the research objective; (ii) identification of the target audience that will respond to the survey; (iii) survey design; (iv) survey evaluation; (v) survey application; and (vi) results analysis and presentation.

Research objective: the main objective of this survey is to provide insight from software testing professionals on the practical application of KM in software testing.

Target audience: 39 software development companies were invited to participate in this survey. The authors contacted the companies directly inviting them to participate in the survey. Only companies that develop software and conduct some software testing process were invited. Thus, the sampling method was non-probabilistic. For privacy reasons, names of the companies are not mentioned here. However, some of their characteristics are: the companies are located in Brazil; there are micro, small, medium and large software companies; the main products developed include critical systems, such as electronic scales receipt and metrology, customized systems to meet the needs of customers in several segments (aviation, pharmaceuticals, automotive parts), hospital systems and Enterprise Resource Planning (ERP). Companies specialized in software testing that has as main service the outsourcing of software testing also participated.

Survey project: We used a questionnaire with sixteen questions divided into two parts. The first part of the questionnaire includes questions to identify the participant profile, such as experience time and position, and company features, namely company size and segment. The second part gathers information about the respondent's insight on employing KM in software testing, such as which software testing activity KM is more useful, test artifacts more appropriate for reuse, and what testing knowledge types are more important in software testing process. Questions were divided into multiple choice (with more than one option) and questions with answers that ranged from "very important" to "not important" on a scale based on the Likert Scale method [14]. The final average score represents the overall level of achievement or attitude toward a subject. Table 1 presents the Survey Questions (SQ)[1].

Table 1: Survey Questions

PART 1 - Participant's current profile
SQ1-SQ6. Name, Position (e.g., tester, test analyst, test designer, among others), Experience in this position (in years), Company Name (confidential), Company Size (micro, small, medium, large), Company Segment
PART 2 - Respondent's Perception
SQ7. In which software testing process activities does KM prove to be more useful?
SQ8. In which activities of testing planning does KM prove to be more useful?
SQ9. The test environment of a project is comprised of, among others, human, software and hardware resources that will be used to carry out the tests. Which of these features are most important to have available knowledge when defining the test environment?
SQ10. In which testing level do you consider KM more useful?
SQ11. Which knowledge type do you consider more important in the software testing process?
SQ12. Tacit knowledge can be made explicit, giving rise to explicit knowledge. In relation to the knowledge item types, indicate the degree of importance of generating explicit knowledge from tacit knowledge.
SQ13. With respect to test artifacts, indicate the degree of importance of knowledge reuse of these artifacts.
SQ14. Why KM is important for software testing (purposes)?

[1] *https://goo.gl/KHgzRK* - presents the complete questionnaire, with its questions and the answers format.

SQ15. What benefits does KM bring to software testing activities within your team?
SQ16. Would you consider applying KM in Software Engineering, especially in software testing process?

These questions were adapted from Souza et al. [7]. In [7], the questions were defined taking into account the results of a systematic mapping on KM in software testing [3] as well as in the conceptualization described by a software testing ontology, called ROoST: Reference Ontology on Software Testing [15].

The survey sample in [7] is a non-probabilistic sample, since the authors made the questionnaire available to groups of social networks interested in software testing and they also sent a direct e-mail to students, teachers and area researchers known to the authors. In total, 86 participants answered the survey [7]. The target audience in [7] did not provide a completely realistic view of the use of KM in software testing in practice in software development companies, since the participants are of different profiles, including, for example, undergraduate students. This fact became a motivation for our research. We applied the questionnaire in a specific target audience of professionals working with software testing in software development companies to gain their opinion into the application of KM in software testing.

Survey evaluation: before being made available, the questionnaire was validated by means of a pilot test. For this, a small sample was selected from the target audience to respond the survey. The questionnaire was also evaluated by an experienced researcher in Software Engineering and KM. The purpose of these assessments was to mitigate potential threats to validity (for example, identify possible difficulties that participants might have in understanding the questions) and correct any errors. After these assessments, the questions have been improved to make them clearer.

Survey application: The survey was made available directly to the 39 companies invited for a period of five months. In the end, 75 software testing professionals answered the questionnaire.

The last phase is the results analysis and presentation. This phase is presented in the next section.

3.1 Survey data analysis

As previously mentioned, 39 software companies participated in this research. Analyzing the first part of the questionnaire (*SQ1-SQ6*), the companies fell into the following categories: micro (9.33%), small (8%), medium (45.33%) and large (37.33%) companies. From the 39 companies, 75 employees answered the questionnaire, with an average of 2 respondents per company. Out of these 75 participants, 42.6% are testing analyst; 16% are testers; 12% are quality analysts; 8% work with agile development and apply Test Driven Development (TDD); and 21.3% perform other functions, such as quality assistant, test architect, test coordinator, and test manager. On average the participants have experience in software testing of 5.8 years with a standard deviation of 11.46 years.

Concerning the second part of the questionnaire, Figure 1 presents a comparative between the results obtained in [7] and the results obtained in the survey presented here, regarding the most appropriate testing process activities to apply KM (*SQ7*). In this question, the following testing activities were considered: (i) Test Planning; (ii) Test Case Design; (iii) Test Code; (iv) Test Execution; and (v) Test Result Analysis. For software companies "Test Planning" (74.66%) was considered the testing activity in which KM is most useful. This perception is a few different from the survey conducted by Souza et al. [7], where "Test Case Design" (98.8%) and "Test Planning" (96.5%) were considered the most appropriate testing activities to apply KM. An explanation for this is that our survey was conducted only with professionals and 42.66% of the participants were test analysts. One of the main activities of test analysts is to plan how tests will be conducted. In order to have a more precise view of what testing activities are pointed out by participants from different positions, we present the graph in Figure 2. Note that most testing analysts point to Test Planning as most appropriate to apply KM.

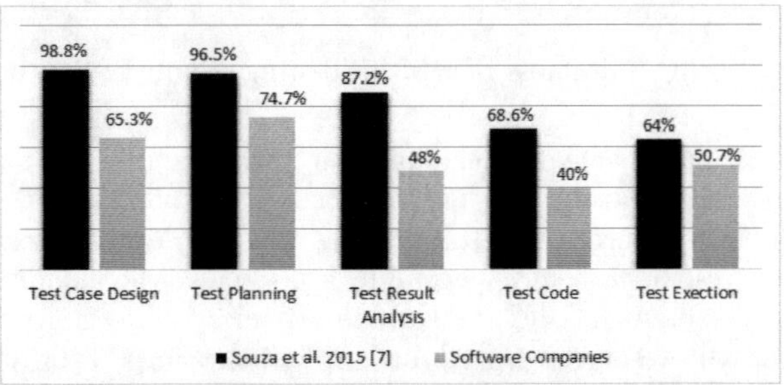

Fig. 1: Importance of KM to Software Testing Process Activities

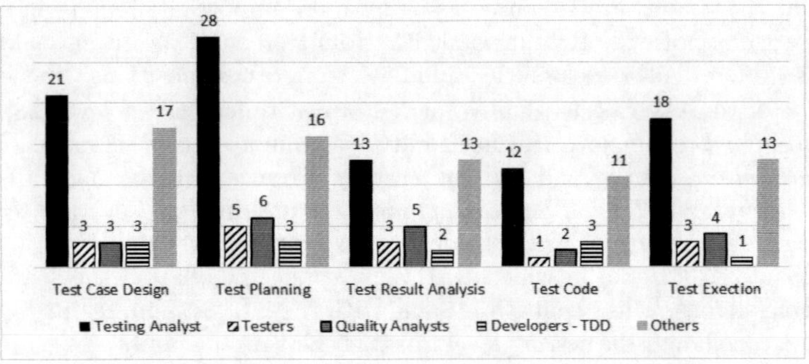

Fig. 2: Testing activities in relation to professionals

Regarding *SQ8*, we are interested in knowing in which activities of Test Planning does KM prove to be more important in the professionals insight, such as Testing Technique Selection, Test Environment Structuring, Test Plan Elaboration. As Figure 3 shows, "Test Plan Elaboration" (41.3%) was considered by companies that the testing planning sub-activity in which KM is most useful. Again, an explanation for this is that 42.66% of the participants were test analysts. On the other hand, in [7], "Testing Technique Selection" (41%) and "Test Environment Structuring" (36%) were considered the most appropriate testing planning sub-activities to apply KM.

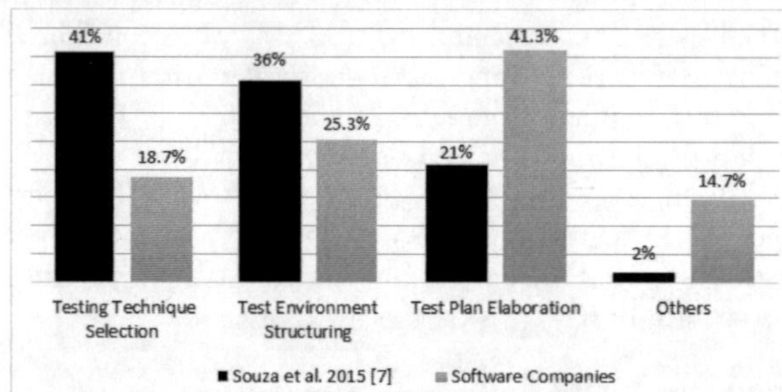

Fig. 3: Usefulness of KM in Testing Planning Sub-activities

The test environment considers both hardware and software, as well as the human resources involved in testing, that is, encompasses the entire structure where the test is performed [15]. With respect to *SQ9*, we asked about the most important resource to have available knowledge when defining the test environment. As Figure 4 shows, "Human resource" and "Software Resource" are considered the resources from which it is most important to have knowledge available at the time of setting the test environment in the perception of both the studies: software companies and Souza et al. [7]. However, there is a greater concern on the part of the companies in relation to software resources (50.6%). Based on these professionals' perspective, we analyzed the professionals profiles that chose Software Resource as being more important: 72% from testing analyst chose Software Resources; 66.6% from testers; 55.5% from quality analysts; 33.3% fom agile development; and 25% from others positions.

Software testing is usually carried out at different test levels [8]. The three most cited testing levels in the literature are made explicit, namely: *Unit Testing*, *Integration Testing* and *System Testing*. However, there may be others, such as *Regression Testing* and *Acceptance Testing*. In *SQ10*, we try to identify in which testing level KM is considered more useful. "System Testing" (73.3%) was considered the one in which KM more applies in relation the software testing professionals. This result is the same with the [7]. "System Testing" (48.8%) was also considered the testing level in which KM most applies.

Similarly to [7], *SQ11*, *SQ13*, and *SQ14* relate to types of knowledge items that are typically managed in the context of software testing and to the conver-

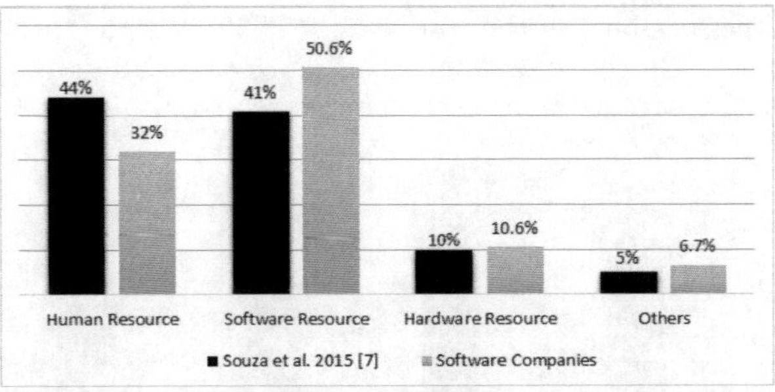

Fig. 4: Importance of KM to Testing Environment Definition.

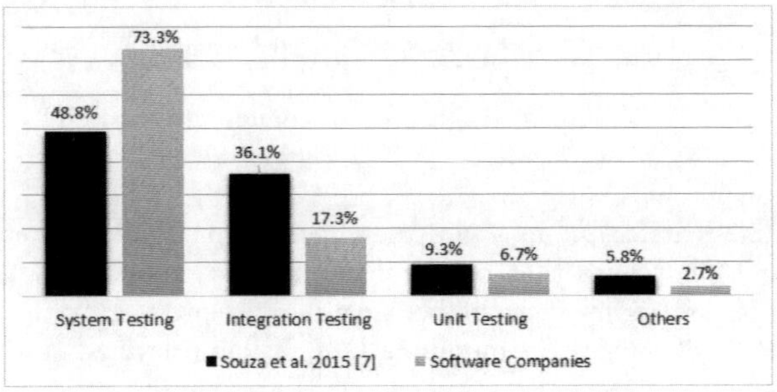

Fig. 5: Importance of KM to Test Levels.

sion of this knowledge. Souza et al. [7] reproduced the same aspects investigated in the systematic mapping about KM and software testing [3] to see if the survey participants confirm or deny the findings of the mapping. We have also conducted this analysis, however, as already mentioned, our target audience are just test professionals working in software development companies.

In *SQ11*, the aim is to highlight which knowledge type is most important to software companies. The participants considered explicit knowledge (74.66%) more important than tacit knowledge (25.33%). This is in line with the result obtained in [7]. However, according to one of the companies that participated in our research, the most important for a company is on how to transform the knowledge from tacit to explicit, that is, the explicit knowledge is more important, but as long as it is converted from tacit, so that it can be stored and reused. Another company also stressed that the conversion of tacit to explicit knowledge is more important, since it make the knowledge sharing easier. Furthermore, when new members are integrated into the team, learning becomes faster if knowledge is already stored.

Since the conversion of tacit knowledge to explicit is more important for companies, from *SQ12*, we try to identify which types of tacit knowledge items seem to be most important to be made explicit. As Figure 6 shows, "Communications between the members of the test team" (73.33%) is the most important to be made explicit. On the other hand, in [7], in general, all items of knowledge were considered important to become explicit.

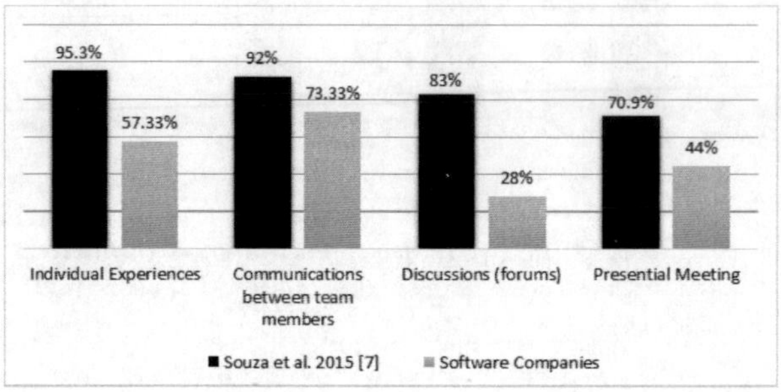

Fig. 6: Making tacit knowledge explicit.

Communication among team members, in particular, is strongly related to KM. Many companies that participated in the survey use agile methods. Agile methods prioritize interactions between people, promoting the face-to-face communication between team members [16]. In agile teams, the focus is the tacit knowledge and transforming this knowledge into explicit is considered a valuable asset for the organization. This statement corroborates the research results in questions *SQ11* and *SQ12*.

Regarding testing artifacts (*SQ13*), "Test Case" (70.66%) is considered the most reusable ones by the professionals, as shown in Figure 7. These results match what many researchers point out in test case reuse terms, as shown in systematic mapping conducted by [3]. [3] shows that the selection of regression test cases depends mainly on the experience of the testers and in order to provide a greater learning, it is important to have more detailed information on test cases.

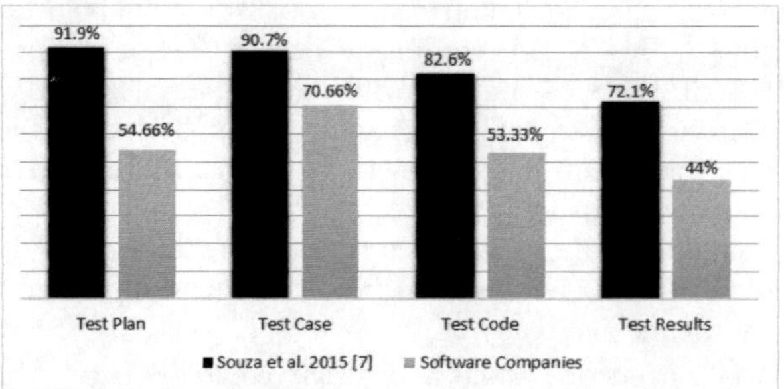

Fig. 7: Artifacts considered more appropriate for reuse.

Although in [7] the target audience is more generic, the results showed that "Test Plan" (91,9%) and "Test Case" (90,7%) are the most reusable artifacts. The authors also analyzed only the answers of professionals who work directly with software testing, and the result is that the most reusable artifacts are also "Test Cases" (94%).

In *SQ14* and *SQ15*, we intend to investigate how the purposes and benefits of applying KM in software testing were perceived as important by the software companies. For the companies, "Improving the quality of results" (68%) is the main purpose of applying KM in software testing, as presented in Figure 8. In [7], "Improving the quality of results" (28%) and also "Reducing costs, time and effort" (26%) were considered the main purposes.

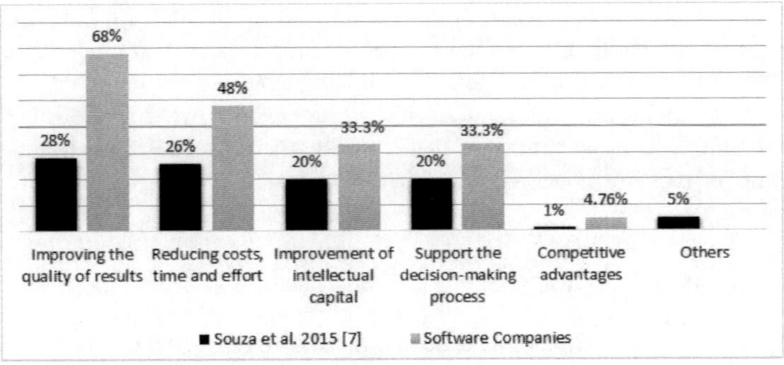

Fig. 8: Purpose of applying KM in Software Testing.

With respect to the benefits, "Increasing the testing process efficiency" (85.33%) and "Selecting and applying more suitable testing techniques" (61.33%) are considered by companies the main benefits of applying KM in software testing (see Figure 9). The same result was obtained in [7].

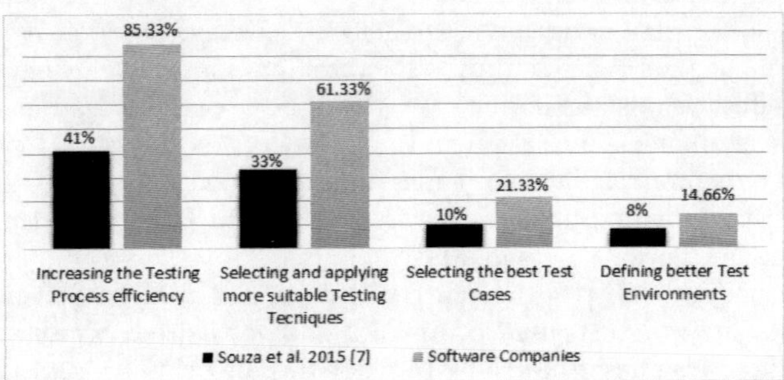

Fig. 9: Expected benefits of applying KM in Software Testing.

Applying KM in software companies is still a challenge, as there are still some barriers, such as KM systems are not appropriate yet, employees are normally reluctant to share their knowledge and increased workload [3]. In the survey question *SQ16*, we entirely leave to the participant's discretion to make any consideration about KM practices. Some comments corroborate exactly with the results of the systematic mapping conducted in [3] on KM in software testing.

According to the companies that participated in the research, applying 100% of the knowledge management process is not always possible. The employers need to meet aggressive deadlines and are pressed for results. This causes the team to be professionally overloaded, which leads to an emotional wear and dismay with the profession. Thus, processes that improve communication, reuse of information and working time become paramount for success.

Other comments emphasize that what is important is not only to implement KM practices, but also to be able to keep KM updated. The larger the company, greater is the challenge. The software testing area has gained prominence with the advent of several agile methods and frameworks. Agile practices can benefit organizations in the management and transfer of knowledge produced. According to participants, agile practices can become an important instrument to improve KM initiatives in software companies. However, companies still do not know how to reconcile these agile practices with KM practices to get better gains.

4 Related Work

As previously mentioned, the study conducted by Souza et al. [7], is a work directly related to ours, since we adapted and reapplied the survey conducted by Souza et al. [7]. However, we analyze only answers from software testing professionals working in Brazilian software development companies. A detailed results comparison of both studies is presented in the Section 3.1.

Tiwana [17] conducted a large-scale empirical study in 232 software development projects in 232 software companies. Three countries participated in the survey; Ireland, Russia, and India. The total number of responders was 54 from Ireland, 59 from Russia and 119 from India. As a result, Tiwana has identified that knowledge integration has a statistically significant effect on software development performance. With respect to software quality, knowledge integration lowers the density of warrant stage defects, lowers defect density throughout the development trajectory, improves software development efficiency, and increases design effectiveness. As in our case, this study conducted an empirical study in software companies in relation to the knowledge generated. However, our study focused only on Brazilian companies and in the context of software testing. Even so, regarding the findings on software testing and KM, both studies converge to the same perceptions about KM benefits.

In Aurum et al. [18], the current practice of KM in Software Engineering processes in two Australian companies is investigated. Similarly to our study, the authors also describes the KM activities and KM process used in Software Engineering practice. A total of 12 people were interviewed and answered a questionnaire in order to capture qualitative and quantitative data about aspects of

KM practices in four projects. One of the main findings in this study is that while KM was considered to be important, the tools, techniques and methodologies currently employed for software development were inadequate to address effective management of knowledge in these organizations; a uniform model of the KM process did not exist; and it is still necessary to encourage the sharing of tactical and explicit knowledge.

In a more recent study [19], Kuusinen et al. presents the results of a survey with 81 responses on organizational knowledge sharing in a multinational agile company. The survey concentrates on knowledge sharing practices, ease of knowledge sharing and motivation for knowledge sharing. Results show that using agile practices improves ease of knowledge sharing within teams. This confirms findings from our survey. In our survey, in *SQ16*, some participants mentioned the agile practices as facilitators for knowledge transfer. In fact, KM has been used to explain the distinctiveness of the agile approach.

5 Conclusions

In this paper, we reported on the results from an analysis related to the software testing professionals perception on the use of KM initiatives in software engineering companies. For this, we adapted and reapplied the survey conducted by Souza et al. [7]. From the survey results, we drew the following main conclusions: (i) Test Planning is considered the most important activity for using KM initiatives; (ii) Communications between the members of the test team is the type of tacit knowledge item most important to be made explicit; and (iii) Test Case is an artifacts that has received more attention by companies in terms of reuse. A strategic planning and the reusing existing test cases has a potential to significantly reduce software development costs and time.

One initial threat to internal validity in this work could be poor instrumentation, which could affect understanding the questions. For this reason, a pilot study was conducted as well as a survey validation by a KM and software testing researcher, so problems could be identified and corrected. Based on these threat, we intend to conduct interviews in software companies and compare the results. A second threat of this research concerns the sample size and representativeness. The sample had 75 valid answers among 39 software companies and a large concentration in Brazil's south and southeast regions, which affect both conclusion and external validity. The results cannot be generalized to a nationwide and world scale. Therefore, we intend to replicate this survey in other regions of Brazil and also in an international context.

A richer investigation with better mechanisms to perception about KM in software companies forms part of future work. We also intend to plan to complement our research with other empirical methods, for example, case studies based on real project data.

Acknowledgment

The authors would like to acknowledge the experts that agree to answer the survey.

References

1. Bjørnson, F.O., Dingsøyr, T.: Knowledge management in software engineering: A systematic review of studied concepts findings and research methods used. Information and Software Technology **11**(11) (2008) 1055–1068
2. Levy, M., Hazzan, O.: Knowledge management in practice: The case of agile software development. In: ICSE Workshop on Cooperative and Human Aspects on Software Engineering. (2009) 60–65
3. Souza, E.F., Falbo, R.A., Vijaykumar, N.L.: Knowledge management initiatives in software testing: A mapping study. Information and Software Technology **57** (2015) 378–391
4. Vasanthapriyan, S., Tian, J., Xiang, J.: A survey on knowledge management in software engineering. In: IEEE International Conference on Software Quality, Reliability and Security - Companion. (2015) 237–244
5. O'Leary, D., R., S.: Knowledge management: an interdisciplinary approach. Intell. Syst. **16**(1) (2001) 24–25
6. Itkonen, J., Mantyla, M., Lassenius, C.: The role of the tester's knowledge in exploratory software testing. IEEE Trans. Software Engineering (2013) 707–724
7. Souza, E.F., Falbo, R.A., Vijaykumar, N.L.: Using the findings of a mapping study to conduct a research project: a case in knowledge management in software testing. In: 41st Euromicro Conference on Software Engineering and Advanced Applications. (2015) 208–215
8. Abran, A., Bourque, P., Dupuis, J.R., Moore, W.: Guide to the software engineering body of knowledge - swebok. Joint technical report, A project of the IEEE Computer Society Professional Practices Committee (2004)
9. Spender, J.C.: Making knowledge the basis of a dynamic theory of the ïňĄrm. Strategic Management Journal **17** (1996) 45–62
10. Markkula, M.: Knowledge management in software engineering projects. In: 11th International Conference on Software Engineering and Knowledge Engineering. (1999) 20–27
11. Nonaka, I., Takeuchi, H.: The knowledge-creating company. 1 edn. Oxford University Press, Oxford, USA (1997)
12. Ciolkowski, M., Laitenberger, O., Vegas, S., Biffl, S.: Practical experiences in the design and conduct of surveys in empirical software engineering. Lecture Notes in Computer Science **2765** (2003) 104–128
13. Kitchenham, B., P.S.L.: Guide to Advanced Empirical Software Engineering. Personal Opinion Surveys. Chapter 3. Springer-Verlag London (2008)
14. Likert, R.: A technique for the measurement of attitudes. Archives of Psychologyy **22**(140) (2010) 1–55
15. Souza, E.F., Falbo, R.A., Vijaykumar, N.L.: ROoST: Reference Ontology on Software Testing. Applied Ontology **12**(1) (2017) 59–90
16. Crispin, L., Gregory, J.: Agile testing:a practical guide for testers and agile teams. Pearson Education, Boston, MA (2009)
17. Tiwana, A.: An empirical study of the effect of knowledge integration on software development performance. Information and Software Technology (2004)
18. Aurum, A., Daneshgar, F., Ward, J.: Investigating Knowledge Management practices in software development organisations - An Australian experience. Information and Software Technology **50** (2008) 511–533
19. Kuusinen, K., Gregory, P., Sharp, H., Barroca, H., Taylor, K., Wood, L.: Knowledge sharing in a large agile organisation: A survey study. In: International Conference on Agile Software Development. (2017) 135–150

Knowledge Management in Agile Testing Teams: a Survey

Glauco Antonio Ruiz[1,3], Patrick Rodrigo da Silva[1], Érica Ferreira de Souza[1], Nandamudi L. Vijaykumar[2], Katia Romero Felizardo[1], Giovani Volnei Meinerz[1]

Department of Computer, Federal Technological University of Paraná – UTFPR[1]
Cornélio Procópio/PR - Brazil
glauco.ruiz@unoeste.br,patricksap@hotmail.com,{ericasouza, katiascannavino,giovanimeinerz}@utfpr.edu.br
Lab. of Comp. and Applied Math., National Institute for Space Research – INPE[2]
São José dos Campos/SP - Brazil
vijay.nl@inpe.br
Department of Computer, University of Western São Paulo - UNOESTE[3]
Presidente Prudente/SP - Brazil

Abstract. Context: Software testing activities are considered as knowledge intensive and therefore Knowledge Management (KM) principles and techniques can be applied to efficiently manage the knowledge generated. In agile development, agile testing practices can benefit the companies in terms of KM, specially in the knowledge sharing. However, there is still little empirical knowledge about the state of practice as well as contemporary problems with respect to agile testing and KM. **Objective:** This study aims to understand how knowledge is shared in Brazilian companies that incorporated agile methodology. **Method:** In order to create an empirical basis on the aspects of agile testing and KM, a survey was conducted with professionals working with agile tests. The survey received 150 replies. **Results:** The results with more highlight are: knowledge is, in fact, shared into the team (89.3%), informal communication is most used (52%), tools are used to share knowledge, the future decisions are based on past problems (88%) and the success stories are stored by team (70.9%). **Conclusion:** Knowledge is recognized as extremely important in any area. Its extraction and publication are of fundamental importance, as can be proven in this research. Agile practices support companies to make use of KM principles.

1 Introduction

In the last years, the agile methods have been received considerable appreciation. The agile developers claim that knowledge sharing is one of the solutions to problems and challenges of software development today [1]. Advances in technology and the emergence of increasingly complex and critical applications require using better strategies, as the software testing, in order to achieve high quality and reliability of software products. In agile development, testing practices are considerably different than in traditional processes. First, agile development recognizes that testing is not a separate phase, but an integral part of software development. Agile is iterative and incremental, so this means that testers test each increment of coding as soon as it is finished. Programmers never get ahead of the testers. In an agile project, there is a quick testing feedback. The agile tester should look for unique ways to facilitate communication in the team [2].

Regardless of the approach, traditional or agile development, software testing activities are considered a knowledge intensive process and, therefore Knowledge Management (KM) principles and techniques can be applied to efficiently manage the knowledge generated. During software testing, a significant amount of information and knowledge are generated becoming important to provide support for tasks of acquiring, processing, analyzing and disseminating testing knowledge for reuse. In this context, testing knowledge should be captured and represented in an affordable and manageable way, and therefore, could make use of principles of KM [3].

The incorporation of KM in software testing has been deployed aiming knowledge items reuse (e.g., lessons learned or test cases) to improve the enactment of software processes [3, 4]. Since several studies show that agile practices and KM principles have an important connection [1], we want to understand this relation in the agile testing activities, mainly with respect to knowledge sharing. However, there is still little empirical knowledge about the state of the practice as well as contemporary problems with respect to agile testing and knowledge sharing.

A clear understanding of the practice state of agile teams and its problems would be needed to steer future research. Therefore, this work has an objective to understand how knowledge is shared in Brazilian companies that incorporated agile methodology in software testing teams. Furthermore, in this research, we try to understand the practices, tools and factors that assist in the storage and share of knowledge in the agile test domain. In order to achieve the proposed objective, a survey was conducted with employees from different companies working with agile tests. The survey received 150 replies in order to provide a deep understanding of their answers. We believe that this study should be interested to industry practitioners as well as academics whose interests are software testing from KM perspective, since the discussion is around how the knowledge is shared, the communication type most used in the team, the tools used to provide knowledge storageand sharing, among other aspects.

The remainder of this paper is structured as follows. Section 2 presents a brief overview of KM and agile testing, as well as related research. Section 3 presents the methods and procedures used to conduct the research. Section 4 shows the results and discussions with respect to survey. Section 5 presents a general discussion to highlight some points of our research. Finally, Section 6 presents conclusions, the potential threats to the study validity and future directions for this research.

2 Background

In this section, the main concepts of this study and related works are discussed briefly.

2.1 Knowledge Management

The main goal of KM is to promote knowledge storage and sharing, as well as the emergence of new knowledge [5]. KM formally manages knowledge resources in order to facilitate access and reuse. KM can be viewed as the development and leveraging of organizational knowledge to increase organization's competitive advantage [6]. In general, KM entails formally managing the increase of knowledge in organizations, in order to facilitate access and reuse of this knowledge, typically by using more efficacious information systems or Knowledge Management Systems (KMS) [7].

There are two main types of knowledge [8]: tacit and explicit. Tacit knowledge typically remains only in people's minds involving intangible factors such as beliefs, perspectives, values and intuition. Tacit knowledge covers knowledge that is unarticulated and associated to the senses, movement skills, physical experiences, intuition, or implicit rules of thumb. On the other hand, explicit knowledge can be documented, and, thus can be shared by several individuals.With respect to KM in software development, the main difference between agile and traditional methods, is the traditional method acts mainly on managing explicit knowledge, while the agile methods, primarily rely on managing tacit knowledge [9].

The concept of "knowledge conversion" explains how tacit and explicit knowledge interact along a continuum [10, 8]. According to Nonaka [8], the creation of knowledge can be considered as a continuous and dynamic interaction between tacit and explicit knowledge. This iteration can occur by four different modes of knowledge conversion: Socialization (transmission of tacit knowledge from one individual to another); Externalization (transformation of tacit knowledge into explicit knowledge through the symbolic representation); Combination (combining different sets of explicit knowledge to generate new explicit knowledge); and Internalization (incorporation of explicit knowledge to tacit knowledge).

Organizational knowledge creation aims at making knowledge created by individuals available and amplifies it as well as materializes and connects it to an organization's knowledge system [10]. Bukowitz and Williams [11] conclude that KM is the process by which the organization generates wealth from its knowledge or intellectual capital. Simply put, KM is the process through which organizations generate value from their intellectual assets (tacit and explicit knowledge). Most often, generating value from such assets involves sharing them among employees, departments and even with other companies in an effort to devise best practices.

In the context of software testing, KM has recently been heavily investigated and new approaches to managing software test knowledge have been proposed [3, 4]. KM can be used to capture knowledge generated during software testing activities in order to share and consequently improve the software development processes. In this work, we want to understand the relationship between KM and software testing in the context of agile development, mainly in relation to knowledge sharing.

2.2 Agile Testing

In the context of Agile Software Development (ASD), software testing is carried out iteratively during the entire development process instead of only during a closed phase in the end. In agile projects, testers do more than just perform tasks of testing. Agile testing involves all members of a cross-functional agile team, with special expertise contributed by testers, to ensure delivering the business value desired by the customer at frequent intervals, working at a sustainable pace [2].

Agile approach describes the testers as professionals who embrace change, collaborate well with both technical and business people, in special the customer, and understand the concepts of using tests to document requirements and drive development. In addition, agile testers know how to collaborate with team. This professional is ready to gather and share information on project progress to everyone [2].

Agile values and principles promote a focus on the people involved in a project and how they interact and communicate. Crispin and Gregory [2] discuss the following principles as being important for an agile tester: provide continuous feedback, deliver value to the customer, enable face-to-face communication, have courage, keep it simple, practice continuous improvement, respond to change, self-organize, focus on people and enjoy. In particular, the communication principle is strongly related to KM, and in agile teams the focus is the tacit knowledge.

On the practices used by agile teams in software testing, the agile programmers use Test-Driven Development (TDD) to write the testing before writing the code. TDD strategy helps in better understanding the system under development and when teams practice TDD, they minimize the number of bugs that could appear later on. Most unit-level bugs are prevented by writing the test before the code. The testers test each increment of coding as soon as it is finished in an iterative and incremental form [2]. Another practice used in the context of agile tests is Acceptance Test Driven Development (ATDD). ATDD is a development methodology based on communication among the business customers, the developers, and the testers. Instead of creating code-focused tests from the developer's perspective (which is the focus of TDD), ATDD advocates that the test be an acceptance test with a direct view of the business from a user's point of view [12].

2.3 Related Work

In the last years, the research in KM and ASD has drawn lot of attention in both industrial and academia. Some of this research is presented below.

In [13], Kuusinen et al. present the results of a survey with 81 responses on organizational knowledge sharing in a multinational agile company. The survey focuses on knowledge sharing practices, ease of knowledge sharing and motivation for knowledge sharing. Some results found by Kuusinen et al. are: knowledge sharing with team members is easier than with customers; using agile practices improves ease of knowledge sharing within teams but not with customers or colleagues; sharing knowledge with colleagues is most often done informally whereas with customers the most common means is in meetings; respondents cited more motivators for sharing with team members than with company colleagues or customers; the regression analysis shows that using agile techniques improves ease of knowledge sharing within agile teams but not with company colleagues or with customer; and knowledge sharing is easier if face-to-face and informal contact is used, whereas one-way presentations decrease the perceived ease of knowledge sharing. Similarly to Kuusinen et al., we also deal with aspects of knowledge sharing, but in agile test teams.

In Andriyani [14], specific knowledge types (i.e. product, project and process knowledge) were investigated in agile practices day to day. KM strategies applied by agile teams and actual knowledge involved in the meetings also were investigated. A case study was conducted using data collected from interviews of sixteen software practitioners from four agile teams and observations of their retrospective meetings. The study showed that identifying and discussing obstacles, discussing feelings, analyzing previous action points, identifying background reasons, identifying future action points and generating a plan are important aspects involved in a retrospective meeting, which is useful for agile team reflection. In our study, we also have the intention of identifying KM and everyday agile practice in software companies. However, our scope is limited to agile testing domain.

In relation to software testing domain, Souza et al. (a) [3] presented a systematic mapping on KM initiatives in software testing, in order to identify the state of the art in the area as well as the future research. Aspects such as purpose, types of knowledge, technologies and research type were investigated. As main results, the mapping study presented that reuse of test cases is the perspective that has received more attention. From the KM point of view, most of the studies discuss aspects related to providing automated support for managing testing knowledge by means of a KM system. Moreover, as a main conclusion, the results show that KM is pointed out as an important strategy for increasing test effectiveness, as well as for improving the selection and application of suited techniques, methods and test cases. Out of the 15 studies returned in the mapping conducted by Souza et al., only one mention agile development. In this study returned in the mapping, Xu-Xiang and Wen-Ning [15], present a PDCA-based testing improvement framework based on the analysis of agile process, benchmarking process and KM.

Finally, Souza et al. (b) [4] presented a survey in order to identify the main knowledge items to be shared and reused in software testing. The purpose of the survey was to identify which is the most appropriate scenario in the software testing domain, from the point of view of testing stakeholders, for starting a KM initiative. From the survey results, Souza et al. presented the following conclusions: (i) test cases and test plans are considered the most useful artifacts to be reused; and (ii) explicit knowledge was considered more important than tacit knowledge. In a similar way this study approached, we also conducted a survey on KM and software testing. However, our focus was on understanding how Brazilian companies are using KM practices in order to share the knowledge in agile testing team.

3 Research Planning

Survey is an empirical study method to provide a description of a specific population during the process of collecting data from questions [16]. A survey is carried out to identify the opinion of a specific population. We conducted the survey following the phases proposed by Kitchenham and Pfleeger [16]: (i) research objective definition; (ii) target audience identification that will respond to the survey; (iii) sampling planning, that is, how the questionnaire will be applied; (iv) survey design (definition of questionnaire type, questions and structure); (v) survey application; and (vi) results analysis and presentation. The following are the main survey characteristics conducted in this work:

Research objective: the main objective of this survey is to understand how Brazilian companies that incorporated agile methodology are using KM practices in order to share the knowledge in agile testing team.

Target audience: professionals who work with software testing in environments that use agile development process.

Sampling: groups interested in ASD were invited to answer the survey in the following ways: (i) personal e-mails were sent to ASD professionals and the participants were asked to share the survey with their acquaintances; and (ii) a request was sent to *LinkedIn*[1] network focusing in ASD professionals. *LinkedIn* is considered the world's largest professional network on the Internet.

Survey project: Fifteen questions were created and divided in four parts. The first part of the survey was composed of questions in order to identify the participants' profile. The second part gathers information about the testing team's profile. The third part identifies how the transformation and sharing of test knowledge occurs within the company in which the survey participants works. Finally, the fourth part is composed of one discursive question to complement the other parts. The format for answering the questions were open and closed questions. All questions used for this study are summarized in Table 1. The complete survey can be seen through the link *https://goo.gl/aJHXHt* (in Portuguese).

Is important to note that this study is part of a master's research project. This project involves the use of KM in agile development. Several secondary studies (systematic reviews or systematic mapping) have been considered as the basis for this project, for example, the reviews conducted in [17] and [18]. The research questions generated to conduct our survey in agile testing teams were based on the main findings of these secondary studies.

---

[1] http://www.linkedin.com/

Table 1: Survey Questions

PART 1 - Participant's current profile
1. Education level: (high school, specialization, undergraduate, MSc, PhD)
2. Job title (e.g., tester, test analyst, test designer, among others)
3. Time experience (in years)
4. Knowledge level in agile development (basic, intermediate and advanced)
5. Knowledge level in software testing (basic, intermediate and advanced)
PART 2 - Test team's current profile
6. Agile method used (XP, Scrum, others)
7. Test team size
8. Frequency of team meetings (Daily, weekly, fortnightly, monthly, never)
PART 3 - Knowledge sharing
9. Do you have an overview of what the other team members are doing?
10. Do team members transfer the acquired knowledge?
11. How is knowledge transferred within the team?
12. What are the tools used to record testing information?
13. Are success stories recorded?
14. Are future decisions made based on past problems?
PART 4 - General question
15. In your opinion, what could be done to improve KM in software testing in your team?

Survey application: Before making it available on the Web, the survey was validated by means of a pilot test. For this, a small sample was selected from the target audience to answer the survey. The questionnaire was also evaluated by one experienced researcher in software engineering and KM. The goal of this validations was to mitigate potential threats to validity (e.g., identifying possible difficulties users could have) and correcting eventual mistakes. After these evaluations, questions were improved to make them clearer. The survey was available for answers during April and May 2017. At the end, 150 ASD professionals answered our survey.

4 Research Outcomes

In the following, we describe the main outcomes, according to the parties highlighted in Table 1.

4.1 PART 1 - Participant's current profile

The answers to questions of Part 1 were used to assure that respondents were representative of the population study. Out of 150 survey participants, 91 (60.7%) are undergraduate, 48 (32.0%) specialization, 7 (4.7%) masters and 4 (2.7%) have selected others. In relation to job title, 102 (68.0%) work as test analyst, 17 (11.3%) are managers, 5 (3.3%) are testers, 15 (10.0%) are system analysts, 7

(4.7%) are quality analysts and 4 (2.7%) said that they work in other functions, such as consultants, for example. Participants have an average of 5.4 years of experience in the positions they occupy. However, this aspect changes when we question the experience time with agile development which results in 2.3 years.

From the analysis made in relation to the participant's current profile in Part 1, 8 (5.3%) participants mentioned to have a basic level of knowledge regarding agile development, 113 (75.3%) answered to possess an intermediate knowledge and 29 (19.3%) participants mentioned advanced knowledge in agile development. Regarding the knowledge level in software testing, 2 (1.3%) participants answered to have a basic level, 101 (67.3%) intermediate knowledge and 47 (31.3%) advanced knowledge in software testing.

4.2 PART 2 - Test team's current profile

In survey Part 2, we analyzed the test team's current profile. Among the existing agile development methods, Scrum is the most adopted by the participants (Question 6). Scrum method was mentioned by 137 (91.3%) participants as a method adopted in the company in which they work. 8.7% of participants mentioned other methods, such as XP, Kanban and Scrumban. Regarding the test team size (Question 7), 22 (14.7%) participants mentioned working alone, that is, they apply practices related to agile testing. 54 (36%) work in a team with three members. 23 (15.3%) work in a team consisting of 5 members and 51 (34%) responders work on test teams composed of more than 5 members.

In order to know the level of communication among test team members through meetings (face-to-face), we asked how often these meetings are held. Figure 1 presents the results of this question. Most participants mentioned that they hold meetings daily (53%). However, while agile guidelines support the communication efficiency when conducted face-to-face, 17 (11%) mentioned that they never held meetings. We have decided to identify whether these 17 respondents are related to responders who work alone in Question 7. 9 of them responded that they worked alone, therefore, it makes sense that there are no team meetings. However, there are still 8 responders who are part of a team (teams with 3 and 5 members) and still responded that they never had formal meetings. This is, in fact, a result of concern, since these 9 people do not follow one of the main agile principles: face-to-face conversation. The face-to-face conversation is the most efficient and effective method of conveying information within a development team. However, it is worth pointing out that our question is in relation to face-to-face meetings, and this does not mean that these 9 people do not hold informal meetings.

4.3 PART 3 - Knowledge sharing

Part 3 of this survey is directly related to KM. From the questions of this part it was possible to identify how actions related to the knowledge sharing among agile test teams occur in practice. First, we tried to identify whether the participant was aware of what the other test team members were working on. With respect

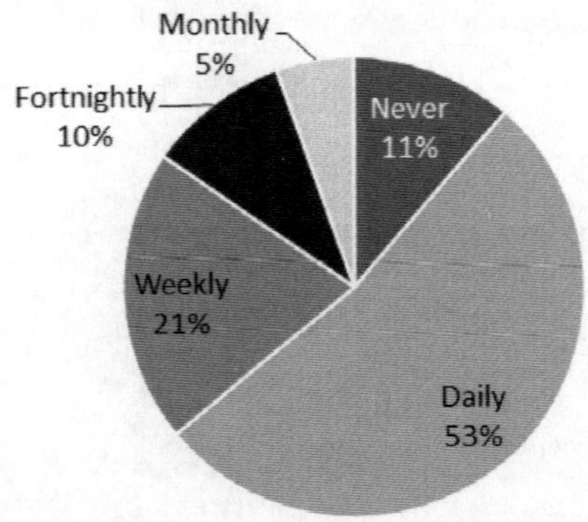

Fig. 1. Frequency that occurs in team meetings

to Question 9, 88.7% of participants responded that they have knowledge about what everyone on the test team is doing. This is a valuable result, since the agile tester is part of a self-organizing agile team and prioritize the communication. The communication and interaction between team members reduces the time spent on non-oral communication [2, 19].

Regarding Question 10, we asked if all team members shared the knowledge they gained. 134 (89.3%) respondents said yes and 16 (10.7%) responded that team members do not pass on knowledge to be shared. Although it seems to be a small number, 16 participants confirmed that team members do not share their knowledge. In the study conducted by Souza et al. (a) [3] about KM and traditional software testing, the authors concluded that employees are normally reluctant to share their knowledge, that is, the experiences are grasped by only a few people and not become public knowledge. This fact disables knowledge transfer in testing.

In relation to how knowledge can be shared, in Question 11 we tried to identify which approaches or tools are used for this purpose. Figure 2 shows the approaches and tools mentioned by the participants. Most of them mentioned approaches such as: informal communication (52%), formal meetings (17%) and systems for management and defect tracking (17%). No team works well without communication (formal or informal) to share experience or lessons learned [3]. This result corroborates the study conducted by Kuusinen et al. [13] which showed in their survey that the most common techniques for knowledge sharing in general were informally, in meetings, and by email. Today, when so many teams are distributed in multiple geographical locations, communication is even more vital and more of a challenge. The agile tester should look for unique ways to facilitate communication.

Systems for management and defect tracking that were mentioned are important to manage the life cycle of a defect. However, many agile practitioners say that it is not necessary to do this anymore, since it is possible to track defects based on user cards or some other simple mechanism proposed by ASD practices

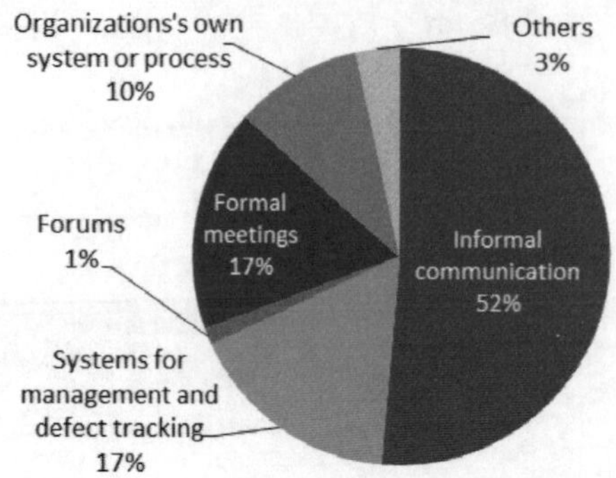

Fig. 2. Approaches and tools used to share knowledge

On the other hand, 17% of practitioners said there were reasons to prefer using a tool to record defects and track how they were fixed. One of the main reasons for preferring tools for this purpose is to create a knowledge base. Systems for management and defect tracking can be used to transfer and share information, turning it into a knowledge base. The information in knowledge base can be used for several purposes, such as to track defect rates in order to generate metrics or traceability to link defects to test cases.

Crispin and Gregory [2] describe that systems for management and defect tracking certainly do not promote communication between programmers and testers, and that ASD provides other practices and principles that help reducing the need for systems for management and defect tracking. Although these systems have not been created for this purpose, the number of participants who mentioned this type of system was considerable. So, from the pilot test results of the survey, we decided to add a new question about which tools are used to record information about the test management and defect tracking (Question 12). A variety of tools were mentioned. Most participants mentioned using tools such as Mantis, TestLink and Jira. The list of tools, purpose of each one and number of participants who mentioned the tool are presented in Table 2. It is worth mentioning that some respondents used more than one tool.

One of KM's main principles is to store knowledge for reuse, especially successful actions. According to Souza et al. (a) [3], KM entails formally managing knowledge resources in order to facilitate access and reuse of knowledge. Based on this context, in Question 13, we asked if success stories are recorded. 105 (70.9%) of respondents said yes in recording success stories. Many of them mentioned that success stories are often presented at meetings and are often recorded in some of the tools presented in Table 2 or informal notes. In a new agile team, for instance, past experiences from user stories will also affect the success of company. Past experiences can be recorded for reuse. This statement is directly related to our survey in Question 14. 132 (88%) participants said that future decisions are made based on past problems.

Table 2: Systems for management and defect tracking

Tools	Purpose	Amount
Jira Software	Bug Tracker	44
TestLink	Test Management	33
Mantis	Bug Tracker	29
Rational Quality Manager (RQM)	Test Management	15
HP Application Lifecycle Management (HP ALM)	Test and Defect Management	10
Team Foundation Server (TFS)	Test Management	9

4.4 PART 4 - General question

Finally, in the last part we composed a single long question, to be answered in writing a text and not a multiple choice, in order to externalize the participants opinion about what could be done to improve KM of software testing in their team. Many participants mentioned that they did not have knowledge about KM as a research area, but they knew the importance of working with the knowledge generated in the test teams. The following are some of the most mentioned actions by the participants to improve KM in software testing: (i) necessity to acquire the culture of sharing information; (ii) maintain traceability of information, such as lessons learned and suggestions for improvement; (iii) create an internal Wiki with the main project evidence; (iv) offer training on how to manage knowledge generated in the company; (v) create a knowledge base aimed at storing good practices and lessons learned; and (vi) create a process for sharing and reusing information about software testing.

5 Discussion

Software has become more and more widespread and indispensable in critical and complex application domains, making testing knowledge increasingly important. Sharing knowledge and experience can provide several benefits. Agile practices can benefit organizations in terms of KM, mainly in the management and transfer of knowledge produced. Some respondents mentioned the importance of KM and suggested that the adoption of practices and methodologies for tasks of acquiring, processing, analyzing and disseminating testing knowledge for reuse could help in the acceptance of this practice so that the knowledge was not only among the people who participate in the meetings, but also enable others to explore this knowledge in the future.

From conducting this survey, we realize that in practice many of the values advocated by the ASD community have helped testing teams to improve work with knowledge, such as: enable communication, especially face-to-face from daily meetings; depend on a self-organizing team that knows what each one is doing; share knowledge; store knowledge; give value to past experiences and information reuse. However, we still found results that were negative drawing attention. For example, some participants said they did not hold meetings and others said that there were team members who were reluctant to transfer knowledge.

Although it is not considered an agile practice by some authors [2], it is still widely common employing management test and defect tracking tools. It was possible to verify by the survey that the use of a subject tracking system is very important to software project. These tools maintain knowledge bases to keep track of not only the defect but also the priorities, severities, and status, and to see to whom they are assigned.

Several survey participants, knowledgeable of agile practices, emphasized the importance of values such as communication, self-organizing teams and knowledge sharing. This confirms findings from Kuusinen et al. [13], that provide evidence to support claims that knowledge sharing is easier within agile teams. Communication and knowledge sharing, in particular, are of the most important principles of KM [3]. Communication is directly related to tacit knowledge transfer. According to Nonaka and Takeuchi [8], tacit knowledge really is hard to be acquired, and it requires good strategies to acquire and process this knowledge; however, it is much more valuable.

Communication and dialog allow the organization to have a more complete world-view, and to appreciate a richer sense of the existing realities in the organization as well as the external environment, bringing the unknown to the surface [20]. In the survey it was possible to perceive that there is reluctance for a dialog and transmit knowledge. The participants mentioned that they try to minimize this problem with constant meetings, but they lack the knowledge of dealing with KM processes to improve this problem.

Based on the results, it is noticeable that agile testing team, in fact, uses in practice the values defended by agile methodologies, although some traditional practices are still recognized by them as important, for example, the use of defect tracking systems. Furthermore, the participants in the survey recognize that agile practices can support companies to make use of KM principles.

6 Conclusion

In this paper, we showed how knowledge is shared in Brazilian companies that incorporated agile methodology in testing teams. In order to attain this objective, an empirical analysis was conducted. The method used was a survey that received 150 answers.

From the analysis of the survey' answers, the aspects most mentioned by participants were: knowledge is shared into the team (89.3%), informal communication is most used (52%), tools are used to share knowledge (e.g. Jira, TestLink, Mantis), future decisions are based on past problems (88%) and success stories are stored (70.9%). The participants of this survey acknowledge the importance that agile practices can bring to the company in relation to KM. However, it is still necessary to promote a culture so that these practices are given a major importance within companies.

The results of this survey can be used by researchers and professionals in the field in order to develop studies and solutions on the addressed issues. Evaluating the practices effectiveness used for KM mentioned in the research responses can point out to results that promote, for example, an adaptation of existing agile methods to highlight where to stress or prioritize the application of KM in companies.

6.1 Threats to Validity

One threat to validity in this work could be poor instrumentation, which could affect subjects' understanding of concepts and questions. For this reason, a pilot study was performed as well as a survey validation by a KM researcher, so any problem could be identified and corrected before the survey was opened for answers.

Concerning survey project validity, the questions were created based in systematic literature reviews about KM in agile software projects, such as the reviews conducted by [17] and [18]. In additional, one open text question was included to allow triangulating the results.

The agile philosophy has a very fuzzy notion. No company faithfully follows all the agile principles. It is natural that customizations are made according to the profile of each organization, and this can influence the participant responses. Although our goal in the survey is broader in the sense of knowing the ways of knowledge sharing, it is still important to deepen this research in order to better understand if the companies and/or project characteristics could influence the research responses. Thus, as future work we intend to conduct interviews in companies to obtain a better understanding of the practices, techniques and approaches used by a agile testing team. We intend to apply interviews in the companies because we believe that this can enrich even more the results obtained in the research as a whole and evidence us important facts that in a research maybe not arise.

Acknowledgments

The authors would like to acknowledge agile testing professionals that agreed to answer the survey.

References

1. B., C., de la Barra C.L., R., S., M., D., E., M.: The role of knowledge management in agile software development. In: Communications in Computer and Information Science. Volume 373. (2013) 17–21
2. Crispin, L., Gregory, J.: Agile testing: a practical guide for testers and agile teams. Pearson Education, Boston, MA (2009)
3. Souza, E.F., Falbo, R.A., Vijaykumar, N.L.: Knowledge management initiatives in software testing: A mapping study. Information and Software Technology **57** (2015) 378–391

4. Souza, E.F., Falbo, R.A., Vijaykumar, N.L.: Using lessons learned from mapping study to conduct a research project on knowledge management in software testing. In: 41st Euromicro Conference on Software Engineering and Advanced Applications (SEAA), Madeira, Portugual (2015) 208–215
5. O'Leary, D., Studer, R.: Knowledge management: an interdisciplinary approach. IEEE Intelligent Systems **16, No. 1** (2001)
6. Zack, M., Serino, M.: Knowledge management and collaboration technologies, Butterworth, Knowledge, Groupware and the Internet (2000) 303–315
7. Herrera, R.J.G., Martin-Bautista, M.J.: A novel process-based KMS success framework empowered by ontology learning technology. Engineering Applications of Artificial Intelligence **45** (2015) 295–312
8. Nonaka, I., Takeuchi, H.: The knowledge-creating company. 1 edn. Oxford University Press, Oxford, USA (1997)
9. Bjørnson, F.O., Dingsøyr, T.: Knowledge management in software engineering: A systematic review of studied concepts, findings and research methods used. Information and Software Technology **50** (2008) 1055–1068
10. Nonaka, I., Krogh, G.: Tacit knowledge and knowledge conversion: controversy and advancement in organizational knowledge creation theory. Organization Science **30** (2009) 635–652
11. Bukowitz, W., Williams, R.L.: The knowledge management fieldbook. Financial Times Prentice Hall, Great Britain (1999)
12. : TEST DRIVEN, Practical TDD and Acceptance TDD for Java Developers
13. Kuusinen, K., Gregory, P., Sharp, H., Barroca, H., Taylor, K., Wood, L.: Knowledge sharing in a large agile organisation: A survey study. In: International Conference on Agile Software Development. (2017) 135–150
14. Andriyani, Y.: Knowledge management and reflective practice in daily stand-up and retrospective meetings. In: International Conference on Agile Software Development. (2017) 285–291
15. Xu-Xiang, L., Wen-Ning, Z.: The pdca-based software testing improvement framework. In: International Conference on Apperceiving Computing and Intelligence Analysis (ICACIA). (2010) 490–494
16. Kitchenham, B., P.S.L.: Guide to Advanced Empirical Software Engineering. Personal Opinion Surveys. Chapter 3. Springer-Verlag London (2008)
17. Paredes, J., Anslow, C., Maurer, F.: Information visualization for agile software development teams. In: IEEE Working Conference on Software Visualization. (2014) 157–166
18. Cabral, A.R.Y., Ribeiro, M., Noll, R.P.: Knowledge management in agile software projects: A systematic review. Journal of Information & Knowledge Management (2014)
19. Levy, M., Hazzan, O.: Knowledge management in practice: The case of agile software development. In: Workshop on Cooperative and Human Aspects on Software Engineering. (2009) 60–65
20. Ikujiro, H., Nonaka, T.: Hitotsubashi on Knowledge Management. John Wiley & Sons (2004)

Gender Gap in Computing: A Preliminary Empirical Study

Geovanny Raura[1], Efraín R. Fonseca C.[1], John W. Castro[2], Tatiana Gualotuña[1], Rebeca Mejía C.[1], Mónica Santillán T.[1], Claudia Pons[3], and Oscar Dieste[4]

[1]Departamento de Ciencias de la Computación, Universidad de las Fuerzas Armadas ESPE, Sangolquí, Ecuador
[2]Departamento de Ingeniería Informática y Ciencias de la Computación, Universidad de Atacama, Copiapó, Chile
[3]Facultad de Informática, Universidad Nacional de La Plata, La Plata, Argentina
[4]Escuela Técnica superior de Ingenieros Informáticos, Universidad Politécnica de Madrid, Madrid, España

{jgraura,erfonseca,tmgualotunia,crmejia,mlsantillan}@espe.edu.ec
john.castro@uda.cl
claudia.pons@lifia.info.unlp.edu.ar
odieste@fi.upm.es

Abstract. The presence of women is significantly lower in the work and academic context regarding computer science. The scarce empirical evidence based on experiments and the lack of conclusive results in this regard motivates us to ask ourselves if: Are there differences in programming skills associated with gender?. In order to answer this question, we statistically analyzed the data obtained from seven experimental replications. These replications corresponding to an experiment in which the code external quality is analyzed through the application of test-driven development in contrast to traditional techniques. We concluded that the gender does not have an influence on the programmers' effectiveness.

Keywords: gender gap, empirical study, software engineering

1 Introduction

Even though the present trend is toward gender equity, this principle has anecdotally weakened in computing and therefore in their environment. Female gender presence in computing is significantly lower [16], it is even claimed that there is a backward in terms of inclusion and equality of opportunities [9]. In the sixties, for example, female gender participation in the programmers' community of USA was approximately of 65%; however, this percentage declined by a 40% in 2012 [2].

This trend is not exclusive of computing, a similar behavior has been identified in other engineering careers [12]. In fact, the presence of female gender in this field does not exceed 10% worldwide [2], this may reflect, among other aspects, that technical careers have traditionally been considered only within male stereotype [7,16].

There are several studies about this subject, which have been performed from different approaches. Low demand for computing career by female gender [16] has been the most controversial issue. Furthermore, the perception of computing career, as both scientific discipline and professional field, has been analyzed from the gender point of view [7] and based on society impact [15]. Nevertheless, some studies conclude that gender does not influence this trend [1,8]; whereas other studies show just the opposite [12]. On the other hand, there are very few studies reporting the results of experimental instances in computing [8].

The lack of experimental studies, conflicting findings and inconclusive results of studies reviewed motivated us to perform a *Post Hoc* analysis of 7 experimental replications from the gender point of view. We replicated an experiment originally conducted by N. Juristo and her team in the FidiPro project ESEIL [11], which explored the effectiveness of using test-driven development (TDD) as opposed to the developers' usual programming approach. The replications were performed in both academic and industrial environments with a total of 160 participants, 25 of whom were women.

All experimental instances were individually designed and analyzed without taking the gender perspective into account. However, during the period in which replications were made (2015 - 2017) we were struck by the notorious gender imbalance within groups.

Our results suggest that gender does not influence programmers' productivity. It has to be mentioned nonetheless that our study has to be validated with new proposals focused on gender.

The paper is organized as follows. Section 2 introduces the environment in which the phenomenon was observed and related works. Research methodology is described in Section 3. Section 4 presents the results obtained from this study. Threats to validity are briefly discussed in Section 5. Finally, a discussion of the results and the main contributions are summarized in Section 6.

2 Background and Related Works

The minority shareholding of female gender in engineering careers is a real and touchable fact. However, this matter has worsened over the last 20 years in computing, particularly in software development [10]. The relative absence of female gender within development teams contributes to such gender be underestimated in software development; but, women consider that the result of development tasks made by men are worse than those obtained by them [9].

Moreover, it was argued that gender inequality constitutes a threat to the software product obtained [10]. Some alternatives based on agile development, collaboration and quality, have been proposed as a framework for instilling a more social and committed vision of software developer in order to encourage female gender to opt for computing and make better this industry [10].

The gender gap has been extensively documented in the literature at least from three different points of view. First, there are studies about factors that influence the students' decision when choosing an engineering or computing career [2,17,3,6]; followed by those who study gender inequality within the environment of software development [10]. Secondly, studies dealing with how computing perception varies depending on gender [13,7]. Finally, studies about programming skills by gender in high school [12] and those who study the productivity by gender in programming activities [8,5].

2.1 Factors influencing the selection of engineering careers

It is a fact that the presence of female gender in engineering sciences programs is much lower than male gender. For example, Alejos et al. [2] studied the perception and influence of gender in students when choosing a university career. The authors analyzed data collected from 2 universities of Spain (the University of Vigo and the Public University of Navarra). In both cases, a clear asymmetry was observed in the proportion of male and female students enrolled in engineering. The observation of and data collection shows that social or tradition conditions remain that determine the choice when students choose between one or other studies.

Sullivan et al. [17] examined CodePlus, a programming club based on the Bridge21 model, which was set up in three female-only schools. Students worked together on activities including computational thinking, computers in society and programming using Scratch. Pre and post-questionnaires were designed to measure the students' prior exposure to Computer Science and their attitudes to Computer Science in terms of future study and career choices. Several factors influencing the decision of a teenager when choosing one or another computing career were identified as a result of this study: Exposure to computing, motivation at home or in the school environment, student's perception of their own ability to solve problems, understanding the various applications of computing and related professional careers and the potential social impact.

Denner et al. [6] analyzed data collected from 191 female students enrolled in an introduction to programming class at one of 15 community colleges in California (USA). Results show that women with the high intention of pursuing computing were more avid computer users in their teens and currently play more video games. They also have a positive view of computer programming and place greater value on computing, related to an interest in solving challenging problems and financial motives, rather than an interest in using computing for the social good. Authors concluded that there is no relationship between environment influence and the decision of choosing a career in computing.

2.2 Perception of computing by gender

Funke et al. [7] performed a study to investigate how young men and women differ regarding (1) their perceptions of computing as a scientific discipline respectively as a professional field and (2) the experiences that had influenced their choice of major subject. For that purpose, a biographical study of computing freshmen was conducted at the university. A total of 217 students (54 female, 163 male) participated in the survey. A qualitative analysis showed that young men and women have different viewpoints on computer science. While male students tend to focus on technical aspects of hardware, mathematics, or logical issues; female students are attracted rather by creativity, communication, or job opportunities.

Lehman et al. [13] explore background characteristics, career aspirations, and self-perceptions of 1636 female first-year college students in the United States who intend to major in computing and compares them with 4402 male computing aspirants as well as with 26642 women planning to major in other science, technology, engineering and mathematics (STEM) sub-fields. The findings reveal a unique profile of women who pursue the computing major and notes many significant differences between men and women in computing and between women in computing and those in other STEM fields. Authors concluded that the fact that women in computing are reporting high levels of artistic abilities suggests that women's perceptions of computing as a field may be broadening, such that many women see computing as a creative field where artistic talents are an asset. In addition, they conclude that understanding characteristics of women in computing will help inform policies and recruitment programs designed to address the gender gap in computing.

2.3 Programming skills and productivity by gender in programming activities

Kiss [12] made an analysis of programming skills by gender in secondary grammar schools with the help of a web-based informatics test. Over 60 teachers from different towns of Hungary used the test to see the knowledge level of more than 1000 students have answered the questions. Significant divergence by gender was found regarding programming skills. Students have to put everything in source code when learning programming. It seems this method is more favorable for boys. Girls have problems finding syntax errors in source code or understand it at all. Boys were better at recognizing errors and find the correct answers.

The empirical study of Choi [5] included quantitative and qualitative analyses of different gender combinations within a pair programming environment. Using a pool of university programming course students as the experiment participants, the study examined three gender pair types: female-female, female-male, and male-male. On the quantitative analysis, the result reported no significant gender difference, but on the qualitative analysis, there were significant compatibility and communication level differences between same gender pair and mixed gender pair. Choi suggested that efforts aimed to increase the number of females in the programming world would also be helped by a better understanding of gender and its effect.

Gómez et al. [8] run a controlled experiment in an academic setting to assess the productivity (lines of code per hour) produced by different gender pair configurations (Female-Female, Female-Male, and Male-Male). The results suggest that productivity is not affected by the different gender pair types. Nevertheless, the programming assignments may impact on the productivity. The productivity is not affected by the relationship between gender pair types and the programming assignments. Mixed gender pairs tend to show major variability than pairs of the same gender.

Summarizing, the interest in studying the influence of gender in computing activities has become increasingly widespread in recent years within the scientific community, especially in software development productivity. However, it is quite clear that are needed more empirical studies to have a better understanding of gender dynamics on this activities and given the lack of experimental studies identified, conflicting findings and inconclusive results of the current studies reviewed.

This leads us to pose the following research question:

RQ: Are there gender differences in programmers skills within software development sector?

3 Methodology

This study was conducted for determining whether gender has an impact on programmers skills. With this purpose, we analyze the results of a series of experiment replications. The base experiment [11] was proposed by N. Juristo and her team, which explores the effectiveness of Test Driven Development (TDD) [14] in comparison to other development techniques. The most relevant aspects of this work are described below, since it constitutes the methodological foundation from which the replications were made, both in the academic and industrial environments.

The experiment basis for replications had a 3 × 2 fractional factorial design, using repeated measures. The factors were: the approach to development (*programming approach*) and the description level of experimental task (*slicing*). The levels used for the *programming approach* factor are: Iterative Test Last Development (ITLD), TDD and development strategy that the programmer knows (typically test last development [TLD], but not necessarily), which we have designated "Your Way" (YW).

The response variables defined for the original experiment were: the code external quality (QLTY), the programmers' productivity (PROD) and the amount of work done (TUS). TUS was necessary to calculate QLTY and PROD.

$QLTY$ represents the software quality measured in terms of compliance with software requirements developed by the experimental subjects through acceptance tests. $QLTY$ is defined as:

$$QLTY = \frac{\sum_{i=1}^{\#tus} QLTY_i}{\#TUS} \tag{1}$$

where $QLTY_i$ is the quality of the i-th user story; consecutively, $QLTY_i$ is defined as:

$$QLTY_i = \frac{\#Assert_i(Pass)}{\#Assert_i(All)}. \quad (2)$$

While #TUS is the *amount of work done*. It is measured as the number of *tackled* user stories. A user story is defined as *tackled* when at least one assertion of one test case has successfully passed. #TUS is defined as:

$$\#TUS = \sum_{i=1}^{\#us} \#Assert_i(Pass) \geq 0 \mapsto True \quad (3)$$

In both cases (eq. 2 and 3), $\#Assert_i(Pass)$ represents the number of passed assertions for the i-th user story.

PROD represents the *amount of work done* satisfactorily by the subjects and is defined as:

$$PROD = \frac{\#Assert(Pass)}{\#Assert(All)}. \quad (4)$$

Only the variable PROD was analyzed in this study, due to QLTY, PROD and TUS variables are calculated based on the comparison of the pass and fail assertions. Hence, we considered that our objective could be achieved only through the results obtained.

The experimental tasks were *MarsRover API* (MR), *Bowling Scorekeeper* (BSK) and *Spread Sheet* (SS), which are commonly used in the agile development community. The experimental tasks were performed using Java as the programming language, JUnit as the tests framework and IDE Eclipse as the development platform. For all experimental tasks, a basic code structure was delivered in order to guide the subject in the writing of the tests to solve problems.

Based on the mentioned experiment we made 7 replications: 5 in the academic environment and 2 in the industry environment, as can be seen in the Table 1.

Table 1. Experimental Instances

No	Experiment	Environment	Organization	Subjects	Country	Year
1	ESPE2015	Academic	ESPE	Graduate	Ecuador	2015
2	UADY2015	Academic	UADY	Graduate	Mexico	2015
3	UNLP2015	Academic	UNLP	Postgraduate	Argentina	2015
4	ESPE2016	Academic	ESPE	Graduate	Ecuador	2016
5	BABEL2016	Industry	Babel Software	Professionals	Costa Rica	2016
6	QUITO2016	Industry	AESOFT - FFAA	Professionals	Ecuador	2016
7	UTN2017	Academic	UTN	Postgraduates	Ecuador	2017

Different experimental protocols were followed, depending on the characteristics of each context. Table 2 shows the experimental protocols (Treatment (T)) applied.

Table 2. Experimental protocol

Session 1		Session 2		Session 3	
T1	T2	T3	T4	T5	T6
Training: Unit Testing	Experimental session: YW	Training: ITL/Slicing techniques	Experimental Session: ITL	Training: TDD technique	Experimental Session: TDD

More specifically, in replications 1, 2, 3, 4, 5, 7 was applied a cross-over design of repeated measures, using *programming approach* (with *ITLD* and *TDD* as levels, and MR and BSK as experimental tasks) and *slicing* as factors; whereas the replication 6 used the original design described above.

It should be noted that a training session was performed before each experimental task within each replication. A six-day workshop (2 hours per day) was organized for replications 1, 4; in replications 2, 3, 5, 6 a five-day workshop (4 hours per day) was performed; whereas, replication 7 had a four-day workshop (6 hours per day).

Two experimental tasks of 2.5 hours (one per day) were performed for replications 1, 2, 3, 4, 5, 7; whereas, replication 6 had an additional experimental session for *YW*.

Finally, training material and experimenters were the same of the original experiment in order to reduce potential threats to validity.

4 Results

4.1 Overview

A column of demographic data with gender información was added into data of each replication, in order to carry out *post hoc* analyses. Afterwards, the information from all replications was consolidated in an unique set of data. Starting from this new data structure we performed new analyses of the PROD variable. Table 4.1 shows the results obtained from gender perspective.

A total of 300 experimental units were reached as a result of the data rearrangement, from which 15.67% (47) correspond to women and 84.33% (253) to men. The distribution of experimental units between experiments was as follows: ESPE2015 76 (17F, 59M), UADY2015 67 (6F, 61M), UNLP2015 17 (0F, 17M), BABEL2016 16 (2F, 14M), ESPE2016 15 (1F, 14M), QUITO2016 56 (6F, 50M) y UTN2017 53 (15F, 38M).

PROD by gender is different between experiments. For example, men are relatively more productive than women in the ESPE2015 experiment (33.64 vs 22.55); while, on the contrary, productivity is slightly higher in women than in men (34.73 vs 31.21) in the UTN2017 experiment.

Standard deviation (sd) behaviour is simillar as PROD. For example, men sd is higher than women (30.28 vs 24.27) in the ESPE2015 experiment. On the contrary, women sd is higher than men (33.78 vs 30.18) in the UTN2017 experiment.

Table 3. Gender productivity achieved in the experiments

	Experiment	Gender	N	PROD	sd
1	ESPE2015	F	17	22.5494117647059	24.2732722017933
2	ESPE2015	M	59	33.6383050847458	30.2836307867709
3	UADY2015	F	6	52.27	35.7492970560262
4	UADY2015	M	61	49.3586885245902	30.5525071243703
14	UNLP2015	F	0		
5	UNLP2015	M	17	57.2794117647059	30.3475801075202
6	BABEL2016	F	2	14.285	20.2020407384997
7	BABEL2016	M	14	14.885	16.2573390527762
8	ESPE2016	F	1	0	
9	ESPE2016	M	14	14.6064285714286	28.8762283407445
10	QUITO2016	F	6	8.13333333333333	10.8645306694153
11	QUITO2016	M	50	15.1696	14.2676494295626
12	UTN2017	F	15	34.7293333333333	33.7815193489548
13	UTN2017	M	38	31.2118421052632	30.1798080748347

4.2 Isolation of possible causes

It appears that productivity isn't related with gender. Figure 1 presents a Boxplot which shows the experiments' productivity obtained by subjects from gender perspective.

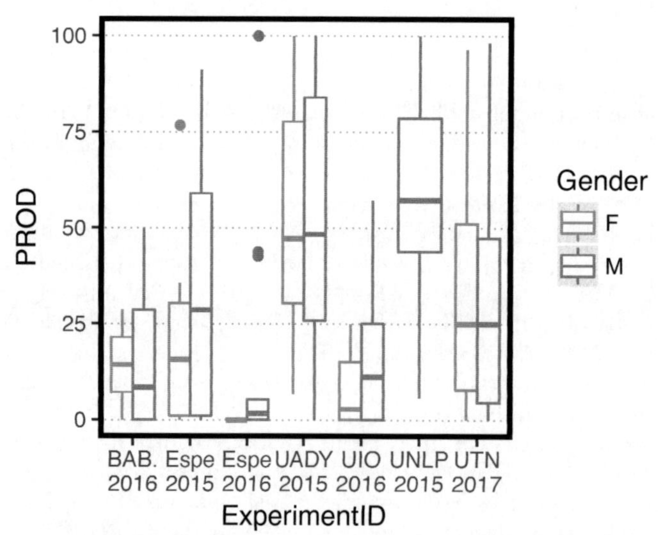

Fig. 1. Experiments productivity from gender perspective

PROD behaviour doesn't respond to a pattern between experiments (see Figure 1). There are no cases in which the difference of PROD by gender is marked. For example, PROD is less than 25% in the BABEL2016 experiment, where women slightly above men. On the contrary, PROD is around 25% in the UTN2017 experiment, but there is no difference by gender.

PROD dispersion is wide in most experiments for both genders; hence, productivity is not stable neither by experiment nor by gender. It is also noted that PROD average (Q2) is below 25% in most experiments (for men and women), except for the experiments UADY2015 and UNLP2015 that are a little better, but do not exceed 50%.

All experiments show the same phenomenon regarding gender, that is, a low presence of female gender. Two diagrams were generated for perform a detailed analysis regarding this issue, one single (see Figure 2) and one including the standard deviation of the data distributions of each experiment (see Figure 3). These diagrams show the experiments average productivity achieved by each gender.

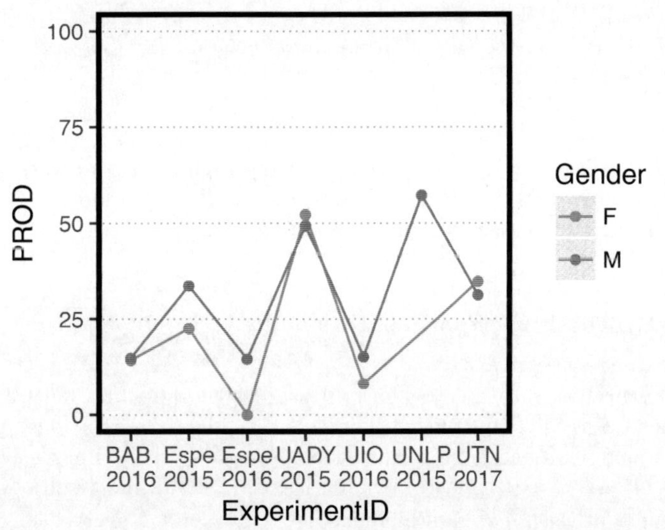

Fig. 2. Average Productivity achieved in the experiments by gender

The results of Figures 2 and 3 show that PROD in male gender is slightly lower than female gender, but this difference isn't significant. In fact, PROD of female gender is minimally better than male gender in two inflection points (UADY2015 y UTN2017).

A cause-effect relationship between PROD and gender is not posible because of results were inconclusive. This, together with the fact that the sample size of

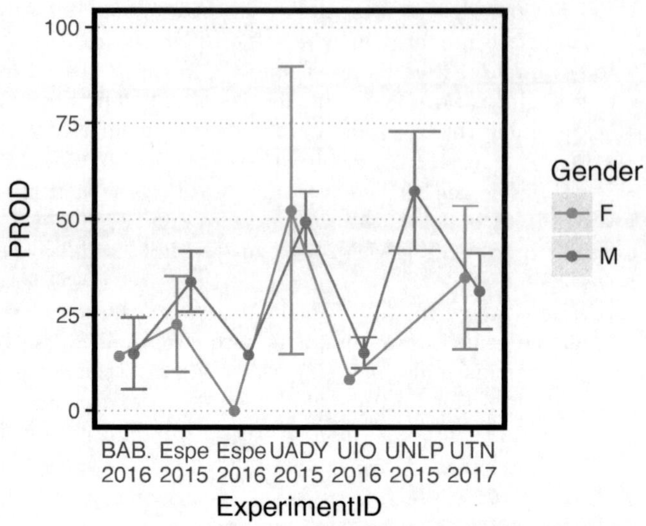

Fig. 3. Average productivity with standard deviation achieved in the experiments by gender

female gender for each experiment is not representative, motivates us to suppose that an individual experimental analysis by gender could result in unreliable findings. Hence, additional analyses are needed.

4.3 Synthesis of experimental results

The natural way to analyze several studies of the same nature is through a synthesis of results, even more so in this case given the relationship between the experiment instances. We choose the Meta-Analysis technique [4] for perform our synthesis of experimental results. Figure 4 shows the results of this analysis.

Our synthesis of results included 7 experiments. Nevertheless meta-analysis technique discards experiments that do not provide comparison elements. Hence, UNLP2015 and ESPE2016 experiments were not considered due to the first one has no experimental units corresponding to the female gender, and the second one has only one experimental unit (which is also not valid since the variance can not be calculated with a single experimental unit).

We considered Cohen conventions [18] to interpret the meta-analysis results. The effect size of the comparison between male and female gender is -0.38, which is statistically significant since the confidence interval does not touch the vertical axis 0. Therefore, male gender has a higher average productivity in this experiment.

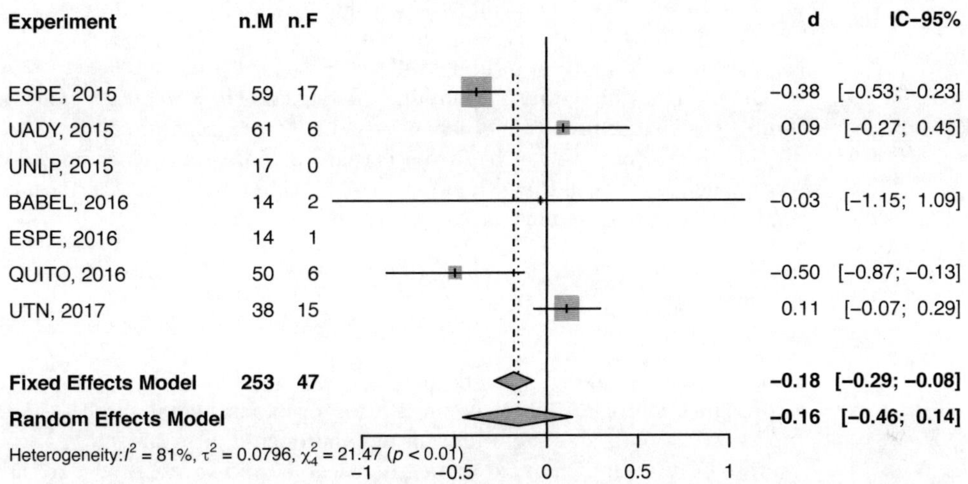

Fig. 4. Meta-analysis by gender

The effect size of the QUITO2016 experiment is -0.50, which is statistically significant for the same reason as above; hence, male gender has higher average productivity in this experiment too.

The effect size of remaining experiments (i.e.: UADY2015, BABEL2016 y UTN2017) isn't statistically significant since their confidence intervals touch the vertical axis 0.

There is statistical heterogeneity ($p < 0.01$) since two experiments show that male gender is less productive than female (ESPE2015 and QUITO2016) and two others (UADY2015 and UTN2017) demonstrate the opposite. The BABEL2016 experiment showed that productivity is the same for both genders.

The fixed effect should not be interpreted due to the presence of heterogeneity. On the contrary, the random effect should be analyzed, which indicates that the average male gender is more productive than the female with an effect of -0.16. However, the random effect rhombus touches the vertical axis of effect 0, which indicates that the result of the random effect is not significant. That is to say, experiments indicate that the male gender is more productive than the female gender, but with a minimal difference and with no significant results.

On the basis of the results obtained, alongside the threats to validity concerning the reduced number of female gender, the aggregation of tasks and the disjoint treatments; we can be deduced that our data series does not allow observe, much less affirm that, there is a marked difference in the performance by gender in the programming tasks performed.

5 Threats to validity

Some threats to validity may have affected the results of this study. This includes Duration of training, the motivation of experimental subjects, previous experience in programming, duration of experimental sessions, etc. All of these limitations are common in experimental research, and we acknowledge their potentially adverse effects.

A specific threat to internal validity should be emphasized for this study. This limitation is related to the imbalance of groups by gender. Only 15.63% (25) of a total of 160 experimental subjects belong to the female gender.

This situation could have affected the apparent performance of the female gender both positively and negatively. That is, for example, if a single experimental subject of female gender had a worse performance than the rest, it may have negatively affected the performance of the whole group. This limitation can be corrected by making new replications with homogenous groups from the gender perspective.

Finally, *post hoc* analyses cannot detect causal relationships. Thus, the influencing variables that were identified should be considered as working hypotheses only, which require future testing in empirical studies. However, these hypotheses can only be evaluated by examining large data sets obtained from comparable experimental replications and other types of empirical studies.

6 Discussion and conclusions

The presence of female gender in technical disciplines like computing is noticeably scarce. This fact has been tried to explain from different perspectives: (i) Students' decisions influenced by social or traditional conditions when they choosing a university career, (ii) environment's influence level (home and/or school) in relation to computing, (iii) family and friends' encouragement, and (iv) interpretation level of computer applications and their related professional careers; but, one of the main reasons argued is the supposed lower ability or intervention of the female gender in certain computer tasks, such as programming.

We analyzed the impact of gender on programmers effectiveness using the data obtained from seven experiments, which explored the effectiveness of TDD as opposed to the developers' usual programming approach. The experiments were performed by professionals, undergraduate, and graduate students, with programming knowledge. However, we observed a low female representation within each experiment instance. Only 25 out of a total of 160 developers were women. This situation motivated us to consider a gender point of view analysis of results, in order to contrast the results of several studies regarding this subject.

The results of the meta-analysis show a low effect size (d = 0.16) in terms of programming productivity by gender (male slightly better than female), but it is not significant for meta-analysis of random effects. On the other hand, individual analyses of experiments show conflicting results regarding programming productivity by gender; i.e., in some cases, male gender is better than female, but in others female gender is better.

Taking into account the sample imbalance from the gender perspective and the contradictory nature of the results, we could say that programming does not represent a handicap for the female gender. This is a fact observed daily in many companies and universities around the world, where performance by gender apparently does not show differences. This conclusion is also based on the fact that our results are in agreement with some existing studies in the literature, which state no productivity difference by gender.

Nevertheless, our study was conducted around several threats to validity. The most important ones are, probably, the low number of programmers who participated in each experiment and the imbalance of groups from a gender perspective. This situation invites a greater research effort in this area.

Acknowledgment

This work was supported by the "Laboratorio Industrial en Ingeniería del Software Empírica (LI2SE)", and the "Análisis Experimental de la Efectividad de Test Driven Development en Función de las Características Particulares de los Programadores a Nivel Personal" ESPE research projects.

References

1. Akinola, S.O.: Computer programming skill and gender difference: An empirical study. American Journal of Scientific and Industrial Research 7(1), 1–9 (2015)
2. Alejos, A.V., Sanchez, M.G., Milagros, M.P., Falcone, F., Sanchís, P., López-Martín, A.: The influence of gender in the adoption of engineering studies. In: 2014 XI Technologies Applied to Electronics Teaching (TAEE). pp. 1–4 (June 2014)
3. Beyer, S.: Why are women underrepresented in computer science? gender differences in stereotypes, self-efficacy, values, and interests and predictors of future cs course-taking and grades. Computer Science Education 24(2-3), 153–192 (2014)
4. Borenstein, M., Hedges, L.V., Higgins, J.P.T., Rothstein, H.R.: Introduction to Meta-Analysis. Wiley & Sons, Ltd (2009)
5. Choi, K.S.: A comparative analysis of different gender pair combinations in pair programming. Behaviour & Information Technology 34(8), 825–837 (2015)
6. Denner, J., Werner, L., O'Connor, L.: Women in community college: Factors related to intentions to pursue computer science. NASPA Journal About Women in Higher Education 8(2), 156–171 (2015)
7. Funke, A., Berges, M., Hubwieser, P.: Different perceptions of computer science. In: 2016 International Conference on Learning and Teaching in Computing and Engineering (LaTICE). pp. 14–18 (March 2016)
8. Gómez, O.S., Solari, M., Calvache, C.J.P., Ledezma-Carrizales, A.C.: A controlled experiment on productivity of pair programming gender combinations: Preliminary results. In: CIbSE 2017. pp. 1–8 (May 2017)
9. Guo, C., Tsang, M.C., Ding, X.: Gender disparities in science and engineering in chinese universities. Economics of Education Review 29(2), 225 – 235 (2010)
10. Judy, K.H.: Agile values, innovation and the shortage of women software developers. In: 2012 45th Hawaii International Conference on System Sciences. pp. 5279–5288 (Jan 2012)
11. Juristo, N., Others: A test-driven development experiment at ericsson (2015), unpublished
12. Kiss, G.: A comparison of programming skills by genders of hungarian grammar school students. In: 2010 7th International Conference on Ubiquitous Intelligence Computing. pp. 24–30 (Oct 2010)
13. Lehman, K.J., Sax, L.J., Zimmerman, H.B.: Women planning to major in computer science: Who are they and what makes them unique? CSE 26(4), 277–298 (2016)
14. Madeyski, L.: Extreme Programming and Agile Processes in Software Engineering, pp. 65–74 (2006)
15. Nelson, B.: The data on diversity. Commun. ACM 57(11), 86–95 (Oct 2014)
16. Stanko, T., Zhirosh, O., Krasnikhin, D.: Why girls with an interest in it in high-school do not choose an it career. In: 2014 International Conference on Interactive Collaborative Learning (ICL). pp. 131–137 (Dec 2014)
17. Sullivan, K., Byrne, J.R., Bresnihan, N., O'Sullivan, K., Tangney, B.: Codeplus - designing an after school computing programme for girls. In: 2015 IEEE Frontiers in Education Conference (FIE). pp. 1–5 (Oct 2015)
18. Wuensch, K.: Cohen's conventions for small, medium, and large effects. Tech. rep., East Carolina University (Revised July, 2015)

An Exploratory Study of Academic Architectural Tactics and Patterns in Microservices: A systematic literature review

Felipe Osses, Gastón Márquez, and Hernán Astudillo

Toeska research group
Universidad Técnica Federico Santa María
Valparaíso, Chile
felipe.osses@sansano.usm.cl, gaston.marquez@sansano.usm.cl,
hernan@inf.utfsm.cl

Abstract. Microservices are becoming a leading architectural choice in the service-oriented software industry. This approach proposes to develop applications as a suite of small services, each running on its own process and intercommunicating with lightweight mechanisms. Currently, there is still no clear perspective of emerging recurrent solutions (architectural patterns) or design decisions (architectural tactics) that influence microservices. This article describes an exploratory study, based on a systematic review, of academic literature related to architectural patterns and tactics proposed for microservices. The review yield 1067 initial studies, which reported: 44 architectural patterns of microservices; architectural tactics related to microservices dependent on other disciplines; and it was also found that most of architectural patterns and tactics are associated to five quality attributes: scalability, flexibility, testability, performance, and elasticity. Added to that, it was noticed that most microservices are reported in articles related to DevOps and IoT. Finally, a new proposal of microservices pattern taxonomy is suggested.

Keywords: Microservices, architectural patterns, architectural tactics, taxonomy, systematic literature review

1 Introduction

Service-oriented architecture (SOA) has emerged as a medium of developing distributed systems based on components as services. Along with SOA, cloud computing is gaining popularity among mid-size and small business allowing the emergence of new trends in software engineering, such as *microservices*. A microservice architectural style is an approach to developing a single application as a suite of small services, each running in its process and communicating with lightweight mechanisms. These services are built around business capabilities and independently deployable by fully automated deployment machinery [16].

Although microservices have emerged from industry [18], academic research has put the focus of interest in this approach. To understand microservices, some studies have been conceived, like [10] [24] [3] [11]. These studies reveal that there is a great interest and emerging trends in microservices, but they do not describe those recurring solutions (*architectural patterns*) or design decisions (*architectural tactics*) that are emerging in this approach. Architectural patterns describe an abstract high-level system structure and its associated behavior, and a architectural tactic is a design decision that influences the achievement of system requirements [6]. According to [6], architectural tactics are "architectural building blocks" from which architectural patterns are created. Therefore, the objective of our study is to explore what architectural patterns and tactics have been described through a systematic review of the literature limited to academic papers to know what kind of proposals have been proposed.

The rest of the article is structured as follows: in Section 2 we describe the motivation and we illustrate those contributions related to systematic reviews that have been accomplishing for microservices. Subsequently, in Section 3 we mention the planning of the study that we have done with the objective of describing in Section 4 the results and the analysis obtained. In Section 5 we detail our proposal of taxonomy for microservices architectural patterns. In Section 6 we outline the threats to the validity of our research, and finally in Section 7, we detail the conclusions of our study.

2 Motivation and related work

The microservice architectural style is becoming a preferred industrial approach to develop applications as suites of small services, each running in its process and communicating with lightweight mechanisms [18] [16]. One of the *avant-garde* companies in adopting the microservice architecture approach is Netflix [1] handling about two billion API edge requests every day composed of approximately 500 microservices. On the other hand, Uber has about 1300 microservices to improve reliability and scalability [2].

There is an interesting set of reviews in the field of microservices. Di Francesco et al. [10] contributes to the study of microservices with a reusable framework for classifying, comparing, and evaluating architectural solutions, methods, and techniques for microservices. Proposals like [24], [3], [19], and [11] not only analyze the emerging standards in microservices but also the types of research conducted and the practical motivations around carrying out the microservices architecture. There are other proposals for microservices architectural patterns in industry such as patterns language [21] and others; but we have focused on academic papers for this review. The previous works show the current evidence on microservices, but none of them describe the architectural patterns and tactics proposed for this discipline. Therefore, this gives us the motivation to perform this systematic review.

[1] https://www.netflix.com/

[2] http://www.theserverside.com/feature/How-microservices-patterns-helped-Uber-systems-perform-better

3 Review planning

In this section, we will describe the research method executed in this study. This is based on procedures for performing systematic reviews of Barbara Kitchenham [14], who propose appropriate guidelines for systematic reviews for software engineering researchers [15]. The research planning is defined in Figure 1. To reduce the possibility of bias, the review was developed by three researchers. The execution of the protocol was done between June 1st and November 30th.

3.1 Research questions

To establish the research questions, we set up meetings with experts using the brainstorming technique[3] focused on the next keywords: "software architecture", "microservices", "quality attributes", "patterns" and "tactics". In those meetings we establish the next research questions:

RQ1: *What architectural patterns have been proposed for microservices?*

RQ2: *What architectural tactics have been proposed for microservices?*

RQ3: *What are the quality attributes associated with architectural patterns and tactics in microservices?*

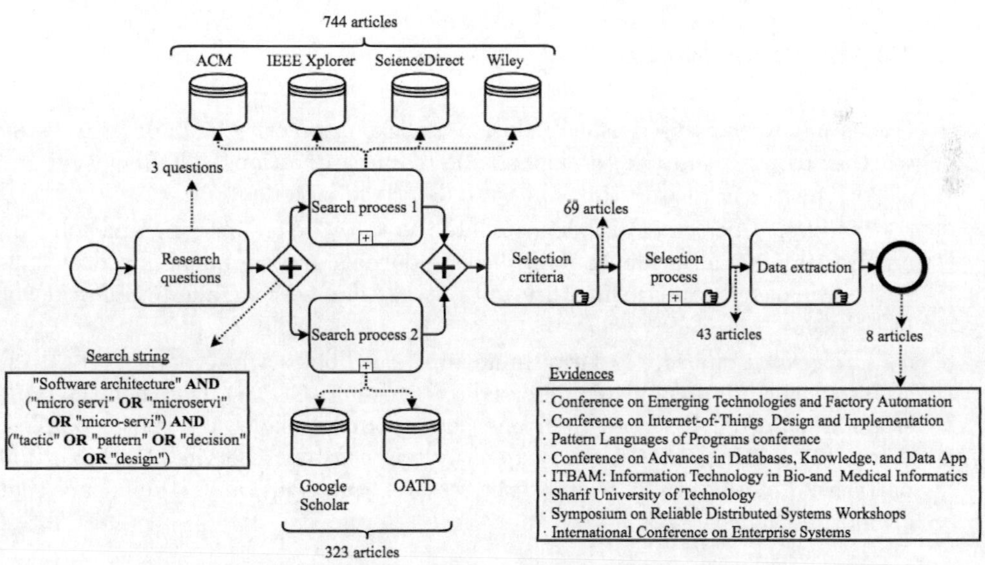

Fig. 1. Planning overview

[3] https://www.mindtools.com/brainstm.html

3.2 Search process

In this process, we establish the search string related to the research questions. Therefore, we use the following search terms to find relevant studies, using and combining all the terms by the boolean AND/OR operators. In the search strings, there are two-word bases: *software architecture* and *microservices*, which should be included in all the questions. Thus, it was decided not only use "tactic" and "patterns" words but also we decided to expand the search string using the words "decision" and "design." For microservices, we included in the string the words "micro servi", "microservi" or "micro-servi" (see Figure 1).

The following step on the search process is to establish where the search would be performed. In this study was decided to concentrate the efforts of search on academic studies on the most important databases of journals and conferences in the area of software engineering. 744 papers were obtained using the next databases (Search Process 1): ACM Digital Library[4], IEEE Xplore[5], ScienceDirect-Elsevier[6], and Wiley InterScience[7]. However, due to the novelty of the microservices and the intention to expand the search and increase the knowledge, it was decided to performed a second search in the following databases, obtaining 323 new papers (Search Process 2): Google Scholar[8], and OATD - Open Access Thesis Databases[9]. In total, 1067 papers were obtained from digital libraries.

3.3 Selection criteria

Each study was analyzed using inclusion and exclusion criteria, in order to verify whether paper is suitable to respond the research questions. The inclusion and exclusion criteria used in this study are described as follows:

Inclusion Criteria:(1) Evidence related to software engineering and software architecture, (2) all evidence published in journals and conferences proceedings in the field of software architecture and software engineering, and (3) all evidence in English.

Exclusion Criteria: (1) Gray literature (e.g. books, white papers, etc.), (2) studies which address only commercial-off-the-shelf (COTS), (3) when the same study is reported by more than one paper, only consider the most complete study, (3) evidence that do not explicitly relate to microservices, architectural patterns or tactics or not relate to the research questions, and (4) evidence that are not in English.

[4] http://portal.acm.org
[5] http://www.ieee.org/web/publications/xplore/
[6] http://www.elsevier.com
[7] http://www3.interscience.wiley.com
[8] https://scholar.google.com/
[9] https://oatd.org/

3.4 Selection Process and Data extraction

The selection of studies was performed based on the next sequence: (a) The first step was to search and identify relevant studies in the selected databases using the search terms, (b) after obtaining the relevant studies, the inclusion and exclusion criteria were applied, (c) the third step was manually excluded studies based on the title, abstracts, introduction, and conclusion of the papers, and (d) finally, we obtain the last list of papers.

Once we apply the selection criteria and process, we use a spreadsheets to extract relevant data used (you can consult the sheet in the next link[10]). For each selected paper, we fill the next fields: paper ID, publication year, paper title, authors, type of study (conference, journal, etc.), and keywords. At the time of manually analyzing each paper, we realized that the vast majority of papers did not offer the complete information to answer our RQs. Therefore, we analyze each paper in depth and discard those that did not meet our expectations. This manual process involved a considerable reduction of the evidence.

4 Results and analysis

We found academic literature evidence in several events (see Figure 1). ICSA (International Conference on Software Architecture) and ECSA (European Conference on Software Architecture) were considered in the first phases of our revision, but we didn't find evidence on architectural tactics and pattern in microservices in these conferences. To be sure of this lack of evidence, we review the papers related to these conferences in IEEExplore and ACM digital library manually (from 2010 to 2017). Then, we will proceed to answer the research questions created for this study.

RQ1: What architectural patterns have been proposed for microservices? Table 1 summarize the 44 architectural patterns of microservices found in our review. We have decided to summarize them using as reference the schema proposed in [2], which are: reference, ID (MSP, MicroService Pattern), name, context, problem and solution.

Although the patterns evidenced in this review are directly or indirectly related to microservices, we will describe those patterns that we have verified that belong directly. The selection of these patterns is based on their contribution to the development of microservice architecture.

- Name: **Microservices Architecture**
  - *Context*: Is required an modular application, and the modules should be independent.
  - *Problem*: How do the architect an application as a set of independent modules?

[10] https://drive.google.com/open?id=1sxbPsYxe8ZtptP7vZKjG5XRUEr03LA6hCJmR6S1ADnk

Table 1. Architectural patterns in microservices in academy

Ref.	ID	Name	Ref.	ID	Name
	AMSP1	*Modern Web Architecture*		**AMSP23**	*Service discovery*
	AMSP2	*Single Page Application*		**AMSP24**	*service discovery client*
	AMSP3	*Native Mobile Application*		**AMSP25**	*Internal load balancer*
	AMSP4	*Near Cache*		**AMSP26**	*external load balancer*
	AMSP5	*Microservices Architecture*		**AMSP27**	*Intro. circuit breaker*
	AMSP6	*Business Microservice*	[4]	**AMSP28**	*Intro. config. server*
	AMSP7	*Backend for Frontend*		**AMSP29**	*Intro. edge server*
	AMSP8	*Adapter Microservice*		**AMSP30**	*Containerize the Services*
[7]	**AMSP9**	*Results Cache*		**AMSP31**	*Deploy Cluster*
	AMSP10	*Page Cache*		**AMSP32**	*Monitor the system*
	AMSP11	*Scalable Store*		**AMSP33**	*Self-containment of services*
	AMSP12	*Key Value Store*		**AMSP34**	*Circuit Breaker*
	AMSP13	*Document Store*		**AMSP35**	*Load Balancer*
	AMSP14	*Microservices DevOps*	[8]	**AMSP36**	*Container*
	AMSP15	*Log Aggregator*		**AMSP37**	*Handling diff. service*
	AMSP16	*Correlation ID*		**AMSP38**	*Blue green deployment*
	AMSP17	*Service Registry*		**AMSP39**	*Canary release*
	AMSP18	*Enable Continuous Integra.*	[17]	**AMSP40**	*Database is the service*
	AMSP19	*Recover the Current Arch.*		**AMSP41**	*IoT edge provisioning*
[4]	**AMSP20**	*Decompose the Monolith*	[20]	**AMSP42**	*IoT edge code deployment*
	AMSP21	*Decom. based on data*		**AMSP43**	*IoT edge orchestration*
	AMSP22	*Change code depen.*		**AMSP44**	*IoT edge diameter of things*

  - *Solution*: Design the application with a set of modules where each is an independent business function with its own data, developed by a separate team and deployed in a separate process.
- Name: **Backend for Frontend**
  - *Context*: The Business Microservices, that encapsulate individual business functions, do not map cleanly to the channel-specific needs of the client applications.
  - *Problem*: How to represent a channel-specific service interface that is consistent with an overall microservices architecture but allows enough uniqueness that it can be adapted to the needs of a specific client type?
  - *Solution*: Build a Backend for Frontend (BFF) that acts as a single API for a client. Implement differents BFFs for different types of clients, each with an API customized to what that client type needs.
- Name: **Microservices DevOps**
  - *Context*: Is neccesary to put a system into production.
  - *Problem*: How to balance the needs of developers (which want to work on small, easy-tomodify artifacts) and operations teams, which need to minimize the impact of changes on critical systems in order to maintain availability?
  - *Solution*: Isolate each microservice as much as possible, while being able to easily and quickly identify and resolve issues with the microservices.

Applying unique CI/CD pipelines to each microservice will allow you to build and deploy each microservice individually.

– Name: **Service Registry**
  - *Context*: Many different business microservices comprising an application.
  - *Problem*: How to decouple the physical address (IP address) of a microservice instance from its clients so that the client code will not have to change if the address of the service changes?
  - *Solution*: Map between a unique identifier and the current address of a service instance in order to decouple the physical address of a service from the identifier.

– Name: **Change Code Dependency to Service Call**
  - *Context*: A software system has been decomposed to a set of small services to use microservices architectural style. There is a component in the system that is acting as a dependency to another services or components.
  - *Problem*: When it is appropriate to change this code-level dependency to service-level dependency? And when it is not?
  - *Solution*: Try to keep the services code as separate as possible. When services shares code as a dependency there is a high chance that a service developer can fail the build process of another service by changing the shared code.

– Name: **Deploy into a Cluster and Orchestrate Containers**
  - *Context*: A software system has been architected based on microservices architectural style, and a continuous integration pipeline is in place and is working.
  - *Problem*: How to deploy a service's instances into a cluster? How to orchestrate the deployment and re-deployment of all of the services with the least effort?
  - *Solution*: There should exists a system that can manage a cluster of computing nodes. This management system should be able to deploy the services container images on-demand, with specified number of instances and on different nodes. Additionally, it should handle the failure of instances and restart the failed nodes or instances in case.

– Name: **Container**
  - *Context*: Individual services can be hosted as a single container.
  - *Problem*: How to simplify deploying applications?
  - *Solution*: The use of containers enclose the microservice itself, including all required libraries and data, which also supports the requirement of self-containment. This in turn provides several advantages: better testability, ease of service deployment better scalability.

– Name: **Database is the Service**
  - *Context*: The addition of new behaviors and business logic at the database level may be a possible approach to reduce complexity, and thus the related risks, and also to gain improvements in terms of speed and scalability.

- *Problem*: If each scalable service has its own database (cluster), is there any way to reduce the complexity of the architecture and the related risks, while also gaining more improvements in terms of speed and scalability?
- *Solution*: Create a service whose sole responsibility will be to keep the databases in sync.

– Name: **REST Integration**

- *Context*: Intuitive way of integrating microservices
- *Problem*: How to synchronize information between microservices?
- *Solution*: Dedicated REST endpoint that other services can use to notify them.

Given the volume of architectural patterns in microservices found in this review, we performed a quality assessment with the objective to illustrate those architectural patterns that, under our criteria, satisfy the following four quality criteria (QC) questions. Each QCs was evaluated using a adaptation of the York University, Centre for Reviews and Dissemination (CDR) Database of Abstracts of Reviews of Effects (DARE) criteria [1]. Some contributions of Kitchenham et al. [15] [13] recommend applying this type of evaluations with the objective of appraise their quality and highlight strengths and weaknesses of the contributions (in our case, the architectural patterns).

QC1: The architectural pattern describes the *context* in which it is applied? Y (yes), the architectural pattern clearly describes the context in which it is located; P (partly), the architectural pattern partially describes the context in which it is located; and N (no), the architectural pattern vaguely describes the context.

QC2: The architectural pattern describes the *problem* it is trying to solve? Y, the architectural pattern openly describes the problem it is trying to solve; P, the architectural pattern does not directly describe the problem to be solved; N, Unable to visualize which problem the architectural pattern is trying to solve.

QC3: The architectural pattern describes the *solution* regarding the context and problem? Y, the architectural pattern clearly describes the solution proposed; P, the architectural pattern partially describes the proposed solution; N, It can not be described what solution the architectural pattern proposes.

QC4: Is the architectural pattern related to one or more quality attributes? Y, the architectural pattern allows one or more quality attributes to be identified in the description; P, the architectural pattern allows identifying at most one attribute of quality in the description; N, it is not possible to identify attributes of quality in the pattern.

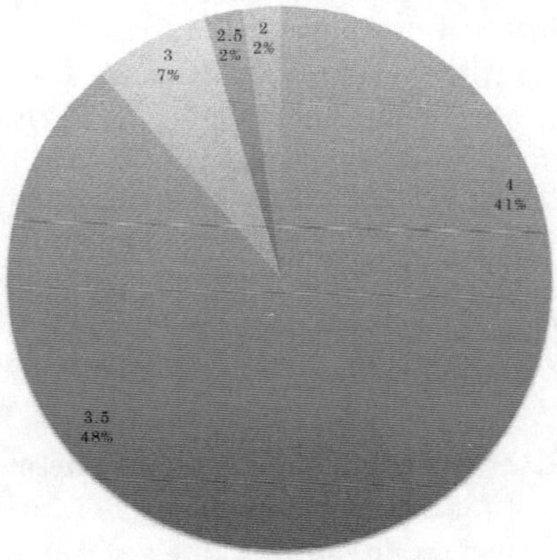

Fig. 2. Total scores distribution

Table 2. Quality evaluation of MSPs

ID	QC1	QC2	QC3	QC4	Total score	ID	QC1	QC2	QC3	QC4	Total score
MSP1	Y	Y	Y	P	3.5	MSP23	Y	Y	Y	P	3.5
MSP2	P	Y	Y	Y	3.5	MSP24	Y	Y	Y	P	3.5
MSP3	Y	Y	Y	Y	4	MSP25	Y	Y	Y	Y	4
MSP4	Y	Y	Y	P	3.5	MSP26	Y	Y	Y	Y	4
MSP5	Y	Y	Y	P	3.5	MSP27	Y	Y	Y	P	3.5
MSP6	Y	Y	Y	Y	4	MSP28	Y	Y	Y	P	3.5
MSP7	Y	Y	Y	Y	4	MSP29	Y	Y	Y	P	3.5
MSP8	Y	Y	Y	P	3.5	MSP30	Y	Y	Y	Y	4
MSP9	Y	Y	Y	P	3.5	MSP31	Y	Y	Y	Y	4
MSP10	Y	Y	Y	P	3.5	MSP32	Y	Y	Y	P	3.5
MSP11	Y	Y	Y	Y	4	MSP33	Y	P	Y	P	3
MSP12	P	Y	Y	Y	3.5	MSP34	Y	P	Y	Y	3.5
MSP13	Y	Y	Y	Y	4	MSP35	N	P	Y	Y	2.5
MSP14	Y	Y	Y	P	3.5	MSP36	Y	N	Y	Y	3
MSP15	Y	Y	Y	P	3.5	MSP37	Y	P	N	P	2
MSP16	Y	Y	Y	Y	4	MSP38	Y	P	Y	Y	3.5
MSP17	Y	Y	Y	Y	4	MSP39	P	P	Y	Y	3
MSP18	Y	Y	Y	Y	4	MSP40	Y	Y	Y	Y	4
MSP19	Y	Y	Y	P	3.5	MSP41	Y	Y	Y	P	3.5
MSP20	Y	Y	Y	Y	4	MSP42	Y	Y	Y	Y	4
MSP21	Y	Y	Y	Y	4	MSP43	Y	Y	Y	P	3.5
MSP22	Y	Y	Y	Y	4	MSP44	Y	Y	Y	Y	4

The scoring procedure was $Y = 1$, $P = 0.5$, $N = 0$. Table 2 describe the final results of the quality evaluation of the architectural patterns. The trend shows that a total of 18 of 44 architectural patterns satisfy our quality criterias, which is equivalent to 48% of the total (See Figure 2). This gives us to understand that almost half of the architectural academic patterns have a complete description. However, those patterns with low score (between 2 and 2.5) that are equivalent to 4% of the MSPs call our attention. These architectural patterns are **MSP35** and **MSP37**. Although the authors of these architectural patterns describe their potential, it does not satisfy our quality criteria since they do not clearly show their contributions.

Key finding (1): *The academy is joining microservices architectural patterns to other disciplines, for example DevOps and IoT*

RQ2: What architectural tactics have been proposed for microservices? The architectural tactics found in this review are not directly related to microservices. We note that architecture tactics for microservices as such do not exist in academia. However, there are architectural tactics that complement each other with other disciplines, such as DevOps (Development and Operations) [9] [5].

Another article found in the review dealing with architectural tactics indirectly is [26]. In the investigation, they describe two indications to what may be architectural tactics: (1) *scaling* and (2) *independence.* From one side, (1) detail that a microservice must be independently deployable with each microservice having its deployment architecture; and not share its resources like containers, caches, datastores with other enterprise software components. On the other side, (2) is complemented by (1) and detail that scaling of one microservice is independent of other microservices; and increasing the capacity of a microservice, by moving its hosted target or by increasing the number of instances, should not have any impact on its consumers. Both (1) and (2) are not architectural tactics directly. However, the authors refer to these words as decisions in microservice architecture. Therefore, we consider that they may be potential of unexplored architectural tactics.

Key finding (2): *In the academic field, not exist sufficient evidence on architectural tactics for microservices*

RQ3: What are the quality attributes associated with architectural patterns and tactics in microservices? Since on the architectural tactics side we do not find enough evidence, we focus our efforts on architectural patterns. To rescue the quality attributes (QA) associated with the 44 architectural patterns found in our studies, we used information retrieval techniques, such as the Rapid Automatic Keyword Extraction (RAKE) algorithm [22]. After apply some manual filters from the keywords obtained by the algorithm, the QAs with the highest score were: scalability, flexibility, testability, elasticity, and performance.

The most prevalent QAs are are scalability and performance. For scalability, the architectural patterns reveal that exists demand and a need for scalability with microservices, just as there are with a traditional IT architecture and software systems deployment. On the performance side, it is clear that this QA is related to scalability. But, despite the obvious importance of a sufficient level of performance, there is still a lack of performance engineering approaches and architectural patterns explicitly taking into account the particularities of microservices [12].

Key finding (3): *Scalability and performance are trends in microservices architectural patterns*

5 Microservices architectural pattern taxonomy

The contribution of our taxonomy is based on naming, describing and classifying the architectural patterns for microservices find in this revision. To create our taxonomy, we follow the strategy proposed by Velardi et al. [23] which is an automated procedure to achieve a significant speed-up factors (in our case, categories) in the development of resources (architectural patterns) with human validation and refinement. Next, we will proceed to describe the classification for architectural patterns in microservices (see Figure 3):

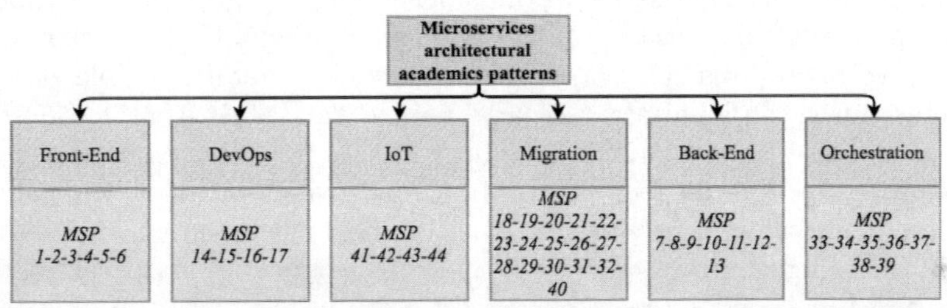

Fig. 3. Proposed taxonomy

IoT patterns: The descriptions of the patterns reveal that microservices and virtualization have changed the industry bringing agility and innovation in this domain.

DevOps patterns: Microservice architecture emerged from a standard set of DevOps ideologies. The evolution of both microservices and DevOps was not just limited to transforming monolithic applications into decomposed services.

Front-End patterns: Our revision reveals that all front-end functionalities are part of a single application and communicate with the back-end that is split into microservices.

Back-End patterns: This category is closely related to the Front-End category. This category describes the layer between the user experience and the resources it calls on.

Orchestration patterns: The orchestration is a concept inherited from SOA. When a service-oriented architecture uses an orchestration pattern for communication, there are point-to-point connections between the services.

Migration patterns: According to [4], the difficulties around the decomposition of a system into small services, and monitoring and managing these services are among the other important factors that make migrating to microservices a non-trivial and cumbersome task.

The taxonomy allows us to visualize those tendencies that academy describe when illustrating recurring solutions in the discipline of microservices.This information gives a practitioner an array of tried and tested solutions to common problems, thus reducing the technical risk to the project by not having to employ a new and untested design.

6 Threats to validity

In this section, we will as a reference the threat list defined in [25] to conduct studies. To minimize the threats to internal validity, the research team that performed the revision discussed each article found based on a scheme, which has the following structure: paper ID, full paper summary, introduction summary, description of the proposal, brief description of the sections of the article, and observations and comments. Some cases, such as the **MSP30** and **MSP36** patterns have a lot of similarity in the name. However, the authors define architectural patterns differently, so we must to include them. On the side of external validity, we have discarded those works that have not been able to validate concretely both the architectural patterns and tactics. In that sense, we were rigorous, because the scientific community is categorical in requesting evidence of the proposals described in the articles. Also, we excluded the so-called *grey literature* (e.g., white papers, editorials, etc.); nevertheless, this issue did not affect our study significantly since we considered papers have undergone a rigorous review process.

Finally, to reduce the selection bias, three researchers made the selection of papers during our revision. Two researchers applied the inclusion and exclusion criteria, compared results and resolved conflicts following the definitions stated in the research protocol. A third person was in charge of managing the selection and participating whenever a resolution is hard to make by the other two. The same three researchers followed the same inclusion/exclusion criteria. Therefore, there was no new confounding factor in the selection of relevant sources from either the included journals/conferences.

7 Conclusions

This article exhibits a summary of architectural patterns and tactics proposed for microservices. To perform the exploratory study, a systematic literature review was performed revealing 8 significant papers. For architectural patterns, the review reported 44 architectural patterns for microservices allowing us to propose a taxonomy based on them. This taxonomy provides a categorization of the 44 architecture patterns for microservices based in Front-End patterns, Back-End patterns, Orchestration patterns, Migration Patterns, IoT patterns and DevOps patterns. On the side of architectural tactics, we did not find tactics related to microservices, allowing us to know and understand that it is an unexplored area. About quality attributes, we found that most of architectural patterns and tactics are associated with five quality attributes: flexibility, testability, elasticity, performance and scalability, the latter two being the most dominant of them.

For researchers, the analysis reveal that there are still significant challenges and issues for future research in the area of architectural patterns/tactics and quality attributes related to microservices. For practitioners, future work is expected to tighten ties between microservices, DevOps and IoT.

Acknowledgments

This work has been financially supported by (1) Comisión Nacional de Investigación Científica (CONICYT) CONICYT-PCHA/Doctorado Nacional/2016-21161005 and (2) FONDECYT regular 1140408. We also appreciate the support of the Chilean Navy.

References

1. Effectiveness matters. the database of abstracts of reviews of effects (dare). United Kingdom: The University of York. https://www.york.ac.uk/media/crd/em62.pdf (2002)
2. Alexander, C., Ishikawa, S., Silverstein, M., i Rami, J.R., Jacobson, M., Fiksdahl-King, I.: A pattern language. University of California, Berkeley (1977)
3. Alshuqayran, N., Ali, N., Evans, R.: A systematic mapping study in microservice architecture. IEEE 9th International Conference on Service-Oriented Computing and Applications (SOCA) pp. 44–51 (2016)
4. Balalaie, A., Heydarnoori, A., Jamshidi, P.: Microservices migration patterns. Technical Report No. 1, Automated Software Engineering Group, Sharif University of Technology (2015)
5. Bass, L., Weber, I., Zhu, L.: Devops: A software architect's perspective. Addison-Wesley Professional (2015)
6. Bass, L., Clements, P., Kazman, R.: Software Architecture in Practice (3rd Edition). SEI Series in Software Engineering (2013)
7. Brown, K., Woolf, B.: Implementation patterns of microservices architectures. Conference on Pattern Languages of Programs (PLoP) (2016)
8. Butzin, B., Golatowski, F., Timmermann, D.: Microservices approach for the internet of things. IEEE 21st International Conference on Emerging Technologies and Factory Automation (ETFA) pp. 1–6 (2016)
9. Chen, H.M., Kazman, R., Haziyev, S., Kropov, V., Chtchourov, D.: Architectural support for devops in a neo-metropolis bdaas platform. IEEE 34th Symposium on Reliable Distributed Systems Workshop (SRDSW) pp. 25–30 (2015)
10. Di Francesco, P., Malavolta, I., Lago, P.: Research on architecting microservices: Trends, focus, and potential for industrial adoption. IEEE International Conference on Software Architecture (ICSA) pp. 21–30 (2017)
11. Dragoni, N., Giallorenzo, S., Lluch-Lafuente, A., Mazzara, M., Montesi, F., Mustafin, R., Safina, L.: Microservices: yesterday, today, and tomorrow. CoRR (2016)

12. Heinrich, R., van Hoorn, A., Knoche, H., Li, F., Lwakatare, L.E., Pahl, C., S., S., Wettinger, J.: Performance engineering for microservices: Research challenges and directions. Proceedings of the 8th ACM/SPEC on International Conference on Performance Engineering Companion pp. 223–226 (2017)
13. Kitchenham, B., Pearl Brereton, O., Budgen, D., Turner, M., Bailey, J., Linkman, S.: Systematic literature reviews in software engineering – A systematic literature review. Information and Software Technology 51(1), 7–15 (2009)
14. Kitchenham, B.: Procedures for performing systematic reviews. Tech. rep., Keele University (2004)
15. Kitchenham, B., Charters, S.: Guidelines for performing Systematic Literature Reviews in Software Engineering. Engineering 2, 1051 (2007)
16. Lewis, J., Fowler, M.: Microservices-a definition of this new architectural term. https://martinfowler.com/articles/microservices.html (2014)
17. Messina, A., Rizzo, R., Storniolo, P., Urso, A.: A simplified database pattern for the microservice architecture. The Eighth International Conference on Advances in Databases, Knowledge, and Data Applications (DBKDA) (2016)
18. Newman, S.: Building microservices: designing fine-grained systems. O'Reilly Media, Inc. (2015)
19. Pahl, C., Jamshidi, P.: Microservices: A systematic mapping study. Proceedings of the 6th International Conference on Cloud Computing and Services Science CLOSER 1, 137–146 (2016)
20. Qanbari, S., Pezeshki, S., Raisi, R., Mahdizadeh, S., Rahimzadeh, R., Behinaein, N., Mahmoudi, F., Ayoubzadeh, S., Fazlali, P., Roshani, K., Yaghini, A., Amiri, M., Farivarmoheb, A., Zamani, A., Dustdar, S.: Iot design patterns: Computational constructs to design, build and engineer edge applications. IEEE First International Conference on Internet-of-Things Design and Implementation (IoTDI) pp. 277–282 (2016)
21. Richardson, C.: A pattern language for microservices. http://microservices.io/patterns/ (2017)
22. Rose, S., Engel, D., Cramer, N., Cowley, W.: Automatic keyword extraction from individual documents. Text Mining: Applications and Theory pp. 1–20 (2010)
23. Velardi, P., Cucchiarelli, A., Petit, M.: A taxonomy learning method and its application to characterize a scientific web community. IEEE Transactions on Knowledge and Data Engineering 19(2) (2007)
24. Vural, H., K.M., Guney, S.: A systematic literature review on microservices. International Conference on Computational Science and Its Applications pp. 203–217 (2017)
25. Wohlin, C., Runeson, P., Hst, M., Ohlsson, M.C., Regnell, B., Wessln, A.: Experimentation in software engineering. Springer Science Business Media (2012)
26. Xiao, Z., Wijegunaratne, I., Qiang, X.: Reflections on soa and microservices. 4th International Conference on Enterprise Systems (ES) pp. 60–67 (2016)

Software Measurement and Estimation: A Case Study in the Financial Services Industry

Juan Cubillos[1] and Jairo Aponte[1]

[1] Universidad Nacional de Colombia, Bogotá, Colombia
{jmcubillosa, jhapontem}@unal.edu.co

Abstract. Software measurement and estimation continue being central aspects of the planning and management of software projects. This research aims to know in detail the evolution and dynamics of those topics in a Colombian financial company, which is highly involved on software development and maintenance projects that are fundamental for its own operation. The instruments used to gather information were an interview and an exploratory survey on software measurement and estimation. The results show although there has been a culture of software measurement with a specific knowledge level, there is a need to design and implement a software measurement and estimation model that integrates the individual activities that are currently carried out, within a much broader conceptual and operational framework. Such a model must include techniques, tools, standards and methodologies, and should be seen not just as an additional management task, but as an essential tool for project planning and optimization aimed at achieving more successful software projects.

Keywords: Software Measurement, Software Estimation, Function Points, SNAP Points, Project Management.

1 Introduction

Research and practical evidence have shown that software size has a direct effect on overall development cost, effort, and schedule [1] . That is why software sizing has gained more and more prominence over time, and nowadays, it is considered as one of the most significant and challenging activities for project planning and management. Although all the inherent drawbacks in providing early and accurate estimations have not yet been resolved, there have been proposed many promising approaches for measuring functional and non-functional requirements [2] [3] [4] [5]. The IFPUG Function Point methodology is one of those techniques that provide an accurate and objective project-sizing measure, suitable for assisting project managers when planning and estimating a new software endeavor.

The main objective of this work is to perform an analysis of the current state of the software measurement and estimation process within the Information Technology (IT) area of a financial company in Colombia, South America. The organization under study has used the IFPUG Function Point methodology for more than 10 years. Likewise, the same method has been used to estimate effort, duration and costs of both new development and maintenance software projects carried out in the company.

In order to perform the desired analysis of the current state of the software measurement and estimation process, we collected and analyzed data from four main areas of interest: (1) the knowledge level of the people involved in that process; (2) the existing measurement and estimation practices and their associated documentation; (3) the tools that support the process; and (4) the usefulness of the current measurement scheme, regarding the project management and software engineering models used in software projects.

The data collection instruments applied in this study included an interview and a survey. They allowed us to gather information related to several facets of the functional and non-functional measurement and estimation activities, in addition to the demographic information of people who play various technical and managerial roles.

The paper is organized as follows: section 2 presents the background of software measurement and estimation as well as a general description of the organization under study. Section 3 describes in detail the interview and the survey used for data collection. Section 4 presents the most significant results extracted from the collected data. Section 5 discusses the key findings, and finally, section 6 presents the conclusions of the study and proposes alternatives to extend this initial work.

2 Background

This section summarizes the most important concepts related to software measurement and estimation that are relevant for the study. Contextual information about the organization under study is also included.

2.1 Software Measurement

Software measurement is an essential component of software engineering. Some authors such as Fenton and Bieman [6] state that technology cannot work without measurement, since it is required in many systems that govern our lives. Measurement helps us understand and interact with our environment and improves our quality of life. Measurement in software engineering has become a well-known and accepted practice. Because some projects fail or do not meet scope, time or cost restrictions, new tools and techniques have emerged to improve both the process and the products generated by projects. Although the software metrics scope is broad, as far as this study is concerned, the most relevant issue is related to software measurement as an essential component for estimating the effort, time and cost in software development and maintenance projects.

With the advent of large-scale software development in the mid-1960s, the software engineering community recognized the need for a better control over the economic aspects surrounding the production and maintenance of software systems. A key aspect was the design of complex procedures to quantify software, so that engineers and project managers be able to have more control and understanding of the multiple factors characteristic of large-scale production [7]. It was at that point, where software measurement started. According to Trendowicz and Jeffery [1], the software size is the main driver for estimating the effort required for its construction. There are two types of software size recognized in the industry: functional and non-functional (also called technical size).

Software functional size is used to measure software from a user perspective. It is independent of technical development and implementation decisions; it can also be used to compare technologies' productivity [7]. Other authors such as Bundschuh and Dekkers [8] define functional size as "a software size derived from the quantification of functional user requirements (FUR)". FURs are defined as a subset of user requirements, which describe what the software should do in terms of functions and services.

Non-functional sizing is used to measure software from a developer perspective. Generally speaking, it addresses quality attributes such as security, performance, reliability, maintainability and portability.

There are multiple industry standards that define the functional software measurement process [9]. Similarly, there are standardized methods such as IFPUG Function Points Method [5], COSMIC Points [2], MK II Function Points Analysis [3], FiSMA [4] and NESMA [10]. Regarding the non-functional component, at the time of this study, there is no industry standard broadly adopted. Instead, there are worldwide recognized methods that are gradually becoming de facto standards such as SNAP Points [11]. In addition, preliminary studies have attempted to integrate functional and non-functional software measurement into a single process, such as the approach proposed by IFPUG [11] [12].

2.2 Software Estimation

The Project Management Institute (PMI) defines "estimate" as a quantitative valuation of a probable quantity or result. It is usually applied to the project costs, resources, effort and duration. It is often preceded by a modifier that clarifies somehow its strength or scope (e.g. preliminary, indicative, feasible, and definitive) [13].

There are different approaches and classifications of software estimation. According to Hill [14], the two principal approaches are macro-estimation and micro-estimation. Macro-estimation (e.g. equations, comparisons and analogies) is mainly used for indicative estimates when there is little information and a high-level estimate is the only feasible alternative. Micro-estimation applies when the project scope is well defined and a Work Breakdown Structure (WBS) can be used to make estimates at the work package level, including activities to produce those work packages. Hence, the overall estimate is the aggregate sum of all estimates of the WBS components.

Abran [15] and other authors classify estimation approaches in two categories: expert judgment and engineering methods. Expert judgment approach is frequently used in software industry; however, it does not have much documentation that supports parameters taken into account and does not provide traceability. Furthermore, it is difficult to measure this model performance since it is not objectively quantified or standardized. Engineering-based approaches are supported by mathematical models and their drivers are parameters managed through clearly defined mathematical equations.

Nguyen's contributions [16] to effort estimation models include a broad description of estimation models such as SLIM, SEER-SEM, PRICE-S, KnowledgePlan, and COCOMO. In addition, there have been studies [17] aimed at comparing the most representative estimation models (e.g., COCOMO II, SEER-SEM, SLIM and True Planning).

2.3 Organization under Study

The organization under study is a company of the financial sector in Colombia - South America. We will refer to it as "XYZ". This company is in the 2000-3000 employees range and has presence all over the country. At the time of this study, the software project portfolio has 20 software development projects and Commercial-Off-The-Shelf (COTS) customization projects as well as 80 software maintenance projects focused on enhancement and defect correction on existing software applications. To support this portfolio, there is an IT area with more than 166 people distributed as shown in Figure 1. It is important to note that part of this staff also carries out ongoing activities related to infrastructure provision services, which are not part of the software project portfolio. Figure 2 shows the most important technologies for each portfolio component in XYZ.

In XYZ, project management and software development methodologies rely on industry standards. For instance, the project management methodology is based on the Project Management Body of Knowledge (PMBOK) created by PMI [18]. In regards to software development process, XYZ uses mostly waterfall and in some cases incremental, and iterative models.

For software measurement and estimation, XYZ has used the IFPUG method [19] [5] for more than 10 years. Prior to the use of this technique, the expert judgment method was the only approach used for the software measurement process. Its results were often considered unsatisfactory, in terms of time, cost and quality. That was why some of the most experienced IT project leaders, from the quality assurance area, proposed the IFPUG Function Points technique to carry out software measurement and estimation activities.

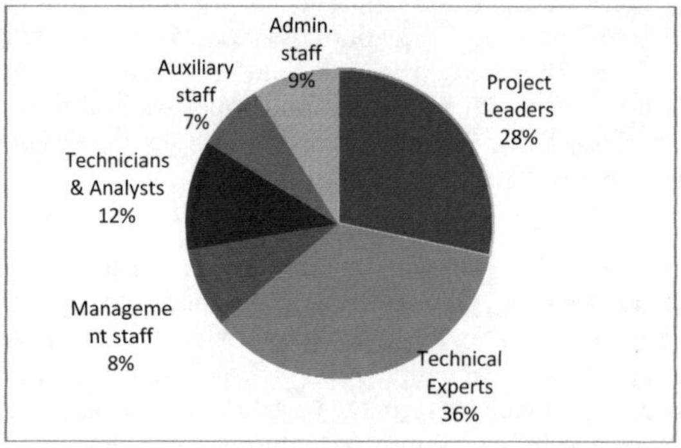

Fig. 1. Staff Distribution.

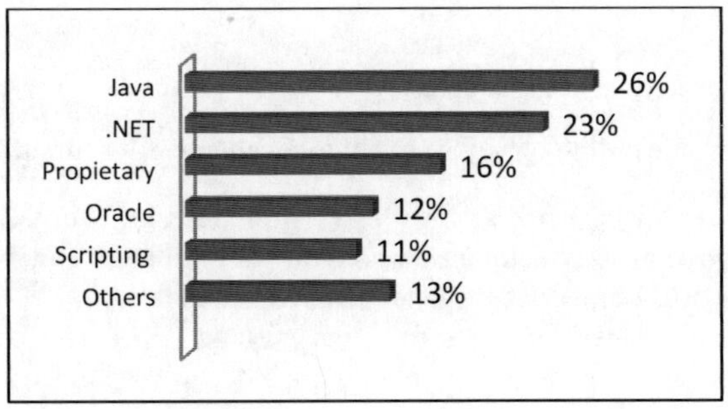

Fig. 2. Software Products by Technology.

The non-functional estimation was initially performed by using the Value Adjustment Factor (VAF) provided by the function points method [20]. Subsequently, this approach was replaced by the expert judgment technique. In addition, XYZ has an outsourcing model for software development and End User Acceptance Testing (UAT). Companies that perform these activities are well known in the local and regional software development market and have extensive experience in the local industry.

3 The Experimental Study

To perform the analysis of the current state of the software measurement and estimation process within XYZ, an in-person interview and an online survey were the two instruments used for data collection.

3.1 The Interview and the Interviewees

The first author of this paper, who is an employee of XYZ, conducted the personal interview. The interviewees were three XYZ employees who have led the software measurement and estimation processes within the company, and two project managers from outsourcing companies that provide software construction services to XYZ and must apply measurement and estimation techniques, as required by XYZ. The interview comprised eleven (11) questions addressing nine (9) topics related to measurement and estimation of software projects in XYZ (i.e., Measurement and estimation process, measurement and estimation parametric techniques for requirements specification, measurement and estimation parametric techniques for software testing, data repositories, measurement and estimation in maintenance projects, outsourcing models for software measurement and estimation, tools for measurement and estimation, documentation availability and knowledge level in measurement and estimation). Since the aim was to encourage a full, meaningful answer using the interviewees' own knowledge and experience, these were open-ended questions that sought the opinion of experts on the subject. The interview was designed in Google Forms and is available on-line [21]. The information collected in the interviews was used to get an overview of the software measurement and estimation process in XYZ. Likewise, it was the main input for performing the qualitative analysis presented in section 4.4.

3.2 The Survey and the Respondents

On the other hand, the online survey was sent to 56 people divided into two groups:

- IT Project leaders who work at XYZ and are or have been involved in measurement and estimation activities for new software development and maintenance projects. The potential number of respondents in this population was 36 people.
- Developers and business analysts from outsourcing firms who perform software measurements and estimates. The potential number of respondents in this population was 20 people. This number could be higher; however, project managers from these firms just provided a list of the 20 people who could respond the survey.

The survey has 26 questions distributed in 5 sections. The first section, related to the demographic profile, inquiries about profession, educational level, age, gender, and software development experience of the respondents. The second, third, and fourth sections are all related to functional and non-functional measurement, and software estimation. These sections request information about knowledge level in terms of methods, techniques, tools and standards; experience in software measurement and estimation process; training, documentation and certification expectations.

The final section has questions about other facets of software measurement and estimation that include opinions on its current documentation, possibilities of making estimation on additional software life cycle stages such as software requirements and software testing. The survey was designed in Qualtrics and the questionnaire is available on-line [22].

The survey was available for three weeks and during this period we got 33 complete responses. They correspond to 58.9% of the sample initially planned. **Table 1** shows the responses distributed by organization type.

Table 1. Respondents' distribution by organization type.

Organization Type	Initial Sample	Respondents	Respondent Percentage
XYZ	36	19	57.58%
Software Provider (Outsourcing)	20	14	42.42%

Other relevant statistics on the respondents' demographic profile are the following:

- 100% of the people involved in software measurement and estimation have a bachelor degree in computer science. 24% of them own a master degree, and 43% have a specialist degree. 30% do not have postgraduate studies. Only one person has doctoral studies.
- The two most representative age ranges are 30-35 years (49% of respondents) and more than 45 years (21% of respondents).
- 72% of respondents are men and 28% are women.

- About 60% of respondents have more than 5 years of experience in software analysis, design and implementation.

4 Results

The following sections present the main findings regarding software measurement and estimation, once the interview and the survey were applied and the results were analyzed. The results described in sections 4.1 and 4.2 refer to the survey, while 4.3 cover findings from both the interview and the survey analysis.

4.1 Software Measurement

In terms of software measurement and estimation, **Table 2** shows the experience reported by the respondents.

Table 2. Respondents' experience in software measurement and estimation

Experience	Percentage
No Experience	3%
0-1 years	9%
1-2 years	21%
2-3 years	24%
3-4 years	21%
More than 5 years	21%

- It is worth noting that 88% of those involved in measuring and estimating software have at least one year of experience.
- About 75% of the respondents have carried out software measurement and estimation on three software projects or less.
- 75% of the respondents have been trained in software functional measurement. The average training period is 9.34 hours per person. 39% of this population has less than 5 hours of training, 22% between 5 and 10 hours, 30% between 10 and 15 hours, and the remaining 9% more than 20 hours.
- Only 12% of the respondents have counted more than 2000 function points. This finding is particularly important because the software measurement industry requires, for instance, to have at least 2500 function points as a mandatory requirement to take the CFPS examination (Certified Function Point Specialist). CFPS is currently the most renowned certification in software measurement, offered by the IFPUG. In the same token, only 9% of the respondents are interested in obtaining certifications on software measurement.
- No more effective software measurement approaches are known than those currently used based on functional measurement. Only 9% of respondents consider that expert judgment is more effective than software measurement based on functionality.

- 71% of the respondents think that functional measurement is appropriate only for new software development projects, while the remaining 29% believe it is useful for both software development and maintenance projects. None of the respondents believes that functional measurement is useful only for maintenance projects.
- 25% of the respondents acknowledge having applied the IFPUG method for software measurement. The remaining 75% neither recognize the IFPUG acronym nor the standard endorsed by this organization.
- 94% of the respondents apply expert judgment for software non-functional measurement. One of the respondents applies a proprietary model and another one does not use measurement methods for non-functional measurement. The respondents are not aware of more effective techniques for non-functional sizing. Only one respondent is interested in getting a non-functional certification.

The main findings regarding the measurement techniques used and the problems when applying them are the following:

- The most recognized measurement techniques are functional measurement, by using the IFPUG method, and counting lines of code. In a few cases and possibly due to a lack of knowledge, some respondents reported COCOMO and Use Cases as software measurement methods.
- The major drawbacks reported in applying software functional measurement rules are listed in **Table 3**. The percentages on the right column allow an assessment of the importance and criticality of the problems reported, according to the participants' experience. For instance, the drawback defined as "The rules do not work well for all types of software" is the most significant problem and was reported by 51.6% of respondents.

Table 3. Major drawbacks reported by the respondents

Drawback	Percentage
The rules do not work well for all types of software	51,6%
The measurement rules are ambiguous	41,9%
Requirements do not have the appropriate quality	38,7%
The rules lexicon is confused or it is inappropriate	29,0%
The learning curve is very long	29,0%
Lack of required business knowledge	25,8%
The documented examples are not practical	25,8%
The official manual differs from internal documentation	6,4%
Access to additional documentation is difficult	3,2%

4.2 Software Estimation

Regarding software estimation and specifically concerning to effort, cost and duration, the salient results are:

- The most recognized model for software estimation is COCOMO II (42%). Regression models (13%) and Planning Poker (16%) are also known. 38% of respondents do not know any software estimation method.
- 90% of respondents use expert judgment in order to estimate time, duration, and effort for software construction. Curiously, the remaining 10% reported that they use function points method for estimating, which technically speaking is not an estimation method but a software measurement approach.

4.3 Other Findings

With regards to the documentation that supports the measurement and estimation processes, 65% of the respondents consider that the documentation available in the organizations, both in XYZ and outsourcing firms, is not enough. Furthermore, 61% of the respondents consider that the existing documentation is useful while the remaining 39% believe otherwise. Apart from that, 7% of the respondents do not know the associated documentation.

Regarding the attitude of the respondents with respect to the importance of maintaining and strengthening measurement and estimation practices, it is remarkable that 90% of the respondents believe that measurement and estimation techniques should be implemented to measure and estimate requirements specification effort, duration and costs. Moreover, 97% of the respondents believe that measurement and estimation techniques should be implemented to measure and estimate software testing, duration and costs.

4.4 SWOT Analysis

This section presents the results of a SWOT analysis (**S**trengths – **W**eaknesses – **O**pportunities -**T**hreats) [23]. SWOT is a qualitative analysis carried out by an organization to identify and understand its internal strengths and weaknesses, as well as its external opportunities and threats. The input for this analysis was the information collected through the interviews, along with part of the survey answers that complemented a few factors of the SWOT model.

Strengths

- Despite the multiple difficulties reported by the participants in this study, the use of functional measurement for more than 10 years, using the IFPUG method, is a clear strength of XYZ.
- XYZ has a membership to the most recognized organizations such as ISBSG and IFPUG, which allows XYZ staff to keep well-informed of advances in software measurement and estimation.
- Software development and maintenance contracts are performed with Service Level Agreements (SLAs) by using functional measurement and productivity based on IFPUG function points standard.

Weaknesses

- In spite of experience on software measurement, key areas of software measurement and estimation are unknown or not completely dominated by both internal XYZ staff and externally in companies that provide software development services.
- The measurement body of knowledge based on function points is not internalized in many people involved in measurement and estimation tasks. Thus, the knowledge is very unevenly spread over the employees.
- There are no methods other than expert judgment for non-functional software measurement and estimation.
- There is no repository to record software measurements and estimates history from previous projects.
- There are no formal methods to measure and estimate software testing processes, activities and tasks.
- Most of the time software measurement and estimation documentation is not used.
- Software measurement and estimation documentation is out-of-date.
- Mainly due to the lack of knowledge, there are different interpretations when the rules of software measurement and estimation are applied.
- Corrective software maintenance is carried out without using any parametric method to measure the size of software to be modified or to estimate the effort required to make those modifications.

Opportunities

- XYZ is interested in a software measurement and estimation model implementation, which will expand through various software life cycle stages. Furthermore, the model will address the issues detected in this study.
- XYZ recognizes the importance of implementing measurement and estimation practices for non-functional software components by using new techniques to replace expert judgment and improve the accuracy of measurement and estimation activities.
- XYZ is willing to analyze possibilities for implementing a parametric measurement and estimation model for corrective, adaptive and preventive software maintenance in order to plan and control in a better way this phase of the software lifecycle.
- XYZ has identified the need and strategic value of reinforcing processes and documentation according to the industry standards, in regards to software measurement and estimation to support the training strategy and accuracy of the results.
- XYZ considers it is essential to create a common lexicon for all stakeholders involved in software measurement and estimation as a first step of maturity in a continuous improvement process.
- For XYZ, creating a software measurement and estimation training program is fundamental for maintaining and improving people's knowledge and skills over time.

- For XYZ, implementing a software measurement and estimation approach for requirements specification is considered the basis for a better project planning and control in this phase of the software lifecycle.
- For XYZ, implementing a measurement and estimation scheme for software testing activities will improve project planning and control in this phase of the software lifecycle.

Threats

- Expert judgment as the only non-functional software estimation method. In many scenarios, the estimator is a person who lacks experience and knowledge to make estimates with acceptable error margins.
- Outdated and incomplete documentation leads to misapplication of measurement and estimation principles and rules.
- The absence of a repository to store the history of measurement and estimation does not allow having key indicators of quality, time and costs associated with software development.
- The risks involved in the increasing use of expert judgment to estimate the effort, cost and lifespan of software projects.

5 Discussion

Although there have been significant efforts to implement a software measurement and estimation model in XYZ, the staff turnaround and the use of fragmented procedures and instruments have caused that the measurement and estimation activities have been partially carried out in most of the cases, and without a clear benefit to the organization. The original project, conceived about 10 years ago, was probably well implemented in its initial phase. However, the evidence from this analysis shows that, over time, the level of knowledge of employees has been gradually decreasing, and consequently, the measurement and estimation practices have not been done with the necessary rigor.

Since the knowledge level of the employees about software measurement and estimation is neither uniform nor good enough, for some of them the tasks required for measurement and estimation activities are not perceived as a project planning and optimization tool, but as additional tasks that do not add value to the software engineering process or project management.

The review of the measurement processes carried out within the company reveals that there have been cases in which for the same measurement scenario, the results obtained by two different teams may differ by up to 50% (in the industry, differences up to 10-15% are acceptable). Thus, there are evidences that software counts and subsequent estimates have been highly subjective. This type of discrepancies might have been resulted in a loss of confidence in the measurement and estimation techniques. Based on the information collected in this study, we believe that the main causes of this problem are the lack of knowledge about measurement and estimation and ongoing training and research around measurement and estimation issues, both internally in XYZ and externally in outsourcing firms.

Based on the gathered evidences from the interviews in regards to lack of appropriate tools to support the software measurement and estimation process in XYZ, it is necessary to conduct a market research study about tools that support the measurement and estimation of software. The focus of such a study should be on software projects measurement and estimation repositories and software estimation tools that implement proprietary or open models. A suggested starting point could be reviewing the research conducted by Buglione and Ebert about estimation tools and techniques [24].

In order to improve the entire measurement and estimation process and their outcomes, we think it is critical to build a productivity model that supports the software estimation processes. This model should include the data collected from previous projects, so that it serves as an essential component for estimating the effort, cost and duration of new software projects.

Overall, this study uncovers opportunities for improvement in the majority of facets that require measurement and estimation associated with software development activities, ranging from requirements specification to software testing. It is also important to use tools that enable tracking of historical information as well as others that support the estimation effort process. Furthermore, current contracting practices in regards to outsourcing software construction must be complemented to include relevant aspects of measurement and estimation. Finally, yet importantly, XYZ must analyze and improve the current training approach and the available documentation that involves software measurement. This may lead to the idea of implementing an integral model where the findings described above are articulated for solving XYZ needs and problems related to software measurement and estimation. Attacking each problem in isolation could lead once again to results similar to those related to the implementation of the functional points: Fragmented knowledge, gradual loss of knowledge and lack of connection with other software development facets.

6 Conclusions and Future Work

We present an empirical study aimed at evaluating the software measurement and estimation practices implemented in a Colombian financial company, which is involved on software development and maintenance projects. The instruments used to gather information were an interview and an exploratory survey. The interviewees were three XYZ employees who have led the software measurement and estimation processes within the company, and two project managers from outsourcing companies that provide software development services to XYZ. 19 project leaders of XYZ, and 14 developers and business analysts from outsourcing firms answered the online survey.

The study results indicate that using the functional point technique over a specific period of time is not enough to ensure that software measurement practices add value to the entire software development process and contribute to the success of the projects. Our findings show that in XYZ the software measurement and estimation process is fragmented and it has only certain strength in functional measurement, by using IFPUG function points, although many of those involved on this process neither recognize the IFPUG acronym nor fully understand the rationale behind the process steps.

Moreover, measures and estimates in other software development cycle phases such as non-functional measurement and software testing are great opportunities for improvement. That is even more interesting since in those phases the only technique used is the expert judgment, and in some cases, those involved in its application are not experts in the technology, the software that supports the business, or in the use of the technique itself.

Although the results of this analysis are specific to the company and the findings are difficult to generalize, this study can be useful for other organizations in terms of the process carried out to get the results: using traditional instruments such as interviews and surveys. Subsequently analyze statistical information and finally, perform a SWOT analysis to structure findings and conclusions.

Future studies might be focused on structuring integral software measurement and estimation models as a result of company's needs and requirements analysis that operate in a multi-software project environment.

Overall, the results highlight the importance of designing and implementing a software measurement and estimation model for organizations like XYZ, with a multi-project environment. Such a model should encompass components that act on the different scenarios where measurement and estimation play an important role for project planning, control and decision making processes. The major model components should be related to measurement and estimation on main software engineering phases such as requirements specification, software construction and testing. The model must be applicable to software development and maintenance projects.

References

[1] A. Trendowicz and R. Jeffery, *Software Project Effort Estimation: Foundations and Best Practice Guidelines for Success*.: Springer Publishing Company, 2014.

[2] ISO, *ISO/IEC 19761:2011. COSMIC: A functional size measurement method*. Geneva, Switzerland.: International Organization for Standardization, 2011.

[3] ISO, *ISO/IEC 20968:2002. MK II Function Point Analysis – Counting Practices Manual*. Geneva, Switzerland.: International Organization for Standardization, 2002.

[4] ISO, *ISO/IEC 29881:2010. FiSMA 1.1 functional size measurement method*. Geneva, Switzerland.: International Organization for Standardization, 2010.

[5] ISO, *ISO/IEC 20926:2009. IFPUG functional size measurement method*. Geneva, Switzerland: International Organization for Standardization, 2009.

[6] N. Fenton and J. Bieman, *Software Metrics. A Rigorous and Practical Approach*. Boca Raton, Florida: CRC Press, 2015.

[7] Alain Abran, *Software Metrics and Software Metrology*. Hoboken, New Jersey USA: IEEE Computer Society, 2010.

[8] M. Bundschuh and C. Dekkers, *The IT Measurement Compendium*.: Springer Verlag Berlin Heidelberg, 2008.

[9] ISO, *ISO/IEC 14143:2012. Functional Size Measurement*. Geneva, Switzerland.:

International Organization for Standardization, 2012.

[10] ISO, *ISO/IEC 24570:2005. NESMA functional size measurement method versión 2.1*. Geneva, Switzerland.: International Organization for Standardization, 2005.

[11] IFPUG, *Integrating Procedures for Function Point Analysis and the Software Non-functional Assessment Process (SNAP) - Part 1*. Princenton Juntion, NJ USA: The International Function Points Users Group, 2016.

[12] IFPUG, *Integrating Procedures for Function Point Analysis and the Software Non-functional Assessment Process (SNAP) - Part 2*. Princenton Juntion, NJ USA: The International Function Points Users, 2017.

[13] PMI, *Practice Standard for Project Estimating*. Newtown Square, Pennsylvania USA.: Project Management Institute, 2010.

[14] P. Hill, *Practical Software Project Estimation. A toolkit for Estimating Software Development Effort & Duration*. New York USA: ISBSG, 2011.

[15] A. Abran, *Software Project Estimation: The Fundamentals for Providing High Quality Information to Decision Makers*, 1st ed. New Jersey, USA: Wiley, 2015.

[16] V. Nguyen, "Improved Size and Effort Estimation Models," University of Southern California, Los Angeles, USA, PhD Thesis 2010.

[17] Derya Toka and Oktay Turetken, "Accuracy of Contemporary Parametric Software Estimation Models," *2013 39th Euromicro Conference Series on Software Engineering and Advanced Applications*, pp. 313-316, 2013.

[18] PMI, *Project Management Body Of Knowledge*, Project Management Institute, Ed. Newtown Square, PA, USA, 2013.

[19] IFPUG, *IFPUG International Function Points Group Website*. Princenton Juntion, NJ USA: International Function Points Users Group, 2016. [Online]. http://www.ifpug.org

[20] IFPUG- The International Function Points Users Group, *Function Point Counting Practices Manual Release 4.3.1*, 431st ed. Princenton Juntion, New Jersey , USA: IFPUG, 2010.

[21] Juan Cubillos and Jairo Aponte. (2017) Interview. [Online]. http://www.it-jmca.com/UN/Paper1/Interview.pdf

[22] J. Cubillos and J. Aponte. (2017) Survey. [Online]. http://www.it-jmca.com/UN/Paper1/Survey.pdf

[23] I. Onyebuchi, J. Nzekwe, and I. Osita, "Organization's stability and productivity: the role of SWOT analysis an acronym for strength, weakness, opportunities and threat," *International Journal of Innovative and Applied Research*, vol. 2, no. 9, pp. 23-32, 2014.

[24] L. Buglione and C. Ebert, "Estimation Tools and Techniques," *IEEE Software*, vol. 28, no. 3, pp. 91-94, 2011.

Towards a Developer's Reputation Model Based on Source Code Features

Óscar Garavito, Jairo Aponte, Felipe Restrepo-Calle, and Fabio González

Universidad Nacional de Colombia, Bogotá, Colombia
{ojgaravitom, jhapontem, ferestrepoca, fagonzalezo}@unal.edu.co

Abstract. Recruiting software developers is an expensive and time-consuming task. To simplify and expedite this process, code challenges, traditionally used in programming contests, are being used to assess coder skills in recruitment platforms. Reputation in programming contest platforms is earned obtaining a good performance, i.e., solving coding challenges. However, studies collected from current literature do not propose any relationship between reputation and code styling or quality features. This paper presents a novel strategy to build a developer's reputation model for programming contest platforms based on source code analysis. The steps followed to accomplish this goal are: selection of a platform reputation model, extraction of source code features, and creation and evaluation of a new reputation model. To evaluate the proposed strategy, a pilot experiment was designed using the Codeforces platform. It was aimed at the classification of developers in either advanced or beginner, analyzing their code style. In the study two methods were used for classification, random forest and neural networks, obtaining an accuracy around 70%.

Keywords: reputation, source code analysis, neural network, random forest, developer recruitment

1 Introduction

Processes for recruiting people are usually expensive and time-consuming [5], and many companies have several problems filling vacancies [1]. Today, it is common to see traditional recruitment processes to hire software developers where managers still use interviews as integral part of the applicant evaluation [12]. However, it is difficult for an interviewer to assess the required skills within a conversation of a few minutes. Furthermore, paying for third party recruiters is not a definitive solution, since costs are high and it may be inevitable to evaluate a considerable number of people who do not meet the desired profiles [13].

Some technological platforms have recently appeared offering developer recruitment services. These Internet-based platforms aim at assessing people from a technical perspective, using code challenges. Examples of this kind of platforms include Codility[1], Toptal[2], and Kattis[3]. In addition, recent studies have shown the importance of such platforms in developer recruitment processes [8].

Nowadays, it is a common practice that recruitment platforms use code challenges from programming contests such as Codeforces[4], HackerRank[5], among others. Thus, one can argue that well ranked developers in competitive programming platforms may have the required coding skills in recruitment processes.

In open source communities and collaborative platforms, developers use to be ranked based on their contributions. Nevertheless, in programming contest environments, programmers are classified using their results in each competition they join in. This concept is known as reputation, which is defined as the set of opinions and ideas that a community or part of it has about a person or company [2]. By the same token, Hendrikx et al. [6] stated that reputation is the perception created by an actor, with each performed action, concerning to its aims and rules.

Several researchers have investigated different aspects that influence developer's reputation in coding platforms. In Hu et al. [7], several social factors are analyzed to determine the main motivations of developers to positively grade their peers in collaborative open source platforms. They found that developers are directly influenced by social aspects when grading their peers. Among the most influential factors are: working together in previous projects; sharing the same languages, both natural and programming; and belonging to the same country or community. Surprisingly, this study completely dismisses technical factors, and only takes into account human interactions.

On the other hand, Méndez-Durón [10] shows that reputation is more influenced by the performance of the individuals than by social interactions. Notwithstanding, this study does not deep into source code features related to code quality measures, such as design complexity or code efficiency, which were excluded from the analysis. The author admits that source code features could be important to determine some aspects of reputation.

Although some studies have tried to relate reputation with source code characteristics [2, 4, 7, 10], they have not performed an in deep analysis of the source code written by developers, when considering their reputation. Most of them only consider indirect traits, such as amount of contributions [2, 7] or final project success [4, 10]. A surprising conclusion found in literature is that it is difficult to build a reputation measure that takes technical factors into account [9].

In this context, we propose an emerging idea to explore source code features to determine their relationship to developer's reputation. This paper presents a strategy to build a developer's reputation model based on source code characteristics, within programming contest platforms. This may constitute the cornerstone of a reputation model to assess the technical skills of a developer, based on

[1] https://codility.com
[2] https://www.toptal.com
[3] https://open.kattis.com
[4] http://codeforces.com
[5] https://www.hackerrank.com

qualifications provided by a platform. It could be eventually used in recruitment processes.

The rest of this paper is organized as follows. Section 2 explains the process to describe developer's reputation based on features extracted from their source code. Next, Section 3 describes the proposed strategy and the preliminary results obtained in a pilot experiment. Finally, Section 4 concludes the paper and gives directions for future work.

2 Developer's reputation based on source code analysis

In order to build a developer's reputation model that considers objective and technical aspects, i.e., source code features, we focus our research on programming contest platforms. These platforms offer several useful features for our purposes: they allow us to isolate developer's code and review code through time; they have built-in reputation rankings to be used as input for the new reputation model construction; and their coding challenges have begun to be used in recruitment processes.

We propose a methodology comprised of four steps to develop the model (Figure 1). The first one is the classification of reputation models used in programming contest platforms. The second stage involves the selection of source code features, suitable for building a reputation model. In the third stage we design and implement a predictive model for reputation using machine learning techniques. Lastly, we validate the model in an empirical way.

In the first phase, the main development competition platforms are selected and their reputation models are analyzed. Information useful for this study is analyzed and categorized, extracting the main characteristics of several reputation rankings. To do that, a literature review is carried out, looking for a variety of reputation models. Furthermore, a comparison among these reputation models is performed, which is the input for the next stages.

Not only reputation models are important to this research, but also another factors, such as source code availability, historical reports of both source code and ranks, supported languages, and size of the code database. With that classification at least one platform is selected to perform experiments on there, taking ranks and code to build a new reputation model.

In addition, a code dataset is built in a database or repository, along with some metadata, such as the author of the code snippet, date of submission, and author's reputation scale. Moreover, the extracted code must satisfy some

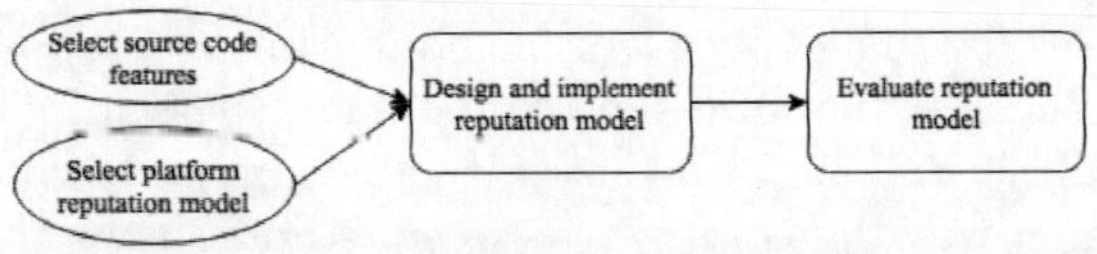

Fig. 1. Building a developer's reputation model based on source code features.

criteria: only accepted solutions are taken into account; programming language version has to be recent; code must be written for the same kind of contest or practice. The dataset size has to be defined at this point.

The aim of the second phase is to select source code features to be used for building a reputation model. At this point, a literature review is required to extract a list of features, used in the state of the art for source code analysis, which describe developers code styling. Works related to other applications of source code analysis can be taken into account as well.

With the previous information, a predictive model for developer's reputation is implemented in the third stage. Firstly, a theoretical model is described based on the findings of previous stages. Secondly, it is implemented in a programming language that results appropriate to perform repeatable experiments, with a set of parameters as input, and the reputation assessment as output.

The final stage is required to assess the precision and recall of the model and validate its results on a testing dataset.

3 Pilot experiment

The goal of the experiment is to construct a prototype to initially explore the relationship between reputation and code features in programming contest platforms. The experiment is conducted through three main steps (Figure 2): source code extraction and analysis, feature representation, and classifier learning and evaluation.

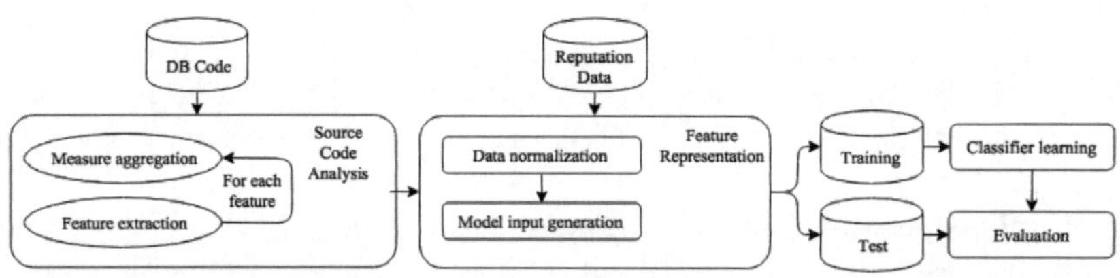

Fig. 2. Experimental setup: source code analysis, feature representation, classifier learning and evaluation.

3.1 Dataset: *CodeForces*

To build a dataset for this experiment, as stated in the purposed methodology, the first step is the selection of the programming contest platform. To do so, a comparative analysis was performed with the most prevalent platforms.

Table 1 summarizes the comparative results and shows the set of relevant traits for the goals of this research. This table indicates whether the platform has an Application Programming Interface (API) to extract the information (Y

- Yes, S - Only Submission, P - Can obtain user data, and N - No). The third column indicates whether the source code can be extracted. The fourth column contains a list of the main supported languages. Finally, it also describes how the rankings are calculated; this represents the reputation model of each platform.

Platforms reputation models are mainly divided in two categories. The first one implies that competition platforms apply a formula to obtain a numerical rank for each contestant. In this group an ELO ranking is commonly used. The second classification uses a simpler approach, taking competition results as a number and summing up those values to the developers' reputation directly. Apart from these numerical rankings, two platforms use badges to give an additional qualitative information, but they were not considered for this paper purposes.

Table 1. Summary of programming contest platforms. The information includes whether the platform provides an API, if there is code available to be downloaded, supported languages, and the reputation model used

Platform	API	Code Avail	Supported Language	Reputation model
Codeforces	Y	Y	C++, Java, Python, C#	Ranking Elo
HackerRank	S	Y	C++, Java, Python, C#	Ranking Elo + badges
TopCoder	Y	N	C++, Java, C#, VB .Net	Ranking Elo
HackerEarth	S	Y	C++, Java, Python, C#	Ranking Elo
Coderbyte	N	Y	C++, Java, Python, C#	Simple counting
SPOJ	N	Y	C++, Java, Python, C#	Formula
Codechef	N	Partial	C++, Java, Python, C#	Simple counting
Codeeval	N	Unknown	C++, Java, Python, C#	Simple
Codewars	P	Unknown	C++, Java, Python, C#	Simple
Exercism	N	Y	C++, Java, Python, C#	No one, uses GitHub.
CodinGame	N	Already solved	C++, Java, Python, C#	Simple + badges

The selected platform for this experiment was CodeForces. It was chosen among all the possibilities due to several practical reasons. For instance: developer's code is available; it supports Java, which is the preferred language for this research; it records developer's reputation over time; it contains a global and centralized history; and its aggregation method for the reputation assessment is not a simple count, but it is calculated using the Elo rating system.

Only Java code was considered in this experiment, to simplify the pilot test execution. We extracted solutions from the competition exercises, which means that they were developed within a contest that had time restrictions. Code snippets are completely functional submissions for one problem in the platform. In this way, it is guaranteed that these programs successfully compile and run.

To classify developers using the Codeforces reputation system, we use the ranking value that each one has after competitions. The new ranking value, achieved by developers, is used to arrange the source code in two categories. Beginner coders were considered up to 1,900 points, and expert ones were taken from 2,300 points onwards. Table 2 shows basic information about the dataset. It constitutes the database input for the first step shown in Figure 2. In total, 4,723 code snippets were obtained, from which 2,363 correspond to beginners and

2,360 to advanced coders. The authors of these snippets of code were distributed as 338 beginners and 26 advanced. Almost 75% of the data was used in training step and 25% remaining for evaluation.

Table 2. Summarization and characterization of dataset. It is divided by usage, developer reputation and Java versions.

	Evaluation		Training		Developers	
	Beginner	Advanced	Beginner	Advanced	Beginner	Advanced
Total	566	587	1,797	1,773	338	26
	1,153		3,570		364	

3.2 Source code analysis

The basis of our predictive model is a set of source code features that accurately reflect a developer's reputation. As a starting point to determine such a feature set, we consider the work by Caliskan-Islam et al. [3], where authors came up with a set of code features that reveal the coding style of a developer. In the implementation of our model, for each feature, each code snippet was analyzed, and a specific measure was extracted from the Abstract Syntax Trees (AST). The features considered are briefly described below.

Average identifier length (AIL). The sum of the lengths of all the identifiers is divided by the total number of identifiers of the code snippet.

Average line length (ALL). Length of lines of code in average for the entire code. Blank lines are also counted because they might delimit small readable blocks of code.

Average of methods by class (AMBC). For each class a number of methods is counted; then, an average is calculated among the number of classes.

Average method cyclomatic complexity (AMCC). Number of branches created by control flow statements and cycles is counted for each method. After that, an average is calculated.

Maximum depth in nested blocks (MDNB). All control flow sentences and cycles are evaluated in each method. Then, the deeper structure is extracted and the height of the tree is calculated.

Number of AST nodes (NASTN). Number of AST nodes is extracted.

Number of Java keywords (NOJK). Amount of Java keywords used in code for versions 1.7 and 1.8. It allows repetition of words.

Number of lines of code (NLOC). The number of lines of code is counted here. Blank and comment lines are ignored.

Size. A discrete measure of the file size, in terms of lines of code. Ranges used were: very small [<50], small [50-100] medium [100-200], large [200-350], and extra-large[>350].

Usage of Java API (UJAPI). All method invocations to the Java API are counted. This metric aims to indicate the usage of the Java API, which could indicate the level of expertise using Java [11].

3.3 Feature representation

In order to build a prediction model, the extracted characteristics need to be properly represented. All feature measures were represented numerically in their own scales, and then some of them were normalized, i.e., they were transformed into a zero-one scale. These features are the input for the neural network and random forest classifiers.

These actions fit into the second step depicted in Figure 2, as well as the reputation information taken from dataset, which is used for model training. This information is also useful to assess the model precision and recall, by comparing model's output and extracted reputation.

3.4 Classifier learning and evaluation

The models for predicting the reputation level of the developer were trained to extract knowledge between the reputation information and the source code features. To do so, we used two different classifiers: a 6-layer artificial neural network (ANN); and a random forest with 3,000 trees. In addition, both models were compared to a dummy classifier, in order to establish a baseline for comparisons.

To train the models, the input generated in previous steps was used jointly with the reputation data, which corresponds to a label that indicates if each developer is beginner or advanced. As it is shown in Table 2, 75% of the dataset is used to train the model and the remaining 25% is used to evaluate it.

As it was previously said, the ANN has 6 layers, with only two different activation functions: *sigmoid*, used for input and output, and *relu*, used for hidden layers; and learning rate was set to 0.01. Random forest parameters were 3,000 trees and the number for the minimum samples required to be at a leaf node was set to 1,000. These configurations were chosen according to their performance.

Table 3 presents the obtained results for the baseline and the two models. Two metrics were taken into account, F1 and accuracy. Best results were obtained by the random forest classifier with 69.8% of accuracy and 73.5% of F1. The ANN achieves 67.8% of accuracy and 67.5% of F1. Both results were higher than the result obtained by the dummy classifier for around 20%.

The proposed model is able to predict the developers' reputation from source code features, in a considerable amount of the cases. It is worth noting that it is feasible to infer the developer's level only based on his/her code styling. This result opens up the door to future research with bigger datasets, and it also demonstrates that it is possible to build a reputation model using technical factors.

Table 3. Classification report: precision and recall by developer reputation.

	Dummy classifier	Neural network (ANN)	Random forest
Accuracy	0.489	0.678	0.698
F1	0.492	0.675	0.735

4 Conclusions and future work

The strategy for developer's reputation forecast, presented in this paper, shows a preliminary evidence about a feasible way to predict the coder's level using source code features. It also uncovers positive relationships between the developer's reputation and their code styling. This represents a promising step towards a model for developer's reputation, based on source code analysis, that can be used in recruitment processes. However, further studies are needed, for instance, to assess the impact of each code feature on the reputation score and to validate the model in more real scenarios.

Thus, the future work will be focused on refining the prediction model and the experimental setup. In addition, this study requires more statistical validation to support findings. In particular, we plan to use more platforms and a more comprehensive set of source code features.

References

1. S. Alamro, H. Dogan, and K. Phalp. Forming Enterprise Recruitment Pattern Based on Problem-Oriented Conceptual Model. *Procedia Computer Sci*, 64:298–305, jan 2015.
2. Yuanfeng Cai and Dan Zhu. Reputation in an open source software community: Antecedents and impacts. *Decision Support Systems*, 91:103–112, 2016.
3. A. Caliskan-Islam, A. Liu, R. Harang, A. Narayanan, C. Voss, F. Yamaguchi, and R. Greenstadt. De-anonymizing Programmers via Code Stylometry. In *USENIX Security Symposium*, pages 255–270, 2015.
4. Rosalva E. Gallardo-Valencia, Phitchayaphong Tantikul, and Susan Elliott Sim. Searching for reputable source code on the web. *Proceedings of the 16th ACM international conference on Supporting group work - GROUP '10*, page 183, 2010.
5. J. Grabara, S. Kot, and L. Pigoń. Recruitment process optimization: chosen fi ndings from practice in Poland. *Journal of International Studies*, 9(10), 2016.
6. Ferry Hendrikx, Kris Bubendorfer, and Ryan Chard. Reputation systems: A survey and taxonomy. *Journal of Parallel and Distributed Comp.*, 75:184–197, jan 2015.
7. Daning Hu, J. Leon Zhao, and Jiesi Cheng. Reputation management in an open source developer social network: An empirical study on determinants of positive evaluations. *Decision Support Systems*, 53(3):526–533, 2012.
8. Grzegorz Jakacki, Marcin Kubica, and Tomasz Walé N. Codility. Application of Olympiad-Style Code Assessment to Pre-Hire Screening of Programmers. *Olympiads in Informatics*, 5:32–43, 2011.
9. Eduard Kuric. Estimation of Student ' s Programming Expertise. In *ESEM '14 Proceedings of the 8th ACM/IEEE International Symposium on Empirical Software Engineering and Measurement*, number 1, 2014.
10. R. Méndez-Durón. Do the allocation and quality of intellectual assets affect the reputation of open source software projects? *Info. & Manag.*, 50(7):357–368, 2013.
11. Dong Qiu, Bixin Li, Earl T. Barr, and Zhendong Su. Understanding the syntactic rule usage in java. *Journal of Systems and Software*, 123:160–172, 2017.
12. Steve Tockey. Insanity, Hiring, and the Software Industry. *Computer*, 48(11):96–101, nov 2015.
13. Joshua Tyler. *Building Great Software Engineering Teams: Recruiting, Hiring, and Managing Your Team from Startup to Success*. Apress, 2015.

Privacy by Design in Software Engineering: a Systematic Mapping Study

Miguel Ehécatl Morales-Trujillo[a], Erick Orlando Matla-Cruz[b], Gabriel Alberto García-Mireles[c] and Mario Piattini[d]

[a] Computer Science and Software Engineering Department, University of Canterbury, Christchurch, New Zealand

miguel.morales@canterbury.ac.nz

[b] Posgrado de la Facultad de Medicina, Universidad Nacional Autónoma de México, Av. Universidad 3000, Ciudad Universitaria, 04510, Mexico City, Mexico

ematla@fmposgrado.unam.mx

[c] Departamento de Matemáticas, Universidad de Sonora, Hermosillo, México

mireles@mat.uson.mx

[d] Alarcos Research Group, University of Castilla – La Mancha, Paseo de la Universidad 4, 13071, Ciudad Real, Spain

mario.piattini@uclm.es

Abstract. Privacy by Design (PbD) is becoming a relevant issue that challenge the way software is developed. The objective of this paper is to determine the extent to which PbD has been applied in software development endeavors. A Systematic Mapping Study was carried out to identify primary papers that describe the way PbD is considered in software engineering, which principles or goals pursues, and what PbD practices or techniques are used in software development efforts. As a whole, we identified a deficiency of sound PbD-related research in the area of software development. The selected primary papers address PbD from a general experience-based perspective. However, good PbD-related practices are neither fully developed nor validated. Furthermore, we observed a strong tendency toward following principles rather than explicit practices.

Keywords: privacy by design, software engineering, software development, systematic mapping study, GDPR

1 Introduction

According to Warren and Brandeis [1], privacy is a state of social withdrawal or the right to be 'left alone'. Altman [2], Nissenbaum [3], Palen and Dourish [4] state that privacy is not just a state of withdrawal, but a contextual, situated, practically achieved matter of boundary management. This means that the context in which information is disclosed and the mechanisms to handle it are essential to determine the extent privacy is addressed in a particular situation [A1]. In this document, square bracket references that contain the letter 'A' refer to the primary papers in this SMS, full reference list can be consulted in the additional material (https://goo.gl/iKTLLr).

In the context of people, personal data is sensitive data that must be safeguarded on two fronts: by technological means and by legal means [5]. Almost any up-to-date system whose goal is to automate and speed up processes stores sensitive data. Being concerned about data privacy should, therefore, be part of any software development, regardless of the industry for which it is intended. In software development efforts, the protection of data is usually resolved through the use of encryption and security applications frameworks. These solutions are, however, applied in the last stages of software development and, moreover, developers must be aware of the usage and exposure of data that the system manipulates or extracts.

Several data protection laws supported by governmental bodies have been created. One example of these is the recent General Data Protection Regulation (GDPR) (Regulation EU 2016/679), which is supported by the European Parliament, the Council of the European Union (EU) and the European Commission and was brought into being with the intention of strengthening and unifying data protection for all individuals within the EU. This regulation incorporates data protection rules that cover design, safety and security measures, and conduct policies; it also defines a special role in charge of evaluating and analyzing data privacy measures.

The concept of Privacy by Design (PbD) has become important in this environment, and has been highly advocated by policy makers; it was conceived in order to mitigate privacy threats from the very beginning, by creating a process that designs information systems in a privacy-respectful manner [A2]. The PbD approach is relatively new and has been unanimously acclaimed as a global privacy standard by the body of International Data Protection Commissioners[1]. In fact, the lack of robust privacy methodologies has led to an increasing acceptance of PbD [A3], which seeks to influence technology design, business practices, and physical infrastructure by embedding privacy protection at its core [A4].

The existent research addresses the PbD approach; however, good PbD-related practices and tasks are not, as yet, fully developed. According to [6], the next stage of PbD evolution is to translate its "7 Foundational Principles" into more prescriptive requirements, specifications, standards, best practices, and operational-performance criteria. Indeed, IT practitioners cannot find appropriate methodological support to implement PbD in software development [A5] and there is a lack of tools to support the design and construction of privacy-friendly systems [A6].

We believe that introducing PbD into software developments is both viable and useful because it is a potential means of including best practices that address data protection in information systems. Moreover, PbD is ideally focused on or targeted at technology developers/providers/designers and manufacturers [7]. The objective of this paper is, therefore, to carry out a systematic mapping study (SMS) in order to determine

[1] https://icdppc.org/

the State of the Art of PbD and its best practices as regards use in software development endeavors.

This paper is organized as follows: Section 2 describes the background of PbD, while Section 3 describes the design of the SMS and its results. The discussion is presented in Section 4. Finally, our conclusions are covered in Section 5.

2 PbD Background

2.1 Towards Understanding Privacy by Design

"Privacy by design" is a concept developed in the 1990s whose purpose is to embed privacy into the design of technology [A7]. The PbD concept relies on a set of seven principles that provide a framework for addressing privacy and data protection throughout all stages of IT and information systems development, including IT design, operation, and management [A7] [8]. The PbD principles are: privacy as default, end-to-end security, respect for user privacy, openness and transparency, proactive not reactive, privacy embedded into design, and full functionality [8] [9]. These principles were derived from the Fair Information Practices [A7] which serve to translate privacy and data protections objectives to law, policy and technologies [8].

Relevant concepts in PbD that need to be described are privacy and data protection. Privacy is related to the control that individuals have over the collection, use, and disclosure of personally identifiable information [9]. Informational privacy is defined as "the ability to maintain control over the use and dissemination of one's personal information" [9]. On the other hand, data protection refers to "an individual's information rights, along with the legal structures that enable them and impose obligations on organizations that process personal data" [8]. Comparing with data protection scope, PbD approach is broader and look for "the highest possible global standard of privacy" [8].

Working with privacy goals in developing information systems and software requires that security safeguards were included during system design and construction. Indeed, assuring privacy requires assuring security [8] [10]. On the one hand, security protection goals - confidentiality, integrity and availability - are driving factors for assessing the risks and potential consequences if their desired level is not achieved [11]. On the other hand, privacy protection goals should consider security protection goals as well as unlinkability, transparency and intervenability [11] [12]. However, several papers address privacy requirements as a special case of security requirements, but this approach overlooks fundamental privacy goals [13]. Thus, this work is centered on mapping current published research on privacy protection goals when software and information systems are developed.

2.2 Literature reviews on PbD

Literature reviews on the "privacy by design" approach are seldom published. However, if we widen the search for papers addressing the "privacy" concept for software engineering endeavors, we find that several literature reviews focused on specific domains have been published. In the case of "privacy by design" search, there is one paper that addresses the topic of ontologies for privacy requirements [13]. The authors report a set of papers addressing privacy by design concepts and relations. Based on the selection of key concepts, a meta-model for addressing privacy requirements is provided, with specific privacy terms such as notice, anonymity, and transparency.

In the case of a wider search, there are several papers that address privacy in different domains, such as healthcare systems and Internet of Things (IoT) technologies, among others. In these reviews, the main topic is understanding the extent to which privacy goals, principles, mechanisms, or stakeholders' privacy concerns are addressed in the systems under consideration. In the domain of healthcare systems, the literature reviews have been focused on cross-organizational data sharing [14], cloud-assisted systems [15], and factors that trigger privacy concerns [16]. However, none of these literature reviews analyses what software development practices were used to develop those systems.

In the context of IoT, Loukil et al. [10] found that data protection and privacy needs deal more with current deficiencies. Privacy should be considered in each data phase to protect sensitive data of an individual, group, or organization [10]. Thus, current privacy-related literature reviews address several systems privacy properties, mainly in usage stage, without focusing on the practices needed to build system software based on the "privacy by design" approach.

3 SMS methodology and results

3.1 Planning the SMS

The purpose of this SMS is to determine the State of the Art of PbD, find out its principles and analyze the best practices that the authors of the papers have addressed. This paper seeks to respond to the following question, which guides this SMS:

What is the State of the Art of PbD when applied to software engineering?

In this section, we present the methodology of the study, which is developed as follows. We start by defining relevant research questions, after which we expand on the data extraction resources employed, and finally, we discuss the evaluation and classification criteria applied to the primary papers. The SMS was carried out following the suggestions presented in [17] and [18].

3.1.1. Research methods and questions. The research questions seek, on the one hand, to define the term PbD, its objective and its principles, and, on the other, to identify its best practices. The research questions and the motivation behind each one are presented in Table 1.

Table 1. Research questions and their motivation

Research Question		Motivation
RQ1	What is PbD?	Defining the concept of PbD.
RQ2	What are the principles/goals of PbD?	Identifying the principles or goals that PbD pursues.
RQ3	Which are the PbD practices or techniques?	Identifying software development practices or techniques that address PbD.

3.1.2. Data sources and search strategy. The search string was built using two major search terms: "privacy by design" and "software engineering". These terms were selected because they are the most general possible and are the main topic of the SMS, since the objective is to know and expand PbD in software engineering. As synonyms to "software engineering", "software development", "information systems" and "requirements engineering" were used.

It is important to highlight that synonyms for "privacy by design" were not used in order to avoid the issue highlighted by [13], in which privacy is seen as a special case of security. This misguides to believe that security covers privacy aspects by default. However, a system may be considered secured and may still not address privacy aspects.

The search scope is focused on peer-reviewed research papers published in journals, academic conferences and workshops. We decided to use Scopus, IEEE Xplore Digital Library and ACM Digital Library as the main search engines in order to preserve the quality of the studies. The fields used were title, abstract and keywords (Scopus); and title and abstract (IEEE Xplore and ACM Digital Libraries).

The search was carried out only for papers written in English. The search date was December, 10th 2017.

The SMS included papers if they addressed PbD in software engineering and reported it as a theoretical or empirical study; and if it was a paper, a book chapter or a poster.

The SMS excluded papers if they reported research that did not deal with PbD in software engineering endeavors; if the document was neither a paper, a book chapter nor a poster, and if the paper was duplicated or unavailable.

The selection criteria for papers were developed by the first two authors; peer-debriefing sessions were developed in order to solve disagreements. The last step, validating how the criteria were applied, was done by the third author.

The data collection was carried out using a table that registered papers' metadata (title, authors, year of publication, type), exclusion details, which research questions were targeted and the actual response to the questions such as definitions, principles, goals, practices or techniques discovered in the papers. This work was done by the first two authors and validated by the third and fourth. The inconsistencies were solved through peer-debriefing.

3.1.3. Classification. The search results were refined by carrying out a classification based on 3 categories. These categories were defined according to the research questions:

1. **PbD definition:** Papers in this category contain an explicit definition of PbD. This category is related to RQ1.
2. **PbD principles or goals:** Papers in this category were classified according to the principles or goals that PbD pursues. This category is related to RQ2.
3. **PbD practices or techniques:** Papers in this category were classified according to the practices or techniques they discuss. This category is related to RQ3.

3.2 Results of the SMS

The search was developed according to the steps and criteria described in the previous section. 92 papers were retrieved from databases. After removing duplicates (16) and applying selection criteria, 35 primary papers were identified. The comparison of the number of documents by year is shown in Figure 1. It will be observed that the interest in this topic has increased since 2011, and of the 35 primary studies found, 31 were published in the period 2011 to 2017 (until December). The full list of primary studies is presented in additional material (https://goo.gl/iKTLLr).

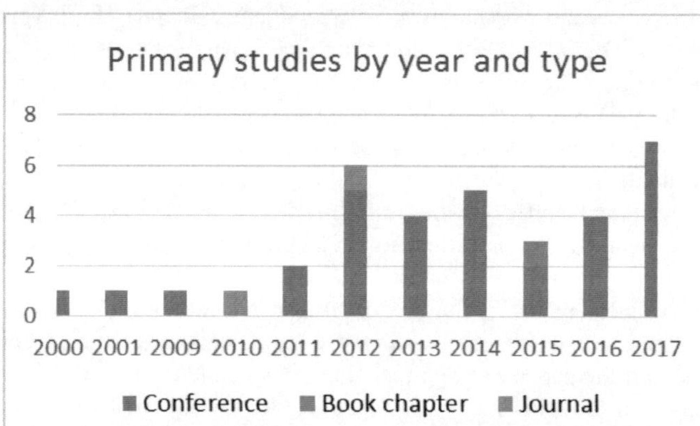

Fig. 1. Distribution of the primary studies by year

The first primary study was published in 2000; it describes obstacles as regards designing technology that could be used to protect civil liberties and, in particular, the difficulties involved in creating and deploying liberty-protecting software [A8]. In 2001, [A9] establishes that no definition is possible for the concept of privacy, and, instead, offers its description from three different angles: its history, its legal status, and its utility.

33 papers have been published since that time, they describe particular cases of compliance with privacy requirements in health care systems [A10] [A11], Internet of Things [A12] [A13], mobile phones [A14] and e-commerce [A15]. Or they provide

guidelines that can be used to include PbD in information systems [A16] and [A17] in the form of patterns. 13 of 35 are experience reports while 22 are theoretical proposals. Following sections describe the main findings considering the research questions.

3.2.1 RQ1. What is PbD?

The primary results led us to define PbD from two perspectives: establishing its scope and objectives, or determining its characteristics and principles.

According to [A2], PbD is "an example of an approach highly advocated by policy makers, intended to mitigate privacy threats from the very beginning, by creating a process that designs information systems in a privacy-respectful way".

Similarly, [A18] establishes that "PbD is an approach to protecting privacy by embedding it into the design specifications of information technologies, accountable business practices, and networked infrastructures, right from the outset".

Three authors cited [6] in connection with the concept of PbD:

- "PbD is an approach that argues building privacy into technologies as a default" [A3].
- "the concept of PbD, aiming at enhancing privacy to IT systems, from the very start of their inception or design, has emerged as an imperative to privacy protection" [A19].
- "PbD is an engineering and strategic management approach that commits to selectively and sustainably minimize information systems' privacy risks through technical and governance controls" [A20].

We found similar definitions that strongly recommend considering privacy during the software design process:

- "PbD approach integrates privacy requirements into the design process right from the beginning" [A21].
- "PbD designates a software design approach that incorporates privacy requirements from the beginning and throughout the software development process, instead of considering them as an afterthought", respectively [A5]

These statements are reinforced by [A22], which points out that "security and privacy by design can be achieved only by design".

However, there is a wider opinion regarding the inclusion of privacy practices in the whole development process. As [A23] states, "PbD incorporates privacy protections into an organization's practices, and maintains comprehensive data management procedures throughout the lifecycle of their products and services". A similar definition is used in [A24]: "PbD is the embedding of privacy awareness throughout all stages of a technology's design and implementation lifecycle". Wohlgemuth [A25] provides a similar definition: "PbD postulates to consider IT security requirements in all phases of software development to reduce vulnerabilities".

Colesky and Ghanavati [A26] provide a related definition and return to Ayalon [A2] and Rowan's [A23] ideas: "PbD is an approach to software development which protects privacy from the early/concept stages of the software development life cycle". Another paper [A6] states that "PbD philosophy "bakes-in" privacy throughout the system development lifecycle".

Moreover, [A4] declares that "PbD seeks to influence technology design, business practices, and physical infrastructure by embedding privacy protection at its core". "The general philosophy of PbD is that privacy should not be treated as an afterthought but rather as a first-class requirement during the design of a system" [A27].

We have used all the aforementioned definitions as a basis to propose a unified definition:

PbD is an approach whose objective is to discover, represent, implement and manage the rules and tasks that preserve the data privacy of any stakeholder of a software system. PbD should be considered from the project inception phase and throughout the entire software lifecycle.

3.2.2 RQ2. What are the principles/goals of PbD?

The second criteria according to which the papers were classified and data were extracted were the principles or goals of PbD. The essential objectives as regards determining whether PbD is involved in software development are stated as the following 7 principles [6]:

1. Proactive not reactive; preventative not remedial.
2. Privacy as the default setting.
3. Privacy embedded into design.
4. Full functionality positive-sum, not zero-sum.
5. End-to-end security, full life-cycle protection.
6. Visibility and transparency- keep it open.
7. Respect for user privacy, keep it user-centric.

These principles are also mentioned by [A12], [A15], [A19] and [A28].

Furthermore, [A29] proposes the following privacy goals: anonymity, pseudonymity, unlinkability, undetectability and unobservability. The author of the paper in question formulates the principles in the form of a pattern and proposes a set of techniques by which to implement each of them in an information system.

PbD lacks of systematic methodologies that address privacy issues and support the translation of its principles into engineering activities [A30]. However, it is important to mention that authors refer to some practices that can be carried out in order to achieve privacy. For example, "PbD means to embed privacy proactively in the design process of a technical system by data minimization techniques" [A28]. However, methodological support for developing software systems belong to the category of guidelines.

The most frequently goals mentioned by the authors are the following:

Minimize (in 8 primary studies) recollection and access to data is defined by [A6] [A26] as "limiting usage as much as possible by excluding, selecting, stripping, or destroying any storage, collection, retention or operation on personal data, within the constraints".

Anonymization and pseudonymization (6 and 5 times respectively) are defined by [A29] as "a characteristic of information that does not permit a personally identifiable information principal to be identified directly or indirectly".

Separation (5) is "personal data should be processed in a distributed fashion, in separate compartments whenever possible" by the same author [A19].

Control (5) is defined by [A6] [A26] as "providing as abundant means as possible for consenting to, choosing, updating, and retracting from storage, collection, retention, sharing or operation on personal data, in a timely manner, within the constraints of the agreed upon purposes".

Consent (5) which is defined as only processing the personal data for which explicit, freely-given, and informed consent is received [A6].

Other 51 goals appear four or less times in the primary studies. The full list is presented in additional materials (https://goo.gl/iKTLLr).

3.2.3 RQ3. Which are the PbD practices or techniques?

In 2010, [A22] stated categorically that security and privacy are two distinct disciplines with two common factors: both need to receive more explicit and direct attention from research and education and can be achieved only by design. In [A21], a PbD process that aims to support privacy requirements engineering is presented, in addition to which a formal method to evaluate the realization of the specified privacy constraints is proposed.

Kost et al. define a four-phase process with which to include and validate privacy in the development of systems:

1. Identify high-level privacy requirements.
2. Map the high-level privacy requirements onto a formal description.
3. Outline the formal requirements and model the system.
4. Match the formal requirements with the formal model system.

In [A30] three privacy requirement engineering methods are analyzed. The framework for Privacy-Friendly Systems Design (PFSD) is a methodology that aims to incorporate privacy into a software development process through three steps [19]:

- Elicit privacy-related goals;
- Analyze the impact of privacy goals on the process; and
- Identify the techniques that best support/implement the aforementioned process.

According to [A30], PFSD is not accompanied by guidelines on how to identify privacy expectations in a structured manner.

The second is LINDDUN, a privacy threat analysis framework for supporting the elicitation and fulfilment of privacy requirements [20]. And the third is the PriS method, which aims to integrate privacy requirements into the early stages of the design process by modelling privacy requirements as organizational goals [19].

Diamantopoulou et al. [A29] claim that moving from a design (in which the privacy requirements of an information system have been elicited) to an implementation that fulfils those requirements is a challenging task in the context of PbD. It can be observed that the integration of PbD into the software development process must include almost all of its phases [A23] [A25].

Furthermore, and with regard to the project management activities, Ali [A31] mentions that negotiation and agreements with the clients should be made by: "Obtaining explicit consent", "Maintaining privacy audit trails", "Creating and maintaining privacy policies", and "Privacy negotiation".

Martín [A5] suggests gathering stakeholders from different communities and defining a collection of roles that are involved in the provision of privacy requirements. In addition, [A5] emphasizes the need to identify, analyze and structure privacy requirements from the requirements specification phase.

With regard to the software development activities, in [A4], an extension to UML Use Case diagram is proposed, which implies that privacy restrictions should still be dealt with at the requirements specification stage.

As expected, in the majority of the papers PbD is included in the design and construction phase by, as stated in [A28] and [A32], embedding "privacy proactively in the design process"; "heightening sensitivity to privacy issues during design" [A1]; applying privacy patterns has been identified as a feasible way in which to support the design of such systems [A29] [A33]. An architectural model based on access control policies is proposed in [A34], and this approach is also implemented at the design phase.

In the case of software verification and validation phase, Oetzel and Spiekermann [A35] present a six-step privacy assessment methodology that could be useful as regards validating how systems manage privacy requirements. In [A12] a set of guidelines that incorporate PbD principles in order to guide software engineers in the systematic assessment of the privacy capabilities of IoT applications and platforms is presented.

However, the authors of [A21] establish that "a comprehensive approach for privacy requirement engineering, implementation, and verification is largely missing", which emphasizes the lack of privacy support in the development process as a whole.

4 Discussion

Our study revealed that the objective of PbD is, according to [A18], to ensure privacy and gain personal control over one's information and, for organizations, to gain a sustainable competitive advantage. We also determined that organizations are forced to deal with data privacy in order to comply with national and international legislation and perceive it as an obligation rather than an advantage for their business and clients.

As can be observed in the results shown in the previous section, on the one hand, the issue of data privacy involves developers, stakeholders and users. On the other, in the majority of cases, it involves discussing questions concerning social privacy rights rather than applying and following best practices and standards.

PbD has not yet been established as either a widespread approach or as a widespread engineering practice [A2]. In addition, most of the proposed methodologies target the treatment of privacy during construction or during early design activities, while none treats privacy as a separate design criterion [19]. Moreover, PbD in itself lacks concrete tools to help software developers design and implement privacy friendly systems. It also lacks clear guidelines regarding how to map specific legal data protection requirements onto system requirements [A6].

Moreover, *minimize the collection and access to data* is the most frequent goal. This goal can be paraphrased as *do not collect or store data that is not needed or will not be used.*

If we analyze the practices that were found during the SMS, it will be noted that they are not yet best practices but rather suggestions and pieces of advice in order to facilitate or comply with data privacy requirements, which denotes that the status of including PbD in the software development process is still preliminary.

We consider that PbD is in its initial stage; its foundations and principles are in the process of being established and a former set of practices, whose intention to follow the principles, has been proposed recently. The next step for PbD is to create more practices and prove their usefulness and applicability in software developments.

In this scenario, we firmly believe that it is important to integrate best PbD practices into software development processes. The objective of this integration is to strengthen systems that are and will be developed by organizations. In addition, it will unify the best practices that guide the software development with PbD, which will, in turn, protect the privacy of sensitive data in the current ever-growing systems.

A first step towards this goal is to integrate PbD practices into particular process models, for example, the ISO/IEC 29110 Software Implementation process. Another example is to create a set of interrelated PbD practices adding a new profile.

4.1 Validity threats

A SMS protocol was built to address the selection bias. Search terms were identified based on influential papers in the field. Given that privacy requirements are treated in a narrow perspective as security requirements [13], and to determine the extent privacy is addressed in SE literature, we focused only on the perspective of "privacy by design" proposed by Cavoukian since it is recognized as an approach to address privacy in software systems [A5].

Databases used in this review are recommended for conducting mapping studies in software engineering [17] and only peer-reviewed articles, including conference proceedings that belong to grey literature [21], were selected. Since sound empirical studies about practices on software engineering were lacking, a literature review that considers both peer-reviewed and grey literature would provide a comprehensive view of issues that practitioners face [22]. In addition, snowballing procedures should be applied to enhance the completeness of the search process [17].

Human error is another aspect that can impact any paper selection. Thus, search and selection procedures were kept in a log to avoid potential issues. Two authors participated in selecting primary papers, while a third verified the selection of a subset of primary papers. Selection inconsistencies were discussed among all researchers. Finally, a template was built to extract verbatim data from each primary paper. The extraction data was verified by the third and fourth authors in a subset of selected primary papers. Obtained data let us develop a classification approach, derived from data, to aggregate data in order to answer the research questions.

5 Conclusions and future work

This paper presents a mapping study that has been conducted in order to determine the State of the Art as regards PbD in software development. –We found little support for embed privacy during software development. Majority of proposals deal with privacy requirements, but they lack of methodological support for dealing with all stages of software development.

We perceived in the results of the SMS that the two types of systems that appeared more frequently in the primary results were social networks and health-care systems. Further research focused on the empirical results of using PbD practices or techniques in industry is needed in order to provide an idea of the real presence of practices in industry.

Moreover, PbD is related not only to developing systems, but also to processes and physical features [23], signifying that privacy regulations and laws oriented toward information systems should be created and disseminated between users and the developers' community. We believe that a well-informed community will create a better understanding of the fact that considering privacy in the whole development process as an inherit aspect, rather than a characteristic, brings a direct benefit to the system.

As a further work, we propose to develop a conceptual framework to address both privacy concerns and provide support for developing privacy-aware systems. In addition, practices for incorporating privacy into software system should be surveyed in companies to identify those practices considered most relevant in the context of privacy. Moreover, a validation of these proposals should be carried out in industrial settings.

Acknowledgements

This work has been developed within the SEQUOIA Project, funded by Fondo Europeo de Desarrollo Regional FEDER and (Ministerio de Economía y Competitividad, (TIN2015-63502-C3-1-R) (MINECO/FEDER).

The authors would like thank the Postgraduate Program of the Medical Faculty (DEP-FM) at the National Autonomous University of Mexico (UNAM).

References

1. Warren, S. and Brandeis, L.: *The Right to Privacy*. Harvard Law Review, Vol. 4, No. 5, pp. 193-220 (1890)
2. Altman, I.: *Privacy: A Conceptual Analysis*. Environment and Behavior, Vol. 8, No. 1, pp.: 7-29 (1976)
3. Nissenbaum, H.: *Privacy in Context: technology, Policy, and the Integrity of Social Life*. Stanford University Press, ISBN: 978-0-8047-5236-7 (2010)
4. Palen, L. and Dourish, P.: *Unpacking "Privacy" for a Networked World*. In Proceedings of CHI, ACM, Ft. Lauderdale, Florida, USA, ISBN: 1-58113-630-7/03/0004 (2003)
5. Hildebrandt, M. and Koops, B-J.: *The challenges of ambient law and legal protection in the profiling era*. Mod Law Rev 73(3):428–460 (2010)
6. Cavoukian, A.: *Privacy by Design: The 7 Foundational Principles*. Information and Privacy Commissioner of Ontario (2009)
7. Klitou, D.: *Privacy-Invading Technologies and Privacy by Design*. Information Technology and Law Series, Vol. 25, pp 27-45, 978-94-6265-026-8 (2014)
8. Cavoukian A.: Privacy by Design: Leadership, Methods, and Results. In: Gutwirth S., Leenes R., de Hert P., Poullet Y. (eds) European Data Protection: Coming of Age. Springer, Dordrecht, pp. 175-202 (2013)
9. Cavoukian, A.: *Operationalizing privacy by design: A guide to implementing strong privacy practices*. Information and Privacy Commissioner, Ontario, Canada. Retrieved on Dec, 6, 2017 from: http://www.ontla.on.ca/library/repository/mon/26012/320221.pdf (2012)
10. Loukil, F., Ghedira-Guegan, C., Benharkat, A. N., Boukadi, K., and Maamar, Z.: *Privacy-Aware in the IoT Applications: A Systematic Literature Review*. In OTM Confederated International Conferences" On the Move to Meaningful Internet Systems" (pp. 552-569). Springer, Cham (2017)
11. Hansen M.: *Top 10 Mistakes in System Design from a Privacy Perspective and Privacy Protection Goals*. In: Camenisch J., Crispo B., Fischer-Hübner S., Leenes R., Russello G. (eds) Privacy and Identity Management for Life. Privacy and Identity 2011. IFIP Advances in Information and Communication Technology, Vol. 375, pp. 14-31 (2012)
12. Meis, R., and Heisel, M.: *Computer-Aided Identification and Validation of Intervenability Requirements*. Information, Vol. 8, No. 1, 30 (2017)
13. Gharib M., Giorgini P. and Mylopoulos J.: *Towards an Ontology for Privacy Requirements via a Systematic Literature Review*. In: Mayr H., Guizzardi G., Ma H., Pastor O. (eds) Conceptual Modeling. ER 2017. Lecture Notes in Computer Science, Vol. 10650, pp. 193-208 (2017)
14. Azarm-Daigle, M., Kuziemsky, C. and Peyton, L.: *A Review of Cross-Organizational Healthcare Data Sharing*. Procedia Computer Science, Vol. 63, pp. 425-432, DOI: https://doi.org/10.1016/j.procs.2015.08.363 (2015)
15. Sajid, A. and Abbas, H.: *Data Privacy in Cloud-assisted Healthcare Systems: State of the Art and Future Challenges*. Journal of Medical Systems archive, Vol. 40, No. 6, pp. 1-16, DOI: 10.1007/s10916-016-0509-2 (2016)
16. Rahim, F., Ismail, Z. and Samy, G.: *Privacy Challenges in Electronic Medical Records: A Systematic Review*. In Proceedings of the Knowledge Management International Conference (KMICe) 2014, pp. 12-15 (2014)

17. Petersen, K., Vakkalanka, S. and Kuzniarz, L.: *Guidelines for conducting systematic mapping studies in software engineering: An update*. Information and Software Technology, Vol. 64, pp. 1-18, (2015)
18. Kitchenham, B.A. and Charters, S.: *Guidelines for Performing Systematic Literature Reviews in Software Engineering*. Technical Report EBSE-2007- 01, School of Computer Science and Mathematics, Keele University (2007)
19. Kalloniatis, C., Kavakli, E. and Gritzalis, S.: *Addressing privacy requirements in system design: the PriS method.* Requirements Eng. 13(3), 241–255 (2008)
20. Deng, M., Wuyts, K., Scandariato, R., Preneel, B. and Joosen, W.: *A privacy threat analysis framework: supporting the elicitation and fulfillment of privacy requirements*. Requirements Eng. Vol. 16, No. 1, pp. 3–32 (2011)
21. Adams, R.J., Smart, P. and Huff, A.S.: *Shades of Grey: Guidelines for Working with the Grey Literature in Systematic Reviews for Management and Organizational Studies*. International Journal of Management Reviews, Vol. 19, pp. 432-454, doi:10.1111/ijmr.12102 (2017)
22. Garousi, V., Felderer, M. and Mäntylä, M.: *The need for multivocal literature reviews in software engineering: complementing systematic literature reviews with grey literature*. In Proceedings of the 20th International Conference on Evaluation and Assessment in Software Engineering (EASE), 26 (2016)
23. Schartum, D.: *Making privacy by design operative*. International Journal of Law and Information Technology, No. 24, 151–175, DOI: 10.1093/ijlit/eaw002 (2016)

Elicitación de requisitos de interoperabilidad desde la perspectiva de las necesidades del negocio: Una revisión sistemática de la literatura

Daniel Eduardo Paz Perafán [1,*], Francisco Jose Pino Correa[1], Sandra Lorena Buitron[1]

[1] Universidad del Cauca, Cauca, Colombia
{danielp, fjpino, sandrabr}@unicauca.edu.co

Resumen. Durante el desarrollo de aplicaciones software (AS) que apoyan el quehacer de las organizaciones, la elicitación de los requisitos de interoperabilidad (RI) realizada de forma alineada a las necesidades de los procesos de negocio puede generar AS compatibles entre sí y a la estructura organizacional, permitiendo un efectivo cumplimiento de los objetivos de negocio. Inicialmente la interoperabilidad ha estado centrada exclusivamente en el intercambio de datos pero se ha ampliado de una manera holística hasta incluir aspectos conceptuales, semánticos y organizacionales para apoyar la gestión del negocio de las empresas. En este sentido, el objetivo de este artículo es presentar una revisión sistemática de la literatura que pretende identificar, categorizar y analizar propuestas que consideran los procesos de negocio de las organizaciones como referencia para la elicitación de RI dentro de un proyecto software. Como resultado se han sintetizado un conjunto de elementos que permiten identificar y establecer RI a partir de la gestión del negocio y además se han determinado oportunidades de investigación en este campo. Una oportunidad de investigación que se está trabajando es la definición de una temprana, formal y sistemática elicitación de RI centrada en el proceso de negocio.

Palabras clave: interoperabilidad empresarial, elicitación de requisitos de interoperabilidad, interoperabilidad de procesos de negocio, necesidades de procesos de negocio.

1 Introducción

Las organizaciones están cambiando de una visión de gestión por áreas funcionales, a una visión de gestión por procesos de negocio transversales a las áreas [1][2], en consecuencia asumen como reto una integración coordinada de sus procesos de negocio, recursos humanos y de TIC involucrados en la entrega de un producto o servicio, independiente de su ubicación geográfica, infraestructura y demás aspectos logísticos, corporativos y tecnológicos [3][4]. Al mismo tiempo las organizaciones desean facilitar, optimizar y mejorar las interacciones del trabajo colaborativo en sus procesos internos y externos [5].

En los proyectos de integración y colaboración obligatoriamente debe existir la interoperabilidad como atributo de calidad [6][7], la cual proporciona a dos o más sistemas de la misma organización o de diferentes organizaciones e independientemente de su ubicación, la capacidad de intercambiar o compartir información, utilizar esa información y acceder a funcionalidades dentro de un entorno distribuido y ambiente heterogéneo [8]. Inicialmente su implementación se consideraba exclusivamente como un problema técnico [9], no obstante actualmente es necesario analizarla bajo un enfoque sistémico a partir de múltiples perspectivas relacionas con aspectos: organizacionales (p. ej., ¿quién hace qué, cómo, cuándo y quién es responsable de qué? ...); conceptuales (p. ej., ¿los datos que se intercambian utilizan un Modelo de datos? ...); semánticos (p. ej., ¿ existe un entendimiento común de la información transmitida? …) entre otros. [10][11][12][13].

En este sentido, en los últimos años se han desarrollado diversos trabajos de investigación alrededor de la interoperabilidad con el objetivo de estructurar su concepto, así como su implementación técnica, medición, evaluación y estandarización en sectores específicos del mercado [5][14], no obstante pocos trabajos abordan la captura, especificación y verificación de RI, y además no se cuenta con un análisis sistemático sobre cuestiones de negocio asociadas [15][16]. Este aspecto es relevante si tenemos en cuenta que dentro del proceso de elicitación de requisitos los stakeholders (usuarios finales, de dirección de la organización y técnicos) generalmente no logran articular RI acordes a las necesidades del negocio [17][18], debido a que analistas y diseñadores se enfocan en aspectos técnicos de las soluciones en lugar de realizar sistemáticamente un análisis holístico de la interoperabilidad y su relación con aspectos del negocio [19]. Este inconveniente da como resultado el desarrollo de AS aisladas, frecuentemente incompatibles con los sistemas de las otras áreas funcionales e inconsistentes con las necesidades de intercambio y uso de información entre procesos de negocios [20].

Por la relevancia de los aspectos mencionados, el objetivo y principal contribución de esta revisión sistemática es identificar, categorizar y analizar propuestas que consideran los procesos de negocio de las organizaciones como referencia para la elicitación de RI. La comprensión de estas propuestas incluye la investigación de cómo se han validado y en qué contexto se han aplicado.

Este artículo está organizado de la siguiente forma: la sección 2 presenta el diseño de la revisión sistemática, la sección 3 expone las propuestas encontradas, la sección 4 presenta un análisis de las propuestas encontradas describiendo los enfoques utilizados para elicitar RI y las brechas de investigación identificadas. Finalmente la sección 5 muestra las conclusiones de la revisión sistemática.

2 Diseño de la revisión sistemática

Una revisión sistemática es una forma de identificar, evaluar e interpretar la investigación disponible relacionada con una pregunta de investigación, área, temática o fenómeno, la cual busca reunir evidencias para fundamentar conclusiones que permitan apoyar o contradecir las afirmaciones de investigadores, identificar brechas en la investigación existente, motivar nuevas investigaciones y proporcionar un contexto para la investigación [21]. Esta revisión fue organizada según el enfoque propuesto por Kitchenham [22] el cual establece tres actividades principales: (i) Planificación de la Revisión, (ii) Realización de la Revisión, y (iii) Reporte de la Revisión. La planificación permitió definir un protocolo que tenía como finalidad reducir la parcialidad de los investigadores, el cual fue realizado por un autor y analizado por los autores restantes para evitar un sesgo en la revisión. Los elementos que componen el protocolo son descritos a continuación:

Preguntas de Investigación. ¿Cuáles propuestas han considerado los procesos de negocio de las organizaciones como referencia para la elicitación de RI? ¿Cuáles son los alcances y características de estas propuestas? ¿Qué dimensiones y/o perspectivas de la interoperabilidad se deberían considerar durante el análisis de las necesidades del negocio con el fin de elicitar RI?

Criterios de inclusión.

- Estudios que plantean dimensiones y/o perspectivas a considerar durante la elicitación de RI, O estudios que tratan los procesos de negocio como fuente de RI, O estudios que utilizan los procesos de negocio para representar RI.
- Estudios publicados en Workshop, conferencias, revistas o reportes técnicos.
- Estudios publicados entre el año 1990 y 2017.

Criterios de exclusión

- Estudios que no tratan necesidades, problemas o requisitos de interoperabilidad.

Fuentes de búsqueda. Las fuentes electrónicas utilizadas en el proceso de búsqueda fueron las siguientes: Scopus, ScienceDirect, Springer, ACM, IEEE y Engineer Ingvillage. Google Scholar fue también explorado con el objetivo de obtener literatura relevante.

Cadenas de búsqueda. Para su creación se identificaron los términos principales de las preguntas de investigación y sinónimos alternativos, con los cuales se lograran obtener el mayor número de estudios primarios relevantes. Como resultado se establecieron las siguientes cadenas de búsqueda:

("Interoperability Requirements Elicitation" OR "Interoperability requirements specification" OR "Interoperability requirements" OR "non functional Requirements Elicitation" OR "non functional requirements specification" OR "non functional requirements" OR "NFRs") AND ("business processes model" OR "business processes")

("Interoperability elicitation" OR "Interoperability Requirements Elicitation" OR "Interoperability requirements specification") AND (solution OR method OR technique OR model OR methodology OR framework OR architecture OR infrastructure OR approach)

El término "non functional" ha sido insertado dentro de las cadenas de búsqueda debido a que la interoperabilidad con mucha frecuencia es considerada como requisito no funcional y por tanto, podrían existir referencias a la interoperabilidad dentro de los trabajos basados en requisitos no funcionales.

Evaluación de la calidad. Fue desarrollado un cuestionario de calidad, basado en los estudios [23] [24] [25], para evaluar la relevancia de las publicaciones seleccionadas. La Tabla 1 presenta las preguntas de evaluación, cada una de las preguntas podría puntuar 1 punto si la respuesta fue "Sí", 0.5 si la respuesta fue "Parcial" o 0 si la respuesta fue "No". Usando este sistema, cada publicación podría obtener una puntuación de 0 a 12 puntos. Se utilizó el primer cuartil (12/4 = 3) como punto de corte, si una publicación obtuvo menos de 3 se excluye de la lista de publicaciones finales para evitar trabajos de baja calidad.

Tabla 1. CheckList para evaluar la calidad de las publicaciones seleccionas.

No	Pregunta
1	¿Están claramente especificados los objetivos del estudio?
2	¿Se diseñó el estudio para lograr estos objetivos?
3	¿Los resultados están claramente explicados?
4	¿Se responde adecuadamente la pregunta de investigación?
5	¿Se especifican las limitaciones del estudio?
6	¿Se presentan resultados negativos (si los hay)?
7	¿Tiene el estudio un número adecuado de promedio de recuento de citas por año?
8	¿Qué tan claros son los vínculos entre los datos, la interpretación y las conclusiones?
9	¿El proceso de elicitación de RI está definido de forma clara?
10	¿Existe un caso de estudio o ejemplo claro de la propuesta?
11	¿El análisis realizado en el estudio se basa en evidencia?
12	¿La propuesta es validada?

Dimensionamiento de la investigación. Para clasificar los diferentes estudios encontrados se determinaron las siguientes dimensiones:

- **Dimensión del tipo de contribución.** Define el tipo de contribución que realizan los autores. En esta dimensión se encuentra: (i) Herramienta: instrumentos concretos que se crean y utilizan para soportar, apoyar, entender y realizar algún proceso específico, (ej. Framework, Marco, Modelo), (ii) Enfoque: dirigidos en detallar conceptualmente un asunto puntual de un proceso con el objetivo de resolver problemas o aclarar dudas de manera efectiva, (iii) Propuesta metodológica: disponen etapas, pasos o procedimientos para realizar una tarea en particular (ej. Método, Técnica,

Metodología, guía), (iv) Estudio: analizan y resumen las características de otros trabajos de investigación desde una perspectiva específica.

- **Dimensión del Tipo de validación realizada**. Define la forma en que se validan los estudios. En esta dimensión se encuentra: (i) Estudio de caso, (ii) Encuesta, (iii) Experimento, (iv) Experiencia, (v) Validación teórica e (vi) Ilustración.
- **Dimensión del objetivo de las propuestas.** Define el objetivo de las propuestas respecto al proceso de elicitación de RI. En esta dimensión se encuentra: (i) Clasificar RI, (ii) Representar o especificar RI, (iii) Guiar la obtención de RI y (iv) Establecer elementos para una correcta obtención de RI.

Estrategia para la selección de la literatura y extracción de datos. El proceso de selección de las publicaciones relevantes siguió la estrategia de búsqueda mostrada en la fig. 1. Cada etapa fue realizada por el primer autor y su resultado fue revisado por el segundo y tercer autor para evitar un sesgo de investigación. Las divergencias en los análisis de los investigadores fueron resueltas en reuniones donde llegaron a un consenso. En la etapa 1 de la estrategia, a partir de la ejecución de las cadenas de búsqueda en las bases de datos, fueron encontradas 1241 publicaciones. En la etapa 2, de 1241 publicaciones, 95 cumplieron los criterios de inclusión y exclusión después de una revisión del título, resumen y conclusiones. En la etapa 3, realizada paralelamente a la 2, de 95 publicaciones, 47 permanecieron posteriormente a eliminar los duplicados, estas publicaciones se denominaron como "publicaciones potenciales". En la etapa 4, de 47 publicaciones, 17 cumplieron los criterios de inclusión y exclusión después de una revisión completa del texto. En la etapa 5, 15 pasaron la evaluación de calidad, lo que representa una reducción del 98,79% en comparación con el conjunto inicial de 1241 documentos. Las referencias de las publicaciones finales y sus respectivas dimensiones son mostradas en la tabla 2.

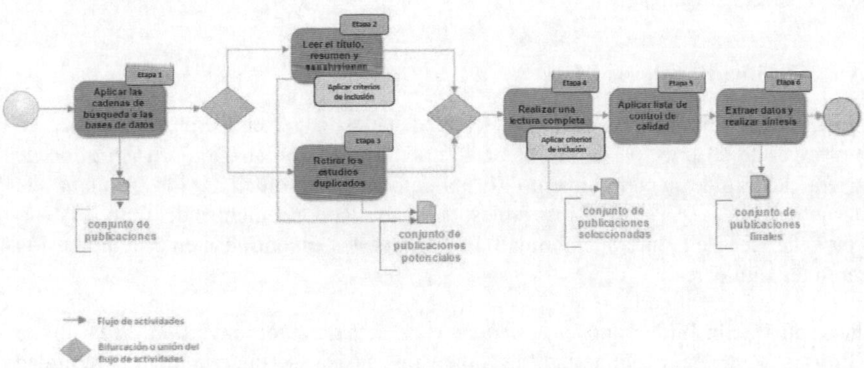

Fig. 1. Estrategia de búsqueda utilizada en la revisión sistemática.

Tabla 2. Publicaciones finales y sus dimensiones.

Ref.	Tipo de contribución	Validación	Objetivo de la propuesta
[26]	Framework	Ilustración	Clas y repres de RI
[27]	Metodológica	Est de caso	Representación de RI
[28]	Framework	Ilustración	Guía para obtención de RI
[29]	Modelo	Est de caso	Elem para obtención de RI
[30]	Framew/Métodologia	Est de caso	Clasificación de RI
[3] y [31]	Metodología	Ejemplo	Guía para obtención de RI
[32]	Framework	No valida	Elem para obtención de RI
[33]	Metodología	Ilustración	Guía para obtención de RI
[34]	Enfoque conceptual	Ilustración	Guía para obtención de RI
[35]	Enfoque conceptual	Ilustración	Representación de RI
[36]	Estudio	Est de caso	Elem para obtención de RI
[37]	Metodología	Est de caso	Elem para obtención de RI
[5]	Enf conc/Framework	Ilustración	Clasificación de RI
[38]	Enf conc/Framework	Ilustración	Guía para obtención de RI

3 Resultados

Esta sección analiza cómo cada propuesta encontrada abordó el tema de la elicitación de RI. El análisis está dividido según el objetivo de las propuestas respecto a los RI el cual puede ser: clasificarlos, representarlos, guiar su obtención o proponer elementos para su correcta obtención.

3.1 Clasificación de los RI

A partir de los trabajos encontrados los RI pueden clasificarse en 7 dimensiones, según: (i) el nivel de abstracción de la interacción dentro de la organización, (ii) el tipo de barrera que impide su cumplimiento, (iii) el enfoque para solucionar los problemas de interoperabilidad, (iv) si son RI medibles, (v) si son RI dependientes del tiempo, y (vi) el ciclo de vida de la interoperabilidad. Las propuestas encontradas en esta dimensión fueron las siguientes:

Chen and Daclin [30] proponen un framework actualmente convertido en la norma (CEN/ISO 11354), el cual define tres dimensiones básicas donde la interoperabilidad puede ser abordada: barreras, niveles y enfoques. Identifican 4 niveles de interoperabilidad: Datos, Servicios, Procesos y Negocio. Transversal a cada nivel se encuentran las barreras o incompatibilidades que impiden el logro de la interoperabilidad, las cuales son: conceptuales, tecnológicas y organizativas. Por lo tanto, el framework establece que los niveles y barreras constituyen el espacio del problema en el cual se pueden identificar necesidades de interoperabilidad que podrían ser resueltas por un RI, comenzando por el nivel superior del negocio hasta llegar al nivel de los datos, analizando trasversalmente los aspectos conceptuales, tecnológicos y organizacionales. Otro aspecto mencionado en el framework son los enfoques integrado, unificado y federado, propuestos por la norma ISO 14258, los cuales representan las diferentes maneras en que se pueden eliminar las barreras descritas anteriormente.

De acuerdo con Camara et al. [26] la especificación de los RI se basa en características de calidad medibles y no medibles. Los requisitos medibles son aquellos que se pueden verificar en la actividad de prueba. De hecho, de acuerdo con [39], los requisitos no funcionales deben ser escritos cuantitativamente, siempre que sea posible, para que puedan ser objetivamente probados. Los RI medibles permiten establecer el nivel de interoperabilidad deseado para cada uno de los procesos de negocio como resultado de la implementación del sistema de información colaborativo. Estos requisitos medibles de acuerdo con Cornu et al. [40] se relacionan con tres aspectos para medir la interoperabilidad: el tiempo medio transcurrido, el coste medio y el porcentaje de fallos. Por otra parte los RI no medibles son aquellos que pueden ser validados en la actividad de prueba pero no verificados debido a su naturaleza no mensurable, consisten en representar directamente problemas de interoperabilidad en modelos de procesos de negocio.

Por otra parte Mallek et al. [5] define cuatro categorías de RI según el ciclo de vida de la interoperabilidad: (i) Compatibilidad, característica considerada invariable a lo largo de la colaboración y relacionada con las barreras de interoperabilidad para cada nivel de interoperabilidad según el enfoque previamente presentado en [30], (ii) Interoperación, característica variable durante la colaboración, relacionada con el desempeño de la interacción, (iii) Autonomía, capacidad de los socios para mantener su independencia mientras están involucrados en un proceso de colaboración, y (iv) Reversibilidad, capacidad de un socio para volver a su estado original en términos de rendimiento después de la colaboración. Además, la investigación plantea que un requisito puede ser a-temporal, es decir independiente del tiempo, o temporal cuando es verificable sólo en ciertas etapas del ciclo de vida de la colaboración.

En el mismo sentido, Daclin and Mallek [17] presentan un framework que ayuda a estructurar los RI a partir de varias dimensiones compuestas de perspectivas. Las dimensiones propuestas son: abstracción, relacionada con la perspectiva conceptual, organizacional y tecnológica presentadas en [30]; de análisis, relacionada con la perspectiva de rendimiento, estabilidad e integridad; y ciclo de vida de la interoperabilidad relacionada con la perspectiva de compatibilidad, interoperación, autonomía y reversibilidad presentadas anteriormente en [5].

3.2 Representación de los RI.

Las propuestas analizadas en esta dimensión plantean que BPMN (Business Process Model and Notation) es una notación adecuada para representar RI, pero son necesarios nuevos artefactos, notaciones y modelos complementarios para describir las características propias de la interoperabilidad. Las propuestas encontradas en esta dimensión fueron las siguientes:

Camara et al. [26] propone que los problemas de interoperabilidad deben ser representados en los modelos de procesos de negocio utilizando la notación BPMN. La representación debe distinguir entre actividades de negocio y aquellas que no agregan un valor (NAV). Las actividades NAV se definen como los componentes de los procesos de negocio que representan esfuerzos entre socios para lograr la interoperabilidad. De la misma forma Pavlovski y Zou [35] establecen que los requisitos no funcionales (RNF), como los RI, no se modelan fácilmente por medio de BPMN, por lo tanto proponen dos nuevos artefactos como extensiones de BPMN que permiten modelar las restricciones asociadas con un proceso de negocio: la condición operativa para denotar una restricción del proceso de negocio y el caso de control para definir criterios de control para mitigar el riesgo asociado con una condición operativa.

Desde otro punto de vista, Chandramohan et al. [27] plantean el uso de BPMN para obtener un perfil de modelo común de información el cual permite realizar un acuerdo sobre el contenido de la información que se intercambia entre aplicaciones. En este mismo sentido Daclin et al. [38] y Mallek et al. [5] para escribir y verificar los RI dentro de un proceso de colaboración utilizan BPMN y además, plantean una notación para clasificar un RI la cual está compuesta de tres partes: las barreras y niveles propuestos en [30], y el ciclo de vida de la interoperabilidad descrito en [5].

3.3 Proceso para la obtención de RI.

Las propuestas analizadas en esta dimensión convergen en que el análisis de un RI debe empezar desde el negocio hasta detallar los datos que se deben compartir. Sin embargo los enfoques propuestos carecen de una guía clara, completa y sistemática para identificar RI analizando las interacciones e intercambios de información que ocurren en los procesos de negocio e involucrando a las partes interesadas, clientes líderes y usuarios finales para entender y externalizar sus necesidades de calidad. Las propuestas encontradas fueron las siguientes:

Dentro del proyecto Athena [33] se establece un procedimiento para extraer RI a partir de casos de negocio. El procedimiento plantea la siguientes actividades: (i) definir un conjunto de principios básicos a fin de evitar problemas de comunicación entre los stakeholders, (ii) establecer y comprender los procesos de negocio, (iii) identificar instancias de casos de negocio en los que es necesaria la interoperabilidad, (iv) analizar cada caso de negocio confrontando la situación actual y un escenario previsto, con el fin de obtener un conjunto de RI que permiten que el escenario previsto se logre.

Qureshi et al. [28] propone un framework para identificar y establecer RI a partir del análisis de las intenciones de los usuarios y de 3 dimensiones de variabilidad: Humana Tecnología y Calidad. Plantean que la variabilidad tiene una influencia sustancial sobre la interoperabilidad ya que permite establecer las preferencias de los usuarios y las necesidades de interoperabilidad en términos de servicios, recursos, y calidad. A lo largo de las dimensiones de la variabilidad el marco explota dos vistas: intencional (contiene objetivos y preferencias de los usuarios) y de procesos de negocio (contiene las necesidades del negocio).

Daclin et al. [3] presentan una metodología para la expresión de las necesidades de interoperabilidad hasta la implementación de soluciones. El primer paso de la metodología consiste en la definición de objetivos y necesidades de interoperabilidad. En cuanto a los objetivos, los socios deben identificar los niveles, planteados por [31], en los que se implementara la interoperabilidad y el desempeño que se busca. En un segundo paso se identifican actores, aplicaciones y sistemas que están involucrados, y las barreras que impiden el logro de la interoperabilidad. La metodología plantea la detección de problemas de interoperabilidad de forma anticipada, enfoque utilizado en la propuesta de Daclin et al.[38], extensión de la investigación presentada en [5], en la cual plantean un repositorio de RI predefinidos derivados de un análisis bibliográfico sobre interoperabilidad y una encuesta realizada en la industria, los cuales pueden utilizarse como guía para identificar tempranamente otros RI.

Desde el punto de vista de los RNF, Jaramillo [34] presenta una guía para facilitar la obtención temprana y sistemática de RNF. La guía utiliza procesos de negocio y modelos de cuestionario en los cuales se realizan preguntas como "¿por qué se necesita el sistema?" y "¿cómo el sistema previsto cumpliría los objetivos de la organización?", las cuales contribuyen a que los RNF estén alineados con las necesidades del negocio. En el mismo sentido Bittencourt y Araujo [37] definen un método para la obtención de RNF a partir de los objetivos del negocio y modelos de procesos de negocio. El método se divide en 5 fases: (i) identificación de las necesidades de calidad del negocio; (ii) análisis del flujo de trabajo presente en los procesos de negocio con el fin de elaborar un cuestionario que guiara la interacción con los usuarios; (iii) identificación de la calidad esperada de los usuarios utilizando como instrumentos de comunicación el cuestionario y el modelo de procesos de negocio; (iv) construcción de un grafo con los RNF confirmados o denegados; y (v) aclaración de conflictos y derivación de otros RNF.

3.4 Elementos para una correcta obtención de RI.

Las propuestas plantean un conjunto de elementos necesarios que se deben presentar durante la obtención de RI independientemente del enfoque utilizado para modelar los procesos de negocio y el método de elicitación. Las propuestas identificadas fueron las siguientes:

Ullberg et al.[41] identifican y estructuras un conjunto de barreras genéricas de interoperabilidad bajo la guía de la norma (CEN/ISO 11354) [30]. Establecen que durante la captura de RI se debe pensar primero en cuáles son las incompatibilidades que impiden la interoperabilidad. En este mismo sentido, Alemany et al. [32] propone un conjunto potencial de RI necesarios para lograr correctamente la colaboración. Los RI se han clasificado utilizando los niveles de interoperabilidad propuestos en [31].

Bittencourt y Araujo [37] plantean que independientemente del enfoque utilizado para modelar los procesos de negocio, los elementos de negocio necesarios para garantizar una elicitación exitosa de RNF son: objetivos, actividades, actores, artefactos, eventos y reglas de negocio, además identifican que debe preexistir un modelo de objetivo de negocio y otro modelo de procesos de negocio donde se observe el flujo de trabajo. De la misma forma Otto et al. [29] establecen un conjunto de componentes que debe tener un modelo de negocio para desarrollar servicios de interoperabilidad, establecen que un requisito previo importante para lograr la interoperabilidad es la construcción de asignaciones entre esquemas de los sistemas involucrados.

En [36] se realizaron tres estudios exploratorios para determinar la aplicabilidad del método presentado en el estudio [37], concluyendo que la obtención de RNF sin contacto permanente con expertos del dominio conduce al predominio de la visión del desarrollador, en consecuencia, gran parte del conocimiento del dominio, las prioridades del negocio y las necesidades no se pueden obtener. De la misma forma Daclin et al. [42] plantea que cuanto más precisa sea la identificación o nivel de detalle del objeto afectado por la interoperabilidad, más se adaptarán y se optimizarán las soluciones seleccionadas e implementadas por los socios.

4 Análisis de las propuestas encontradas

4.1 Enfoques utilizados para elicitar RI

El análisis de las propuestas revela que existen diferentes enfoques para apoyar la elicitación de RI teniendo en cuenta las necesidades del negocio, entre los cuales se han identificado los siguientes: un repositorio de RI y barreras, los cuales pueden utilizarse como guía para elicitar otros RI; instancias de casos de uso e hipótesis, utilizados para confrontar la situación actual y el escenario previsto, con el fin de generar RI que permitan que suceda el escenario; las intenciones de los usuarios; modelos de procesos de negocio, objetivos del negocio y el flujos de trabajo; cuestionarios para guiar a los participantes en la lectura de los diagramas de proceso; la identificación de los niveles y perspectivas en los cuales puede estar presente la interoperabilidad y el enfoque para desarrollar la interoperabilidad.

4.2 Discusión y brechas de investigación

Al analizar los resultados de la revisión sistemática se observa que son mínimas las propuestas claras y sistemáticas, como [33], [34] y [37], que tienen como fin realizar la elicitación de RI considerando su relación con las necesidades de negocio de las organizaciones. Por otra parte propuestas como [3], [17], [28] y [30] plantean que el análisis de la interoperabilidad, teniendo como referencia las necesidades del negocio, debe abordarse desde varios niveles y en conjunción con múltiples perspectivas. Desde otro punto de vista, las propuestas encontradas no establecen que elementos particulares de los procesos de negocio se deben analizar para obtener problemas, necesidades y expectativas de los stakeholders, las cuales posteriormente derivan en RI. Principalmente se observa en las publicaciones analizadas la utilización de artefactos, como por ejemplo: cuestionarios, escenarios de negocio, hipótesis y plantillas como apoyo a los modelos de procesos de negocio dentro de un método de elicitación. Por otra parte, estableen que BPMN no es suficiente para representar los RI, por lo tanto las propuestas plantean nuevos artefactos, notaciones y modelos para describir las características propias de la interoperabilidad.

La validación de las propuestas es otro aspecto crucial, como se muestra en la tabla 2 como método de validación 8 estudios utilizan la ilustración, 5 el estudio de caso, 1 el ejemplo, 1 no valida la propuesta y ninguno utiliza los experimentos. Por lo tanto, podemos establecer que la evidencia generada al utilizar la ilustración como método de validación no tiene el mismo rigor de un experimento o estudio de caso, por consiguiente se ve amenazada la confiabilidad de los resultados. De igual forma cabe destacar que los trabajos que presentan estudios de caso no muestran evidencias para verificar si los RI crearon un impacto positivo en el producto final, y no existen métricas explícitas que determinen el nivel de interoperabilidad logrado. Además, se observa un mínimo porcentaje de propuestas que han sido aplicadas en el ámbito industrial.

Respecto a la dimensión tipo de contribución, 7 son herramientas (6 framework, 1 modelo), 4 son enfoques conceptuales, 5 son propuestas metodologías, y 1 es un estudio. Se observa que la mayoría de propuestas se catalogan como frameworks o enfoques conceptuales, los cuales respectivamente ofrecen instrumentos concretos para soportar el proceso de elicitación de RI y establecen un conjunto de conceptos relacionados al dominio de interoperabilidad dentro del contexto de ingeniería del software. Por el contrario únicamente 5 metodologías fueron encontradas para soportar la elicitación de RI, por lo tanto hacen falta propuestas que se enfoquen en guiar la elicitación de RI de forma alineada a las necesidades de los procesos de negocio.

Por otra parte, los resultados de este estudio pueden tener algunas amenazas a su validez. En primer lugar, puede haber un sesgo en la selección de los documentos por parte de un investigador. Con el objetivo de mitigar esta amenaza, el segundo y tercer autor analizaron y debatieron los resultados. Además, la definición del protocolo y la cadena de búsqueda, así como el no acceso a la descarga de algunos artículos pueden no permitir obtener todos los estudios relevantes. Para mitigar este riesgo otros investigadores revisaron el diseño de la revisión; la cadena de búsqueda fue generada identificando los términos principales de las preguntas de investigación y ajustándola de acuerdo a la precisión de los resultados; y las bases de datos seleccionadas permitieron obtener una visión general del área de investigación de RI desde la perspectiva de las necesidades del negocio.

Debido a las anteriores brechas de investigación, actualmente dentro del grupo de investigación IDIS de la universidad del Cauca se están desarrollando propuestas para guiar a los analistas en la búsqueda de RI, junto con los clientes y usuarios finales. La elicitación utiliza los modelos de procesos de negocio como un instrumento de comunicación. El enfoque seguido plantea que los elementos de negocio ayudan a cuestionar las expectativas de los usuarios y clientes, a los usuarios en entender por qué se están realizando las preguntas dentro del proceso de elicitación, al analista del sistema a justificar el desarrollo de los RI y fundamentalmente para alinear los RI con las necesidades de los procesos de negocio de uso e intercambio de información.

5 Conclusiones

En este trabajo es presentada una revisión sistemática para identificar, categorizar y analizar propuestas que consideran los procesos de negocio de las organizaciones como referencia para la elicitación de RI. El análisis de cada propuesta seleccionada fue dividido en varias dimensiones como: tipo de propuesta, forma de validación, y objetivo respecto a la elicitación de RI. A partir de los resultados obtenidos se identificó que pocos enfoques consideran la relación entre los RI y las necesidades de negocio. Al realizar un análisis de las propuestas encontradas fueron identificados diferentes enfoques para realizar la elicitación de RI, formas de representar estos requisitos y brechas de investigación. Como resultado, se plantea que el conocimiento sobre la temática de RI y su alineación con las necesidades del negocio es escaso y disperso en la literatura, por consiguiente es necesario llevar a cabo estudios para promover una mejor comprensión y avances en este campo de investigación.

6 Referencias

1. Meng, J., Su, S.Y.W., Lam, H., Helal, A., Xian, J., Liu, X., Yang, S.: DynaFlow: a dynamic inter-organisational workflow management system. Int. J. Bus. Process Integr. Manag. 1, 101–115 (2006)
2. Bae, J., Bae, H., Kang, S.-H., Kim, Y.: Automatic control of workflow processes using ECA rules. IEEE Trans. Knowl. Data Eng. 16, 1010–1023 (2004)
3. Daclin, N., Chen, D., Vallespir, B.: Developing enterprise collaboration: a methodology to implement and improve interoperability. Enterp. Inf. Syst. 10, 467–504 (2016). doi:10.1080/17517575.2014.932013
4. Soomro, T.R., Awan, A.H.: Challenges and future of enterprise application integration. Int. J. Comput. Appl. 42, 42–45 (2012)
5. Mallek, S., Daclin, N., Chapurlat, V.: The application of interoperability requirement specification and verification to collaborative processes in industry. Comput. Ind. 63, 643–658 (2012). doi:10.1016/j.compind.2012.03.002
6. Chen, D., Doumeingts, G.: European initiatives to develop interoperability of enterprise applications - Basic concepts, framework and roadmap. Annu. Rev. Control. 27 II, 153–162 (2003). doi:10.1016/j.arcontrol.2003.09.001
7. Panetto, H., Zdravkovic, M., Jardim-Goncalves, R., Romero, D., Cecil, J., Mezgár, I.: New perspectives for the future interoperable enterprise systems. Comput. Ind. 79, 47–63 (2016)
8. Vernadat, F.B.: Technical, semantic and organizational issues of enterprise interoperability and networking. IFAC (2009)
9. Rezaei, R., Chiew, T.K., Lee, S.P., Aliee, Z.S.: Interoperability evaluation models: A

systematic review. Comput. Ind. 65, 1–23 (2014)
10. Cenci, K., Estevez, E., Fillottrani, P.R.: Facilitating Data Interoperability in Science and Technology: A Case Study and a Technical Solution. In: Proceedings of the 18th Annual International Conference on Digital Government Research. pp. 407–415. ACM (2017)
11. Javanbakht, M., Rezaie, R., Shams, F., Seyyedi, M.: A new method for decision making and planning in enterprises. In: Information and Communication Technologies: From Theory to Applications, 2008. ICTTA 2008. 3rd International Conference on. pp. 1–5. IEEE (2008)
12. Kajan, E.: Electronic Business Interoperability: Concepts, Opportunities and Challenges: Concepts, Opportunities and Challenges. IGI Global (2011)
13. Kuziemsky, C.E., Weber-Jahnke, J.H.: An ebusiness-based framework for ehealth interoperability. J. Emerg. Technol. Web Intell. 1, 129–136 (2009)
14. Chen, D., Doumeingts, G., Vernadat, F.: Architectures for enterprise integration and interoperability: Past, present and future. Comput. Ind. 59, 647–659 (2008). doi:10.1016/j.compind.2007.12.016
15. Legner, C., Wende, K.: Towards an excellence framework for business interoperability. BLED 2006 Proc. 29 (2006)
16. Motta, R.C., de Oliveira, K.M., Travassos, G.H.: Characterizing Interoperability in Context-aware Software Systems. In: Computing Systems Engineering (SBESC), 2016 VI Brazilian Symposium on. pp. 203–208. IEEE (2016)
17. Daclin, N., Mallek, S.: Capturing and Structuring Interoperability Requirements: A Framework for Interoperability Requirements. In: Mertins, K., Bénaben, F., Poler, R., and Bourrières, J.-P. (eds.) Enterprise Interoperability VI: Interoperability for Agility, Resilience and Plasticity of Collaborations. pp. 239–249. Springer International Publishing, Cham (2014)
18. Przybylek, A.: A business-oriented approach to requirements elicitation. In: Evaluation of Novel Approaches to Software Engineering (ENASE), 2014 International Conference on. pp. 1–12. IEEE (2014)
19. Abukwaik, H., Rombach, D.: Software Interoperability Analysis in Practice: A Survey. In: Proceedings of the 21st International Conference on Evaluation and Assessment in Software Engineering. pp. 12–20. ACM (2017)
20. Harmon, P.: The State of Business Process Management 2018 - BPTrends. (2018)
21. Williams, B.J., Carver, J.C.: Characterizing software architecture changes: A systematic review. Inf. Softw. Technol. 52, 31–51 (2010)
22. Kitchenham, B.: Procedures for performing systematic reviews. Keele, UK, Keele Univ. 33, 1–26 (2004)
23. Kitchenham, B., Charters, S.: Guidelines for performing Systematic Literature reviews in Software Engineering Version 2.3. Engineering. 45, 1051 (2007). doi:10.1145/1134285.1134500
24. Neiva, F.W., David, J.M.N., Braga, R., Campos, F.: Towards pragmatic interoperability to support collaboration : A systematic review and mapping of the literature. 72, 137–150 (2016). doi:10.1016/j.infsof.2015.12.013
25. Ormeño, Y.I., Panach, I.J., Pastor, Ó.: Elicitación De Requisitos De Usabilidad: Un Estudio Sistématico. 2011. 9 (2011)
26. Camara, M.S., Dupas, R., Ducq, Y.: Validation and Verification of Interoperability

Requirements BT - Enterprise Interoperability: 6th International IFIP Working Conference, IWEI 2015, Nîmes, France, May 28-29, 2015, Proceedings. Presented at the (2015)

27. Chandramohan, L.S., Ravikumar, G., Member, S.: Business Process Model for Deriving CIM Pro fi le : A Case Study for Indian Utility, (2015)
28. Qureshi, N.A., Nguyen, C.D., Perini, A.: Analyzing interoperability requirements for adaptive service-based applications: A goal-oriented approach. Proc. - Int. Comput. Softw. Appl. Conf. 239–244 (2010). doi:10.1109/COMPSACW.2010.49
29. Otto, B., Ebner, V., Baghi, E., Bittmann, R.M.: Toward a business model reference for interoperability services. Comput. Ind. 64, 887–897 (2013). doi:10.1016/j.compind.2013.06.017
30. Chen, D., Daclin, N.: Framework for enterprise interoperability. In: Proc. of IFAC Workshop EI2N. pp. 77–88. sn (2006)
31. Daclin, N., Chen, D., Vallespir, B.: Methodology for enterprise interoperability. IFAC (2008)
32. Alemany, M.M.E., Alarcón, F., Lario, F.C., Poler, R.: Conceptual Framework for the Interoperability Requirements of Collaborative Planning Process. Enterp. Interoperability IV. 25–34 (2010). doi:10.1007/978-1-84996-257-5_3
33. ATHENA: PDE1. Introduction to Dynamic Requirements Definition. (2004)
34. Jaramillo, A.: Non-functional requirements elicitation from business process models. … Challenges Inf. Sci. (RCIS), 2011 …. 1–7 (2011). doi:10.1109/RCIS.2011.6006824
35. Pavlovski, C.J., Zou, J.: Non-Functional Requirements in Business Process Modeling. Proc. 5th Asia-Pacific Conf. Concept. Model. 79, 103–112 (2008)
36. Bittencourt, R., Araujo, R., Cappelli, C., Ferreira, J., Engiel, P.: Experiences on the use of business models for identifying quality requirements for information systems. Proc. - 7th Int. Conf. Qual. Inf. Commun. Technol. QUATIC 2010. 192–197 (2010). doi:10.1109/QUATIC.2010.41
37. Bittencourt, R.V., Araujo, R.M. De: Using business models to identify expected quality for information systems. Int. J. Bus. Process Integr. Manag. 5, 159 (2011). doi:10.1504/IJBPIM.2011.040207
38. Daclin, N., Daclin, S.M., Chapurlat, V., Vallespir, B.: Writing and verifying interoperability requirements: Application to collaborative processes. Comput. Ind. 82, 1–18 (2016). doi:10.1016/j.compind.2016.04.001
39. Ian, S.: Software Engineering. Addison-Wesley, Reading (2011)
40. Cornu, C., Chapurlat, V., Quiot, J.-M., Irigoin, F.: Customizable Interoperability Assessment Methodology to support technical processes deployment in large companies. Annu. Rev. Control. 36, 300–308 (2012). doi:http://dx.doi.org/10.1016/j.arcontrol.2012.09.011
41. Ullberg, J., Chen, D., Johnson, P.: Barriers to enterprise interoperability. Enterp. Interoperability. 13–24 (2009)
42. Daclin, N., Mallek-Daclin, S.: Towards a sustainable implementation of interoperability solutions: Bridging the gap between interoperability requirements and solutions. In: International IFIP Working Conference on Enterprise Interoperability. pp. 73–82. Springer (2015)

Challenges in System of Systems Development: A Systematic Mapping

Diego de Lima Nascimento[1] and Rosana Teresinha Vaccare Braga[1]

Institute of Mathematics and Computer Science
University of São Paulo
São Carlos-SP, Brazil
diego.lnasc@usp.br, rtvb@icmc.usp.br

Abstract. System Of Systems (SoS) is an emerging field of research whose main purpose is the interoperability of constituent systems. SoS communicate through a variety of existing and independent systems, but achieving the interoperability of these systems is not trivial. This paper presents a systematic mapping (SM) that aims to classify and analyze the challenges that occur during the development of SoS. The studies of this SM were identified through a protocol and planning criteria already described in the literature. Furthermore, the SM found 39 studies in five sources that indexed different journals and conferences. After the analysis, it was possible to identify the main challenges that occur during the development and use of SoS. Therefore, the SM has found recent discussions on the most common challenges found during SoS development. The studies were categorized into nine areas with the purpose of highlighting the major problems and better characterizing the scope of SoS development. In short, most studies belong to the integration and management categories, because of the enormous difficulty of interoperating heterogeneous systems, and managing or finding engineers with the knowledge to work in the field. Finally, this SM can help researchers working with SoS integration, as they can benefit from the mapping we have provided correlating the difficulties in SoS development to the studies that address them.

Keywords: System of Systems, Interoperability, Challenge, Systematic Mapping

1 Introduction

The need to gather information in real time, integrating business partners to reduce end-to-end delivery times, resulted in organizations that are increasingly dependent on interconnected systems, which provide capabilities not found in single systems [40].

Therefore, software-intensive systems have become increasingly ubiquitous and complex, arising from the cooperation of several operationally independent and geographically distributed systems, often developed with different technologies and for different platforms. This cooperation is essential to solve larger and more complex missions that could not be solved by systems working separately [3].

Given growth of size and complexity, software systems are moving towards the so-called System of Systems (SoS). This class of systems has a diverse collection of large-scale components that work independently, but operate together to achieve a common goal. Thus, the integration of different components (constituent systems) offers a new capability based on the individual elements. According to DoD [41], SoS is a set or arrangement of systems that results when independent and useful systems are integrated into a larger system that has a specific capability.

A SoS is usually found in large scale and heterogeneous systems, although they can be differentiated from other traditional or complex systems through their distinguishing properties [42–44]: (i) operational independence: Any constituent system that is part of the SoS is independent, and is capable of operating normally if the SoS ceases to exist; (ii) managerial independence: Constituent systems collaborate with other members of the SoS, but each constituent is managed individually; (iii) geographic distribution: The constituent systems can be distributed geographically, but they can still cooperate with the SoS; (iv) emergent behavior: behavior arises during the collaboration of the constituent systems in the SoS, since the synergism cannot be assigned and/or achieved by each constituent individually; and (v) evolutionary development: the SoS is never complete, i.e., evolutionary development defines that objectives and functionalities are constantly changing and can be added, modified or removed. Thereby, some examples of SoS's are defense systems [42], emergency [45] or even intelligent transportation systems [42].

These intrinsic properties make a SoS distinctive and challenging, but very promising for this era of system inter-operation. Although there are many works regarding SoS development, we could not find a secondary study where the problems/challenge of developing SoS are clearly identified and discussed. Therefore, the main objective of this paper is to investigate the challenges that occur in the development of SoS. This is done by conducting a systematic mapping on this subject and discussing the results found.

The remainder of this paper is organized as follows. Section 2 describes the systematic mapping and how it was conducted. Section 3 presents the planning and protocol details. Section 4 summarizes the results. Section 5 presents threats to validity. Finally, Section 6 concludes the paper.

2 Systematic Mapping

Before starting a research, authors usually seek means to verify the scope, gaps and relevance of the proposed study. To help in this process, we can mention, among other techniques, literature reviews and rigorous reading methods that aid in the validation of the study. More specifically in the software engineering area, Evidence-Base Software Engineering (EBSE) promotes the use of two main methods, systematic review (SR) and systematic mapping (SM) [46]. Both methods are based on the same methodological principle, but a SR is able to reach a greater depth in the topic researched, based on specific research questions (RQ) and rigorous criteria during the selection of studies. On the other hand, an SM aims to analyze literature in a broader way, with less specific research questions, thus providing an overview of the state of the art [47, 48].

Planning, conducting and analyzing are the three main steps to perform a SR or SM. Each step is executed after the previous one, establishing a dependency and order between each one. The steps are defined as:

- Planning: a protocol for conducting the review is defined. This planning/protocol is based on why the SR/SM is necessary, thus research questions that seek to elucidate the theme are created. The protocol also contains important criteria to be followed, so this initial part should be carefully planned.
- Conduction: Beginning of review. At this stage the studies are properly searched, by means of criteria defined in the execution protocol.
- Report: Completion of the review. The results are discussed and evaluated in order to answer the main objective of the systematic review.

3 Planning

The first step of the SM consists of a well-defined plan that must contain fundamental parts from the beginning to the end of execution. In this stage, we have defined the research questions, search strategies and criteria for classification of the studies found. This protocol should elucidate the importance of the SM and its purpose, therefore, it needs well defined and structured research questions, as well as strategies that result in studies of the area with the purpose of extracting the maximum to enrich these issues.

Search Strategy and Engines The SM was conducted with the objective of answering two research questions, which have been directed to problems that occur with the development of SoS:

- RQ1: What are the challenges faced during the development of SoS?
- RQ2: Is there any solutions or at least considerations/discussions for the challenges encountered?

The RQs have keywords that can assist in the search for primary studies. Thus, the following main terms were used: *System-of-Systems*, *Problem* and *Development*, as well as the corresponding synonyms for the definition and refinement of a search string. The string used in this SM is shown below:

("System-of-Systems" OR "System-of-System" OR "Systems-of-Systems") AND ("Development" OR "Software Development" OR "Software Engineering") AND ("Problem" OR "Difficulty" OR "Challenge")

It is important to note that synonyms, related terms, or alternative spellings are incorporated with the Boolean OR operator; and the main terms with the Boolean operator AND. Subsequently, this string was adapted to the five search engines that can be visualized in Table 1. The most relevant engines for computer science and engineering have been chosen, among the various ones, as they index the main conferences of the research theme. The availability of the studies was also essential for the researchers [47].

Table 1. Selected Engines

Engine	Address
IEEEXplore	http://ieeexplore.ieee.org
ACM DigitalLibrary	http://dl.acm.org
Scopus	http://www.scopus.com
Web of Science	http://sub3.webofknowledge.com
Science Direct	http://www.sciencedirect.com

3.1 Inclusion and Exclusion Criteria

A well-executed SM must be based on a well structured string that improves the chance of a successful search, returning all the studies needed to respond the RQs. However, the string should not be very broad so as to return unnecessary studies. Regardless of the effort employed on defining the string, the returned studies need to be classified methodically, so that the best ones are filtered and better analyzed. To help on this issue, we have specified criteria to evaluate whether a study should be included or not (IC and EC: inclusion and exclusion criteria, respectively). For our particular SM, it is important to understand how SoS are being used and the difficulties found to use them, so only one inclusion criterion was defined, as well as three exclusion criteria:

- IC1: Primary studies that explicitly highlight problems/challenges during the use of SoS.
- EC1: The study is not in Portuguese or English.
- EC2: The study is not complete or the researcher cannot have access to the publication.
- EC3: The study is not related to SoS or does not point out problems/challenges.

3.2 Conduction

The search performed during our SM resulted in 900 initial studies. The procedure was initiated in August 2016. The selection of the studies was performed in two stages, (i) at first, a reading of the studies title and abstract was done to classify them according to their relevance. If positive, the study would move on to the next stage, also stressing that the study should be relevant to the inclusion criteria to be accepted. Otherwise, the study was removed by some exclusion criteria. However, a change was made after reading a few studies because it was difficult to identify the problems/challenges only by reading the title and abstract. Consequently, the reading of the conclusion was also included in order to mitigate this problem. (ii) The second stage, called extraction, was performed with the same inclusion and exclusion criteria, but a diagonal reading of the papers was also performed, as this reading technique has a greater focus on the most relevant parts of the text, more specifically introduction and conclusion.

It is common to obtain a substantial number of repeated studies, because some search engines index the same conference or journal. In the case of this SM, a total of 194 duplicate studies were found, and of the remaining 706, 580 were rejected by some exclusion criterion. Therefore, most of the studies did not go through the first inclusion criterion, because they did not make clear the problem/challenge faced during the development of SoS. Hence, 126 studies were approved for the initial stage, but only 39 remained after reading the second stage.

The extraction and synthesis phase started after finishing the two initial stages of selection. The 39 selected studies were completely read and the following information was obtained: (i) demographic data; (ii) identification of the different domains of use of SoS; (iii) identification of the types of studies applied in the context of SoS and in different domains, for example architecture, framework, among others; (iv) identification of the problems/challenges encountered during the use of SoS; (v) determination of whether or not the author proposes a solution/consideration to the challenge described.

4 Results

In this SM, no studies prior to 2003 have been included in the results summary, even without using year filtering to help verifying specific events or how the area is behaving in recent years. The reason for not finding studies before 2003 is justified by the fact that, although systems with SoS characteristics have been discussed for a long time, their definitions and particularities were defined explicitly only in 1998 by [42]. Consequently, it is common that problems aroused or began to be discussed only a few years after, as shown in Fig 1.

It is worth noting that the search was made in the middle of 2016, so the smaller number of studies in 2016 is due to the fact that this year was not considered in its entirety, besides the natural delay for newly published papers to be indexed by the search engines.

4.1 Domains and Types of Studies

The extraction activity has the purpose of verifying if there is any relation between the problems encountered and the different domains of SoS development. In addition, it has the objective of knowing which area is using this class of systems more frequently. The results are shown in Table 2.

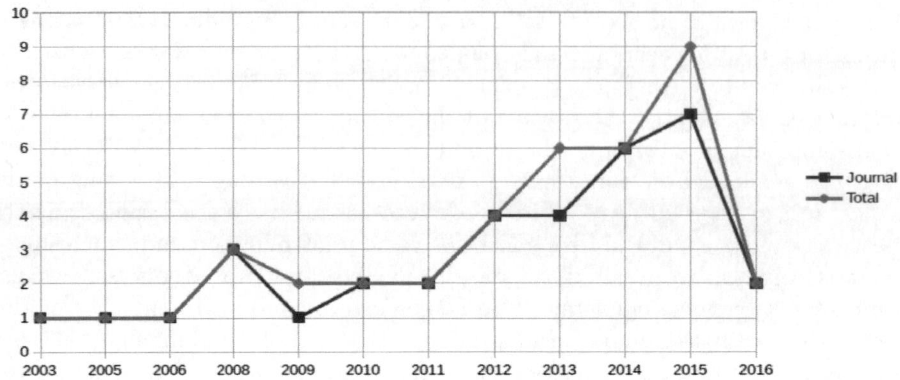

Fig. 1. Distribution of Studies

It can be observed that most studies (61.53 %) do not refer to a specific domain, however, they use as an example big systems such as those described in the remaining domains, resulting in a more general discussion about SoS or SoS Engineering (SoSE). Some studies cite examples to elucidate concepts about SoS, however, these cases are for explanation only, so they are classified in the "no specific domain" category.

Table 2. Classification of Application Domains

ID	**Amount**	**Domain**
S1[1], S3[3], S7[7], S9[9], S10[10], S11[11], S12[12], S14[14], S15[15], S17[17], S20[20], S21[21], S22[22], S23[23], S26[26], S27[27], S28[28], S31[31], S32[32], S33[33], S34[34], S37[37], S38[38], S39[39]	24(61,5%)	No specific domain
S5[5], S18[18], S19[19], S24[24]	4(10,2%)	Industrial automation
S13[13], S16[16]	2(5,1%)	Earth observation system
S30[30], S36[36]	2(5,1%)	Department of Defense (DoD)
S2[2], S29[29]	2(5,1%)	Public sector
S4[4], S35[35]	2(5,1%)	Maritime
S6[6], S8[8]	2(5,1%)	Physically coupled
S25[25]	1(2,5%)	Automotive, rail and avionics

The search results were classified and categorized (Table 3) with the main purpose of visualizing the growth of the area and, subsequently, to verify if there was any relation between the domains and types with the problems found. For the classification, the types were defined and the studies were classified according to each definition, right after reading. In this sense, the first type of study found is related to secondary studies where a systematic literature mapping or review (SR or SM) has been presented. The two retrieved studies in this category are related to the SoS context, but with emphasis on different uses. The first is related to integration, while the second regards the development of SoS based on IoT. Both of them presented difficulties related to SoS.

Ten "Framework" studies have also been found, which address processes, tests, techniques and/or methodologies proposed by the researchers. Studies classified in the "Architecture" category propose standards, define concepts or cover some difficulties related to the SoS research line. They can also refer to modeling and/or the development process, e.g. activities related to validation, requirements or something more specific such as integration.

We have also found studies that discuss the SoS or SoSE area itself, explaining concepts, definitions and common problems related to specific SoS types or not. Such studies were grouped in the "Approach" category. Researches that discuss a more specific domain or have a more limited scope of the problem, in a way that characterizes an application environment, have been classified as a "case study". Finally, there is the "Ontology" category, in which a specific study discusses and defines specific terms of SoS integration (SoSI).

4.2 Conclusions of the Research Questions

In this step, the results are presented according to the research questions defined in the protocol. **RQ1**. The purpose of this question is to extract the problems/challenges encountered in SoS development. The result of this question was achieved after analyzing the 39 studies and summarizing them to get an overview of the main open problems found. First, all studies were read and summarized, and all types of problems, challenges and other interests were identified. Subsequently, all the challenges were analyzed and categorized in large areas of "Challenge", which are summarized in the following:

Table 3. Type of Studies

ID	Amount	Type
S1, S12	2(5,1%)	SR or SM
S6, S8, S10, S14, S16, S23, S27, S30, S35, S36	10(25,6%)	Framework
S3, S21, S22, S37	4(10,2%)	Architecture
S4, S7, S9, S11, S15, S17, S18, S19, S20, S28, S32, S33, S34, S38, S39	15(38,4%)	Approach
S2, S5, S24, S25, S26, S29, S31	7(17,9%)	Case study
S13	1(2,5%)	Ontology

- **Integration**: SoS integration is not a trivial task. According to [13], integration must be handled during the development of SoS, so that it is present throughout the life cycle. Studies in this category mainly portray that integration is still a challenge because of the lack of specific knowledge about each constituent system; the variety of implementations (the constituents do not have standardization of interfaces); managerial and operational independence can be a problem when information protection is needed; difficulty in coordinating the SoS or the constituent; geographical distribution of the constituents can cause problems with communication and information sharing; and difficulty to interoperate heterogeneous systems in an effective and transparent manner. The difficulty in system integration is nothing new, and it is easy to note the variety of problems that occur, since these problems (standardization, interdependence, interoperability, and complexity) are also found in other software engineering areas.

- **Management**: Management difficulties start when looking for qualified engineers to work in the SoS area. This happens due to the high need of specific knowledge about systems in general (or about a particular system) and is worsened by the necessity of controlling several stakeholders who present different objectives and communication problems. Moreover, several risks can be present and future uncertainties of the SoS must be managed.
- **Documentation**: The SoS requires communication and sharing abilities in order to evolve properly. The lack of documentation implies that no guidelines are available to assist engineers during the development process. This affects growth as a whole, causing problems of dependence on engineers that know the system and how to make them interoperate with new systems. The lack of documentation can affect other subareas, since it makes communication more difficult, e.g., when hiring engineers to evolve or integrate new systems.
- **Evolution and Maintenance**: Evolutionary development [42] is one of the main features of SoS, but doing so in real time is extremely complex. Therefore, collaboration in a SoS can be compromised due to the difficulty in evolving the system as a whole. According to [21], the evolution of SoS can undermine its performance, as new harmful emerging behaviors may arise, and consequently, this unique feature of SoS may render unreliable the generalization of experiments. In this context, there is also a study [20] which describes that components can be added and removed at all times, since independence and evolution over time is a predominant feature of SoS, and as such, the interaction and composition of the constituent elements of the SoS is carried out to accomplish the shared mission.
- **Architecture and Modeling**: According to [22] it is very difficult to model and analyze a SoS by conventional means, especially how to represent SoS in detail, because the complete details of the constituent systems may not be readily available. Therefore, in this category, discussions about architecture and modeling were classified in the context of SoS, starting from the low mobility of the community in the evolution of existing reference architectures until the difficulty of representing the characteristics of a SoS and how to represent it in a single model.

- **Requirements and Quality**: According to [20], quality is a key issue to SoS success, as inconsistencies and ambiguities can arise when quality attributes are overlooked in the SoS architecture. In this category we have included studies that discuss the importance of quality and the difficulty of applying requirements engineering in the context of SoS.
- **Test**: SoS can present problems in its current context, but the problems can be found in the interfaces with constituents or in the constituents themselves, so testing challenges are amplified [24]. Only two studies portrayed test challenges within SoS.
- **Dynamic Reconfiguration and Monitoring**: Three studies addressed problems related to the SoS reconfiguration at run time, especially in the context of structural changes and SoS composition.
- **Behavior**: Finally, several studies that discuss problems related to interactions, consequences and effects of emergent SoS behavior.

Table 4. Problem Categorization

ID(Paper linked to the Challenge)	**Challenge**	**Considerations**
S1, S5, S8, S9, S11, S12, S13, S17, S18, S21, S28, S32, S35, S38, S39	Integration	S27
S1, S5, S10, S17, S18, S21, S29, S32, S34, S36, S39	Management	S7
S1, S3, S12, S13, S20	Documentation	
S1, S3, S11, S20, S21, S22, S32, S34, S37, S39	Evolution and Maintenance	S19, S27
S1, S3, S11, S20, S22, S31, S37, S39	Architecture and Modeling	S4, S6, S14, S15, S16, S23, S27, S33
S20, S26, S28, S32, S37	Requirements and Quality	S2, S7, S25
S24, S35	Test	S30
S11, S20, S35	Dynamic Reconfiguration and Monitoring	S5, S16, S19
S1, S5, S11, S21, S28	Behavior	

It is not possible to observe a relationship between challenge and domain in the studies (Table 2 and Table 4), i.e., there are no evidences that a particular domain would present specific challenges, in short, there is no correlation. However, it is possible to notice the lack of tools to ease SoS development and the lack of experience of stakeholders in the SoS area. This can be partially justified by the fact that there is a big proportion of closed and unavailable projects, resulting in a higher learning curve for engineers, besides leading to the lack of standardization of architectures and models.

RQ2. This RQ aimed at investigating the studies in which the problems/challenges already have a proposed solution or, at least, considerations or discussions are presented by the authors. In this sense, this question was focused on evidencing the state of the art concerning SoS. To facilitate this investigation, one of the reading criteria was to examine the studies in descending order, i.e., from 2016 to 2003.

In general, this RQ is complex to be analyzed. Researchers always (or generally) point out considerations or ways to mitigate problems in their area, however, in SoS studies, they tend to propose specific solutions to challenges encountered during the development of their research or ongoing projects. Thus, we have decided to make a correspondence of studies that present relevant considerations to the subareas described above (Table 4). This is done in the "Considerations" column of the table. In this paper, these considerations correspond to researches that present ideas (research, methods, frameworks, among others) of how such challenges can be smoothed. Thereby, the researches that are in the column "Considerations", present somehow solutions that can aid in the described problem. It is important to emphasize that such research does not mitigate the problems/challenges, only aid in their control.

Finally, it is worth observing that SoS often refers to large enterprise systems or proprietary projects, resulting in frameworks and approaches that are not available to the community. Consequently, most of the studies mention lack of communication and availability to the community and stakeholders, i.e., the area needs more cooperation and sharing to make possible to derive standards and to achieve progress in the near future.

5 Threats to Validity

This SM was conducted in August 2016 and is limited to studies that discuss SoS development. It is important to emphasize that no filter was used in the search engines and no type of gray literature has been included. Therefore, the main threats to the validity of this research are related to the selection and extraction bias of the studies.

First, the entire process was structured from the RQs and the protocol defined in Section 2. This protocol was written by the first author, but was also revised and refined by the second author, improving the coherence and accuracy of the SM with the RQs. The selection of the studies was carried out strategically (following the inclusion and exclusion criteria), using the systematic review tool "State of the Art through Systematic Review" (StArt) [49], which aims to assist the execution of SM and organize the selection of studies, and automatically remove duplicate studies.

It is important to note that in this paper the peer review process was not performed, however, the second author was always consulted in case of doubts. Additionally, each study underwent two rigorous classification phases (subsection 3.2), in which all 39 studies were accepted twice by the inclusion criterion. Nevertheless, although the databases are the most relevant in the area [47], some studies might not have been analyzed because of limitations of the search engines or lack of authors' access to the work.

The bias in the extraction of the studies was also controlled by the establishment of a protocol based on the RQs. However, not all the studies had well-defined responses to the SM RQs, so they needed to be interpreted and categorized by the authors of this work.

6 Conclusion

SoS fosters a new form of benefiting from the functionality of existing systems, so interoperation of resources allows new visions to be realized to achieve broader goals. However, the integration of different systems is a challenging task, since they were not developed with the purpose of working together, which poses numerous challenges.

The present SM discusses the major challenges that researchers face during the development of SoS. Thus, several studies in different contexts and domains were found between 2003 and 2016, but often have similar problems. Therefore, it was possible to categorize the challenges in nine specific areas, in which integration and management were the most pointed by the researchers. In fact, SoSI was and still is a subject of enormous debate, so it was to be expected that most of the challenges would be present in this category. Surprisingly, management was also a category that presented several problems, whose key factors were qualified (experienced) engineers and control of various stakeholders.

However, this SM points out essential characteristics for researchers working with SoSE, since problems are not only categorized but also correlated with the state of the art considerations. In addition, several studies present solutions targeted to specific projects and SoS, and often these solutions are valid for other studies and research, even though the contexts are different, so they can and should be analyzed.

Acknowledgment

We are thankful to Fundação de Amparo à Pesquisa do Estado de São Paulo (FAPE- SP), process number 2016/05129-0, to Coordenação de Aperfeiçoamento de Pessoal de Nível Superior (CAPES), and to the University of São Paulo (USP) for supporting the execution of this research.

References

1. Vargas, I. G., Gottardi, T., Braga, R. T.: Approaches for Integration in System of Systems: A Systematic Review. In Proceedings of the 4th International Workshop on Software Engineering for Systemsof-Systems (SESoS 16). ACM, New York, NY, USA, 32-38. (2016)
2. Larsson, J., Borg, M., Olsson., T.: Testing Quality Requirements of a System-of-Systems in the Public Sector - Challenges and Potential Remedies. CoRR abs/1602.05618. (2016)

3. Nakagawa, E. Y., Oquendo, F., Avgeriou, P., Cuesta, C. E., Drira, K., Maldonado, J. C. , Zisman, A.: Foreword: Towards Reference Architectures for Systems-of-Systems. In 2015 IEEE/ACM 3rd International Workshop on Software Engineering for Systems-of-Systems. ACM, Florence, Italy, 1-4. (2015)
4. Hachem, J. E.: Towards Model Driven Architecture and Analysis of System of Systems Access Control. In 2015 IEEE/ACM 37th IEEE International Conference on Software Engineering, Vol. 2., Florence, Italy, 867-870. (2015)
5. Rabiser, R., Vierhauser, M., Grnbacher, P.: Variability Management for a Runtime Monitoring Infrastructure. In Proceedings of the Ninth International Workshop on Variability Modelling of Software-intensive Systems (VaMoS 15). ACM, New York, NY, USA, 35–42. (2015)
6. Chiprianov, V., Gallon, L., Salameh, K., Munier, M., Hachem, J. E.: Towards security software engineering the Smart Grid as a System of Systems. In 2015 10th System of Systems Engineering Conference (SoSE). IEEE, San Antonio, TX, USA, 77-82. (2015)
7. Safwat, A., Senousy, M.B.: Addressing Challenges of Ultra Large Scale System on Requirements Engineering. Procedia Computer Science 65, 442-449. (2015)
8. Kampert, D., Nazari, S., Sonntag, C., Epple, U., Engell, S.: A Framework for Simulation, Optimization and Information Management of Physically-Coupled Systems of Systems. IFAC-PapersOnLine 48, 3, 1553-1558. (2015)
9. Pennock, M. J., Wade, J. P.: The Top 10 Illusions of Systems Engineering: A Research Agenda. Procedia Computer Science 44, 147-154. (2015)
10. Fang, Z., DeLaurentis, D.: Multi-stakeholder Dynamic Planning of System of Systems Development and Evolution. Procedia Computer Science 44, 95-104. (2015)
11. Nielsen, C. B., Larsen, P. G., Fitzgerald, J., Woodcock, J., Peleska, J.: Systems of Systems Engineering: Basic Concepts, Model-Based Techniques, and Research Directions. ACM Comput. Surv. 48, 2, 18–41. (2015)
12. Maia, P., Cavalcante, E., Gomes, P., Batista, T., Delicato, F. C., Pires, P. F.: On the Development of Systems-of-Systems Based on the Internet of Things: A Systematic Mapping. In Proceedings of the 2014 European Conference on Software Architecture Workshops (ECSAW 14). ACM, New York, NY, USA, 23:1-23:8. (2014)
13. Madni, A. M., Sievers, M.: System of Systems Integration: Key Considerations and Challenges. Systems Engineering 17, 3 (2014), 330-347. (2014)
14. Chiprianov, V., Falkner, K., Gallon, L., Munier, M.: Towards modelling and analysing non-functional properties of systems of systems. In 2014 9th International Conference on System of Systems Engineering (SOSE). IEEE, Adelade, SA, Australia, 289-294. (2014)
15. Chiprianov, V., Falkner, K., Szabo, C., Puddy, G.: Architectural Support for Model-Driven Performance Prediction of Distributed Real-Time Embedded Systems of Systems. Springer International Publishing, Cham, 357-364. (2014)
16. Vierhauser, M., Rabiser, R., Grnbacher, P., Danner, C., Wallner, S., Zeisel, H.: A Flexible Framework for Runtime Monitoring of System-of-Systems Architectures. In 2014 IEEE/IFIP Conference on Software Architecture. IEEE, Sydney, Australia, Australia, 57-66. (2014)
17. Keating, C. B.: Governance implications for meeting challenges in the system of systems engineering field. In 2014 9th International Conference on System of Systems Engineering (SOSE). IEEE, Adelade, SA, Australia, 154-159. (2014)
18. Papatheocharous, E., Axelsson, J., Andrersson, J.: Issues and Challenges in Ecosystems for Federated Embedded Systems. In Proceedings of the First International Workshop on Software Engineering for Systems-of-Systems (SESoS 13). ACM, New York, NY, USA, 21-24. (2013)

19. Vierhauser, M., Rabiser, R., Grnbacher, P., Danner, C., Wallner, S.: Evolving Systems of Systems: Industrial Challenges and Research Perspectives. In Proceedings of the First International Workshop on Software Engineering for Systems-of-Systems (SESoS 13). ACM, New York, NY, USA, 1-4. (2013)
20. Batista, T.: Challenges for SoS Architecture Description. In Proceedings of the First International Workshop on Software Engineering for Systems-of-Systems (SESoS 13). ACM, New York, NY, USA, 35-37. (2013)
21. Henshaw, M., Siemieniuch, C., Sinclair, M., Henson, S., Barot, V., Jamshidi, M., Delaurentis, D., Ncube, C., Lim, S. L., Dogan, H.: Systems of Systems Engineering: A research imperative. In 2013 International Conference on System Science and Engineering (ICSSE). IEEE, Budapest, Hungary, 389-394. (2013)
22. Kalawsky, R. S., Joannou, D., Tian, Y., Fayoumi, A.: Using Architecture Patterns to Architect and Analyze Systems of Systems. Procedia Computer Science 16 (2013), 283–292. (2013)
23. Alexander, R., Kelly, T.: Supporting systems of systems hazard analysis using multi-agent simulation. Safety Science 51, 1, 302-318. (2013)
24. Ali, N. b., Petersen, K., Mntyl, M.: Testing highly complex system of systems: An industrial case study. In Proceedings of the 2012 ACM-IEEE International Symposium on Empirical Software Engineering and Measurement. ACM, New York, NY, USA, 211-220. (2012)
25. Penzenstadler, B., Eckhardt, J.: A Requirements Engineering content model for Cyber-Physical Systems. In 2012 Second IEEE International Workshop on Requirements Engineering for Systems, Services, and Systems-of-Systems (RESS). IEEE, Chicago, IL, USA, 20-29. (2012)
26. Hallerstede, S., Hansen, F. O., Holt, J., Lauritsen, R., Lorenzen, L., Peleska, J.: Technical challenges of SoS requirements engineering. In 2012 7th International Conference on System of Systems Engineering (SoSE). IEEE, Genoa, Italy, 573-578. (2012)
27. Griendling, K., Salmon, J., Mavris, D.: Elements of a decision-making framework for early-phase system of systems acquisition. In 2012 IEEE International Systems Conference SysCon 2012. IEEE, Vancouver, BC, Canada, 1-8. (2012)
28. Ncube, C.: On the engineering of systems of systems: Key challenges for the Requirements Engineering community. In 2011 Workshop on Requirements Engineering for Systems, Services and Systems-of-Systems. IEEE, Trento, Italy, 70-73. (2011)
29. Liu, S.: Employing System of Systems Engineering in China's Emergency Management. IEEE Systems Journal 5, 2 (June 2011), 298-308. (2011)
30. Dahmann, J., Lane, J. A., Rebovich, G., Lowry, R.: Systems of systems test and evaluation challenges. In 2010 5th International Conference on System of Systems Engineering. IEEE, Loughborough, United Kingdom, United Kingdom, 1-6. (2010)
31. Jamshidi, M.: From Large-Scale Systems to System of Systems Control Challenges for the 21st Century1. IFAC Proceedings Volumes 43, 8 , 13–19. (2010)
32. Lewis, G. A., Morris, E., Place, P., Simanta, S., Smith, D. B.: Requirements engineering for systems of systems. In 2009 3rd Annual IEEE Systems Conference. IEEE, Vancouver, BC, Canada, 247-252. (2009)
33. Despotou, G., Alexander, R., Kelly, T.: Addressing challenges of hazard analysis in systems of systems. In 2009 3rd Annual IEEE Systems Conference. IEEE, Vancouver, BC, Canada, 167-172. (2009)
34. Smith, D., Lewis, G.: Systems of Systems: New challenges for maintenance and evolution. In 2008 Frontiers of Software Maintenance. IEEE, Beijing, China, 149-157. (2008)

35. Gonzalez, A., Piel, E., Gross, H. G., Glandrup, M.: Testing Challenges of Maritime Safety and Security Systems-of-Systems. In Testing: Academic Industrial Conference - Practice and Research Techniques. IEEE, Windsor, UK, UK, 35-39. (2008)
36. Dahmann, J. S., Baldwin, K. J.: Understanding the Current State of US Defense Systems of Systems and the Implications for Systems Engineering. In 2008 2nd Annual IEEE Systems Conference. IEEE, Montreal, Que., Canada, 1-7. (2008)
37. Cole, R.: The changing role of requirements and architecture in systems engineering. In 2006 IEEE/SMC International Conference on System of Systems Engineering. IEEE, Los Angeles, CA, USA, 1–5. (2006)
38. Ring, J., Madni, A. M.: Key challenges and opportunities in 'system of systems' engineering. In 2005 IEEE International Conference on Systems, Man and Cybernetics, Vol. 1. IEEE, Waikoloa, HI, USA, 973-978 Vol. 1. (2005)
39. Chen, P., Clothier, J.: Advancing systems engineering for systems-of-systems challenges. Systems Engineering 6, 3 (2003), 170183. (2003)
40. Lewis, G., Morris, E., Simanta, S., Smith, D.: Service Orientation and Systems of Systems. IEEE Software 28, 1, 58-63. (2011)
41. DOD. Systems Engineering Guide for Systems of Systems. Available at: <http://www.acq.osd.mil/se/docs/SE-Guide-for-SoS.pdf>(2008)
42. Maier, M. W.: Architecting principles for systems-of-systems. Systems Engineering 1, 4, 267-284. (1998)
43. Firesmith, D.: Profiling Systems Using the Defining Characteristics of Systems of Systems (SoS). Technical Report CMU/SEI-2010-TN-001. Software Engineering Institute, Carnegie Mellon University, Pittsburgh, PA. http://resources.sei.cmu.edu/library/asset-view.cfm?AssetID=9269 (2010)
44. Jamshidi, M.: Systems of systems engineering: principles and applications. CRC press, sn. (2008)
45. Lane, J. A.: What is a system of systems and why should i care? . Technical Report. University of Southern California, Los Angeles, CA, USA. (2013)
46. Dyba, T., Kitchenham, B. A., Jorgensen, M.: Evidence-based software engineering for practitioners. IEEE Software 22, 1, 58-65. (2005)
47. Kitchenham, B., Charters, S.: Guidelines for performing systematic literature reviews in software engineering, Technical Report EBSE-2007-01, School of Computer Science and Mathematics, Keele University. (2007)
48. Petersen, K., Feldt, R., Mujtaba, S., Mattsson, M.: Systematic Mapping Studies in Software Engineering. In Proceedings of the 12th International Conference on Evaluation and Assessment in Software Engineering (EASE08). BCS Learning & Development Ltd., Swindon, UK, 68-77. (2008)
49. Zamboni, A., Thommazo, A. D., Hernandes, E., Fabbri, SCPF.: StArt uma ferramenta computacional de apoio à revisão sistematica. In Proc.: Congresso Brasileiro de Software (CBSoft10), Salvador, Brazil. CBSoft, Salvador, Brazil, 91-96. (2010)

Factores asociados a prácticas de desarrollo y pruebas de *software* en Costa Rica: Un estudio exploratorio

Christian Quesada-López, Marcelo Jenkins

Universidad de Costa Rica, San Pedro, Costa Rica
{cristian.quesadalopez, marcelo.jenkins}@ucr.ac.cr

Resumen. La industria de desarrollo de *software* costarricense se desenvuelve en entornos cambiantes y competitivos. Para enfrentar los continuos desafíos adoptan distintas prácticas ingenieriles que les permitan cumplir las metas de calidad establecidas e incrementar la productividad. Este estudio realiza un análisis cruzado de factores entre las prácticas de ingeniería de *software* utilizadas en la industria versus los factores demográficos de los profesionales. Para esto, exploramos las relaciones y patrones identificados para las prácticas de desarrollo y pruebas de *software*. Nuestro análisis considera las respuestas de 135 profesionales que participaron en una encuesta basada en el cuerpo de conocimiento en la ingeniería del *software* (*SWEBOK*). En nuestra investigación encontramos que no existe una asociación significativa entre el tamaño de la organización y las metodologías de desarrollo. Además, un conjunto de asociaciones identificadas con distintos factores de contexto son discutidas. Los resultados sugieren que las organizaciones y sus equipos de desarrollo adaptan las prácticas ingenieriles en sus procesos de acuerdo a las necesidades específicas y el contexto de negocios en el que desarrollan sus proyectos. Se requieren estudios similares que analicen las tendencias de uso y adopción de las prácticas de la ingeniería del *software* en distintos contextos.

Palabras clave. Análisis cruzado de factores, prácticas en la industria, proceso de desarrollo y pruebas, Costa Rica, encuesta, ingeniería de *software*.

1 Introducción

En la actualidad existe una gran cantidad de prácticas ingenieriles que las organizaciones de desarrollo de *software* pueden adoptar para enfrentar los continuos desafíos a los que se enfrentan [1, 2]. Estas organizaciones se desenvuelven en entornos cambiantes y competitivos [2] en los cuales deben cumplir metas de calidad establecidas e incrementar su productividad [3]. Para entender las prácticas y técnicas en la industria es necesario explorar los factores que afectan cuando los profesionales las utilizan, además del nivel de éxito que estas les proveen [1]. El estudio de estos factores permite un mejor entendimiento de cómo cada una de las prácticas se adaptan a los distintos ambientes de operación. Por ejemplo, como los ingenieros de *software* adoptan distintos procesos de desarrollo de acuerdo a su contexto de negocio [4]. La caracterización y entendimiento de los factores asociados a las prácticas utilizadas en la industria puede ayudar a los profesionales e investigadores en el mejoramiento de los retos que enfrenta la ingeniería del *software* en la práctica [1].

El objetivo de este estudio es explorar los factores demográficos asociados a las prácticas de la ingeniería del *software* (SE) utilizadas en la industria. Para esto se realiza un análisis de las relaciones y patrones identificados entre las prácticas de desarrollo y pruebas de *software* y los distintos factores demográficos de los profesionales. Asimismo, nuestro estudio analiza la asociación entre estas prácticas ingenieriles. El análisis se realiza bajo un enfoque exploratorio [5]. Los datos para este estudio incluyen las respuestas de 135 profesionales de la ingeniería del *software* en Costa Rica que participaron en una encuesta [3] basada en el cuerpo de conocimiento en la ingeniería del *software* (*SWEBOK*) [6, 7]. En dicha encuesta se reportó el análisis individual de las prácticas de la ingeniería del *software*. El análisis realizado en este trabajo se basa en los estudios reportados en [1, 8] y compara algunas de las tendencias reportadas previamente en dichos estudios.

La estructura de este artículo es la siguiente: la Sección 2 discute brevemente los trabajos relacionados, la Sección 3 describe el diseño del estudio, los resultados obtenidos se presentan en la Sección 4. La Sección 5 resume los resultados y discute las lecciones aprendidas y finalmente, la Sección 6 presenta las conclusiones y el trabajo futuro.

2 Trabajo relacionado

Múltiples estudios han realizado análisis de factores asociados a las prácticas de la ingeniería del *software* en la industria [1]. Blackburn et al. [9] analizan factores asociados en la velocidad y productividad de los desarrolladores tales como las fases del ciclo de desarrollo y el tamaño de los equipos. Herbsleb et al. [10] analizan los factores relacionados entre los retrasos en las solicitudes de modificaciones y el número de involucrados, la magnitud de los cambios y su tamaño y severidad. Jiang et al. [11] analizan 15 factores de desempeño en los proyectos y su relación con la madurez de los procesos de desarrollo. Los autores analizan los datos recolectados de ingenieros de *software* y reportan las actividades con mayor influencia en la madurez de los procesos. Chow et al. [12] realizan un estudio con datos de 109 proyectos ágiles para identificar los factores asociados al éxito percibido en proyectos de desarrollo ágiles. Los resultados soportan 10 hipótesis que determinan dichos factores de éxito.

Dagenais et al. [13] analizan las características de los proyectos con los cuales se enfrentan los desarrolladores al incorporarse en un nuevo proyecto. Los autores analizan los datos de 18 profesionales e identifican las principales características de un nuevo proyecto junto con los aspectos clave de orientación para finalmente determinar los principales aspectos que impactan su integración a los proyectos. Garousi et al. [1] analizan las asociaciones de múltiples factores demográficos en el uso de las prácticas de ingeniería del *software* en la industria. Los autores analizan las respuestas de 202 participantes e identifican relaciones entre factores de la organización, tipos de proyectos, perfil de los participantes y las prácticas en la industria tales como la relación entre el tamaño de las organizaciones y las metodologías de desarrollo. Kuhrmann et al. [2]

realizan un estudio enfocado metodologías de desarrollo de *software* híbridas y analizan factores de contexto asociados al uso y combinación de las distintas metodologías. Los autores examinan las respuestas de 69 participantes y determinan que no existe relación entre distintos factores de contexto y las metodologías de desarrollo híbridas utilizadas. Akdur et al. [14] analizan las prácticas de modelado versus factores demográficos en la industria de *software* embebido. Los autores recolectaron datos de 627 participantes y determinaron las principales relaciones con las prácticas de modelado.

Nuestro estudio se basa en el reportado en [1] y se limita al análisis de un subconjunto de las prácticas de ingeniería versus factores demográficos que agregan evidencia para la caracterización de las prácticas de desarrollo y pruebas en la industria.

3 Descripción del estudio

Este estudio explora las relaciones y patrones identificados entre las prácticas de la ingeniería del *software* utilizadas en la industria y distintos factores demográficos de los profesionales. El estudio es una replicación parcial externa, sin interacción con los investigadores originales, en la industria de *software* de Costa Rica que se basa en el estudio publicado en [1] y considera las recomendaciones detalladas en [2]. El estudio incluye el análisis de factores para los datos recolectados en la encuesta publicada en [3] y su comparación con estudios previos [1, 2].

El objetivo del estudio es explorar los factores asociados a las prácticas de desarrollo y pruebas de la ingeniería del *software* utilizadas en la industria de *software* costarricense. Con base en este objetivo, se definen las siguientes preguntas de investigación:

- RQ1. ¿Cuál es la relación entre las metodologías de desarrollo de *soft*ware y los factores demográficos de los profesionales?
- RQ2. ¿Cuál es la relación entre las prácticas de pruebas del *soft*ware y los factores demográficos de los profesionales?

Las preguntas de investigación se basan en un sub conjunto de las presentadas en [1, 2] que investigan factores potenciales que pueden relacionarse entre factores demográficos de los profesionales y las prácticas de la ingeniería del *software*. Las RQ's se clasifican en la categoría de "Relación" <<*¿Está el factor X relacionado con el factor Y?*>> [15]. El Cuadro 1 muestra los factores demográficos recolectados en la encuesta y que son considerados para este estudio. El Cuadro2 detalla las relaciones estudiadas para cada una de las preguntas de investigación. El Cuadro 1 y Cuadro 2 representan las secciones de la encuesta realizada en [3] que son de interés para este estudio. Las prácticas de la ingeniería del software para las cuales se analiza su relación con factores demográficos se encuentran marcadas con (×). El detalle del estudio original que detalla el cuestionario se encuentra en el reporte técnico descrito en [3].

Diseño del instrumento de encuesta. Se diseñó un cuestionario electrónico basado en el instrumento propuesto en [1, 8] y la estructura del *SWEBOK* [6, 7]. Los datos para este estudio incluyen las respuestas de 135 profesionales de la ingeniería del *software* en Costa Rica que participaron en la encuesta reportada en [3].

Cuadro 1 Factores demográficos considerados en el estudio

No.	Per.	Pregunta	Esc.	#	No.	Per.	Pregunta	Esc.	#
1	PO	Sector	SM	18	5	PY	Tipos	SU	4
2	PO	Tamaño	SU	9	6	PY	Tipo de cliente	SU	4
3	PO	Capital	SM	3	7	PY	Software desarrollado	SM	5
4	PO	Unidad de proyectos	YN						

Perfil: PO = Organización, PY = Proyectos. Escala: SM= Selección múltiple, SU= Selección única, YN=Sí/No.

Procedimiento de recolección de datos. El cuestionario electrónico fue puesto en línea mediante la herramienta *LimeSurvey* durante 4 meses, de julio a octubre del 2016. Para la selección de los participantes se utilizó un muestreo no probabilístico, donde los participantes fueron contactados por medios electrónicos y participaron de manera voluntaria y anónima. El muestreo por conveniencia [16] es uno de los más utilizados en el área de la ingeniería del *software*. Todos los participantes fueron invitados por medio de distintas instituciones relacionadas con la industria de *software* en Costa Rica.

Procedimiento de análisis. Se utilizaron distintos métodos para responder las preguntas de investigación. Para todas las preguntas se utilizaron estadísticas descriptivas y se aplicaron pruebas de hipótesis. Se realizaron las pruebas estadísticas *Pearson's* χ^2 $(p \leq 0.05)$ para analizar la asociación entre variables que se encuentran en escala categórica y *Spearman's rank correlation* $(p \leq 0.05)$ para analizar la correlación entre variables con escala de intervalo y ordinal. Nuestras pruebas estadísticas fueron realizadas de acuerdo con las recomendaciones presentadas en [1, 2].

Amenazas a la validez. Las limitaciones en nuestro estudio son las comúnmente reportadas en estudios de encuesta en el área de la ingeniería de *software* [1, 2, 3, 8]. *Validez de la conclusión.* Para cada pregunta de investigación se realizó un procesamiento de datos estadístico y trazable a través de la información analizada. Cuando se ejecutan las pruebas de hipótesis, el estudio está sujeto al problema del *multiple testing*. En nuestro estudio no se aplican correcciones de la taza de error para múltiples pruebas lo que constituye una amenaza a la validez. Los análisis estadísticos para cada uno de los factores se analizan por separado. *Validez interna.* El sesgo de la selección de los participantes es una amenaza por ser una muestra a conveniencia no aleatoria. Nuestros participantes fueron invitados por correo electrónico mediante las principales instituciones que tienen relación con el área de estudio. Se enviaron recordatorios periódicos a los participantes y se permitió guardar la encuesta para continuar su llenado posteriormente. La participación del sector privado fue limitada (organizaciones pequeñas y transnacionales), al igual que la participación de ingenieros jóvenes. Durante el llenado del cuestionario, algunos participantes dejaron preguntas sin responder y otros abandonaron el cuestionario. Después del pre procesamiento de datos, se analizan las respuestas de 135 profesionales, 48% de las respuestas originales. Los resultados que se reportan se basan en todas las respuestas incluyendo las respuestas parciales. *Validez del constructo.* Se utilizó el *SWEBOK* y se procesaron los datos de acuerdo a las recomendaciones e instrumentos recomendados en [1, 8]. Los instrumentos fueron validados en el contexto de la industria de *software* costarricense, dado que este estudio utilizó los instrumentos validados en [1, 8] no se realizaron validaciones adicionales a las preguntas del cuestionario. La invitación indicó explícitamente que la participación era anónima y los resultados serían publicados de manera agregada sin afectar la privacidad. *Validez externa.* Se aplicaron diferentes estrategias para minimizar el sesgo de la población. Sin embargo, los resultados solo pueden generalizarse a los datos demográficos que se describen. Los resultados no pueden generalizase sin realizar un análisis crítico que los evalúe de acuerdo con las características de los profesionales y de las organizaciones específicas. Los resultados deben ser interpretados con cautela dado el sesgo que puede introducirse por la muestra. Los resultados deben ser interpretados bajo esta condición y no pueden ser asociados a las organizaciones o a sus proyectos de *software* [8].

Cuadro 2 Asociaciones investigadas

						Factores demográficos						
No	**Grp**	**Pregunta**	**Esc**	**#**	*****	**1**	**2**	**3**	**4**	**5**	**6**	**7**
8	CV	Metodologías de desarrollo	SM	9	*	×	×	×	×	×	×	×
9	PR	Tipos y niveles	L	5	*		×					
10	PR	Automatización	L	5	*		×					

*=relación con ella misma. Prácticas: CV= Ciclo de vida y prácticas organizacionales, PR= Pruebas. Escala: SM= Selección múltiple, L=Likert.

4 Análisis de resultados

4.1 Características de los participantes del estudio

En total, se analizan 135 respuestas completas. El Cuadro 3 muestra las frecuencias de los participantes por cada uno de los roles que desempeñan dentro de su organización. El Cuadro 4 muestra la distribución en que los profesionales se encuentran por sector. Los participantes indicaron sus roles con la posibilidad de realizar selección múltiple por lo que se totalizan todas las posiciones reportadas por cada uno de ellos. Del mismo modo, se totalizan los sectores por organización donde los participantes pueden estar activos en múltiples sectores. Con respecto a los tamaños de las organizaciones, los datos contienen respuestas que abarcan todos los rangos, pero principalmente de participantes que laboran en organizaciones grandes (64%). En el caso del rol del participante, los administradores y/o líderes de proyectos representan un 11%, al igual que los desarrolladores, seguido por los ingenieros de requerimientos y profesionales relacionados con la docencia (10%). Finalmente, los arquitectos y diseñadores representan un 9%. En el caso de los sectores representados, los participantes se encuentran principalmente en organizaciones de gobierno y sector público (29%), seguido por el sector banca y finanzas y educación superior (14%) y el sector de servicios de TI (11%).

4.2 Metodologías de desarrollo de *software* versus factores demográficos

La RQ1 busca determinar las asociaciones entre el uso de las distintas metodologías de desarrollo de *software* y los factores demográficos de los profesionales y sus organizaciones. Para esto se plantean un conjunto de hipótesis que se analizan para determinar si existen estas relaciones. Para realizar las pruebas se utilizan las categorías de metodologías de desarrollo: tradicionales (que incluye cascada, prototipos, incremental y espiral) y ágiles (*agile* o *lean*, *extreme programming*, *scrum*), posteriormente se realiza el análisis de cada una de las subcategorías para determinar si existen otras asociaciones.

Cuadro 3. Roles de los participantes

Tamaño	Q	%	R1	R2	R3	R4	R5	R6	R7	R8	R9	R10	R11	R12	R13	R14	R15	R16
1-5	6	4	-	-	-	2	-	-	-	-	-	2	2	3	2	-	-	1
6-10	6	4	6	6	6	6	6	-	-	-	-	6	6	-	6	-	-	-
11-20	4	3	2	1	1	-	2	-	1	-	1	1	1	2	-	1	1	1
21-30	3	2	2	2	2	2	-	-	-	-	2	3	-	2	3	-	-	-
31-50	2	1	-	-	1	-	-	-	-	-	-	1	-	-	1	1	-	1
51-100	8	6	3	5	1	1	3	2	-	3	1	2	-	-	3	-	-	-
101-200	12	9	2	6	-	1	3	2	4	-	2	-	2	3	2	1	-	-
201-500	7	5	-	1	1	1	2	-	2	-	2	1	1	3	5	1	-	-
501+	87	64	23	29	32	31	39	13	35	4	26	23	6	22	28	11	5	5
Total	135	100	38	50	44	44	55	17	42	7	34	39	18	35	50	15	6	8
		%	8	10	9	9	11	3	8	1	7	8	4	7	10	3	1	2

R1: Analista, R2: Ingeniero de Req., R3: Arquitecto, R4: Diseñador, R5: Desarrollador, R6: Tester, R7: Ingeniero de *software*, R8: "QA lead", R9: Administrador de pry., R10: Líder de proyecto, R11: Gerente, R12: Soporte técnico, R13: Docente, R14: Investigador, R15: Vendedor, R16: Otro. Q: Cantidad.

Cuadro 4. Participantes por sector de la organización

Tamaño	Q	%	S1	S2	S3	S4	S5	S6	S7	S8	S9	S10	S11	S12	S13	S14	S15	S16	S17
1-5	6	4	-	2	2	-	-	1	-	-	2	-	1	-	-	-	-	-	-
6-10	6	4	-	6	6	-	-	-	-	-	-	-	-	-	-	-	-	-	-
11-20	4	3	1	1	1	2	-	-	-	1	-	-	2	1	1	1	1	-	1
21-30	3	2	2	-	2	-	-	-	-	1	-	-	-	-	-	-	-	-	-
31-50	2	1	1	-	-	-	-	-	-	2	-	-	-	-	-	-	-	-	-
51-100	8	6	5	6	6	4	-	-	-	-	-	-	-	-	-	-	-	-	-
101-200	12	9	-	1	1	8	-	-	-	2	-	2	2	-	-	1	-	-	1
201-500	7	5	-	-	-	4	-	-	1	1	2	-	-	-	-	-	-	-	-
501+	87	64	6	1	7	51	3	32	3	25	6	3	2	1	1	-	2	2	3
Total	135	100	15	17	25	69	3	33	4	32	10	5	7	2	2	2	3	2	5
		%	6	7	11	29	1	14	2	14	4	2	3	1	1	1	1	1	2

Q: Cantidad. S1: Desarrollo a la medida, S2: Paquetes, S3: Servicios TI, S4: Gobierno y sector público, S5: Manufactura o ingeniería, S6: Banca o finanzas, S7: Seguros, S8: Educación o Universidad, S9: Educación, S10: Salud, S11: Comercio, S12: Administración y negocios, S13: No gubernamental, S14: Organismo internacional, S15: Telecomunicaciones, S16: Asociación, S17: Otro.

Uso de varias metodologías en un mismo contexto. El análisis explora la combinación de uso de diferentes metodologías de desarrollo en un mismo contexto. Para esto utilizamos la prueba *Pearson* χ^2 $(p \leq 0.05)$ para cada par de diferentes metodologías de desarrollo. A continuación se listan los principales resultados:

- No se encuentra una asociación significativa entre las metodologías tradicionales y ágiles $\chi^2(1, N = 135) = 2.208, p = .137$. Sin embargo, analizando las sub categorías se encuentra una asociación significativa entre cascada y prototipos $\chi^2(1, N = 135) = 4.495, p = .034$ denotando que si una de las prácticas es usada (o no usada) es probable que la otra práctica sea usada (o no usada) también.

- Basado en la proporción del uso de cascada y prototipo (18/24)/(23/70), el uso de la metodología de prototipos es 2.3 veces más alto si las organizaciones usan cascada.
- Se encuentra una asociación entre espiral y prototipos $\chi^2(1, N = 135) = 13.125, p = .000$ que indica que el uso de espiral influencia el uso de prototipos, sin embargo no se puede concluir ya que no se cumple con una de las suposiciones de la prueba.
- Se encuentra una asociación significativa entre *scrum* y el desarrollo incremental $\chi^2(1, N = 135) = 7.834, p = .005$ donde el uso de la metodología incremental es 3.8 veces más alto si las organizaciones usan *scrum* (14/39)/ (7/75).
- Existe una asociación entre *agile* o *lean* y espiral $\chi^2(1, N = 135) = 12.132, p = .000$ que indica que el uso de *agile* o *lean* influencia el uso de espiral, sin embargo no se puede concluir ya que no se cumple con una de las suposiciones de la prueba.
- Al igual que lo reportado en [1] se encuentran asociaciones entre *agile* o *lean* tanto con *scrum* $\chi^2(1, N = 135) = 24.628, p = .000$ como *extreme programming* $\chi^2(1, N = 135) = 3.506, p = .061$. El uso de *extreme programming* y *scrum* es de 4.6 [(4/39)/(2/90)] y 6.9 [(30/13)/(23/69)] veces más respectivamente si la organización utiliza las metodologías *agile* o *lean*.

Tamaño de la organización. El análisis busca identificar si el uso de una metodología de desarrollo se relaciona con el tamaño de la organización para lo cual se utilizó la prueba *Pearson* χ^2 $(p \leq 0.05)$ donde los participantes votan si usan o no cada una de las metodologías de desarrollo. Para realizar las pruebas se utilizan las categorías de tamaño de organización: pequeña (1 a 50 empleados que incluye micro de 1 a 10 y pequeña de 11 a 50), mediana (51 a 200 empleados) y grande (201 o más empleados). Las agrupaciones por tamaño se realizan para cumplir con el mínimo N requerido por la prueba estadística. A continuación se listan los principales resultados:

- Los resultados indican que no existe una asociación significativa entre el tamaño de la organización y las metodologías tradicionales $\chi^2(2, N = 135) = 4.069, p = .131$. Esto es, la decisión de las organizaciones de utilizar las metodologías tradicionales no depende de su tamaño.
- No encontramos una asociación significativa entre el tamaño de la organización y las metodologías ágiles $\chi^2(2, N = 135) = 1.604, p = .448$.
- Por cada una de las sub categorías de las organizaciones pequeñas, micro y pequeña, se obtienen similares resultados para ambos enfoques de desarrollo: tradicional $\chi^2(3, N = 135) = 4.649, p = .199$ y ágiles $\chi^2(3, N = 135) = 2.176, p = .537$.
- Las pruebas para cada una de las subcategorías de las metodologías de desarrollo encuentran que no existe una asociación significativa entre el tamaño de la organización y cascada $\chi^2(2, N = 135) = .266, p = .875$, prototipos $\chi^2(2, N = 135) = 5.204, p = .074$ e incremental $\chi^2(2, N = 135) = .649, p = .723$.
- En el caso de la metodología de espiral sí se encuentra una asociación $\chi^2(2, N = 135) = 23.010, p = .000$ que indica que aunque las organizaciones parecen no utilizar esta metodología, las pequeñas son las más anuentes a utilizarla en comparación con las medianas y grandes.
- Las organizaciones de tamaño micro reportan un 50% de utilización de un total de 12 respuestas. Sin embargo, con este resultado en particular no es posible concluir

sobre su asociación dada la cantidad de respuestas de algunas de las categorías de tamaño que no cumplen una de las suposiciones de la prueba.

- Las pruebas para las subcategorías *agile* o *lean* $\chi^2(2, N = 135) = 3.202, p = .202$ y *extreme programming* $\chi^2(2, N = 135) = 2.438, p = .296$ no encuentran una asociación significativa, pero en el caso de la metodología *scrum* $\chi^2(2, N = 135) = 13.183, p = .001$ sí se encuentra una asociación significativa. Las organizaciones grandes son las más anuentes a utilizar esta metodología (49%) en comparación con las pequeñas (10%) y medianas (25%).
- Aunque los resultados reportados en [1] presentan algunas tendencias relacionadas al tamaño de la compañía, nuestros resultados no identifican una relación entre el uso de las metodologías de desarrollo y el tamaño de las organizaciones. En este caso, estos resultados mantienen correspondencia con los reportados en [2]. En nuestro caso, la tendencia de la metodología *scrum* se invierte con respecto a lo reportado en [1].

Sector objetivo y tipos de proyectos. Este análisis explora si el uso de una metodología de desarrollo se relaciona con el sector objetivo del *software* que una organización desarrolla para lo cual utilizamos la prueba *Pearson* χ^2 $(p \leq 0.05)$. Para realizar las pruebas se utilizan las categorías de sector objetivo: gobierno y sector público, manufactura o ingeniería, banca y finanzas, seguros, educación superior, salud y comercio. Al observar los resultados podemos identificar que para la mayoría de combinaciones no se encuentra una asociación significativa entre los sectores y las metodologías de desarrollo. A continuación se listan algunos ejemplos representativos de los principales resultados:

- Para el sector gobierno y las metodologías tradicionales no encontramos asociaciones significativas, $\chi^2(1, N = 135) = .666, p = .414$ y para las ágiles $\chi^2(1, N = 135) = .194, p = .659$.
- El sector banca y finanzas y las metodologías agiles presentan una asociación $\chi^2(1, N = 135) = 28.447, p = .000$ donde en este sector se adoptan estas metodologías en un 85% de las veces, caso contrario su adopción se acerca a un 35%. Del mismo modo con la metodología incremental $\chi^2(1, N = 135) = 6.174, p = .013$ para la cual su adopción es del 28% en el sector banca y caso contrario es de solo el 10%. En el caso de *agile* o *lean* $\chi^2(1, N = 135) = 14.032, p = .000$ la adopción es del 55% y solo del 22% si no es una organización del sector. Del mismo modo para *scrum* $\chi^2(1, N = 135) = 48.872, p = .000$ con un 85% de uso contra solo el 20% si no es del sector.
- Se encuentra una asociación con el sector de seguros y metodologías ágiles $\chi^2(1, N = 135) = 5.234, p = .022$, cascada $\chi^2(1, N = 135) = 4.187, p = .041$ y *scrum* $\chi^2(1, N = 135) = 4.103, p = .043$. En el caso de ágiles la adopción es del 79% en el sector de seguros y caso contrario es de solo el 46%. Para la metodología de cascada la adopción es del 7% contra un 34% si no es del sector. La adopción para *scrum* es del 64% en este sector y caso contrario es del 36.4%.
- En el sector de salud la tendencia se invierte, se encuentran asociaciones entre este sector y metodologías ágiles $\chi^2(1, N = 135) = 5.725, p = .017$, cascada $\chi^2(1, N = 135) = 4.554, p = .033$ y *scrum* $\chi^2(1, N = 135) = 5.282, p = .022$. Sin embargo, para este sector la adopción de las metodologías ágiles es solo del 17%

y del 53% en caso contrario. La adopción de *scrum* es del 8% contra el 43% y cascada del 58% contra solo un 28% si no es del sector.

- Analizando el uso de las metodologías por sector confirmamos parcialmente los reportado en [1]. Las metodologías *product line development*, espiral y *extreme programming* no son muy populares entre los distintos sectores, las metodologías ágiles son muy utilizadas en el sector de banca y seguros y las metodologías tradicionales, como cascada, son muy utilizadas en el sector de salud y manufactura e ingeniería.

Asimismo, se realiza un análisis para explorar si el uso de una metodología de desarrollo depende del tipo de proyectos que se desarrollan en las organizaciones. Para realizar las pruebas se utilizan las categorías de proyectos: *in-house*, paquetes para un sector de industria, paquetes de uso general para negocios y desarrollo a la medida. A continuación se listan los principales resultados:

- Se identifica una asociación significativa entre los proyectos *in-house* y las metodologías tradicionales $\chi^2(1, N = 135) = 5.138, p = .023$. En este tipo de proyectos se utilizan estas metodologías un 64% contra un 44% en el caso de que el proyecto no sea *in-house*.
- Existe una asociación en proyectos *in-house* y metodologías ágiles $\chi^2(1, N = 135) = 20.228, p = .000$ donde la adopción es del 65% para este tipo de proyectos y 26% en caso contrario. Se identifica una asociación con la metodología prototipos $\chi^2(1, N = 135) = 4.256, p = .039$ para la cual su adopción es del 37% en el caso que el proyecto sea *in-house* y del 20% caso contrario. Igualmente, se encuentra una asociación con las metodologías *agile* o *lean* $\chi^2(1, N = 135) = 12.035, p = .001$ y *scrum* $\chi^2(1, N = 135) = 19.264, p = .000$. En el caso de *agile* o *lean* la adopción es del 43% para este tipo de proyectos y caso contrario es de solo el 15%. En el caso de *scrum* la adopción es del 54% y solo del 17% caso contrario.
- Para el desarrollo de paquetes de un sector de industria no se identifica una asociación significativa con las metodologías tradicionales $\chi^2(1, N = 135) = 3.729, p = .053$. Sin embargo, si se identifica una asociación con las metodologías ágiles $\chi^2(1, N = 135) = 8.429, p = .004$ donde la adopción es del 69% para este tipo de proyectos y 42% en caso contrario.
- En el caso del desarrollo de paquetes de uso general para negocios no se identifica una asociación significativa con las metodologías tradicionales $\chi^2(1, N = 135) = 3.497, p = .061$ y tampoco para las metodologías ágiles $\chi^2(1, N = 135) = 2.695, p = .101$. Para la metodología *scrum* se identifica una asociación significativa $\chi^2(1, N = 135) = 5.429, p = .020$. En *scrum* la adopción es del 61% para este tipo de proyectos y solo del 35% en caso contrario.
- Para el desarrollo a la medida se identifica una asociación significativa con las metodologías tradicionales $\chi^2(1, N = 135) = 4.565, p = .033$ con una adopción del 65%. En el caso de las metodologías ágiles $\chi^2(1, N = 135) = 2.682, p = .102$ no se identifica una asociación significativa. Para la metodología cascada se identifica una asociación significativa $\chi^2(1, N = 135) = 4.235, p = .040$. En cascada la adopción es del 39% para este tipo de proyectos y solo del 23% en caso contrario.

Otros factores demográficos. Este análisis busca identificar si el uso de una metodología de desarrollo se relaciona con otros factores demográficos de los profesionales.

Para esto utilizamos la prueba *Pearson* χ^2 $(p \leq 0.05)$. Realizamos el análisis para las categorías de tipo de capital de la organización: nacional, extranjero o ambos. A continuación se listan los principales resultados:

- Este factor no influye en el uso de las metodologías tradicionales $\chi^2(2, N = 131) = 2.163, p = .339$.
- Encontramos una asociación entre el tipo de capital y las metodologías ágiles $\chi^2(2, N = 131) = 10.339, p = .006$. Las organizaciones de capital nacional tienden a tener una menor adopción de metodologías agiles (45%) que las de capital extranjero (72%) y ambas (87%). Con respecto a este resultado en particular no es posible concluir sobre su asociación dada la cantidad de respuestas que no cumplen una de las suposiciones de la prueba.
- No encontramos una asociación entre la existencia de una unidad de proyectos en la organización y la adopción de las metodologías tradicionales $\chi^2(1, N = 128) = .307, p = .580$.
- Se encuentra una asociación significativa con el uso de las metodologías ágiles $\chi^2(1, N = 128) = 5.175, p = .023$ donde la existencia de una unidad de proyectos muestra un uso del 60% y en caso contrario solo del 40%. En el caso de la metodología *scrum* se identifica la misma asociación $\chi^2(1, N = 128) = 12.764, p = .000$ donde las organizaciones con una unidad de proyectos (54%) parecen utilizar con mayor frecuencia esta metodología que las que no la tienen (22%).

Se analizan las asociaciones para los tipos de clientes de las organizaciones (internos, externos o ambos):

- No existe una asociación entre el tipo de cliente y el uso de las metodologías tradicionales $\chi^2(2, N = 122) = .244, p = .885$.
- Se encuentra una asociación significativa con el uso de las metodologías ágiles $\chi^2(2, N = 122) = 10.170, p = .006$ donde para clientes internos su uso es del 40%, para clientes externos del 27% y si cuentan con ambos tipos de cliente es del 66%. Tanto el desarrollo con las metodologías *agile* o *lean* $\chi^2(2, N = 122) = 8.332, p = .01$ y *extreme programming* $\chi^2(2, N = 122) = 12.923, p = .002$ presentan asociaciones significativas con el tipo de cliente.
- La metodología *scrum* $\chi^2(2, N = 122) = 3.695, p = .158$ es igualmente adoptada independiente del tipo de cliente.

4.3 Prácticas de pruebas de *software* versus factores demográficos

La RQ2 busca determinar las asociaciones entre el uso de las distintas prácticas de calidad del *software* y los factores demográficos de los profesionales. Para esto se plantean un conjunto de hipótesis que se analizan para determinar si existen estas relaciones.

Tipo y nivel de pruebas versus tamaño de la organización. El análisis busca identificar si los distintos tipos y niveles de pruebas se relacionan con el tamaño de la organización para lo cual se utilizó la prueba *Spearman's rank correlation* $(p \leq 0.05)$. Además se analiza las correlaciones entre distintos tipos y niveles de pruebas. Los tipos y niveles de pruebas son: pruebas de unidad, de integración, aceptación, pruebas funcionales, de sistema, de rendimiento, pruebas de carga y estrés, pruebas de seguridad y de usabilidad. Las categorías de tamaño de organización: pequeña (1 a 50 empleados que incluye micro de 1 a 10 y pequeña de 11 a 50), mediana (51 a 200 empleados) y grande (201 o más empleados). Las agrupaciones por tamaño se realizan para cumplir con el mínimo N requerido por la prueba estadística. A continuación se listan los principales resultados:

- Se identifica que el tamaño de la organización presenta una correlación positiva débil con las pruebas funcionales $r_s(88) = .239, p = .027$ y una correlación positiva débil con las pruebas de carga y estrés $r_s(88) = .230, p = 0.31$. Al realizar las pruebas, todos los valores son cercamos a cero lo que indica la ausencia de una correlación entre el tamaño de las organizaciones y los tipos y niveles de pruebas.
- Las tendencias muestran que si el tamaño de la organización crece, incrementa la probabilidad de realizar pruebas funcionales y de sistema.
- Existen correlaciones entre los distintos tipos y niveles de pruebas que indican que si una organización decide realizar un tipo o nivel de pruebas podría decidir realizar el otro tipo o nivel de pruebas. Los resultados se muestran en el Cuadro 5.

Cuadro 5 Correlaciones significativas entre tipo y nivel de pruebas

Tipos y niveles	$r_s(88)$	p	Correlación
Pruebas funcionales y de sistema	.948	.000	Positiva muy fuerte
Pruebas de integración y de sistema	.756	.000	Positiva fuerte
Pruebas de unidad y pruebas de integración	.751	.000	Positiva fuerte
Pruebas de integración y pruebas funcionales	.701	.000	Positiva fuerte
Pruebas de rendimiento y pruebas de carga y/o estrés	.690	.000	Positiva fuerte
Pruebas de aceptación y pruebas de sistema	.666	.000	Positiva fuerte
Pruebas de aceptación y pruebas funcionales	.665	.000	Positiva fuerte
Pruebas de unidad y pruebas funcionales	.614	.000	Positiva fuerte
Pruebas de seguridad y pruebas de usabilidad	.612	.000	Positiva fuerte
Pruebas de integración y pruebas de aceptación	.611	.000	Positiva fuerte
Pruebas de sistema y pruebas de usabilidad	.606	.000	Positiva fuerte

Pruebas automatizadas y pruebas manuales. El análisis busca identificar si las pruebas automatizadas y manuales se relacionan con el tamaño de la organización para lo cual se utilizó la prueba *Spearman's rank correlation* ($p \leq 0.05$). Además se analiza las correlaciones entre distintos tipos y niveles de pruebas con la realización de pruebas manuales o automatizadas. A continuación se listan las principales asociaciones:

- El tamaño de la organización no presenta una correlación con la realización de pruebas manuales o automatizadas.
- Se identifica una correlación positiva débil entre las pruebas manuales y pruebas de integración $r_s(93) = .236, p = .023$, pruebas de aceptación $r_s(93) = .289, p = .005$ y pruebas funcionales $r_s(84) = .304, p = .005$.
- Se identifica una correlación positiva débil entre las pruebas automatizadas, las pruebas de carga y estrés $r_s(94) = .269, p = .009$ y las pruebas de seguridad $r_s(94) = .252, p = .014$.

5 Discusión

5.1 Resumen de resultados

- Las organizaciones de desarrollo de *software* adaptan las prácticas ingenieriles de sus procesos de acuerdo a sus necesidades específicas y el contexto de negocios en el que desarrollan sus proyectos, las que son muy diversas, y no existen patrones generalizables a todas ellas que expliquen cuáles son los factores que influyen en sus decisiones.
- En este estudio encontramos que no existe una correlación significativa entre el tamaño de la organización y las metodologías de desarrollo que utiliza, por lo que el tamaño, en número de empleados, no es uno de los factores que expliquen la adopción de metodologías específicas.
- Tampoco encontramos una asociación significativa entre el uso de metodologías tradicionales o de metodologías ágiles, con respecto a los factores demográficos.
- Las metodologías ágiles son actualmente las más utilizadas, principalmente *Scrum*. Sin embargo las metodologías tradicionales tales como cascada y desarrollo por prototipos también son populares en la industria.
- Las metodologías ágiles son más utilizadas en el sector de banca y seguros y las metodologías tradicionales, tales como cascada, son más utilizadas en el sector de salud y manufactura. Determinar las razones de este fenómeno requiere una investigación más profunda para determinar las causas del porqué de estas tendencias.
- Determinamos que no existe una correlación significativa entre el tamaño de las organizaciones y los tipos y niveles de pruebas que realizan, y tampoco entre el tamaño y si realizan pruebas manuales o automatizadas. En otras palabras, el nivel de automatización de las pruebas no se puede predecir con base en el tamaño de las organizaciones.
- Se identifican correlaciones fuertes entre pruebas funcionales y de sistema, integración y sistema, unidad e integración, integración y funcionales, rendimiento y carga/estrés, aceptación y sistema, aceptación y funcionales, unidad y funcionales, seguridad y usabilidad, integración y aceptación, y finalmente, sistema y usabilidad.
- Finalmente, los datos sugieren que la no adopción de las prácticas en la ingeniería del software no solo se debe a aspectos técnicos sino a la falta de recursos en las organizaciones. Debemos ahora investigar por qué los desarrolladores hablan de falta de recursos, aun en organizaciones grandes. Situación que se presente principalmente en el sector público gobierno.

5.2 Lecciones aprendidas durante la ejecución del estudio de encuesta

La mayor cantidad de preguntas sin contestar se relacionan con las secciones de las prácticas específicas en la ingeniería del software. Los factores que pueden influenciar esta tendencia son: (1) la cantidad de preguntas del cuestionario y (2) el que algunos de los participantes son reservados acerca de las prácticas específicas en sus organizaciones.

Aunque nuestro instrumento se basa en estudios previos y sigue la estructura del *SWEBOK*, el pilotaje con profesionales permitió depurar y mejorar la estructura y el contenido del mismo. Es importante realizar una validación de los instrumentos en el contexto donde se conduce el estudio y utilizando el idioma nativo de los profesionales. El instrumento se aplicó en el lenguaje español y los investigadores fueron los responsables de realizar las traducciones respectivas.

La comparación de las tendencias entre estudios se dificulta dada la variedad del contexto donde se desarrollaron los estudios. Para una comparación más rigurosa es necesario contar con los datos crudos de los estudios previos para poder realizar el análisis correspondiente. Al ser este estudio una replicación externa se dificulta este proceso.

6 Conclusiones y trabajo futuro

El presente estudio realizó un análisis exploratorio sobre los factores demográficos de los profesionales asociados a las prácticas de la ingeniería del *software* utilizadas en la industria costarricense. En nuestro estudio discutimos las asociaciones de estos factores demográficos con las prácticas de desarrollo y pruebas de *software*. Nuestra investigación indica que no existe una asociación entre el tamaño de la organización y las metodologías de desarrollo. Los resultados sugieren que las organizaciones de desarrollo adaptan las prácticas ingenieriles en sus procesos de acuerdo a las necesidades específicas y el contexto de negocios en el que realizan sus proyectos. Estas prácticas son muy diversas, y no existen patrones generalizables a todas ellas que expliquen cuáles son los factores que influyen en sus decisiones.

Cómo trabajo futuro, se requieren realizar análisis adicionales sobre los factores asociados a las prácticas de la ingeniería. Existen múltiples relaciones adicionales que pueden ser exploradas con los datos de la encuesta original [3]. Planeamos complementar este estudio para analizar las tendencias de adopción de otras prácticas de la ingeniería a partir de los factores demográficos de los profesionales. Finalmente, nuestro estudio no pretende generalizar los resultados para cualquier contexto de desarrollo. Por el contrario, este trabajo tiene como objetivo aportar en el entendimiento del uso y adopción de las prácticas de la ingeniería en la industria. Se requieren futuros estudios que exploren las tendencias de adopción de las prácticas en contextos específicos y estudios particulares con organizaciones de desarrollo para lograr dicho entendimiento y proveer recomendaciones para los profesionales con respecto a lo que se puede mejorar en sus procesos y prácticas.

Agradecimientos. Agradecemos a todos (as) los (as) profesionales que participaron anónimamente en la encuesta y a las instituciones que colaboraron con su difusión. Este estudio fue apoyado por el Ministerio de Ciencia, Tecnología y Telecomunicaciones (MICITT) y la Universidad de Costa Rica (No. 834-B5-A18).

Referencias

1. Garousi, V., Coşkunçay, A., Demirörs, O., Yazici, A.: Cross-factor analysis of software engineering practices versus practitioner demographics: An exploratory study in Turkey. Journal of Systems and Software, 111, 49-73 (2016).

2. Kuhrmann, M., Diebold, P., Münch, J., Tell, P., Garousi, V., Felderer, M., & Prause, C. R. (2017, July). Hybrid software and system development in practice: waterfall, scrum, and beyond. In Proceedings of the 2017 International Conference on Software and System Process (pp. 30-39). ACM.
3. Quesada-López, C., y Jenkins, M. (2017). Un estudio sobre las prácticas de la ingeniería del software en Costa Rica: Resultados preliminares. Proceedings of the XX Ibero-American Conference on Software Engineering (CibSE 2017). Buenos Aires, Argentina, 22-23 May 2017.
4. Kalus, G., & Kuhrmann, M. (2013, May). Criteria for software process tailoring: a systematic review. In Proceedings of the 2013 International Conference on Software and System Process (pp. 171-180). ACM.
5. Runeson, P., & Höst, M. (2009). Guidelines for conducting and reporting case study research in software engineering. Empirical software engineering, 14(2), 131.
6. Abran, A., Moore, J., Bourque, P., Dupuis, R. (Eds): Guide to the Software Engineering Body of Knowledge: 2004 version. IEEE Press, CA, USA (2004).
7. Bourque, P., Fairley, R. (Eds): Guide to the Software Engineering Body of Knowledge: Version 3.0. IEEE Press, CA, USA (2014). Recuperado de http://www.swebok.org.
8. Garousi, V., Coşkunçay, A., Betin-Can, A., Demirörs, O.: A survey of software engineering practices in Turkey. Journal of Systems and Software, 108, 148-177 (2015).
9. Blackburn, J. D., Scudder, G. D., & Van Wassenhove, L. N. (1996). Improving speed and productivity of software development: a global survey of software developers. IEEE Transactions on Software Engineering, 22(12), 875-885.
10. Herbsleb, J. D., Mockus, A., Finholt, T. A., & Grinter, R. E. (2001, July). An empirical study of global software development: distance and speed. In Proceedings of the 23rd international conference on software engineering (pp. 81-90). IEEE Computer Society.
11. Jiang, J. J., Klein, G., Hwang, H. G., Huang, J., & Hung, S. Y. (2004). An exploration of the relationship between software development process maturity and project performance. Information & Management, 41(3), 279-288.
12. Chow, T., & Cao, D. B. (2008). A survey study of critical success factors in agile software projects. Journal of systems and software, 81(6), 961-971.
13. Dagenais, B., Ossher, H., Bellamy, R. K., Robillard, M. P., & De Vries, J. P. (2010, May). Moving into a new software project landscape. In Proceedings of the 32nd ACM/IEEE International Conference on Software Engineering-Volume 1 (pp. 275-284). ACM.
14. Akdur, D., Garousi, V., & Demirörs, O. (2017, June). Cross-factor analysis of software modeling practices versus practitioner demographics in the embedded software industry. In Embedded Computing (MECO), 2017 6th Mediterranean Conference on (pp. 1-5). IEEE.
15. Easterbrook, S., Singer, J., Storey, M. A., & Damian, D. (2008). Selecting empirical methods for software engineering research. Guide to advanced empirical software engineering, 285-311.
16. Wohlin, C., Runeson, P., Höst, M., Ohlsson, M. C., Regnell, B., & Wesslén, A. (2012). Experimentation in software engineering. Springer Science & Business Media.

Using Automatic Refactoring to Improve Energy Efficiency of Android Apps

Luis Cruz[1] and Rui Abreu[2]

[1] University of Porto / HASLab, INESC TEC, luiscruz@fe.up.pt
[2] Instituto Superior Técnico, University of Lisbon / INESC-ID, rui@computer.org

Abstract. The ever-growing popularity of mobile phones has brought additional challenges to the software development lifecycle. Mobile applications (apps, for short) ought to provide the same set of features as conventional software, with limited resources: such as, limited processing capabilities, storage, screen and, not less important, power source. Although energy efficiency is a valuable requirement, developers often lack knowledge of best practices. In this paper, we study whether or not automatic refactoring can aid developers ship energy efficient apps. We leverage a tool, *Leafactor*, with five energy code smells that tend to go unnoticed. We use *Leafactor* to analyze code smells in 140 free and open source apps. As a result, we detected and fixed code smells in 45 apps, from which 40% have successfully merged our changes into the official repository.

1 Introduction

In the past decade, the advent of mobile devices has brought new challenges and paradigms to the existing computing models. One of the major challenges is the fact that mobile phones have a limited battery life. As a consequence, users need to frequently charge their devices to prevent their inoperability. Hence, energy efficiency is an important non-functional requirement in mobile software, with a valuable impact on usability.

A study in 2013 reported that 18% of apps have feedback from users that is related with energy consumption [25]. Other studies have nonetheless found that most developers lack the knowledge about best practices for energy efficiency in mobile applications (apps) [17, 23]. Hence, it is important to provide developers with actionable documentation and toolsets that aim to help deliver energy efficient apps.

Previously, we have identified code optimizations with significant impact on the energy consumption of Android apps [4]. However, certify that code is complying with these patterns is time-consuming and prone to errors. Thus, in this paper we study how automatic refactor can help develop code that follows energy best practices.

There are state-of-the-art tools that provide automatic refactoring for Android and Java apps (for instance, *AutoRefactor*[3], *Walkmod*[4], *Facebook pfff*[5], *Kadabra*[6]). Although these tools help developers creating better code, they do not feature energy related patterns for Android. Thus, we leverage five energy optimizations in an automatic refactoring tool, *Leafactor*, which is publicly available with an open source license. In addition, the toolset has the potential to serve as an educative tool to aid developers in understanding which practices can be used to improve energy efficiency.

On top of that, we analyze how Android developers are addressing energy optimizations and how an automatic refactoring tool would help ship more energy efficient mobile software. We have used the results of our tool to contribute to real Android app projects, validating the value of adopting an automatic refactoring tool in the development stack of mobile apps.

In a dataset of 140 free and open source software (FOSS) Android apps, we have found that a considerable part (32%) is released with energy inefficiencies. We have fixed 222 anti patterns in 45 apps, from which 18 have successfully merged our changes into the official branch. Results show that automatic refactoring tools can be very helpful to improve the energy footprint of apps.

This work is an extension of a previous two-page tooldemo that introduces *Leafactor* [5]. The remainder of this paper is organized as follows: Section 2 details energy refactorings and corresponding impact on energy consumption; in Section 3, we present the automatic refactor toolset that was implemented; Section 4 describes the experimental methodology used to validate our tool, followed by Sections 5 and 6 with results and discussion; in Section 7 we present the related work in this field; and finally Section 8 summarizes our findings and discusses future work.

2 Energy Refactorings

We use static code analysis and automatic refactoring to apply Android-specific optimizations of energy efficiency. In this section, we describe refactorings which are known to improve energy consumption of Android apps [4]. Each of them has an indication of the energy efficiency improvement (🍃) and the fix priority provided by the official *lint* documentation[7]. The priority reflects the severity of a pattern in terms of performance and is given in a scale of 1 to 10, with 10 being the most severe. The severity is not necessarily correlated with energy performance. In addition, we also provide examples where the refactorings are applied. All refactorings are in Java with the exception *ObsoleteLayoutParam* which is in XML — the markup language used in Android to define the user interface (UI).

[3] *AutoRefactor*: https://goo.gl/v5im9X (March 2, 2018).
[4] *Walkmod*: https://goo.gl/LmsUDX (March 2, 2018).
[5] *Facebook pfff*: https://goo.gl/NG1PTE (March 2, 2018).
[6] *Kadabra*: https://goo.gl/A5PsZf (March 2, 2018).
[7] *Lint* is a tool provided with the Android SDK which detects problems related with the structural quality of the code. Website: https://goo.gl/RA2EVC (March 2, 2018).

2.1 ViewHolder: View Holder Candidates

Energy efficiency improvement (🍃): 4.5%. Lint priority: |||||||||| 5/10.

This pattern is used to make a smoother scroll in *List Views*, with no lags. When in a *List View*, the system has to draw each item separately. To make this process more efficient, data from the previous drawn item should be reused. This technique decreases the number of calls to the method `findViewById()`, which is known for being a very inefficient method [14]. The following code snippet provides an example of how to apply *ViewHolder*.

```
// ...
@Override
public View getView(final int position, View convertView, ViewGroup parent) {
  convertView = LayoutInflater.from(getContext()).inflate( ❶
    R.layout.subforsublist, parent, false
  );
  final TextView t = ((TextView) convertView.findViewById(R.id.name)); ❷
// ...
```

Optimized version:

```
// ...
private static class ViewHolderItem { ❸
        private TextView t;
}

@Override
public View getView(final int position, View convertView, ViewGroup parent) {
  ViewHolderItem viewHolderItem;
  if (convertView == null) { ❹
    convertView = LayoutInflater.from(getContext()).inflate(
      R.layout.subforsublist, parent, false
    );
    viewHolderItem = new ViewHolderItem();
    viewHolderItem.t = ((TextView) convertView.findViewById(R.id.name));
    convertView.setTag(viewHolderItem);
  } else {
    viewHolderItem = (ViewHolderItem) convertView.getTag();
  }
  final TextView t = viewHolderItem.t; ❺
// ...
```

❶ In every iteration of the method `getView`, a new `LayoutInflater` object is instantiated, overwriting the method's parameter `convertView`.

❷ Each item in the list has a view to display text — a `TextView` object. This view is being fetched in every iteration, using the method `findViewById()`.

❸ A new class is created to cache common data between list items. It will be used to store the TextView object and prevent it from being fetched in every iteration.

❹ This block will run only in the first item of the list. Subsequent iterations will receive the `convertView` from parameters.

❺ It is no longer needed to call `findViewById()` to retrieve the `TextView` object.

One might argue that the version of the code after refactoring is considerably less intuitive. This is in fact true, which might be a reason for developers to ignore optimizations. However, regardless of whether this optimization should be taken care by the system, it is the recommended approach, as stated in the Android official documentation[8].

2.2 DrawAllocation: Allocations within drawing code

🍃 1.5%. Lint priority: |||||||||| 9/10.

Draw operations are very sensitive to performance. It is a bad practice allocating objects during such operations since it can create noticeable lags. The recommended fix is allocating objects upfront and reusing them for each drawing operation, as shown in the following example:

```
public class DrawAllocationSampleTwo extends Button {
  public DrawAllocationSampleTwo(Context context) {
        super(context);
  }
  @Override
  protected void onDraw(android.graphics.Canvas canvas) {
      super.onDraw(canvas);
      Integer i = new Integer(5);❶
      // ...
      return;
  }
}
```

Optimized version:

```
public class DrawAllocationSampleTwo extends Button {
  public DrawAllocationSampleTwo(Context context) {
        super(context);
  }
  Integer i = new Integer(5);❷
  @Override
  protected void onDraw(android.graphics.Canvas canvas) {
    super.onDraw(canvas);
    // ...
    return;
  }
}
```

❶ A new instance of `Integer` is created in every execution of `onDraw`.

❷ The allocation of the instance of `Integer` is removed from the drawing operation and is now executed only once during the app execution.

2.3 WakeLock: Incorrect wake lock usage

🍃 1.5%. Lint priority: |||||||||| 9/10.

Wake locks are mechanisms to control the power state of a mobile device. This can be used to prevent the screen or the CPU from entering a sleep state. If an application fails to release a wake lock, or uses it without being strictly necessary, it can drain the battery of the device.

The following example shows an Activity that uses a wake lock:

[8] *ViewHolder* explanation in the official documentation: https://goo.gl/tgy7xL visited in March 2, 2018.

```
extends Activity { private WakeLock wl;

  @Override
  protected void onCreate(Bundle savedInstanceState) {
    super.onCreate(savedInstanceState);

    PowerManager pm = (PowerManager) this.getSystemService(
      Context.POWER_SERVICE
    );
    wl = pm.newWakeLock(
      PowerManager.SCREEN_DIM_WAKE_LOCK | PowerManager.ON_AFTER_RELEASE,
      "WakeLockSample"
    );
    wl.acquire();❶
  }
}
```

❶ Using the method `acquire()` the app asks the device to stay on. Until further instruction, the device will be deprived of sleep.

Since no instruction is stopping this behavior, the device will not be able to enter a sleep mode. Although in exceptional cases this might be intentional, it should be fixed to prevent battery drain.

The recommended fix is to override the method `onPause()` in the activity:

```
//...
@Override protected void onPause(){
  super.onPause();
  if (wl != null && !wl.isHeld()) {
    wl.release();
  }
}
//...
```

With this solution, the lock is released before the app switches to background.

2.4 Recycle: Missing `recycle()` calls

0.7%. Lint priority: 7/10.

There are collections such as `TypedArray` that are implemented using singleton resources. Hence, they should be released so that calls to different `TypedArray` objects can efficiently use these same resources. The same applies to other classes (e.g., database cursors, motion events, etc.).

The following snippet shows an object of `TypedArray` that is not being recycled after use:

```
public void wrong1(AttributeSet attrs, int defStyle) {
  final TypedArray a = getContext().obtainStyledAttributes(
    attrs, new int[] { 0 }, defStyle, 0
  );
  String example = a.getString(0);
}
```

Solution:

```
public void wrong1(AttributeSet attrs, int defStyle) {
  final TypedArray a = getContext().obtainStyledAttributes(
    attrs, new int[] { 0 }, defStyle, 0
  );
  String example = a.getString(0);
```

```
  if (a != null) {
    a.recycle();❶
  }
}
```

❶ Calling the method `recycle()` when the object is no longer needed, fixes the issue. The call is encapsulated in a conditional block for safety reasons.

2.5 ObsoleteLayoutParam (OLP): Obsolete layout params

0.7%. Lint priority: 6/10.

During development, UI views might be refactored several times. In this process, some parameters might be left unchanged even when they have no effect in the view. This causes useless attribute processing at runtime. As example, consider the following code snippet (XML):

```
<LinearLayout>
  <TextView android:id="@+id/name"
    android:layout_width="wrap_content"
    android:layout_height="wrap_content"
    android:layout_alignParentBottom="true"> /* DeleteMe */ ❶
  </TextView>
</LinearLayout>
```

❶ The property `android:layout_alignParentBottom` is used for views inside a `RelativeLayout` to align the bottom edge of a view (i.e., the `TextView`, in this example) with the bottom edge of the `RelativeLayout`. On contrary, `LinearLayout` is not compatible with this property, having no effect in this example. It is safe to remove the property from the specification.

3 Automatic Refactoring Tool

In the scope of our study, we developed a tool to statically analyze and transform code, implementing Android-specific energy-efficiency optimizations — *Leafactor*. The toolset receives a single file, a package, or a whole Android project as input and looks for eligible files, i.e., Java or XML source files. It automatically analyzes those files and generates a new compilable and optimized version.

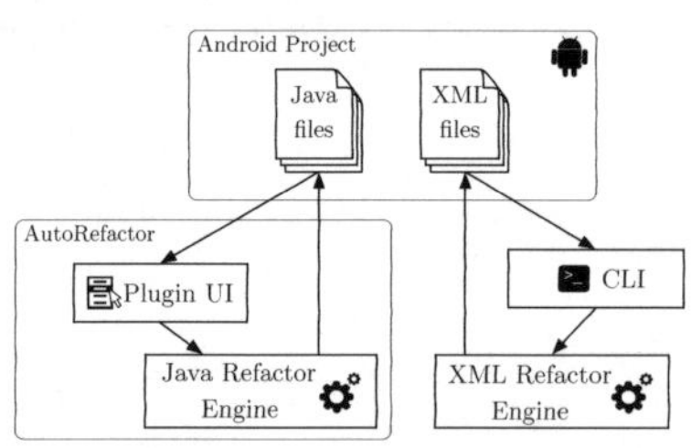

Fig. 1. Architecture diagram of the automatic refactoring toolset.

The architecture of *Leafactor* is depicted in Figure 1. There are two separate engines: one to handle Java files and another to handle XML files. The refactoring engine for Java is implemented as part of the open-source project *AutoRefactor* — an *Eclipse* plugin to automatically refactor Java code bases.

AutoRefactor provides a comprehensive set of common code cleanups to help deliver “smaller, more maintainable and more expressive code bases”[9]. Eclipse Marketplace[10] reported 2884 successful installs of *AutoRefactor*. A common use case is presented in the screenshot of Figure 2. Under the hood, *AutoRefactor* integrates a handy and concise API to manipulate Java *Abstract Syntax Trees* (ASTs). We contributed to the project by implementing the Java refactorings mentioned in Section 2.

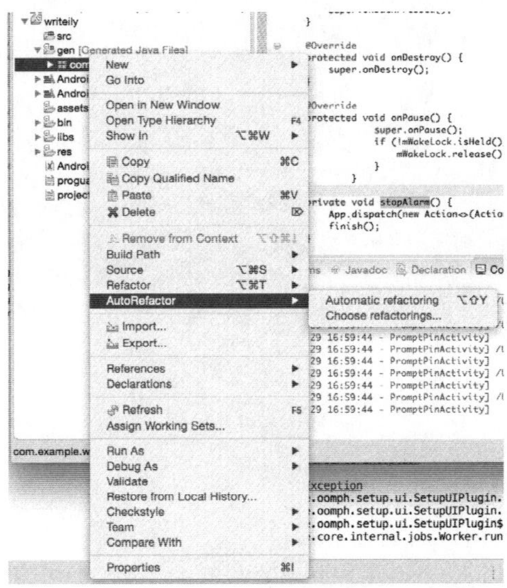

Fig. 2. Developers can apply refactoring by selecting the “Automatic refactoring” option or by using the key combination ⌥ + ⇧ + Y.

Since XML refactorings are not supported by *AutoRefactor*, a separate refactoring engine was developed and integrated in *Leafactor*. As detailed in the previous section, only a single XML refactoring is offered — *ObsoleteLayoutParam*.

4 Empirical evaluation

We designed an experiment with the following goals:

- Study the benefits of using an automatic refactoring tool within the Android development community.
- Study how FOSS Android apps are adopting energy efficiency optimizations. Improve energy efficiency of FOSS Android apps.

[9] As described in the official website, visited in March 2, 2018: https://goo.gl/v5im9X

[10] *Eclipse Marketplace* is an interface for browsing and installing plugins for the Java IDE Eclipse: https://goo.gl/QkTcWm visited in March 2, 2018.

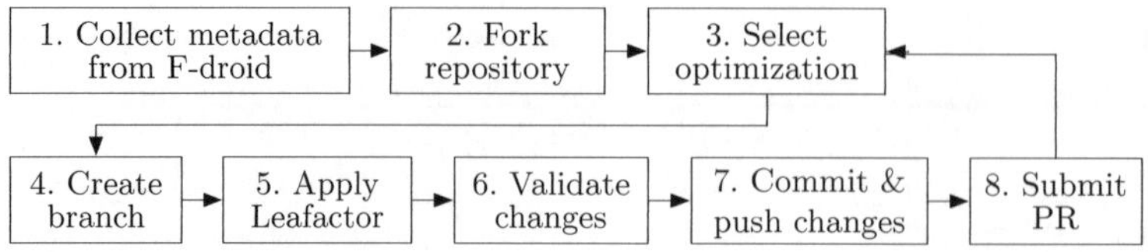

Fig. 3. Experiment's procedure for a single app.

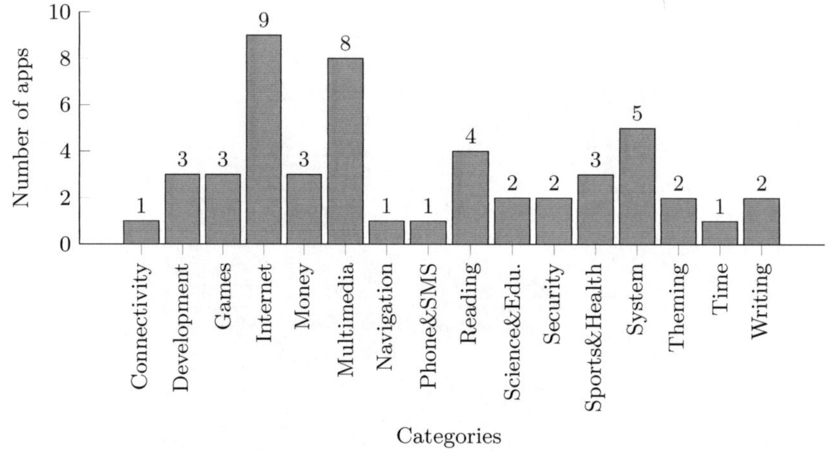

Fig. 4. Number of apps per category in the dataset.

We adopted the procedure explained in Figure 3. Starting with step *1*, we collect data from the *F-droid* app store[11] — a catalog for free and open-source software (FOSS) applications for the Android platform. For each app we collect the git repository location which is used in step *2* to fork the repository and prepare it for a potential contribution in the app's official project. Following, in step *3* we select one refactoring to be applied and consequently initiate a process that is repeated for all refactorings (steps *4–8*): the project is analyzed and, if any transformation is applied, a new *Pull Request* (PR) is submitted to be considered by the project's integrator. Since we wanted to engage the community and get feedback about the refactorings, we manually created each PR with a personalized message, including a brief explanation of commited code changes.

We analyze 140 free and open-source Android apps collected from *F-droid*[12]. Apps are selected by date of publish (i.e., it was given priority to newly released apps), considering exclusively Java projects (e.g., *Kotlin* projects are filtered out) with a *Github* repository. We select only one git service for the sake of simplicity. Apps in the dataset are spread in 17 different categories, as depicted in Figure 4.

[11] F-droid repository is available at https://goo.gl/cj8fC8 visited in March 2, 2018.
[12] Data was collected in Nov 27, 2016 and it is available here: https://goo.gl/CrmUEz

The largest project in terms of Java files is *TinyTravelTracker* (1878), while *NewsBlue* is the largest in terms of XML files (2109). Table 1 presents descriptive statistics for the source code and repository of the projects in the dataset. In total we analyzed 6.79GB of Android projects in 4.5 hours, totaling 15308 Java files and 15103 XML files.

Table 1. Descriptive statistics of projects in the dataset.

	Java Files	XML Files	Github Forks	Github Stars	Contributors
Mean	103	102	65	179	15
Min	0	4	0	0	1
25%	13	23	3.75	7.75	2
Median	38	48	9	24	3
75%	106	97	39	111	10
Max	1678	2109	1483	4488	323
Total	15308	15103	9547	26484	2162

5 Results

Our experiment yielded a total of 222 refactorings, which were submitted to the original repositories as PRs. Multiple refactorings of the same type were grouped in a single PR to avoid creating too many PRs for a single app. It resulted in 59 PRs spread across 45 apps. This is a demanding process, since each project has different contributing guidelines. Nevertheless, by the time of writing, 18 apps had successfully merged our contributions for deployment.

Table 2. Summary of refactoring results

Refactoring	ViewHolder	DrawAllocation	Wakelock	Recycle	OLP*	Any
Total Refactorings	7	0	1	58	156	222
Total Projects	5	0	1	23	30	45
Percentage of Projects	4%	0%	1%	16%	21%	32%
Incidence per Project	1.4×	-	1.0×	2.5×	5.2×	4.8×

*OLP — ObsoleteLayoutParam

Table 2 presents the results for each refactoring. It shows the total number of applied refactorings, the total number of projects that were affected, the percentage of affected projects, and the average number of refactorings per affected project.

ObsoleteLayoutParam was the most frequent pattern. It was applied 156 times in a total of 30 projects out of the 140 in our dataset (21%). In average, each affected project had 5 occurrences of this pattern. *Recycle* comes next, occurring in 16% of projects (58 refactorings). *DrawAllocation* and *Wakelock* only showed marginal impact. In addition, Table 2 also presents the combined results for the occurrence of any type of refactoring (*Any*). In addition, Figure 5

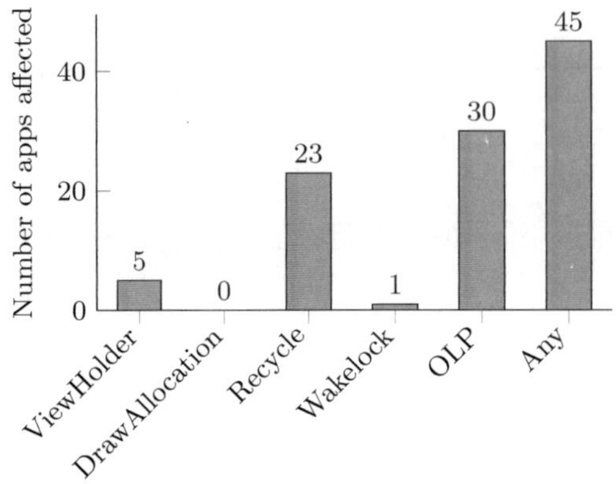

Fig. 5. Number of apps affected per refactoring.

presents a plot bar summarizing the number of projects affected amongst all the studied refactorings.

For reproducibility and a clarity of results, all the data collected in this study is publicly available[13]. All the PRs are public and can be accessed through the official repositories of the apps. As example, the PR for the refactoring *ViewHolder* performed in the app *Slide*[14] can be found in the *Github* project `ccrama/Slide` with reference `#2346`[15].

6 Discussion

Results show that an automatic refactoring tool can help developers ship more energy efficient apps. A considerable part of apps in this study (32%) had at least one energy inefficiency. Since these inefficiencies are only visible after long periods of app activity they can easily go unnoticed. From the feedback developers provided in the PRs, we have noticed that developers are open to recommendations from an automated tool. Only in a few exceptions, developers expressed being unhappy with our contributions. Most developers were curious about the refactorings and they recognized being unaware of their impact on energy efficiency. This is consistent with previous work [17, 23].

In a few cases, code smells were found in code that does not affect the energy consumption of the app itself (e.g., test code). In those cases, our PRs were not merged. Nevertheless, we recommend consistently complying with these optimizations in all types of code since new developers often use tests to help understand how to contribute to a project.

The code smell related with *ObsoleteLayoutParam* was found in a considerable fraction of projects (21%). This relates with the fact that app views are

[13] Spreadsheet with all experimental results: https://goo.gl/CrmUEz.

[14] *Slide*'s website: https://goo.gl/8HuJ6g visited in March 2, 2018.

[15] PR of the *ViewHolder* of app *Slide*: https://goo.gl/P2gFBx visited in March 2, 2018.

often created in an iterative process with several rounds of trial and error. Since some parameters have no effect under very specific contexts, useless lines of specification can go unnoticed by developers.

Recycle is frequent too, being observed in 16% of projects. This pattern is found in Android API objects that can be found in most projects (e.g., database cursors). Although a clean fix is to use the Java *try-with-resources* statement[16], it requires version 19 or earlier of Android SDK (introduced with Android 4.4 Kitkat). However, developers resort to a more verbose approach for backwards compatibility which requires explicitly closing resources, hence prone to mistakes.

Our *DrawAllocation* checker did not yield any result. It was expected that developers were already aware of *DrawAllocation*. Still, we were able to manually spot allocations that were happening inside a drawing routine. Nevertheless, those allocations are using dynamic values to initialize the object. In our implementation, we scope only allocations that will not change between iterations. Covering those missed cases would require updating the allocated object in every iteration. While spotting these cases is relatively easy, refactoring would require better knowledge of the class that is being instantiated. Similarly, *WakeLocks* are very complex mechanisms and fixing all misuses still requires further work.

In the case of *ViewHolder*, although it only impacted 4% of the projects, we believe it has to do with the fact that 1) some developers already know this pattern due to its performance impact, and 2) many projects do not implement dynamic list views. *ViewHolder* is the most complex pattern we have in terms of lines of code (LOC) — a simple case can require changes in roughly 35 LOC. Although changes are easily understandable by developers, writing code that complies with *ViewHolder* pattern is not intuitive.

A positive outcome of our experimentation was that we were able to improve energy efficiency in the official release of 18 Android apps.

7 Related Work

Energy efficiency of mobile apps is being addressed with many different approaches. Some works opt by simplifying the process of measuring energy consumption of mobile apps [26, 18, 19, 9, 6, 3]. Alternatively, other works study the energy footprint of software design choices and code patterns that will prevent developers from creating code with poor energy efficiency [13, 11, 12, 15, 16, 20].

Automatic detection of anti-patterns for Android has been studied before. Fixing code smells in Android has shown gains up to 5% in energy efficiency [4]. Code was manually refactored in six real apps and energy consumption was measured using an hardware based power monitor. Our work extends this research by providing automatic refactoring to the resulting energy code smells.

The frequency of anti-patterns in Android apps was studied in previous work [10]. Patterns were automatically detected in 15 apps using the tool *Paprika*

[16] Documentation about the Java *try-with-resources* statement: https://goo.gl/5TmSkc visited in March 2, 2018.

which was developed to perform static analysis in the bytecode of apps. Although Paprika provides valuable feedback on how to fix their code, developers need to manually apply the refactorings. Our study differs by focusing on energy related anti-patterns and by applying automatic refactoring to resolve potential issues.

Previous work has also studied the importance of providing a catalogue of bad smells that negatively influence specific quality requirements, such as energy efficiency [22, 21]. Although the authors motivate the importance of using automatic refactoring, their approach lacks an extensive implementation of their catalogue. In this work, we validate our refactorings by applying *Leafactor* in a large dataset of real Android apps. Moreover, we assess how automatic refactoring tools for energy can positively impact the Android FOSS community.

Other works have detected energy related code smells by analyzing source code as *TGraphs* [8, 7]. Eight different code smell detectors were implemented and validated with a navigation app. Fixing the code with automatic refactoring was discussed but not implemented. In addition, although studied code smells are likely to have an impact on energy consumption, no evidence was presented.

Previous work have used the event flow graph of the app to optimize resource usage (e.g., GPS, Bluetooth) [2]. Results show significant gains in energy efficiency. Nevertheless, although this process provides details on how to fix the code, it is not fully automated yet.

Other works have studied and applied automatic refactorings in Android applications [23, 24]. However, these optimizations were not mobile specific.

Besides refactoring source code, other works have focused in studying the impact of UI design decisions on energy consumption [15]. Agolli, T., et al. have proposed a methodology that suggests changes in the UI colors of apps. The new UI colors, despite being different, are almost imperceptible by users and lead to savings in the energy consumption of mobile phones' displays [1]. In our work, we strictly focus on changes that do not change the appearance of the app.

8 Conclusion

Our work shows the potential of using automatic refactoring tools to improve energy efficiency of mobile applications. We have analyzed 140 FOSS Android apps and as an outcome we have fixed 222 energy related anti-patterns. In total, we improved the energy footprint of 45 apps.

As future work, we plan to study and support more energy refactorings. In addition, it would be interesting to integrate automatic refactoring in a continuous integration context. The integration would require two distinct steps: one for the detection and another for the code refactoring which would only be applied upon a granting action by a developer. One could also use this idea with an educational purpose. A detailed explanation of the code transformation along with its impact on energy efficiency could be provided whenever a developer pushes new changes to the repository.

Acknowledgments

This work is financed by the ERDF European Regional Development Fund through the Operational Program for Competitiveness and Internationalization - COMPETE 2020 Program and by National Funds through the Portuguese funding agency, FCT - Fundação para a Ciência e a Tecnologia within project POCI-01-0145-FEDER-016718. Luis Cruz is sponsored by an FCT scholarship grant number PD/BD/52237/2013.

References

1. Agolli, T., Pollock, L., Clause, J.: Investigating decreasing energy usage in mobile apps via indistinguishable color changes. In: Proceedings of the 4th International Conference on Mobile Software Engineering and Systems. pp. 30–34. IEEE Press (2017)
2. Banerjee, A., Roychoudhury, A.: Automated re-factoring of android apps to enhance energy-efficiency. In: Proceedings of the International Workshop on Mobile Software Engineering and Systems. pp. 139–150. ACM (2016)
3. Couto, M., Carção, T., Cunha, J., Fernandes, J.P., Saraiva, J.: Detecting anomalous energy consumption in android applications. In: Brazilian Symposium on Programming Languages. pp. 77–91. Springer (2014)
4. Cruz, L., Abreu, R.: Performance-based guidelines for energy efficient mobile applications. In: Proceedings of the 4th International Conference on Mobile Software Engineering and Systems. pp. 46–57. IEEE Press (2017)
5. Cruz, L., Abreu, R., Rouvignac, J.N.: Leafactor: Improving energy efficiency of android apps via automatic refactoring. In: Proceedings of the 4th International Conference on Mobile Software Engineering and Systems. pp. 205–206. MOBILESoft '17, IEEE Press (2017)
6. Di Nucci, D., Palomba, F., Prota, A., Panichella, A., Zaidman, A., De Lucia, A.: Petra: a software-based tool for estimating the energy profile of android applications. In: Proceedings of the 39th International Conference on Software Engineering Companion. pp. 3–6. IEEE Press (2017)
7. Ebert, J., Riediger, V., Winter, A.: Graph technology in reverse engineering–the tgraph approach. In: Proc. 10th Workshop Software Reengineering. GI Lecture Notes in Informatics. Citeseer (2008)
8. Gottschalk, M., Josefiok, M., Jelschen, J., Winter, A.: Removing energy code smells with reengineering services. GI-Jahrestagung 208, 441–455 (2012)
9. Hao, S., Li, D., Halfond, W.G., Govindan, R.: Estimating mobile application energy consumption using program analysis. In: Software Engineering (ICSE), 2013 35th International Conference on. pp. 92–101. IEEE (2013)
10. Hecht, G., Rouvoy, R., Moha, N., Duchien, L.: Detecting antipatterns in android apps. In: Proceedings of the Second ACM International Conference on Mobile Software Engineering and Systems. pp. 148–149. IEEE Press (2015)
11. Li, D., Halfond, W.G.: An investigation into energy-saving programming practices for android smartphone app development. In: Proceedings of the 3rd International Workshop on Green and Sustainable Software. pp. 46–53. ACM (2014)
12. Li, D., Halfond, W.G.: Optimizing energy of http requests in android applications. In: Proceedings of the 3rd International Workshop on Software Development Lifecycle for Mobile. pp. 25–28. ACM (2015)

13. Li, D., Hao, S., Gui, J., Halfond, W.G.: An empirical study of the energy consumption of android applications. In: Software Maintenance and Evolution (ICSME), 2014 IEEE International Conference on. pp. 121–130. IEEE (2014)
14. Linares-Vásquez, M., Bavota, G., Bernal-Cárdenas, C., Oliveto, R., Di Penta, M., Poshyvanyk, D.: Mining energy-greedy api usage patterns in android apps: an empirical study. In: Proceedings of the 11th Working Conference on Mining Software Repositories. pp. 2–11. ACM (2014)
15. Linares-Vásquez, M., Bernal-Cárdenas, C., Bavota, G., Oliveto, R., Di Penta, M., Poshyvanyk, D.: Gemma: multi-objective optimization of energy consumption of guis in android apps. In: Proceedings of the 39th International Conference on Software Engineering Companion. pp. 11–14. IEEE Press (2017)
16. Malavolta, I., Procaccianti, G., Noorland, P., Vukmirović, P.: Assessing the impact of service workers on the energy efficiency of progressive web apps. In: Proceedings of the 4th International Conference on Mobile Software Engineering and Systems. pp. 35–45. IEEE Press (2017)
17. Pang, C., Hindle, A., Adams, B., Hassan, A.E.: What do programmers know about the energy consumption of software? PeerJ PrePrints 3, e886v1 (2015)
18. Pathak, A., Hu, Y.C., Zhang, M.: Where is the energy spent inside my app?: fine grained energy accounting on smartphones with eprof. In: Proceedings of the 7th ACM european conference on Computer Systems. pp. 29–42. ACM (2012)
19. Pathak, A., Hu, Y.C., Zhang, M., Bahl, P., Wang, Y.M.: Fine-grained power modeling for smartphones using system call tracing. In: Proceedings of the sixth conference on Computer systems. pp. 153–168. ACM (2011)
20. Pereira, R., Carção, T., Couto, M., Cunha, J., Fernandes, J.P., Saraiva, J.: Helping programmers improve the energy efficiency of source code. In: Proceedings of the 39th International Conference on Software Engineering Companion. pp. 238–240. IEEE Press (2017)
21. Reimann, J., Aβmann, U.: Quality-aware refactoring for early detection and resolution of energy deficiencies. In: Proceedings of the 2013 IEEE/ACM 6th International Conference on Utility and Cloud Computing. pp. 321–326. IEEE Computer Society (2013)
22. Reimann, J., Brylski, M., Aßmann, U.: A tool-supported quality smell catalogue for android developers. In: Proc. of the conference Modellierung 2014 in the Workshop Modellbasierte und modellgetriebene Softwaremodernisierung–MMSM. vol. 2014 (2014)
23. Sahin, C., Pollock, L., Clause, J.: How do code refactorings affect energy usage? In: Proceedings of the 8th ACM/IEEE International Symposium on Empirical Software Engineering and Measurement. p. 36. ACM (2014)
24. Sahin, C., Pollock, L., Clause, J.: From benchmarks to real apps: Exploring the energy impacts of performance-directed changes. Journal of Systems and Software 117, 307–316 (2016)
25. Wilke, C., Richly, S., Gotz, S., Piechnick, C., Aßmann, U.: Energy consumption and efficiency in mobile applications: A user feedback study. In: Green Computing and Communications (GreenCom), 2013 IEEE and Internet of Things (iThings/CPSCom), IEEE International Conference on and IEEE Cyber, Physical and Social Computing. pp. 134–141. IEEE (2013)
26. Zhang, L., Tiwana, B., Qian, Z., Wang, Z., Dick, R.P., Mao, Z.M., Yang, L.: Accurate online power estimation and automatic battery behavior based power model generation for smartphones. In: Proceedings of the eighth IEEE/ACM/IFIP international conference on Hardware/software codesign and system synthesis. pp. 105–114. ACM (2010)

Structuring and Accessing GoF Design Patterns with Kuaba Ontology

Patrick. H. A. Belem [12] and Adriana P. de Medeiros [1]

[1] Science and Technology Institute
Federal Fluminense University (UFF), Rio das Ostras - RJ, Brazil
[2] Superintendence of Information and Communication Technology (SuperTIC)
Federal University of Rio de Janeiro (UFRJ), Macaé – RJ, Brazil
patrickbelem@tic.ufrj.br, adrianamedeiros@id.uff.br

Abstract. Design patterns have been proposed to support developers to choose design alternatives that make software reusable. However, many developers still have difficulties in using them due to how information about patterns is structured, usually in the catalog form. This paper presents a new way of structuring and accessing GoF design patterns using the Kuaba Ontology. The aim is to facilitate the visualization of the patterns available for a particular design problem so that the developers can compare them and decide which one to use. An initial evaluation of the work showed that the proposed structure can facilitate the understanding of the GoF patterns and promote their use in software development.

Keywords: Design Pattern, GoF Patterns, Design Rationale, Kuaba Ontology.

1 Introduction

Design patterns have been proposed to help developers choose design alternatives that make a system reusable, and avoid alternatives that compromise reuse [1]. Patterns encode proven solutions to recurring design problems, thus they represent a valuable contribution to the theory and practice of software development [2]. However, many developers still have difficulties in using design patterns.

In order to verify the use of design patterns by professionals in software development, a survey was applied in the Information Systems Administration of the Federal University of Rio de Janeiro (UFRJ). It was conducted via online form answered by 45 professionals and showed that 89% of them know the subject design patterns, but only 49% declare they use patterns, against 40% that not use. Those who do not use patterns, 29% claim that they do not know how to use them, 24% that access to information of the patterns is difficult and time-consuming, 22% that it is difficult to identify when to use a certain pattern, 20% who saw no advantage in using them and 7% claimed other reasons. Finally, 78% of the professionals answered that the way of accessing the patterns information directly affects their use.

These difficulties are largely related to how information about design patterns is structured, usually in the catalog form. According to Budgen [3], the effectiveness of using design patterns requires much more than a catalog, however good it may be. In addition, Jalil and Noah [4] comment that although the patterns classification and availability proposed in [1] are quite detailed, there is still a lack of understanding about the relationships existing among them. There are also difficulties in identifying the right pattern for a design problem and making sure that this pattern is the best choice for this problem. In the catalog it is unclear what the problem is being addressed and which set of patterns addresses each specific problem. Thus, the problem investigated in this work is how to structure design patterns in order to facilitate the identification of the right pattern for a given design problem.

Design Rationale (DR) describes the reasons behind design decisions, including the problems analyzed, the different solution alternatives considered, the pros and cons of these alternatives and the decisions made [5]. This work presents a new approach for structuring and accessing GoF (Gang of Four) design patterns using the DR schema defined by the Kuaba Ontology [6]. Using this schema to organize and relate design patterns permits the rapid identification of the design problem at hand, and the visualization in a single place of all patterns that address that problem in some way, in addition to the advantages and disadvantages of each. The goal is to make it easier to visualize the available patterns for a particular problem, so that the developer can compare them and decide which pattern to use. Therefore, it is expected to facilitate the understanding of the design patterns and promote their use in software design.

An initial evaluation of this work showed that the proposed approach can indeed help developers compare the GoF patterns and choose one to solve a specific design problem, since it guides them to first identify the design problem in hand and only then visualize in a DR graph those patterns that solve it.

2 Related Work

A framework that combines DR and design patterns to develop reusable software is proposed in [7]. It allows recording and retrieving the knowledge acquired during the development. A goal-oriented approach is presented in [8] for documenting design patterns, in order to push the designer to focus on design decisions enclosed in patterns rather than on the solutions. In [9] an approach is proposed to support the suitable usage of design patterns and the documentation of each decision taken in the software process. The main idea is creating a patterns catalog, in which each pattern has general questions about the proper way to use it. According the authors, this approach allows the most appropriate usage of patterns, the documentation of decisions on the patterns use, and the elicitation of the requirements, which are directly related to these decisions and are obtained from the answers to the questions for each pattern.

DR *Graph* (DRG) [10] and *Design Patterns Rationale Graph* (DPRG)[11] are presented in order to facilitate understanding and improve the design patterns use. In [10] a tool was developed to automatically create the DRG from the information in the pattern text and in [11] other tool was developed to create the graph from the source code of a pattern. The authors observe that DPRG provides a graphic representation of a design pattern text, making explicit the relationship among design concepts in a pattern and supporting the identification of these concepts in the implemented code.

Although such works relate DR and design patterns, none of them use a DR schema to organize patterns by design problems, so that a developer can easily identifies the problem and compare the patterns available for it to decide which pattern to use.

3 Kuaba Ontology

Kuaba Ontology defines a set of elements (classes, properties, relations e restrictions) that express the DR domain [6]. Fig.1 shows the reasoning elements of the ontology utilized to organize the design patterns information in this work. An UML-like graphical notation is used to help visualization (see http://www.uml.org).

Briefly described, the reasoning elements represent the design problems (questions) that the designer should deal with, the possible solution alternatives (ideas) for these problems and the arguments for or against the presented ideas, which record the knowledge that designers have employed in the design. The acceptance or the rejection of an idea as a solution to a question is recorded by the element Decision [12].

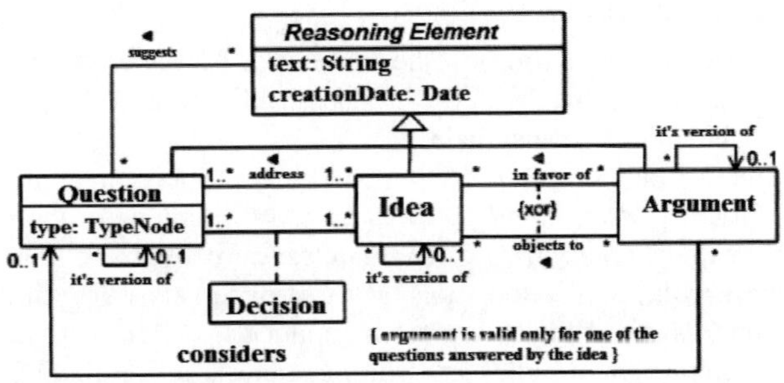

Fig. 1. Reasoning Elements and their Relations in Kuaba Ontology [12]

4 Structuring GoF Design Patterns Using Kuaba Ontology

In the catalog presented in [1], GoF design patterns are classified by two criteria: purpose (what a pattern does) and scope (if the pattern applies primarily to classes or objects). Each GoF pattern is described according to a template, divided into sections such as pattern name, intention, motivation, applicability and consequences, among others. There is not a section that clearly describes the design problem resolved. Moreover, it is not easy identify the problem in the intention section. Consider as an example the *Command* pattern intent described in [1]: "*Encapsulates a request as an object, in this way allowing you to parameterize clients with different requests, queue or log requests and support operations that can be undone*." This description is clear as to the solution that the *Command* pattern proposes, that is, it encapsulates a particular request, allows it to parameterize clients, and even queues, registers, and supports operations, but does not make clear what the design problem addressed by the pattern.

The correct identification of the object oriented design problem in hand facilitates the search for GoF patterns, because it does not require the developer to have prior knowledge of the available patterns. This section shows how the design problems addressed by GoF patterns have been selected, grouped and related to each problem in a DR graph using the reasoning elements of the Kuaba ontology.

4.1 Mapping Design Problems and Structuring GoF Patterns

GoF design patterns are applied to object-oriented (OO) software. Thus, the major design problems addressed by them are common problems to OO development, such as the definition of objects granularities, specification of objects interfaces, coupling, inheritance and reuse mechanisms. To identify the design problems addressed by the GoF patterns, each pattern is analyzed to understand how concepts and good practices of object orientation are used. Then, similar purpose patterns are analyzed in order to define the common OO design problem addressed by them.

To exemplify this mapping, consider specification of interfaces as a means of reducing coupling, a good practice used in many patterns. An interface represents a set of operations common among the classes that implement it and this causes the client objects to reference these operations in the same way, from the interface. Therefore, the use of interfaces avoids that the objects refer directly to each other, in other words, avoids the strong coupling between them.

The direct collaboration (dependency) among objects is a common design problem addressed by *Chain of Responsibility*, *Command*, *Mediator* and *Observer* patterns, since they deal with different forms of communication between emitter and receiver objects to process requests. The intentions of these patterns indicate the treatment of this collaboration to avoid the coupling between objects. All of them use interface to implement the communication between emitting objects and receiving objects. So, from this analysis it is possible identify the design problem: "*How to decouple emitter objects from receiving objects?*" and define the solutions proposed by patterns *Chain of Responsibility*, *Command*, *Mediator* and *Observer* as alternative solutions to this problem. Other design problems identified in the mapping are illustrated in Fig. 2.

The design problems identified in the mapping and the respective patterns that address them are organized using the reasoning elements of the Kuaba ontology. Each design problem is represented as a *Question*. The patterns that address a certain problem are represented as *Ideas* for the respective question and the advantages and disadvantages of using each pattern as a solution to the question are represented as *Arguments* for or against each solution idea. Fig. 3 shows an example of this structure, a DR graph, generated from the reasoning elements of the Kuaba ontology.

The example shows the design question "*How to decouple emitter objects and receiving objects in an application*?" (represented as rectangle), the solution ideas *Chain of Responsibility*, *Command*, *Mediator*, and *Observer* (represented as ellipses) that somehow address the question. It also shows the pros and cons arguments (represented as dashed rectangles) of using each pattern for the defined question. This visualization of available patterns for a particular design problem and their respective arguments in a single structure helps the developer compare them and decide which pattern to use.

According to Gamma et al [1], design patterns help to choose design alternatives that make a system reusable and avoid alternatives that compromise reuse. The structure presented in Fig. 3 facilitates the task of the developer to choose and avoid alternatives, since the alternative patterns for a given problem can be visualized together. As each question is exactly a design problem, the proposed structure helps to increase the contact of professionals with recurring design problems, mentioned in [13] as being one of the obstacles for beginners. Arguments guide the developer in choosing the pattern and can be considered a possible solution to one of the problems described in [4], where the authors cite the lack of a classification or organization that allows a developer to more easily choose the correct pattern and make sure that it is the best choice.

5 Access To GoF Patterns

A web application (in Portuguese: http://patrick.ison.com.br/) has been developed to support access to GoF design patterns using the Kuaba Ontology. In this application the user can search information about the patterns in two ways: from a design problem or using the categories of the catalog defined in [1]. By clicking on the "Search by problem" option in the main page, the user will have access to the "Design Problems" index, shown in Fig. 2, which presents the design problems defined in the mapping described in section 4. These problems are presented as questions, according to the Kuaba ontology. For each design problem the number of patterns that address somehow that problem is displayed. For example, the problem "*How to decouple emitter objects and receiving objects in an application?*" is addressed by four (4) design patterns.

When selecting one of the design problems listed in this index, the user has access to a new index containing all the GoF patterns that address the selected problem. This index is displayed as a DR graph, as shown in Fig. 3. Each design pattern represents a solution idea to the selected question. Each argument describing the advantages or disadvantages of each pattern is displayed as a pop-up window when the user clicks on the dashed rectangle. The name of each pattern in the DR graph has an associated anchor that allows navigation for detailed information about the pattern.

Fig. 4 shows the page with the pattern *Command* information displayed after the user selects it in the DR graph of Fig. 3. It displays the proposed solution by the pattern, advantages and disadvantages, examples and an index of related patterns. The examples include the UML class diagram and the code of a real application of the pattern in a given domain, not just the pattern structure as in the catalog in [1].

The user can still browse the other patterns using the "Previous" and "Next" navigation buttons displayed at the bottom of the page, following the order of presentation of these patterns in the DR graph (index) in Fig. 3. In this way, the user can navigate the information of the patterns that addressed the same design problem and compare the solutions proposed by them.

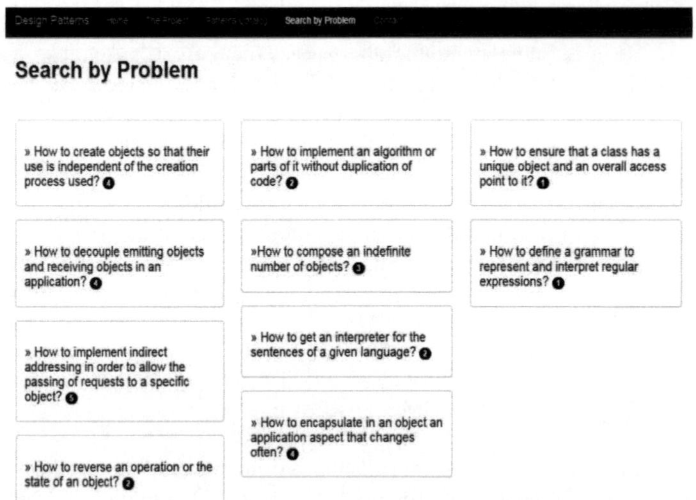

Fig. 2. Page with the Design Problems Index

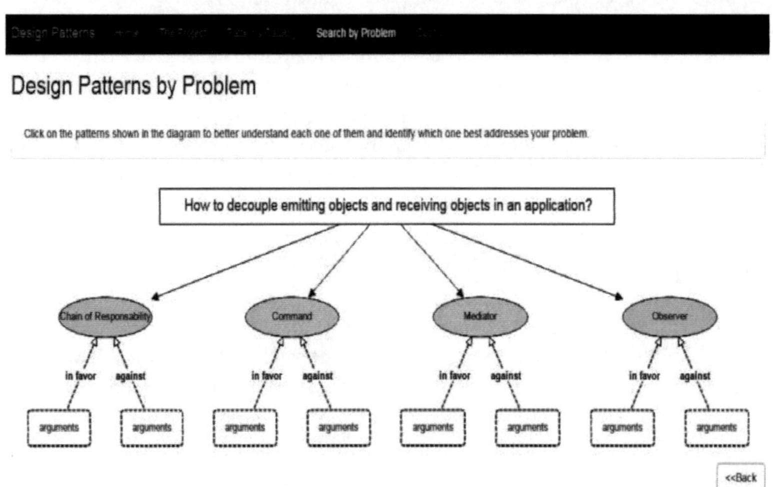

Fig. 3. DR Graph representing the GoF Patterns Index for the selected Design Problem.

6 Evaluation

A test activity was elaborated to evaluate the approach including two scenarios with OO design problems that can be solved with GoF patterns. Twenty-three participants with some knowledge in object orientation and design patterns performed the test: eighteen software developers, three teachers and two undergraduate students in Computing. The evaluation was done anonymously via a web form. The participants were asked to analyze two scenarios and, using the "Search by Problem" option of the Web application developed in this work, identify which design pattern could be used in each scenario and report on the evaluation form which GoF pattern should be used as a solution and which design problem they searched. After, the participants answered five questions regarding the new approach: four in open-ended format about the search and selection of patterns with the DR graph; and one question using Likert scale about the new form of access compared to the access in books and web sites.

The data obtained show that most of the participants were able to correctly identify the design problems in scenarios 1 (69.6%) and 2 (60.9%). Identifying the design problem correctly and using the DR graph permit participants analyzing only the patterns directly related to the problem identified, without having to previously know a certain pattern or searching all twenty three patterns of the catalog presented in [1].

Considering the questions answered about the approach and Web application, 87% of participants claimed that the "Search by Problem" option facilitated the search for design patterns, 78% that the proposed structure facilitates the visualization and comparison of patterns, 91% that the arguments are useful for their analysis and selection, and, lastly, 83% claimed that the information available for each pattern helped to understand it. Finally, 48% of participants rated the form of access in the Web application as very good compared to that available on books and Internet sites, 30% rated as good and 22% as optimal. None of them rated as bad or very bad.

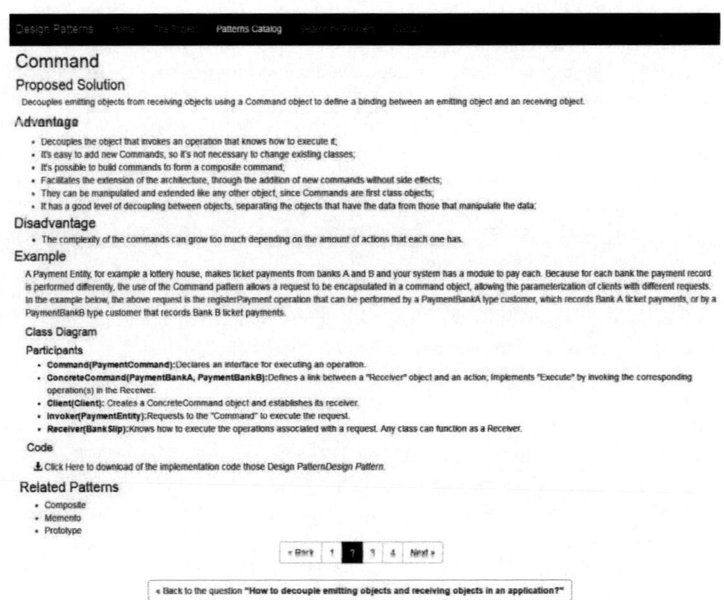

Fig. 4. Command pattern information in the context “Design Patterns by Problem”.

7 Conclusion

This work presents a new approach for structuring and accessing the GoF design patterns, using the DR schema defined by the Kuaba Ontology. The goal is to assist developers in choosing which pattern to use for a particular design problem, without having to know or search all GoF patterns. The initial evaluation results show that the proposed approach can indeed help a developer in comparing the GoF patterns and choosing one to solve a specific design problem. This is possible because the approach guides the developer to first identify the OO design problem in hand and only then visualize in a DR graph those patterns that solve this problem. The results also indicate that the arguments in the pattern information, which show its advantages and disadvantages, aid the developer to choose the most appropriate pattern for the analyzed design problem. However, this initial evaluation is still limited. An ongoing work is the design of an experiment that permit compare the approach proposed with the search of GoF patterns using others resources as books, web sites, wikis, etc.

References

1. GAMMA, E.; VLISSIDES, J.; HELM, R.; JOHNSON R. (1995) - Design Patterns: Elements of Reusable Object Oriented Design. Addison-Wesley.
2. EL BOUSSAIDI, G., & MILI, H. (2012). Understanding design patterns — what is the problem?, Journal of Software: Practice and Experience, Vol. 42, Issue 12, p. 1495–1529.
3. BUDGEN, D. (2013). Design Patterns: Magic or Myth?. IEEE software, p. 87-90, 2013.
4. ABDUL JALIL, M.; NOAH, S. A. M. (2007). The difficulties of using design patterns among novices: An exploratory study. In: ICCSA 2007. IEEE, p. 97-103.
5. LEE, J (1997). Design Rationale Systems: Understanding the Issues, IEEE Expert Volume 12, No. 13, p. 78-85.
6. MEDEIROS, A. P., SCHWABE, D., and FEIJÓ, B. (2005). Kuaba ontology: Design rationale representation and reuse in model-based designs. ER 2005, LNCS 3716, 241–255.
7. PEÑA-MORA, F.; VADHAVKAR, S (1996). Design rationale and design patterns in reusable software design. In: Artificial Intelligence in Design'96. Springer. p. 251-268.
8. SABATUCCI, L., COSSENTINO, M., SUSI, A. (2015). A goal-oriented approach for representing and using design patterns. The Journal of Systems and Software 110. 136-154.
9. DURDIK, Z.; REUSSNER, R. (2013). On the appropriate rationale for using design patterns and pattern documentation. In: Proceedings of the 9th international ACM Sigsoft conference on Quality of software architectures. ACM. p. 107-116.
10. BANIASSAD, E.; MURPHY, G.; SCHWANNINGER, C. (2002). Understanding Design Patterns with Design Rationale Graphs. Technical report T2-2002-01, Department of Computer Science, University of British Columbia.
11. BANIASSAD, E. L.; MURPHY, G. C.; SCHWANNINGER, C (2003). Design pattern rationale graphs: Linking design to source. ICSE 2003. IEEE Computer Society, 352-362.
12. MEDEIROS, A. P.; SCHWABE, D. (2008). Kuaba approach: Integrating formal semantics and design rationale representation to support design reuse. AIDAM, v. 22, 04, p. 399-419.
13. THOMASSON, B., RATCLIFFE, M. and THOMAS, L. (2006), "Identifying Novice Difficulties in Object-Oriented Design." Proceedings of the ITiCSE'06, Bologna, Italy.

An Ontology-Based Approach to Identify Developers in a Software Ecosystem Based on Their Skillset

Marcio Tadeu de Oliveira Júnior[1], Regina Maria Maciel Braga Villela[1], José Maria Nazar David[1], Marco Antônio Pereira Araújo[1], Victor Stroële de Andrade Menezes[1] and Fernanda Cláudia Alves Campos[1]

[1] Federal University of Juiz de Fora, Juiz de Fora MG, 36036-900, Brazil
mtojunior@ice.ufjf.br
regina.braga@ufjf.edu.br
jose.nazar@ice.ufjf.br
marco.araujo@ice.ufjf.br
victor.stroele@ice.ufjf.br
fernanda.campos@ice.ufjf.br

Abstract. [Background] Software ecosystems are composed of a set of actors who share a common market around some software platform, allowing a high degree of co-innovation through collaboration, and information and values sharing, thus creating a virtuous cycle of generation of values and artifacts. For better enjoying this market, its participants need to be aware of its network of collaborators and related actors, in order to comprehend the skills of the members of their network, for a better use of these skills. [Method] This work specifies an ontology-based approach able to provide knowledge related to the network of actors in a software ecosystem through ontological rules, allowing the identification of skills of these actors, leading to the discovery of developers who fit a certain role, through services that use such ontology. [Results] In order to demonstrate the validity of the proposed approach in providing the knowledge about the network of related actors, a service that obtains information from repositories in Github was created. By populating the ontology, it has been able to infer the profiles of the users who have the role of a developer in some repository, considering the languages used in this repository. [Conclusion] The developed approach allowed information about the participating developers in the ecosystem to be inferred. This enables its application on social networks to support software ecosystems, enabling recommendation systems to utilize the ecosystem information by indicating developers to a repository, based on their skills.

Keywords: Software Ecosystems, Social networks, Ontology, SECO, Developers.

1 Introduction

Software ecosystems (SECO) can be defined as "a set of actors that function as a unit, interacting with a shared market for software and services, along with the relationships among them. These relationships are frequently underpinned by a common technological platform or market and operate through the exchange of information, resources and artifacts" [10]. Typically, SECO have a common software platform, developed by a keystone developer, with niche agents, which can develop custom software that extends that platform, thereby adding value to the ecosystem.

Software ecosystems can be seen as a natural evolutionary response to the difficulty encountered by keystone developers in supporting the high demand for customized solutions by their end users. In facing this high demand, keystone developers find themselves in a situation in which, by opening the platform, a production of customized solutions that meets the demand of the end users can be achieved by involving external developers making the development of these solutions more feasible and affordable [4].

For growth in an ecosystem, it is critical for an actor to comprehend its relative position over the rest of the ecosystem, so that it can make better decisions by comprehending the relationships within the SECO. Therefore, one problem faced by actors is the lack of awareness of their positioning within SECO, so developers may not be able to take advantage of being participants in an ecosystem to grow, evolve or get profit. A mechanism is then needed to help the developers be aware of their surroundings, to better position themselves in the market. At this moment, it turns out that an approach based on the social network analysis is able to strongly support the developers to position themselves within the SECO. In this work it is presented an ontology-based approach to support developers within an SECO by analyzing their social networks and finding potential collaborators for theirs projects.

This work is divided as follows: section 2 brings theoretical background of this work, section 3 presents the proposed ontology and a generic architecture for applying the ontology on knowledge discovery, section 4 brings a service that implements the proposed approach to analyze projects hosted on github[1] and find potential collaborators for projects based on the knowledge inferences made by the service. In section 5 ,the related works are discussed, and finally, in section 6, the results are discussed, and future works are presented.

2 Background

Software ecosystems may appear as a natural evolution of software product lines (LPS), whose traditional products have had a significant high demand for new features and customization, to the point that the company that offers such a product cannot handle such demand due to limitations with research and development of technologies [4]

On both cases, the company cannot meet the demands for new features, and also cannot offer interoperability of its product with a variety of other products and services. In this vein, the company responsible for the product sees itself in a position, in which

[1] Available at https://github.com/

by opening the platform, external developers may meet such demand. This characteristic becomes an economically viable option for the keystone developer as the product becomes the platform of a new ecosystem.

In addition to the advantages of meeting users' demands, other advantages can be offered by establishing an ecosystem around a software platform [4], such as: increased value of the features offered; increased attractiveness to new users; increased adhesion to the platform; acceleration of innovation through co-innovation, including the collaboration with partners to share innovation costs, as well as the joint solutions developed by partners to the platform; reduction of the cost of acquisition and maintenance of features developed for partners, among others.

SECO can be studied from different perspectives. Campbell and Ahmed [7] study SECO from a three-dimensional view, the dimensions being:

- Architectural dimension: it focuses on the platform and its engineering. It deals with the architectural model, variability models, interoperability, domain engineering process and other topics related to platform architecture.
- Transactional dimension: it focuses on transactions between actors through business negotiation, projects, strategic planning, acquisition of solutions and other topics related to transactions between actors.
- Social dimension: it focuses on the relations between actors, promotion, sharing and acquisition of knowledge and other themes related to the relationships of actors existing in the ecosystem.

In this work, we adopt the definition for software ecosystem by Manikas and Hansen [11], which conducted a systematic review of the SECO´s literature, combining previous definitions, redefining software ecosystems as:

"[...] the interaction of a set of actors on top of a common technological platform that results in a number of software solutions or services. Each actor is motivated by a set of interests or business models and connected to the rest of the actors and the ecosystem as a whole, with symbiotic relationships, whilst, the technological platform is structured in a way that allows the involvement and contribution of the different actors" [11].

On the other hand, social networks are a set of people or a set of group of people with some pattern of contact or interactions with each other [12]. Social networks can be represented through graphs where nodes represent the entities and edges represent their relationships. Both entities and edges can have different types and attributes.

Social networks of developers are a subset of social networks, in which the entities represented are individual developers; development companies; groups of developers; consortia; OSS organizations; among other entities that develop software. Likewise, the edges can identify different types of relationships, such as software supply; collaboration, interests in common; among others.

Social network sites (SNS) are "web based services that allow individuals to (1) construct a public or semi-public profile within a bounded system, (2) articulate a list of other users with whom they share a connection, and (3) view and traverse their list of connections and those made by others within the system " [6].

Social networking sites support the discovery of other participants and the establishment of relationships between them, in addition to establishing connections with known participants from other place than the site itself, thus supporting the social network of the participants. In this way, social networking sites are of great importance for understanding and maintaining the social networks they support.

According to Seichter et al. [15], there are eight key elements that should be supported on social networking sites, so people can extract value from their relationships:

- Profiles: information about social network participants;
- Murals: are part of user profiles, where users can post their statuses. It is optional for users to be able to post on the murals of other users;
- News Feeds: These are personal resources that bring information of interest to users;
- Information sharing: it is one of the points that generates greater interaction within social networking sites;
- Teaming: refers to the possibility of people connecting in different ways, not only by a single type of relationship;
- Search: refers to the search for participants of interest;
- Suggestions: it is the suggestion resource of participants, groups and information of interest of the participants;
- Message exchange: this is the feature that allows two participants to communicate, whether through discussion forums, status comments, instant messages, etc.

Socio-technical networks are networks between actors of a SECO that involve the relationships of the social and transactional dimensions of the ecosystem. In addition to the actors, socio-technical networks also include the relationships between artifacts and knowledge [8]. The importance of understanding socio-technical networks is due to the possibility of inferring key information for the strategies adopted within a SECO. In this work, we adopt this strategy in order to help developers to position themselves within the SECO.

3 Proposed approach

This section presents an ontology-based approach to model the socio-technical network of a software ecosystem along with an architecture, named DevSECOSocialNet to support the operation of developers' social network site within a SECO. This approach aims to provide the architecture features, according to Seichter et al. [15], i.e., Profiles, Murals, News Feeds, Information Sharing, Teaming, Search, Suggestions and Message Exchange.

3.1 Ontology definition

Initially, a model for the SECO´s socio-technical network is necessary. To model the network, as stated before, we used the definition of software ecosystems given by Manikas and Hansen [11].

The proposed model uses ontologies considering that with its uses, it is possible to share and reuse knowledge between different sources, in addition to the power of expressing concepts that can be processed by inference engines to derive implicit knowledge. Besides that, considering that it is expected to connect the Social Network Site (SNS) to other services, it is expected to perform matching operations with ontologies from other sources, thus expressing external concepts in concepts computable by our proposal.

Considering the idea that ontologies are also useful for reuse, we searched for ontologies from the domain of social networks and software ecosystems. Finally, one social network ontology was found that was expanded to include the SECO´s elements as well as concepts related to developer´s social network. The original ontology for social networking is the Semantically-Interlinked Online Communities (SIOC)[2], represented in Figure 1.

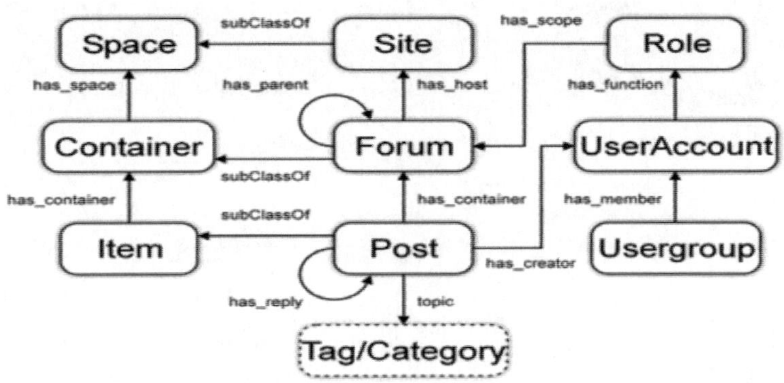

Fig. 1. SIOC Ontology

By extending this ontology, an ontology created to represent the social dimension of software ecosystems. Its main classes, object properties and properties chains are presented in Figure 2. Elements in red represent the participants of the SNS (note that the software is also a participant due to the fact it may have its own profile); elements in blue represent characteristics of the individuals; the orange elements represent subclasses of software, and the green represent the spaces. The ontology was created using the OWL standard, in RDF description in XML format, through the Protégé tool[3]. This representation of the ontology omits some information, e.g. attributes, since it would unfold in a large diversity of information, making it hard to have a clear understanding of its core principles.

[2] Available at http://rdfs.org/sioc/spec/

[3] https://protege.stanford.edu/

The *Space* class had its meaning extended to any shared space where actors can interact, be it a forum, chat or mural for example. In this way, the *Forum* class was removed, along with *Item* and *Site* classes, since a space, in this case, is always at a site. Likewise, the *Post* class has become a subclass of *Message*, which represents every type of message sent in any shared space. For the extended ontology, the role of the user within the social network was rethought, being redefined by the *actor's role* in the socio-technical network.

The *Tag / Category* class is now considered to be the *Skill* that a *Space* deals with, for example, a post in a forum on ruby development, should be linked to the "ruby development" skill.

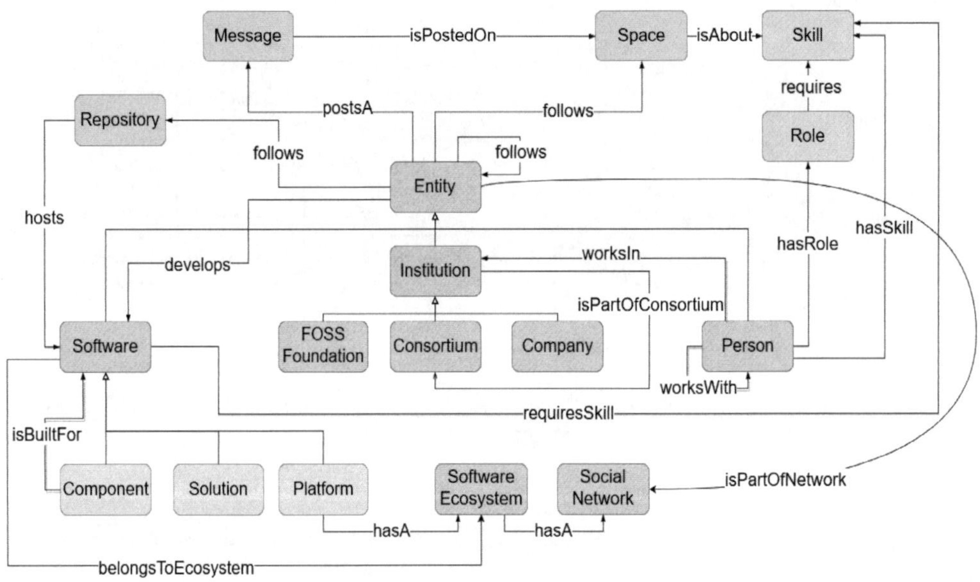

Fig. 2. Ontology representing the socio-technical network of a SECO

The ontology addresses each of the elements highlighted by Seichter et al. [15] as follows:

- Profiles: every participant should have a profile. The type of profile depends on the subclass of the entity;
- Murals: linked to each profile;
- News feeds: provide information based on the actors' relationships with other actors. For instance, people who work in an institution (*worksIn*) may receive news of whom became part of the institution;
- Information sharing: occurs through shared spaces;

- Teaming: inferred through the connections between individuals in the same repository (*worksWith*);
- Search: any entity in the socio-technical network can be searched in the ontology;
- Suggestions: roles can be suggested based on an individual's abilities (*Skills*);
- Message exchange: performed through shared spaces.

It is noticeable that not only the social aspects of the software ecosystem are represented, but its transactional aspects are represented as well in the ontology, by incorporating concepts of software supply networks (SSN) according to the definition of SSNs given by Boucharas et. al [5], whereas a single software supply network is represented by software that are required by the product of interest (POI), including recursively their dependencies and those that require it, directly or indirectly. By required software, it is considered the software that is a component of other, e.g. libraries, or co-required software for operation of the software of interest. The ontology also expands the representation given by SSN, by stating the tree of dependencies of the softwares that require the POI along the others that have common requirements to the POI. Figure 3 shows how SSNs are typically represented, whilst Figure 4 shows how the ontology approach can expand this representation, without losing information and context, but adding even more information to the network. Note that the non-dependent software are not originally included in the SSN representation, whilst the ontology representation can include them, allowing new ways to discover information from the ecosystem.

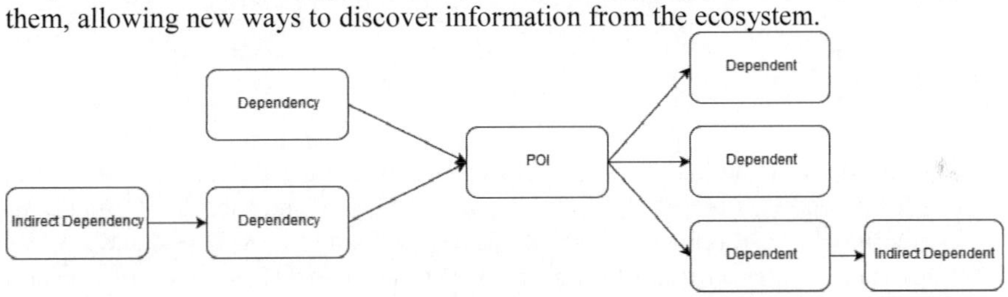

Fig. 3. Example of typical representation by SSN

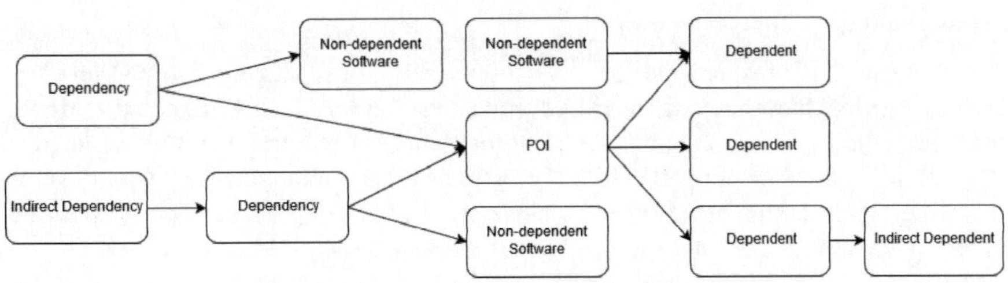

Fig. 4. Example of representation by ontology

Some of the object properties must be given as direct input, while some of them will be inferred from those that are given as input. For instance, property chain *worksWith*, which explicit the cooperation between two people of the class *Person* is inferred whenever these two people work in the same company, in turn a person works for a company, if this person develops the software that this same company owns. Another example is the property chain *belongsToEcosystem*, for instance, a component is part of the ecosystem if it is built for (*isBuiltFor*) a solution which in turn is built for the platform that is the ecosystem's platform. For this work, an important property that is the *mayWorkWith* property chain, which represents the skills that a person has, based on the repository they collaborate, represented in the Protégé syntax as:

hasSkill o isNeededBy,

or in SWRL syntax by

hasSkill(?person, ?skill) ^ isNeededBy(?skill, ?repository) -> mayWorkWith(?person, ?repository)).

The object property *hasSkill* itself can be inferred based on the information gathered. In the next section it is considered that a developer / GitHub user has the skill to develop in the language the repositories they collaborate are developed. Therefore, *hasSkill* may be directly an input or it may be inferred.

The *belongsToEcosystem* and *isPartOfNetwork* are closely related. Every *Entity* that is somehow related to the platform or other software that belongs to the ecosystem are considered as part of the social network and belonging to de SECO.

3.2 DevSECOSocialNet architecture

Based on the defined ontology, an architecture that supports the actors involved in software development was defined. It follows the Model-View-Controller (MVC) and Data Access Objects (DAO) architectural standards. By following the MVC standard, View is in charge of the presentation of the SNS, whilst the Controller has control over the Web Service, which in turn has access to the ontology data through the DAO classes. These in turn have direct access to the ontology through an ontology library capable of making automatic inferences.

The controller is responsible for receiving requests for retrieving information from the web service. It does it by receiving a request via the service's API, then it retrieves the information from the external services, for example, by retrieving a list of interest repositories and developers related to a project or related to another developer. Then, this information is processed by the class assigned for that API call, populating the ontology with the minimum of information necessary through the DAO classes.

After populating the ontology, the controller class uses a reasoner to infer the information into the ontology. By executing queries to retrieve information from the inferred ontology, the controller processes the information depending on the called service, and then it returns it to be consumed by the SNS or another service that had called the web service.

The architecture can be seen in Figure 5, and an example of its use is presented in the next section.

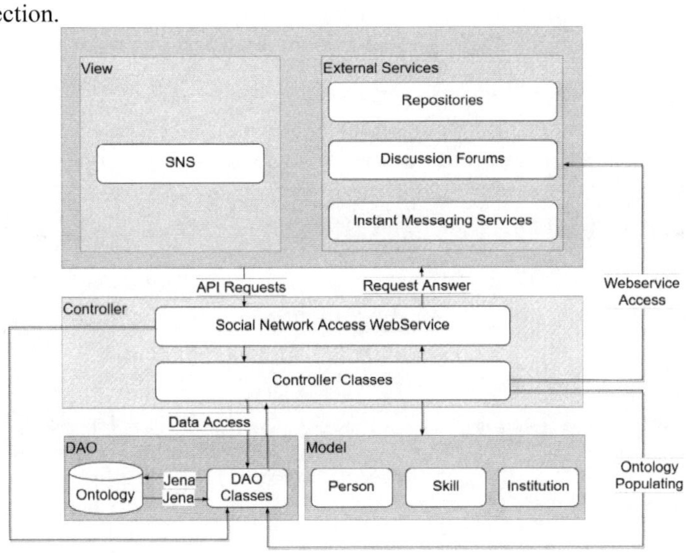

Fig. 5. DevSECOSocialNet Architecture

4 DevSECOSocialNet in Action

Aimed at verifying the applicability of this architecture, especially in the domain of software development, we use the architecture together with the Github ecosystem, as a proof of concept. Github is an open source software ecosystem (OSSECO), according to Manikas et al. [11], which hosts more than 10 million projects [1], most of them hosting software projects. This proof of concept consists on finding the users that may be suitable to work in a determined repostitory, takin in account the users and projects in its close social network.

Initially the Github's public repository were accessed by its API [9], along with related repositories, extracting their owners, collaborators, followers and implementation platforms. Here are taken into consideration the followers of the repository of interest, its collaborators, the collaborator's followers, and other repositories that those people collaborate, along the languages that are used in each repository.

Due to limitations to the number of requests per time, the extracted information was stored in a MySQL database. Figure 6 presents the database model used to store this information.

After downloading the relevant information, the DevSECOSocialNet service receives a repository as input, and access the database, loading a set of correlated users and repositories, by exploring this repository's collaborators and the repositories where these collaborators also collaborate in. Then, it is executed a search to gather the social network of the repository, considering the relationships of collaboration and followers.

The ontology considers that two developers collaborate with each other whenever those two contribute at least in one common repository. Also, it is considered a follower of an actor in this social network, whomever follows a user or a repository.

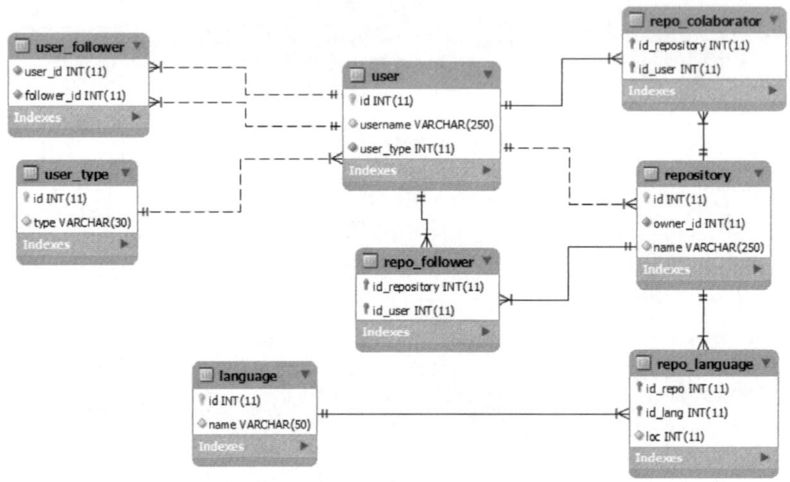

Fig. 6. Database model to store the extracted data

All the users, repositories and relationships are then added to the ontology as individuals and object properties via Jena library[4]. Jena is a Java library capable of modeling ontologies into graphs to use inference mechanisms to retrieve new information from those ontologies. Some information is then inferred based on ontological rules, so that it is possible to use SPARQL queries to search for the individuals that represent the actors close to the repository.

When the closest users are identified, their skills are inferred based upon the repositories they collaborate with. Then the skillset of each user is matched against the skillset required by the repository. Then they are classified in three groups, the first one is that of the users who have all the skills required by the repository, the second one is that of users who matched at least one of the required skills but have not matched all, the third group is that of users who have matched none of the required skills.

To narrow the developers to those that are capable of working in a repository, the solution uses the property chain *mayWorkAt*, which is defined by those developers that knows at least on language used in the repository of interest.

The DeveSECOSocialNet service then returns with the list of the first group of users along some other extra skills they may have, with a list of the second group along a list with their extra skills and the skills they lack.

In the Figure 7 is possible to verify the output of the web service responsible for verifying the developers who are capable of collaborating in a repository based on the languages used in its hosted software implementation.

[4] Available at http://jena.apache.org/

The web service answers with the languages required for the repository, and the two sets of developers that may work in the repository, those that have all skills and those whom have only some, which are retrieved by inferring their skills based on their collaboration in other repositories.

The answer also states the skills that the developers lack or have as extra skills considering those expected. As the service also can discover new developers for a repository, it also allows the requester discover developers that may work with new technologies to be added to the project hosted on the repository.


```
▼Role:
  ▼RequiredSkill:
    ▼0:
       Skill:        "Ruby"
    ▼1:
       Skill:        "JavaScript"
  ▼URI:              "http://www.semanticweb.o…cial-network#wycats+merb-core-developer"
▼HaveSomeSkills:
  ▼0:
    ▼LackingSkills:
      ▼0:
        ▶URI:        "http://www.semanticweb.o…cial-network#JavaScript"
     username:       "stephank"
    ▼ExtraSkills:
      ▼0:
        ▶URI:        "http://www.semanticweb.o…cial-network#ApacheConf"
      ▶1:            {…}
▼HaveAllSkills:
  ▼0:
     username:       "brainopia"
    ▼ExtraSkills:
      ▼0:
        ▶URI:        "http://www.semanticweb.o…cial-network#ApacheConf"
      ▶1:            {…}
      ▶2:            {…}
```


Fig. 7. Web services' output

5 Related Works

In this section are presented some works that have previously been published concerning software ecosystems modelling, mainly focusing on their social and transactional aspects.

Goal-oriented I* modelling, proposed by Sadi et. al [13], is a representation that takes into account the goals of the actors in the software ecosystem. It consists on gathering the actors in the SECO socio-technical network. The actors' technical and non-technical requirements are specified, so that it may reflect their motivations, expectations and criteria to join the SECO. This information is then analyzed to be specified as requirements for the SECO. These requirements are then used to classify the actors to reflect the roles in the software ecosystem. This representation identifies the meta-model for each SECO's socio-technical network via strategic dependencies that reflect socio-technical aspects, e.g. the dependency external developers have for an API being provided by the keystone developers. A drawback of this type of modeling is that it is basically exclusive to human interpretation, not allowing automatic processing by applications to interpret and obtain value from it.

Boucharas et. al [5] present a modelling technique that focus in the transactional aspects of a socio-technical network, by representing an actor's software supply network. It consists on identifying the technical dependencies of a software or multiple software of an actor with other software. Thus, it is necessary to identify the software dependencies and their dependents along their suppliers and users. For each software's dependency it is expected a trade relationship. It is possible to interpret these relationships by a machine, since it is well formalized in [5] and may be translated into mathematical representation.

Software ecosystems may also be represented by complex networks [2][3][14]. This type of representation often examines only one aspect of the socio-technical network per model, which in turn allow one type of relationship to be examined without context loss. For example, it may analyze the software supply network previously discussed by representing actors as nodes and software supplying as edges that may carry information, e.g. currency exchange for a software bought. This type of representation allows machine interpretation depending on which relationships are modeled into the graph. So, it is possible to extract information from the graph that represents the socio-technical network by analyzing some graph metrics for example, e.g. finding the main players in the socio-technical network by measuring their centrality in the graph.

The representation through an ontology facilitates the machine interpretation, since ontologies were designed for computer representation and comprehension. It allows a free representation of the concepts and their relationships. This type of representation is able to express concepts of any domain and process inferences to derive implicit information. An ontology model also has the advantage to be reused and extended, so that it may be used by different users and services, yet maintaining the meaning of the described contents. Therefore, we consider that the use of ontologies is the main differential of our approach. With ontologies, we can derive implicit information about developer´s skills, better positioning them in the SECO platform. Although it's expected that the ontology offers a greater power to describe domains, including the software ecosystem domain, by allowing to represent its concepts, it's still necessary to conduct studies to validate the use ontology as the strongest way to model SECO, by showing that it can encompass all the other modeling techniques in itself. Future studies aim to validate the viability of using ontologies as a more powerful resource to model SECO.

6 Conclusions

This work presented an architecture, named DevSECOSocialNet, based on the use of ontologies and social-technical network. It aims to provide actors with an environment that allow them to obtain value from their social networks, by extracting implicit information from it. Although Github already provide information that could be easily inferred by humans, our main objective is to provide automatic processing of this implicit information in order to be processed by applications that participates in a SECO platform. As a pilot case study, we used the architecture together with GitHub system in order to extract information to build a social-technical network considering implicit information. The results sound promising.

As future works, we look forward to using the architecture in other software ecosystems contexts, such as Educational and Scientific SECOs. In addition, it is under development the extraction of developers´ skills based on their commits to Github. Another future work lies within the clustering technique. The current one takes into account every single relationship that is within a restrict degree of distance from the source. So, a new way to extract the developers' candidates for a skillset must be developed to improve performance and still provide a good set of candidates.

References

1. 10 Million Repositories, Github Blog, https://github.com/blog/1724-10-million-repositories, last access 2017/12/13.
2. Angeren, J. Van; Alves, C.; Jansen, S. Can we ask you to collaborate? analyzing app developer relationships in commercial platform ecosystems. Journal of Systems and Software , Elsevier, v. 113, p. 430–445, (2016).
3. Angeren, j. Van; jansen, s.; brinkkemper, s. Exploring the relationship between partnership model participation and interfirm network structure: An analysis of the office365 ecosystem. In: SPRINGER. International Conference of Software Business, p. 1–15 , (2014).
4. Bosch, J. From software product lines to software ecosystems. In: Proceedings of the 13th International Software Product Line Conference, Carnegie Mellon University, Pittsburgh, PA, USA, p. 111–119, (2009).
5. Boucharas, V.; Jansen, S.; Brinkkemper, S. Formalizing software ecosystem modeling. In: Proceedings of the 1st International Workshop on Open Component Ecosystems - IWOCE, p. 41–50, (2009).
6. Boyd, D. M., Ellison, N. B.: Social network sites: Definition, history, and scholarship. Journal of Computer-Mediated Communication , Wiley Online Library, v. 13, n. 1, p. 210– 230, (2007).
7. Campbell, P. R. J.; Ahmed, F. A three-dimensional view of software ecosystems. In: Proceedings of the Fourth European Conference on Software Architecture: Companion Volume, ACM, New York, NY, USA, p. 81-84, (2010).
8. dos Santos, R. P.; Werner, C. M. L. "Treating social dimension in software ecosystems through ReuseECOS approach," *2012 6th IEEE International Conference on Digital Ecosystems and Technologies (DEST)*, Campione d'Italia, pp. 1-6, (2012).
9. Github API, https://developer.github.com/v3/, last access 2017/12/13.

10. Jansen, S.; Finkelstein, A.; Brinkkemper, S. A sense of community: A research agenda for software ecosystems. In: 2009 31st International Conference on Software Engineering - Companion Volume , p. 187–190, (2009).
11. Manikas, K.; Hansen, K. M. Software ecosystems – a systematic literature review. Journal of Systems and Software , v. 86, n. 5, p. 1294 – 1306, (2013).
12. Newman, M. E. The structure and function of complex networks. SIAM review , SIAM, v. 45, n. 2, p. 167–256, (2003).
13. Sadi, M. H.; Dai, J.; Yu, E. Designing software ecosystems: How to develop sustainable collaborations? In: SPRINGER. International Conference on Advanced Informa- tion Systems Engineering , p. 161–173, (2015).
14. Scacchi, W.; Feller, J.; Fitzgerald, B.; Hissam, S.; Lakhani, K. Understanding free/open source software development processes. Software Process: Improvement and Practice, Wiley Online Library, v. 11, n. 2, p. 95–105, (2006).
15. Seichter, D.; Dhungana, D.; Pleuss, A.; Hauptmann, B. Knowledge management in software ecosystems: software artefacts as first-class citizens. In: ACM. Proceedings of the Fourth European Conference on Software Architecture: Companion Volume, ACM, p. 119–126 , (2010).

Towards using task similarity to recommend Stack Overflow posts

Gláucia Melo[1], Ulisses Telemaco[1], Toacy Oliveira[1], Paulo Alencar[2], Don Cowan[2]

[1] COPPE – Systems Engineering and Computer Science Department
UFRJ – Federal University of Rio de Janeiro
Rio de Janeiro – RJ – Brazil

[2] David R. Cheriton School of Computer Science
University of Waterloo
Waterloo – ON – Canada

{gmelo, utelemaco, toacy}@cos.ufrj.br, {palencar, dcowan}@cs.uwaterloo.ca

Abstract. Software development depends on diverse technologies and methods and as a result, software development teams often handle issues in which team members are not experts. In order to address this lack of expertise, developers typically search for information on web-based Q&A sites such as Stack Overflow, a well-known place to find solutions to specific technology-related problems. The access to these web-based Q&A locations is currently not integrated into the software development environment, and because the associations between software development processes and the supporting sources of known solutions, usually referred to as knowledge, is not explicitly modeled and recorded, software developers often need to search for solutions to similar recurring issues multiple times. Moreover, this lack of integration hampers the implementation of a proactive recommender system that can point developers to knowledge that is relevant to their development processes. This research aims at proposing a solution that explicitly associates process elements (such as project tasks) to Stack Overflow posts and presents a recommender system that proactively recommends Stack Overflow posts to developers based on the similarity of project tasks. A literature review was used to find the concepts to define a meta-model for project tasks. This research paper advances the area of software development knowledge reuse by reporting on both the model and the results of experiments performed with real project development data.

Keywords: software process; software development; project task; stack overflow; recommender system.

1 Introduction

Software development is a knowledge-intensive collaborative activity [1], [2]. Currently, the development environment constantly changes with the variety of technologies in use, and because of this, new knowledge must be constantly obtained and software engineers need to engage in tasks that are related to knowledge management, such as learning, capturing and reusing collaborative knowledge during a software project [2]. Software development tasks are systematized through a software development process and executed by people. During the execution of a software development process (the act of working on tasks related to software development), software engineers often share and transfer knowledge [2].

There are a number of components that support software development, such as code editors and debuggers [22]. The software development environment is usually an integrated system of these components with which developers interact to build a software product. In order to acquire external support (e.g. code snippets), developers frequently switch between a development environment and browsers [4]. Further, software development processes and supporting sources of known solutions, usually referred to as knowledge, are not closely coupled. Developers must leave the development environment, reason about relevant and accurate terms for searches, open a browser, verify the results of the search, check if the source is reliable and only then transfer the knowledge obtained into the software and test the code or information [3], [4]. Without help from external sources, it is common to spend much valuable time in tasks that are peripheral to project goals [5]. Such activity usually occurs more than once, as software projects are large-scale organized processes.

When knowledge often needed and used by developers is not associated with specific development tasks, that information tends to get lost or diluted. The possibility of associating relevant knowledge to software development environments through appropriate tools would save developers time that they could spend on searching for what needs to be used during development. This approach could bring more productivity to the development process by reducing interruptions to process development flow [4], [5]. In addition, associating knowledge with project tasks could enrich the process definition, which might allow previously unknown knowledge to be synthesized within the software development process.

Important sources of knowledge for developers are Question and Answer (Q&A) websites. These websites receive questions and people who have already worked on the matter can provide an answer to a specific question. Many Q&A websites have voting and reputation systems implemented to ensure users are likely to get valuable content [6]. One famous Q&A site for software engineers is Stack Overflow, a community of millions of users that has become a main source of knowledge for developers because it is focused on getting detailed answers about development issues. The content available on Stack Overflow is completely focused on technically related material. This repository is mostly used during the development phase that comprises coding and testing. On Stack Overflow, developers place questions regarding problems they have encountered so anyone can attempt to answer the questions. Even though Stack Overflow participants might not be aware of specific details of a project or company, as long as the developer provides enough information for the problem to be understood or reproduced, one or more persons will likely work on an answer.

Although Stack Overflow is widely used during software development, there are still issues about associating a software development process and knowledge obtained from a Stack Overflow post. Researchers have identified the lack of an explicit association between knowledge gained from Stack Overflow and a software development task as a serious problem. The research reported in this paper aims at bridging this gap by integrating Stack Overflow posts with the software development process. A secondary objective of this research is that, by acknowledging that a process is a systemic entity with several activities executed over project phases that require various types of knowledge, processes may be used to generate development recommendations through the identification of similar project tasks.

In order to further the area of software development knowledge reuse, this paper proposes an association between project tasks and Stack Overflow posts used by developers to solve tasks. With this integration, the recommendation of Stack Overflow content will be provided once similar tasks are identified. Similar tasks will be identified by the definition of their context, which is a contribution of this research.

The remainder of this paper is organized as follows. In Section 2, the proposed solution is presented. Section 3 describes the study to test recommendation through similar tasks in a real industry software development environment. Related work is presented in Section 4 and Section 5 presents some conclusions, examines the validity of the research, and discusses possible future work.

2 Proposed Solution

Developers rely on Q&A websites (such as Stack Overflow) in order to resolve technology-related issues while working on project tasks [7]. During a project task, the developer with a problem often searches for online information to help resolve technological issues. Developers use keywords that help retrieve posts of a similar or even identical problem. Once the developer finds a likely solution, it is implemented and tested, ensuring that the application works as required, and the developer completes or resolves the project task. The information that was used to complete the project task is not saved and indexed anywhere and therefore is not associated with the project. If in the future the developer or other members of the team have the same or similar problem, they will have to redo the Stack Overflow search, repeating all the steps, including reasoning about a search string and searching for the post that helped with the initial problem. This paper proposes to address this problem of knowledge reuse by (1) associating knowledge (Stack Overflow posts) used to complete a project task with that task; (2) setting a task context and developing a solution that uses this context in order to relate project tasks, and (3) proactively providing developers with recommendations of Stack Overflow posts when similar tasks are identified. The goal is to deliver what developers might need from Stack Overflow based on task similarity, and understand how context can influence the similarity between tasks and therefore the recommendation provided.

2.1 Overview of Concepts

There are some key concepts needed to address the issues with finding and retaining information for future reuse, which are described next.

Software Processes are an important concept to be used during software development, in order to work toward the goal of appropriate quality. Processes, which are the steps toward achieving a goal [8], have been applied to the construction of software products. There are definitions, such as Rocha's [9], which suggest that software development involves a transformation between Process Planning and Execution, each with characteristics of its own. The former defines essentially a process and the latter provides the steps to be executed as part of that process. This transformation is represented in **Fig. 1**, which demonstrates how software concepts can be viewed primarily as a *Concept Cloud*, through concepts that are not materialized yet, such as quality standards, maturity models and software development methodologies, as well as technological or software architectural related concepts. Once this *Concept Cloud* is reified, process models are created, containing information about process activities and their relations, among other elements. After instantiation, project tasks are produced as part of the *Project Work Plan* creation. At this stage, it is possible to work on project tasks, which can use Stack Overflow posts in order to be completed. Thus, this is the phase that supports the association of Stack Overflow content with project tasks. Other authors have found this approach to Software Process transformation useful for Process Representation [24], Process Tailoring [23] and Process Mining [10], [11].

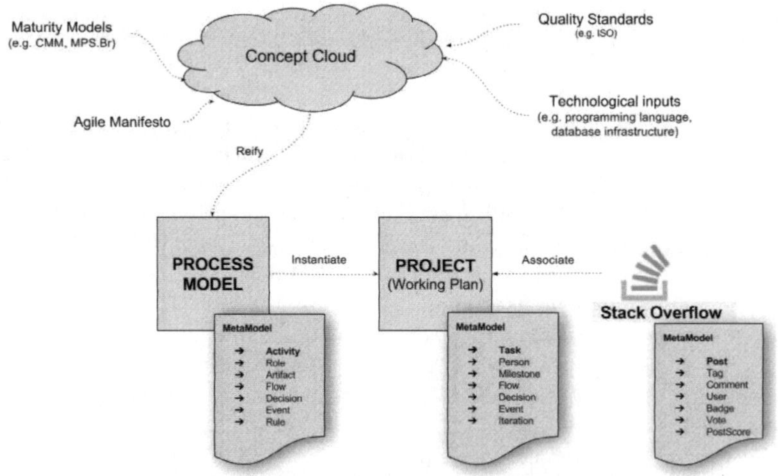

Fig. 1. From process concept to project execution.

Question and Answer (Q&A) websites are online communities where people with specific interests post questions and other users attempt to provide answers. There has been an evolution of such Q&A sites and often participants in a site have substantial expertise in specific domain areas, thereby increasing the value of the content. Given this value for some Q&A sites and with the addition of mechanisms that monitor the quality of the questions and the answers, these sources of knowledge have become significant assets in supporting professional use. As developers work, they often need to access knowledge repositories to support the execution of their project tasks. Software developers have their own source of technical knowledge within the Q&A website Stack Overflow, and this site is considered to be one important source of such knowledge. Thus, Stack Overflow could be viewed as a significant knowledge base for highly technical software development [6]. Therefore, this knowledge source is considered as a foundation for this research, although there are other important sources of information for software developers, such as product manuals and guides, maturity models, Wikis and even a software developer's own experience (i.e., tacit knowledge). Each Stack Overflow post comprises one question, and one or more answers. One post can also receive comments. It is possible to vote for questions or answers, based on the quality of the content, and these votes are transformed into scores for the authors of the content.

Recommender Systems for Software Engineering (RSSE) are software applications that provide valuable information in support of a software engineering task [5]. According to Robillard et al. [5], the architecture of a typical RSSE comprises at least three basic characteristics: a data-collection mechanism, recommender engine and an interface for a user to give and receive recommender inputs and outputs. Recommender systems deal with problems such as the cold-start problem, which addresses the lack of content to be recommended on initial states of the system, when there are little or no available data.

2.2 Knowledge to task association

In order to recommend Stack Overflow posts based on task similarity, once the developer identifies a Stack Overflow post that helped solve a task, then the developer should associate this post with that task. This solution assumes that similar tasks might have the need for knowledge from similar Stack Overflow posts, so the knowledge associated with a project task might be used to solve another similar issue. The proposed solution stores these Stack Overflow posts and associates them with the task helped by that specific post. An explicit association between Stack Overflow posts and project tasks is proposed in this research. This association should be initially the developer's responsibility, in order to avoid the cold-start problem. Then, as similar tasks are found, this associated knowledge should be recommended proactively. The solution stores the post related to the task and also the association between Stack Overflow knowledge and project task. The proposed solution should be a tool that will be integrated into the project management platform where project tasks are stored, once these platforms contain task information relevant to this solution.

2.3 Context Definition

Knowledge context was discussed by Rus and Lindvall [1], who explored two types of knowledge for the software development process: technical knowledge and knowledge about the application domain of a system. The former refers to design, programming and software processes. The latter refers to knowledge about aspects of a specific application. This research does not consider application domain knowledge, because the solution should be applied to any software development business context; it only considers the first type of knowledge, namely the technical knowledge needed to complete software tasks.

The proposed solution infers context as the information related to project tasks in the software development. Based on the assumptions that context is process and technological information, a meta-model for a Task is presented in **Fig. 2**. This information will be considered when searching for task similarity, as this is what comprises task context. Stack Overflow package in **Fig. 2** represents the external information that will be attached to the Task's and context data.

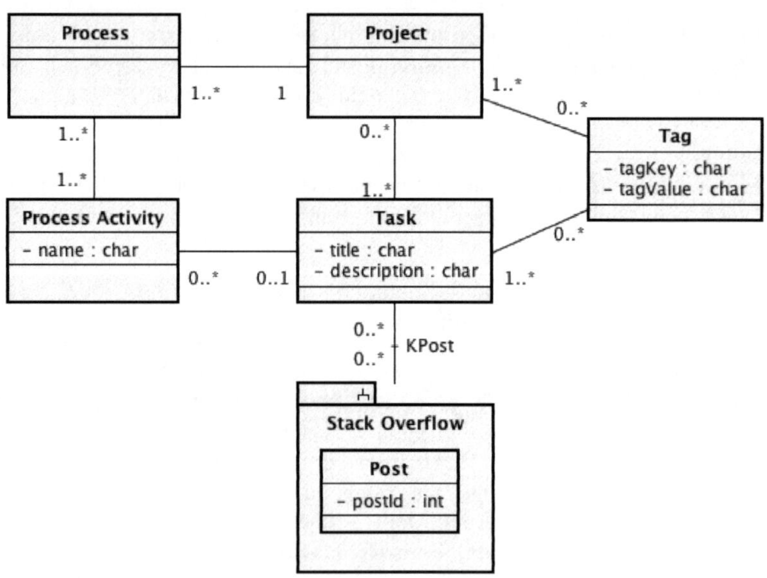

Fig. 2. Task Context Diagram.

2.4 Similarity Strategy

Once the context is defined and the stored knowledge is available, the final step is to define what is meant by similarity between tasks. A literature search was conducted to investigate similarity solutions that might be suited for defining task similarity.

Some approaches for recommender systems use distance-based similarity calculations in a multi-dimensional feature space, known as content-based recommendation. Some of the more popular distance-based similarity calculations used [12] for comparing two documents (text fragments) are: Cosine [13], Jaccard [14] and Levenshtein [15].

Considering that our approach to task similarity involves looking for features that are shared between texts, and not missing features, the algorithm that counts the number of steps for one text to be transformed into another seems the most appropriate. Because the commonly used Levenshtein distance [15] is defined as the minimum number of edits needed to transform one string or text into the other, and is therefore compatible with our approach, it was selected as the proposed similarity strategy to discover similarities between project tasks. Note that the Levenshtein distance was originally intended to be used in the development of self-correcting binary codes.

This approach to a distance metric checks the minimum effort required to transform one string into another, counting the number of insertions, deletions and substitutions, and then generates a numerical index. The project task similarity is inversely proportional to the distance; a distance of zero (0) implies maximum similarity. In this research, task similarities are compared and their similarity is presented at different levels or degrees.

3 Case Study Validation

To analyze if the same Stack Overflow post could be used during the resolution of similar tasks, a study was conducted at a Brazilian software development company. This company was founded in 1998 and is focused on software solutions for companies with a wide range of application needs in both the private and public sectors in Brazil. For the last 10 years, the company has mostly developed software for logistics and cargo transportation in container ships and trucks.

We collected data from the company's project management tool with the help of two of the most experienced developers in the company. They were asked to associate project tasks with Stack Overflow posts and describe the posts. After executing a similarity search, the developers were asked if the same Stack Overflow posts could be reused during the resolution of similar tasks that were discovered. Project tasks from one project were used. The developers defined the context for this project and its tasks. The developers suggested the project to be analyzed in this case study, based on the fact this was the oldest project in the company and had been using the SCRUM process successfully.

The tasks descriptions (e.g., title, context) are in Portuguese, and were not translated into English during the similarity search in order to keep the original text and because this proposal is intended to be multilingual.

The developers associated three Tasks with Stack Overflow Posts. The associations are presented in **Table 1**.

Task ID	Task Title (Portuguese) + Task Context	Task Context	Task Title (English)*[1]	Stack Overflow Post
Task1	[2.10.2] Evolutiva 39 - Inclusão de combo no campo E-mail envio NFS-e + Construir e testar código	Construir e testar código	[2.10.2] Evolution 39 - Inclusion of combo in E-mail sending NFS-e field	29174164
Task2	[2.10.13.1] [Recepção] [Cheio] Sistema não registra ocorrência de envio de email ao criar pedido	Construir e testar código	[2.10.13.1] [Reception] [Full] System does not record occurrence of email sending when creating order	25636091
Task3	[2.10.2] Erro ao subir aplicação em homol após inclusão do campo listaEmailNFSe	Construir e testar código	[2.10.2] Error uploading test application after inclusion of lis-taEmailNFSe field	25996758

Table 1. Manual association between Task and Stack Overflow posts.

Each of these three (3) tasks was compared to all tasks from the same project using Levenshtein distance; the most similar ones (>= 50% similar) are presented in **Table 2**, **Table 3** and **Table 4**. After compiling the table, the company's software architect provided an opinion about reusing the same Stack Overflow post to complete the similar project tasks that have been discovered. Answers are tabulated in **Table 2**, **Table3** and **Table 4** for each compared task.

% of similarity (rounded)	Description	Can possibly use the same Stack Overflow post?
52%	[HOMOL][Evolutiva] Envio de e-mail – Interceptor	Yes
51%	[HOMOL] Alteração do texto do e-mail Meio Ambiente	No
51%	[TESTE] Alteração do texto do e-mail Meio Ambiente	No
52%	[TESTE][Evolutiva] Envio de e-mail - Interceptor	Yes
50%	[Tela 3] - Criticar exclusão de transportador do pedido	No
50%	[2.2] Alteração do nome de procedure de DTC	No
50%	[HOMOL 2.2] Evolutiva na Consulta Boletim de Pesagem	Yes
50%	[DTC] E-MAIL - Envio de e-mail com PDF	No
51%	[RETIRADA] Importação - Alteração do formato do campo CE Mercante para string	No

[1] For information purposes only.

51%	[2.5.0]Erro ao finalizar Recepção Vazio Embarque Direto	No
51%	[2.3.8] HPU - Alteração do nome do bloqueio	No
50%	[Navis] Validação da solução de envio multiThreads	No

Table 2. Levenshtein similarity calculations and developer's opinion about Stack Overflow post reuse – Task1.

% of similarity (rounded)	Description	Can possibly use the same Stack Overflow post?
51%	[Reprogramar Recepção] Sistema está exibindo mensagem de erro ao reprogramar	Yes
53%	[ConsultaPedidoRecepçãoCheio] TESTAR Rever acesso do Botão Editar Pedido	No
54%	[Criar Pedido CHEIO] SIstema não gera ocorrencia de criação de HPU (BLOQUEIO NAVIS) na criação do PEDIDO CHEIO	Yes
51%	[HOMOL_2.3.8] Recepção Vazio Embarque Direto - Envio e-mail PDF	No
50%	[2.5.0] Recepção Cheio e Vazio - Alteração de restrição de utilização de container	No
54%	[PRODUÇÃO] RECEPÇÃO - Sistema não exibe mensagem de taxa não paga ao aprovar	No
54%	[TRUNK] RECEPÇÃO - Sistema não exibe mensagem de taxa não paga ao aprovar	No
51%	[RECEPÇÃO] Registrar no LOG que o usuário cancelou o envio de email automático	No

Table 3. Levenshtein similarity calculations and developer's opinion about Stack Overflow post reuse – Task2.

% of similarity (rounded)	Description	Can possibly use the same Stack Overflow post?
51%	[Tela 2] Erro como Administrador do Sistema	Yes
51%	[Tela 1] - Aplicar Exceção E4 como pré-condição da tela 1	No
50%	[2.5.0]Erro ao finalizar Recepção Vazio Embarque Direto	Yes

Table 4. Levenshtein similarity calculations and developer's opinion about Stack Overflow post reuse – Task3.

3.1 Discussion

According to the company's software architect, for all three tasks, there was at least one similar task that could possibly reuse a Stack Overflow post. As shown in **Table 2** the Task1 scenario encountered 12 tasks that are at least 50% similar to Task1, and from this group of 12 similar tasks, a quarter of them can possibly reuse the associated Stack Overflow post. In the Task2 scenario, shown in **Table 3**, from 8 similar tasks, 2 can possibly reuse the same Stack Overflow post associated with Task2. Task3 has 3 similar tasks and 2 of them could have reused the associated Stack Overflow post, as presented in **Table 4**.

The presented study result provides posts that are relevant to developers executing specific tasks. Preliminary, though modest, results indicate that, through the proposed solution, it is possible to couple development process and Stack Overflow posts, reusing posts whenever similar tasks are found, reducing development process interruption. This proposed solution considers the task context and discovers relations related to the task's text, and although positive results were obtained, the approach should be refined to improve context usage. The proposed approach was able to generate recommendations within all analyzed scenarios. According to an experienced software architect, the recommended Stack Overflow post could be useful for the execution of at least 30% of similar tasks.

4 Related Work

There are several papers discussing the idea of reusing information generated during the software development process in order to support future steps in the same or other processes. Our motivation is similar. However, the approach reported in this paper uses the reuse of Stack Overflow posts during the resolution of project tasks to complete subsequent task issues. A literature search found related work with approaches that use code, development artifacts or information to leverage the development process.

The idea of using Stack Overflow during software development is discussed in approaches such as Seahawk [18] and Prompter [3], which during the coding phase suggest Stack Overflow code snippets based on the context inside Eclipse. Both Seahawk and Prompter are designed as Eclipse plugins only and recommend code, while any development tool can use what is proposed in this research. Seahawk allows developers to drag & drop pieces of code into Eclipse. The approach proposed by Souza et al. [21] classifies Stack Overflow pairs of question/answers, comparing the pairs with the developer's code through text similarity, and also focuses on retrieving code snippets. Fishtail [16] has the same limitations, although it searches all over the web, not just Stack Overflow.

The Android "Issue Tracker" has been associated with Stack Overflow in the research described in Wang et al. [17], which proposes Crosslink, a solution that aims at automatically associating issues with Stack Overflow posts. The issues mentioned are uniquely from Android "Issue Tracker".

There is also research conducted by Kochhar et al. [7], which uses development artifacts to search for Stack Overflow posts during the testing phase. The work of Rahman et al. [20] states that looking for Stack Overflow posts, switching between IDE and browsers, can be distracting and time-consuming. Their research focuses on code exceptions and errors, considering context and the results show that context can have a major influence on recommendations.

The solution proposed in this research is agnostic to software or IDE, meaning the results can be used wherever Stack Overflow can be applied in software development. In addition, this proposal does not focus uniquely on code snippets, as it can recommend any kind of knowledge available in a Stack Overflow post which has been associated with a project task. This approach also considers process information and other identified task context while looking for similar tasks, which appears to be significantly beyond the scope of some of the related work.

5 Conclusions

The solution proposed in this paper aims to help developers extract knowledge from Stack Overflow requests, using project task context. The solution integrates Stack Overflow with tasks and identifies similar tasks, recommending the same knowledge used and associated with that similar task. This approach provides the developer proactively with information they will probably need, as that person will not have to leave the development environment to search for such knowledge.

This paper used Stack Overflow, because it is a Q&A site that is frequently used by software developers searching for information on knowledge-intensive development processes. Although Stack Overflow supports software development, this platform has no clear connection to project tasks during the development process, and the knowledge acquired is not normally stored, even when that knowledge was vital for subsequent task solution. This recommender tool addresses this problem, allowing developers to store useful knowledge, and therefore they are more likely to receive recommendations of useful Stack Overflow posts that can be used to complete a project task. Using process and technical context, the tool gathers similar tasks and recommends related posts. The case study indicates that such an approach is definitely worth pursuing further.

Although this research has examined the most commonly used strategies for text similarities, there is no similar research for software development or other processes to which we can compare the results. Future work might involve the automatic discovery of Stack Overflow posts, the incorporation of rating mechanisms for recommendations and the definition of a relevance rating of a Stack Overflow post with respect to the task. A more sophisticated method for the similarity strategy using the task context is also planned as future work.

References

1. M. Lindvall and I. Rus, "Knowledge Management for Software Organizations", in *Managing Software Engineering Knowledge*, Springer Berlin Heidelberg, 2003, pp. 73–94.
2. S. Vasanthapriyan, J. Tian, and J. Xiang, "A Survey on Knowledge Management in Software Engineering", in *2015 IEEE International Conference on Software Quality Reliability and Security - Companion*, 2015.
3. L. Ponzanelli, G. Bavota, M. D. Penta, R. Oliveto, and M. Lanza, "Mining StackOverflow to turn the IDE into a self-confident programming prompter", in *Proceedings of the 11th Working Conference on Mining Software Repositories - MSR 2014*, 2014.
4. A. N. Meyer, L. E. Barton, G. C. Murphy, T. Zimmermann, and T. Fritz, "The Work Life of Developers: Activities Switches and Perceived Productivity", *IEEE Transactions on Software Engineering*, pp. 1–1, 2017.
5. M. P. Robillard and R. J. Walker, "An Introduction to Recommendation Systems in Software Engineering", in *Recommendation Systems in Software Engineering*, Springer Berlin Heidelberg, 2013, pp. 1–11.
6. A. Anderson, D. Huttenlocher, J. Kleinberg, and J. Leskovec, "Discovering value from community activity on focused question answering sites", in *Proceedings of the 18th ACM SIGKDD international conference on Knowledge discovery and data mining - KDD 12*, 2012.
7. P. S. Kochhar, "Mining testing questions on stack overflow", in *Proceedings of the 5th International Workshop on Software Mining - SoftwareMining 2016*, 2016.
8. P. H. Feiler and W. S. Humphrey, "Software process development and enactment: concepts and definitions.", in *Proceedings of the Second International Conference on the Software Process-Continuous Software Process Improvement*, 1993.
9. A. R. C. da Rocha, J. C. Maldonado, and K. C. Weber, *Qualidade de software: teoria e prática*. Sao Paulo: Prentice Hall., 2001.
10. A. M. Valle, E. A. P. Santos, and E. R. Loures, "Applying process mining techniques in software process appraisals", *Information and Software Technology*, vol. 87, pp. 19–31, Jul. 2017.
11. R. M. S. Santos, T. C. Oliveira, and F. B. e Abreu, "Mining software development process variations", in *Proceedings of the 30th Annual ACM Symposium on Applied Computing - SAC 15*, 2015.
12. Y.-S. Lin, J.-Y. Jiang, and S.-J. Lee, "A Similarity Measure for Text Classification and Clustering", *IEEE Transactions on Knowledge and Data Engineering*, vol. 26, no. 7, pp. 1575–1590, Jul. 2014.
13. J. Han, J. Pei, and M. Kamber, *Data mining: concepts and techniques*. Elsevier, 2011.
14. M. S. P. Tan and V. Kumar, *Introduction to Data Mining*. Addison Wesley, 2005.
15. E. S. Ristad and P. N. Yianilos, "Learning string-edit distance", *IEEE Transactions on Pattern Analysis and Machine Intelligence*, vol. 20, no. 5, pp. 522–532, May 1998.
16. N. Sawadsky and G. C. Murphy, "Fishtail", in *Proceeding of the 1st workshop on Developing tools as plug-ins - TOPI 11*, 2011.
17. T. Wang, G. Yin, H. Wang, C. Yang, and P. Zou, "Linking stack overflow to issue tracker for issue resolution", in *Proceedings of the 6th Asia-Pacific Symposium on Internetware on Internetware - INTERNETWARE 2014*, 2014.
18. L. Ponzanelli, A. Bacchelli, and M. Lanza, "Seahawk: Stack Overflow in the IDE", in *2013 35th International Conference on Software Engineering (ICSE)*, 2013.

19. D. ˆCubranic, G. C. Murphy, J. Singer, and K. S. Booth, "Learning from project history", in *Proceedings of the 2004 ACM conference on Computer supported cooperative work - CSCW 04*, 2004.
20. M. M. Rahman, S. Yeasmin, and C. K. Roy, "Towards a context-aware IDE-based meta search engine for recommendation about programming errors and exceptions", in *2014 Software Evolution Week - IEEE Conference on Software Maintenance Reengineering, and Reverse Engineering (CSMR-WCRE)*, 2014.
21. L. B. L. de Souza, E. C. Campos, and M. de A. Maia, "Ranking crowd knowledge to assist software development", in *Proceedings of the 22nd International Conference on Program Comprehension - ICPC 2014*, 2014.
22. R. Minelli, A. Mocci, and M. Lanza, "I Know What You Did Last Summer – An Investigation of How Developers Spend Their Time," Proceedings of ICPC 2015 (23rd IEEE International Conference on Program Comprehension), pp. 25—-35, 2015.
23. Raquel M. Pillat, Toacy C. Oliveira, Paulo S.C. Alencar, Donald D. Cowan, "BPMNt: A BPMN extension for specifying software process tailoring, In Information and Software Technology", Volume 57, 2015, Pages 95-115, ISSN 0950-5849, https://doi.org/10.1016/j.infsof.2014.09.004.
24. Andre L. N. Campos, Toacy C. de Oliveira: "Software Processes with BPMN: An Empirical Analysis". PROFES 2013: 338-341.

Um Estudo Qualitativo sobre o *Crowdsourcing*: Análise da Colaboração na plataforma TopCoder

Ricardo Melo[1], Letícia Machado[2], Rafael Prikladnicki[2], Cleidson de Souza[1]

[1] Universidade Federal do Pará (UFPA) – Belém – PA – Brasil
[2] Pontificia Universidade Católica do Rio Grande do Sul – Porto Alegre – RS – Brasil

Abstract. In crowdsourcing a task is split into small pieces carried out by members of the crowd. Crowdsourcing in software engineering means this task is a software development task. TopCoder is the world's largest software engineering crowdsourcing platform with hundreds of thousands of registered developers. Tasks are called challenges, and winners of a TopCoder challenge receive financial compensation. This article describes a qualitative analysis of the collaboration between coders on the TopCoder platform. We analyzed forum messages between participants of the challenges that took place in July 2017. This analysis included two codifications. First, the type of the message, and second the related theme associated with that message type. Results suggest that although this is a competition, there are different types of collaboration among participants. These results can be used to suggest mechanisms that encourage the collaboration among participants in the platform.

1 Introdução

A geração atual da internet, chamada de geração 3.0, cria conteúdo, colabora espontaneamente com causas e marcas [1]. O crowdsourcing (CS) aproveita essa cultura colaborativa e canaliza a mesma para a realização de uma determinada tarefa, seleciona o vencedor, remunera e organiza todo este processo em uma plataforma na internet [2].

É possível identificar na abordagem de crowdsourcing um grande potencial para lidar com uma força de trabalho flexível que atenua desafios como a escassez de mão de obra especializada ou limitações geográficas. Sob a perspectiva dos indivíduos dessa multidão, o crowdsourcing cria novas oportunidades de renda e mobilidade social [3].

Com mais de um milhão de coders cadastrados, o TopCoder se tornou a maior plataforma de crowdsourcing na área de Engenharia de Software, conforme é apresentado em seu site. Esta plataforma realiza desafios de programação e os ganhadores são recompensados financeiramente [4].

Assim, é objetivo deste trabalho analisar a colaboração entre os coders em desafios no TopCoder. Para cada desafio existe um fórum relacionado, e cada fórum, por sua vez, é organizado em tópicos, denominados threads. A análise da colaboração aqui apresentada se refere à participação por meio das mensagens enviadas pelos competidores nos fóruns dos desafios no mês de Julho de 2017. Esta análise tem como intuito verificar a existência e classificar a colaboração entre os coders envolvidos nas competições do TopCoder. Desta forma, pretende-se contribuir neste estudo para o entendimento sobre como a colaboração ocorre em um ambiente competitivo de desenvolvimento de software crowdsourcing.

2 *Crowdsourcing* e Engenharia de Software

2.1 Visão Geral

Diversos aspectos têm sido estudados no contexto de crowdsourcing, incluindo como o mesmo pode trazer ganhos para as atividades de desenvolvimento de software [5]. Neste contexto, SW CS pode ser definido como "uma realização de determinadas tarefas de desenvolvimento de software em nome de uma organização por um grande grupo indefinido de pessoas externas com os conhecimentos técnicos especializados através de um chamado aberto" [6]. Essa abordagem usa uma multidão online para terceirizar tarefas, incluindo especificação de requisitos, projeto, codificação, testes, evolução e documentação [7].

O crowdsourcing no desenvolvimento de software normalmente envolve três tipos de atores: (i) os clientes, que possuem tarefas a serem realizadas; (ii) os programadores, que realizam as atividades; e (iii) as plataformas, que provêm um ambiente online para clientes e programadores [8]. Em outras palavras, as plataformas são os intermediadores entre clientes e desenvolvedores. A próxima seção irá justamente explorar uma destas plataformas.

2.2 A plataforma TopCoder

A plataforma TopCoder é um dos exemplos mais famosos de crowdsourcing para desenvolvimento de software. Criada em 2001 [9], a plataforma reúne especialistas do mundo todo em design, desenvolvimento, testes entre outras áreas da engenharia de software. O objetivo é beneficiar tanto os coders quanto os clientes. Os coders têm a oportunidade de serem reconhecidos profissionalmente, de melhorar suas habilidades e receber recompensas por seus conhecimentos. Por outro lado, os clientes buscam soluções alternativas produzidas rapidamente e com menor custo.

A comunidade do TopCoder constrói softwares para diversos clientes diferentes. Isto é acompanhado por testes contínuos e processos de gestão, assim, a plataforma coloca para seus usuários uma nova forma de resolução de problemas alcançada através de desenvolvedores espalhados ao redor do mundo. Na prática, o TopCoder "quebra" os projetos de seus clientes em pedaços e oferece os mesmos para a multidão como desafios competitivos [10]. Um desafio representa uma tarefa de software tal como: *Specification, Design, Development, Code*, etc [5].

Os coders da crowd se comunicam na plataforma TopCoder de maneira assíncrona via fóruns. Nos fóruns é possível enviar mensagens e visualizar mensagens entre os coders ativos nas discussões. Existem também os copilotos que desempenham papéis importantes durante o período em que a competição está ocorrendo. Eles atuam como facilitadores, solucionando dúvidas, incentivando a participação dos coders, obtendo feedback, intermediando solicitações do cliente do projeto, dentre outras atividades.

3 Metodologia

3.1 Coleta de Dados

Para analisar a colaboração entre os coders em desafios da plataforma TopCoder, é necessária a análise das mensagens trocadas nos fóruns dos desafios. Assim, o Web Scraper foi utilizado para extração dos dados destes fóruns. Entretanto, para realizar esta extração foi necessário o registro nos desafios de desenvolvimento, em tarefas do tipo *Code*. Isto se deu, pois o TopCoder só permite acesso a seus fóruns aos participantes registrados. Assim, a segunda autora se registrou nos fóruns do mês de Julho que atendiam aos critérios estabelecidos na Tabela 1. Somente depois disso, os dados dos fóruns foram extraídos e transformados em resultados textuais.

Tabela 1. Critérios definidos para análise de dados no TopCoder.

Definição	Métrica	Descrição
Período de análise	Julho de 2017	Desafios registrados em Julho de 2017; De acordo com a demanda e oferta em diferentes períodos do ano [5].
Coders registrados	> 25	Número de coders registrados no desafio.
Recompensa financeira	> $500	Valor que o solicitante do desafio está disposto a pagar.
Status	Aberto	Indica o status (Aberto, Submissão, Revisão, etc.).
Categoria	Desenvolvimento	Indica a área (design, development e data science).
Subcategoria	*Code*	Organiza por tarefas (conceptualization, design, code...).

3.2 Análise de Dados

O conceito de codificação existente na abordagem qualitativa foi utilizado para analisar os dados. Isso envolveu as atividades de separar, examinar, comparar, conceituar e categorizar os dados que foram sumarizados em um código ou categoria [11]. Mais especificamente, a análise das mensagens dos fóruns considerou dois tipos de codificação: a primeira identifica a categoria e a segunda o tema da mesma.
Baseado na percepção dos autores a primeira codificação foi das categorias descritas na Tabela 2. Na segunda codificação, o assunto abordado na mensagem é apresentado, complementando, assim, a primeira codificação. As Tabelas 2 e 3 evidenciam estas duas codificações.

Tabela 2. Classificação evidenciada na primeira codificação.

Categoria	Mensagem
i - Anúncio Público	*"[...] The purpose of this document should be to train the ML system to identify data in the schedule."*
ii - Dica	*"But just a heads up, the numerical problems aren't free from errors, you better have a calculator nearby"*
iii - Pedido de Ajuda	*"All sections of the specification document seem to have a good purpose, except section 9.3. Should we use the formulas in section 9.3? How?"*
iv - Pedido de Confirmação	*"[...] Also it should cover restrictions and data types for fields, right?"*
v - Pedido de Convite	*"please Invite me to [...]"*
vi - Problema Identificado	*"[...] I'm experiencing the same problem [...] Don't really know what it could be though..."*
vii - Resposta de Ajuda	*"[...] After all Qk* are calculated, you can calculate Qlam by summing up [...]"*
viii - Resposta de Confirmação	*"Yes, you are right, it is fine to use d3js for such auxiliary calculations."*
ix - Resposta de Convite	*"You have been invited"*
x - Resposta de Problema	*"You should first add corresponding class into .scss file, save that, and only then use it in .jsx [...]"*

Tabela 3. Classificação evidenciada na segunda codificação.

Tema	Mensagem
i - Acesso	*"Is it possible to get access to the ios repo? [...]"*
ii - Biblioteca	*"Do you really need D3JS here? Why don't you want just render svg elements using the standard ReactJS?"*
iii - Conexão	*"Can you provide sample user name and password for connect app, since it is redirect to [...]"*
iv - Deadline	*"Is it possible to provide an additional extension of just 24h? I am definitely going to submit this"*
v - Entradas	*"Yes, we've been discussing the metal nu parameter, so if it's not used in the metal calculation, it can be an optional parameter."*
vi - Estilo	*"Try to wrap the content of _reset.scss into :global {} [...]"*
vii - Processamento	*"I'm having some trouble with my android studio and i am not able to build the app.Will work at it. Thanks for the help."*
viii - Requisitos	*"In the specification it is given, the program shall use a standard directory as follows [...]"*
ix - Saída	*"To clarify, do you mean that we should output a txt file containing data in the format of the sample file?"*
x - Scorecard	*"I appreciate that there's a custom scorecard for this challenge"*
xi – Unidades	*"It seems that they are considering a ton = 1000 Kg, i.e. ton = tonne. Not like in [...]"*

4 Resultados

De um modo geral, 408 mensagens foram analisadas. Estas mensagens foram enviadas por 56 coders ativos nos fóruns, distribuídos entre 97 threads em 9 desafios da categoria desenvolvimento e subcategoria *Code* durante o período analisado. As mensagens foram classificadas em 10 categorias e 11 temas.

Os resultados apresentam a análise dos usuários ativos nas discussões que mais enviaram mensagens nos fóruns dos desafios. A Fig. 1 mostra a quantidade de mensagens enviadas pelos 10 coders que mais enviaram mensagens. Além disso, a relação entre a quantidade de coders e mensagens enviadas foi analisada. A Fig. 2 mostra a relação entre a quantidade de coders e de mensagens enviadas. Pode-se também observar que quanto maior o número de mensagens enviadas, menor o número de coders que enviam a mensagem, ou seja, existe uma concentração de mensagens enviadas por apenas alguns poucos coders.

A Fig. 2 revela também a quantidade de mensagens apresentadas pelos coders, destacando em parêntesis a quantidade de mensagens enviadas apenas por copilotos. Quanto ao tipo de pergunta realizada pelos coders, foram consideradas na codificação as seguintes: Pedido de Ajuda, Pedido de Confirmação e Problema identificado. Quanto ao tipo de resposta, foram identificadas apenas: Dica, Resposta de Ajuda, Resposta de Confirmação e Resposta de Problema.

Por fim, a quantidade dos coders ativos que participaram por fórum de desafios no mês de Julho foi analisada. A Fig. 3 mostra a quantidade de coders ativos, a quantidade de soluções submetidas e a quantidade de coders registrados por desafio.

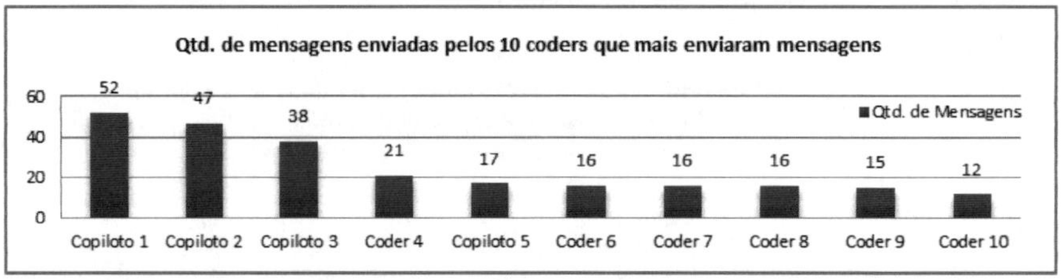

Fig. 1. Quantidade de mensagens enviadas pelos 10 coders que mais enviaram mensagens nos fóruns dos desafios no mês de Julho.

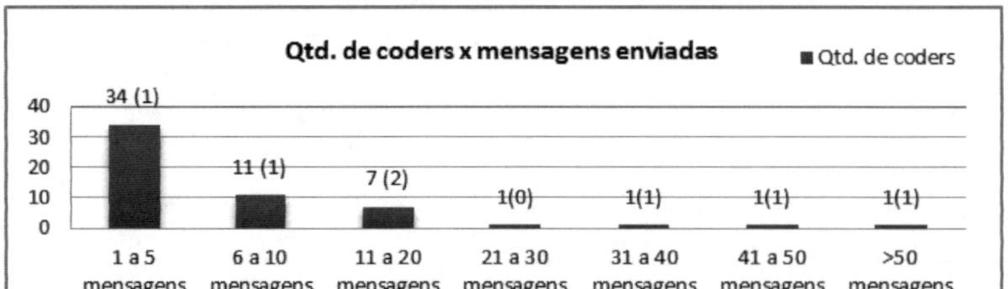

Fig. 2. Relação entre a quantidade de coders e quantidade de mensagens enviadas nos fóruns dos desafios no mês de Julho. Em parêntesis os copilotos.

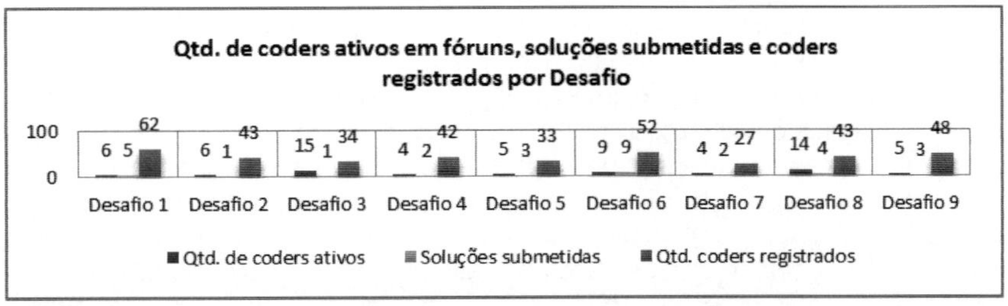

Fig. 3. Quantidade de coders ativos em fóruns, soluções submetidas e coders registrados por desafio no mês de Julho.

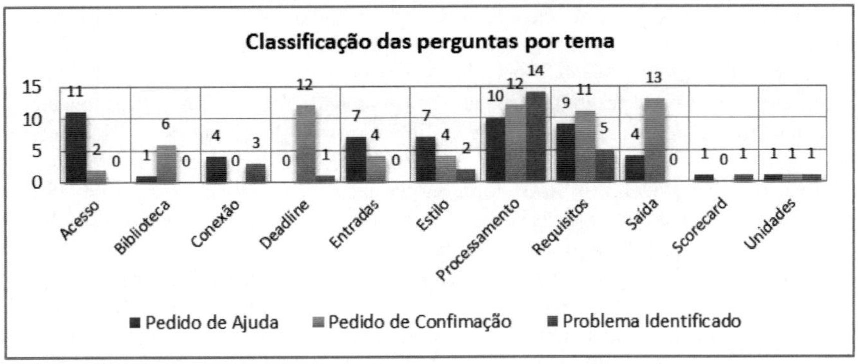

Fig. 4. Tema das perguntas realizadas pela crowd no mês de Julho.

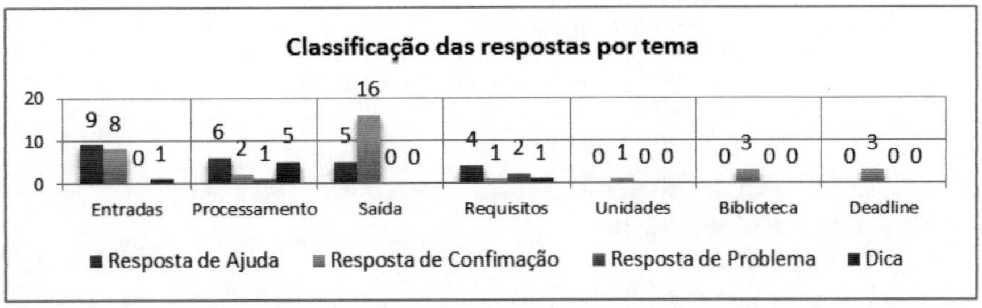

Fig. 5. Tema das respostas realizadas pela crowd no mês de Julho.

5 Discussão

Ainda que se trate de uma competição, Gray [12] observa que existe colaboração em crowdsourcing ao relatar três formas de colaboração: (i) compartilhamento com a crowd da sobrecarga administrativa para reduzir os custos; (ii) busca por informações de oportunidades de tarefas para compartilhar com a crowd; e, por fim, (iii) auxilio aos outros membros da crowd para avançar ou terminar uma determinada tarefa.

A quantidade de coders que estão competindo para submeter as suas soluções também é reduzida durante o desafio. Isso é evidenciado pelo número de mensagens enviadas nos fóruns de cada desafio (Fig. 3), onde poucos coders trocam mensagens sobre as tarefas. No entanto, é possível perceber que 9 coders ativos submeteram suas soluções para o desafio 6. A maioria dos coders enviou entre 1 a 5 mensagens (Fig. 2). É possível observar que os desafios iniciam com uma média alta de coders registrados. No entanto, ao final do desafio, poucas soluções são submetidas (Fig. 3). Em alguns casos (desafios 2 e 3), apenas uma solução é submetida.

Um exemplo de colaboração foi identificado em uma thread onde 3 coders pertencentes a crowd interagem entre si durante a condução de um desafio, representados na Fig. 1, como coders 4, 6 e 7. Os coders estão trocando informações sobre a especificação da tarefa e dessa forma colaborando entre si, mesmo em um ambiente competitivo.

Quanto ao tema das perguntas trocadas entre os participantes dos fóruns, destacou-se como maior registro a categoria definida como Problema Identificado com mensagens relacionadas ao tema Processamento. Na categoria Pedido de Confirmação, destacaram-se as perguntas relacionadas ao tema de Saída, Processamento, Deadline e Requisitos. Os temas Processamento e Requisitos foram destaques na categoria Pedido de Ajuda (Fig. 4).

Em relação ao tema das respostas, destacou-se como maior registro a categoria Resposta de Confirmação, relacionadas ao tema de Entrada e Saída. Na categoria Resposta de Ajuda, destacaram-se as respostas relacionadas ao tema de Entradas, Processamento, Saídas e Requisitos. Nas categorias Dica e Resposta de Problema a incidência foi maior em Processamento e Requisitos, respectivamente (Fig. 5).

Os resultados sugerem que, apesar dos desafios serem realizados em um formato de competições, onde a premiação é financeira, existem diferentes tipos de colaboração entre os coders. Assim, um estudo sobre a colaboração entre a crowd no TopCoder pode sugerir mecanismos que permitam incentivar a colaboração dos coders na plataforma.

6 Trabalhos Relacionados

Alguns autores [4] analisaram os fatores que levam à um maior ou menor esforço por parte dos coders na comunidade da Topcoder. Para isso, foram consideradas diferentes medidas, entre elas, Incentivo em dinheiro, Habilidade da equipe, Tempo e Atividade da equipe (enviar mensagem ou submeter solução). Os resultados sugerem que os níveis de esforço são movidos por incentivos financeiros e da interação de outros coders. O estudo contribui para identificar os fatores que motivam a colaboração, no entanto, não classificam as interações (mensagens) qualitativamente.

No contexto brasileiro, outros autores [15] apresentam uma análise de como as empresas brasileiras estão usando as plataformas de crowdsourcing para colaboração e inovação aberta. Os resultados indicaram que os projetos brasileiros de crowdsourcing têm sido bem sucedidos nesta área.

7 Conclusão

Essa pesquisa buscou contribuir para o tema de crowdsourcing no desenvolvimento de software colaborativo através de um estudo sobre a colaboração nos fóruns da plataforma TopCoder. Foram coletados dados sobre mensagens trocadas entre os coders a partir dos fóruns em desafios no mês de Julho. As mensagens foram codificadas em 10 categorias e 11 temas. Após análises, concluímos que, apesar desta ser uma competição, existem diferentes tipos de colaboração entre os coders. A análise contínua destes dados em um espaço mais longo de tempo poderá revelar como a participação e colaboração nos fóruns evolui, por exemplo, existe um aumento da participação dos coders nos fóruns em cada mês? Pretendemos realizar esta análise em um futuro próximo.

8 Agradecimentos

Os autores gostariam de agradecer à CAPES pela bolsa de mestrado do primeiro autor e ao CNPq pelo apoio financeiro (processos 406692/2013-0, 440880/2013-0, 310468/2014-0 e 420801/2016-2).

Referências

1. Kommers, P., et al: The Evolution of the Internet in the Business Sector: Web 1.0 to Web 3.0. Advances in e-business research series. Editora IGI Global (2014)
2. Howe, J.: Crowdsourcing: How the Power of the Crowd Is Driving the Future of Business. Random House. (2008)
3. Kittur, A., et al.: The Future of Crowd Work. In Proceedings of the 2013 conference on Computer Supported Cooperative Work. USA, San Antonio, 1301-1318. (2013)
4. Boudreau, K., et al.: From Crowds to Collaborators: Initiating Effort & Catalyzing Interactions Among Online Creative Workers. Social Science Research Network. (2014)
5. Dubey, A., et al.: Dynamics of software development crowdsourcing, Proc. IEEE 11th International Conference on Global Software Engineering. (2016)
6. Stol, K. and Fitzgerald, B.: Two's company, three's a crowd: a case study of crowdsourcing software development. ICSE. (2014)
7. Leicht, N., et al.: Crowdsourcing in Software Development: A State-of-the-Art Analysis. 28th Bled eConference. Bled, Slovenia. (2015)
8. Zhao, Y. and Zhu, Q.: Evaluation on crowdsourcing research: Current status and future direction. Inf Syst Front. (2012)
9. Lunden, I.: Appirio Buys TopCoder To Add More Crowdsourcing, And 500K Developers And Designers, To Its CloudSpokes Network. (2013)
10. Malone, T., et al.: The big idea. The age of hiperspecialization. Havard Business. (2011)
11. Strauss, Anselm L.; Corbin, Juliet: Basics of Qualitative Research: Grounded Theory, Procedures and Techniques. Newbury: SAGE. (1990)
12. Gray, L. et al.: The crowd is a collaborative network. In: Proceedings of the 19th Computer Supported Cooperative Work Conference. ACM. p. 134-147. (2016)
13. Mattos, C., et al.: The Use of Collaborative Platforms for Improved Open Innovation: Brazilian Context. International Conference on Industrial Engineering. (2013)

Improving the Decision-Making Support in Context-Aware Applications: The Case of an Adaptive Virtual Education Learning Management System

Jose Bocanegra[1], Luis H. Garcia Paucar[2], Jaime Pavlich-Mariscal[1], and Nelly Bencomo[2]

[1] Systems Engineering Department, Pontificia Universidad Javeriana
Bogotá, Colombia
{jose_bocanegra, jpavlich}@javeriana.edu.co
[2] School of Engineering and Applied Science, Aston University
Birmingham, U.K.
{garciapl, n.bencomo}@aston.ac.uk

Abstract. An application is context-aware if it uses context information to provide the user with relevant information or services. Generally, the process of making decisions about what information should be presented to the user taking into account a certain context is performed at design time. However, as the context usually changes during the execution of the system, the relevance of the information with respect to the context may be affected while the system is running. Therefore, new approaches that take into account these dynamic changes during the decision-making process at runtime for context-aware applications are required. The authors of this paper argue that a decision-making process based on the runtime reassessment of context-based relevance can be used to improve the information or services provided to the user under uncertain conditions which were not totally foreseen previously. The services can be in the form of suggested system adaptations. In order to demonstrate the feasibility of our approach, we present a novel case study from the domain of virtual education, which involves an adaptive context-aware learning management system. We demonstrate positive improvements to the autonomous decision-making support for this kind of systems.

1 Introduction

A context-aware application uses context to provide the user with relevant information or services [9]. An important class of context-aware applications is a learning management system (LMS) [25]. LMS are ubiquitous now due to the fact that both feedback and assessment is autonomously performed by software systems and, also, distance education become increasingly common in educational systems around the world [16].

M. Genero, M. Kalinowski (Eds.): CIbSE 2018, Bogotá - Colombia, 2018

LMS use context to provide the students with computer-assisted adapted learning plans in order to improve the learning experience based on the singularities associated to the students and their own learning progress and capabilities. The application supporting the learning process determines the student's characteristics (*e.g.*, learning style and personality), the access device, and the place in which student and application are interacting. Based on the above, the application provides students with tailored learning activities.

Depending on the context, the information that is provided to the user, in this case the student, should change accordingly. For instance, it is not the same to provide information to a student who is starting his training process than to a student at a more advanced stage, or to a student who presents specific challenges or progress. Usually, the type of the information that is provided to the user is specified at design time. However, due to the changes in the context during the learning process of the program taken by the student (*e.g.*, when the student gets a lower grade in an evaluation) the relevance and nature of the information provided to the student may be affected. In this case, the information is relevant only if it helps the student to achieve his/her learning goals (for instance, developing new skills).

In this paper we argue that the decision-making process in context-aware applications can be improved using automatic runtime re-appraisal and update of relevances [18]. In our case study, relevances of the information in context-aware applications correspond to weights and or preferences in decision-making processes [17] and adapted learning plans correspond to adaptations and reconfigurations. The approach to support the reassessment is ARRoW, a method that has been originally applied in the context of the reappraisal of weights of non-functional requirements during the decision-making for self-adaptive systems [22].

The work presented in this paper is motivated through a case study in the area of virtual education. In the case study, ARRoW has been used to modify, at runtime, the information that is provided to the student when his/her performance in a particular skill is not in the desired level. The benefit is that the final learning plan is adapted according to the needs and characteristics of the student and his/her learning progress.

This paper is structured as follows: Section 2 describes the motivating scenario. The rationale behind the approach presented is outlined in Section 3. Section 4 details the initial experiment and discusses the preliminary results. Section 5 covers the analysis of the related work. Finally, the conclusions and the future research directions are presented in Section 6.

2 Motivating Scenario

To illustrate the need for improving the decision-making support in context-aware applications, this section introduces the ASHYI-EDU [19] project, which is a context-aware virtual learning environment developed by the interdisciplinary research group ISTAR at the *Pontificia Universidad Javeriana* in Bogotá, Colombia.

The main goal of the ASHYI-EDU project is to use context information for performing dynamic adaptive planning that best suits the student's requirements according to their performance and singularities.

The process starts with the creation of an adaptive plan. At this initial stage, the teacher defines a set of skills to be met by the students by the end the execution of the virtual course. To achieve each skill, the teacher creates a set of learning plans that are composed by several academic activities.

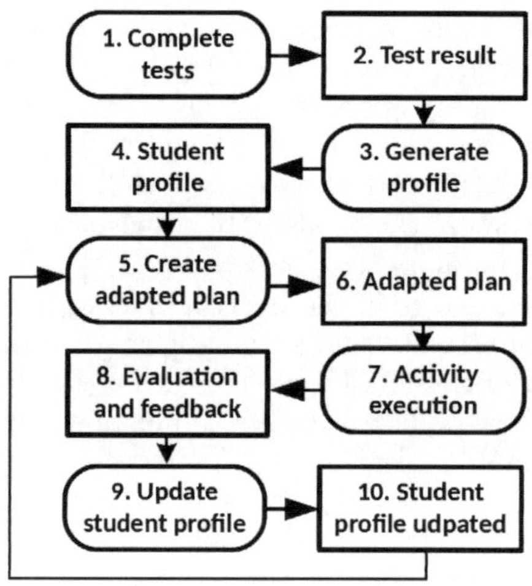

Fig. 1. Process in ASHYI-EDU

When the student interacts with the application for the first time, the application uses context information such as the student's learning styles and personality. As is depicted in Fig. 1, this information is measured by using a set of predefined tests. With the results of the tests, the application creates a user profile. Then the profile is used to select the most suitable plan for the student.

In ASHYI-EDU other context information is also selected to personalize the activity. For instance, the application detects the access device and the connection type. In a slow connection and in a small size screen device the application provides the student with basic textual information, while in a high-speed connection and in desktop device the student will be provided with enriched multimedia information.

A relevant issue in the case study is that the relevance of the learning plan, based on a specific context, is determined at design time. This design-time task is usually performed by experts in education and pedagogy [14].

When the experts detect that the learning plan may not helping to improve the required skill anymore (e.g, when the student get a lower grade in an evaluation), the plan needs to be adjusted to ensure that the information provided to the student is still relevant for helping to acquire the skill. Adjusting and monitoring the execution of a learning plan for a single student may be a complex and time consuming activity [14]. Therefore, the process for adapting and monitoring, for instance, 20 different plans for a group of 20 heterogeneous students may turn to be even more challenging.

This scenario describes the potential opportunities for improving the decision-making support. An example of an opportunity for improvement is when the same application may use context information (e.g., the performance nominator that stores information about measured performance of a learner through an academic activity [23]). In this case, if the value is not the targeted value, the application can therefore readjust autonomously, the learning plan to be provided to the student. This process is scalable, as it can be done for both a single student or for a large group of them.

3 Background Information

This section describes the main topics that support the ideas developed in the paper, specifically we cover context-aware applications and the reappraisal of weights in decision-making of self-adaptation.

3.1 Context-Aware Applications

As stated by Dey et al. in [9], a new challenge for software engineers is to enhance the behaviour of any application by using their context. Context is referred to any information that characterises the situation of entities that are considered relevant to the interaction between a user and an application, including the user and the application themselves.

Some examples of contexts are related to technology issues such as network, hardware, software; others are related to location, time, physical conditions (e.g. heat, light, sound), activity, user, and social relations [23].

Context-aware applications are part of a new generation of smart and autonomous applications that are able to collect and sense context information and use it to make adaptation decisions [1] or to provide the user with relevant information or services [2]. In other words, the behaviour of these kinds of applications is context dependent.

Figure 2 provides a simplified view of a context-aware application. In the example, the user interacts with the application; the application senses the context (or reacts to its changes). Then, the application is able to use that context data to provide the user with specially-tailored information or services. The LMS described in Section 2 is an example of a context-aware application.

One of the main goals of context aware applications is that they can monitor the context and they act accordingly with minor human mediation. To Alegre et al. [2], "the aim of having an autonomous system is to reduce the user intervention, easing its use and decreasing user distraction", what is one of our aims in arrow.

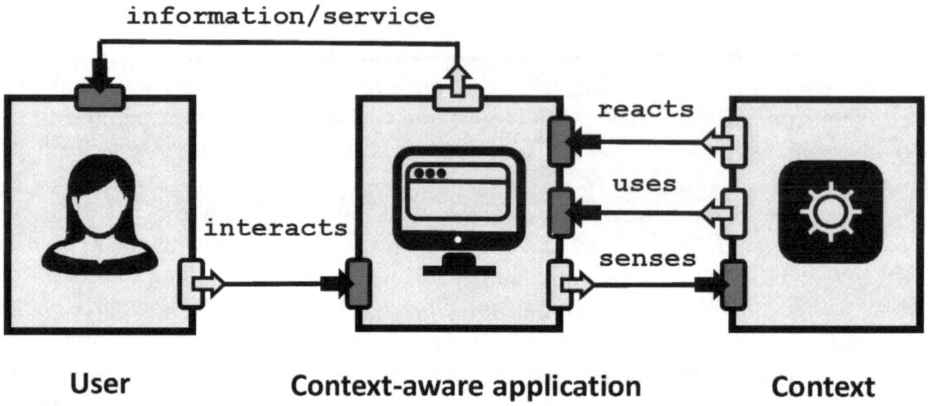

Fig. 2. Scheme of a context-aware application

However, sometimes the process of making decisions about what information should be presented to the user, and taking into account a certain context, is still performed with mayor human mediations and at design time [3]. Therefore, new approaches that tackle these issues and facilitate the decision-making process are required in the area of context-aware applications.

An approach to use to tackle these issues identified above is the *reappraisal of weights in decision-making of self-adaptation* [17,18], which is explained in the next subsection.

3.2 The Reappraisal of Weights in Decision-Making of Self-Adaptation During Runtime

The goal of the dynamic reappraisal of weights in decision-making of self-adaptation (ARRoW) [17,18] is to monitor, at runtime, the satisfaction level of a set of non-functional requirements (NFR) to update the weights or preferences of the choices during runtime accordingly. If the satisfaction level of the NFR is not in the desired range due to unsuitable preferences, ARRoW is able to improve the decision-making of the system and its behaviour by reappraising and updating incongruous initial weights of NFR to therefore, match the new found conditions and contexts.

Upper and lower bounds for NFRs. On the basis of information provided by the system's experts, at the beginning of the application of ARRoW, upper and lower bounds of the satisfaction level for each NFR are identified (See Table 1).

The upper and lower bounds previously identified, allow the classification of the satisfaction level for each NFR into three categories: *poor*, *suitable*, and *optimal*. The satisfaction level for each NFR is monitored at runtime. Based on its monitored values, how important the NFR should be is affected and updated

Table 1. Categories for the satisfaction of NFRs

NFR Ranges of Satisfaction (%)	[0%, lower bound%]	[lower bound%, upper bound%]	[upper bound%, 100%]
Categories of Monitored Values	Poor	Suitable	Optimal

in the decision-making objective functions. The idea is to improve the levels of satisfaction of the NFRs with *poor* values with respect to NFRs that present *suitable* values and, also improve the levels of satisfaction of the NFRs with *suitable* values with respect to NFRs with *optimal* values.

ARRoW process. *ARRoW* is applied over different time slices during the execution of the system. The approach aims to improve the decision-making in SASs by reappraising and updating unsuitable weights of NFRs in a Temporal Model for Decision Making (TMDM), using, for example, Dynamic Decision Networks (DDN) [5] while finding new contexts at runtime. Fig. 3 presents a diagram that overviews the *ARRoW* process. The steps involved are as follows:

- Step 1: Detecting NFRs within poor category. This step is performed at runtime to detect if at least one NFR has a satisfaction value labeled within the poor category (i.e., probability $P(NFR = True)$). If so, the following step will follow.
- Step 2: Balancing weights of NFRs. The comparison and prioritization of the NFRs is performed by using Primitive Cognitive Network Process (P-CNP) and a given scale of comparison [17,18]. Higher importance is assigned to NFRs with monitored values of satisfaction within the *poor* category. For instance, if the monitored values of satisfaction for two NFRs are NFR1 within the *suitable* category and NFR2 within the *poor* category, the results will show that NFR2 is more important than NFR1 given their current runtime satisfaction values.

3.3 Adapting ARRoW to Context-Aware Applications

The decision-making in the case of context-aware applications, and specifically the case of the LMS, can be framed as a problem to be tackled by ARRoW while reassessing the weights and preferences (i.e. relevances) of choices during the decision-making for self-adaptive systems. Accordingly, the following mapping has been defined between the concepts used in the *reappraisal of weights in decision-making of self-adaptation* (1) and the case study in *context-aware applications* (2).

- The *non-functional requirements* in (1) have been mapped to *student's skills* in (2). The current satisfaction level (specified as probability values) for each

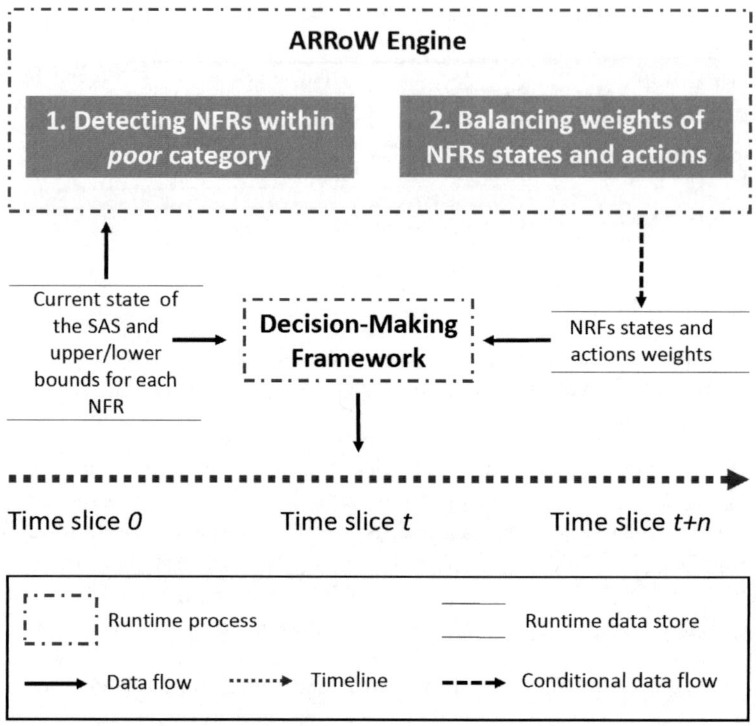

Fig. 3. ARRoW process at runtime

student's skill will be monitored and involved in the decision-making process of the system.

- The *environment* in (1) corresponds to the *context information* in (2). The *context information* is represented by the evaluations and assessments performed to the students in order to measure the acquired skills.
- The *time slices* in (1) are mapped to an *activity execution and evaluation* in (2). The execution and evaluation of these activities may have different temporal frequencies (*e.g.*, daily or weekly). Time slices correspond to days and weeks.
- The *monitored values* in (1) corresponds to the *grade* or marks obtained by the student with respect to each acquired skill. The obtained *grade* has an impact on the current satisfaction level of the *student's skill.*

4 Experiments and Preliminary Results

This section details the initial experiment and discuses the preliminary results.

4.1 Experiments

Based on the case study presented in Section 2, in the experiment we have defined three elements of the context which need to be monitored: *critical thinking* (CT), *problem solving* (PS), and *assertive communication* (AC). These context elements corresponds to three student's skills (i.e. NFR).

The experiment also defines three activities to improve the above mentioned skills. These activities are *essays, presentations*, and *simulations*. The experts who elaborated the case study have determined that each activity helps to increase a specific skill. For example, the preparation of an essay helps to strengthen critical thinking, a presentation may be developed to improve assertive communication, and the elaboration of simulations helps to increase problem solving skills.

The skills are monitored by the application by taking into account the results obtained when the teacher evaluates each activity developed by the student.

Table 2. Ranges of satisfaction levels for each skill in the ASHYI-EDU case study

Skill	**Ranges of satisfaction levels**		
	Basic	**Intermediate**	**Advanced**
CT	[0%, 40%]	[41%, 70%]	[71%, 100%]
PS	[0%, 30%]	[31%, 75%]	[76%, 100%]
AC	[0%, 20%]	[21%, 70%]	[71%, 100%]

For each skill, several ranges of satisfaction has been defined. These ranges are detailed in Table 2. The goal of defining the satisfaction ranges is that when a student is evaluated and his/her grade is in a range that has been defined as *basic*, the application would evaluate the possibilities and benefits of modifying its own behaviour by suggesting a different activity to help the student improving their own performance in that particular skill. Thus, the application would monitor the context and adjust the relevance of the information to be provided accodingly.

As the ARRoW approach is based on temporal models such as Dynamic Decision Networks [4,5] and POMDPs [11], we need to stablish, at design time, the (i) transition model, the (ii) observation model, and the (iii) initial decision maker preferences (weights) for each combination among state nodes (skills) and decision nodes (activities).

The transition model (i), summarized in Table 3, indicates the probability of getting a suitable or unsuitable degree in an skill given that in the previous time slice the student had developed that skill, and in the current time slice the student is developing a specific activity. For example, in the first row, the probability or getting a suitable degree in the *critical thinking* skill, developing the *essay* activity, and having a suitable degree in the same skill in the previous time slice is 60%. As opposite, the probability or getting a suitable degree in the critical *thinking skill*, developing the *essay* activity, but having a unsuitable degree in the same skill in the previous time slice is 50%.

Table 3. Transition Model

Skill	Activity	Probability
CT	P(CT t = true | ESS, CT t-1 = true)	0,6
	P(CT t = true | ESS, CT t-1 = false)	0,5
	P(CT t = true | SIM, CT t-1 = true)	0,4
	P(CT t = true | SIM, CT t-1 = false)	0,3
	P(CT t = true | PRE, CT t-1 = true)	0,5
	P(CT t = true | PRE, CT t-1 = false)	0,4
AC	P(AC t = true | ESS, AC t-1 = true)	0,5
	P(AC t = true | ESS, AC t-1 = false)	0,4
	P(AC t = true | SIM, AC t-1 = true)	0,4
	P(AC t = true | SIM, AC t-1 = false)	0,3
	P(AC t = true | PRE, AC t-1 = true)	0,6
	P(AC t = true | PRE, AC t-1 = false)	0,5
PS	P(PS t = true | ESS, PS t-1 = true)	0,4
	P(PS t = true | ESS, PS t-1 = false)	0,3
	P(PS t = true | SIM, PS t-1 = true)	0,6
	P(PS t = true | SIM, PS t-1 = false)	0,5
	P(PS t = true | PRE, PS t-1 = true)	0,5
	P(PS t = true | PRE, PS t-1 = false)	0,4

The observation model (ii), summarized in Table 4, indicates the probability of getting a grade in a specific range given that in the previous time slice the student had developed that skill, and in the current time slice the student is developing a specific activity. For example, in the first row, the probability or getting a grade less than r (40% according to the ranges defined in Table 2) in the *critical thinking* skill, developing the *essay* activity, and having a suitable degree in the same skill in the previous time slice is 20%. Notice that due to space limitations the probabilities for other skills (*problem solving* and *assertive communication*) are not included in this paper.

The set of the initial weights for the DDN (iii) are given in Table 5. These initial weights are updated at runtime when the applications detects changes in the context. In our case study, these changes correspond to a low grade (located in the basic range) obtained by the student.

4.2 Preliminary Results

In the initial scenario, the student has interacted with the application and has developed the suggested activities. At the end of the activity, the evaluation indicates that his/her grade for the *problem solving* skill is located in the basic range. This means that for the next iteration, the application should suggest an activity that helps strengthen that skill.

Table 4. Observation Model

Skill	Activity	Probability
CT	P(var < r | CT = true, ESS)	0,2
	P(var in[r,s] > | CT = true, ESS)	0,6
	P(var >= s | CT = true, ESS)	0,2
	P(var < r | CT = false, ESS)	0,25
	P(var in[r,s] > | CT = false, ESS)	0,55
	P(var >= s | CT = false, ESS)	0,2
	P(var < r | CT = true, SIM)	0,3
	P(var in[r,s] > | CT = true, SIM)	0,5
	P(var >= s | CT = true, SIM)	0,2
	P(var < r | CT = false, SIM)	0,35
	P(var in[r,s] > | CT = false, SIM)	0,45
	P(var >= s | CT = false, SIM)	0,2
	P(var < r | CT = true, PRE)	0,25
	P(var in[r,s] > | CT = true, PRE)	0,55
	P(var >= s | CT = true, PRE)	0,2
	P(var < r | CT = false, PRE)	0,3
	P(var in[r,s] > | CT = false, PRE)	0,5
	P(var >= s | CT = false, PRE)	0,2

Table 5. Utility node initial weights in the ASHYI case study. Key: Ai=alternative i; CT=critical thinking; PS problem solving; AC=assertive communication; ESS=essay; SIM=simulation; PRE=presentation

Ai	Activity	CT	PS	AC	Weight	Ai	Activity	CT	PS	AC	Weight
A1	SIM	T	T	T	0,0519	A13	ESS	F	T	T	0,0421
A2	SIM	T	T	F	0,0467	A14	ESS	F	T	F	0,0369
A3	SIM	T	F	T	0,0467	A15	ESS	F	F	T	0,0369
A4	SIM	T	F	F	0,0414	A16	ESS	F	F	F	0,0317
A5	SIM	F	T	T	0,0414	A17	PRE	T	T	T	0,0517
A6	SIM	F	T	F	0,0362	A18	PRE	T	T	F	0,0468
A7	SIM	F	F	T	0,0362	A19	PRE	T	F	T	0,0467
A8	SIM	F	F	F	0,0310	A20	PRE	T	F	F	0,0413
A9	ESS	T	T	T	0,0525	A21	PRE	F	T	T	0,0414
A10	ESS	T	T	F	0,0473	A22	PRE	F	T	F	0,0363
A11	ESS	T	F	T	0,0473	A23	PRE	F	F	T	0,0362
A12	ESS	T	F	F	0,0421	A24	PRE	F	F	F	0,0311

Following the process proposed by ARRoW, the first step is to balance the initial weights depicted in Table 5.

The new values (detailed in Table 6) suggest that in the next iteration the student must perform not the *essay* (suggested by the initial weights in Table 5) but the *simulation* activity, which according to what the experts have established, is the activity that helps to develop the *critical thinking* skill.

Table 6. Adjusted weights in the ASHYI case study. Key: Ai=alternative i; CT=critical thinking; PS problem solving; AC=assertive communication; ESS=essay; SIM=simulation; PRE=presentation

Ai	Activity	CT	PS	AC	Weight	Ai	Activity	CT	PS	AC	Weight
A1	SIM	T	T	T	0,0530	A13	ESS	F	T	T	0,0421
A2	SIM	T	T	F	0,0477	A14	ESS	F	T	F	0,0369
A3	SIM	T	F	T	0,0477	A15	ESS	F	F	T	0,0369
A4	SIM	T	F	F	0,0425	A16	ESS	F	F	F	0,0317
A5	SIM	F	T	T	0,0425	A17	PRE	T	T	T	0,0506
A6	SIM	F	T	F	0,0373	A18	PRE	T	T	F	0,0458
A7	SIM	F	F	T	0,0373	A19	PRE	T	F	T	0,0456
A8	SIM	F	F	F	0,0321	A20	PRE	T	F	F	0,0402
A9	ESS	T	T	T	0,0525	A21	PRE	F	T	T	0,0404
A10	ESS	T	T	F	0,0473	A22	PRE	F	T	F	0,0353
A11	ESS	T	F	T	0,0473	A23	PRE	F	F	T	0,0352
A12	ESS	T	F	F	0,0421	A24	PRE	F	F	F	0,0301

From the results obtained in this initial experiment it is observed that the application has the skill to adjust the relevance of an activity when there is evidence that the student has not achieved the required skill. These decisions, which initially had to be taken by the teacher who conducts the virtual course, is now taken automously by the application. Several similar experiments have been performed with similar results.

Using the novel case study with ARRoW has brought up new insights about the broader kind of applications that can be tackled with the ARRoW approach. For instance, different from the usual self-adaptive systems [7] that use very short time-slices measured in seconds with strict time-related constrains, LMS applications offer the opportunity to use longer time-slices that can be measured in days and weeks. This allows the use of ARRoW with different constrains allowing us to relax constrains associated with the time-based constrains and to take longer time while performing the approximations. Also, applications such as LMS, provide new context for the capabilities of Bayesian learning using with decision-making infrastructure that support ARRoW [4,21,11]. Accordingly, we are studying the use of Bayesian learning to make conclusions about the learning skills of students, to therefore, for example, define singular profiles that describe the generic learning skills of students based on their previous performance using our approach. In other words, using Bayesian learning the LMS system can learn and therefore make conclusions about the way students could perform in the future, including other modules based on the probability values associated. This is an exciting research line that we did not foresee before.

5 Related Work

Although the area of decision making for context aware applications has several related initiatives, most of the existing approaches predefine the decision making support at design time, which prohibits any dynamic modification [10], [12].

Authors in [24] have proposed a set of predefined workflows that are instantiated in response to runtime context changes. When a change occurs, the most suitable workflow is selected, as in our case, using based on a Markov Decision Process. A similar situation occurs in the Apto [13] approach, in which an adaptation fragment is selected and applied to the process to cope with the context situation. However, in both approaches describe previously the adaptation are specified at design time and the services provided cannot be changed at runtime. Further, in [24], authors use off-line Markov Decision Process, in our case we are using as well on-line Markov Decision Process [21] what certainly facilitates the dynamic assessment of relevances and solve scalability issues. Off-line algorithms are not scalable while on-line algorithms provide approximations that tackle scalability issues.

Other proposals such as [8] only analyse the context and model the uncertainty at the requirements and design phases. The main issue of these proposals is that the models created at design time do not evolve at runtime. In [20], runtime changes are specified directly into the source code of the applications while in [15] the runtime changes are specified textually as adaptation actions. As consequence, specifying the runtime changes in that way is a complex, time consuming and error prone activity.

6 Conclusions and Future Work

This paper has explored the correlation between automatic runtime re-appraisal and update of relevances and context aware applications. In particular, we have used the ARRoW approach for improving the decision making process for a case study in the area virtual education, in which the information provided to students need to be adapted according to changes in the context. In this initial iteration the preliminary results obtained are positive and encouraging.

Part of the future work is to integrate the decision in a specific framework for context-aware software. In that context, we are already making progress to be able to use ARRoW as part of the MiDAS framework [6], which is a model-driven approach aimed to ease the specification and development of context-aware applications. The goal of the integration is to use the decision making in other context-oriented domains different from the educational domain.

Acknowledgements

This work has been partially supported by the *Pontificia Universidad Javeriana* through the research project MiDAS (code SIAP1774), by the *Departamento Administrativo de Ciencia, Tecnología e Innovación (Colciencias)* through a doctorate scholarship, and by the Systems Analytics Research Institute (SARI) at Aston University.

References

1. Ahmed Al-alshuhai and François Siewe. An extension of the use case diagram to model context-aware applications. In *SAI Intelligent Systems Conference (IntelliSys), 2015*, pages 884–888. IEEE, 2015.
2. Unai Alegre, Juan Carlos Augusto, and Tony Clark. Engineering context-aware systems and applications: a survey. *Journal of Systems and Software*, 117:55–83, 2016.
3. Germán H Alférez and Vicente Pelechano. Dynamic evolution of context-aware systems with models at runtime. In *MoDELS*, pages 70–86. Springer, 2012.
4. Nelly Bencomo and Amel Belaggoun. Supporting decision-making for self-adaptive systems: from goal models to dynamic decision networks. In *International Working Conference on Requirements Engineering: Foundation for Software Quality*, pages 221–236. Springer, 2013.
5. Nelly Bencomo, Amel Belaggoun, and Valérie Issarny. Dynamic decision networks for decision-making in self-adaptive systems: a case study. In *Proceedings of the 8th International Symposium on Software Engineering for Adaptive and Self-Managing Systems, SEAMS 2013, San Francisco, CA, USA, May 20-21, 2013*, pages 113–122, 2013.
6. Jose Bocanegra, Jaime Pavlich-Mariscal, and Angela Carrillo-Ramos. MiDAS: a model-driven approach for adaptive software. In *Proceedings of the 11th International Conference on Web Information Systems and Technologies - Volume 1: WEBIST*, pages 281–286. INSTICC, SciTePress, 2015.
7. Betty H. Cheng and et al. Software engineering for self-adaptive systems. chapter Software Engineering for Self-Adaptive Systems: A Research Roadmap, pages 1–26. Springer-Verlag, Berlin, Heidelberg, 2009.
8. Shang-Wen Cheng and David Garlan. Handling uncertainty in autonomic systems. *International Workshop on Living with Uncertainty*, 2007.
9. Anind K Dey, Gregory D Abowd, and Daniel Salber. A conceptual framework and a toolkit for supporting the rapid prototyping of context-aware applications. *Human-computer interaction*, 16(2):97–166, 2001.
10. Nicolas Ferry, Franck Chauvel, Hui Song, and Arnor Solberg. Towards meta-adaptation of dynamic adaptive systems with models@ runtime. In *Proceedings of the 5th International Conference on Model-Driven Engineering and Software Development, Port, Portugal, February 19-21, 2017*, 2017.
11. Luis Garcia and Nelly Bencomo. Re-storm: Mapping the decision-making problem and non-functional requirements trade-off to partially observable markov decision processes. In *Proceedings of the 8th International Symposium on Software Engineering for Adaptive and Self-Managing Systems, SEAMS*, 2018.
12. Mahmoud Hussein, Jun Han, Jian Yu, and Alan Colman. Enabling runtime evolution of context-aware adaptive services. In *Services Computing (SCC), 2013 IEEE International Conference on*, pages 248–255. IEEE, 2013.
13. Zakwan Jaroucheh, Xiaodong Liu, and Sally Smith. Apto: a mdd-based generic framework for context-aware deeply adaptive service-based processes. In *Web Services (ICWS), 2010 IEEE International Conference on*, pages 219–226. IEEE, 2010.
14. James H McMillan. *Classroom Assessment: Pearson New International Edition: Principles and Practice for Effective Standards-Based Instruction.* Pearson Higher Ed, 2013.
15. Peyman Oreizy, Nenad Medvidovic, and Richard N Taylor. Architecture-based runtime software evolution. In *Proceedings of the 20th international conference on Software engineering*, pages 177–186. IEEE Computer Society, 1998.

16. Ashish Pant. Distance learning: History, problems and solutions. *Advances in Computer Science and Information Technology (ACSIT)*, 1(2):65–70, 2014.
17. Luis Hernan Garcia Paucar and Nelly Bencomo. Arrow: Tool support for automatic runtime reappraisal of weights. In *Requirements Engineering Conference (RE), 2017 IEEE 25th International*, pages 458–461. IEEE, 2017.
18. Luis Hernan Garcia Paucar, Nelly Bencomo, and Kevin Kam Fung Yuen. Juggling preferences in a world of uncertainty. In *Requirements Engineering Conference (RE), 2017 IEEE 25th International*, pages 430–435. IEEE, 2017.
19. Jaime Pavlich-Mariscal, Yolima Uribe, Luisa Fernanda Barrera León, Nadia Alejandra Mejia-Molina, Angela Carrillo-Ramos, Alexandra Pomares Quimbaya, Monica Brijaldo, Martha Sabogal, Rosa Maria Vicari, and Hervé Martin. ASHYI-EDU: applying dynamic adaptive planning in a virtual learning environment. In *Proceedings of the 7th International Conference on Computer Supported Education - Volume 1*, CSEDU 2015, pages 52–63, Portugal, 2015. SCITEPRESS - Science and Technology Publications, Lda.
20. Mario Pukall, Christian Kästner, and Gunter Saake. Towards unanticipated runtime adaptation of java applications. In *Software Engineering Conference, 2008. APSEC'08. 15th Asia-Pacific*, pages 85–92. IEEE, 2008.
21. S Ross, J Pineau, S Paquet, and B Chaib-Draa. Online planning algorithms for pomdps. *J. Artificial Intelligence Research, 32(1)*, 2008.
22. Mazeiar Salehie and Ladan Tahvildari. Self-adaptive software: landscape and research challenges. *ACM TAAS*, 4(2):14, 2009.
23. Katrien Verbert, Nikos Manouselis, Xavier Ochoa, Martin Wolpers, Hendrik Drachsler, Ivana Bosnic, and Erik Duval. Context-aware recommender systems for learning: a survey and future challenges. *IEEE Transactions on Learning Technologies*, 5(4):318–335, 2012.
24. Hongbing Wang, Xuan Zhou, Xiang Zhou, Weihong Liu, Wenya Li, and Athman Bouguettaya. Adaptive service composition based on reinforcement learning. *Service-Oriented Computing*, pages 92–107, 2010.
25. Shu-Lin Wang and Chun-Yi Wu. Application of context-aware and personalized recommendation to implement an adaptive ubiquitous learning system. *Expert Systems with applications*, 38(9):10831–10838, 2011.

Ufahamu: Um Framework para Aplicações Móveis Android Conscientes de Contexto

Rafael Nascimento de Souza e Cleidson R. B. de Souza

Universidade Federal do Pará, Belém, Pará, Brasil – 66075-110
nascimento.rsouza@gmail.com
cleidson.desouza@acm.org

Abstract. This paper describes Ufahamu, a Java framework for Android that facilitates and simplifies the development of context-aware applications. This framework was built to address limitations of previous frameworks since it was built using the Context-Rule-Action approach. Ufahamu's approach and design are presented in details, as well as its implementation and an initial evaluations. Two evaluations were conducted, one through the development of an app using the proposed framework and another one comparing the proposed framework with 3 other frameworks from a code complexity point of view. These results suggest the Ufahamu framework does simplify the development of context-aware applications.

Keywords: Context-aware computing; ubiquitous computing; framework; Java; Context-Rule-Action.

1 Introdução

A chamada computação ubíqua não diz respeito apenas a computadores de vários formatos que podem ser embutidos em diferentes locais, mas a uma nova maneira de pensar sobre computadores no mundo; uma maneira que considera o ambiente natural no qual o usuário está inserido e permite que o computador "desapareça" no segundo plano e habilite o usuário a focar em novos objetivos [18].

Um campo da computação ubíqua que tem se destacado na última década é a Computação Consciente de Contexto [1]. Sistemas conscientes de contexto são capazes de adaptar suas operações ao ambiente (contexto) em que o usuário está inserido sem a intervenção explícita do mesmo, aumentando a usabilidade e a efetividade dessas operações ao considerar informações adicionais importantes [1]. Por exemplo, um aplicativo que reconhece que o usuário está dirigindo e, de alguma forma, muda a interface gráfica do mesmo para evitar distrações do usuário. Percebe-se, assim, que a Computação Consciente de Contexto é um dos principais meios para a criação de "computadores invisíveis" [13]. Para isso, a consciência de contexto deve ir além da simples modelagem, implementação e fornecimento de contexto; ela requer, fundamentalmente, o entendimento do ambiente e da situação dos usuários, ou seja, do contexto, e da utilização desta informação pelos computadores [13].

Desde o seu surgimento, a infraestrutura necessária para a computação consciente de contexto apresenta um acelerado passo de evolução: *smartphones*, *smartwatches*, *smartglasses*, entre outros dispositivos ubíquos, crescem cada vez mais em termos de capacidade, poder de processamento e recursos. Tal avanço incentivou o surgimento e a consolidação de muitas aplicações, API's e frameworks interessantes e relevantes para a área. Com isso, torna-se fundamental, continuar desenvolvendo estudos e aplicações e incentivar o surgimento de novas aplicações conscientes de contexto. Por exemplo, a API *Awareness* da Google [9] unificou as principais capacidades de sensoriamento já presentes nos dispositivos Android e otimizou o seu acesso para permitir o desenvolvimento de novas aplicações conscientes de contexto para estes dispositivos..

Dey e colegas [4] argumentam que um dos motivos para a construção de aplicações conscientes de contexto ser difícil é a falta de abstrações para que os engenheiros de software possam pensar no conceito de contexto. Diante disso, este trabalho apresenta uma nova abordagem que visa facilitar o desenvolvimento de tais aplicações. Ele visa auxiliar desenvolvedores de software a atingirem o objetivo fundamental da computação ubíqua: tornar os dispositivos computacionais invisíveis em meio às tarefas cotidianas do usuário. Isto será feito ao permitir que novos tipos de contexto sejam definidos e utilizados em dispositivos Android de maneira simples, a critério do desenvolvedor da aplicação consciente de contexto. Assim, este trabalho apresenta o framework Ufahamu[1] que permite a um desenvolvedor de aplicações móveis para Android definir contextos e ações baseadas em tais contextos utilizando um modelo de simples entendimento e utilização. Exemplos de contextos definidos pelo desenvolvedor incluem uma ligação perdida de um contato favorito, o momento de uma reunião de trabalho, o momento em que o usuário entra e sai de sua casa, entre outros. Além da descrição do framework Ufahamu, este trabalho também descreve a avaliação inicial do mesmo. Para isto, o framework foi utilizado para implementar uma aplicação sensível ao contexto com funcionalidades de um aplicativo relativamente conhecido: o Motorola Assist [11]. Este aplicativo permite a configuração de automações, ou regras, quando o usuário está em determinados contextos, como por exemplo, dirigindo ou em reunião. Os quatro contextos e regras existentes no Motorola Assist foram implementados no Ufahamu. A segunda avaliação comparou o Ufahumu com 3 outros frameworks para desenvolvimento de aplicações concientes de contexto do ponto de vista de complexidade de código, isto é, de quão complexo seria para desenvolvedores externos implementares aplicações usando o Ufahamu. Os resultados das duas avaliações sugerem que o framework Ufahamu é

[1]O vocábulo Ufahamu vem da língua africana suaíle, oficial em alguns países da África. O termo sugere a ideia de ciência, no sentido discutido por este trabalho, isto é, conhecimento, noção, percepção do contexto.

adequado para a construção de aplicações sensíveis ao contexto pois facilita o desenvolvimento destas.

O restante deste trabalho está organizado como segue. A seção 2 apresenta os conceitos fundamentais da área de Computação Consciente de Contexto. A seção 3 apresenta a metodologia adotada neste trabalho. A seção 4 descreve o framework Ufahamu, enquanto que a seção 5 apresenta alguns trabalhos relacionados relevantes que são utilizados em uma das validações aplicadas ao Ufahamu. A seção 6 apresenta duas avaliações iniciais conduzidas com este framework. Finalmente, a seção 7 conclui o artigo discutindo também algumas idéias para trabalhos futuros.

2 Computação Consciente de Contexto

Desde que nascemos, a nossa interação com o ambiente produz conhecimento que nos permite um comportamento inteligente com os dados que coletamos sensorialmente; a habilidade de predizer a reação que uma certa ação causará é um exemplo de tal comportamento [13]. Quando as pessoas interagem, elas podem usar informações implícitas do ambiente ao seu redor para enriquecer a comunicação entre elas. Infelizmente, essa habilidade de processar dados implícitos não é trivial para a interação de pessoas com máquinas. No modelo tradicional de interação humano-computador, usuários dispõem de mecanismos de comunicação – dispositivos de entrada e saída, como teclados, mouses, tela, entre outros – que não capacitam as máquinas a obter tudo aquilo que o contexto da interação pode oferecer [5]. Para modificar esse cenário, é necessário aumentar o acesso da máquina ao contexto em que o usuário está inserido, o que permitiria a disponibilização de serviços computacionais melhores e mais úteis [5]. Esta é a chamada Computação Consciente de Contexto ou Computação Sensível ao Contexto.

O termo Consciência de Contexto foi introduzido na literatura por Schilit e Theimer [12], que definiram Computação Consciente de Contexto como a habilidade de aplicações de computação móvel de descobrir e reagir a mudanças no ambiente em que estão inseridos. Dey e Abowd [5] analisaram as definições de computação consciente de contexto cunhadas até então e propuseram uma definição mais abrangente: "um sistema é consciente de contexto usa o contexto para fornecer informação e/ou serviços relevantes para o usuário, onde a relevância depende da tarefa do usuário". Por exemplo, um *smartphone* pode se autoconfigurar no modo silencioso ao saber que o usuário está entrando em uma reunião.

Dey, Abowd e Salber [4] identificaram três funções que uma aplicação consciente de contexto precisa implementar: (i) apresentação de informações e serviços, (ii) a execução automática de serviços e (iii) a etiquetagem. A apresentação se refere a funções que mostram informações de contexto para usuários ou usam contexto para propôr seleções de ações apropriadas ao usuário. A execução automática de serviços descreve funções que disparam um comando ou reconfiguram o sistema sem a intervenção do usuário de acordo apenas com mudanças de contexto. Finalmente, a etiquetagem ou anotação denota funções

– de crucial importância para aplicações conscientes de contexto – que coletam, marcam e organizam dados de sensores para serem processados e entendidos posteriormente.

Um aspecto fundamental da computação consciente de contexto é a frequente mudança do ambiente de execução da aplicação; à medida que o usuário se move, o conjunto de objetos com os quais a aplicação interage muda e, portanto, a localização é um fator essencial, ou ainda, a localização é considerada como um dos principais tipos de contextos sendo utilizada em diversas aplicações descritas na literatura [12, 14, 18].

3 Metodologia

A primeira etapa deste trabalho foi a condução de uma revisão da literatura para identificar trabalhos relacionados para embasamento teórico e também para efeito de comparação de resultados. Os trabalhos pesquisados foram obtidos a partir da literatura de computação consciente de contexto. De maneira particular, buscou-se trabalhos que discutissem frameworks para a área, os quais serão apresentados na seção 5.

Paralela à revisão da literatura, foi conduzida uma pesquisa sobre o que foi, por falta de um termo melhor, genericamente chamado de "tipos de contexto" que um *smartphone* é capaz de identificar com o seu conjunto de sensores. Por exemplo, com GPS, acelerômetro e giroscópio, um *smartphone* é capaz de acertar com alguma precisão a localização do usuário. Assim, esta localização é um tipo de contexto. Tal pesquisa considerou *os* sistemas operacionais Android e iOS. Então, passou-se a pesquisar sobre API's existentes para estes sistemas operacionais que disponibilizassem funcionalidades capazes de lidar com o maior número de "tipos de contexto" encontrados possível.

Após o estudo de API's, a API *Awareness* foi escolhida para ser estendida e aprimorada, de acordo com alguns critérios, tais como flexibilidade, suporte, manutenção, número de usuários do sistema operacional em que ela é suportada e código-fonte aberto. Então, uma *app* consciente de contexto inicial para Android foi implementada com o intuito de aprender a utilizar a API e permitir uma melhor definição da arquitetura proposta. A partir da implementação desta *app* inicial, o framework Ufahamu começou a ser definido para permitir o acréscimo de novos tipos de contexto à API *Awareness*, podendo ir desde um simples novo sensor até a junção de diversas aplicações que monitorem o contexto do usuário. Este framework é discutido em detalhes a seguir.

4 O Framework Ufahamu

4.1 Visão Geral

O framework Ufahamu foi idealizado como um modelo de Contexto-Regra-Ação: uma *Regra* é uma condição que monitora um ou mais *Contextos* e executa uma ou mais *Ações* quando todos os contextos forem verdadeiros. Este modelo é baseado no paradigma de programação *trigger-action*. Neste paradigma, o usuário especifica o comportamento do sistema como um evento (*trigger*) e a ação (*action*) correspondente a ser executada sempre que o evento ocorrer [16]. Tanto o evento quanto a ação podem conter parâmetros para customizar seu comportamento.

O website IFTTT – "*if this than that*" – é uma das primeiras consolidações do paradigma *trigger-action* e conta atualmente com milhões de usuários [10]. Ele permite que usuários escrevam algoritmos bem simples que conectam vários serviços, sites de mídia social e dispositivos físicos. Assim, por exemplo, quando um usuário atualiza sua foto de perfil do Facebook, para corresponder, o IFTTT atualiza a foto de perfil do Twitter imediatamente, se o usuário estiver utilizando tal regra.

4.2 Arquitetura

O framework Ufahamu foi escrito na linguagem de programação Java e foi projetado para sistemas Android. Ele encapsula a API *Awareness* da Google, disponibilizando sua funcionalidade de modo que um desenvolvedor interessado em escrever uma aplicação sensível ao contexto escreva o mínimo possível de linhas de código. Além disso, ele permite a criação de novos tipos de contexto, regras e ações. Estas funcionalidades não existem na API *Awareness*.

A Figura 1 mostra o diagrama de classes do framework (neste diagrama, as classes contêm apenas os seus principais métodos). As classes Context, Rule e Action são classes abstratas, assim como as classes AwarenessAPIContext e NewContext. A estrutura das classes Context, Rule e Action foi modelada a partir do modelo *trigger-action*. Neste caso, a classe Rule impõe uma regra entre o evento e a ação. A criação da classe Context traz a vantagem de abordar o problema exposto por Dey, Abowd e Salber [4], e discutido anteriormente, sobre a dificuldade de desenvolvedores em abstrair o conceito de contexto. O modelo definido pelo Ufahamu também é baseado nas funções que uma aplicação consciente de contexto deveria implementar discutidas na seção 2.

De modo particular, a classe Context foi projetada para encapsular a API *Awareness* e ao mesmo tempo estendê-la. Por isso a necessidade das classes AwarenessAPIContext e NewContext. Um objeto AwarenessAPIContext deve necessariamente utilizar um dos tipos de contexto pré-definidos pela API *Awareness*. Por outro lado, um objeto NewContext deve necessariamente implementar um novo tipo de contexto.

A classe Context pode possuir um conjunto de objetos independentes da classe Rule. A classe Rule possui uma lista de objetos Context e uma lista de objetos Action de modo que todos estão relacionados, isto é, apenas quando todos os objetos Context forem verificados como acontecendo, os objetos Action serão executados. A classe Action não possui atributos, mas recebe o objeto Rule como parâmetro do seu único método. ContextState, por sua vez, é usado apenas como valor para o estado do contexto, por isto ContextState é um Enum Java.

É importante ressaltar que o padrão de projetos Observer [8] é implementado no contexto da relação entre as classes Rule e Context, assim, quando um objeto (Rule ou Context) muda de estado, todos os seus dependentes (Rule ou Context) são notificados e atualizados automaticamente.

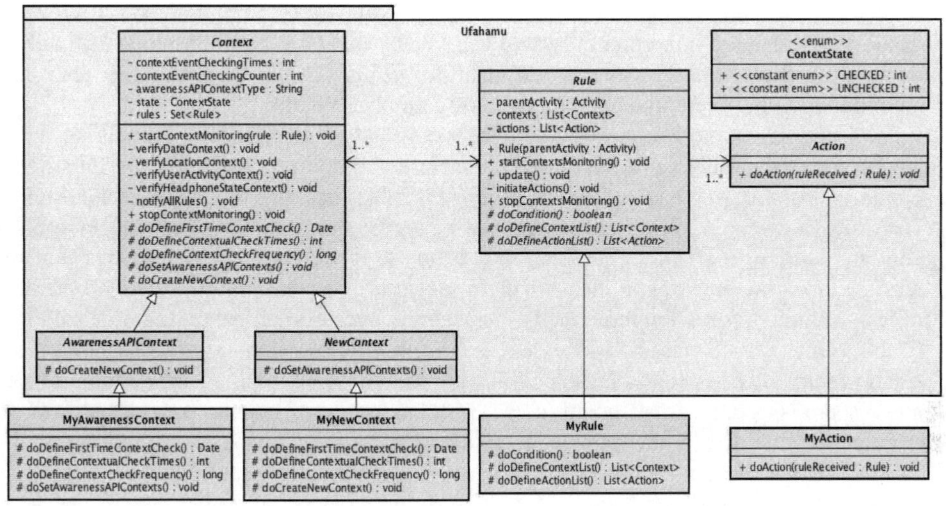

Figura 1. Diagrama de classes do framework Ufahamu.

4.3 Utilização do framework

O framework pode ser usado de duas maneiras: na primeira, o foco está na criação de novos tipos de contextos; na segunda, o foco está na criação de nova ações para contextos existentes. Assim, no primeiro modo, o desenvolvedor deve implementar uma classe que estenda AwarenessAPIContext ou NewContext. Isto é, duas opções existem: (1) se o desenvolvedor deseja usar um tipo de contexto já existente dentre os pré-definidos pela API *Awareness* – data/hora, localização, atividade do usuário ou estado do *headphone* –, ou (2) se deseja definir um novo tipo de contexto. Para a opção (1), o desenvolvedor deve estender a classe AwarenessAPIContext. Neste caso, ele terá que implementar quatro métodos abstratos: *doDefineFirstTimeContextCheck*, que definirá a primeira vez que o contexto deve ser verificado – uma data e uma hora específicas ou, se indefinido, imediatamente –; *doDefineContextualCheckTimes*, que definirá quantas vezes o contexto deve ser verificado – se for definido 0, o contexto é verificado infinitamente, se for definido um número maior que 0, este será o número exato de vezes da verificação –; *doDefineContextCheckFrequency*, que definirá a frequência com que o contexto deve ser verificado – em milissegundos, de uma em uma hora, de um em um dia, etc –; e *doSetAwarenessAPIContexts*, que deve definir um dos contextos pré-determinados na API *Awareness* já discutidos. Por outro lado, para o caso (2), o desenvolvedor deve estender uma classe a partir da classe NewContext e implementar também quatro métodos abstratos: os três primeiros já mencionados – *doDefineFirstTimeContextCheck*, *doDefineContextualCheckTimes*, *doDefineContextCheckFrequency* – e o método *doCreateNewContext*, o qual se dedicará à lógica do novo contexto requerido.

No segundo modo, para a criação de ações diferentes para contextos existentes, o desenvolvedor deve implementar uma classe que estenda a classe Action. Esta subclasse deve implementar apenas um método abstrato: *doAction*, que executa uma ação quando chamado por um objeto instância da subclasse da classe Rule.

Em ambos os modos, o desenvolvedor deve também criar uma subclasse de Rule. Neste caso, a subclasse deve implementar três métodos: *doCondition*, que define a condição para que todas as ações sejam tomadas quando todos os contextos forem verificados; *doDefineContextList*, que define os contextos aos quais aquela regra está condicionada; e *doDefineActionList*, que define as ações que serão tomadas por aquela regra. Em outras palavras, a classe Rule é a classe que conecta um objeto Context a um objeto Action. Após a implementação das classes necessárias, basta que o desenvolvedor chame o método *startContextsMonitoring* em um objeto instância de Rule para (i) iniciar o monitoramento dos contextos especificados nos objetos Context associados a esta regra através dos sensores do dispositivo, e (ii) executar as Actions associadas a esta regra, quando os contextos forem verificados como acontecendo.

Na Figura 1, tais classes concretas estão representadas, respectivamente, por MyAwarenessContext, MyNewContext, MyAction e MyRule.

Ao criar um novo contexto pela implementação do método *doCreateNewContext*, o desenvolvedor deve definir duas condições mutuamente exclusivas: uma em que o contexto é verificado como "acontecendo" e outra em que ele é verificado como "não acontecendo". Assim, ao iniciar o monitoramento, a seguinte lógica será seguida:

1. Quando o contexto for verificado como "acontecendo", o código implementado deve definir o estado do contexto como *CHECKED.*
2. No momento em que o estado do contexto é definido como *CHECKED* e se o estado anterior foi *UNCHECKED*, o contexto notifica todas as regras ligadas a ele – um contexto pode ter uma ou mais regras, como mostra a Figura 1.
3. Quando uma regra recebe a notificação de um de seus contextos, ela deve verificar se todos os seus contextos definidos estão no estado *CHECKED.* Se estão, todas as suas ações definidas são executadas. Caso contrário, a regra não faz nada e continua esperando o contato de um contexto.
4. Quando o contexto for verificado como "não acontecendo", o código implementado deve definir o estado do contexto como *UNCHECKED.*

Mais especificamente, quando um contexto é iniciado, uma *thread* é criada para executar o código definido no método *doSetAwarenessAPIContext* ou no método *doCreateNewContext*. Essa *thread* executará um dos dois métodos periodicamente com a frequência definida pelo desenvolvedor no método *doDefineContextCheckFrequency*. Além disso, em *doDefineFirstTimeContextCheck,* o desenvolvedor pode definir a primeira vez que a *thread* deve começar a verificar o contexto e, em *doDefineContextualCheckTimes*, quantas vezes ela deve fazer tal verificação, como já mencionado. As decisões de projeto de limitar o número e a frequência de verificações da *thread* se deram para que o desenvolvedor otimize o consumo de recursos – como bateria – do dispositivo Android.

5 Trabalhos Relacionados

A seguir são apresentados trabalhos relevantes da literatura que também apresentam uma abordagem para a otimização da implementação de funcionalidades de consciência de contexto. Em todos os trabalhos é feita uma comparação do mesmo com o Ufahamu.

Dey, Abowd e Salber [4] são os primeiros autores a apresentarem algum mecanismo de auxilio ao desenvolvimento de aplicações sensíveis ao contexto. Eles apresentaram o *Context Toolkit*, um framework para facilitar o desenvolvimento de aplicações conscientes de contexto. Este framework contém uma combinação de características e abstrações para dar suporte a desenvolvedores de aplicações conscientes de contexto. As três abstrações principais são: *widget* de contexto (para recuperar dados de sensores), interpretador de contexto (para transformar dados brutos de sensores em informação de contexto usando diferentes técnicas) e agregador de contexto.

É importante ressaltar que o trabalho de Dey, Abowd e Salber está focado no conceito de contexto em seu sentido mais amplo não se limitando a aplicações de *smartphones*. O Ufahamu, por outro lado, utiliza os sensores embutidos de dispositivos Android, especialmente *smartphones*. Portanto, ele não dá suporte a algumas das características apresentadas por Dey, Abowd e Salber [4], como comunicação distribuída e armazenamento de histórico de contexto.

Bardram [2] discute o framework Java JCAF cujo propósito é ter um conjunto robusto e simples de interfaces a serem estendidas por desenvolvedores para criar aplicações conscientes de contexto. O JCAF possui três aspectos característicos: (i) uma infraestrutura distribuída e orientada a serviço baseada na ideia de disponibilizar aquisição e gerenciamento de contexto em uma rede; (ii) uma arquitetura segura, de propósito geral, robusta, modificável em tempo real e baseada em eventos; e (iii) um modelo de programação genérico e extensível para o desenvolvimento de aplicações conscientes de contexto. Enquanto o JCAF é um framework que suporta aplicações conscientes de contexto em qualquer escopo, o Ufahamu foi desenvolvido para dispositivos Android.

Van Wissen e colegas [17] discutem os requisitos de um framework de contexto para um *smartphone* a fim de facilitar a programação de aplicações conscientes de contexto e reduzir o uso ineficiente de recursos. Além disso, é apresentado o ContextDroid, um framework que preenche todos os requisitos definidos pelo trabalho. Estes autores definem o conceito de *Entidade de Contexto*, como uma coleção de informações relacionadas. Por exemplo, a localização atual do usuário, expressa em latitude, longitude e altitude é uma entidade de contexto. Para usar isso, é necessário usar condições de contextos cujas propriedades e detalhes adicionam complexidade ao trabalho do desenvolvedor de aplicações. Diferente do ContextDroid, a utilização do Ufahamu requer apenas que o programador se adeque à estrutura Regra-Contexto-Ação.

Carlson e Schrader [3] introduzem o Dynamix, um framework que permite que capacidades avançadas de sensoriamento de contexto sejam implantadas dinamicamente em dispositivos móveis Android como *plug-ins*. O framework é executado como um serviço em *background*, usando o próprio dispositivo móvel como uma plataforma de sensoriamento, processamento e comunicação de informações de contexto. Isto é, aplicações Dynamix são aplicações Android que incorporam funcionalidades de modelagem de contexto provenientes do serviço Dynamix. Dynamix disponibiliza suporte para *plug-ins* de contexto externos que podem ser manualmente instalados no serviço Dynamix ou implantados automaticamente em *background*. Em relação ao Ufahamu, o Dynamix é um framework mais robusto por incluir uma camada de segurança e possibilitar o acesso a repositórios externos de *plug-ins*.

Doukas e Antonelli [6] apresentam o COMPOSE, um framework que habilita o desenvolvimento de consciência de contexto ao disponibilizar algumas ferramentas. Tais ferramentas são: para coleta de informações contextuais em dispositivos inteligentes; para comunicação com recursos externos à aplicação; para hospedar dados e processamento; e um *marketplace* aberto e escalável onde não apenas aplicações mas também serviços podem ser compartilhados e negociados. Ao contrário do COMPOSE que disponibiliza diversas ferramentas, o Ufahamu consiste apenas de um único e simples framework integrado utilizado pelo desenvolvedor em código-fonte para otimizar funcionalidades de consciência de contexto.

Elmalaki, Wanner e Srivastava [7] apresentam o CAreDroid, um framework Android que torna o desenvolvimento de aplicações conscientes de contexto mais fácil e eficiente modularizando funcionalidades, mapeamento e monitoramento e integrando adaptação ao contexto em tempo de execução. O framework é dividido em três elementos principais: (i) um conjunto de métodos polimorfos, (ii) um sistema de monitoramento de contexto e (iii) um mecanismo de adaptação que muda diferentes métodos baseado no monitoramento do contexto. Um arquivo de configuração deve ser criado pelo desenvolvedor com o preenchimento de algumas tags em formato XML. Neste arquivo, o desenvolvedor define regras para cada método, como por exemplo, se a conectividade WiFi está ligada. O framework possui um módulo que continuamente obtém informações de contexto. Ainda, para escolher a implementação polimórfica adequada ao contexto atual, CAreDroid usa um mecanismo de adaptação baseado-no no arquivo de configuração XML. Em comparação ao Ufahamu, o CAreDroid é muito mais complexo por influenciar até mesmo o processo de compilação do código. E, embora os dois compartilhem o mesmo objetivo – simplificar o trabalho do desenvolvedor –, as duas opções são bem distintas, no que tange a abordagem. O CAreDroid apresenta uma abordagem que requer que o programador crie um arquivo XML, além do código-fonte. O Ufahamu, por sua vez, apresenta uma estrutura simples a ser implementada no próprio código-fonte.

Em 2016, a empresa Google publicou sua plataforma especializada em contexto: a API *Awareness* [9]. Segundo a Google, a API *Awareness* é uma plataforma de sensoriamento unificada e otimizada que habilita aplicações que rodam em Android a "tomarem consciência" de múltiplos aspectos do contexto do usuário, consumindo recursos de hardware de maneira ótima [15].

Tabela 1. Apresenta a comparação dos pontos fortes dos trabalhos discutidos nesta seção com o Ufahamu.

TRABALHOS RELACIONADOS	UFAHAMU
As três abstrações principais do *Context Toolkit* são: *widget* de contexto, interpretador de contexto e agregador de contexto. [4]	O Ufahamu utiliza os sensores embutidos de dispositivos Android, especialmente *smartphones*.
O framework Java JCAF [2] suporta aplicações conscientes de contexto em qualquer escopo.	O Ufahamu dá suporte apenas no escopo de dispositivos Android.
O ContextDroid [17] utiliza o conceito de *Entidade de Contexto*, que é uma coleção de informações relacionadas. Para a utilização desta entidade, é necessário usar condições de contextos que adicionam complexidade ao trabalho do desenvolvedor de aplicações.	A utilização do Ufahamu requer apenas que o programador se adeque à estrutura Regra-Contexto-Ação, simplificando o seu trabalho.
O Dynamix [3] permite que capacidades avançadas de sensoriamento de contexto sejam implantadas dinamicamente em dispositivos móveis Android como *plug-ins*. O framework é executado como um serviço em *background*.	Em relação ao Ufahamu, o Dynamix é um framework mais robusto por incluir uma camada de segurança e possibilitar o acesso a repositórios externos de *plug-ins*.
O COMPOSE [6] é um framework que habilita o desenvolvimento de consciência de contexto ao disponibilizar algumas ferramentas, como: coleta de informações contextuais em dispositivos inteligentes; comunicação com recursos externos à aplicação; e hospedagem de dados e processamento.	Ao contrário do COMPOSE que disponibiliza diversas ferramentas, o Ufahamu consiste apenas de um único e simples framework integrado utilizado pelo desenvolvedor em código-fonte para otimizar funcionalidades de consciência de contexto.
O CAreDroid [7] é um framework Android que modulariza funcionalidade, mapeamento e monitoramento e integra adaptação ao contexto em tempo de execução.	Em comparação ao Ufahamu, o CAreDroid é muito mais complexo internamente pois requer que o programador crie um arquivo XML, além do código. O Ufahamu apresenta uma estrutura a ser implementada apenas como código-fonte.

6 Resultados Iniciais

6.1 Validação via programação

Uma validação inicial do framework foi conduzida através da implementação dos "modos" de trabalho que existem no aplicativo Motorola Assist. Este aplicativo automatiza tarefas do *smartphone* usando o modelo *trigger-action* também utilizado no IFTTT [11]. Quatro funcionalidades foram implementadas: o modo *Sleeping*, que silencia o telefone em um intervalo de tempo definido pelo usuário e mostra ligações apenas de favoritos ou de quem ligou mais de uma vez em um intervalo de tempo; o modo *Driving*, que anuncia em voz alta quem está ligando, quem enviou mensagem de texto e a mensagem recebida, se o usuário estiver dirigindo; o modo *Home*, que anuncia em voz alta quem está ligando, quem enviou mensagem de texto e a mensagem recebida, se o usuário estiver na sua casa; e, finalmente, o modo *Meeting*, que silencia o telefone e envia respostas automáticas por mensagem de texto para ligações perdidas de favoritos, se o usuário estiver em reunião.

Para a implementação das funcionalidades do Motorola Assist, nove regras, nove contextos e dez ações diferentes foram implementados. Ressalta-se a reutilização de um mesmo objeto Contexto (por exemplo, Localização) em várias regras diferentes. Uma interface Android para o usuário configurar as regras também foi desenvolvida. A implementação total consistiu de: 339 linhas de código Java de classes que estenderam a classe Rule; 517 linhas de código Java de classes que estenderam Context; e 328 linhas de código Java de classes que estenderam Action. Ou seja, um pequeno número de linhas de código foi necessário para implementar quatro regras de contexto diferentes.

Em trabalhos futuros, além de coletar a métrica de número de linhas de código, pretende-se também coletar métricas sobre a complexidade e o tempo necessários para o desenvolvimento da aplicação. É importante ressaltar que esta validação foi realizada pelo mesmo desenvolvedor do framework Ufahamu. Esta constitui uma limitação desta validação. Assim, uma segunda validação, descrita na próxima seção, foi conduzida.

6.2 Validação via ferramenta Metrix

A segunda validação foi conduzida utilizando a ferramenta Metrix [19], uma ferramenta que, a partir do arquivo compilado de uma API qualquer, analisa esta API e calcula a complexidade da mesma. Mais especificamente, uma medida de complexidade para cada método da API é calculada e, baseado nessa informação, a complexidade da classe, do pacote e da API como um todo são derivadas.

Na Metrix, as medidas de complexidade são apresentadas em 3 possíveis visualizações. Neste trabalho a visualização TreeMap foi escolhida. Esta visualização mostra as classes como retângulos cujo tamanho e cor são proporcionais à complexidade da classe, calculada pela própria ferramenta. As cores variam dentro de dez intervalos de verde claro a vermelho, o que diferencia classes menos complexas e mais complexas, respectivamente, de acordo com a legenda apresentada pela ferramenta. O usuário da

Metrix, ao analisar uma API, pode escolher algumas métricas de análise de código disponibilizadas. A métrica utilizada para este trabalho foi apenas a métrica Tamanho da Interface [19].

Uma comparação do Ufahamu com alguns dos trabalhos relacionados apresentados na seção 2.2 foi feita na Metrix, mostrando resultados satisfatórios. A Figura 2 apresenta a visualização em TreeMap de cada uma das seguintes API's, nesta ordem, da esquerda para a direita, de cima para baixo: ContextToolkit, JCAF, Dynamix e Ufahamu. As API's da seção de trabalhos relacionados ContextDroid, COMPOSE e CAreDroid não entraram na análise uma vez que seus códigos-fonte não foram encontrados disponíveis na Internet.

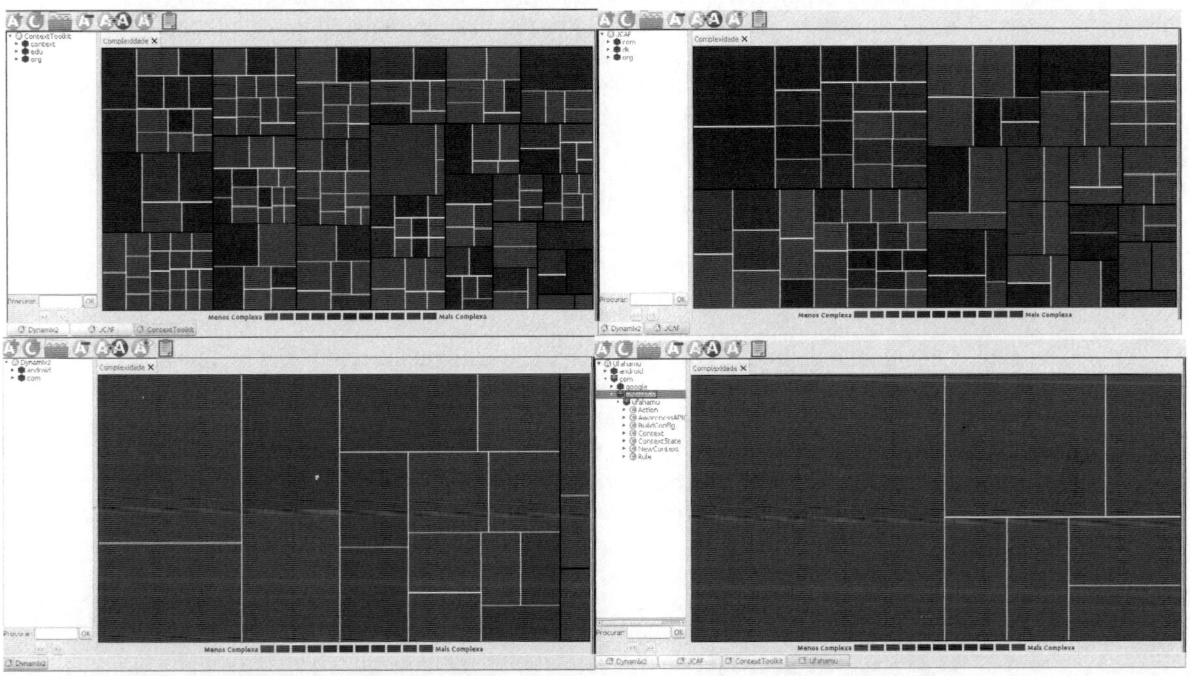

Figura 2. Comparação das API's (da esquerda para direita, de cima para baixo) ContextToolkit, JCAF, Dynamix e Ufahamu na ferramenta Metrix [19].

A visualização da complexidade da API ContextToolkit na Metrix (canto superior esquerdo da Figura 2) mostra muitos retângulos – o que significa muitas classes – e a cor predominantemente vermelha – isto é, com a maioria das classes com uma alta complexidade. A visualização da complexidade da API JCAF na Metrix (canto superior direito da Figura 2) mostra um número menor de classes em relação à ContextToolkit, com menos classes vermelhas. A visualização da complexidade da API Dynamix na Metrix (canto inferior esquerdo da Figura 2) mostra um número menor de classes em relação à ContextToolkit e à JCAF e apenas tons de verde, significando classes menos complexas. Por fim, a a complexidade da API Ufahamu (canto inferior direito da Figura 2) mostra a API mais simples de todas na comparação, evidente tanto no número de classes quanto na cor das mesmas. Isto comprova a simplicidade de código e, por conseguinte, simplicidade e facilidade de uso e entendimento do framework em relação aos outros framworks relacionados a este.

Uma vez que a ferramenta Metrix tem o propósito de justamente analisar a complexidade e demonstrar através visualizações a análise de uma API, a sua utilização na validação do Ufahamu e os resultados atingidos apresentados na Figura 2 justificam e legitimam a conclusão alcançada de que o Ufahamu possui uma estrutura de código simples de ser utilizada por desenvolvedores de aplicações conscientes de contexto.

Antes de se utilizar a Metrix, foi necessária uma calibração da mesma para que ela pudesse avaliar corretamente aplicações desenvolvidas para Android (*.apk) e assim poder trazer resultados significativos na avaliação do framework Ufahamu. Devido a limitações de espaço, este processo não será detalhado neste artigo.

7 Conclusões e Trabalhos Futuros

Este trabalho apresentou o framework Ufahamu, que facilita o desenvolvimento de aplicações conscientes de contexto para dispositivos Android. Para isso, o Ufahamu implementa um modelo de Contexto-Regra-Ação, que facilita a abstração da situação de contexto com a qual o desenvolvedor deverá lidar. Uma avaliação inicial do framework é apresentada através da implementação das funcionalidades da aplicação Motorola Assist utilizando o Ufahamu visando demonstrar como o mesmo facilita o trabalho de um desenvolvedor de aplicações. Neste caso, uma limitação é que esta implementação foi realizada pelo primeiro autor, projetista do framework Ufahamu. Assim, uma segunda avaliação considera a complexidade da API do Ufahamu e de três outros frameworks similares foi realizada. Novamente, os resultados sugerem que o Ufahamu é adequado para o desenvolvimento de aplicações conscientes de contexto.

É um plano futuro conduzir avaliações sistematizadas do framework através de experimentos ou quasi-experimentos com desenvolvedores de software interessados em desenvolver aplicações conscientes de contexto usando o Ufahamu.

8 Agradecimentos

Os autores gostariam de agradecer à CAPES pela bolsa de mestrado do primeiro autor e ao CNPq pelo apoio financeiro (processos 440880/2013-0, 310468/ 2014-0, e 420801/2016-2).

Referências

1. Baldauf, M.; Dustdar, S.; Rosenberg, Florian. A Survey on Context-Aware Systems. Int. J. Ad Hoc Ubiquitous Comput.. Interscience Publishers, Switzerland, p. 263-277. jun. 2007.
2. Bardram, J. E.. The Java Context Awareness Framework (JCAF) - A Service Infrastructure and Programming Framework for Context-Aware Applications. In *Pervasive Computing*. 2005.
3. Carlson, D.; Schrader, A. Dynamix: An Open Plug-and-Play Context Framework for Android. In *International Conference on the Internet of Things*: IEEE, 2012.
4. Dey, A. K.; Abowd, G. D.; Salber, D. A conceptual framework and a toolkit for supporting the rapid prototyping of context-aware applications. *Journal Human-computer Interaction*. Hillsdale, p. 97-166. dez. 2001.
5. Dey, A. K.; Abowd, G. D. Towards a Better Understanding of Context and Context-Awareness. In *Proceedings of the 1st International Symposium on Handheld and Ubiquitous Computing*, 1999.
6. Doukas, C.; Antonelli, F. COMPOSE: Building Smart & Context-Aware Mobile Applications utilizing IoT Technologies. In *IEEE Global Information Infrastructure & Networking Symposium*, 5., IEEE, 2013.
7. Elmalaki, S.; Wanner, L.; Srivastava, M. CAreDroid: Adaptation Framework for Android Context-Aware Applications. *Proceedings of the Annual International Conference on Mobile Computing and Networking*; 2015:386-399.
8. Gamma, E. et al. Behavioral Patterns. Design Patterns. Addison-wesley, 1994. p. 293-303.
9. GOOGLE.Google Awareness API. Disponível em: <https://developers.google.com/awareness/>. Acesso em: 14 ago. 2016.
10. IFTTT INC.Disponível em: <https://ifttt.com/>. Acesso em: 10 jun. 2016.
11. MOTOROLA MOBILITY. Como utilizar o aplicativo Assist? Disponível em: <https://motorola-global-portal-pt.custhelp.com/app/answers/detail/a_id/100937>. Acesso em: 15 fev. 2017.
12. Schilit, B. N.; Theimer, M. M. Disseminating Active Map Information to Mobile Hosts. *IEEE Network: The Magazine Of Global Internetworking*. p. 22-32. set. 1994.
13. Schmidt, A. *Ubiquitous Computing - Computing in Context*. 2002. 312 f. Tese de Doutorado - Curso de Computer Science, Lancaster University, 2002.
14. Spreitzer, M.; Theimer, M. Providing Location Information in a Ubiquitous Computing Environment. In *Symposium on Operating Systems Principles*, 14., 1993, p. 270 - 283.
15. The Cheese Factory Co. Google's Awareness API in action. Make your application be User's Context-Aware.Disponível em: <https://inthecheesefactory.com/blog/google-awareness-api-in-action/en>. Acesso em: 14 ago. 2016.
16. Ur, B. et al. Practical trigger-action programming in the smart home. In *Conference on Human Factors in Computing Systems*, 14., 2014,
17. Van Wissen, B. et al. ContextDroid: an Expression-Based Context Framework for Android. In *International Workshop on Sensing for App Phones*, 2010, Zurique. Workshop.
18. Weiser, M. The Computer for the 21st Century. *Sigmobile Mobile Computing and Communications Review*. p. 3-11. jul. 1999.
19. SOUZA, Cleidson R. B. de; BENTOLILA, David L. M.. Automatic Evaluation of API Usability using Complexity Metrics and Visualizations. In: ICSE, 31., 2009, Vancouver.. 2009. p. 1 - 8.
20. Android Drawer. Disponível em: <https://www.androiddrawer.com/>. Acesso em: 30 out. 2017.

Sýntixi – A Generative Approach to Dynamic Fusion of Software Components *

Juan-Alberto Hernández-Martínez[1], Ulises Juárez-Martínez[1], and Nicolás Cardozo[2]

[1] Instituto Tecnológico de Orizaba, Orizaba, México
{jhernandezm,ujuarez}@ito-depi.edu.mx
[2] Universidad de Los Andes, Bogotá, Colombia
n.cardozo@uniandes.edu.co

Abstract. Current software applications are often updated by software developers due to unforeseen changes in user requirements as well as the emerging needs in different industrial sectors. To address such issues, developers perform many tasks to adapt and evolve the applications' behavior. However, the increasing technological complexity makes such tasks harder to carry out in a manual manner, which has a counter-productive impact on time and effort applied by developers. An interesting alternative to solve such issues resides in the use of generators whose capabilities allow to minimize human intervention and automate software component implementation and modification tasks, especially when applications cannot stop their execution. In this sense, current paper provides an overview of Sýntixi, a generator based on Generative Programming techniques to fuse software components at run-time from high-level specifications as a support to dynamic software adaptation and evolution.

Keywords: Generators, Dynamic Fusion, Dynamic Adaptation, Dynamic Evolution

1 Introduction

Nowadays, computing represents an indispensable area for several organizations and industrial sectors due to the support it provides to perform complex tasks quickly and efficiently through the using of software [1]. This importance, from developers' perspective, represents a challenge considerably complex since it is necessary to perform many tasks for implementing, adapting or evolving software applications before the constant inclusion of new domains, emerging technologies, or unforeseen user requirements, which increases time and effort applied as well as error-proneness [2, 3]. In this sense, it is an important issue of current software development the establishment of suitable mechanisms for improving

* The authors would like to thank CONACyT for providing the facilities to realize the current research.

the software development speed, minimizing human intervention during such tasks, as well as dynamically changing applications' behavior [4, 5].

Generative Programming is an interesting alternative to solve such issues since its goal is designing and implementing exchangeable software modules to generate specialized and highly optimized applications by using generators to fulfill a specific requirement [6]. The importance of generators resides in the ability to automate software components and systems development and bridging the gap between high intentionality and desired executable.

Based on the above, current paper presents a generator based on Generative Programming techniques, which allows the dynamic fusion of software components as support to dynamic software adaptation and evolution. Thus, the main contributions of this paper are the following:

1. A generator for fusion of software components at run-time based on Generative Programming techniques and MAPE-K loop as support to dynamic software evolution.
2. A set of fusion alternatives for avoiding unnecessary functionality inside software components.

The remainder of the paper is structured as follows: Section 2 provides an overview of the Sýntixi generator from its architecture to its working. Section 3 presents the related work. Finally, in Section 4 concluding remarks and future work are outlined.

2 Sýntixi: A Generator for Fusion of Software Components

Sýntixi is a generator whose main goal is the dynamic fusion of software components from high-level specifications. This generator obeys fusion model principles [7], which establishes the following points basically: 1) each atom corresponds to a software component, 2) each atom provides its elements partially or completely, and 3) each molecule corresponds to a new adaptation or generation of software components. Accordingly, Sýntixi uses Generative Programming techniques and the MAPE-K control loop to support such fusion principles.

On the one hand, the generator applies a strategy commonly used by generators in Generative Programming context, which consists of receiving a high-level requirement specification, verifying the system or component buildability, completing the specification by calculating default values and assembly the involved components to get a concrete system [6]. On the other hand, the generator incorporates the principles established by MAPE-K control loop, which allows Sýntixi including dynamic features to minimize human intervention during the fusion process as well as providing support to dynamic software adaptation and evolution [8, 9]. Figure 1 presents an overview of Sýntixi's generation process supported by MAPE-K control loop.

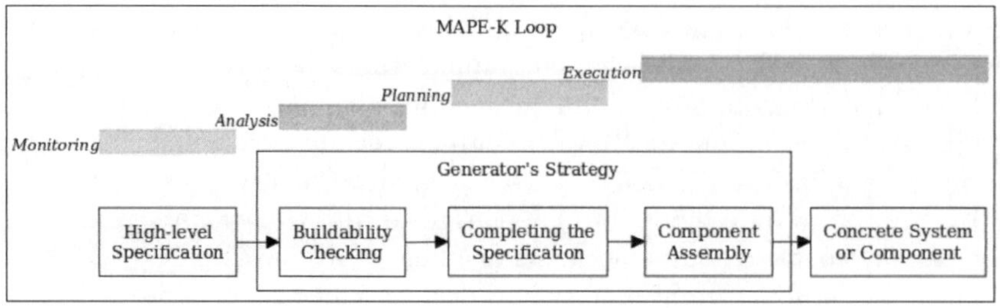

Fig. 1. Sýntixi's generation process supported by generative strategies and MAPE-K control loop

2.1 Layered Architecture

Sýntixi generator is implemented in Java programming language and its architecture obeys the Virtual Machine architectural style, which allows organizing a system hierarchically where each layer exposes an interface that lower layers use [10]. In this sense, Sýntixi consists of three layers: *Input*, *Fusion*, and *Instrumentation*, as shown in Fig. 2.

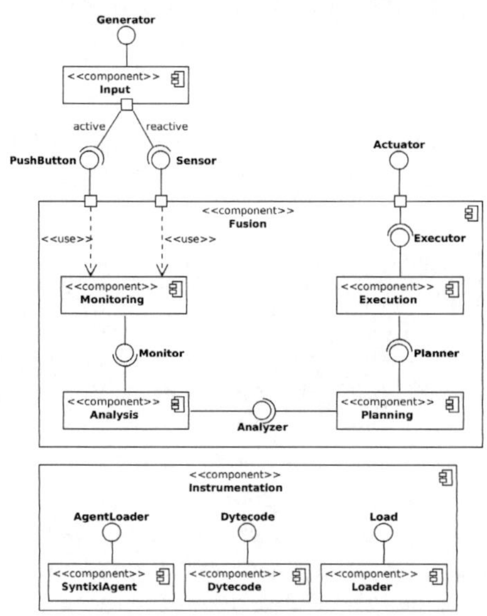

Fig. 2. Sýntixi's architecture based on the Virtual Machine architectural style

Input Layer Represents the generator starting point. This layer exposes an interface called *"Generator"*, which allows the user to interact with Sýntixi generator by using two execution commands: `active` and `reactive`.

The `active` command sets the generator to finish its working after generating *fused components*, which satisfies a user requirement completely. This command controls the fusion process explicitly. However, it is mandatory that user requirements exist in the generator's workspace before starting the fusion process. On the other hand, the `reactive` command sets the generator's working indefinitely until the user finishes it explicitly by using the `Ctrl + C` keystroke. By using the `reactive` command, Sýntixi responds to new user requirements automatically. Therefore, it is not mandatory such requirements exist in the generator's workspace before starting its execution.

Fusion Layer This layer includes the MAPE-K principles to generate, adapt and evolve dynamically software components. Also, this layer exposes three interfaces: *Sensor*, *PushButton*, and *Actuator*.

Sensor interface encapsulates a physical sensor's functionality able to monitor both execution environment and the generator's workspace to respond to new user requirements automatically. This interface is related to `reactive` command and its implementation consists of a finite state machine based on the MAPE-K control loop, as shown in Fig. 3.

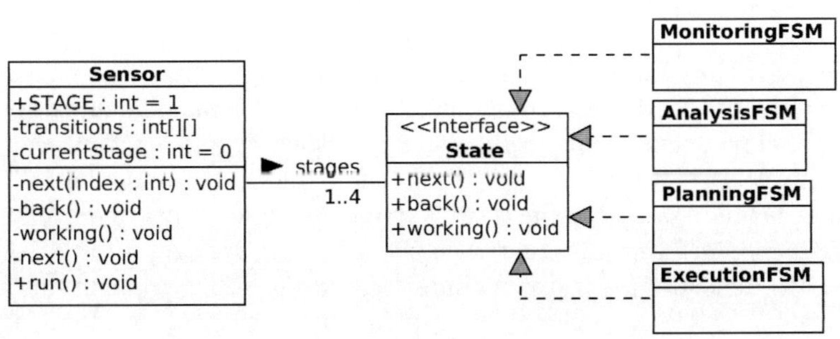

Fig. 3. Sensor interface implementation

In general, in *Sensor* interface context each MAPE-K loop stage implements three possible states: `back`, `working`, and `next`. Firstly, *monitoring* stage starts in `working` status and remains operating until the generator fulfills established goals. Then, the finite state machine changes to `next` status and go forward to the following MAPE-K loop stage, taking into account the basic interaction between stages: Monitoring → Analysis → Planning → Execution.

It is noteworthy that the finite state machine allows the user to add more stages and modify the transition between them if necessary, as well as go back between stages using the `back` state.

PushButton interface encapsulates a pushbutton functionality able to execute specific tasks every time is pressed. This interface is directly related to `active` execution command and its implementation obeys the *Template Method* design pattern [11], as shown in Fig. 4.

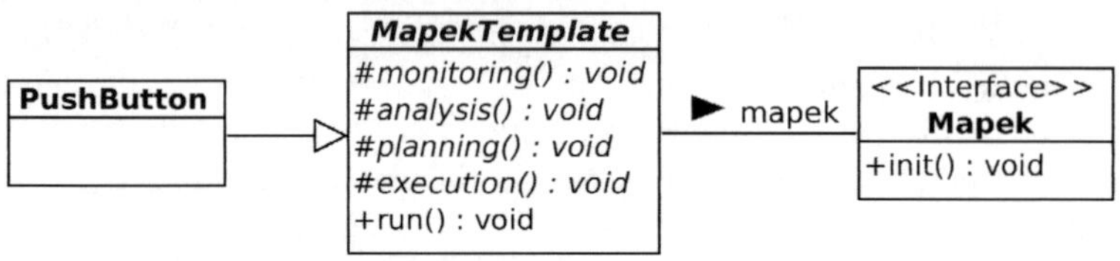

Fig. 4. PushButton interface based on the Template Method design pattern

Using the *PushButton* interface allows Sýntixi to start the *monitoring* stage and go forward to each MAPE-K loop stage based on a predefined transition sequence that cannot be modified.

Finally, *Actuator* interface encapsulates a physical device functionality able to generate an effect over an automated process. Its main goal is to provide to the user all resulting components the from fusion process, i.e., fused components. This interface establishes communication with *execution* stage related to the MAPE-K loop as well as Sýntixi's dynamic loader.

Instrumentation Layer Stores information from generated components in the *Fusion* layer and loads them dynamically in Java Virtual Machine. This layer consists of three components: *SýntixiAgent*, *Dytecode*, and *Loader*.

SýntixiAgent is a dynamic agent aimed at retrieving and storing information from loaded classes in the Java Virtual Machine. This agent exposes the *AgentLoader* interface to interact with the following features: SýntixiAgent execution both at load-time and run-time, coupling to other applications by using a process ID (PID) to perform instrumentation tasks and calculating the similarity between strings through the Levenshtein algorithm. Each one of these features results in a relevant option to the *analysis* mechanism to find and select components that fulfill a specific user requirement dynamically.

Dytecode is a component responsible for dynamically loading bytecode in the Java Virtual Machine. In general, this component consists of two elements: *compiler*, which is responsible for compiling source code from `java` files as well as source code as `string` variable statements, and *loader*, which is responsible for dynamically loading the generated bytecode. *Dytecode* is important due to the ability to compile and load bytecode without `class` files, as well as testing components dynamically before implementing them in class files.

Finally, *Loader* allows Sýntixi loading *fused components* at run-time. The main difference between *Loader* and *Dytecode* is that *Loader* extends the capabilities of Java class loader to work with `class` files.

2.2 Requirements to Fuse Components

Sýntixi works by using two main elements: high-level specifications and software components described as follows.

High-level specifications correspond to XML files by which the user describes new requirements. The main purpose of using this specification is to provide a flexible means to specify the component's functionality and delegate complex tasks, such as code analysis and implementation to Sýntixi generator decreasing time and effort applied by developers. Each XML specification consists of a description, a functionality, and a fusion alternative, as shown in Code 1.1.

```xml
<?xml version="1.0" encoding="UTF-8"?>
<fusion>
        <component id="1">
                <description>
                        <name>Calculator</name>
                        <goal>Performs math operations</goal>
                </description>
                <functionality>
                        <keywords>sqrt</keywords>
                        <input>double</input>
                        <output>double</output>
                </functionality>
                <functionality>
                        <keywords>sum</keywords>
                        <input>int,int</input>
                        <output>double</output>
                </functionality>
                <alternative>GCC</alternative>
        </component>
</fusion>
```

Code 1.1. XML specification in the fusion context

Based on the above, the `description` tag allows users to indicate what is desired at the end of the fusion process, specifying the component's name and its goal. The `functionality` tag allows user to specify the set of operations that a final component must have, describing the `keywords` to identify each functionality and the `input` and `output` data types. Finally, the `alternative` tag allows users to specify the fusion type to be made, i.e., by generating components and connectors, generating components without connectors, using the original components through connectors or using the original components without using connectors. On the other hand, Sýntixi works with Java components, which follow the Design by Contract methodology as well as including an API formed by annotations established by the Sýntixi generator, as shown in Code 1.2.

```java
@Component(goal="Performs sum operations", keywords="operations",
     requiredInterfaces=0, providedInterfaces=1)
public class Sum {
    @Interface(goal="Sum of two positive integers",
        keywords={"sum","addition"}, parameters=2, returnType="int",
        type=Interface.InterfaceType.PROVIDED,
        importance=Interface.Measure.MEDIUM,
        susceptible=Interface.Measure.MEDIUM)
    @Pre(expr="(a > 0) && (b > 0)", message="Invalid numbers.")
    @Post(expr="_returns > 0", message="Number less than zero.")
    public int sum(int a, int b){
        return a + b;
    }
```

```
9 }
```

Code 1.2. Fusionable Component `Sum.java`

With `@Pre` and `@Post` annotations, Sýntixi has an adequate means to determine the component correctness before, during and after the fusion process, because specific entry and exit conditions must be met. These annotations are provided by the OVal (Object Validation) framework, an external tool for Design by Contract methodology, which supports to Sýntixi generator.

The `@Component` annotation enriches a traditional component with information that allows knowing its purpose as a whole, the keywords for identifying its functionality, the importance that it has within a particular context and how susceptible it is to undergo implementation changes. The `@Interface` annotation is intended to enrich methods, interfaces, and constructors. The only difference regarding the @Component annotation is the interface type specification that each element represents within the component context.

Fusion Alternatives Sýntixi uses the following alternatives to adapt and evolve components at run-time: *OCC* (Original Components and Connectors), *GCC* (Generate Components and Connectors), *OCWC* (Original Components Without Connectors), and *GCWC* (Generate Components Without Connectors). These alternatives propose deleting unnecessary or irrelevant behavior from components to meet a specific requirement. Such resulting components are known in the fusion context as "thin components". To reach this goal, Sýntixi generator performs dynamic class instrumentation tasks by manipulating components directly, generating new components or by using connectors. In general, Sýntixi executes the following steps to address the proposed alternatives:

1. Monitoring the execution environment to detect components.
2. Analysis components' annotations through reflection and Levenshtein algorithm to calculate the similarity between strings.
3. Selection of components compatible with user requirement specification.
4. Introspection of compatible components to find the suitable behavior according to user requirement specification by using techniques as mentioned in step 2.
5. Making adjustments by adding or deleting behavior.

The previous steps represents the fusion alternatives commonality. However, step 5 has some differences depending on the alternative applied since each one of them works over different components, i.e., originals or generated components. In this sense, the most relevant information about each alternative is described as follows.

OCC Alternative This alternative uses the original components and connectors, as shown in Figure 5.
The main idea behind this approach is communicating components by using connectors to establish a similar way to molecule creation. This alternative involves interaction between original components, which in turn remain

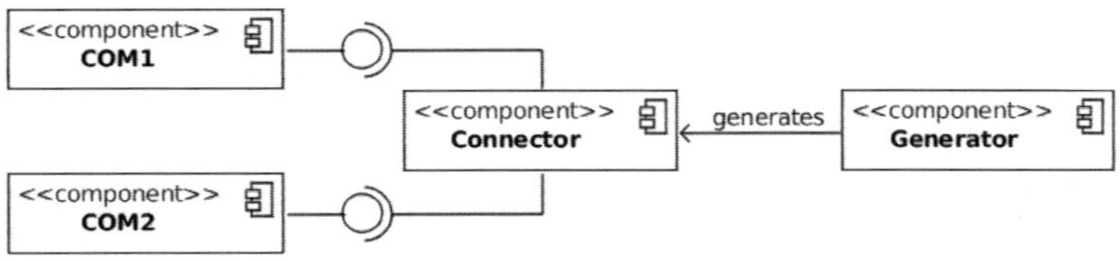

Fig. 5. OCC fusion alternative using original components and connectors

in the resulting component to provide a new functionality. To achieve this type of adaptation, the generator dynamically implements a connector with information that fulfills a user requirement and then communicates each component involved in the fusion process to provide a new behavior.

GCC Alternative This alternative focuses on generating new components from original components' most important features, as shown in Figure 6.

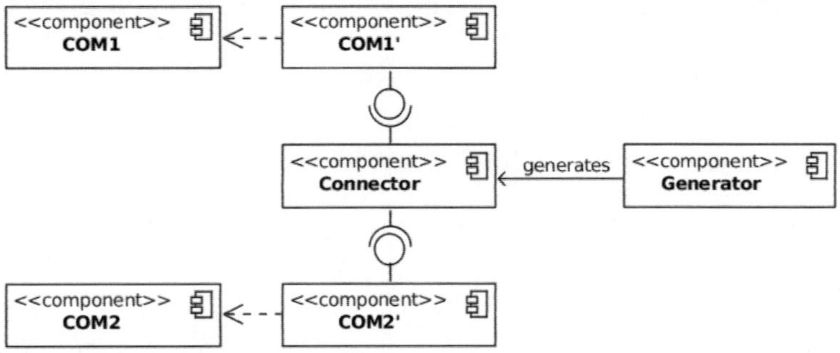

Fig. 6. GCC fusion alternative generating new components and connectors

This approach tries to keep original elements unchanged such that they stay available to new fusion processes with their original behavior as well as generate new components and connectors to allow their communication. This alternative has a similar purpose to a letters template where it is possible to take only the necessary letters to define new words. To achieve this result, generator implements dynamically a new component for each fusionable component involved in the fusion process whose behavior is formed by information obtained earlier. Finally, the generator implements the necessary connectors to assemble the generated components. This alternative results in support to component versioning, which is suitable for situations where it is necessary to get a previous version in case of anomalous behavior.

It is noteworthy that both OCC alternative and GCC alternative, the using of connectors results in support to minimize dependencies between components, gather design decisions to improve software analysis and maintenance, and separate communications mechanism among components.

OCWC Alternative This alternative establishes communications between original components without using intermediary connectors, as shown in Figure 7.

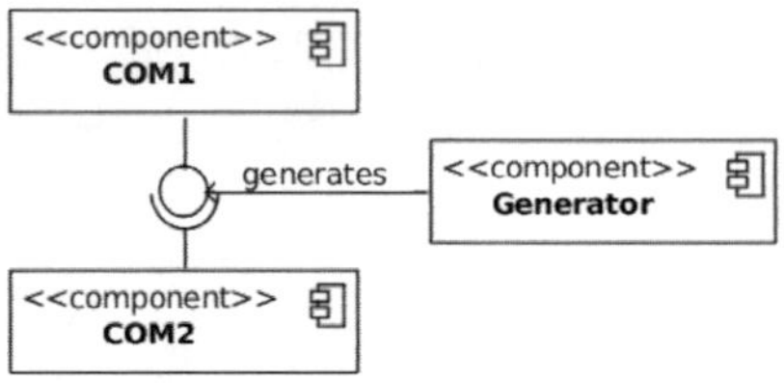

Fig. 7. OCWC fusion alternative using original components without connectors

To achieve this kind of adaptation, the generator performs dynamic changes in original components' bytecode, specifically generating and/or modifying interfaces to communicate involved components. Later, the generator dynamically loads the modified components.

It is noteworthy that although this type of interaction between components is commonly used in software development, the main difference resides in the selection of elements that each component provides.

GCWC Alternative This alternative allows generating a unique component without using connectors, as shown in Fig. 8.

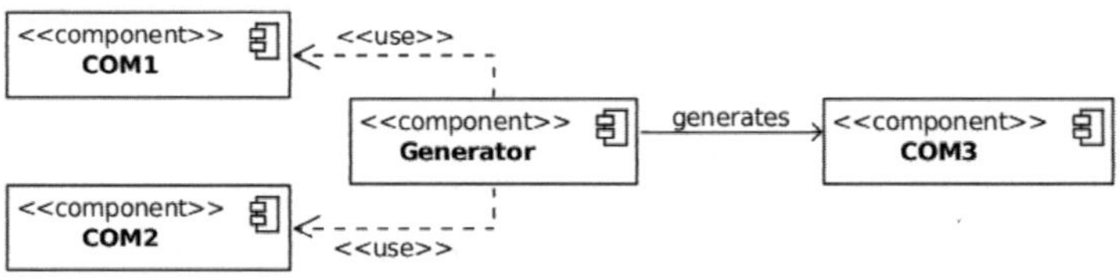

Fig. 8. GCWC fusion alternative to generating new components without connectors

Unlike previous approaches, this alternative does not use connector components to achieve its goal, does not make modifications on the involved components and there is no dynamic generation of components for each fusionable component involved in the fusion process. In this approach, the generator implements a new and unique component with different features from the suitable behavior that satisfies a user requirement. This alternative is useful to generate components similar to plugins where all the functionalities remain in a single entity.

2.3 Sýntixi Internals: MAPE-K as Fusion Support

Sýntixi's core is based on the MAPE-K control loop due to it is widely used in autonomous contexts, such as self-adaptation and dynamic software evolution. This control loop allows modularizing a system implementation, adaptation and/or modification through four related stages: monitoring, analysis, planning, and execution.

In Sýntixi context, *monitoring* stage implementation uses the *Observer* design pattern [11] since it provides a flexible mechanism to define `1-N` dependencies between objects, such that whenever specific object changes, all their dependent objects receives a notification. Therefore, the monitoring mechanism is responsible for monitoring both execution environment for finding new user requirements and components running into Java Virtual Machine by using reflection capabilities. Concretely, the *monitoring* mechanism updates a list of components and requirements detected. These lists remain available to the *analysis* mechanism in order to get the most relevant information for each element, i.e., classes, interfaces, components' goal, class hierarchy, among others. Figure 9 presents an overview of Sýntixi's monitoring mechanism.

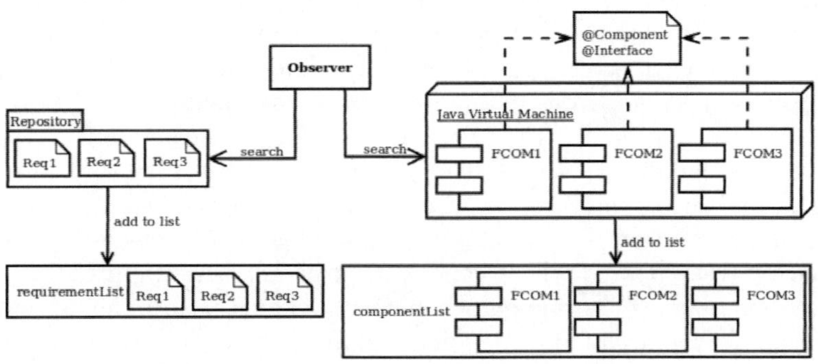

Fig. 9. Sýntixi's monitor mechanism

The *analysis* stage is implemented by a set of classes whose main goal is the introspection of components and requirements detected by monitoring mechanism through reflection capabilities. Firstly, analysis mechanism creates Java object instances for each requirement detected, which contain both the requirement structure and a checklist to verify the functionalities solved during the fusion process. Secondly, Sýntixi performs an analysis of fusionable components, which consist of retrieving the information described in the user's specification and comparing such information to component's annotation by using reflection and Levenshtein algorithm to calculate the similarity between them. In case of fusionable components do not fulfill the requirement, the analysis mechanism searches for compatible components within Java API and then updates the checklist to keep a trace of functionalities solved at this point. Figure 10 presents an overview of Sýntixi's analyzer mechanism.

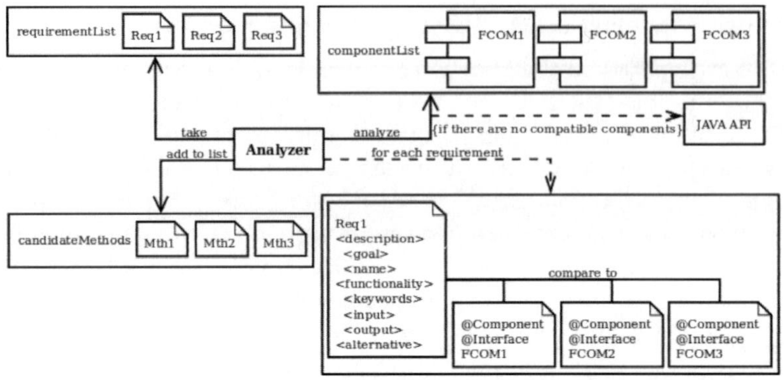

Fig. 10. Sýntixi's analyzer mechanism

The *planning* stage is implemented by using the *Strategy* design pattern [11] since it focuses on reaching a specific goal under the premise that a strategy is a plan. In this sense, based on the checklist updated in previous stages, the planning mechanism determines which components and which elements fulfill every functionality described in the user requirement. Also, the planning mechanism determines if the components involved provide their functionality partially or completely, and generates or modify such components according to the fusion alternative specified by the user. At this point, the generator is responsible for correct decision-making to solve dynamically issues, such as addition, modification, and incompatibility of elements, as well as the order and priority of components to perform the fusion. So far, the following elements to determine the priority are proposed: the component with the most important operation, the component less susceptible to behavioral changes, and the component of the most class hierarchy. These points establish a flexible mean to prioritize the involved components and make fusion process easier. Finally, the planning mechanism builds the components necessary, which contain a set of annotations with information related to the new functionality through dynamic bytecode generation. Figure 11 presents an overview of Sýntixi's planning mechanism.

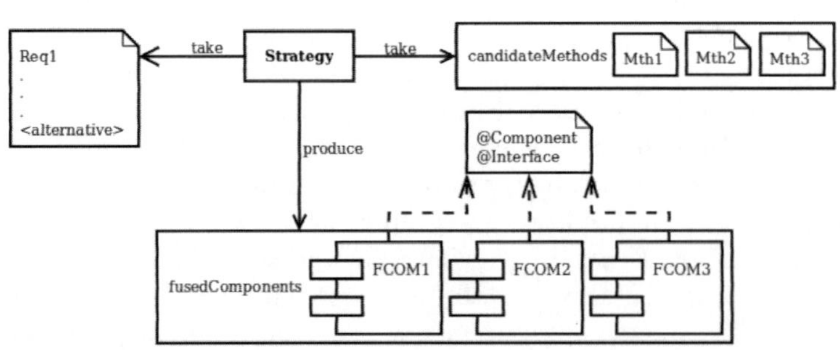

Fig. 11. Sýntixi's planning mechanism

Execution stage is implemented by using the *Abstract Factory* design pattern [11] since it allows creating sets or family of objects commonly known as products through an interface. In this stage, the generator fuses the selected components by using class instrumentation techniques with Javassist to generate class files at run-time, dynamic class loading by using hot-swapping techniques and dynamic loaders, such as the *Loader* and *Dytecode* components. Figure 12 presents an overview of Sýntixi's execution mechanism.

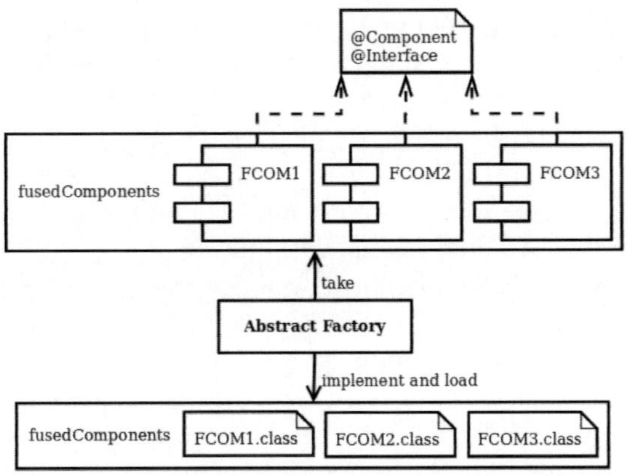

Fig. 12. Sýntixi's execution mechanism

In order to get a clearer perspective of the elements involved in Sýntixi's implementation, Table 1 presents the most relevant information.

Table 1. Sýntixi generator

Layer	Interface	Design	Stage related	Interaction	Technology
Input	Sensor	Finite State Machine	Monitoring	JVM, Workspace	Reflection, Executor
	PushButton	Template Method			Reflection
Fusion	Monitor	Observer	Analysis	JVM, Workspace	Reflection, VirtualMachineDescriptor
	Analyzer	-	Planning	SýntixiAgent	Reflection, Levenshtein, Instrument
	Planner	Strategy	Execution	Javassist	Javassist, Reflection
	Executor	Abstract Factory	Monitoring	Dytecode, Loader	ClassLoader, Reflection, Hotswap, Javassist
Instrumentation	AgentLoader	-	Analysis	JVM	Instrument
	Dytecode	-	Execution	Bytecode	ClassLoader, Compiler
	Loader	-		Classes	ClassLoader

3 Related Work

In the dynamic evolution context, several authors provide service-oriented tools, such as [12] whose framework allows updating components at run-time specifying such components as provided and required services and communicating them through SOAP, JMS or RPC protocols. Another similar example is reported in [13] whose middleware supports the dynamic evolution of distributed component-based systems by using ontologies for applications' context modeling. Unlike these tools, Sýntixi does not incorporate or use web-oriented mechanisms. Sýntixi is focused on evolving components which are running locally on the Java Virtual Machine. In addition, the communication between components is not predefined or specified by SOAP protocols since the generator is responsible for carrying out such work at run-time.

Some other authors provide tools to work with components locally as mentioned in [14] whose dynamic approach allows composing software components generally represented as JavaBeans without code generation. In addition, a framework to dynamically update Java applications through a lightweight execution system, which is incorporated into an application through bytecode transformation at load-time is presented in [4]. Even though these approaches are similar to Sýntixi, it is noteworthy that Sýntixi tries to get a new behavior taking into account both initial functionality of each component and execution environment where they are. Also, bytecode changes are performed at run-time rather than load-time.

Finally, some approaches apply software evolution techniques through source code modification, adding, changing or deleting classes by call renaming and extending the class loader capabilities as mentioned in [15, 16] and [17]. Although Sýntixi performs these operations to evolve the behavior of one or more components at run-time, such modifications are carried out directly on the bytecode.

4 Conclusions

The use of generators results in an attractive alternative to dynamic software development automation as well as strengthen self-adaptation and dynamic software evolution approaches.

Establishing alternatives for fusion of software components allow programmers to have different adaptation approaches according to the manipulation degree that should be applied to the elements involved in the fusion process. This approach is beneficial in situations where minimizing human intervention to modify original components is required or preserving them without changes to establish a component versioning scheme.

Strengthen existing approaches to implement and evolve software components at run-time, as well as developing new schemes benefit both applications that require changes in its implementation without stopping its execution and applications whose dynamic nature require constant updating.

References

1. Messerschmitt, D.G., Szyperski, C.: Software Ecosystem: Understanding an Indispensable Technology and Industry. MIT Press, Cambridge, MA, USA (2003)
2. Krupitzer, C., Roth, F.M., VanSyckel, S., Schiele, G., Becker, C.: A survey on engineering approaches for self-adaptive systems. Pervasive Mob. Comput. **17**(PB) (February 2015) 184–206
3. Mendoza, P., Davila, A.: A technique based on naming patterns for finding candidates to components from source code. IEEE Latin America Transactions **15**(3) (March 2017) 482–487
4. Gregersen, A.R., Jørgensen, B.N.: Dynamic update of java applications—balancing change flexibility vs programming transparency. Journal of Software Maintenance and Evolution: Research and Practice **21**(2) (2009) 81–112
5. Junior, E.C., Maia, P.H.M., Affonso, F.J.: Sases: A framework for the development of service-based self-adaptive applications. IEEE Latin America Transactions **14**(9) (Sept 2016) 4187–4195
6. Czarnecki, K., Eisenecker, U.W.: Generative Programming: Methods, Tools, and Applications. ACM Press/Addison-Wesley Publishing Co., New York (2000)
7. Hernández-Martínez, J.A., Juárez-Martínez, U.: Model for fusion of software components. In: Companion Proceedings of the 15th International Conference on Modularity. MODULARITY Companion 2016, New York, NY, USA, ACM (2016) 143–145
8. Kephart, J.O., Chess, D.M.: The vision of autonomic computing. Computer **36**(1) (jan 2003) pp. 41–50
9. Huebscher, M.C., McCann, J.A.: A survey of autonomic computing—degrees, models, and applications. ACM Comput. Surv. **40**(3) (August 2008) 7:1–7:28
10. Medvidovic, N., Taylor, R.N.: Software architecture: foundations, theory, and practice. In: 2010 ACM/IEEE 32nd International Conference on Software Engineering. Volume 2. (May 2010) 471–472
11. Gamma, E., Helm, R., Johnson, R., Vlissides, J.: Design Patterns: Elements of Reusable Object-oriented Software. Addison-Wesley Longman Publishing Co., Inc., Boston, MA, USA (1995)
12. Baresi, L., Ghezzi, C., Ma, X., Manna, V.P.L.: Efficient dynamic updates of distributed components through version consistency. IEEE Trans. Softw. Eng. **43**(4) (April 2017) 340–358
13. Zhou, Y., Ma, X., Gall, H.: A middleware platform for the dynamic evolution of distributed component-based systems. Computing **96**(8) (Aug 2014) 725–747
14. Grinkrug, E.: Dynamic component composition. International Journal of Software Engineering & Applications **5**(4) (Jul 2014)
15. Orso, A., Rao, A., Harrold, M.J.: A technique for dynamic updating of java software. In: Software Maintenance, 2002. Proceedings. International Conference on. (2002) 649–658
16. Pukall, M., Kästner, C., Cazzola, W., Götz, S., Grebhahn, A., Schröter, R., Saake, G.: Javadaptor—flexible runtime updates of java applications. Software: Practice and Experience **43**(2) (2013) 153–185
17. Zhang, S., Huang, L.: Research on dynamic update transaction for java classes. Frontiers of Computer Science in China **1**(3) (Jul 2007) 313–321

Quito SmartSafe City Un Sistema en Tiempo Real de Rescate Usando Comunicación IoT

Ana Zambrano[1], Eduardo Ortiz[1], Xavier Calderón-Hinojosa[1], Marcelo Zambrano[2]

[1] Departamento de Electrónica y Redes de Información, Escuela Politécnica Nacional, Quito 170517, Ecuador
[2] Laboratorio de Sistemas Tiempo Real y Distribuido, Universitat Politècnica de València, Valencia 46022, España
{ana.zambrano; eduardo.ortiz; xavier.calderon}@epn.edu.com; oszamvi@doctor.upv.es

Abstract. Uno de los grandes problemas que actualmente tiene que enfrentar la sociedad ecuatoriana y latinoamericana es la inseguridad; en la cual nadie está exento de convertirse en víctima. La propuesta descrita en este artículo, pretende dar el primer paso para vincular al Ecuador dentro de un nuevo modelo de gestión de la seguridad para ciudades inteligentes *(Smartcity),* por medio del uso y aplicación de nuevas tecnologías de la información y comunicación (TICs) como el *Internet of Things (IoT)*, *Machine to Machine (M2M)* y *Cloud Computing*. Se plantea el desarrollo de un sistema de información y comunicaciones en tiempo real, que permita reducir el tiempo de rescate y recuperación de víctimas de un secuestro. La comunidad cercana (ciudadanía, agentes de seguridad y/o transporte público) será notificada del secuestro de una persona, a través de sus *smartphones* y una red de comunicación virtual *M2M* implementada por medio del protocolo *Message Queue Telemetry Transport (MQTT)*, el cual es ideal para aplicaciones de *IoT* en las que el consumo energético es importante. Los *smartphones* son pieza clave para el desarrollo de esta solución, dada su gran difusión y capacidades de comunicación y sensorización, las cuales permiten aprovechar el paradigma de *crowdsensing* (cuanto más sensores existan en la red, mayor eficiencia se logrará). Sin duda alguna, con la fusión de investigación, tecnología y sociedad, es posible lograr una sociedad mejor.

Keywords: Internet of Things, Smart City, Smartphones, Real-time System, Distributed System, Message Queue Telemetry Transport.

1 Antecedentes

Los derechos y necesidades de una comunidad cambian respecto a su ubicación, a la cultura, y otras variables; así por ejemplo, lo que es derecho de una persona a caminar libre por la calle, o permitir a sus hijos jugar en un parque, en Latinoamérica en sí, hoy por hoy, es una necesidad más que un derecho. El derecho a la Seguridad. Según el

Centro Internacional para Niños Desaparecidos y Explotados (CINDE), más de 1,8 millones de niños son víctimas de explotación sexual globalmente; y aunque, afortunadamente, la cifra infantil va disminuyendo en América Latina, la problemática ahora es la trata de niñas y jovencitas de 11 a 22 años, afirma la fundadora de una *Asociación de niños robados y desaparecidos* [1]. De la misma manera, el panorama no es alentador para el Ecuador, que según cifras que ofrece el Ministerio del Interior, dentro del año 2015, hubo 217 casos de secuestros, de los cuales 179 fueron encontrados con vida mientras que el restante no; de los sobrevivientes el 27% fueron encontrados en mismo día de la desaparición, y el 73% fueron encontrados en al menos 7 días de la desaparición [2]. Si bien es cierto, muchos de los casos son resueltos por la *Dirección Nacional de Delitos contra la vida, muertes violentas, desapariciones, extorsión y secuestros* (DINASED), pero ¿Qué significa realmente el que este tiempo de rescate cambie de días a horas? Es necesario tomar en cuenta, el golpe psicológico de sufrir un secuestro, el cual es proporcional al tiempo de estar retenido en contra de su voluntad. Actualmente, el proceso de búsqueda se basa en pasos logísticos y burocráticos que toman demasiado tiempo y además, la comunidad no interviene en el proceso ni colabora con los agentes de búsqueda; comunidad que podría tener información relevante del escenario, del secuestrado, de los secuestradores, etc.

Se presenta una innovadora solución en tiempo real, alojado en la nube, que aprovecha la tecnología y recursos de la comunidad (smartphones), y el protocolo *Message Queue Telemestry Transport* (MQTT) de IoT y M2M, para mejorar tiempos de rescate ante secuestros.

Este artículo está estructurado, primeramente con una clara explicación del problema; segundo se presentan proyectos relacionados con el estado del arte; siguiente se detalla la arquitectura y protocolos a utilizar; el apartado 4 corresponde a los resultados preliminares obtenidos; y finalmente se presentan las conclusiones.

2 Estado del Arte

Existen varios tipos de proyectos realizados en este ámbito, sin embargo aún la gran mayoría se han considerado poco ortodoxos porque no utilizan herramientas tecnológicas para conseguirlo. De los más relevantes, se puede citar a la organización no lucrativa **Natalia Estemirova,** dedicado a derechos humanos con el proyecto "*Bracelets Alert Twitter and Facebook to kidnapping*" [3]. Consta de la distribución de un brazalete que alerta en redes sociales, utilizando una señal móvil un ataque o secuestro y emite la ubicación GPS de la víctima. Sin embargo, el problema más representativo con este proyecto sería la gran inversión económica que representaría el conseguir un brazalete por cada persona. Otro proyecto es "*Child abduction alert system*" [4], el cual se basa en una red *broadcast* que permite alertar la desaparición de niños por diferentes medios de comunicación. Se encuentra extendido por 18 países con grandes presupuestos. Al igual que lo que se espera, se dice que [4], ha mantenido su éxito gracias al gran apoyo policial y ciudadano. En Ecuador, sería la primera ayuda en este campo, al ocupar nuevos estándares de comunicación y a su vez, mejorar tiempos en el rescate inmediato de una posible víctima.

3 Arquitectura

Este artículo propone un sistema en tiempo real capaz de reducir el tiempo de rescate de una persona secuestrada, el cual incluirá a los agentes de seguridad y a la comunidad (transporte público, agentes de policía y personas naturales); permitiendo que estos se involucren como parte de la solución. La Figura 1 y la Figura 2, detallan la cadena logística y la arquitectura técnica del sistema respectivamente.

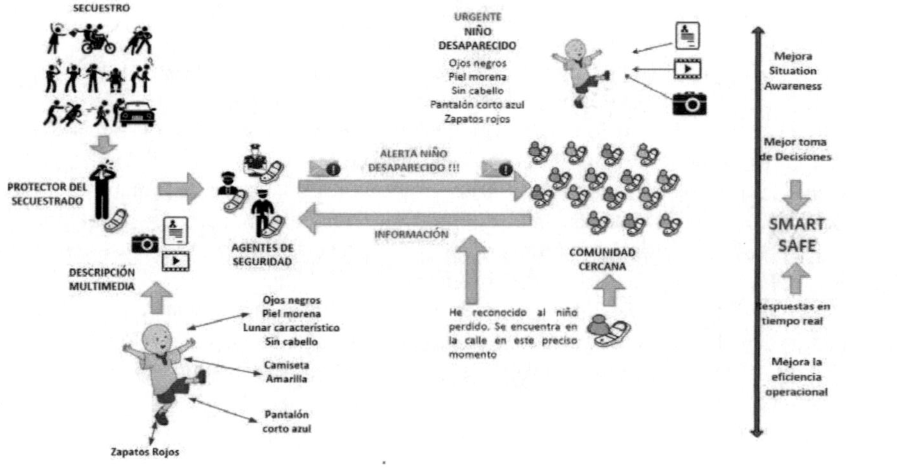

Fig. 1. Cadena logística del sistema.

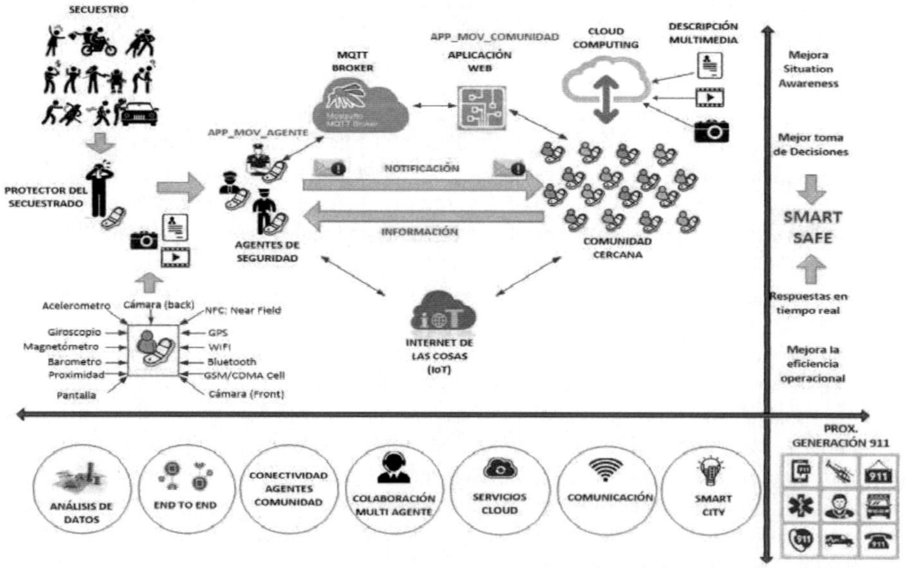

Fig. 2. Bloque técnico del sistema.

3.1 Descripción y cadena logística

Siguiendo la Figura 1, cuando existe un secuestro de una persona vulnerable (niño, anciano o persona discapacitada) es esencial que su protector notifique inmediatamente a un agente de seguridad (policía) y él, mediante la ***APP_MOV_AGENTE*** transmite en tiempo real a la "comunidad cercana", dentro de un perímetro virtual a determinar este acontecimiento. Permite dar a conocer las características de la persona desaparecida, por ejemplo en el caso de un niño: características físicas, color de su vestimenta, e incluso, pudiendo mejorar la descripción con recursos multimedia como fotografías, videos y audios. Es necesario recalcar que el término "comunidad cercana" se refiere a 3 agentes en especial; la primera, consiste en todo miembro de seguridad, generalmente policías; la segunda, toda persona natural cerca del suceso del secuestro; y la tercera, personas al mando de medios de transporte públicos como taxis y buses. De esta manera, la comunidad tiene un papel primordial en la difusión de la información; a través de su *smartphone*; un dispositivo óptimo capaz de transmitir y procesar información al ser adecuado (personalizado) mediante una aplicación ***APP_MOV_COMUNIDAD***, conocida como *opportunistic aplicación* [5]. Por tanto, el *smartphone* es parte primordial del éxito de esta propuesta, y cuantos más dispositivos conformen el sistema, mayor eficiencia podrá alcanzar; esto es conocido como *crowdsensing* [5] [6]. Este proceso pone en alerta a la comunidad de manera inmediata; una vez que la persona anteriormente notificada observa un evento que asemeja a las características detalladas (Ej: un niño de camiseta amarilla, pantaloneta azul, sin cabello, piel blanca, etc.) notifica a los agentes pertinentes mediante la misma aplicación **APP_MOV_COMUNIDAD** que ha identificado el suceso permitiendo la identificación y rescate antes de perder todo rastro de la víctima; incluso, podría brindar características del posible atacante. Es necesario recalcar el hecho de que la desaparición debe ser primeramente reportada a un agente de seguridad con el fin de que los casos sean solamente los validados y no perder credibilidad en el sistema.

3.2 Comunicación y Aplicaciones

Un Sistema en Tiempo Real (*Real-Time System*) es un sistema que procesa cualquier información y debe responder a una entrada o estímulo dentro de un periodo temporal específico y finito. Por ejemplo, para un sistema de detección de sismos [7] este límite (periodo) rondará los 4 segundos. En este escenario, el umbral definido para que la información sea procesada y notificada a la comunidad es de 1 hora, superando anteriores trabajos como [8], que presenta un rango de 1 a 3 horas para este proceso. Además, tomando en cuenta que las primeras horas son críticas, más aún cuando las estadísticas corroboran aduciendo que el 74% de los niños están muertos dentro de las 3 horas posteriores al secuestro [9]. Dados estos antecedentes, se diseña el sistema utilizando el protocolo MQTT, muy utilizando en *SmartCities* [10] gracias a sus amplias ventajas. MQTT es un protocolo ligero de transporte que emplea el modelo publicador/suscriptor permitiendo interactuar con uno o muchos usuarios [11]. MQTT es ideal para aplicaciones móviles tomando en cuenta el bajo uso energético, eficiencia de distribución de la información y mínimo almacenamiento [12].

Se ha escogido al proveedor *Amazon Web Services* [13] por sus amplias y comprobadas ventajas como proveedor de *Cloud Computing,* para crear un servidor Linux Ubuntu 16.04 LTS disponible de manera ubicua. En este servidor se ha instalado una base de datos MySQL 5.5 la misma que se encargará de gestionar la información concerniente a las personas desaparecidas. Se ha escogido emplear el Broker MQTT Eclipse Mosquitto v3.1 cuyo puerto estándar es TCP/IP 1883 / 8883 (SSL) [14]; y un servidor Web Apache 2.4.29 para almacenar eficientemente los recursos multimedia de manera jerárquica en la carpeta */html.* Todo esto mostrado en la Figura 3:

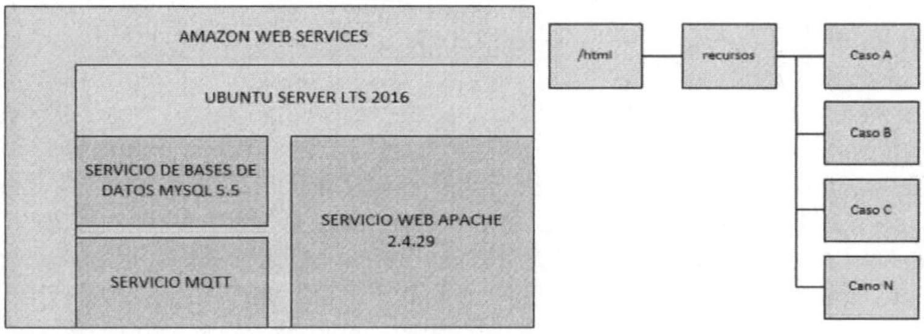

Fig. 3. Diseño de la arquitectura.

4 Resultados Preliminares

4.1 Análisis de la Ciudad de Quito

Un tema importante a validar es el rango de extensión de las notificaciones, en otras palabras, hasta qué rango de distancia (km) las notificaciones deben ser enviadas en un primer aviso. Quito presenta una extensión de 370.39 km^2, y tomando en cuenta primero que, el tráfico promedio es 21 km/h, y el máximo es 42km/h [15]; y segundo que las estadísticas aducen que el 72% de los niños, pasado las 3 horas se encuentran sin vida [16], se ha validado con pruebas reales de campo las posibles distancias máximas alcanzadas por un secuestrador en un límite de tiempo en la ciudad de Quito, mostrados en la Tabla 1. Tras analizar la situación geográfica de Quito [17], se ha determinado subdividir el territorio en áreas de 70 km2. Todo esto mostrado en la Figura 4. De esta manera, la comunidad que conforme el sistema, podrá recibir/enviar notificaciones enviadas de manera eficiente.

Tabla 1. Distancias máximas (km) que un secuestrador podría alcanzar en Quito.

Transporte/Tiempo	0.5 Horas	1 Hora	2 Horas	3 Horas
Público (Buses)	11,89	5,945	11,89	23,78
Público (Taxis)	14,10	7,05	14,11	28,20
Trole Bus	8,68	17,37	34,74	52,11
Particular	14,13	7,06	14,13	28,26

Caminata/Correr	2,175	4,35	8,70	13,05

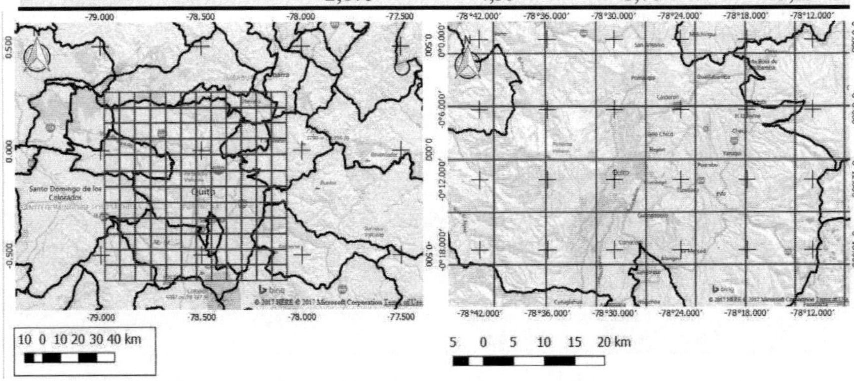

Fig. 4. Rango de sectorización para notificaciones MQTT en la ciudad de Quito.

4.2 Pruebas de funcionamiento

Las aplicaciones móviles se han realizado bajo el IDE Android Studio, siguiendo una estructura en servicios REST [18]. Se ha validado el funcionamiento de las aplicaciones en diferentes escenarios, así como en diferentes dispositivos móviles, como muestra la Figura 5. Como se puede observar, las aplicaciones presentan un consumo de energía mínimo, equiparable a la más utilizada de mensajería instantánea *WhatsApp,* que de la misma manera que esta propuesta, utilizan MQTT para su funcionamiento.

Por otro lado, se ha validado también el tiempo promedio que dura almacenar/descargar archivos multimedia (imágenes y videos) de un caso. Para ello colaboraron 20 personas con las aplicaciones instaladas asumiendo el papel del agente de seguridad, obteniendo los resultados mostrados en la Tabla 2. La Tabla 3, muestra el consumo de batería al utilizar la aplicación ***APP_MOV_AGENTE*** y ***APP_MOV_COMUNIDAD*** bajo el uso del servidor MQTT, usando diferentes tiempos de *heartbeat* (5 minutos – 15 minutos) y diferentes conexiones: WIFI (*download*: 15 Mbps, *upload*: 2Mbps) y 3G (*download*: 2 Mbps, *upload*: 0.7 Mbps).

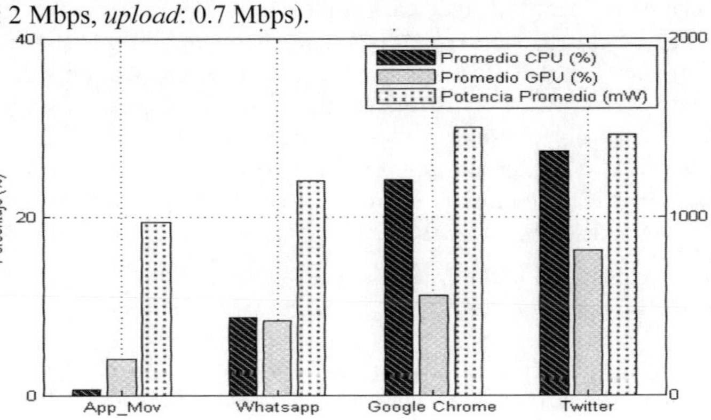

Fig. 5. Cuadro comparativo con otras aplicaciones.

Tabla 2. Tiempos en almacenar/descargar un caso de desaparición.

Tipo de Conexión	WIFI (15 Mbps / 2 Mbps)		3G (2 Mbps / 0.7 Mbps)	
Tipo de Archivo	**Imágenes[a]**	**Video[b]**	**Imágenes[a]**	**Video[b]**
Almacenar (seg)	4.90	23.80	18.40	34.50
Descargar (seg)	1.91	6.87	2.34	26.27

[a] Imágenes de tamaño 3MB [b] Videos de tamaño 5MB

Tabla 3. Consumo de batería móvil usando el protocolo MQTT.

Tiempo *Heartbeat*	5 minutos		15 minutos	
Tipo de Conexión	**3G**	**WIFI**	**3G**	**WIFI**
Consumo de Batería/hora	0.1553	0.0245	0.0021	0.00037

5 Conclusiones

Las cifras de inseguridad en varias ciudades latinoamericanas llegan a ser alarmantes, y este antecedente ha impulsado a los gobiernos a buscar soluciones económicas y eficientes promovidas por las nuevas tecnologías de la información y comunicación, en las que la comunidad esté involucrada de manera directa. Este artículo presenta un caso de investigación aplicada, que permitirá mejorar los tiempos de rescate ante la desaparición de una persona. Además, es importante resaltar que la ejecución de este proyecto tiene una repercusión directa al ***cambio de la matriz productiva del país*** puesto que la inseguridad corrompe y obstaculiza el crecimiento de un país en cualquier ámbito.

Este artículo enfatiza el uso de MQTT como protocolo de comunicación, y una gestión de información en *cloud computing* a través de *Amazon Web Services*. MQTT es un protocolo modelo publicador/suscriptor de Internet de las Cosas (IoT) cuyas características como: el eficiente envío de mensajes de uno a uno y de muchos a muchos, el consumo mínimo de energía y ligera sobrecarga; hacen que los objetivos de un sistema en tiempo real sean cumplidos. Se usa el bróker *MQTT Eclipse Mosquitto v3.1*, con una jerarquía interna de manera de mantener la información de cada caso de desaparición ordenados. El sistema ha sido validado comprobado que las aplicaciones realizadas consumen mínima cantidad de energía con respecto a otras aplicaciones de uso común, aprovechando el *crowdsensing*. Además, el tiempo en desplegar un caso a la comunidad, cumple con los objetivos de tiempos planteados.

A futuro, puesto que se cuenta con la predisposición del Ministerio del Interior del Ecuador, se espera realizar pruebas en un entorno real, de manera de corroborar a ciencia cierta, los beneficios de esta innovadora arquitectura.

Agradecimientos

Se agradece el financiamiento otorgado por la Escuela Politécnica Nacional para el proyecto PII-DETRI-2017-1 "*Ecuador Smart Safe City: Sistema de Rescate anti secuestros en tiempo real utilizando comunicación IoT*".

Referencias

1. Navas M. El drama de los niños desaparecidos de América Latina, http://www.bbc.com/mundo/noticias/2013/11/131106_ninios_perdidos_desaparecidos_explotados_america_latina_men, último acceso 2017/11/26.
2. Ministerio del Interior. Dinased resolvió el 84.8 % de los casos de desaparecidos 2017, http://www.ministeriointerior.gob.ec/dinased-resolvio-el-84-8-de-los-casos-de-desaparecidos-este-ano/, último acceso 2017/11/26.
3. Isaacson B. "Natalia Project" Bracelet Aims To Protect Human Rights Defenders | Huff-Post 2017, https://www.huffingtonpost.com/2013/04/08/natalia-project-bracelet-human-rights-defenders_n_3024220.html, último acceso 2017/11/26.
4. Department of justice. AMBER Alert - America's Missing: Broadcast Emergency Response 2017, https://www.amberalert.gov/ último acceso 2017/11/26.
5. Chon Y, Lane N, Cha H, Zhao F. Automatically Characterizing Places with Opportunistic Crowdsensing Using Smartphones, p. 481–90 (2012).
6. Raghu K, Fan Y, Hui L. Mobile crowdsensing: current state and future challenges. IEEE ;49 (2011).
7. Zambrano A, Pérez I, Palau C, Domingo M. Sistema Distribuido de Detección de Sismos Usando una Red de Sensores Inalámbrica para Alerta Temprana. Rev Iberoam Automática E Informática Ind;12:260–269 (2015).
8. Sakaki T, Makoto O, Yutaka M. Tweet Analysis for Real-Time Event Detection and Earthquake Reporting System Development. IEEE; 25:919–31 (2013).
9. Hanfland A, Keppel D, Weis G. Case Management for missing children Homicide Investigation. U.S.: Department of justice; (1997).
10. Gómez A, Gómez M, María P-M. Turismo inteligente y patrimonio cultural: un sector a explotar en el desarrollo de las smart cities. Int J Sci Manag Tour; 3:389–411 (2017).
11. Hunkeler U, Hong T, Andy S-C. MQTT-S – A Publish/Subscribe Protocol For Wireless Sensor Networks. IEEE (2008).
12. Ferreira D, Kostakos V, Dey AK. AWARE: Mobile Context Instrumentation Framework. Front ICT 2015. https://www.frontiersin.org/articles/10.3389/fict.2015.00006/full, último acceso 2017/11/26.
13. Jackson KR, Ramakrishnan L, Muriki K. Performance Analysis of High Performance Computing Applications on the Amazon Web Services Cloud. IEEE (2011).
14. Banks A, Gupta R. MQTT Version 3.1.1 2014. http://docs.oasis-open.org/mqtt/mqtt/v3.1.1/os/mqtt-v3.1.1-os.html último acceso 2017/11/26.
15. Municipio del DMQ. FlacsoAndes | Plan maestro de movilidad para el Distrito Metropolitano de Quito. FlacsoAndes, http://www.flacsoandes.edu.ec/libros/118765-opac último acceso 2017/11/26.
16. Defensoría del Pueblo. Informe temático sobre las personas desaparecidas en el Ecuador Análisis de respuestas estatales, estadísticas, acceso a la justicia y contexto socio cultural de la problemática 2013-2014 (2017).
17. DMQ. Geoportal SMI-Q. Sist Inf Metrop 2016. http://geoportal.quito.gob.ec/smiq/, último acceso 2017/11/26.
18. Blotski P, Gómez, María Teresa. Desarrollo de Servicio WEB REST y Aplicación Android para Eventos de Ocio. Universidad de Sevilla, (2016).

Towards a Simulation-Based Project Monitoring and Control Learning Approach

Jean Carlo Rossa Hauck[1], Santiago Matalonga[2], Gerardo Matturro[3], Gerardo Quintana[3], Lucas Jacques [1], Christian Galafassi [1] and Rafael Queiroz Gonçalves [1]

[1] Federal University of Santa Catarina, Florianópolis/SC, Brazil
[2] University of the West of Scotland, Paisley, UK
[3] Universidad ORT Uruguay. Montevideo, Uruguay
jean.hauck@ufsc.br, santiago.matalonga@uws.ac.uk, matturro@uni.ort.edu.uy, gquintana@uni.ort.edu.uy, lucas.jacs@gmail.com, chrisitan.galafassi@gmail.com, rafael.q.g@hotmail.com

Abstract. Software project management is a core competency for today's software engineering. However, most undergraduate software project management courses are not prepared for the new generation of software engineers. One reason is that instructors are not giving the students the tools that would enable the development of competencies to apply all knowledge areas covered by a PMBOK-based course. In particular, we are concerned with competencies related to project monitoring and control which are difficult to put into practice in a classroom scenario. This paper presents our experiences and results in designing a software project management course, including project execution simulation. This simulation gives students the opportunity to apply project monitoring and control competencies based on data provided by the project execution simulation. We have piloted the approach and observed positive perceptions towards it by a sample of 19 students.

Keywords: Software engineering, Software project management, Software project management education. Software project simulation

1 Introduction

Software development projects are complex endeavours, and arguably, software project management competencies are necessary for Software Engineering (SE). Software project management is present in both SWEBOK [1] and ACM Curriculum Guidelines for Undergraduate Degree Programs in Software Engineering [2]. On the other hand, students' expectation has changed in the past years. Millennials are now the majority of the undergraduate population, and they expect and demand new approaches for the university classroom [3].

At Universidad ORT Uruguay (ORT) and Universidade Federal de Santa Catarina (UFSC) a module on Software Project Management has been part of undergraduate Software Engineering, computer science and information systems curricula for over a decade. Reflecting upon our teaching practice and reviewing the available literature, we came to the realization that a key missing element in project management education was the possibility to give students opportunities to apply Project Monitoring and Control - PMC (a process required to track, review and regulate project progress and performance and identify and manage changes when needed [4]). We have observed that applying project planning – and related process areas – can be achieved through application-oriented exercises. In contrast, to give the students the opportunity to apply PMC within an undergraduate course could require the introduction of a project execution simulation approach.

As a result, we embarked on a joint effort with the objective of developing and applying a suitable strategy to enable project management students to practice PMC in both universities taking into consideration the available resources.

This paper describes how we have introduced application-oriented exercises and simulation that fulfils the requirement. We have adapted and aligned the curricula of the project management module in both universities and implemented a software tool capable of simulating the execution of the students' project plans. This approach gives students the opportunity to apply PMC in a controlled environment. A differentiating factor of this approach is that we have re-designed a PMBOK[4]-based course, to adopting our simulation approach. As a result, the practical exercises can span multiple weeks throughout the semester – as opposed to one-shot interventions which are currently the norm when serious games or simulations have been introduced in the literature. To evaluate the applicability and the perception of learning of our approach, it was applied to 19 students at UFSC. Overall, our results demonstrate positive perceptions about the proposed approach.

This paper is organized as follows. Section 2 presents the results of our literature review. Section 3 presents the methodology. Section 4, describes the development of the simulation approach, including how it is grounded in the module descriptor (section 4.1) and the technical aspects of the simulation software (section 0). Section 5 presents the results of our pilot implementation. Finally, section 6 presents our conclusions and future work plans.

2 Background - Simulation in Software Engineering Education

This section presents a summary of our research on the application of simulation to SE education. Dörner et al. define a "serious game" as a digital game created with the intention to entertain and to achieve at least one additional goal (e.g., learning or health). These additional goals are named characterizing goals [5]. These authors also define the concept of "educational games" to denote a subgroup of serious games, tackling the formal educational sector from elementary schools to higher education, vocational training, and collaborative workplace training. Educational games focus on formal learning in dedicated educational institutions.

Educational games and simulations have been observed in literature as excellent tools to improve the teaching-learning process because they stimulate and inspire the students, providing a more attractive and ludic way of learning, as multiple experiences have reported [6] [7] [8] [9]. On the other hand, a "simulation game" is one that attempts to copy various activities from real life in the form of a game for various purposes such as training, analysis, or prediction [10]. Well-known examples of simulation games are war games, business games, and role-play simulations.

Claufield et al. present a systematic review of the literature [11] aimed at games or simulations used for educational or training purposes in SE across any of the SWEBOK knowledge areas. The results showed that games were mainly used in the knowledge areas of SE management and development processes. The results also showed that most games in the field have learning objectives aimed at the first level of Bloom's taxonomy (knowledge) [12].

Calderon et al. [13] introduce experiences of integrating a simulation-based serious game for software project management training (ProDeck). ProDeck aims to place the learners in a virtual organization where they can manage software projects and apply their knowledge to real-life scenarios. The achieved outcomes show positive evidence about the learners' motivation, experience and learning acquisition with the use of ProDec.

To contribute to the student´s formation process in Software Project Management, de Souza et al. [8], presents the development and validation of an electronic board serious game named SCRUMI, whose goal is to introduce concepts of the SCRUM framework. They observed positive results and found that games in the classroom are worth exploring.

Simsoft [11] is a serious game at the center of a research project designed to see if and how games can contribute to better SE management education by helping software engineers and project managers explore some of the complexities of the field in a controlled environment.

Go for it! [14] is an educational game for contributing to teaching the ISO/IEC 29110 standard. It is designed for use in conjunction with project management education modules, and helps reinforce concepts presented in up-front teaching environments.

PMG-2D [6] is an educational serious-game that aims to assist in the training of inexperienced software project managers. The game simulates a real software development environment where the player, acting as a project manager, goes through all phases of a software project lifecycle.

DELIVER! [7] is a board game to teach the Earned Value Management (EVM) technique used for monitoring and controlling the execution of a software project. The game is intended to be used as part of a project management course, and its purpose is to reinforce EVM concepts and to exercise its application. The authors argue that the game does not substitute, but complements other instructional strategies such as, expository lessons, to be adopted beforehand to present the basic concepts of EVM.

Schoeffel proposed a simulation game named PizzaMia in a way that he called an experiential dynamics to support teaching and learning in a project management course based on the Project Management Body of Knowledge (PMBOK) [14]. The activity is based on planning and execution of a real meal.

As it was identified by Claufield et al. [11], we found just few references that included systematic evaluations of the results. A review [15] on the use of games-based learning within SE to identify what empirical evidence exists within this literature to support this approach. Authors found that the evaluation of the impact of the simulation-based learning approach is severely limited and in many cases non-existent. They suggest that more research needs to be carried out to evaluate the use of this approach and longitudinal studies are required in simulation-based learning within higher education. In order to evaluate the software engineering educational approaches, [16], present an example of a multi-angled evaluation that showcases the difference between the amount of insight gained through a small pilot study versus that from a more comprehensive evaluation.

Regarding evaluation of serious games, Calderon et al. [15], performed a systematic literature review to summarize the existing evidence on evaluation procedures and methods to assess serious games in different application domains. They found that the educational domain, especially the higher education, is the domain where more studies evidenced assessment experiences, followed by health and wellness, and professional training and learning. They noticed that "computer games" is the type of game that attracts more interest towards assessment. Most of the studies analyzed selected the questionnaire as the main assessment method. Petri and von Wangenheim also present a systematic literature review [9]. Their results show that most evaluations use a simple research design in which, typically, the game is used, and afterwards subjective feedback is collected via questionnaires from the learners. Most of the evaluations are run with small samples, without replication, using mostly qualitative methods for data analysis. We also observed that most studies do not use a well-defined evaluation model or method. The authors conclude that there is a need for more rigorous evaluations as well as methodological support to assist game creators and instructors to improve such games as well as to support decisions on when or how to include them within instructional units. Furthermore, in Petri et al. [14], authors present an analysis of 43 case studies that use MEEGA, a model for educational games evaluation. The analysis provides evidence that digital and non-digital games can yield a positive effect on the learning of SE, providing a pleasant and engaging experience to the students and motivate them.

3 Methodology

This proposed simulation-based project monitoring and control learning approach have been developed and applied to overcome the limitations we had identified in the previous sections, and, in particular, to give students the opportunity to apply project monitoring and control body of knowledge.

Both at ORT and UFSC, we had identified that students were not being given the opportunity to apply PMC competences. While in both universities modules of the body of knowledge for PMC were included in the syllabus, they were only being delivered at the *remember* and *understand* levels of Bloom's taxonomy [12]. In contrast, areas associated with project planning were given at *remember*, *understand* and *apply* levels through the implementation of assigned classroom projects.

Thus, the following activities were undertaken to develop the proposed approach:

- Syllabus alignment: to align ORT and UFSC project management modules, we mapped the topics and learning outcomes for the courses. Even though both courses were based on the Project Management Body of Knowledge, they drifted in the amount of effort devoted to each knowledge area. The result of this work is presented in **Table** 1;
- Learning module piloting: we piloted the module at ORT giving more importance to the PMC knowledge areas. To achieve this, the application exercise involved the planning and management of a simple project. Students were lead to an incremental lifecycle, with three deliveries. First a plan (which should include chapters for all knowledge areas associated with PMBOK initiation and planning). Secondly, they were requested to hand in two progress reports;
- Development of the simulation software: following an incremental Use-Case centered software development approach; we have developed the first version of the project execution simulation software. This is described in section 4;
- Simulation software piloting and evaluation: we piloted the simulation software with a small cohort of students at UFSC. This is described in section 5.

Fig. 1 shows a high-level overview of the activities that we performed during 2016-2017 as a joint effort to define and apply the approach.

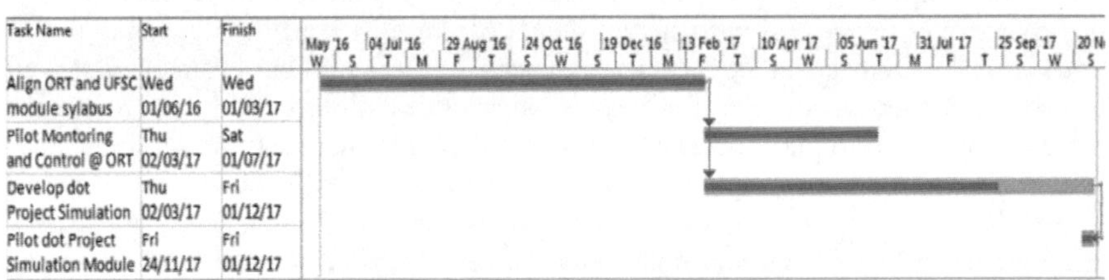

Fig. 1. Overview of the project plan

Thus, the two major results of the development of the approach: the teaching module and the software tool for simulation are presented in the following sections.

4 A project simulation-based approach to educate students in software project management.

The simulation-based project monitoring and control learning approach was developed to address the students' need to apply monitoring and control. In particular, the intention of this approach is to give students opportunity to apply the PMC body of knowledge.

Starting the approach development, our appraisal of the initial situation at both universities was:

- Both courses were based on the PMBOK
- Both covered most of the knowledge areas

- Both were evaluated with an application-oriented exercise and final exams.
- The application-oriented exercise involved extensive planning but required no applied execution nor monitoring and control real practices.

Thus, having this initial scenario, we decided that, to give students the opportunity to apply the processes of the monitoring and control knowledge area, one way was to change the application-oriented practical activities.

These activities include decision-making on significant deviations that may lead to corrective actions, even in the context of the time constraints of an undergraduate project management class course in which it is not possible to develop a real project, and more than half the time of the course is dedicated to the project planning. As the result, a learning plan was developed to achieve the pedagogical objectives defined for a one-semester 72 hours course.

Thus, we also envisioned a simulated software platform, were students would write-in their project plans, while instructors would control the execution, introducing simulated deviations from each student plan. Thereby, allowing students to apply the monitoring and control knowledge they had received during the modules.

4.1 Module delivery strategy

This section presents how we envision the module delivery. **Fig.** 2 presents an overview of the proposed approach.

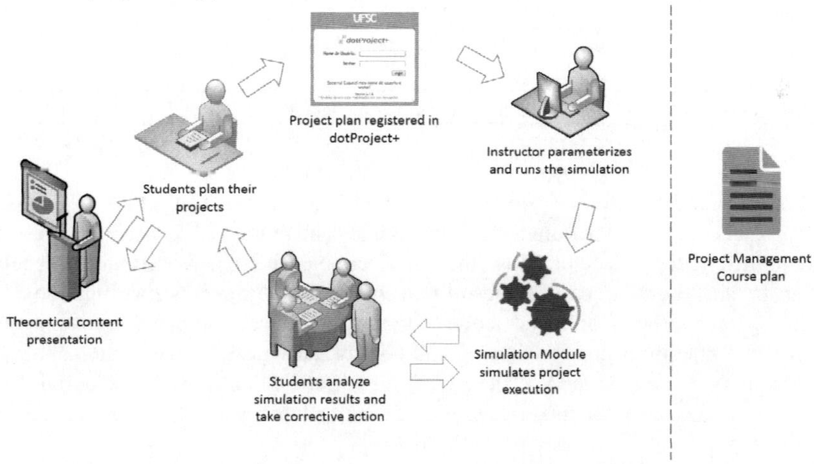

Fig. 2. Simulation-Based Project Monitoring and Control Learning Approach

Each week, a theoretical overview of project management is presented. These presentations cover the project management knowledge areas of Scope, Time, Costs, Quality, Human Resources, Communications, Risks, Acquisitions and Stakeholders, as defined in the teaching plan presented in **Table** 1.

Table 1. Unified Project Management Course Plan

Subject	Learning Objectives	Module milestone
Introduction and Basic concepts	Understand project management basic concepts	
Project Initiation and Planning	Understand project initiation	Application-exercise presented to students.
Project Charter	Develop Project Charter	
Scope, WBS, and Activities	Plan scope and activities	
Resources Estimation	Estimate project resources	
Schedule	Develop project schedule	
Quality, Human Resources and Communications	Plan quality and human resources and communication	
Risk Management	Plan project risk management	
Acquisitions, Costs and budget	Plan project acquisitions, costs and budget	Deadline for project plan delivery
Project monitoring and control	Understand software project monitoring and control concepts	
Simulated project execution	Execute monitoring and control activities	Deadline progress report 1
Monitoring and control practice	Analyze project execution data and take corrective actions	
Project closure	Understand project closure concepts	Deadline final report

For the practical activities, students are asked to form into groups that will make up their project teams for the duration of the module. The practical activities are presented and defined by the instructor. Then, the introduction of the software simulation enables the instructor to present case studies of real software requirements specification documents. Thereby, the breadth and scope of the practical activities are not compromised by the introduction of the monitoring and control activities (as it was the case in the pilot activity carried out at ORT described in section 3). For the practical activity, students are required to document each area of their planning in a project management tool.

We have use dotProject+ [17] as the project management tool to support the approach and as the basis for the development of the project execution simulation because dotProject+ is a free project management tool that has been developed and evolved through improvements in its main features and also by the development of several plugins to support project management education [17]. These improvements in dotProject+ have expanded its functionality by supporting all processes of the PMBOK knowledge areas.

As it has been mentioned, the practical activity results in three deliveries. The first one with the project plan, and two subsequent deliveries with progress reports.

Upon the first deadline, all teams are requested to present their plan to the class and to the instructor, who evaluates the project plans for their technical quality.

The deadline for the delivery of the project plan, coincides with the presentation of the PMC concepts. Thus, the instructor parameterizes dotProject+ to allow students to start simulating the execution of their projects.

The simulation generates progress records and possible risks occurrences with its impacts in terms of effort, costs, deadlines and resource allocation. Following, the students then analyze the project status, based on the management indicators provided by the tool, such as the earned value analysis indicators. Students then decide on possible necessary corrective actions, perform them, and present it to the whole group.

For each of the next three weeks, this cycle of simulation of execution, analysis, taking of corrective actions and presentation, are repeated by the students, using the tool. Next section presents a technical overview of the dotProject+ simulation tool.

4.2 The dotProject+ Project Simulation: technical overview

dotProject+ has been successfully used to support the learning of project management knowledge areas [17]–[19]. One of the most important functionalities for this support is the instructional feedback to the students, which is carried out during the student's project planning (**Fig.** 3). The platform provides immediate feedback about necessary planning steps, incomplete artefacts and tips on how to better carry out each step of the planning. On the instructor's side, the tool provides support to the management of student classes, groups and teams/projects, as well as the artefacts they produce and also performing a semi-automated evaluation of the various artefacts produced, especially in relation to its completeness.

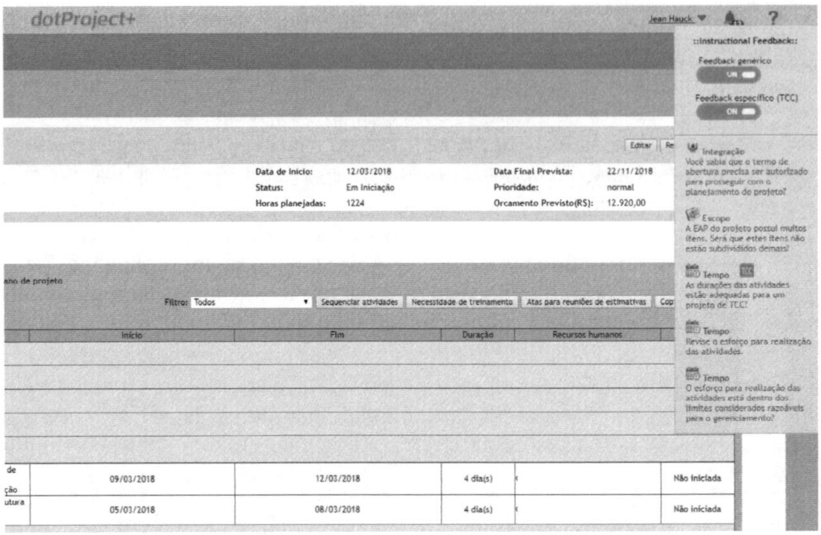

Fig. 3. dotProject+ with instructional feedback supporting Project Management learning

Thus, we decided to use dotProject+ for supporting the software Project Management course, and enhance it by developing a project simulation plugin to fulfil our learning objectives.

Based on our needs, a requirements engineering was performed following an Use-Case based analysis approach. Through this approach, two main actors were identified: Instructor and Student. As can be seen in **Fig.** 4, the Instructor can configure the simulation parameters, generate the execution of the simulation and analyze the results of the simulation. The Student can visualize the results of the project execution simulation and manage the possible corrective actions.

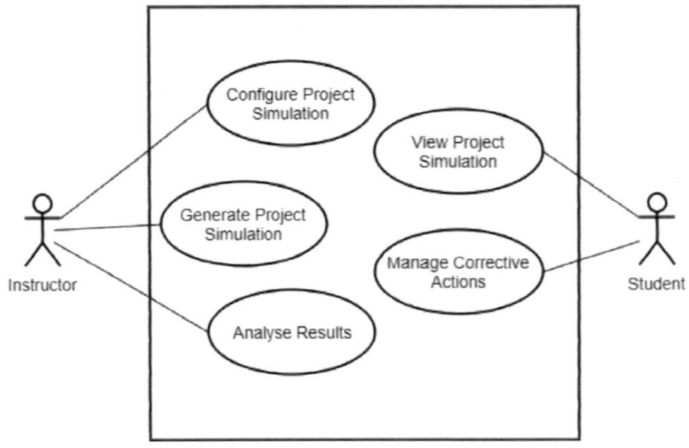

Fig. 4. Simulation plugin Use Cases

Following the process presented in **Fig.** 2, as part of managing students' progress in the dotProject+ tool, the Instructor accesses the tool and views the student groups and their projects from each of the classes in which he or she teaches. In the project simulation screen (**Fig.** 5**a**), after selecting the class, the instructor can parameterize the project simulation, indicating the period of execution to be simulated, the sensibility of the simulation, what types of risks and the projects to be simulated.

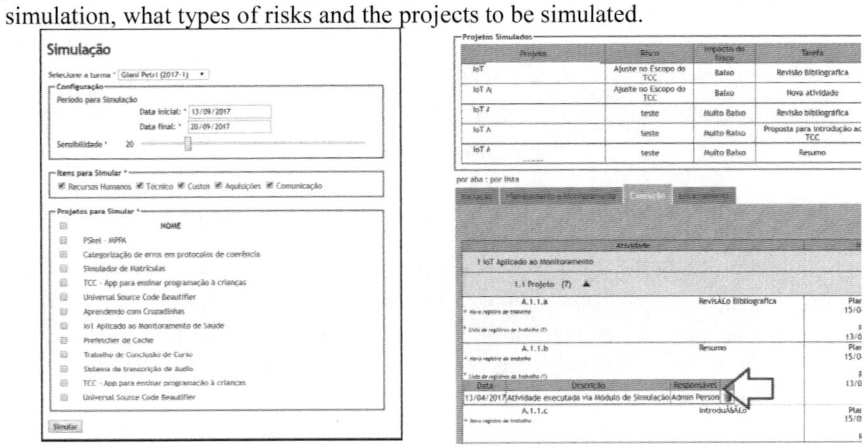

(a) Simulation configuration (b) Simulation results

Fig. 5. Simulation Module

After clicking on "simulate", the system performs the simulation of the project execution and generates execution records of the project, as shown in **Fig.** 5**b**. Then, the Simulation plugin scrolls through the list of planned activities for the simulated period of all selected projects, including tasks not yet finalized from previous periods. Based on this list of tasks, the simulation plugin draws from the planned risks those that may occur in the period, based on a Poisson distribution simulation [19].

Based on the planned risks, classified according to a field-based classification [20], previously prioritized by students based on the calculated exposure factor, the Simulation Plugin then simulates the occurrence of risks, generating the possible impacts, according to each type of risk. **Fig.** 6 shows a high-level description in pseudo-code of the plugin simulation algorithm.

```
function do_simulation($configuration){
        global $projectRisks, $projectTasks, $projectChangedTasks;
        foreach($configuration->selectedProject as $project){
                $projectRisks = selectProjectRisks($project, $configuration);
                $projectTasks = selectProjectTasks($project, $configuration);
                executeSimulation($projectTasks, $projectRisks);
                updateRisks($projectRisks);
                saveTaskLogs($projectChangedTasks);
        }
}
```

Fig. 6. Project Execution Simulation plugin high-level algorithm

Within the `executeSimulation` procedure (**Fig.** 6), the Poisson distribution (**Fig.** 7) was chosen for the possibility of simulating the probability of occurrence of a risk in a possibly large number of tasks executed within a certain range of dates of the projects' planned schedule. Furthermore, the historical probability of occurrence of each type of risk is obtained from a survey conducted by the Brazilian PMI Chapter [21].

$$f(k;\lambda) = \frac{e^{-\lambda}\lambda^k}{k!}$$

Fig. 7. Poisson risk-type probability

The probability of occurrence of each type of risk is calculated, as follows:

- *e* is the basis of the natural logarithm,
- *k!* is the factorial of the number of discrete occurrences of a given type of risk in the planned time interval,
- λ is the expected number of occurrences, taken from the PMI survey [21] , with the sensibility parameter, defined by the instructor on starting the execution simulation.

Currently, the first initial version of the simulation module is implemented and has already been used in the context of a project management course, as presented in the next section.

5 Initial Evaluation

To evaluate the applicability and the perception of learning of our approach, the unified Project Management Course including project execution simulation to support PMC learning was applied in the Project Management class of the Bachelor of Information Systems course at UFSC during the second semester of 2017.

The use of the project execution simulation was evaluated under two perspectives: (i) whether the use of the simulation in the course contributed to the learning of Project Monitoring and Control and (ii) if the simulation module is adequate to be used as support for Project Monitoring and Control learning.

This initial evaluation was conducted using a single group posttest-only design [22]. Nineteen students participated in this initial evaluation. Students participated in the simulation module and after asked to answer a questionnaire. This questionnaire included questions related to the two aspects of learning perception and applicability of the simulation module. Participants were mostly men (85%), all attending the course for the first time and with no previous project management experience. **Fig.** 8 presents initial evaluation results, broken down by the applicability of the module in terms of five categories: easiness to use, usefulness, functional completeness, functional correctness and satisfaction.

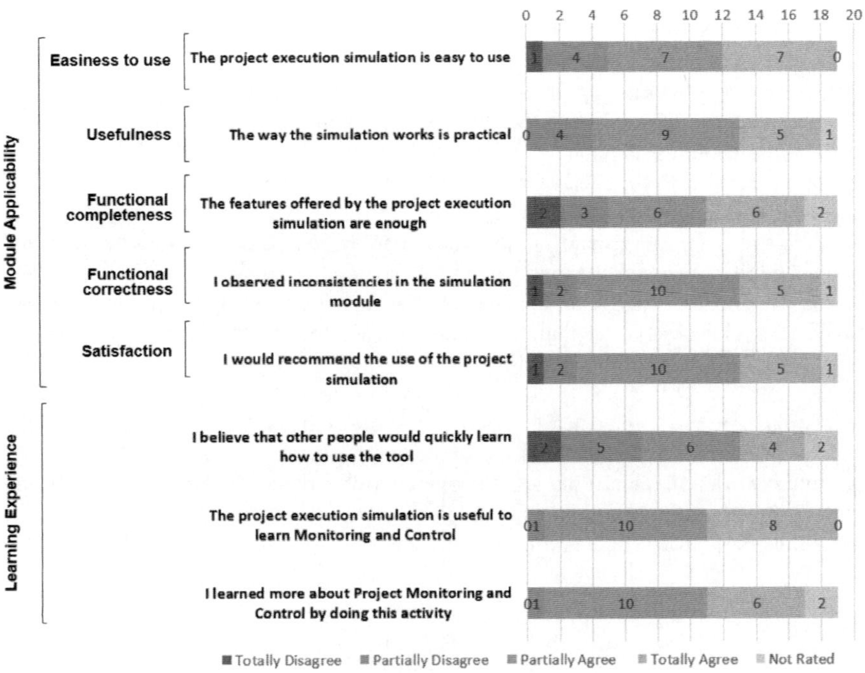

Fig. 8. Initial evaluation results

In terms of the evaluation of the simulation module applicability, it is possible to observe (**Fig.** 8), that most of the participating students agree that the module is easy to use (74%), its use is practical (74%) and that the functionalities offered by the simulation module are enough to support the learning of Project Monitoring and Control process area (70%). As opportunities for improvement, 83% of the students identified inconsistencies in the simulation. A causal analysis of this result revealed a defect in the programming that generated incomplete execution data in some cases.

Regarding the learning perception, the majority of the students (95%) agree that project execution is useful as a support for Project Monitoring and Control learning and most agree (89%) that they had learned more about Project Monitoring and Control using project execution simulation.

Some threats to the validity of this initial evaluation can be observed, such as the small sample of students, which limits the possibilities of generalization of the conclusions. Likewise, the use of single group posttest-only design is naturally subject to maturation and testing threats. Despite these threats to validity, this application is an initial evaluation of the project execution simulation, using a simulation module that is still in development, and the results can raise insights that contribute to the continuity of its development and the possibility of experimentation with larger experimental groups in the future.

6 Conclusions

This paper presented our current approach to teaching software Project Management. This approach focuses on giving the students the opportunity to work at the first three levels of the Bloom's taxonomy. In particular, the motivation with this approach is to provide students with the capacity to apply project monitoring and control knowledge. A key differentiating aspect of our approach is that we have re-designed a PMBOK-based course from the ground up so that technological elements could be seamless integrated into the students′ experience in the module.

As such, the enabler for giving the students the capacity to apply this knowledge is a project execution simulation plugin. This paper presented the development process and main design decisions of this plugin.

Furthermore, we have presented our initial evaluation of the project execution simulation approach. In general, positive responses have been received from the students who have come into contact with the approach.

Our future work will include the full deployment of the redesigned module at ORT and UFSC software project management modules and its evaluation at larger scale to better understand the impact of the proposed approach.

References

[1] A. Abran, J. W. Moore, P. Bourque, R. Dupuis, and L. L. Tripp, *Guide to the Software Engineering Body of Knowledge*, vol. 19759, no. 6. 2004.

[2] M. Ardis, D. Budgen, G. W. Hislop, J. Offutt, M. Sebern, and W. Visser, "SE 2014: Curriculum Guidelines for Undergraduate Degree Programs in Software Engineering," *Computer (Long. Beach. Calif).*, vol. 48, no. 11, pp. 106–109, 2015.

[3] S. Matalonga, G. Mousques, and A. Bia, "Deploying Team-Based Learning at Undergraduate Software Engineering Courses," in *2017 IEEE/ACM 1st International Workshop on Software Engineering Curricula for Millennials (SECM)*, 2017, pp. 9–15.

[4] Project Management Institute, *A guide to the project management body of knowledge (PMBOK ® guide)*. 2013.

[5] S. . W. W. Dörner Ralf; Gobel, *Serious games : foundations, concepts and practice*. Switzerland: Springer, 2016.

[6] J. E. N. Lino, M. A. Paludo, F. V. Binder, S. Reinehr, and A. Malucelli, "Project management game 2D (PMG-2D): A serious game to assist software project managers training," in *2015 IEEE Frontiers in Education Conference (FIE)*, 2015, pp. 1–8.

[7] C. G. Von Wangenheim, R. Savi, and A. F. Borgatto, "DELIVER! - An educational game for teaching Earned Value Management in computing courses," *Inf. Softw. Technol.*, vol. 54, no. 3, pp. 286–298, 2012.

[8] A. Diniz De Souza, R. Duarte Seabra, J. Marinho Ribeiro, and L. E. Da S. Rodrigues, "SCRUMI: A Board Serious Virtual Game for Teaching the

SCRUM Framework," in *2017 IEEE/ACM 39th International Conference on Software Engineering Companion (ICSE-C)*, 2017, pp. 319–321.

[9] G. Petri and C. Gresse von Wangenheim, "How games for computing education are evaluated? A systematic literature review," *Comput. Educ.*, vol. 107, pp. 68–90, Apr. 2017.

[10] K. Jones, *Simulations : a handbook for teachers and trainers*. London New York: Kogan Page Nichols Pub. Co, 1987.

[11] C. Caulfield, J. C. Xia, D. Veal, and S. Paul Maj, "A systematic survey of games used for software engineering education," *Mod. Appl. Sci.*, vol. 5, no. 6, pp. 28–43, 2011.

[12] B. Bloom, "Bloom ' s Taxonomy," *ReVision*, pp. 1–6, 2001.

[13] A. Calderon, M. Ruiz, and E. Orta, "Integrating Serious Games as Learning Resources in a Software Project Management Course: The Case of ProDec," in *2017 IEEE/ACM 1st International Workshop on Software Engineering Curricula for Millennials (SECM)*, 2017, pp. 21–27.

[14] M.-L. Sánchez-Gordón, R. V O'Connor, R. Colomo-Palacios, and S. Sanchez-Gordon, "A Learning Tool for the ISO/IEC 29110 Standard: Understanding the Project Management of Basic Profile," in *Software Process Improvement and Capability Determination: 16th International Conference, SPICE 2016, Dublin, Ireland, June 9-10, 2016, Proceedings*, P. M. Clarke, R. V O'Connor, T. Rout, and A. Dorling, Eds. Cham: Springer International Publishing, 2016, pp. 270–283.

[15] A. Calderón and M. Ruiz, "A systematic literature review on serious games evaluation: An application to software project management," *Comput. Educ.*, vol. 87, pp. 396–422, Sep. 2015.

[16] E. O. Navarro and A. van der Hoek, "Comprehensive Evaluation of an Educational Software Engineering Simulation Environment," in *20th Conference on Software Engineering Education & Training (CSEET'07)*, 2007, pp. 195–202.

[17] C. G. von Wangenheim, J. C. R. Hauck, and A. von Wangenheim, "Enhancing Open Source Software in Alignment with CMMI-DEV," *IEEE Softw.*, vol. 26, no. 2, pp. 59–67, Mar. 2009.

[18] R. Q. Gonçalves, A. Pereira, and C. G. von Wangenheim, "Supporting Time Planning Aligned with CMMIDEV and PMBOK," in *Seventh International Conference on Software Engineering Advances*, 2012.

[19] R. Q. Gonçalves, E. de F. Kühlkamp, and C. Gresse von Wangenheim, "Enhancing DotProject to Support Risk Management Aligned with PMBOK in the Context of SMEs," *Int. J. Inf. Technol. Proj. Manag.*, vol. 6, no. 2, pp. 40–60, Apr. 2015.

[20] D. D. Wu and D. L. Olson, "Computational simulation and risk analysis: An introduction of state of the art research," *Math. Comput. Model.*, vol. 58, no. 9–10, pp. 1581–1587, Nov. 2013.

[21] PMI Chapter Brazil, "PMI survey," 2014. .

[22] L. B. Christensen, R. B. Johnson, and L. A. Turner, "Research Methods, Design, and Analysis," *Araştırma Yöntemleri Desen ve Anal.*, p. 560, 2010.

¿Los estudiantes de pregrado son capaces de diseñar software? Estudio de la relación entre el tiempo de codificación y el tiempo de diseño en el desarrollo de software.

Silvana Moreno[1] and Diego Vallespir[1]

[1] Universidad de la República, Uruguay
smreno@fing.edu.uy, dvallesp@fing.edu.uy

Resumen. El diseño es una actividad fundamental del proceso de desarrollo de software. Durante el diseño se traducen los requisitos en una representación del software cuya calidad puede ser evaluada.
Este trabajo busca, por un lado, conocer el esfuerzo que dedican estudiantes de pregrado a diseñar en relación al que dedican a codificar. Por otro lado, saber cuál es la percepción de los estudiantes respecto al diseño de software y a la enseñanza de esta disciplina durante la carrera.
Se analizan los datos recabados en el contexto de cursos donde los estudiantes desarrollan 8 programas siguiendo un proceso y registrando sus datos en una herramienta. El análisis realizado muestra que los estudiantes dedican al menos 4 veces más de tiempo a la codificación que al diseño de software. Además, pocos estudiantes se dan cuenta que no dedican el tiempo suficiente en etapas tempranas del desarrollo.
Nosotros entendemos que no han incorporado la práctica de elaborar un diseño detallado cuando construyen software. Esto nos invita a repensar la forma en la cual se enseña diseño de software en las carreras universitarias de computación.

Keywords: Software Design, Student Effort, Student Perception, Empirical Study

1 Introducción

El desarrollo de software es una actividad importante y cada vez más compleja en el mundo actual. A pesar de que en las últimas décadas se han hecho avances importantes en la ingeniería de software, lograr desarrollar software de calidad aún no es una tarea sencilla [1].

Entendemos que es necesario fortalecer a la industria del software mediante mejoras en la educación en ingeniería de software. De esta manera, la industria contará con personal mejor calificado. En particular, entendemos que es necesario enseñar (y educar mejor en) las prácticas conocidas que permiten desarrollar software de calidad. De esta forma se puede consolidar una cultura de calidad en los ingenieros de software; cultura que no es evidente se tenga hoy [2].

El diseño de software es una de estas prácticas. Durante el diseño se traducen los requisitos en una representación del software cuya calidad puede ser evaluada. Diversas opiniones coinciden en que el diseño de software es uno de los componentes más importantes para asegurar el éxito de un sistema de software [3],[4].

Lamentablemente, el diseño es un tema difícil de comprender en el pregrado, y el éxito parece requerir un cierto nivel de desarrollo cognitivo que pocos estudiantes alcanzan [4]. Salvo algunas excepciones [5], la mayoría de los investigadores en informática no ven a los estudiantes como diseñadores.

Los estudiantes adoptan normalmente la mala práctica de desarrollo "*code-and-fix*" (codificar y corregir). El *code-and-fix* es poco útil, pero bastante común incluso en la industria [6]. Esta práctica consiste en codificar (programar algo tratando que el resultado proporcione los objetivos deseados), ejecutar pruebas, y luego corregir el código para que funcione (normalmente añadiendo más código, probar y volver a corregir).

El objetivo de este trabajo es conocer el esfuerzo que dedican a diseñar software estudiantes de pregrado. Además, nos interesa conocer la percepción de los estudiantes con respecto al diseño de software a lo largo de la carrera.

El resto del documento se estructura de la siguiente forma: la sección 2 plantea los trabajos relacionados; en la sección 3 se explica la propuesta y metodología de trabajo seguida; la sección 4 presenta el contexto de la investigación; en la sección 5 se realiza el análisis de los datos y en la sección 6 se presenta la percepción de los estudiantes; los hallazgos realizados se discuten en la sección 7 y las amenazas a la validez en la sección 8; por último, la sección 9 resume las conclusiones a las que se llegó durante la realización de este trabajo y los trabajos a futuro.

2 Trabajos relacionados

Con el objetivo de conocer los trabajos relacionados a la enseñanza y aprendizaje del diseño de software realizamos una búsqueda en Scopus aplicando la cadena: (*"software design") and (students or teach or learn*). También se incluyeron artículos mediante la técnica de *backward snowballing*.

Encontramos un conjunto de estudios relacionados que utilizan la misma especificación de requerimientos *("super alarm clock"*) para conocer acerca del diseño de software producido por estudiantes.

El artículo reportado por Tenenberg [7] describe las habilidades que tienen los estudiantes al diseñar software utilizando como datos primarios los diseños elaborados. Tenenberg utilizó los datos recabados por un estudio multi-institucional y multinacional, donde participaron 21 instituciones de 4 países [8]. Los participantes representan tres tipos de categorías dentro de la población de estudio*: First competency students, Graduating students* y *Educators*. Los 314 participantes se clasifican en 28 *educators*, 136 *first-competency* y 150 *graduating students*. Se entrega a cada participante la especificación del "*super alarm clock*" que debe diseñar de forma individual. Al terminar, se les pide que "hablen" de su diseño y describan la función de cada parte. Los resultados indican que con el aumento de categoría, los participantes usan menos notaciones de diseño textual y más notaciones gráficas y estandarizadas. Además son mas conscientes de los problemas con las especificaciones ambiguas. Sin embargo, el nivel educativo parece tener poco efecto en la valoración de los estudiantes sobre las características claves del diseño.

En los estudios presentados por Eckerdal [9, 10] se examinan los artefactos producidos por los estudiantes que participaron del estudio reportado por Tenenberg [7]. Los diseños construidos por los estudiantes son agrupados utilizando una clasificación de diseño (*nothing, restatment, skumtomte, first step, partial design y complete*) propuesta por los investigadores. Los resultados indican un bajo rendimiento en los estudiantes próximos a graduarse. Los porcentajes asociados a las categorías propuestas indican que: un 3% produce *nothing*, un 18% *restatment*, un 41% *skumtomte*, 29% *first step*, 7% *partial design* y 2% *complete*. Además se recogieron los antecedentes académicos y demográficos incluyendo: su edad y sexo; su formación académica y números de cursos. Se utilizaron estos datos para mostrar que existe una correlación positiva entre las categorías de diseño producidas y el número de cursos tomados.

El estudio publicado por Eckerdal [9] fue posteriormente revisado por Loftus [11] en el contexto de un curso que integra el conocimiento del diseño de los estudiantes con el estudio de metodologías ágiles. El objetivo de este trabajo es conocer si los estudiantes próximos a graduarse son capaces de diseñar en grupo y además si son capaces de reconocer diseños buenos y malos producidos por otros. Para evaluar la calidad de los diseños, los autores proponen un sistema de ponderación relativo a cada área de diseño: Análisis, Arquitectura global (estructurales y de comportamiento), el diseño detallado (estructurales, de comportamiento, base de datos, interfaz gráfica de usuario, de seguridad) y la vinculación entre los artefactos de diseño. Los resultados obtenidos confirman los reportados por Eckerdal [4]. Además, señala que las principales cosas que faltaban en los diseños de los estudiantes eran descripciones del comportamiento del sistema y la consistencia entre los diagramas de casos de uso y los diseños implementados. Sin embargo, llegaron a la conclusión de que los estudiantes son capaces de reconocer un buen diseño cuando lo ven. Los autores concuerdan que es posible que la dinámica social de los grupos puede haber impactado en los diseños presentados.

En el estudio reportado por Lynda Thomas [12] se expanden la investigación de Eckerdal [9]; y en lugar de investigar si los estudiantes son capaces de producir un diseño de software, el objetivo es determinar la comprensión de los estudiantes con la instrucción "Producir un diseño". Utilizaron un enfoque fenomenográfico para obtener una visión de los aspectos críticos del fenómeno "Producir un diseño". Recolectaron datos de 35 estudiantes que fueron proyectos finales de un curso. Los autores analizaron todos los diseños y construyeron una lista de características fundamentales que diferencian las distintas formas en que los estudiantes entienden el fenómeno de diseño (*informal design, analysis, static structure, dynamic behavior, multiple related artifacts, expert category*). Los resultados obtenidos no resultan tan malos en el área de las habilidades de diseño de los estudiantes como se reportó inicialmente. Los estudiantes obtuvieron mejores resultados que los reportados por Eckerdal [10] y Loftus [11]. Sin embargo, aunque los estudiantes conocen los mismos métodos / enfoques que los profesionales, carecen de la experiencia necesaria para poder producir diseños elegantes.

Chenglie Hu [13] continúa esta línea de trabajos reportando un experimento en el que 12 estudiantes próximos a graduarse realizan el diseño al mismo problema "*super alarm clock*" de forma individual. En este caso los estudiantes realizaron el ejercicio como parte de un curso avanzado de diseño. Los resultados muestran que alrededor del 80% de los estudiantes pudieron completar un diseño o en su mayoría. Específicamente un 50% de los diseños fueron clasificados en la categoría *partial design* y un 33,3% en la categoría *complete*.

Los trabajos encontrados examinan de diferentes formas los diseños de software producidos en la academia. El primer estudio [7] reporta tendencias a medida que la formación de los estudiantes avanza. Estudiantes con más formación usan menos notaciones de diseño textual y notaciones más gráficas, además que son mas conscientes de las ambigüedades al especificar. Otros estudios examinan los artefactos producidos por los estudiantes para conocer cuanto pueden producir "diseño de software" [9], [10],[11],[13]. Algunos autores concluyen que la mayoría de los estudiantes que se gradúan no son capaces de diseñar un sistema de software. Además, la mayoría de los estudiantes no parecen entender qué tipo de información deberían incluir al diseñar software [9] y [10]. Estos resultados son confirmados posteriormente por Loftus [11]. Chenglie Hu [13] revela resultados que se contraponen con los anteriores estudios, donde el 80% de los diseños producidos corresponden a las categorías *partial design* y *complete*. Desde una perspectiva diferente, Lynda Thomas [12] analiza los artefactos para determinar la comprensión del estudiante al producir un diseño de software. Concluyen que los estudiantes conocen los artefactos de diseño, aunque hace falta experiencia para lograr diseños de expertos.
Los estudios presentados anteriormente utilizan el diseño construido (producto) para examinar, clasificar y concluir sobre cuanto pueden producir diseño de software los estudiantes.

Nuestro trabajo cambia el enfoque, analizando el esfuerzo dedicado por los estudiantes al diseño de software. En particular, nos interesa conocer si los estudiantes consideran importante la fase de diseño de un proceso de desarrollo de software.

1 Metodología de desarrollo

Propusimos y ejecutamos un estudio en el contexto de un curso de la carrera Ingeniería en Computación de la Universidad de la República, Uruguay, durante los años 2012, 2013 y 2014. Durante el curso los estudiantes realizan 8 ejercicios de desarrollo de software siguiendo un proceso establecido y registrando datos de la ejecución del proceso en una herramienta (*Logs*). Las fases del proceso, los *scripts* y el registro de *logs* se presentan en la figura 1. Los estudiantes desarrollaron cada ejercicio de forma individual.

El proceso de desarrollo se divide en las siguientes fases: planificación, diseño, codificación, compilación, testing y postmortem. Para seguir el proceso se brinda un conjunto de *scripts*. Los *scripts* son una guía que establece las entradas, salidas y actividades a realizar en cada fase. Por ejemplo, las actividades de la fase de diseño son: revisar los requerimientos y producir un diseño que lo satisfaga; registrar los defectos encontrados y el tiempo utilizado en dicha fase.

Los ejercicios son de pequeño porte, de baja y similar complejidad por lo que la fase de diseño se refiere a diseño detallado; i.e. identificar clases, atributos, operaciones, escenarios del programa (o componente), cambios de estado y/o pseudo-codigo.

En la fase de postmortem los estudiantes deben realizar una retrospectiva de su trabajo y registrar en la herramienta los problemas encontrados al seguir el proceso y mejoras posibles. Dicho registro se denomina PIP (Propuesta de Mejora de Proceso) y se solicita el mismo desde el ejercicio 2 al 8 de forma obligatoria.

Al finalizar cada ejercicio los estudiantes entregan los registros de la herramienta, el código fuente y una captura de pantalla con las ejecuciones de las pruebas realizadas.

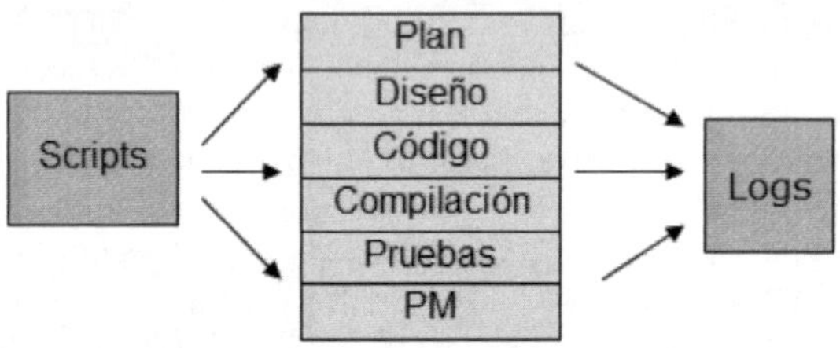

Figura 1. Proceso de desarrollo guiado por *scripts* y registrando datos en los *logs*.

2 Contexto de la investigación

2.1 Objetivos y Métricas

El objetivo de nuestro estudio es conocer el esfuerzo que dedican a diseñar software estudiantes de pregrado. Dicho esfuerzo se mide como el tiempo utilizado en pensar una solución al problema y construir dicha solución antes de codificar. Además, nos interesa conocer cuál es la percepción de los estudiantes frente a los problemas a los que se enfrentan (relacionados al diseño).

Nuestro interés es que los estudiantes resuelvan cada ejercicio a su manera, aplicando sus habilidades y conocimientos. En el curso no se pide que los estudiantes entreguen el diseño realizado. Creemos que una entrega obligatoria del diseño causaría que los estudiantes realizaran un mayor esfuerzo al que normalmente harían para producirlo; lo que estaría sesgando nuestra investigación.

Las variables de respuesta son el tiempo dedicado a diseñar la solución (medido en minutos), el tiempo dedicado a codificar (medido en minutos) y la percepción de los estudiantes respecto al diseño (medido a través del PIP y el cuestionario).

El Personal Software Process (PSP) propone como una de las medidas de la calidad del proceso, indicando como medida indirecta la calidad del diseño, a la relación entre el tiempo de diseño detallado y el tiempo de codificación. Empíricamente se comprobó que cuando esta relación es cercana a 1 a 1 (igual tiempo de diseño que de codificación) se producen productos de una mejor calidad que los producidos cuando esta relación es lejana a 1 a 1 [14], [15].

Nos interesa conocer esta relación en los ejercicios realizados por los estudiantes avanzados de nuestra carrera.

Plantemos la siguiente pregunta de investigación:

RQI: ¿Cuál es la relación entre el esfuerzo dedicado a diseñar con respecto al esfuerzo dedicado a codificar?

Para conocer más sobre la variabilidad de la relación Tiempo de diseño detallado (TDLD) sobre Tiempo de codificación (TCOD) entre estudiantes y de cada estudiante a lo largo de los ejercicios agregamos las siguientes preguntas:

RQ2: ¿Cómo es la variabilidad de la relación (TCOD/TDLD) entre estudiantes?

RQ3: ¿Cómo es la variabilidad de la relación (TCOD/TDLD) a lo largo de los ejercicios que realiza cada estudiante?

Por último, queremos conocer cómo se sienten los estudiante frente a la actividad de diseño, planteando la pregunta:

RQ4: ¿Cuál es la percepción de los estudiante frente al diseño?

2.2 Estudiantes

Participaron un total de 36 estudiantes: 12 en la primera ejecución que se realizó en 2012, 10 en el primera replicación en 2013, y 14 en la segunda replicación en 2014. Estas ejecuciones se llevaron a cabo de la misma manera.

Los participantes son estudiantes de pregrado de Computación de la Universidad de la República, Uruguay. Son estudiantes avanzados que se encuentran en su cuarto o quinto año (último año de la carrera). Todos han aprobado los cursos de Programación 3, Programación 4, Taller de Programación e Ingeniería de software. Durante estos cursos se enseñan técnicas y artefactos de diseño de software, lenguajes de programación, algoritmos y conceptos fundamentales de ingeniería de software. Consideramos que el grupo de estudiantes que participó es homogéneo, ya que son estudiantes en una etapa similar de su carrera.

Los estudiantes dieron su consentimiento por escrito para que los datos que ellos registran durante el proceso puedan ser usados en trabajos de investigación sin nunca revelar la identidad individual de cada uno.

2.3 Procedimiento de recolección de datos y Materiales

El estudio consiste en la realización de 8 ejercicios por parte de un conjunto de estudiantes. Los estudiantes realizan los ejercicios siguiendo los pasos descritos por el conjunto de scritps y recolectan y registran sus datos en la herramienta. Todos los estudiantes desarrollan los mismos ejercicios en el mismo orden. Debido a que el proceso seguido por cada estudiante se mide 8 veces (8 programas), el estudio tiene un diseño de medidas repetidas [16].

El uso de los scripts busca que el estudiante sea disciplinado con su proceso, a través de una serie de pasos. El script de diseño establece revisar los requerimientos y producir un diseño que los satisfaga. La forma (técnica o método) para producirlo es una elección del estudiante.

Los ejercicios los realizan de forma individual en sus casas, pero son monitoreados por un tutor. Durante la realización de cada ejercicio se producen intercambios de correos electrónicos, llamadas telefónicas o reuniones para evacuar consultas. Al finalizar cada ejercicio, el tutor asignado revisa y envía las correcciones necesarias al estudiante. El tutor revisa que el estudiante siga el proceso de forma completa, registrando todos los datos requeridos en los logs y que estos sean consistentes.

Los estudiantes realizan los ejercicios sin límite de tiempo. Limitar el trabajo a la duración de una clase puede distorsionar la forma en la que desarrolla software un estudiante. Esta limitante ocasionaría (quizás) ciertos apuros en algunas fases del proceso o despreocuparse de la calidad del software, entre otras distorsiones posibles.

Antes de comenzar el primer ejercicio cada estudiante debe elegir el lenguaje de programación a utilizar a lo largo del curso. Nuestro interés es recolectar datos de la ejecución del proceso de desarrollo con el uso de un lenguaje que el estudiante domina y no datos del aprendizaje de un lenguaje.

Los 8 programas (ejercicios) realizados por los estudiantes son los mismos utilizados en los cursos del PSP. Son programas sencillos, de soluciones a problemas matemáticos (a excepción del programa 2). Además, si bien pueden resolverse de manera independiente, los requerimientos de los ejercicios permiten y fomentan el reuso de ejercicios anteriores. El cuadro 1 presenta una breve descripción de los programas.

Aunque los programas resulten sencillos, el diseño no deja de ser un aspecto fundamental a considerar. Un buen diseño detallado ayuda a la prevención de defectos y a su testeabilidad [17] así como también al mantenimiento de software. Identificar entidades y relaciones, elaborar el pseudo código de algún algoritmo clave permiten construir las bases bajo las que se implementará y logrará un producto de calidad.

En 2014 incorporamos un cuestionario que los estudiantes responden luego de finalizados los 8 ejercicios. El cuestionario pretende conocer aspectos académicos del estudiante y cuestiones prácticas como, por ejemplo, técnicas de diseño empleadas durante la realización de los ejercicios.

Cuadro 1. Descripción de los ejercicios a realizar

Prog.	Descripción
1	Calcular el promedio y la desviación estándar de un conjunto de números almacenados en una lista enlazada.
2	Contador de líneas de código de una clase y cantidad de métodos.
3	Calcular los parámetros de regresión lineal β0 y β1, así como los coeficientes de correlación r y r2 dado un conjunto de pares de valores.
4	Calcular los tamaños relativos de una clase para los rangos, muy pequeño, pequeño, medio, grande, y muy grande.
5	Integrar numéricamente una función utilizando la regla de Simpson
6	Calcular la función t-student: encontrar el valor de x para el cual integrando la función *t* desde 0 hasta *x* se obtiene el resultado *p*.
7	Calcular la correlación ente dos conjuntos de números X e Y, y la significancia de la correlación. Calcular los parámetros de regresión lineal β0 y β1 para un conjunto de n pares de datos, dar una estimación XK, calcular la proyección YK, donde $Y_K = \beta 0 + \beta 1 . X_K$ Por ultimo, calcular el intervalo de predicción del 70% para esa estimación
8	Calcular los parámetros de estimación (β0, β1, β2, β3) para la regresión múltiple con tres variables.

3 Análisis de Datos

En esta sección se analizan los datos para responder las tres preguntas de investigación planteadas.

RQ1: ¿Cuál es la relación entre el esfuerzo dedicado a diseñar con respecto al esfuerzo dedicado a codificar?

Para responder esta pregunta de investigación estudiamos la proporción que relaciona el tiempo de diseño (TDLD) y el tiempo de codificación (TCOD). Los datos a utilizar consisten de 8 pares de valores (TDLD, TCOD) por estudiante, ya que cada estudiante realiza 8 ejercicios. Participaron un total de 36 estudiantes, por lo que disponemos de 36*8=288 pares de valores.

Analizamos la existencia de outliers utilizando un diagrama *box and whisker*. Se detectan 21 outliers pertenecientes a 8 estudiantes distintos y se analiza uno por uno los datos de cada outlier. A partir de este análisis detectamos que uno de los estudiantes tiene datos que reflejan que no siguió el proceso establecido de forma adecuada. Por lo tanto, eliminamos los 8 pares de datos de ese estudiante del análisis (estos datos tienen 3 outliers). El análisis del resto de los outliers no muestra errores, por lo que contamos con un total de 280 pares de datos.

Para determinar el test estadístico que mejor se ajusta al problema a resolver estudiamos previamente la distribución de los datos, comprobando que los valores no se ajustan a una distribución normal. Por lo tanto, y debido a que el tamaño de la muestra es pequeño utilizamos el test de Wilcoxon [18] de una cola para muestra apareadas. Las muestras están apareadas ya que los pares muestreados (TDLD, TCOD) corresponden a un mismo ejercicio.

Las hipótesis para el test aplicando la relación entre el tiempo de codificación y diseño para cada programa son:

H0: Mediana (TCOD) <= Mediana (TDLD)

H1: Mediana (TCOD) > Mediana (TDLD)

Al ejecutar el test se rechaza la hipótesis nula (p-value < 2.2e-16, el nivel de significancia se toma con valor 0,05), lo que confirma que el tiempo de codificación es mayor al tiempo de diseño.

Para conocer cuánto más o cuál es la relación entre estos tiempos (TCOD = N*TDLD) proponemos aplicar nuevamente el test pero ahora multiplicando el TDLD por un valor N que varía entre 2, 3, 4 y 5, hasta que no se rechace la hipótesis nula.

H0: Mediana (TCOD) <= Mediana (N*TDLD)

H1: Mediana (TCOD) > Mediana (N*TDLD)

La cuadro 2 presenta para los valores de N ejecutados, el p-value obtenido del test.

Cuadro 2 valores resultantes del test de Wilcoxon

N=2	N=3	N=4	N=5
2,2e-16	7,731e-14	0,006118	**0,8629**

Los resultados indican que para N= 2, N=3 y N=4 se rechaza la hipótesis nula (pvalue <= 0,05), por lo que el tiempo de codificación es mayor a 4 veces el tiempo de diseño. Para N= 5 no se logra rechazar la hipótesis nula (pvalue > 0.05). Es decir, estadísticamente podemos comprobar que los estudiantes dedican al menos 4 veces más tiempo a la codificación que al diseño.

RQ2: ¿Cómo es la variabilidad de la relación (TCOD/TDLD) entre estudiantes?

Para conocer la variación entre estudiantes intentamos aplicar la prueba no parametrica de Kruskal-Wallis. Dicha prueba asume que los datos provienen de la misma distribución. Comúnmente, una forma en que se viola ese supuesto es con datos heterocedásticos. Por lo tanto, aplicamos el test de Levene que propone en la hipótesis nula que las varianzas poblacionales son iguales (homocedasticidad) y en la hipótesis alternativa que las varianzas difieren (heterocedasticidad). El p-value resultante de aplicar la prueba de Levene es inferior a 0.05, por lo tanto, rechazamos la hipótesis nula de igualdad de varianzas y concluimos que existe una diferencia entre las variaciones de la relación (TCOD/TDLD) entre estudiantes.

Este resultado no nos permite aplicar la prueba de Kruskal-Wallis por lo que decidimos estudiar la variación entre estudiantes utilizando un diagrama de boxplot presentado en la figura 2. Graficamos 35 valores, correspondientes a cada uno de los 35 estudiantes participantes. Para cada estudiante se calcula la relación TCOD/TDLD promedio de los 8 ejercicios ($\sum TCOD_i / \sum TDLD_i$, para i entre 1 y 8).

La enorme variación entre estudiantes en la relación del esfuerzo dedicado a codificación y diseño puede observarse fácilmente. Para el total de los estudiantes, esto varía desde 1,2 hasta 16,6. Además, el rango intercuartílico (IQR) es 5,2. Esto indica una dispersión importante en los datos. Es decir, los estudiantes se comportan de forma diferente y muy variable en lo que refiere a la relación del esfuerzo entre código y diseño.

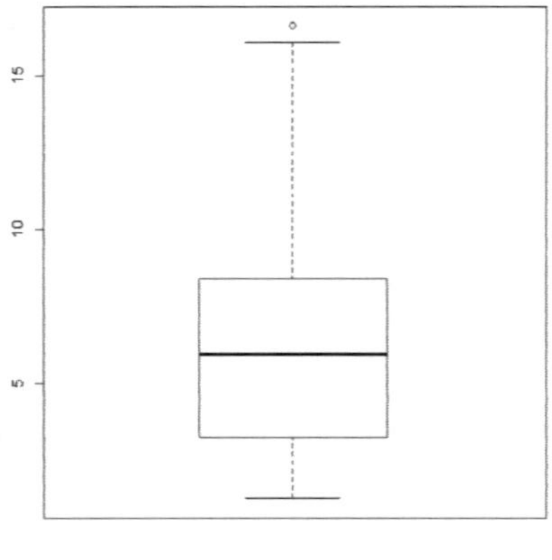

Figura 2. Promedio TCOD/TDLD para cada estudiante.

RQ3: ¿Cómo es la variabilidad de la relación (TCOD/TDLD) a lo largo de los ejercicios que realiza cada estudiante?

Para conocer la variación individual analizamos la relación TCOD/TDLD de cada estudiante en los 8 ejercicios. Esta variación puede analizarse a partir del valor del primer cuartil, tercer cuartil y el rango intercuartílico de cada estudiante que se presenta en el cuadro 3.

Se puede observar que la variación individual es muy dispar. Algunos estudiantes como el 1, el 16 y el 19 tienen poca variación a lo largo de sus ejercicios. En estos casos podríamos decir que los estudiantes son "consistentes" en relación al tiempo que dedican al diseño y a la codificación. Otros casos, por ejemplo los estudiantes 10 y 30 presentan una variación en la relación TCOD/TDLD durante la realización de sus ejercicios bastante dispar. La figura 3 presenta la relación TCOD/TDLD a lo largo de los 8 ejercicios para los estudiantes 1, 10, 16, 19 y 30.

Cuadro 3. valores de Q1, Q3 y IQR por estudiante para los 8 programas

Est.	**1**	**2**	**3**	**4**	**5**	**6**	**7**	**8**	**9**	**10**	**11**	**12**
Q1	1,1	6,4	2,6	1,9	15,2	2,3	4,2	1,5	3,2	13,3	4,6	5,7
Q3	2,7	15,6	6,6	5	23,5	3,9	8,3	2	7,7	31,9	11,8	8,6
IQR	1,5	9,1	4	3,3	8,2	1,6	4	0,4	4,5	18,5	7,1	2,8
Est.	**13**	**14**	**15**	**16**	**17**	**18**	**19**	**20**	**21**	**22**	**23**	**24**
Q1	2,5	6,1	7	1	13,5	2,1	3,3	1,4	1,2	2,5	5,1	7,4
Q3	4,6	9	8,9	1,6	18,5	4,2	3,9	3,3	1,9	3,9	7,3	17,9
IQR	2	2,9	1,9	0,6	5	2	0,5	1,8	0,6	1,3	2,2	10,4
Est.	**25**	**26**	**27**	**28**	**29**	**30**	**31**	**32**	**33**	**34**	**35**	
Q1	2,5	4,1	6,1	4,4	4,4	16,1	3	6,2	3,8	2	7,4	
Q3	5,5	10	16,7	9	11	33,8	4,7	12,2	9,9	7,6	12,6	
IQR	2,9	5,8	10,6	4,6	6,5	17,6	1,6	6	6	5,5	5,1	

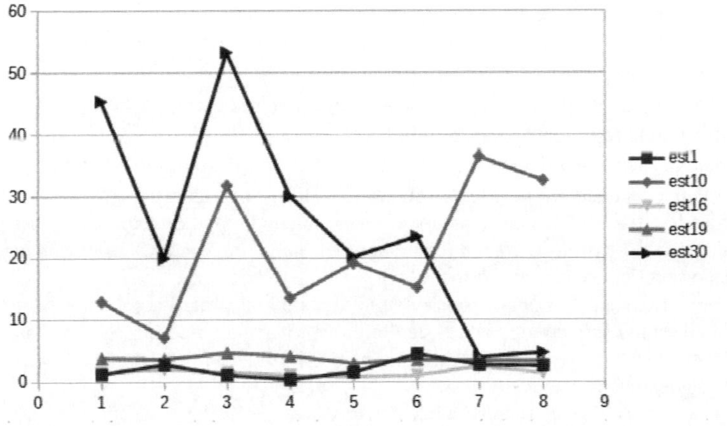

Figura 3. Relación TCOD/TDLD para una muestra de estudiantes a lo largo de los 8 ejercicios

4 Percepción de los estudiantes

Para responder a RQ4 analizamos todos los registros del PIP referentes a la visión de los estudiantes con respecto al diseño y el cuestionario.

RQ4: ¿Cuál es la percepción de los estudiante frente al diseño?

Los registros son completados por los estudiantes de forma obligatoria para los ejercicios del 2 al 8. Sólo 10 registros de PIP de estudiantes distintos (de 245 PIP) describen problemas relacionados al diseño. Los registros presentados en el cuadro 4 muestran cómo estos estudiantes en cierto ejercicio se dieron cuenta que no dedicaron tiempo suficiente en etapas tempranas del desarrollo y los efectos que esto tuvo.

Por otro lado, analizamos parte del cuestionario en papel realizado a partir del curso del año 2014 (14 participantes). El cuestionario contiene una sección de preguntas sobre información académica y profesional del estudiante y una sección de preguntas con relación a la aplicación del proceso. Analizamos las preguntas presentadas en la figura 4 que nos resultan de interés para este trabajo. Con respecto a la pregunta 1, los 14 estudiantes participantes del estudio respondieron que realizaron pseudo código durante la fase de diseño. Además, sólo 1 de los 14 dijo también apoyarse en diagramas de clases y diagramas de colaboración. Para la pregunta 2, se obtuvieron 13 respuestas afirmativas, mientras que 1 estudiante considera que no lo suficiente.

Cuadro 4. Descripciones de PIP recolectadas de la herramienta.

Descripción del PIP
"El problema que encontré fue que le dediqué poco tiempo a la etapa de planificación y al diseño con lo que la etapa de código y testing conllevó más tiempo ya que muchos de los problemas se podrían haber prevenido en esas etapas"
"No se entendió en la etapa de diseño el problema y esto llevó a demorar más en la etapa de codificación al buscar la mejor solución en ese momento"
"Hubo un mal seguimiento de la descripción del método de Gauss, lo que llevó a problemas en la implementación."
"Tuve problemas con la interpretación y el diseño, perdí mucho tiempo para poder resolver un defecto que lo encontré recién en la etapa de UT"
"En la etapa de planificación y diseño leo la tarea y creo entender qué es lo que tengo que hacer, pero en test encuentro problemas que muestran que no entendí"
"Continúo teniendo errores de atención que me cuestan mucho tiempo de retrabajo. Considero que dedico poco tiempo a etapas tempranas del ejercicio como planificación y diseño que luego se refleja en errores costosos"
"Estoy teniendo varios errores por no pensar bien antes de codificar. La solución para esto es hacer un diseño detallado, de manera de definir cada método a desarrollar con sus variables. Esto va a generar más tiempo de diseño, pero disminuye el tiempo de codificación y la cantidad de errores inyectados"
"Gran número de errores (en este caso relacionados con las cuentas del algoritmo) que se descubren recién en la etapa de pruebas"
"Tuve problemas de lógica en las funciones. Debería detenerme más en las etapas de planificación y diseño a entender más al detalle los algoritmos."
"Creo que en no me tomé el tiempo suficiente para comprender a fondo el ejercicio en la etapa de diseño. Esto causó varios inconvenientes a la hora de codificar y hacer el testing, ya que en esas etapas recién me di cuenta que no había comprendido el ejercicio, e incurrí en una pérdida de tiempo y retrabajo evitable."

1. Seleccione cuales de las siguientes actividades realizó durante la fase de diseño □ Pseudo código □ Diagrama de colaboración □ Diagrama de clases □ Otra. Describa brevemente
2. ¿Considera que en la facultad se le enseñó a diseñar?

Figura 4. Preguntas del cuestionario.

5 Discusión

Nuestro estudio sirve para constatar que los estudiantes dedican poco tiempo al diseño en comparación con lo dedicado a la codificación. Esto, suponemos, lleva a pensar la solución al problema durante la codificación, acarreando diversos problemas y empobreciendo la calidad del software.

El no pedir la entrega de diseño elaborado (sólo se pide el registro de tiempo dedicado a la fase) permite conocer el comportamiento normal del estudiante al desarrollar software. Pedir el diseño probablemente sesgaría al estudiante en el seguimiento del proceso.

Estadísticamente los datos muestran que los estudiantes dedican al menos 4 veces más tiempo a la codificación que al diseño. Creemos que esto se puede deber a la falta de conocimiento/conciencia sobre la importancia del diseño en la calidad del software. Por otro lado, la variación individual a lo largo de los ejercicios parece ser signo de una falta de hábito o apropiación del proceso. Los estudiantes, más allá de la naturaleza del problema, no parecen aplicar técnicas o artefactos de diseño de forma habitual.

Los registros del PIP muestran como algunos estudiantes (10/35) son capaces de detectar las consecuencias de no haber diseñado. Creemos que existe una "ansiedad" por comenzar a codificar que interfiere con dedicar el tiempo suficiente a pensar soluciones al problema. Sin embargo, un problema aún mayor es que un numero importante de estudiantes (25/35) ni siquiera son capaces de detectar problemas respecto al diseño.

Los resultados de la encuesta muestran que el 100% de los estudiantes dice que realizan pseudo código, y además 13 de 14 estudiantes consideran que en la facultad se les enseña a diseñar. Resulta un poco inverosímil que hayan hecho pseudo código ya que en muchos casos los registros de tiempos de diseño son de 2 o 3 minutos. Aunque más allá de eso, el dato más interesante es que sólo un estudiante se apoyó en otros artefactos de diseño, lo que revela que realmente no hay una elaboración de la solución durante la fase de diseño del proceso.

6 Amenazas a la validez

Como la mayoría de los estudios empíricos, éstos se ven amenazados por la forma en que la investigación se lleva a cabo. En esta sección se describen las amenazas a la validez que hemos detectado.

Identificamos como una amenaza los problemas de calidad en los datos recolectados. Los registros de tiempos y defectos pueden contener errores de tipeo al registrarlos en la herramienta. Intentamos minimizar esta amenaza con la revisión por parte del tutor, buscando inconsistencias entre los registros de tiempos y defectos, entre otros.

Los estudiantes realizan sus ejercicios desde sus casas lo que provoca un control limitado por parte de los investigadores. Intentamos reducir esta amenaza asignando tutores a los estudiantes de forma de supervisar y atender las consultas durante la realización de ejercicios. Además, el tutor revisa cada ejercicio una vez finalizado y envía feedback con comentarios y correcciones a sus estudiantes.

En tercer lugar, la cantidad de estudiantes en el estudio constituye una amenaza a la conclusión estadística. Los 36 estudiantes en los 3 cursos (2012, 2013 y 2014) resultan ser un tamaño de muestra insuficiente para poder aplicar test paramétricos. Esto provoca la realización del análisis estadístico utilizando test no paramétricos cuya potencia estadística es menor a los test paramétricos [19].

7 Conclusiones

Los resultados de nuestro estudio muestran que los estudiantes dedican poco tiempo al diseño en comparación con el tiempo dedicado a la codificación. Esto nos hace pensar varias cosas. Por un lado, que no han incorporado la práctica de elaborar un diseño detallado cuando construyen software. Por otro lado, deberíamos conocer los motivos de por qué sucede esto y repensar la forma en la cual se enseña diseño de software en las carreras universitarias.

Los estudiantes tienen un comportamiento muy variable entre ellos y también un comportamiento muy variable al desarrollar distintos programas (de similar complejidad y naturaleza). Esto puede estar mostrando una falta importante de hábitos y disciplina al momento de desarrollar software.

El feedback obtenido a través del cuestionario revela que sólo 1 de 14 estudiantes utilizó diagramas de clases y de colaboración. Sin embargo, 13 de los 14 consideró que la facultad le enseñó a diseñar. Si realmente aprenden pero no lo aplican, ¿Qué más podemos hacer como educadores? ¿son necesarios años de experiencia cómo concluye Lynda Thomas [12]?.

Creemos en la necesidad de enfatizar más desde los primeros años de la carrera sobre la importancia y los resultados de la actividad de diseñar en la calidad del software. Esto permitirá no sólo mejores procesos y productos sino mejores ingenieros.

Como trabajo a futuro vamos a estudiar el código entregado por los estudiantes desde el punto de vista de la calidad del diseño. Para esto utilizaremos herramientas que nos permitan detectar anti patrones y *code smells* en el código. Esto nos permitirá entender si los estudiantes que tienen una relación TCOD/TDLD cercano a uno tienen un código más mantenible y con menos problemas de diseño que aquellos que se alejan de esa relación.

También ejecutaremos nuevos estudios con variantes de los aquí presentados. Nos interesa investigar qué sucede si se les pide la entrega obligatoria del diseño. Esto posiblemente provocará un aumento en el tiempo de diseño, pero es interesante conocer si esta entrega mejora la calidad del producto logrado, si el código resultante es más mantenilble, entre otros.

Referencias

1. Chaos, tech. report, Standish Group Int'l (2016)
2. Massood Towhidnejad, Incorporating Software Quality Assurance in Computer Science Education: An Experiment, 32"' ASEE/IEEE Frontiers in Education Conference, Boston, MA (2002).
3. Welcome Message, The 33rd International Conference on Software Engineering, Honolulu, Hawaii, DOI= http://2011. icse-conferences.org/content/welcome (2011).
4. Hu, Chenglie, The Nature of Software Design and Its Teaching: An Exposition, ACM Inroads, New York, NY, USA (2013).
5. Brian A. Danielak, William E. J. Doane.: Studying Students' Early-Stage Software Design Practices ICLS 2014 Proceedings (2014).
6. Steve McConnell., Desarrollo y gestión de proyectos informáticos, Ed.: McGraw-Hill, ISBN: 84-481-1229-6
7. Tenenberg J. et al.: Students Designing Software: a MultiNational, Multi-Institutional Study. Informatics in Education, vol. 4, No. 1, pp 143–162 (2005).
8. T. Chen, S. Cooper, R. McCartney, and L. Schwartzman. The (relative) importance of software design criteria. In Proceedings of the 10th Annual Conference on Innovation and Technology in Computer Science Education, pp 34–38, Monteda Caparica, Portugal (2005).
9. Eckerdal, A., McCartney, R., Moström, J.E., Ratcliffe, M. Zander, C.: Can graduating students design software systems?, Source of the Document Proceedings of the Thirty-Seventh SIGCSE Technical Symposium on Computer Science Education (2007).
10. Eckerdal, A. el al.: Categorizing student software designs: Methods, results, and implications, Computer Science Education vol. 16, Issue 3, pp 197-209 (2006).
11. C. Loftus, L. Thomas, and C. Zander.: Can graduating students design: Revisited. In Proc. SIGCSE '11, pp 105–110, New York, NY, USA, 2011. ACM. (2011).
12. Lynda Thomas; Anna Eckerdal el al.: Graduating Students' Designs – Through a Phenomenographic Lens. Proceedings of the tenth annual conference on International computing education research, pp 91-98, Glasgow, Scotland, United Kingdom (2014).
13. Chenglie Hu. Can Students Design Software? The Answer Is More Complex Than You Think. Proceedings of the 47th ACM Technical Symposium on Computing Science Education, Memphis, Tennessee, USA (2016).
14. W. Humphrey, The Personal Software Process, Tech. Rep. CMU/SEI-2000-TR-022, Software Engineering Institute, Carnegie Mellon University, Pittsburgh, Pa, USA, (2000)
15. W. Humphrey, PSP: A Self-Improvement Process for Software Engineers, Book ,Addison-Wesley, USA, (2005)
16. Juristo, N. Moreno, A.: Basics of Software Engineering Experimentation, Kluwer Academic Press, 1st edition, (2001)
17. McDonald, Marc and Musson, Robert and Smith, Ross, The Practical Guide to Defect Prevention ISBN:9780735622531, Ed.:Microsoft Press, USA. (2007)
18. Gibbons, D, Chakraborti, S, Nonparametric Statistical Inference, Berlin, Heidelberg, isbn=978-3-642-04898-2, (2011)
19. Sheskin, D; Handbook of Parametric and Nonparametric Statistical Procedures, Chapman and Hall/CRC; 5 edition (2011).

Evaluation of source code in ACM ICPC style programming and training competitions

Wilson Julca-Mejia[1], Hugo D. Calderon-Vilca[1] and Flor C. Cárdenas-Mariño[2]

[1] Universidad Nacional Mayor de San Marcos, Lima 01, Perú
hcalderonv@unmsm.edu.pe
[2] Universidad Nacional Tecnológica de Lima Sur, Lima 01, Perú

Abstract. The execution of harmful source code is one of the main problems in the platforms of programming contest. In this research, we propose NinjaCoding, which is a web platform to evaluates the source code in programming contests and training ACM ICPC style. NinjaCoding is designed to be a scalable, safe and economical system. In addition, our proposal ensures the execution of source code through the use of containers and subprocesses. Students can use NinjaCoding to participate in past or active contests and in training problems with live feedback. This system has been tested in several programming contests that have been taken place in various congresses and universities in different Peruvian cities, qualifying more than 1000 presentations in the languages C/C ++, Python and Java. This document describes and discusses the architecture and the implementation that is used in NinjaCoding.

Keywords: Online judge, programming practice, auto grading, programming competition, programming contest, docker, sandbox.

1 Introduction

Annualy ACM ICPC holds contests which are sponsored by IBM, these contests are international programming competitions where universities around the world participate. During the competition, the teams have about 5 hours to solve between 9 and 12 problems. Solutions must be programmed with C, C ++, Java or Python. The programs sent by the teams are compiled and executed with certain input data, if the program fails when calculating the solution, the team is notified and can send the program again or try other problems [15]. The objective of the competitive programming is to produce skilled computer programmers who are well prepared to produce better software or to deal with the most difficult problems in computer science research in the future [22].

Currently, in Peru there are only some platforms for contests and training, each with scalability problems and aimed at a very small community. One of the platforms in Peru is HuahCoding [16] that does not evaluate source code, but only evaluates the final response. Therefore, it does not evaluate if there is compilation error, time limit or memory exceeded. Also, when a programming contest is organized in some events, external platforms such as Uva Judge [17], Timus Online Judge [18], among others, are used. The problem with these is that they provide problems in English language and therefore are not very suitable for students who are just starting college.

In Latin America, especially in Brazil, one of the most used systems to administrate programing contests is BOCA[25]. This system must to be downloaded and configured for the contest.

The manual evaluation in programming competitions that took place in the past lasted days, besides the evaluation systems such as Mooshak, CMS, DOM judge and PC2 had deficiencies in managing the contests, because the collection and classification of shipments, handling of questions and clarifications of competitors, publication of results, and statistics were deficient [3].

The different platforms of programming contests have a main concern: to guarantee the security in the execution of source code, to guarantee this, they use Virtual Machines [7] or Containers [6], and the containers do not incorporate their own kernel, but rather they run directly in the host's core. This shortens the execution route and remove the guest kernel and the virtual hardware layer. In addition, containers can share software resources (libraries) with the host. This action will prevent the code duplication. The absence of kernel and some system libraries make the containers very light, the image sizes can be reduced to a few megabytes, which allows a fast boot process [10].

In this paper, we propose a platform called NinjaCoding that evaluates source code in different programming languages such as C/C ++, Python and Java style ACM ICPC. Its design provides scalability to add other compilers to evaluate presentations in more languages such as Ruby, Php among others. In addition, not only does the platform aim at participants of intermediate or advanced level, but also, participants who are just starting as we provide problems in Spanish and a repository of problems grouped by category and the level of difficulty. NinjaCoding has a mechanism to clarify the contestants about some doubts or problems that may appear during the contest. Also it has roles for the teams, judges, organizers and administrators. These roles have their own interface which is customized according to their necessities. The difference between BOCA[25] and NinjaCoding is that the first one is a system that needs to be downloaded and configured to be used, whereas NinjaCoding is an online system in which it's enough to have an organizer account to organize a programing contest.

For this paper, first we performed the analysis of other programming platforms modules, then an architecture was designed, this architecture not only limit to programming and training contests, but also it is used as a base for adding other modules and functionalities in a way that is scalable and robust. After this design, the implementation stage was carried out. The stack of technologies are Python, Django, Redis, PostgreSQL, Docker, AngularJS, socketIO and deployed in Linux Virtual Private Servers. And finally, it was validated in various online contests, such contests have been organized in various universities since 2016.

In next section is presented the state of the art, in section III we describe the architecture of the system, in section IV the results and discussion are presented, and section V we finalized with the conclusion.

2 Related Works

Systems like Judge.org from [7] and Pythia from [5], provide security against malicious code use Virtual Machines with different approaches. The first one states it takes too long to restart the virtual machines after each correction, so they proceed to restart them after a dozen corrections to amortize the restart time. The second author states that the using of virtual machines that emulate hardware devices such as KVM or VirtualBox, are too slow; which is why he propose a SandBox that executes a very short version of ArchLinux which uses less main memory.

Another component is the Queue, which allows to manage the presentations in the Sandboxes and it is a common component in most of the judges of programming contests [1] [3] [4] [5] [6] [7], it is vital to ensure that a SandBox only takes care of one process at a time, whether it is compiling or executing a single presentation. These queues, according to the approaches of each author, can prioritize certain processes over others; for example, the author [1] prioritizes the compilation processes because it's much faster and this way it provides a much faster feedback to the contestants.

In the architectures of judges of programming contests [1] [2] [3] [4] [5] [7], we observe modules with similar functionalities such as FrontEnd, Grading, Queue Manager, Grading, SandBox and Scoreboard . The FrontEnd is in charge of presenting the challenges or problems to the users and sending the solutions that are made by the contestants and passing them to the evaluation module (grading). The Grading controls the entire classification process by calling the compilers, the sandbox, and it compares the output of the solution with the expected response. The Queue Manager facilitates the evaluation of tasks in parallel, maintains a queue of presentations and distributes them among the SandBox. The Gradding processes the outputs of the executions and compilations made in the SandBox and generates various reports (for example, scorecards, detailed feedback reports for the contestants). The SandBox directs the contestant's solution in a controlled and secure environment, which limits its execution time, consumption of memory and calls to the. The Scoreboard classifies the participants according to the number of solved problems and time of resolution.

3 Architecture of the evaluation system of the source code

This type of system is oriented to reinforce or study specific competitive programming topics and to simulate ACPC ICPC type contests.

The proposed architecture consists of the modules: FrontEnd, Manager, Grader, Queue Manager, SandBox, Problems Repository and Scoreboard.

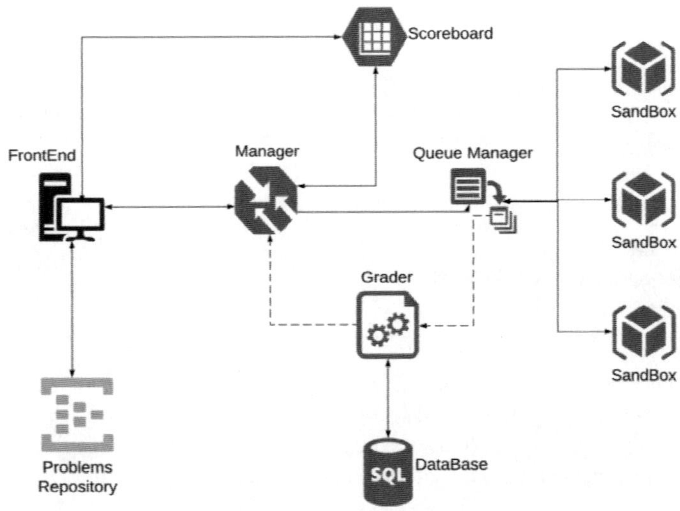

Figure. 1: Architecture of the evaluation system of the source code

3.1 SandBox

This component executes the user's solution in a supervised and secure environment, limiting its execution time, memory consumption and system calls [9]. A SandBox must ensure that the execution of a solution will not damage the system, it must impose time restrictions, memory and network [3].

In our proposal to implement this component, we use Containers through Docker and subprocesses with the Python language.

We use sub-processes because it is a mechanism that allows to execute system commands in a secure way, to initiate processes, to communicate to their input pipes, output and error. Additionally, we use Docker because it allows to isolate processes and control the resources that are going to be used in the execution and compilation of source code such as memory and CPU. It is vital to have this module decoupled from the rest of the modules to ensure the robustness of the platform, because in this component is where the greatest risks will occur when executing or compiling source code that can be harmful to the host system.

In our research the SandBoxs are created from Docker images and these are created from Dockerfiles through subprocesses as shown in Table 1.

Dockerfile is a file that describes how a container image will be constructed, providing a set of instructions to simplify the construction process. All available commands are designed to create images for independent containers [6].

Table 1: Way to create an image from a SandBox

```
command = 'docker build -t {} {}'
subprocess.Popen(command.format(image_name, path_to_dockerfile).split(' '))
```

Each Dockerfile contains the commands to install the necessary compilers of each language supported by the system, this way it's possible to scaled to more gramming languages through this mechanism. For the creation of each SandBox we used, as base, an Alpine image that weighs only 5MB and has access to a package manager apk [19] as we see in Table 2.

Table 2: Contents of a Dockerfile file, commands to install the compilers of C ++ and Python3

```
FROM alpine:3.4
RUN apk add –no-cache python3-dev
RUN apk add g++
```

To execute and compile, we use the docker run command, which is accompanied with the directory route where the source code is stored, the directory within the volume of the container where the command will be executed, the name of the image from which the container will be created, and the command to execute. Table 3.

Table 3: Execution and / or compilation of source code in a container

```
docker run --rm -v {workdir}:/code -w /code {image} {command}
```

The amount of memory that the container will use can be limited to the execution or compilation; an essential requirement for algorithmic problems in optimization, for this reason the -m and --memory-swap parameters are added, followed by the maximum amount of memory to be used. This is used in problems where you need to evaluate the memory that uses some of the proposed presentations. Table 4.

Table 4: Compilation of source code in a container with a memory limit of 15 Megabytes

```
docker run -m 15M --memory-swap 15M --rm -v {workdir}:/code -w /code {image} {command}
```

The memory for the execution or compilation can be limited, as well as the execution time of the process in the container. To do this the timeout command come first and then comes the command in Table 3, followed by the maximum amount of time to execute. This is useful for algorithmic problems where a time limit must be evaluated according to some algorithmic complexity that is posed by the problem setter. Table 5.

Table 5: Execution or compilation of source code in a container with a time limit of 1 second

```
timeout 1 docker run --rm -v {workdir}:/code -w /code {image} {command}
```

3.2 Queue Manager

The function of this module is to administrate the uploading of solutions of the users, whether it's to SandBox or Grader. This module is the one that will know how many SandBox are available, and to which SandBox you will have to send certain solution.

The Queue Manager not only sends the solutions of users to the SandBox, but also the test cases of the problem and the constraints of the problem, Figure 2.

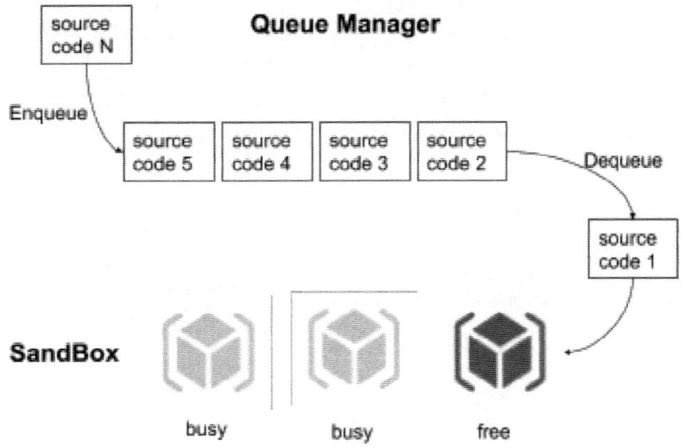

Figure. 2: Queue Manager and how it interacts with the SandBox module

3.3 Grader

It is responsible for evaluating the output generated by the execution of a participant's solution with the expected output that has been posed by the problem setter and it emits a result, this result can be either of success, incorrect answer, correct answer, time limit exceeded, memory limit exceeded or execution error. Also, it evaluates if there were compilation errors at the time of compiling the code, this will be also a result that will be reported to the user. Once evaluated, the answer of user, the Grader notifies the Manager that there is a evaluated presentation ready to be shown to the participant. The evaluation is carried out by comparing the JSON which was generated after the execution or compilation of the source code with the expected JSON. This can be seen in Table 6.

Table 6: JSONs to evaluation

JSON Generate	JSON Expected

{
"completed": Bool,
"stderrGenerate": String,
"stdoutGenerate": String,
"timeGenerate": Double,
"memoryGenerate": Double }
	{
	"stdoutExpected": String,
	"timeExpected": Double,
	"memoryExpected": Double
	}

The evaluation process is based on the algorithm of Figure 3: a) It start by evaluating the stderrGenerate, if it is different from empty, then it means that a compilation error occurred. In this case the state and the generated error are saved in CE. b) It is verified if the evaluation process is complete, if it is negative it is sent to the Queue Manager for its later execution; otherwise, we proceed to evaluate whether the time and memory limits have been exceeded. c) finally proceeds to evaluate the generated output cases, if this generated output is equal to the expected output it is because the proposed presentation is correct and the AC state is saved in the database if it is not the same the state is saved WA.

In the evaluation process, if there was an error in its execution, the state of RTE (Run Time Error) is saved. This evaluation, depending on whether the presentation was made in a compiled or interpreted language, is made in the second or first time you enter the Grader.

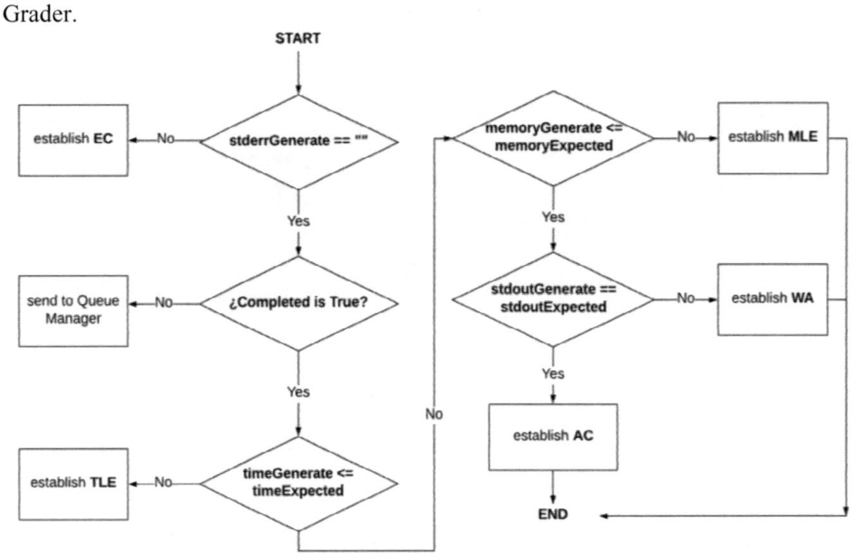

Figure. 3: Evaluation algorithm for a compiled language.

3.4 Manager

The Manager is the core module in the entire architecture, it communicates with most of the modules. It receives the solution through the FrontEnd, then it is forwarded to the Queue Manager, receives the notification of the Grader when a solution has already been evaluated, notifies the Scoreboard for its update and sends the response to the user through FrontEnd, Figure 4.

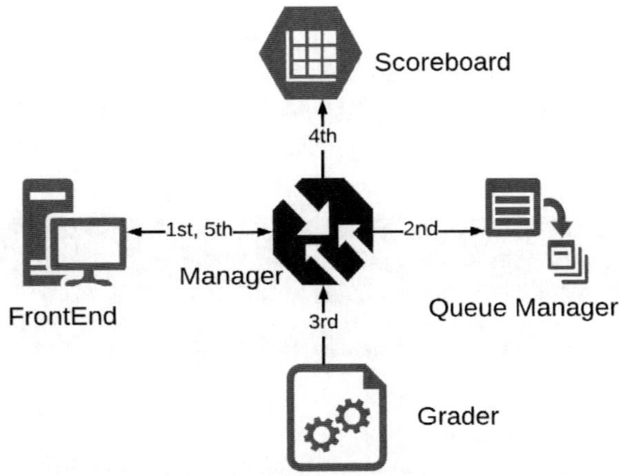

Figure. 4: Interaction of the Manager with other modules

3.5 Scoreboard

This module is responsible for showing the results of all the teams in merit order. The best qualified are at the top and goes downwards decreasing to the worst ones. Figure 5.

This classification is made according to 3 variables: 1) The number of solved problems, 2) How long each problem has been solved and 3) The number of attempts for each solved problem.

For each failed attempt there is a penalty of 20 minutes, so if a problem is solved on the 2nd attempt at 30 minutes, it is as if it had been resolved at 50 minutes.

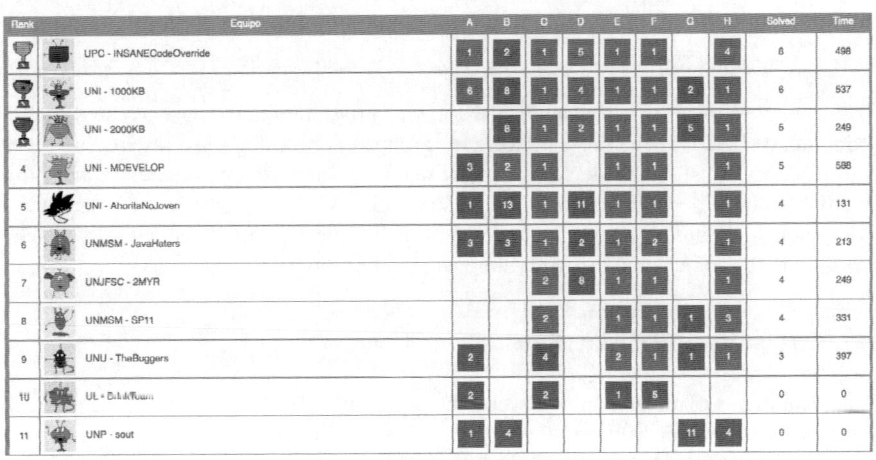

Rank	Equipo	A	B	C	D	E	F	G	H	Solved	Time
	UPC - INSANECodeOverride	1	2	1	5	1	1		4	6	498
	UNI - 1000KB	6	8	1	4	1	1	2	1	6	537
	UNI - 2000KB		8	1	2	1	1	5	1	5	249
4	UNI - MDEVELOP	3	2	1		1	1		1	5	588
5	UNI - AhoritaNoJoven	1	13	1	11	1	1		1	4	131
6	UNMSM - JavaHaters	3	3	1	2	1	2		1	4	213
7	UNJFSC - 2MYR			2	8	1	1		1	4	249
8	UNMSM - SP11			2		1	1	1	3	4	331
9	UNU - ThaBuggers	2		4		2	1	1	1	3	397
10	UL - [illegible]	2		2		1	5			0	0
11	UNP - sout	1	4					11	4	0	0

Figure. 5: Scoreboard of the 2016 CONEISC programming contest.

3.6 FrontEnd

This module is responsible for showing all interfaces to the teams, judges, organizers and administrators. The interfaces are: solutions sent, run status, proposed exercises, problems categories list, current and past competitions, interface for sending solutions, user panel, interface to create problem, interface to create contest, login and register, Figure 6.

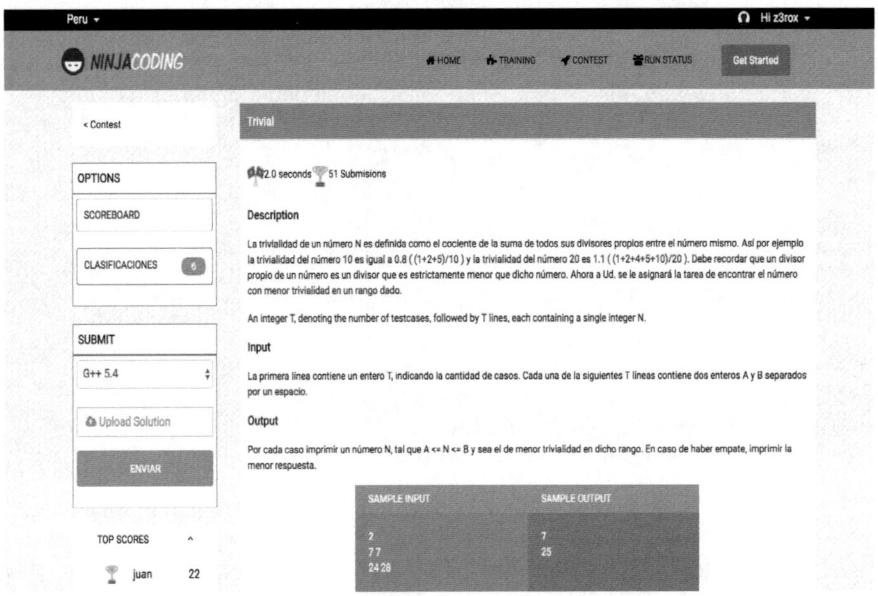

Figure. 6: Visualization of a problem in a contest.

3.7 Problems Repository

This module shows all the problems used in past programming contests created by the community. The way the presentations are grouped is by categories, ordered by level of difficulty and showing statistics of how many solution attempts there are and how many ones have been satisfactory for each problem.
This module would be one of the access points for the training of the participants according to the subject and difficulty they wish to reinforce.

4 Results and discussion

The data in our platform is provided by the problem setters and these can create their own problems or obtain from other sources such as the repositories of past programming contests of the ACM ICPC. All these problems are tested through 4 tests: correct answer test, incorrect answer test, compile error test and exceeded limit time test. After passing these tests, the problems can be used either in contests or become public in the platform's problem repository.

The testing of our system of source code evaluation has been carried out in two phases:

Phase 1 test, 4 problems of the practice contest of the East Central North America 2015 [20] competition were used Table 7. The tests to each one of these problems were deliberated in the following order: Accepted test, test of limit time exceeded, compilation error test and wrong answer test.

Table 7: test problems

Problem	*Title*
A	Bottled-Up Feelings
B	Mastering Mastermind
C	Shuffling Along
D	Towering Problem

Accepted Test:

For this test, we have sent the source code shown in Table 8 to our system. The correct source code was taken from the East Central North America Region 2015 [20] competition.

Table 8: source code

```
// File: bottle1.cpp
#include <iostream>
using namespace std;
int main( ){
   int s, v1, v2;
   cin >> s >> v1 >> v2;
   int t1 = (s/v1)*v1;
   while (t1 >= 0 && (s-t1)%v2 != 0)
      t1 -= v1;
   if (t1 >= 0)
      cout << t1/v1 << ' ' << (s-t1)/v2 << endl;
   else if (s%v2 == 0)
      cout << 0 << ' ' << s/v2 << endl;
   else
      cout << "Impossible" << endl;
return 0;
}
```

In that case, the Queue Manager module first provides the source code to SandBox using the compilation command shown in Table 4, then it goes to the queue again and then, when going to the SandBox, it provides the execution command that is shown in the Table 5.

Table 9: Output of the execution of the source code bottle1.cpp

JSON Generate	JSON Expected

{
"completed": True,
"stderrGenerate": "",
"stdoutGenerate": "108 4",
"timeGenerate":"0.01",
"memoryGenerate": "4802"
}
	{
	"stdoutExpected": "108 4",
	"timeExpected": "0.3",
	"memoryExpected": "25600"
	}

Then, Grader module receives the output that is in JSON see Table 9, compares it with the correct output using the algorithm shown in Figure 3, then the Grader informs the Manager and sends it to FrontEnd to show the verdict as "Accepted". which is shown in Figure 7.

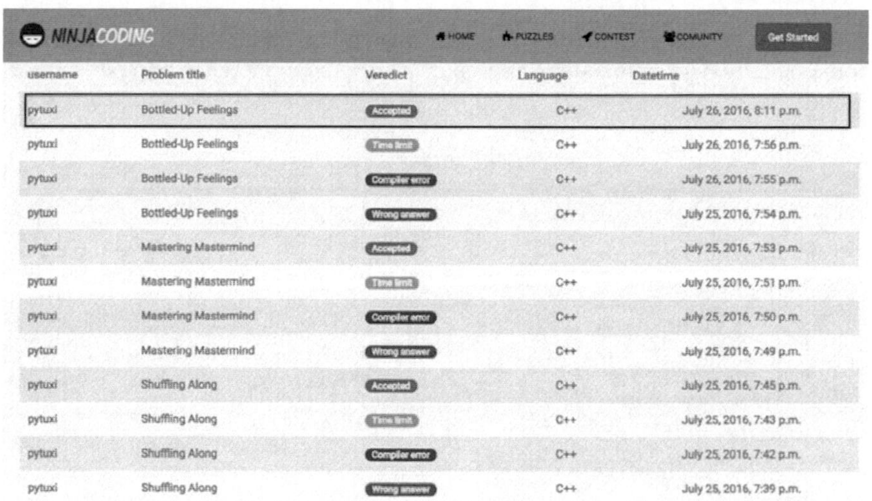

Figure. 7: Result of the accepted test of problem A: Bottled-Up Feelings

Time Limit Exceeded Test:

For this test, the source code shown in Table 10 has been sent as input, which we can clearly see that it has an infinite cycle.

Table 10: source code to Time Limit

```
//File: helloWorldTLE.cpp
#include <iostream>
using namespace std;
int main() {
  while(1){
    cout<<"Hello World"<<endl;
  }
  return 0;
}
```

Like the Accepted Test it was first compiled and then executed. The grader receives the output in JSON and compares it using the algorithm Figure 3 and shows the Time Limit verdict as shown in the second row of Figure 7.

Subsequently, the other tests were carried out: compiler error, wrong answer for each problem stated in Table 7, of the 16 tests performed, all evaluations were exactly the same as expected, this is shown in Figure 7.

Phase 2 test, since 2016, NinjaCoding was tested in several contests in congresses and in different universities and it has graded more than 1000 presentations in different programming languages that are detailed in Table 11.

Table 11: Test results in different events

Event	**University**	**Number of evaluated presentations**	**Number of participants**
CONEISC 2016 (National Congress of Systems and Computer Engineering Students)	Universidad Nacional de Ucayali	224	45 students from differents universities
Selection contest UNI-FIIS Stage I 2016	Universidad Nacional de Ingeniería	97	22 students of UNI
Selection contest UNI-FIIS Stage II 2016	Universidad Nacional de Ingeniería	74	20 students of UNI
Contest in the UNMSM-FISI anniversary	Universidad Nacional Mayor de San Marcos	125	39 students between UNI and UNMSM

In our research as well as the author [6], the Sandbox module was built with Docker, but we are different on the fact that when running Docker we use threads of the Python language. Python threads are a safe way to start processes from the Python language and have a communication method that allows the sending of standard data input (stdin) and read or output data (stdout) and error (stderr) without risk of interlocks [21].

Building SandBox using Virtual Machines the way [7] does it in its Judge.org project, makes the boot of the sandbox much slower, instead in our research we use Docker for the SandBox, where they directly use the host's core which shortening the execution route of system calls, eliminate the guest kernel and the virtual hardware layer that virtual machines [10] use, therefore, it is much faster.

We agree that [4], the resolutions of algorithmic problems should not be forced to be solved in a single programming language, for this reason, in this investigation, the proposed problems, both in contests and trainings, can be solved by using different programming languages.

The research [3] is limited to support traditional programming languages such as C/C++, Java and Pascal, whereas in this research we have taken care of supporting also popular and modern programming languages such as Python and Ruby.

5 Conclusions

In this paper, we presented the architecture and platform of an automatic evaluation system for source code that is used for both programming contests and training. In addition, it was possible to support the required languages for ACPC ICPC type programming contests and to provide scalability to extend the use of other programming languages.

Automatic systems for evaluation acquire more importance thanks to the growing demand for IT programmers. An evaluation system can greatly improve the quality of its solutions for participants, since participants find themselves forced to produce efficient and error-free solutions; in the educational environment, this type of systems also increases the interest and academic performance of students, increasing from 40% to 70% [11].

The most important requirement for the automatic evaluation must be the safe and isolated execution environment of the other modules of the system, since the source code that is being executed can be harmful and dangerous. NinjaCoding was built to meet these requirements for automatic evaluation. Through Docker and Python language threads it ensures the isolation of the execution environment and provides flexibility to add constraints of time and memory and support more programming languages.

Our proposed system has a promising development potential, because we are going to give support to more programming languages according to the tendencies of use of these, we will also develop the educational module so that this platform can be applied in the different programming courses in the various universities. Finally we will provide support to different types of contests such as IOI [23] and Google Code Jam [24] so that there is more diversity of contests.

References

1. S. Maggiolo y G. Mascellani. Introducing CMS: A Contest Management System. Olympiads In Informatics 6, 86 – 99 (2012).
2. J. Fernando y M. M. Liem. Componentes And Architectural Design of an Autograder System Family. Olympiads In Informatics 8, 69 – 79 (2014)
3. M. Jovanov, B. Kostadinov, E. Stankov, M. Mihova y M. Gusev. State Competitions in Informatics and the Supporting Online Learning and Contest Management System with Collaboration and Personalization Features MENDO. Olympiads In Informatics 7, 42 – 54 (2013)
4. L. H. Chávez, A. Gonzáles y J Ponce. omegaUp: Cloud-Based Contest Management System and Training Platform in the Mexican Olympiad in Informatics. Olympiads In Informatics 9, 169 – 178 (2014)
5. S. Combéfis y V.Clément. Teaching Programming and Algorithm Design with Pythia, a Web-Based Learning Platform. Olympiads In Informatics 6, 31 – 43 (2012)
6. F. Spacek, R. Sohlich y T. Dulík. Docker as Platform for Assignments Evaluation. Procedia Engineering 100, 1665-1671 (2015)
7. O. Giménez, J. Petit, S. Roura. Judge.org: An educational Programming Judge. Proceedings of the 43rd ACM technical symposium on Computer Science Education, 445 – 450 (2012)
8. D. J. Malan. CS50 Sandbox: Secure Execution Of Untrusted Code. Proceeding of the 44th ACM technical symposium on Computer science education, 2013.
9. M. Mares y B. Blackham. A New Contest Sandbox. Olympiads in Informatics 6, 100 – 109 (2012)
10. T. Combe, A. Martin y R. Di Pietro. To Docker or Not to Docker: A Security Perspective. IEEE Cloud Computing 3 (5),. 54 – 62 (2016)
11. H. Wu, Y. Liu, L. Qiu y Y. Liu. Online Judge System and Its Applications in C Language Teaching. International Symposium on Educational Technology (2016)
12. D. Bernstein. Containers and Cloud: From LXC to Docker to Kubernetes . IEEE Cloud Computing 1 (5), 81 – 84 (2014)
13. W. Felter, A. Ferreira, R. Rajamony, J. Rubio. An Updated Performance Comparison of Virtual Machines and Linux Containers. IBM Research Report (2014)
14. M. Shams Ul haq, L. Liao, M. Lerong. Design and Implementation of Sandbox Technique for Isolated Applications (2016)
15. ACM ICPC. Available: https://icpc.baylor.edu/compete/problems [Accessed: Nov. 3, 2017]
16. HuahCoding. Available: http://huahcoding.com [Accessed: Oct. 3, 2017]
17. Uva Judge. Available: https://uva.onlinejudge.org/ [Accessed: Oct. 3, 2017]
18. Timus Judge Online. http://acm.timus.ru/ [Accessed: Oct. 3, 2017]
19. Alpine Linux. Available https://alpinelinux.org/ [Accessed: Feb. 10, 2016]
20. East Central North America Region 2015. Available: http://acm-ecna.ysu.edu/PastResults/2015/problemset.html [Accesed: Dec, 15, 2015]
21. Subprocess. Available: https://www.python.org/dev/peps/pep-0324/ [Accessed: Nov, 20, 2016]
22. S. Halim y F. Halim, Competitive Programing 2, pp 1 (2011)
23. IOI. Available: http://www.ioinformatics.org/index.shtml [Accessed: Nov. 3, 2017]
24. Google Code Jam: https://code.google.com/codejam/ [Accessed: Nov. 3, 2017]
25. C. P. de Campos and C. E. Ferreira. BOCA - Um sistema de apoio a competições de programação (2004)

Extending MoWebA for MobileApps with Functions in the Cloud*

Emanuel Sanchiz, Magalí González, Nathalie Aquino, and Luca Cernuzzi

Universidad Católica "Nuestra Señora d e la Asunción" - DEI, Asunción, Paraguay
{emanuel.sanchiz, mgonzalez, nathalie.aquino, lcernuzz}@uc.edu.py

Abstract. Currently, a growing interest is being caused by the mobile applications and the cloud. In this work, we have focused on mobile applications with functions implemented in the cloud (MobileApps-FC). The improvement related to the portability of these applications among different platforms and different service providers is an interesting challenge. Model Driven Development (MDD) constitutes one of the alternatives to address portability issues. Indeed, in this work we propose MoWebA Mobile, an extension of a MDD approach, called MoWebA, for the design and generation of the MobileApps-FC. Specifically, in this work we have focused on a specific aspect of the mentioned applications, which is the network communication between the mobile applications and their functions in the cloud. Furthermore, as a preliminary validation we present a comparative study with MoWebA Mobile regarding to the traditional development and WebRatio Mobile Platform.

Keywords: Mobile applications · Cloud · Network communication · MDD · Portability

1 Introduction

In recent years, the number of users of smartphones and tablets has been increasing quickly, overcoming the number of users of computers and notebooks.[1] Consequently, the interest for the development of mobile applications has also increased,[2] particularly for native applications.[3] Moreover, it is important to consider the current growing market of the cloud, specially the public cloud,[4] and its role as enhancer of the restricted resources of mobile devices [1,2]. Taking into account both perspectives, mobile devices and the cloud, it is worth noting

* This work has been funded by CONACYT through the PROCIENCIA program with resources from "Fondo para la Excelencia de la Educación e Investigación - FEEI" from FONACIDE. This work has been developed under the project "Mejorando el proceso de desarrollo de software: propuesta basada en MDD" (14-INV-056).

[1] Morgan Stanley, link: `https://goo.gl/Ifznvz`

[2] Mobile is all about application, link: `https://goo.gl/tCnZfN`

[3] Native vs hybrid application, link: `https://goo.gl/JH1u7K`

[4] Growing of public clouds, link: `https://goo.gl/WOVYJW`

the growing convergence between them [3]. Hence, the interest of this study is focused on mobile applications which have at least one module or implementation (e.g., procedure, service, database) running in the cloud. We refer to these applications as mobile applications with functions in the cloud (MobileApps-FC).

On one side, the mobile environment can be based on several different platforms, being iOS and Android the most popular ones. These platforms, again, consider different operating systems, programming languages, tools, etc. In most cases, mobile applications must be developed for more than one mobile platform. And due to differences among these platforms, specific application versions must be built for each one of them. Therefore, more effort and time must be employed, resulting in higher costs in the development process. Since the same implementation can hardly be used for different mobile platforms, there is a portability challenge in the mobile environment [3,4,5].

On the other side, the cloud environment is constituted by several different service providers. In a similar way than previously exposed, each of these providers uses its own specific platform (operating systems, programming languages, libraries, etc.). This causes a portability problem, which in the cloud context is known as vendor lock-in. Therefore, tasks such as building an application that is able to run in clouds from different service providers or migrating an application from the cloud of one service provider to another one constitute interesting challenges, since the same implementation can hardly be used in different cloud service providers [6,7].

Therefore, when considering applications that include, at the same time, the mobile and the cloud environments, the portability problem is highlighted. In this sense, Model Driven Development (MDD) emerges as a possible solution. In fact, one of the main motivations of MDD is related to the improvement of portability [8]. MDD focuses efforts on designing domain models that capture the knowledge of the data and functionality that an application must provide independently of the platform in which it will be run.

Therefore, our goal is to propose a model driven approach for the modeling and generation of the MobileApps-FC. In this case, the scope of the modeling and the generation focuses on one aspect of the applications, which is the network communication. We present our proposal as an alternative for addressing the extra effort caused by the difficulty of platform portability.

The model driven approach adopted for this work is MoWebA [11]. Based on MoWebA, we have identified three aspects that could have a positive impact in the portability problem that is found in the MDD development of MobileApps-FC. These aspects are: i) incorporation of an Architecture Specific Model (ASM) as a new modeling layer, in order to keep the portability of the Platform Independent Model (PIM) regarding the different architectures (e.g., RIA, SOA, Mobile); ii) clear separation of the presentation layer with regard to the navigation and behavior layers, would prevent additional complications to the presentation, since, it is the layer that presents more difficulties related to portability; and iii) definition of the navigational structure according to a function-oriented approach, which prevents the modification of the navigation design caused by implementation changes. Such prevention means a saving of effort, which, finally, contribute to alleviate the effects introduced by the portability difficulty. We have studied the adoption of such aspects in the state of the art, through a Systematic Mapping Study (SMS) [9], which results are summarized in the next section.

The rest of the document is structured as follows. Section 2 analyzes the related works. Then, Section 3 presents the proposal, which is the extension of MoWebA through an ASM for the modeling and generation of the network communication aspect. Section 4, describes a comparative study as a preliminary validation of our proposal. Finally, Section 5 presents the conclusions and future works.

2 Related Works

In this section, due to the space limitation, we present a brief summary of the results of a SMS of the state of the art we have done. More details about the study can be found in Sanchiz et al. [9]. In such SMS, we have identified six model driven proposals for the development of MobileApps-FC that address the portability problem. Such proposals are: 1) WebRatio Mobile Platform [4], a framework based on IFML;[5] 2) SIMON [10], a framework including runtime models based on XML; 3) MD^2 [11]; 4) MobiCloud [12] and 5) Steiner et al. [13], which present a textual modeling language based on the Model-View-Controller (MVC) schema; and, 6) Ruokonen et al. [14], which presents a modeling based on business process models. In Table 1, we summarize the differences between the identified proposals and MoWebA, based on the adoption of the three design aspects: i) incorporation of an ASM; ii) clear separation of the presentation layer with regard to the navigation and behavior layers; and iii) definition of the navigational structure according to a function-oriented approach.

Table 1: Comparison based on the design aspects, more details in [9]

Work	**Aspects**		
	ASM	**Clear Separation of Presentation**	**Function Oriented Navigation**
WebRatio Mobile	Yes	No	Yes
SIMON	Partially	No	No
MD^2	No	Yes	Yes
MobiCloud	No	No	No
Steiner et al.	No	No	Yes
Ruokonen et al.	No	No	No

This review showed us that none of the proposals considered includes all the three MoWebA's design aspects, which could have a positive impact on the

[5] IFML - OMG standard; link: `http://www.omg.org/spec/IFML/`

design portability. Consequently, we were motivated to adopt MoWebA and to extend it for the development of the MobileApps-FC. Specifically, in the present study, we are focusing on the extension for the modeling and the generation of the network communication of the MobileApps-FC.

Furthermore, from the mentioned proposals we also have learned some aspects like: i) the use of standard modeling languages. (WebRatio uses IFML models while SIMON uses XML for textual models); ii) the adoption of the MVC schema, (derived from MobiCloud, MD^2 and Steiner et al.); iii) the adoption of a unified modeling (derived from MD^2, MobiCloud and Steiner et al.); iv) the combination of MDD and the open source approach (derived from WebRatio); v) the use of REST as a uniform and portable communication interface, (derived from WebRatio, MD^2, SIMON, MobiCloud); vi) the generation of native mobile applications (generated by MobiCloud, MD^2, SIMON and Steiner et al.). MoWebA considers natively the aspects i) and ii). While the other ones, iii), iv), v) and vi), we are including into MoWebA Mobile, which is the extended version of MoWebA.

3 Extending MoWebA for the Network Communication

In this section, we present the extension of MoWebA to model and to generate the network communications functions for the MobileApps-FC. Furthermore, we describe the extensions we have applied to one of the PIM models' diagrams of MoWebA, the logic one. From such extension we obtain the ASM which enables the modeling of the network communication of the MobileApps-FC. Similarly, we will present the transformation rules which map the ASM with the code to be generated. Moreover, we will explain the modeling and generation process. Finally, we present an example to show the use of our proposal.

3.1 Network Communication Functions

We have focused on the network communication aspect because its implementation necessarily implies working with different platforms and technologies (iOS, Android and the cloud service providers' platforms) of the MobileApps-FC. In this sense, the platform abstraction which proposes a MDD approach is highlighted on the network communication aspect. Starting from the official documentations of Android[6] and iOS[7] (currently, the most popular platforms)[8] we focused on four types of network communication functions. There are more variants of such functions, but we have focused on such four ones to cover some of the most common cases. Those communication functions set the scope of this work for the design and the generation implementation. Following, we describe the types of such functions: i) *light-data*, where the data exchange does not include files (e.g., images, documents, video or audio). In this sense, the data to

[6] Android, `https://goo.gl/LwMLXn`
[7] iOS, `https://goo.gl/3F1ZqW`
[8] Popularity of Android and iOS, `https://goo.gl/ZAu8Ho`

exchange is *light*; ii) *load-image*, to get and to load images in memory for displaying them. Commonly, this function is used for image and video previews; iii) *download-files*, to download files in background; and iv) *upload-files*, to upload files in background.

The mentioned functions include implementations in both sides, the mobile and the cloud, respectively. Such implementation are based on the REST architecture [15].

3.2 MoWebA Mobile: the Network Communication Proposal

The definition process for extending MoWebA for different architectures consists in the following steps [16]: i) define the metamodel using MOF;[9] ii) define the corresponding UML[10] Profile; iii) define transformation rules for elements that can be obtained in an automatic way; iv) apply transformation rules in order to obtain the first version of the ASM from the PIM; v) make necessary manual adjustments to complete the ASM model; vi) generate the target code applying transformation rules; and, vii) include manual adjustments, if necessary.

The scope of this work has focused, on one side, on the steps i) and ii) for defining the ASM metamodel and profile and, on the other side, on the step iii) and vi) for defining model to text transformation rules and to apply them to get the target code from the ASM. It was not necessary the step vii). We have left for future works the automatic transformation from the PIM to the ASM, which includes the steps iv) and v). We illustrate the scope of the extension we have made in Figure 1.

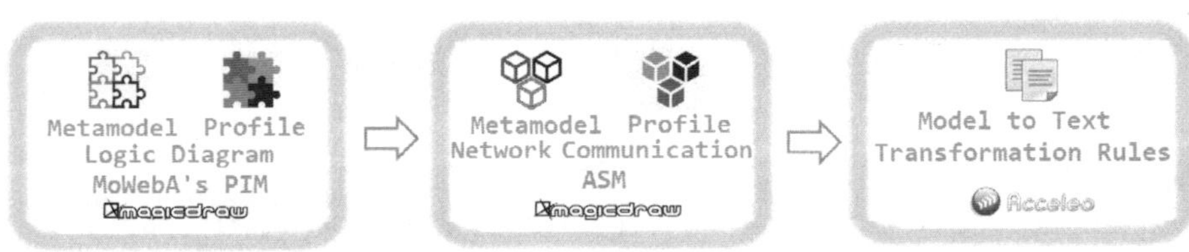

Fig. 1: The extension includes a metamodel, a profile and transformation rules

In this work, we have defined the metamodel and profile for obtaining the network communication ASM. Such metamodel and profile extend the logic diagram of MoWebA. Such logic diagram enables the definition of logic processes. In fact, we consider the network communication as a logic process. The logic diagram contains *TProcesses*, which are the logic processes defined. Such processes include *Services*, which are procedures doing a specific task. Also, the logic diagram has *ValueObjects*, which group attributes of entities and enable the access to the entities' data.

[9] MOF, link: `http://www.omg.org/mof/`
[10] UML, link: `http://www.uml.org/`

Following we describe the extensions we made on the logic diagram. The extensions for obtaining the ASM are based on the REST architecture and on the four types of network communication functions, presented in the previous section. Such elements belong to the metamodel showed in Figure 2.

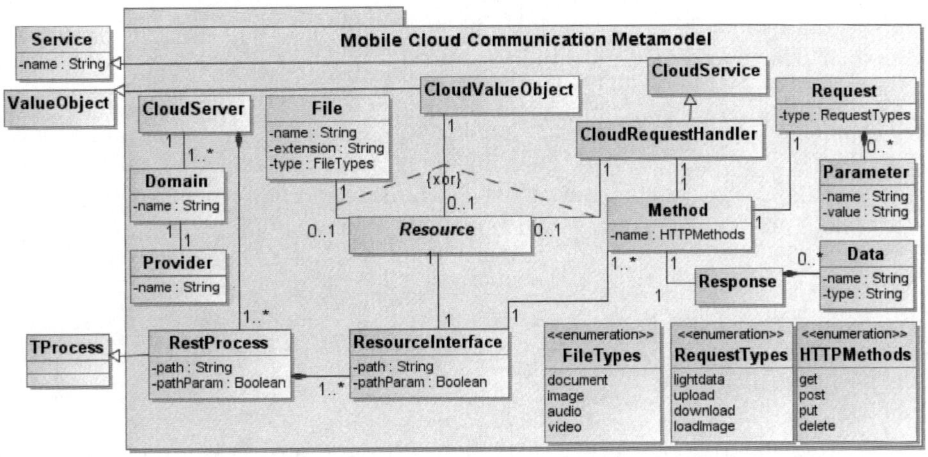

Fig. 2: Metamodel for the network communication ASM

Firstly, it is defined a *CloudServer*, which is accessed through a *Domain*. The *Domain* is provided by a service *Provider*, which enables the recognition of the particular configurations required by each cloud service provider. Then, each *CloudServer* contains a set of logic processes, where each one of them is called *RestProcess*. Such processes modularize the network communication design. Subsequently, each *RestProcess* includes a set of resource interfaces, where each *ResourceInterface* is associated with a *Resource*, one at a time. A *Resource* can be a MoWebA's *ValueObject* called *CloudValueObject* because it is residing in the cloud, a *File* stored or to be store in the cloud or a MoWebA's *Service* called *CloudRequestHandler*, which is executed in the cloud.

Each *ResourceInterface* is associated to a set of methods, where each *Method* defines the operation to be performed on a *Resource*. At the same time, each *Method* is associated to the object *Request* and, in some cases, to the object *Response*. On one side, each *Request* can be associated to a set of parameters, which contains each *Parameter* of the request. On the other side, each *Response* is associated to a set of data expected to receive from a *light-data Request*, operated by the *Method get*.

Following, we will explain the attributes of representative elements described so far. The *RestProcess* has a relative *Path*, which makes the process accessible, and a boolean flag which establish if the *Path* is used as additional data in each *Request*. For instance, the *Path* could be a user identification. The same case is for the attributes of the *ResourceInterface*. About *File*, its attributes specify the *name*, *extension* and the file *type*. The *Name* of *Method* defines the type of HTTP method (*get, post, put, delete*). The four HTTP methods considered are the most common ones. The *Request type* (*lightdata, download, upload, loadImage*) defines the call to be done. In case of *lightdata*, the associated *Method* can be any of the mentioned HTTP methods. Nevertheless, *download* (*get*), *upload* (*post*) and loadImage (*get*) have, each one, a predefined *Method*. The *name* and the *value* of the *Parameter* describe the different parameters of the *Request*. Finally, the *name* of *Data* specify the data to be received from the *Request lightdata* and the *Method get*. Such *name* specifies an attribute of the *CloudValue Object* associated to the respective resource interface.

The described elements of the ASM are represented concretely in the respective profile.[11] The profile contains the definition of the elements (stereotypes, tag values and enumerations), which enable the modeling.

3.3 Transformation Rules

We have defined model to text (M2T) transformation rules in order to generate the target code from the ASM. In order to built the transformation rules, we have followed an approach based on templates. We have used the Model transformation language (MTL) of Acceleo[12] for defining the templates. Similarly, we have used OCL for doing queries to the model. Furthermore, we have built a service in Java to extend the functions of the MTL. We have built the transformation rules based on the classes, properties and operations characterized by the respective stereotypes, tag values and enumerations defined in the ASM's profile. In this sense, such rules perform a mapping between the model elements defined and the target code to be generated. Basically, the generation for both side, mobile and cloud, depends on each combination of a *CloudServer*, a *RestProcess*, *ResourceInterface* and *CloudRequestHandler*.

The target code generated consists, on one side, in native mobile code written in Java[13] for Android, in Swift[14] for iOS, and on the other side, in open source code written in Javascript[15] with Node.js for the Openshift and Amazon Web Services platforms. Additionally, our cloud implementation is based on Docker,[16] which is a container where an application runs. Moreover, Docker is an emerging method developed by the open source community for easing the portability of cloud applications.

---

11 More details about the profile, link: `https://goo.gl/DZY2yk`
12 Acceleo, link: `https://goo.gl/jgCZhu`
13 Java, link: `https://goo.gl/hGBggw`
14 Swift, link: `https://developer.apple.com/swift/`
15 Javascript, link: `https://www.javascript.com/`
16 Docker, `https://www.docker.com/what-docker`

3.4 Modeling and Code Generation with MoWebA Mobile

For modeling we have used MagicDraw,[17] which is a modeling tool of general purpose. Once the model is done, it has to be exported as XMI files. Such files are imported from Acceleo, which is a tool for defining and executing transformation rules. Therefore, in Acceleo, the transformation rules are executed on the imported model. Consequently, the implementation of the network communication is obtained in for every platform considered. See the modeling and generation process in Figure 3.

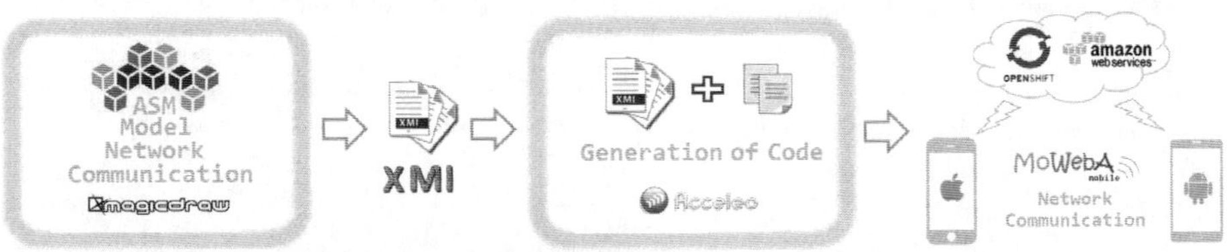

Fig. 3: Modeling and generation process of MoWebA Mobile

The generated code is a running implementation of the network communication. In other words, the generated code is ready to be executed for both mobile platforms, Android and iOS and for both cloud service providers, Openshift and Amazon Web Services.

With the aim of improving the understanding of the design process, we show an example of modeling an application. To see the complete explanation of the example, go to MoWebA Mobile Book.[18]

We have considered a application similar to one presented in Brambilla et al. [4]. The application is a virtual shop for selling products. It is going to be deployed on tablets and cell phones for field agents, i.e., salesman that go to customers for selling the products. This application requires the implementation in mobile and cloud platforms. In this case, the task is focused on the functions of network communication for the data exchange. Basically, the data to be exchanged is about the products (e.g., images, technical sheets, providers). Part of the modeling is shown in Figure 4.

In order to explain the modeling and generation example, we focus on one of the modeled functions, see Figure 5. We consider the load-image function for loading provider logos on the screen. As can be seen in Figure 5, from one model, we can obtain the implementation for every considered platform. The function implies the request on the URL formed from the attributes of the *cloudServer* (the domain server), the relative paths of the *restProcess* and the *resourceInterface*, respectively, and the name of the resource, in this case an image. The function is triggered by a button, when it is touched the image is obtained from

[17] MagicDraw, link: `https://goo.gl/mLPvur`
[18] MoWebA Mobile Book, `https://goo.gl/Qr9367`

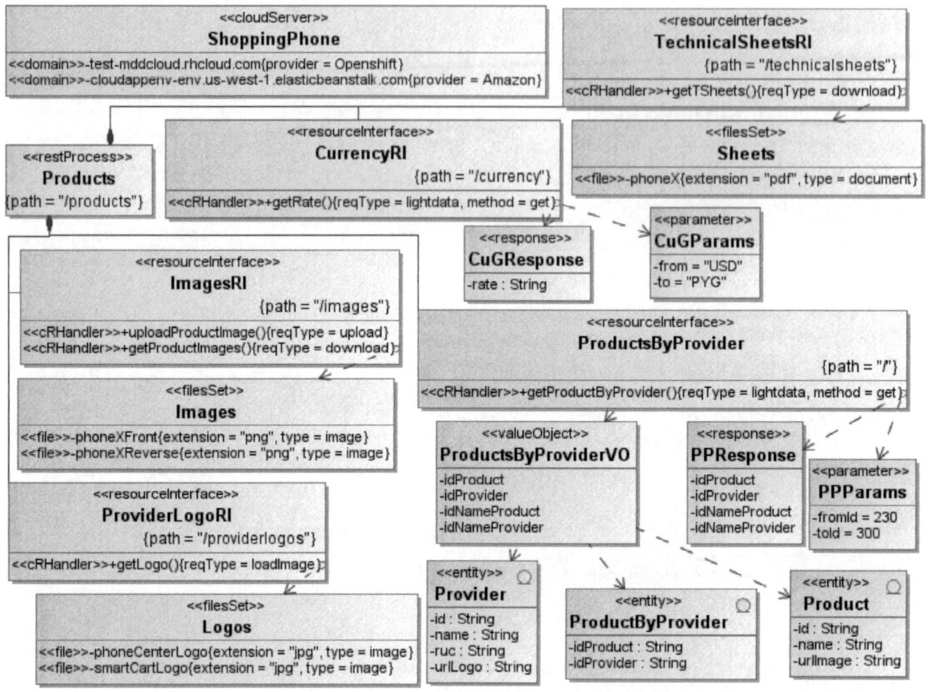

Fig. 4: Example of an application for offering products

the server, then it is loaded in memory and, afterwards, on the screen. The remote function, which handles the requests on the URL is specified in the *resourceInterface*, where it is specified as well, the type of the communication, in this case load-image. The implementation of such request handler function is generated for both cloud service providers' platforms. Similarly, we generate the implementation for every network communication function modeled.

4 Comparative Study with MoWebA Mobile

In this work, we have proposed an alternative to address the portability challenge, which consists in the extra effort introduced in the development of the MobileApps-FC. Specifically, we have focused on the modeling and generation of the network communication aspect. As a preliminary validation of our proposal, we have done a comparative study. In such study, we have measured the effort related to the development of the MobileApps-FC's network communication functions. In order to do the study, basically, we have proceeded as follows: i) we have selected an application as an example to develop its network communication; ii) we have used MoWebA Mobile, WebRatio Mobile Platform (another MDD approach [4]) and the traditional approach to develop independently the network communication; iii) we have measured and registered the development

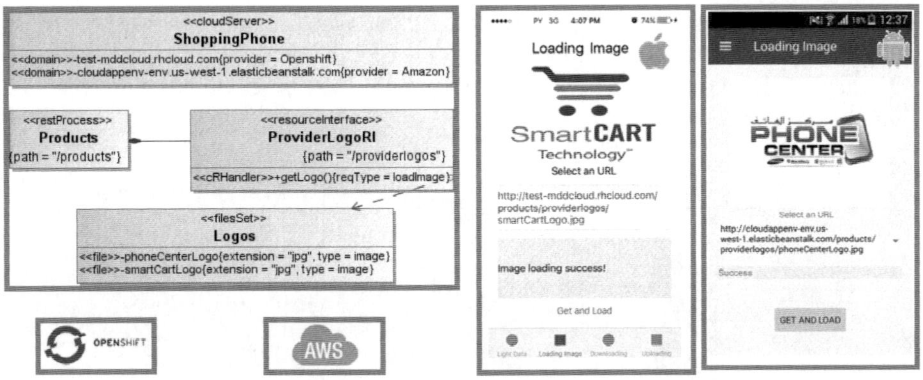

Fig. 5: Example of an application for offering products. Load-image function

times taken by each alternative; iv) in case of the MDD approaches, we have registered and analyzed the modeling and generation differences which could affect the development effort. Following, we describe the study in more details.

We have considered the same application presented in Section 3.4 to develop the network communication functions using the three alternatives. The development have been done in an academic environment. The developer was a computer science student in his last year at the university. In this case, we have had only one developer, which is a limitation of the study. Moreover, the resources used to guide and support the development were those available on-line.

As we have mentioned, we have compared MoWebA Mobile against the traditional approach and WebRatio Mobile Platform. In this case, we have assumed the following research question:

RQ1- How much time of development do the traditional approach, WebRatio Mobile Platform and MoWebA Mobile require to obtain the network communication implementation?

Similarly, we have compared exclusively both MDD approaches, MoWebA Mobile (A) and WebRatio Mobile Platform (B). In this case, we have focused on comparing modeling and generation aspects related to the effort, according to the next research questions:

RQ2- What differences in the modeling process between *A* and *B* could affect the effort required to develop MobileApps-FC?

RQ3- Respectively, how many platforms do A and B generate code for (mobile and cloud)?

Following, we present the results by each research question defined.

RQ1: We have compared MoWebA Mobile against the traditional approach and a consolidated MDD tool to analyze the required effort differences. Obviously, a MDD tool will improve the effort needed following a traditional approach (i.e., the manual development). However, in this case, the aim was to understand how big the difference is. WebRatio Mobile Platform, is used in the industry and it is the most representative MDD tool for the development of the MobileApps-

FC [9]. Therefore, we have compared it with MoWebA Mobile to see how much difference of effort exists with such kind of tool.

The development effort, measured through the development time, is presented in Figure 6.

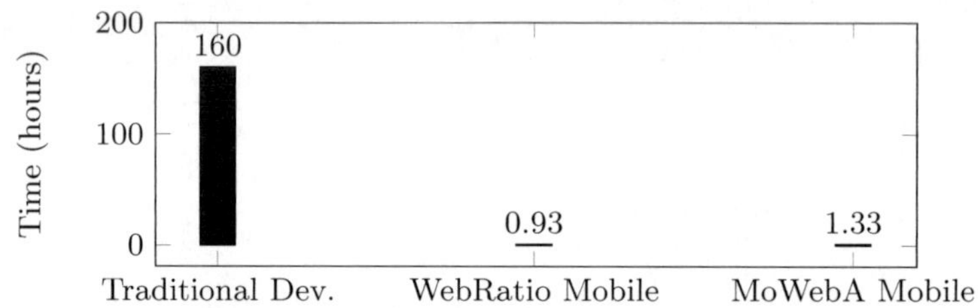

Fig. 6: Comparison of development times

It is worth noting that there exists a substantial difference of effort among the development times of the MDD approaches against the traditional one. For obtaining the same implementation, using WebRatio Mobile Platform and MoWebA Mobile have been necessary 0.93 hours (55 minutes) and 1.33 hours (1 hour 20 minutes), respectively. The traditional approach has taken 160 hours.

On one side, since, the network communication development implies, necessarily, working with several platforms and cloud service providers. In this sense, the developer had to face difficulties like the transition between different development environments (mobile, cloud), the use of different frameworks and programming languages. Such difficulties slowed down the development using the traditional approach.

On the other side, about the MDD approaches, they have several properties which support such difference of time. Firstly, the abstraction of specific details of the different platforms through the models. We highlight two advantages of such abstraction. On one side, it prevents dealing with the difficulty of working with different technologies. On the other side, it allows developers without specific platform and communication knowledge to get specific platform implementation of the network communication of the MobileApps-FC. Secondly, the automatic generation of platform specific code from the built model, which save most of the development time. Third, the generated code is already tested, so the probability to spend time in fixing bugs decreases.

Therefore, we could say that there is a considerable improvement in saving effort using a MDD approach for the development of the network communication of MobileApps-FC.

Comparing the MDD approaches, there is a difference that favors to one of them. First of all, we have to say that WebRatio Mobile Platform has a specific development environment, which eases, makes simple and faster the modeling comparing with MoWebA Mobile. Furthermore, WebRatio Mobile Platform is a robust and mature platform used in the industry. In contrast, in MoWebA

Mobile the modeling and the generation are made with tools of general purpose which slowed down the development process. Therefore, we suppose that if we build a MoWebA Mobile's specific tool, it will help to make more simple and faster the process of modeling and generation. Such eventual reduction could imply equalizing, or even improving, the network communication development time of WebRatio Mobile Platform. Following, we present further differences which reinforce the possible improvement of development time using MoWebA Mobile through a more specific tool. We refer to MoWebA Mobile as *A* and to WebRatio Mobile Platform as *B*.

RQ2: On one side, *A* prescribe all the modeling and configurations in a unified model, while *B* works with two models and projects. One project for mobile, another project for back-end. In case of *A*, the purpose of working with the same project and model for designing the communication is to abstract the developer from individuals settings and modelings by each side (mobile and cloud). In other words, since the communication implies two sides (mobile and cloud), from a unified model, at the moment of generation, the design and settings are replicated in both sides. Therefore, the developer "works once" instead of twice or more, which is the case of *B*. For instance, if a url is modified, then, the developer does not modify it for the cloud side and for the mobile side, the url modification is made only once in the model. Afterwards, thanks to the transformation rules, the change is replicated in both sides, the mobile and cloud ones. In this sense, *A* saves effort in the modeling process and consequently, in the overall process of developing MobileApps-FC.

On the other side, the main difference of MoWebA regarding other MDD approaches is the inclusion of three design aspects which could help to address the portability challenge. Since, in this work, where we have focused on the network communication aspect, we consider one of such aspects, which is the ASM. The relevance of the ASM is to improve the portability of the PIM regarding the different architectures. Even though, WebRatio considers as well the ASM, MoWebA considers, additionally, model to model (M2M) transformation rules, which enable the semi-automatic transition from the PIM to ASM. In fact, there exist such rules for other architectures.[19] Regarding the network communication aspect, we do not have yet such M2M rules. Nevertheless, once available (such rules) we consider that we could accelerate the modeling of MoWebA Mobile, and, consequently, save more time in the modeling process. Such saving of time implies as well a saving of effort in the process of developing MobileApps-FC.

RQ3: On the mobile side, both, *A* and *B*, generate code for iOS and Android, the most popular platforms. While *A* generates native mobile code, *B* generates code for hybrid applications. On the cloud side, *A* generates code for two providers (Openshift and Amazon). *B* generates a Java application just for one provider, that is its own cloud service platform.[20] With *B*, thanks to its development tools, the application can be automatically deployed in the cloud. In case of A, it generates an implementation to run in two different clouds service

[19] M2M transformation rules for RIA, `https://goo.gl/8Lsy6n`

[20] WebRatio Cloud Plans, link: `https://goo.gl/ByQgMp`

provider's (Openshift and Amazon). Even though, we highlight that the code generated using A, is based on Docker,[21] which is a method developed by the open source community. Precisely, one of the main goals of Docker is to ease the cloud application portability. Therefore, the code generated could be ported, more easily, to other providers which include Docker in their services.

A brief summary of the comparative study is shown in Table 2.

Table 2: Brief summary of the comparative study

Aspects	**Approaches**			**Comments**
	MoWebA M. (*A*)	**WebRatio M. (*B*)**	**Traditional**	
Dev. time	1 h 20 min	55 min	160 hs	*A*'s time can be improved using a specific tool
Modeling diff.	Unified model	One model for mobile, another one for cloud	—	In *A*, the network communication is designed in only one model which saves design effort
	It considers M2M semi-automatic rules from PIM to ASM	It does not consider such M2M rules	—	The semi-automatic M2M rules could help to save effort in the modeling process
Number of Gen. Platf.	2 mobile platforms, 2 cloud platforms	2 mobile platforms, 1 cloud platform	—	The cloud code generated by *A* is based on Docker, which eases the code portability

5 Conclusions and Future Works

In summary, we have proposed the adoption of MoWebA for the modeling and generation of MobileApps-FC, based on three design aspects which could improve the portability of such applications. Furthermore, we have focused on extending MoWebA to model and generate the network communication aspect, through an ASM. A as preliminary validation of our work, we have presented a comparative study of MoWebA Mobile versus the traditional approach and the consolidated MDD platform WebRatio Mobile. As expected, we have found a considerable saving of effort in the development of the network communication functions of the MobileApps-FC, using the MDD approaches. Among the MDD approaches, the development time using WebRatio is slightly better than MoWebA Mobile's time. Nevertheless, considering that MoWebA Mobile is implemented through generic tools, we believe that having a MoWebA Mobile's specific and more friendly modeling and generation tool its development time will be improved, which will lead to an additional saving of effort and, consequently, to a better alleviation of the portability challenge effects.

Thus, as future works, we consider: 1) to build a specific tool for making simpler and faster the modeling; 2) to build the transformation rules for the automatic transition from the PIM to the ASM, which includes the steps iv) and v) of the MoWebA extension definition [16]; and, 3) to improve the validation of the proposal with additional rigorous experiments.

[21] Docker, link: `https://www.docker.com/what-docker`

References

1. March, V., Gu, Y., Leonardi, E., Goh, G., Kirchberg, M., Lee, B.S.: Mcloud: Towards a new paradigm of rich mobile applications. Procedia CS **5** (2011) 618–624
2. Sahu, D., Sharma, S., Dubey, V., Tripathi, A.: Cloud computing in mobile applications. International Journal of Scientific and Research Publications **2**(8) (2012) 1–9
3. Abolfazli, S., Sanaei, Z., Gani, A., Xia, F., Yang, L.T.: Rich mobile applications: genesis, taxonomy, and open issues. Journal of Network and Computer Applications **40** (2014) 345–362
4. Brambilla, M., Mauri, A., Umuhoza, E.: Extending the interaction flow modeling language (IFML) for model driven development of mobile applications front end. In: Mobile Web Information Systems - 11th International Conference, MobiWIS 2014, Barcelona, Spain, August 27-29, 2014. Proceedings, Springer International Publishing (2014) 176–191
5. Sanaei, Z., Abolfazli, S., Gani, A., Khokhar, R.H.: Tripod of requirements in horizontal heterogeneous mobile cloud computing. CoRR **abs/1205.3247** (2012)
6. Gupta, P., Gupta, S.: Mobile cloud computing: The future of cloud. International Journal of Advanced Research in Electrical, Electronics and Instrumentation Engineering **1**(3) (2012) 134–145
7. da Silva, E.A.N., Fortes, R.P., Lucrédio, D.: A model-driven approach for promoting cloud paas portability. In: CASCON. (2013) 92–105
8. Pons, C., Giandini, R., Pérez, G.: Desarrollo de Software Dirigido por Modelos. Editorial de la Universidad Nacional de La Plata (EDULP)/McGraw-Hill Educación (2010)
9. Sanchiz, E., González, M., Aquino, N., Cernuzzi, L.: Development of mobile applications with functions in the cloud through the model driven approach: A systematic mapping study. CLEI electronic journal **20**(3) (December 2017)
10. Chondamrongkul, N., Chondamrongkul, N.: Model-driven framework to support evolution of mobile applications in multi-cloud environments. International Journal of Pervasive Computing and Communications **12**(3) (2016) 332–351
11. Heitkötter, H., Majchrzak, T.A., Kuchen, H.: Cross-platform model-driven development of mobile applications with md 2. In: Proceedings of the 28th Annual ACM Symposium on Applied Computing, ACM (2013) 526–533
12. Ranabahu, A.H., Maximilien, E.M., Sheth, A.P., Thirunarayan, K.: A domain specific language for enterprise grade cloud-mobile hybrid applications. In: Proceedings of the compilation of the co-located workshops on DSM'11, TMC'11, AGERE! 2011, AOOPES'11, NEAT'11, & VMIL'11, ACM (2011) 77–84
13. Steiner, D., Turlea, C., Culea, C., Selinger, S.: Model-driven development of cloud-connected mobile applications using dsls with xtext. In: EUROCAST (2). Volume 8112 of Lecture Notes in Computer Science., Springer (2013) 409–416
14. Ruokonen, A., Pajunen, L., Systä, T.: On model-driven development of mobile business processes. In: SERA, IEEE Computer Society (2008) 59–66
15. Richardson, L., Amundsen, M., Ruby, S.: RESTful Web APIs. "O'Reilly Media, Inc." (2013)
16. González, M., Cernuzzi, L., Aquino, N., Pastor, O.: Developing web applications for different architectures: The moweba approach. In: Tenth IEEE International Conference on Research Challenges in Information Science, RCIS 2016, Grenoble, France, June 1-3, 2016. (2016) 1–11

Applying Transformation Templates to Diversify User Interfaces Generated by Model-Driven Engineering *

Nathalie Aquino[1], Luca Cernuzzi[1], and Oscar Pastor[2]

[1] Departamento de Electrónica e Informática,
Universidad Católica "Nuestra Señora de la Asunción",
Tte. Cantaluppi y G. Molinas, Asunción, Paraguay
nathalie.aquino@uc.edu.py, lcernuzz@uc.edu.py

[2] Centro de Investigación en Métodos de Producción de Software,
Universitat Politècnica de València,
Camino de Vera s/n, 46022 Valencia, Spain
opastor@pros.upv.es

Abstract. Model-driven engineering of user interfaces aims to manage the inherent complexity of the development of user interfaces and to decrease the effort needed to develop them. However, from the end-user perspective, user interfaces generated by model-driven engineering usually present usability problems and it is not always easy to customise them. Transformation Templates arise as a means to improve model-driven engineering of user interfaces, providing several design options to customise user interfaces, at a concrete level. In this work we show how to apply Transformation Templates to OO-Method/Integranova, a model-driven engineering approach for the development of information systems. We present different user interface designs that could be generated, targeting the web platform and devices with small screen. Some of these new designs could have better usability properties than the original design.

Keywords: Model-driven engineering, MDE, user interface, transformation templates.

1 Introduction and Motivation

Historically, the development of graphical user interfaces has been challenging in terms of skills, times and resources [1]. Recently, the wide variety of hardware and software platforms from which interactive systems are accessed to, as well as the diversity of languages and tools for their development, have added more difficulties to their implementation [2].

* This work has been funded by CONACYT through the PROCIENCIA program, with resources from "Fondo para la Excelencia de la Educación e Investigación - FEEI", FONACIDE. This work has been developed under the project "Mejorando el proceso de desarrollo de software: propuesta basada en MDD" (14-INV-056).

Model-driven engineering (MDE) of user interfaces helps to manage these difficulties and diversities. In this context, several works can be mentioned, such as UsiXML [3], Maria [4], Just-UI [5], among others. Meixner et al. [6] present an interesting introduction to MDE of user interfaces. Meixner et al. [2] also analyse its past, present and future.

However, the literature also reports issues related to MDE of user interfaces [7, 8]. In general, MDE does not provide the possibility of generating different, customised user interfaces. Instead, generated interfaces are usually always similar to each other, which could be good when standard patterns are important, but which could also be an issue when end-users have special interactive requirements that cannot be satisfied with the MDE process. Furthermore, the literature has also reported usability problems in user interfaces generated by MDE [9–11].

OO-Method [5] is an object-oriented and MDE method that allows the automatic generation of software applications from conceptual models. It is supported by a commercial tool named Integranova M.E.S. In a previous work, we have analysed the usability of the user interfaces generated by OO-Method/Integranova in different platforms (desktop, web) and devices (with small, standard and large screens) [11]. We found that usability could be improved for the web platform and devices with small screen (PDAs, tablets, smartphones, etc.).

Furthermore, we have also previously presented Transformation Templates [12] as a means to improve MDE of user interfaces, providing several design options to customise user interfaces at a concrete level.

Therefore, in this work we show how to apply the Transformation Templates approach in OO-Method/Integranova, in order to show that different types of user interfaces can be generated, considering the web platform and devices with small screen. Some of these new designs could have better usability properties than the original designs.

The rest of this paper is organised as follows: Section 2 briefly describes the OO-Method/Integranova technology and presents the results of a usability evaluation of user interfaces generated with these tools. Section 3 presents the Transformation Templates approach. Section 4 applies the Transformation Templates approach to OO-Method/Integranova and presents alternative user interface designs that could be generated. Finally, Section 5 discusses about benefits of the Transformation Templates approach and the expected improvements in usability.

2 User Interfaces Generated by OO-Method/Integranova

This section presents an MDE software development method named OO-Method and its corresponding tool, Integranova. Furthermore, the Presentation Model of OO-Method is described. The section ends presenting a usability evaluation of the user interfaces generated using this tool.

2.1 OO-Method/Integranova and its Presentation Model

OO-Method [5] is a software development method that is MDE-compliant. It involves models of the future interactive system at different levels of abstraction and provides a transformation mechanism among them. It is supported by a commercial software suite named Integranova M.E.S., which was developed by Integranova Software Solutions [3].

Four system views are specified in the OO-Method development process: 1) the Object Model; 2) the Dynamic Model; 3) the Functional Model; and 4) the Presentation Model. Once these models are achieved, they are submitted to model compilation. For different possible target computing platforms (C# or ASP running on .NET or .NET 2.0; EJB, JSP, or JavaServer Faces running on Java), the source code of a fully functional application is automatically generated and structured according to a three-tiered architecture: interface, application, and persistence.

The OO-Method Presentation Model is composed of interaction units, which, in turn, are composed of elementary patterns.

Interaction units represent the main interactive operations that can be performed on domain objects. There are four interaction units: 1) the Service Interaction Unit (SIU), which allows the modification of objects, their attributes, and relationships; 2) the Population Interaction Unit (PIU), which shows a group of similar objects; 3) the Instance Interaction Unit (IIU), which shows a single object at a time; and 4) the Master/Detail Interaction Unit (MDIU), which shows a hierarchical view of relationships among objects.

Elementary patterns are used to build interaction units and to restrict and specify their behaviour. For example, if a PIU is being specified, then five elementary patterns could be attached to it: 1) the Filter pattern, which filters a set of objects to display only the needed ones; 2) the Order Criterion pattern, that specifies the order in which objects will be shown; 3) the Display Set pattern, that restricts which attributes of objects are going to be presented; 4) the Navigation pattern, which specifies navigation among objects; and 5) the Action pattern, which specifies functions that can be triggered from a selected object.

As an example, Figure 1 presents a PIU generated by OO-Method/Integranova, indicating its corresponding elementary patterns. The example corresponds to an Expenses Report application that allows the expenses of the employees of an organisation to be managed. In particular, this user interface corresponds to a list of all the expense registries.

From the explanation of the OO-Method Presentation Model decomposition, the SIU and PIU can be considered to be the most relevant interaction units of the approach, since the MDIU is a composition of other interaction units, and the IIU is a special case of a PIU in which just one object at a time is shown. Therefore, in this work we focus on SIUs and PIUs.

[3] http://www.integranova.com

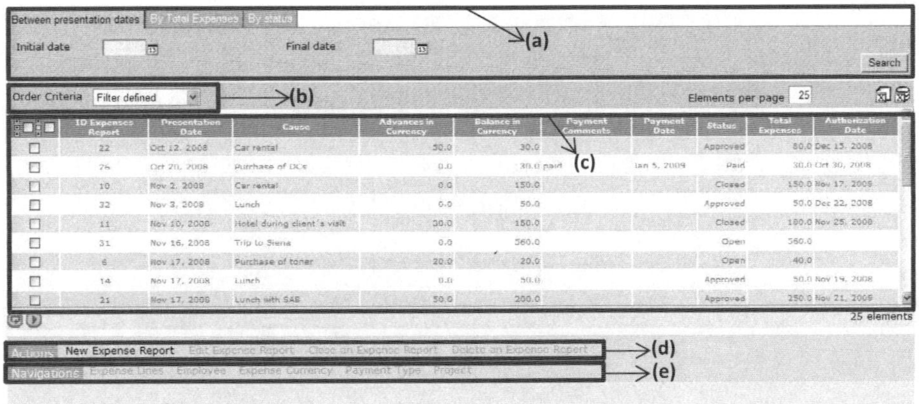

Fig. 1. User interface generated from a PIU with filter (a), order criterion (b), display set (c), actions (d), and navigations (e). Corresponds to the list of expense registries of the Expenses Report application.

2.2 Usability Evaluation of User Interfaces Generated by OO-Method/Integranova

As earlier commented, we have previously evaluated the usability of user interfaces generated by OO-Method/Integranova. An exploratory usability evaluation was carried out in an experimental controlled context. All details concerning this empirical study (motivation, planning, operation, analysis of data, interpretation of results) were reported in [11]. This section presents just a brief description, including a summary of results.

Usability was examined in terms of satisfaction, effectiveness and efficiency. The evaluation focused on interfaces generated from PIUs and SIUs of the previously mentioned Expenses Report application. Furthermore, the evaluation was carried out using different platform versions of the interfaces (web and desktop) and using devices with different screen sizes (small, standard and large).

Figure 2 and Figure 3 present two of the twelve different combinations of interaction unit (PIU, SIU), platform (web, desktop), and screen size (small, standard, large) that were evaluated. Figure 2 corresponds to a PIU that presents the list of expense registries of the Expenses Report application. Figure 3 corresponds to a SIU that allows new expense registries to be added. Both figures correspond to the web platform and the device with small screen (an ultra-mobile PC with 7" screen).

Table 1 summarises the results of this experiment. Perceptions of satisfaction and effectiveness were good, although there is still room for improvements. Efficiency results were most affected by the use of different platforms and devices.

In general, the web platform obtained worse results than the desktop platform. And the device with the small screen obtained worse results than devices with standard or large size screens.

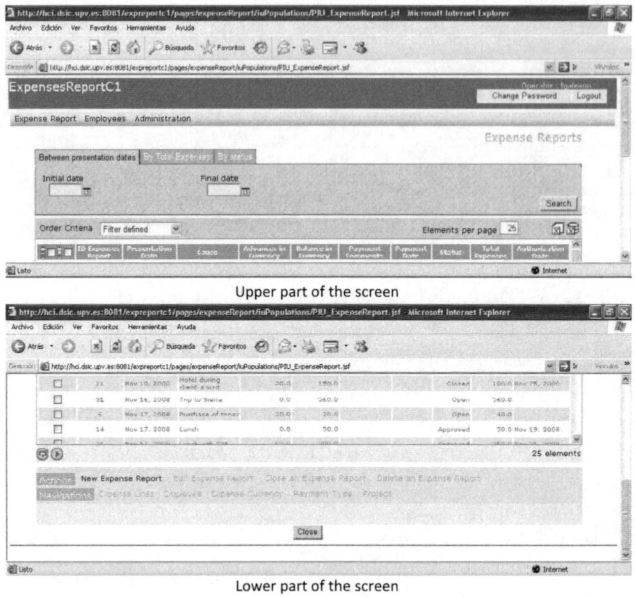

Fig. 2. User interface generated from a PIU that lists the expense registries of the Expenses Report application, as it was seen in the web platform and device with small screen

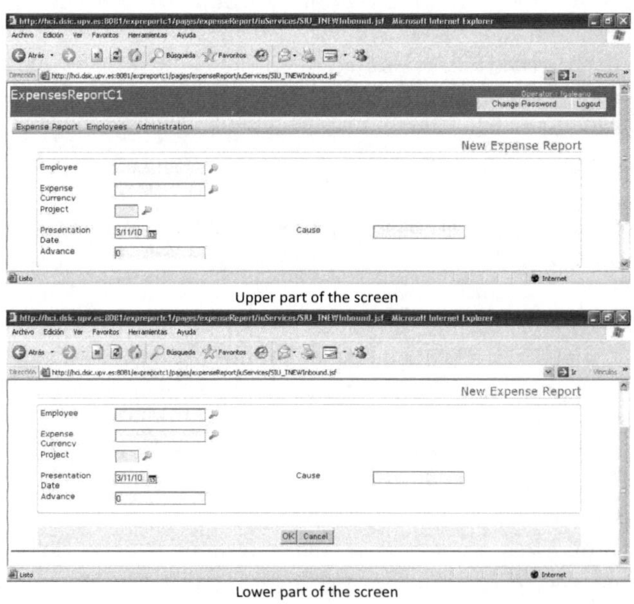

Fig. 3. User interface generated from a SIU that allows new registries to be added in the Expenses Report application, as it was seen in the web platform and device with small screen

Table 1. Summary of results of a usability evaluation of user interfaces generated by OO-Method/Integranova

Usability Aspect	Results
Satisfaction	- The perception of satisfaction was good for user interfaces generated from PIUs and SIUs. - Devices with different screen sizes have not affected the satisfaction perceived using interfaces generated from PIUs or SIUs. - Different platforms have not affected the satisfaction related to user interfaces generated from PIUs. In the case of SIUs, satisfaction was slightly better using the desktop platform than the web platform.
Effectiveness	- Subjects reached high percentages of task completion (means above 80%) when using interfaces generated from PIUs and SIUs. The achieved effectiveness is good. - The effectiveness related to interfaces generated from PIUs has not been affected by the use of devices with different screen sizes or diverse platforms. - The effectiveness related to interfaces generated from SIUs has been affected by different combinations of device and platform. Effectiveness was better using the combination of small screen with desktop platform than using the combination of standard size screen with web platform.
Efficiency	- The efficiency related to interfaces generated from PIUs and SIUs has been affected by the use of devices with different screen sizes. In the case of PIUs, efficiency was better using the large screen than using the small screen. In the case of SIUs, efficiency was better using standard or large screens than using the small screen. - The efficiency related to interfaces generated from PIUs and SIUs has been affected by different platforms. In both cases, efficiency was better using the desktop platform than using the web platform.

Currently, the OO-Method Presentation Model allows a user interface to be specified in a way that is independent from platforms and devices, and the transformation logic is internally defined in the Integranova tool, which generates the user interface code. It can be considered that the tendency to have better results for standard or large screens and for the desktop platform is related to the fact that the OO-Method/Integranova approach is mainly used to develop organisational information systems [5]. It can also be considered that the device with the small screen obtained worst results because the kinds of user interfaces that people are used to using in small devices are different from the types of user interfaces generated with Integranova.

Therefore, the OO-Method/Integranova approach should incorporate enhancements in order to generate multi-device/platform user interfaces with improved usability.

3 Transformation Templates

A Transformation Template [12] aims to explicitly specify the structure, layout, and style of a user interface, according to preferences and requirements of end-users, as well as in line with different hardware and software computing platforms and environments in which the user interface will be used.

The main concepts that characterise the Transformation Templates approach are related to context, to user interface models, and to the Transformation Templates themselves.

Context refers to the context of use of an interactive system. We have defined context according to the Cameleon Reference Framework [13], which is widely accepted in the human-computer interaction community. According to this framework, a context of use is composed of the stereotype of a user, who carries out an interactive task, with a specific computing platform in a given surrounding environment. Conceptualising context, we can define Transformation Templates for different contexts of use.

A *user interface meta-element* represents, in a generic way, any meta-element of a user interface meta-model. A *user interface element* represents an element of a user interface model. These generic representations allow the Transformation Templates approach to be used with different MDE approaches.

A *parameter type* represents a design or presentation option related to the structure, layout or style of the user interface. Defining a parameter type subsumes specifying the list of user interface meta-elements that are affected by it, as well as its value type. The *value type* refers to a specific data type (e.g., integer, URI, colour, etc.) or to an enumeration of the possible values that a parameter type can assume. A parameter type, with all or a set of its possible values, can be implemented in different contexts of use. In order to facilitate decision-making regarding these implementations, we propose that each possible value receive an estimation of its importance level and its development cost for different relevant contexts of use. In this way, possible values with a high level of importance and a low development cost can be implemented first in a given context, followed by the other options if appropriate. Furthermore, for each relevant context of use, usability guidelines can be assigned to each possible value of a parameter type. These guidelines will help user interface designers in choosing one of the possible values by explaining the conditions under which the values should be used.

Table 2 shows an example of the definition of a parameter type named *Filter Widget*. This parameter type is useful for deciding how to present filters in PIUs. Three different possible values have been defined: tabs, combo and accordion. The parameter type has been associated to two contexts of use: desktop and web platforms. Furthermore, Table 3 and Table 4 show that for each context of use and each possible value, importance level and development cost have been estimated, and usability guidelines have been proposed. These usability guidelines were extracted from [14].

A *transformation template* gathers a set of *parameters* for a specific context of use. Each parameter of a Transformation Template corresponds to a parameter

Table 2. Parameter Type: Filter Widget

Name	Description	Affects To	Possible Values	Contexts of Use
Filter Widget	Allows to select the widget to be used to present filters of a PIU	Filter	Tabs Combo Accordion	Desktop Web

Table 3. Parameter Type: Filter Widget - importance level, development cost and usability guidelines for the desktop platform

Value	Importance Level	Development Cost	Usability Guidelines
Tabs	high	low	The number of filters is not too big, less than 8
Combo	low	low	The number of filters is high
Accordion	low	low	The number of panels should be small, less than 8

type and has both, a value and a selector. A *value* is an instance of a value type. The value of a parameter corresponds to a possible value of the corresponding parameter type. A *selector* delimits the set of user interface elements that are affected by the value of a parameter. We have defined different types of selectors that allow the designer to choose a specific user interface element, all the user interface elements of a certain type, the first or last element contained in a specific type of user interface element, or other options.

As a simple example of a transformation template, Table 5 represents a fragment of a transformation template defined for a context of use that addresses a web platform and devices with small screens. This transformation template uses the Filter Widget parameter type to specify that all filters of PIUs will be displayed using accordions (first row), except for the filter with id=12, that will be displayed using a combo (second row).

Transformation Templates add flexibility in MDE approaches because they externalise the design knowledge and presentation guidelines, and make them customisable according to the characteristics of the project being carried out. At the same time, they diversify the kinds of user interfaces that an MDE approach

Table 4. Parameter Type: Filter Widget - importance level, development cost and usability guidelines for the web platform

Value	Importance Level	Development Cost	Usability Guidelines
Tabs	high	low	The number of filters is not too big, less than 8
Combo	low	low	The number of filters is high
Accordion	high	low	The number of panels should be small, less than 8

Table 5. Transformation Template for web platform and devices with small screen

Parameter	Value	Selector
Filter Widget	Accordion	Filter
Filter Widget	Combo	Filter with id=12
...	...	...

Table 6. Parameter Type: PIU Layout

Name	Description	Affects To	Possible Values
PIU Layout	Provides options for positioning elementary patterns of a PIU	PIU	PIU layout 1 PIU layout 2 PIU layout 3

can generate. Furthermore, Transformation Templates defined for one project can later be reused in other similar projects, targeting similar contexts of use.

It is worth noting that Transformation Templates do not replace any implicit transformation logic or explicit transformation languages; instead, they provide a higher-level tier for user interface designers to specify user interface transformations.

4 Applying the Transformation Templates Approach to OO-Method/Integranova

The definition of parameter types is among the first steps of the process to incorporate Transformation Templates in an MDE approach for user interface development. Therefore, this section presents some parameter types defined for OO-Method/Integranova. Then, we use these parameter types to suggest alternative designs for generating PIUs and SIUs, considering the web platform and devices with small screen.

4.1 Parameter Types for OO-Method/Integranova

Besides Filter Widget, which was previously presented, this section introduces four more parameter types for OO-Method/Integranova. For space reasons, estimations of importance level and developments cost, as well as usability guidelines, are omitted.

Table 6 presents the *PIU Layout* parameter type, which allows different configurations for the position of the elementary patterns that conform a PIU (filter, display set, actions, navigations) to be chosen. Figure 4 presents a graphical representation of the possible values.

Table 7 presents the *Display Set Layout* parameter type, which allows to specify if display sets are going to be displayed with tables or using a set of independent fields.

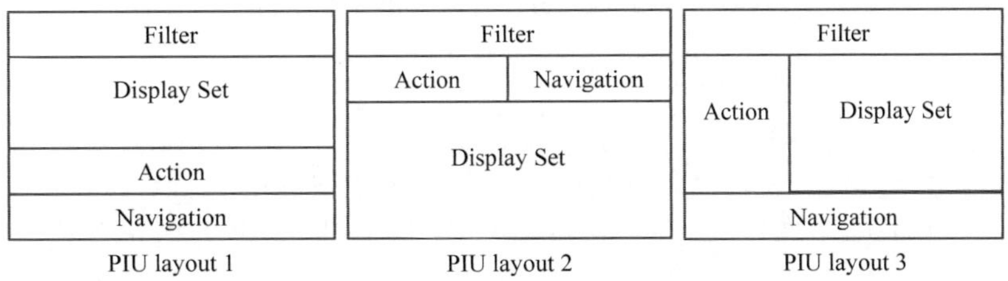

Fig. 4. Graphical representation of the possible values of PIU Layout

Table 7. Parameter Type: Display Set Layout

Name	Description	Affects To	Possible Values
Display Set Layout	Allows to specify if a display set is going to be displayed with a table or with a set of independent fields	Display Set	Table Reduced table Independent fields

Table 8 presents the *SIU Layout* parameter type, which allows to specify if input arguments of a SIU are going to be displayed in one or two columns, or if they are going to be placed according to the current algorithm used by Integranova.

Table 9 presents the *Label Alignment* parameter type, which allows the alignment of a label with regard to an input field to be specified.

4.2 Alternative Designs for PIUs and SIUs

This section presents two alternative designs for PIUs, as well as two for SIUs, targeting a context of use composed by web platform and devices with small screen. These alternative designs could be generated if, in the future, OO-Method/Integranova incorporates the Transformation Templates approach and implements the previously defined parameter types for the considered context of use.

The first alternative design for PIU is presented in parts (a), (b), (c) and (d) of Figure 5. This design is obtained using the following parameters and values:

Table 8. Parameter Type: SIU Layout

Name	Description	Affects To	Possible Values
SIU Layout	Allows to specify if a SIU is going to be displayed in 1 or 2 columns, or following the standard algorithm	SIU	Standard algorithm 1 column 2 columns

Table 9. Parameter Type: Label Alignment

Name	Description	Affects To	Possible Values
Label Alignment	Allows the alignment of a label with regard to an input field to be specified	Filter SIU	Left Up Inside

- *PIU Layout* = *PIU layout 2*, therefore, filters appear on top (in blue), followed by actions (in orange) and navigations (in green) at the same level, and the display set appears at the bottom (see Figure 5(a)).
- *Filter Widget* = *Accordion*, therefore, an accordion is used to present the three different filters of this PIU. In Figure 5(b) and (d) the accordion is closed. In (c) all filter options are displayed. In (b) one filter is open to be used.
- *Display Set Layout* = *Independent fields*, therefore, registries are not displayed using a table, but as a sequence of independent fields (see Figure 5(a)).
- *Label Alignment* = *Inside*, therefore labels of input arguments in the filter appear inside the input texts (see Figure 5(b)).

The second alternative design for PIU is presented in Figure 5(e). This design is obtained using the following parameters and values:

- *PIU Layout* = *PIU layout 3*, therefore, filters appear on top, actions appear to the left, the display set appears to the right, and navigations appear at the bottom.
- *Filter Widget* = *Tab*, therefore, tabbed panels are used to display the three different filters of this PIU.
- *Display Set Layout* = *Reduced table*, therefore, registries are displayed using a table, but only four of a total of ten columns are displayed (see Figure 2), providing also a link to access a different view with the missing columns.
- *Label Alignment* = *Left*, therefore labels of input arguments in the filter appear to the left of input texts.

The first alternative design for SIU is presented in Figure 6(a). This design is obtained using the following parameters and values:

- *SIU Layout* = *1 column*, therefore, input arguments are presented in one column.
- *Label Alignment* = *Inside*, therefore, labels of input arguments appear inside the input texts.

The second alternative design for SIU is presented in Figure 6(b). This design is obtained using the following parameters and values:

- *SIU Layout* = *2 columns*, therefore, input arguments are presented in two columns.
- *Label Alignment* = *Up*, therefore, labels of input arguments appear above input texts.

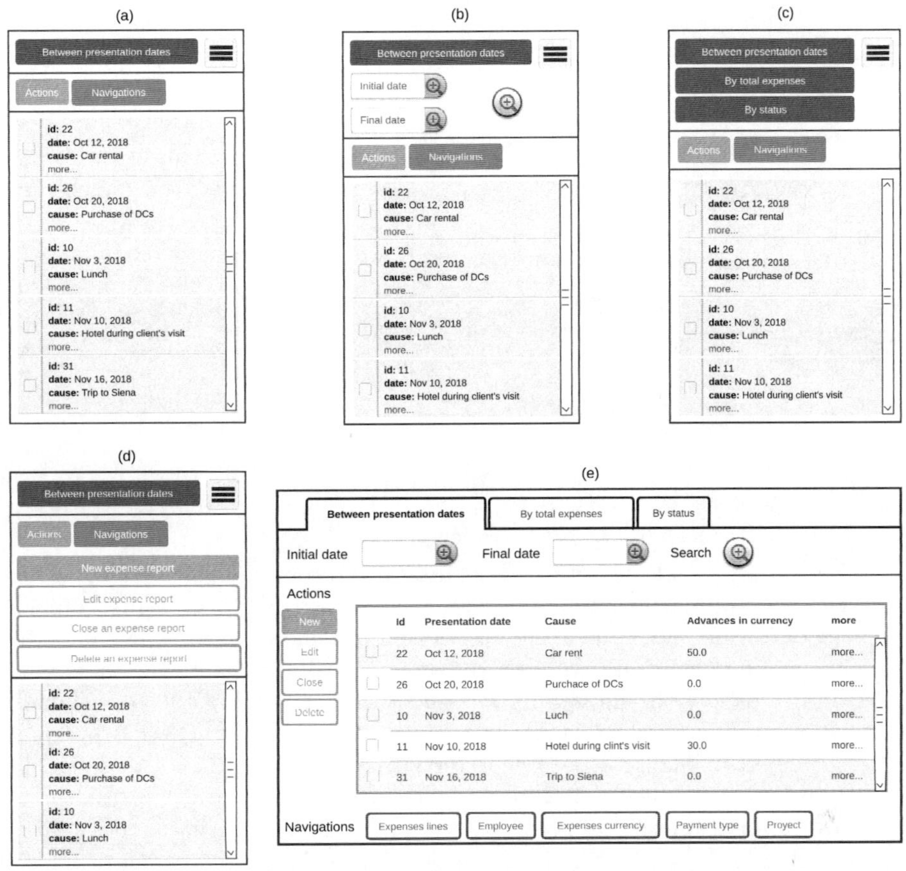

Fig. 5. Alternative designs for PIU

5 Discussion

Applying the Transformation Templates approach to OO-Method/Integranova we can obtain the following consequences: 1) the transformation logic becomes explicit and customisable, since it can be expressed in transformation templates by means of parameters with their corresponding values and selectors; 2) it becomes possible to target specific contexts of use, including specific platforms, since transformation templates implies that a specific context of use must be selected; 3) it becomes possible to generate different types of user interfaces, using the different possible values of parameter types, as presented in Section 4.2; and 4) among the different user interfaces that can be generated using Transformation Templates, some of them could have better usability properties than the original designs, considering a particular context of use. At this point, it is worth noting that currently, the Integranova tool has not implemented yet the Transformation Templates approach, therefore these are expected benefits.

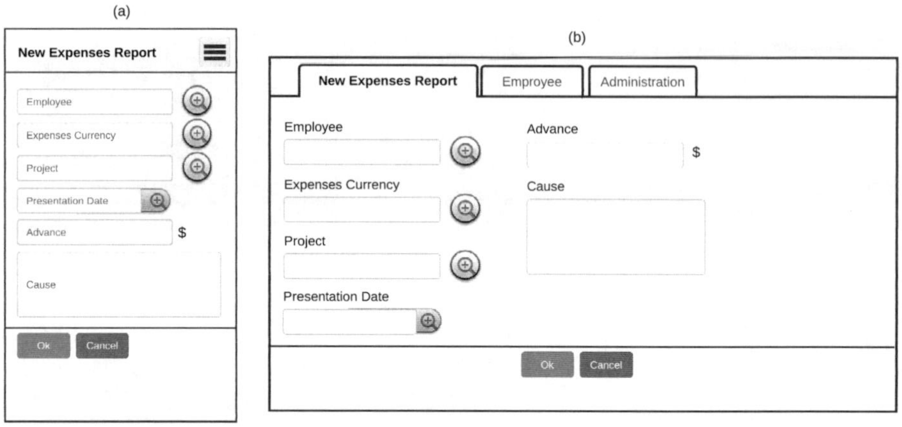

Fig. 6. Alternative designs for SIU

Elaborating a little bit more about usability problems, it is useful to highlight that our approach considers that for each context of use, usability guidelines should be provided for all possible values of a parameter type. Therefore, when defining a transformation template, the designer will be able to see these guidelines and to choose the most appropriate value, considering the corresponding context of use. For instance, it could be possible that the alternative designs for PIU presented in Figure 5 obtain better usability results than the design presented in Figure 2, since usability guidelines for small devices suggest that: 1) the most relevant information (the content of the display set in this case) should be presented first, in upper and central positions; 2) the use of tables should be avoided. As a future work we plan to perform an empirical evaluation in order to formally verify if these new designs improve the usability with regard to the original ones.

Finally, we recognise that currently there is a trend to use responsive web design when targeting to the web. However, it is still valid to follow guidelines for specific hardware or software platforms. Furthermore, it should be taken into account that the Transformation Templates approach is not specific for the web. It can also be applied in desktop or native platforms.

References

1. Myers, B.A., Rosson, M.B.: Survey on User Interface Programming. In Bauersfeld, P., Bennett, J., Lynch, G., eds.: Conference on Human Factors in Computing Systems, CHI 1992, Monterey, CA, USA, May 3-7, 1992, Proceedings, ACM (1992) 195–202
2. Meixner, G., Paternò, F., Vanderdonckt, J.: Past, Present, and Future of Model-Based User Interface Development. i-com **10**(3) (2011) 2–11
3. Limbourg, Q., Vanderdonckt, J., Michotte, B., Bouillon, L., López-Jaquero, V.: USIXML: A Language Supporting Multi-path Development of User Interfaces. In

Bastide, R., Palanque, P.A., Roth, J., eds.: Proc. of 9th IFIP Working Conference on Engineering for Human-Computer Interaction jointly with 11th Int. Workshop on Design, Specification, and Verification of Interactive Systems, EHCI-DSVIS 2004 (Hamburg, July 11-13, 2004). Volume 3425 of Lecture Notes in Computer Science., Springer-Verlag, Berlin (2005) 200–220

4. Paternò, F., Santoro, C., Spano, L.D.: MARIA: A universal, declarative, multiple abstraction-level language for service-oriented applications in ubiquitous environments. ACM Trans. Comput.-Hum. Interact. **16**(4) (2009)
5. Pastor, O., Molina, J.C.: Model-Driven Architecture in Practice: A Software Production Environment Based on Conceptual Modeling. Springer-Verlag New York, Inc., Secaucus, NJ, USA (2007)
6. Meixner, G., Calvary, G., Coutaz, J.: Introduction to Model-Based User Interfaces. Technical report, World Wide Web Consortium (2014) http://www.w3.org/TR/mbui-intro/.
7. Montero Simarro, F., López-Jaquero, V., Vanderdonckt, J., González, P., Lozano, M.D., Limbourg, Q.: Solving the Mapping Problem in User Interface Design by Seamless Integration in IdealXML. In Gilroy, S.W., Harrison, M.D., eds.: Interactive Systems, Design, Specification, and Verification, 12th International Workshop, DSVIS 2005, Newcastle upon Tyne, UK, July 13-15, 2005, Revised Papers. Volume 3941 of Lecture Notes in Computer Science., Springer (2005) 161–172
8. Coutaz, J.: User interface plasticity: model driven engineering to the limit! In Sukaviriya, N., Vanderdonckt, J., Harrison, M., eds.: Proceedings of the 2nd ACM SIGCHI Symposium on Engineering Interactive Computing System, EICS 2010, Berlin, Germany, June 19-23, 2010, ACM (2010) 1–8
9. Abrahão, S., Iborra, E., Vanderdonckt, J.: Usability Evaluation of User Interfaces Generated with a Model-Driven Architecture Tool. In Law, E.L.C., Hvannberg, E.T., Cockton, G., eds.: Maturing Usability - Quality in Software, Interaction and Value. Human-Computer Interaction Series. Springer (2008) 3–32
10. Schramm, A., Preußner, A., Heinrich, M., Vogel, L.: Rapid UI Development for Enterprise Applications: Combining Manual and Model-Driven Techniques. In Petriu, D.C., Rouquette, N., Haugen, Ø., eds.: Model Driven Engineering Languages and Systems - 13th International Conference, MODELS 2010, Oslo, Norway, October 3-8, 2010, Proceedings, Part I. Volume 6394 of Lectures Notes in Computer Science., Springer (2010) 271–285
11. Aquino, N., Vanderdonckt, J., Condori-Fernández, N., Dieste Tubío, Ó., Pastor, O.: Usability Evaluation of Multi-Device/Platform User Interfaces Generated by Model-Driven Engineering. In Succi, G., Morisio, M., Nagappan, N., eds.: Proceedings of the International Symposium on Empirical Software Engineering and Measurement, ESEM 2010, 16-17 September 2010, Bolzano/Bozen, Italy, ACM (2010)
12. Aquino, N., Vanderdonckt, J., Pastor, O.: Transformation Templates: Adding Flexibility to Model-Driven Engineering of User Interfaces. In Shin, S.Y., Ossowski, S., Schumacher, M., Palakal, M.J., Hung, C.C., eds.: Proceedings of the 2010 ACM Symposium on Applied Computing (SAC), Sierre, Switzerland, March 22-26, 2010, ACM (2010) 1195–1202
13. Calvary, G., Coutaz, J., Thevenin, D., Limbourg, Q., Bouillon, L., Vanderdonckt, J.: A Unifying Reference Framework for Multi-Target User Interfaces. Interacting with Computers **15**(3) (2003) 289–308
14. Galitz, W.O.: The Essential Guide to User Interface Design: An Introduction to GUI Design Principles and Techniques. John Wiley & Sons, Inc., New York, NY, USA (2002)

Análisis sobre la adopción de MDSE en empresas de construcción de software del Eje Cafetero colombiano

Fáber D. Giraldo, Diego A. Zabala, Jonathan S. Moncada

Grupo de Investigación SINFOCI, Universidad del Quindío, Colombia
email: fdgiraldo@uniquindio.edu.co,
{dazabalab, jsmoncada_1}@uqvirtual.edu.co

Abstract. La ingeniería de software dirigida por modelos (MDSE por sus siglas en inglés) se ha venido promoviendo como un camino para manejar la complejidad del proceso de construcción de software elevando el nivel de abstracción y automatizando labores intensivas de generación de código. Sin embargo, existe poca evidencia empírica sobre el conocimiento, aceptación y adopción de la MDSE en la industria de construcción de software colombiana. El objetivo de este estudio empírico es investigar cómo están las empresas de construcción de software de la región del Eje Cafetero colombiano en cuanto a la práctica y uso de conceptos relevantes en el MDSE y el análisis de los factores considerados teóricamente importantes para su adopción. La muestra se compone de 16 empresas que participaron de forma voluntaria en este estudio. Los datos recolectados proceden de la aplicación de una encuesta presencial y virtual. Entre los factores detectados se evidencia el desconocimiento del paradigma, y la influencia de la percepción personal, la visión y el tamaño de la organización en la adopción del MDSE. Finalmente, se discuten los desafíos en la adopción del MDSE.

Keywords: MDSE, adopción del MDSE, estudio empírico, empresas de construcción de software, Eje Cafetero colombiano.

1 Introducción

El paradigma de la Ingeniería de Software dirigida por modelos (MDSE) viene promoviéndose como un medio para manejar el desarrollo de sistemas de software altamente complejos. MDSE hace referencia a las metodologías donde los modelos constituyen el artefacto principal y que fomentan el uso eficiente de los mismos durante todas las etapas del proceso de desarrollo del software. MDSE plantea elevar el nivel de abstracción, que permite ocultar detalles específicos de plataformas concretas con el propósito de mejorar la comprensión del sistema, adaptarse a las necesidades específicas de contextos, soportando la formulación de lenguajes específicos de dominio (DSL), y aprovechando la transformación de modelos y la reutilización de componentes para automatizar el trabajo repetitivo y mejorar la calidad del software.

Mientras que MDSE ha sido adoptado e implementado por empresas referentes del sector tecnológico tales como Motorola e IBM [1], otras compañías no han considerado aún la posibilidad de incluir este paradigma como parte de su estrategia para la construcción de productos software. Las motivaciones y desafíos que se deben conocer y afrontar en el proceso de adopción del MDSE en la industria son el problema de estudio en esta investigación. Se analizaron los resultados de un estudio empírico realizado en 4 casos industriales sobre las motivaciones de adoptar MDE [6], y una revisión sistemática sobre su aplicación en la industria [4], para agrupar en dos clases las motivaciones de aplicar MDSE: mejorar la productividad y disminuir el tiempo de desarrollo, y mejorar la calidad del software.

El objetivo de este estudio empírico fue investigar cómo están las empresas constructoras de software de la zona denominada Eje Cafetero colombiano en cuanto a la práctica y uso de algunos conceptos relevantes del MDSE y el análisis de los factores considerados teóricamente importantes para su adopción. La muestra se compone de 16 empresas que participaron de forma voluntaria en este proyecto de investigación y que poseen productos propios o hacen desarrollo de software a la medida que podrían ser analizados y desarrollados utilizando técnicas MDSE. Los datos recolectados proceden de la aplicación de una encuesta presencial o virtual y voluntaria. Ninguna de las empresas involucradas en la investigación había ejecutado previamente proyectos con enfoque MDSE o estaban aplicándolo, mientras tanto siguen en el proceso de familiarización con este enfoque.

El resto del trabajo se organiza de la siguiente manera. La Sección 2 presenta el contexto, se describe el método de investigación y los procedimientos de recolección de datos, una introducción al *Modelo de Aceptación de Tecnología (TAM)* y sus extensiones. Este modelo es utilizado para evaluar los factores percibidos como importantes para la adopción del MDSE. La Sección 3 presenta los resultados que surgieron del análisis de los datos, seguido de las discusiones en la Sección 4. La Sección 5 presenta las conclusiones e implicaciones para el trabajo futuro.

2 Contexto y metodología de la investigación

El estudio presentado en este trabajo fue realizado en la región del Eje Cafetero colombiano, compuesto por las ciudades de Manizales, Pereira, y Armenia. Los investigadores contactaron inicialmente un total de 98 pymes de desarrollo de software, de las cuales 16 decidieron contribuir con la investigación. Algunas de las pymes participantes son sedes de multinacionales, pero que medidas por cantidad de recurso humano e infraestructura siguen perteneciendo a la categoría de pymes. La participación se desarrolló de forma voluntaria. La Tabla 1 presenta la lista de empresas participantes en este estudio clasificadas por ciudad.[1].

[1] Por acuerdos de confidencialidad, los nombres de las empresas no serán referenciados explícitamente durante la presentación de los resultados de nuestro estudio.

Tabla 1: Conformación de la muestra de las empresas participantes en el estudio.

Pymes desarrolladoras de software ubicadas en las capitales del Eje Cafetero colombiano.		
Armenia	Pereira	Manizales
Celuweb	Alpha Tech	Apolo Ingeniería
Catavento Tecnología	Avansis	Aporte médico
Ingeneo	Datacenter	Insoft S.A.S.
Kijho tecnologies	Sedisoft	Sigma Ingeniería
Universidad Gran Colombia		Grupo CI2DT2 (Unicaldas)
TOC		Newshore

Con las pymes de la Tabla 1 se agendaron citas presenciales en sus instalaciones para la explicación, contextualización y aplicación de la encuesta que sustenta la investigación. Las pymes que participación en el proyecto fueron de 5 dominios diferentes, incluyendo aplicaciones empresariales, telecomunicaciones, sistemas de facturación y contable, software médico y sistemas geográficos. La guía de elaboración y posterior evaluación de los resultados obtenidos con la encuesta gira en torno a 5 secciones:

1. *Capabilidades de la Ingeniería de Modelos:* definida como el desarrollo de metodologías y herramientas para modelar sistemas [6]. Esta sección contiene 20 preguntas y abarco los lenguajes de dominio específico o DSL, la interiorización organizacional de los modelos, conocimiento sobre trazabilidad entre modelos y durante el proceso de transformación a otros modelos y generación de código fuente.
2. *Estado actual en la empresa del enfoque MDSE*: esta categoría contiene 19 preguntas y abarca el uso, el propósito y la cantidad de modelos utilizada en la organización, problemas con las herramientas de modelado, mitos relacionados con la metodología, claridad entre lógica y modelado de negocio, reutilización y generación de código fuente.
3. *Visión del profesional sobre el enfoque MDSE*: esta categoría contiene 15 preguntas, donde se busca encontrar cuál es la percepción que posee la organización de este enfoque. Esta área de investigación abarco los beneficios, roles, importancia de los DSL, inversión de tiempo y dinero, fuentes de investigación y conocimiento sobre los problemas y retos afrontados por las empresas que han adoptado MDSE. Por otro lado, se les pregunta a los encuestados si en la organización tienen la intención o han pensado en comprar y/o crear herramientas de modelado, automatizar procesos y por qué creen que un enfoque de desarrollo basado en modelos debería ser tomado en cuenta.
4. *Aspectos organizacionales*: esta categoría contiene 21 preguntas que abarcan pilares organizacionales como la infraestructura, experiencia, recurso humano, ámbito de actuación geográfico, innovación e investigación, gestión de proyectos y definición de roles que unidos permitirán la caracterización de las empresas participantes en la investigación.

5. *Retos y problemas del MDSE*: se compone de 7 preguntas que buscan evaluar sesgos conceptuales, la percepción del encuestado sobre su empresa y conocimiento de los beneficios del enfoque: todo esto permitirá validar la parte 1 sobre capabilidades. Esta sección esta creada para identificar si los integrantes de la muestra poseen dominio del tema y coherencia en las respuestas.

Con el fin de evaluar las secciones del formulario de una manera sistemática se utilizó el enfoque GQM, el cual consiste en definir preguntas de investigación específicas para cada situación que podría reflejar patrones de uso del MDSE y sus métricas de evaluación [7]. Con el fin de proporcionar una plataforma común para la evaluación de MDSE como una metodología, aprovechamos el Modelo de Aceptación de Tecnología (TAM) [6], y algunas extensiones para recopilar los factores importantes percibidos por los desarrolladores para poder usar el MDSE y retos para su uso futuro.

2.1 Comparación con trabajos previos

Respecto a estudios previamente reportados en el estado del arte, este estudio empírico no busca analizar el nivel de aceptación del enfoque MDSE tal como se presenta en [3,2,5,8,9], ya que ninguno de los profesionales aquí encuestados poseía experiencia profesional en el enfoque. Los resultados presentados en los trabajos previos muestran una curva satisfactoria de aceptación del enfoque debido a la adopción paulatina, organizada y planeada del MDSE; sin embargo, las dudas y la resistencia al cambio de paradigma sigue presente en el proceso de adopción del mismo. Por ejemplo, en [8] se reporta las experiencias y factores de éxito/fracaso observados en 17 empresas que decidieron iniciar un proceso de adopción del MDSE. El reporte de la adopción exitosa del MDSE en los trabajos previos ha sido alto porque todos los involucrados desarrollan un sentido de pertenencia por el proceso y desde el inicio son conscientes tanto de las ventajas como del esfuerzo requerido.

2.2 Metodología

Este estudio utiliza la investigación cualitativa donde el investigador recoge a menudo datos emergentes abiertos con la intención primaria de deducir temas y teorías con estos datos. La investigación aplicada en este proyecto es exploratoria [10]. Se recopilan y analizan múltiples tipos de datos categorizados por secciones con el fin de analizar el impacto de la adopción del MDSE en la industria de software del Eje Cafetero colombiano. Es un estudio empírico que permite evaluar la adopción del MDSE y por lo cual no hay un conjunto de datos resultantes. Como se mencionó anteriormente, las empresas desarrolladoras de software que participaron en la investigación fueron contactadas telefónicamente y se les propuso participar de forma voluntaria en el proyecto, de las cuales, hay empresas regionales, nacionales y multinacionales. El perfil de los profesionales que resolvieron la encuesta varía entre Líder de Proyectos, Desarrolladores Senior y

Gerentes administrativos con vasta experiencia en el desarrollo de software, lo que anula la posibilidad de hacer la selección de los casos de estudio por conveniencia.

Los estudios realizados en el proyecto transcurrieron desde el mes de febrero hasta el mes de junio del año 2017 y se clasifica como una investigación para la adopción de MDSE diseñada y realizada por 2 investigadores externos a las empresas y abordando preguntas de investigación que permitieron analizar la adopción del MDSE.

El cronograma de las investigaciones realizadas fue el siguiente: la construcción del instrumento estadístico para recolectar la información se llevó a cabo en los meses de agosto-noviembre del año 2016. Posteriormente se identificaron las empresas legalmente constituidas en la región del Eje Cafetero, y éstas fueron contactadas para establecer la muestra del estudio empírico (febrero-junio del 2017). Cada empresa participó en el proyecto designando un profesional del área del desarrollo de software que fue el encargado de responder la encuesta. La evaluación era una retroalimentación verbal entre encuestador y encuestado durante y después de terminada la encuesta.

La encuesta fue diseñada de acuerdo al enfoque Goal Question Metric (GQM) y los resultados se analizaron basados en el Modelo de Aceptación de Tecnología (TAM) presentado en la siguiente sección. Los resultados de la encuesta son el tema de este documento. La encuesta fue diseñada y conducida por un investigador que no participó en ninguno de los casos de estudio. Cada reunión duró entre 60 y 90 minutos de la cual quedo como constancia el formulario solucionado en formato físico.

El número de respuestas en algunas secciones de la encuesta es demasiado bajo para generar estadística. Los resultados son, sin embargo, importantes cuando se interpretan en el contexto donde se realizó el estudio, sobre todo porque ha habido pocos estudios empíricos realizados en pymes desarrolladoras de software. Por lo tanto, resumimos los resultados de la encuesta por ciudad y los analizamos basados en otros datos recogidos de estudios específicos en grandes empresas que han iniciado el proceso de adopción de MDSE o han evaluado la posibilidad de hacerlo.

2.3 Modelo de aceptación de tecnología

Los autores en [6] presentan el *Technology Acceptation Model - TAM*, un modelo que explica la intención de los usuarios de usar una nueva tecnología (o sistema) a través de dos creencias: la utilidad percibida, que es la medida en que una persona piensa que el uso de un sistema mejorara su desempeño en el trabajo y su facilidad de uso, en pocas palabras es evaluar que tan fácil cree la persona que va a ser el uso del sistema. A continuación, se hablará de factores adicionales a TAM que son relevantes para este proyecto.

En [6] se analizan 5 modelos teóricos que permiten explicar la aceptación de metodologías: TAM, TAM2, Características Percibidas de la Innovación (de sus siglas en ingles PCI), Teoría de Comportamiento Planeado (de sus siglas en ingles TPB) y Modelo de Utilización de Computadoras Personales (de sus

Construct	TAM	TAM2	PCI	TPB	MPCU
Usefulness	Usefulness	Usefulness	Relative advantage	Attitude	Job fit
Ease of use	Ease of use	Ease of use	Complexity		Complexity
Subjective norm		Subjective norm		Subjective norm	Social factors
Voluntariness		Voluntariness	Voluntariness		
Perceived Behavioral Control (PBC)				PBC- External	Facilitating conditions

Fig. 1: Comparación de factores comunes entre modelos de aceptación [6].

siglas en ingles MPCU). La Figura 1 presenta los factores en común que tienen estos 5 modelos teóricos. MPCU evalúa los factores en el entorno que facilitan la utilización de un sistema. PCI incluye, por ejemplo, la compatibilidad de factores, que hace referencia al grado en que una innovación se percibe como consistente con los valores existentes, las necesidades y la experiencia pasada de los posibles adoptantes en una compañía.

En [6] se sugiere que la utilidad percibida y la facilidad de uso eran los factores más importantes para la adopción del MDSE. TAM se seleccionó porque en el trabajo realizado por [6] se demuestra su pertinencia en estudios similares, es útil para describir los elementos que influyen en la aceptación de una tecnología y definen una lista de factores que son relevantes en el procedimiento de evaluación de la adopción del MDSE, los cuales son: utilidad percibida, percepción de la facilidad de uso, compatibilidad percibida con los métodos y prácticas de desarrollo existentes, norma subjetiva y percepción de la madurez de las herramientas del MDE.

En este estudio empírico se optó por no evaluar los siguientes factores dependientes del modelo TAM: el apoyo organizativo, la facilidad de uso, la norma subjetiva y la percepción de la madurez de las herramientas del MDSE ya que las empresas de desarrollo de software involucradas no habían adquirido experiencias en proyectos con este enfoque. Las variables dependientes en el modelo TAM implementado son el uso actual e inconsciente de algunos artefactos y conceptos claves del MDSE y las intenciones de uso futuro. La Figura 2 muestra el modelo que se aplicó en un proyecto de investigación [6] y la adaptación realizada para este análisis empírico.

3 Resultados

En esta sección se describe el estado actual de uso del MDSE en las organizaciones, este uso puede ser consiente: que actúan con conocimiento de que están implementando tareas que pertenecen a este enfoque; o que no es consiente: lo hacen empíricamente. Como se mencionó en un apartado anterior, las empresas son pymes desarrolladoras de software a la medida o con un producto software y las respuestas a la encuesta reflejan el nivel de uso o practica observado por los

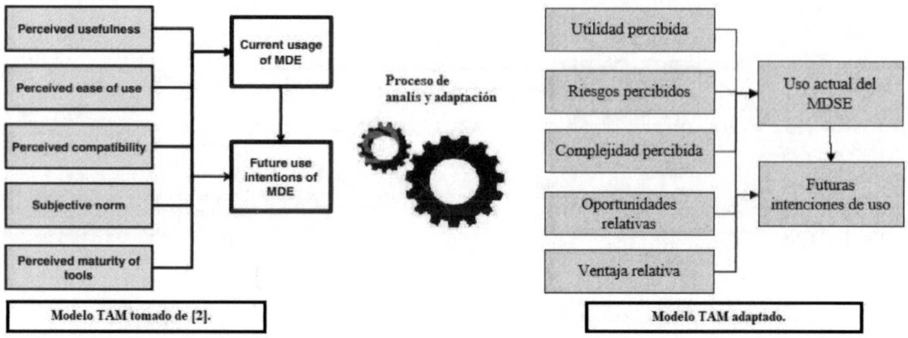

Fig. 2: Modelo TAM parcialmente modificado y adaptado a las necesidades específicas del proyecto.

desarrolladores, y también su conocimiento sobre el enfoque MDSE. El nombre de las empresas es anónimo (en la encuesta se pide con la única finalidad de ordenar los datos) porque así se planteó desde el inicio de la investigación.

En las encuestas, se descubrió que muy pocas de las empresas usan modelos en el proceso de desarrollo de software, especialmente durante las fases de análisis y diseño. Sin embargo, el porcentaje de uso varia significativamente entre las empresas y todas usan modelos sólo con el propósito de guiar y documentar. La Tabla 2 muestra los resultados promediados de la calificación dada al grado de uso (medido en una escala Likert de 1 a 5, donde 1=No se usa, 3= Se usa medianamente, 5=Se usa completamente) de los procesos claves en la adopción y aplicación del enfoque MDSE en las empresas de la muestra.

Tabla 2: Calificación en escala Likert del *grado de uso* de procesos del enfoque MDSE en Armenia, Pereira y Manizales

	Armenia					Pereira					Manizales				
Proceso	1	2	3	4	5	1	2	3	4	5	1	2	3	4	5
Modelado		X								X			X		
Herramientas de modelado		X							X				X		
Modelado del negocio			X						X					X	
Lógica del negocio				X					X					X	
Lenguajes de dominio específico			X						X				X		
Optimización del código				X					X				X		
Reutilización de código fuente				X					X					X	
Reutilización de componentes				X					X					X	
Generación de código fuente		X						X							X

A continuación, se describen los resultados obtenidos para cada uno de los factores independientes del modelo TAM implementado. Los resultados de estos factores se presentan en la Tabla 3[2].

Tabla 3: Promedio de los puntajes dados por las empresas a las preguntas del modelo TAM de la encuesta.

Empresa	Utilidad percibida	Riesgos percibidos	Complejidad percibida	Oportunidad relativa	Ventaja relativa	Futuras intenciones de uso
Pereira						
PER01	3.6	4.11	Difícil	3.3	4.9	5
PER02	2.87	2.33	Difícil	2.5	4.4	2
PER03	4.6	4	Fácil	3	4.4	3
PER04	3.6	3	Difícil	2.1	5	2
Manizales						
MAN01	3.87	2.67	Difícil	2.8	5	4
MAN02	2.37	3.67	———	2.5	4.9	2
MAN03	3.5	2.89	Fácil	4.8	4.5	5
MAN04	2.37	3.33	———	2.2	4.9	———
MAN05	3.87	3.78	Difícil	2.8	5	2
MAN06	3.7	3.89	Fácil	3.3	4.1	2
Armenia						
ARM01	3.6	4.33	Difícil	3.8	3.2	3
ARM02	2.7	3.56	Difícil	2.2	3.1	1
ARM3	4.2	2.33	Fácil	1.3	2.7	2
ARM4	3.87	4.78	Fácil	3.2	4.5	5
ARM05	3.2	3.22	Difícil	3.8	3.8	2
ARM06	4.1	3.56	Fácil	3.3	4.4	3

3.1 Utilidad percibida

La utilidad percibida es el grado en que una persona cree que usar el enfoque MDSE podría mejorar su desempeo laboral [6]. Los resultados arrojan que la mayoría de la muestra está en desacuerdo con que los modelos solo se usen para documentar; en cuanto al porcentaje de código autogenerado y automatizable, los resultados indican que la mayoría está en desacuerdo con que se pueda generar más de un 50%. En cuanto a los DSL, la reutilización y la optimización de procesos con modelos son conceptos que la muestra ve con optimismo.

Las puntuaciones medias de las respuestas dadas a los procesos mencionados previamente se observan en la tabla 2. La agrupación se realiza utilizando los factores independientes en la adopción del MDSE definidos en la Sección 2.

[2] La escala numérica utilizada para las columnas a excepción de la complejidad percibida es *1 = Muy bajo*, *2=Bajo*; *3=Medio*, *4=Alto*, y *5 = Muy alto*. Los valores numéricos son el promedio de los puntajes dados por los encuestados a las preguntas concernientes a cada factor independiente en la adopción del MDSE.

3.2 Riesgos percibidos

El riesgo percibido es el grado en que un profesional encuestado cree que una lista de retos o problemas expuestos en la encuesta, se pueden llegar a materializar en una organización que desee realizar la adopción del enfoque MDSE. Para evaluar este factor independiente se le presentó un caso de estudio sobre adopción del enfoque MDSE en procesos de desarrollo de software, para esto se listaron los problemas hallados en [6] sobre la adopción del MDSE.

3.3 Complejidad percibida

La complejidad percibida es el grado en que un encuestado cree que la adopción del enfoque MDSE puede conllevar a problemas o retos estructurales en su organización. En la encuesta una pregunta cubría la complejidad percibida en la adopción del MDSE. A la pregunta *Cree qué integrar MDE en los procesos internos de la empresa es complejo y conlleva una gran inversión de dinero y tiempo?* 8 empresas contestaron afirmativamente mientras que 5 no y las restantes decidieron no hacerlo por desconocimiento del enfoque MDSE.

3.4 Oportunidad relativa

Las oportunidades relativas tomadas en cuenta en esta investigación son aquellas fortalezas organizacionales, de definición de roles, económicas, profesionales, experiencia en proyectos MDSE, inversión en herramientas de modelado e investigación que posee la empresa. Seis preguntas de la encuesta cubrían este factor y este factor también tiene sus respectivos resultados en la Tabla 3.

3.5 Ventaja relativa

La ventaja relativa en esta investigación es la percibida por los investigadores, donde se busca analizar si las empresas de la muestra cuestionan sus procesos en pro de mejora, si los profesionales se interesan por diversificar sus conocimientos, si la empresa ejecuta actividades laborales y académicas con el fin de mantener actualizado su conocimiento empresarial, si invierten en investigación o en la aplicación de técnicas de desarrollo de software y si la empresa le permite a su recurso humano espacios de estudio y/o capacitación. Otra ventaja relevante en este factor es el estado actual de la empresa en cuanto a infraestructura, planeación estratégica, cultura organizacional, gestión de proyectos, entre otros. En la encuesta, 9 preguntas cubrían la ventaja relativa y este factor también tiene sus respectivos resultados en la Tabla 3.

3.6 Intenciones de uso futuro

Cabe aclarar que las intenciones de uso futuro no representan en este caso ninguna experiencia previa con el enfoque MDSE y sus resultados también se encuentran expuestos en la tabla 3. No se preguntó directamente si desearían usar el MDSE ya que el conocimiento sobre este en las empresas era limitado, por lo cual se formularon preguntas que permitieron deducir implícitamente una motivación/intención para usar en el futuro este enfoque de desarrollo e identificar empresas con la estructura organizacional suficiente para iniciar una posible adopción del MDSE. Las preguntas de la encuesta que cubrían las intenciones de uso futuro fueron 4.

Una hipótesis inicial se fundamenta en el desconocimiento del enfoque, los bajos niveles de oportunidades percibidas y los altos índices de riesgos percibidos. Los profesionales encuestados generalmente pensaron que no les gustaría usar MDSE en un trabajo a futuro, aunque las ventajas relativas son altas las empresas son reacias a usarlo. La muestra es pequea para generar conclusiones estadísticas, aunque las puntuaciones son útiles para comprender los hallazgos.

Al promediar los puntajes obtenidos se encontró que todas las compaías de la muestra se caracterizaron por percibir la utilidad y los riesgos como medio-altos, las oportunidades relativas y el uso futuro del enfoque MDSE obtuvieron una valoración baja-media, aunque las ventajas percibidas estén en un rango alto-muy alto. Las opiniones sobre los DSL, las herramientas utilizadas para modelar y los problemas más frecuentes que se les han presentado (la integración, migración, e inexperiencia) fueron generalmente negativas, lo que también es importante para describir las intenciones de uso futuro.

3.7 Motivaciones y obstáculos para la adopción de MDSE

El 62.5% de las empresas encuestadas no avala la creación de una herramienta de modelado sin embargo en cuanto a comprarlas el 37.5% presenta oposición, lo que establece un interés del 62.5% de mejorar sus procesos de modelado usando herramientas. Manizales y Pereira presentan en su muestra un 50% de no aceptación frente a la compra de herramientas de modelado, pero Manizales con un 66.66% prefiere no crear sus herramientas. Armenia es la ciudad más receptora con un 83.33% de la muestra interesada en comprar herramientas de modelado, porcentaje que desciende a 33.33% si se trata de crear sus propias herramientas de modelado, hallazgo que resulta consistente con la valoración de sus recursos y capacidades.

El 50% de la muestra tomada en Armenia expresa que no ha participado en ningún proyecto cuya solución parte de un modelado y Manizales con un 33.3%, generando una incertidumbre en la forma en que se ejecutan la planeación de sus proyectos.

El aprovechamiento de los modelos es una motivación importante. En los resultados obtenidos el 75% asegura que en sus empresas utilizan modelos, cuyos porcentajes varían según el proyecto o la necesidad que se presente, sin embargo: en Armenia se asegura que los proyectos en los que usaron modelos fueron aprovechados en más de un 11%, Pereira establece un porcentaje de aprovechamiento mayor al 20% y Manizales indica un grado mayor al 70%; cifras que dejan a Manizales como la ciudad que más saca beneficio de los modelos y Armenia en el tercer puesto.

4 Discusión

4.1 Factores de aceptación del MDSE

Utilidad . El 75% de los encuestados encontraron MDSE útil, aunque no hubo opiniones fuertes que sustentaran este fenómeno. Los desarrolladores de empresas que tenían más conocimiento sobre el MDSE y habían trabajado previamente con generación de código y DSL fueron más positivos en cuanto a la utilidad del enfoque. Como se refleja en las encuestas el MDSE no obtuvo una opinión positiva ni negativa, sino que resultó ser una alternativa a evaluar por parte de las empresas. La utilidad es claramente un determinante significativo para utilizar el enfoque y las herramientas del MDSE, por lo tanto, este aspecto fue objeto de varias preguntas de investigación definidas usando GQM para el levantamiento de información en las empresas de la muestra. Algunos ejemplos de métricas definidas para evaluar la utilidad percibida son: Uso, tipo de modelos y perfiles DSL utilizados para resolver un problema; relación entre modelo y generación de código; optimización, reutilización y transformación de modelos; relación entre modelado y lógica de negocio. En [6] también encontraron la utilidad como un factor relevante para analizar la adopción del MDSE.

Riesgos percibidos. Los hallazgos en la encuesta indicaron que el riesgo percibido es un factor significativo en la adopción y que los obstáculos con mayor índice de importancia son: carencia de abstracción, falta de una semántica definida lo que conlleva a que el significado de un modelo a menudo depende de la herramienta, inexperiencia del equipo de trabajo y la falta de escalabilidad de los modelos mientras que por otro lado los profesionales encuestados creen que la falta de herramientas de migración es un problema poco importante.

Complejidad percibida. La complejidad que perciben los desarrolladores de software de un paradigma de desarrollo relativamente nuevo es un factor importante para la adopción del MDSE ya que las empresas expresan su preocupación económica por los riesgos que se deben afrontar y mitigar. Los resultados de la encuesta indican que 8 de las empresas opinan que la adopción de MDSE es un proceso complejo y 8 opinan lo contrario, de las cuales 2 tienen la máxima valoración de uso futuro del enfoque y 2 no dieron su opinión. Los profesionales encuestados mencionaron que las futuras soluciones resultantes de la adopción de este paradigma deben compensar reduciendo algunos costos y/o complejidad en el proceso de desarrollo de software y siendo reutilizables en otros tipos de proyectos. La complejidad percibida también se encontró como un factor importante en la investigación presentada en [6] y hace parte de los modelos PCI y MPCU.

Oportunidades relativas. Las oportunidades relativas son aquellas fortalezas que posee la organización y se percibe como un factor importante ya que permite evaluar los factores del entorno que facilitan la utilización de un sistema [6].

Para caracterizar este aspecto se les pregunto a los profesionales encuestados si en algún momento le corresponde realizar tareas que no competen con su rol o cargo para identificar si la empresa tiene una estructura definida a lo cual 10 profesionales respondieron afirmativamente, los otros consideraron que no debían hacerlo ya que sus responsabilidades estaban bien determinadas. La experiencia en el proyecto muestra que las empresas tienen pocas alternativas de capacitación interna y externa, y el grado promedio de inversión en investigación es 3 (medianamente).

Ventaja competitiva. Una ventaja competitiva relativa es alguna característica presente en la empresa que la diferencie de las demás permitiéndole destacar en una competencia de mercado. Para evitar posibles confusiones cabe aclarar que este factor independiente no es equivalente a la ventaja relativa que compone el modelo PCI. Aunque la ventaja competitiva relativa no está incluida en TAM o modelos similares, los entrevistados mencionaron que era importante evaluar los procesos de autoevaluación internos, capacitaciones, actualidad en tendencias, inversión en investigación, diagnostico organizacional y proyección de la empresa para ofrecer un punto de vista sobre la viabilidad de iniciar un proceso de adopción del MDSE.

4.2 Uso actual y futuro

En cuanto al uso actual, no se identificaron empresas como usuarios principiantes o experimentados en el enfoque MDSE. Algunas de las empresas pudieron identificar áreas donde el MDSE tiene valor agregado en comparación con otros enfoques de desarrollo. En cuanto al uso futuro del enfoque, los hallazgos actuales no respaldan la hipótesis de que el uso actual motiva un uso futuro ya que las puntuaciones y opiniones se encuentran muy dispersas. Sin embargo, las empresas que poseen un alto nivel de modelado (una minoría muestral) percibieron que el MDSE era más fácil de usar, más útil, con un alto índice de riesgo por lo cual poseían las puntuaciones más altas en intenciones de uso futuro. Estos hallazgos se consideran importantes porque permiten indicar que a la mayoría de las empresas no les interesa cambiar de paradigma de desarrollo porque el que usan actualmente les ha funcionado bien y son reacias con el uso del enfoque, la empresa B, que era un usuario de métodos de desarrollo empíricos (lógica y modelado de negocio meramente mental), estaba muy convencida de que no valía la pena arriesgar capital económico por cambiar un proceso y una estructura que ya funcionaba mientras que la empresa C estaba muy convencida de los beneficios del MDSE. Para definir las intenciones de uso futuro, se necesita hacer una investigación con un grupo de empresas que posean conocimientos básicos sobre MDSE y sus desafíos o que estén ejecutando proyectos experimentales de adopción del paradigma donde se puedan evidenciar sus principales beneficios.

5 Conclusiones

Este trabajo presentó los resultados de un estudio realizado sobre pymes de software del Eje Cafetero Colombiano respecto a la adopción del paradigma MDSE en procesos reales de construcción de software. El estudio encontró que, el proceso de desarrollo de software empleado por la mayoría de las pymes de la muestra se estructura como un modelo de negocio que responde a las necesidades existentes en el mercado, donde toma importancia metodologías agiles y por cuestión de retrasos en el cronograma u oportunidades competitivas se dejan de ejecutar fases como el diseño (modelamiento). Por consiguiente, una posible adopción del enfoque MDSE se ve truncada por la desinformación y la polarización de la información, factor que se sustenta en la baja o casi nula participación de los ingenieros encuestados en proyectos que usen este enfoque.

En las empresas de la muestra el desarrollo de software se fundamenta en conocimientos adquiridos y apoyados en la experiencia. Se es consciente de que los modelos son una herramienta multipropósito pero su uso depende del proyecto y el contexto, por lo cual, en la mayoría de los casos se dejan de usar lo que disminuye el nivel de documentación, organización y estructuración que demanda un proyecto de ingeniería.

En cuanto a la capacitación de su personal e inversión en investigación estructuran su funcionamiento de cara a las necesidades inmediatas de la organización, por lo cual, este tema es abordado con cautela y baja o casi nula inversión económica para no perder la estabilidad comercial que posee, lo que permitió hallar desinterés y resistencia al cambio de paradigmas o enfoques de desarrollo.

Como conclusión final, se encontró que la industria de software del Eje Cafetero no posee la madurez necesaria para afrontar la adopción de un enfoque diferente para desarrollar software. Los resultados arrojaron un bajo índice de manejo y conocimiento del enfoque, pero la mayoría de la muestra posee el musculo económico, la infraestructura y la experiencia comercial para iniciar un proceso de adopción del MDSE guiado por un profesional experto en el área.

Como trabajo futuro se puede partir de los resultados obtenidos en este proyecto de investigación empírica para investigar las carencias académicas concernientes al MDSE, crear o ajustar planes de estudio que integren o mejoren los contenidos académicos de este enfoque de desarrollo con la finalidad de mejorar su idoneidad en los programas de pregrado concernientes al área de desarrollo de software. También se plantea analizar el impacto de los espacios académicos relacionados con MDSE impartidos desde el año 2015 en el énfasis en Ingeniería de Software de la Maestría en Ingeniería de la Universidad del Quindío, con el propósito de identificar un eventual incremento en la adopción industrial del paradigma model-driven en la industria local de construcción de software del Eje Cafetero colombiano a partir de los primeros resultados de este programa de posgrado; dicho análisis incluye el aumento de la muestra de empresas participantes.

Agradecimientos

Los autores agradecen a la Vicerrectoría de Investigaciones de la Universidad del Quindío (Colombia) por el apoyo al proyecto mediante la modalidad de *Semilleros de Investigación Fase III 2017-I.* Los autores también agradecen a las empresas encuestadas por su participación voluntaria en el estudio.

Referencias

1. Paul Baker, Shiou Loh, and Frank Weil. *Model-Driven Engineering in a Large Industrial Context — Motorola Case Study*, pages 476–491. Springer Berlin Heidelberg, Berlin, Heidelberg, 2005. ISBN 978-3-540-32057-9.
2. Tony Clark and Pierre-Alain Muller. Exploiting model driven technology: a tale of two startups. *Software & Systems Modeling*, 11(4):481–493, Oct 2012.
3. Jesús Sánchez Cuadrado, Javier Luis Cánovas Izquierdo, and Jesús García Molina. Applying model-driven engineering in small software enterprises. *Science of Computer Programming*, 89:176 – 198, 2014. Special issue on Success Stories in Model Driven Engineering.
4. Parastoo Mohagheghi and Vegard Dehlen. *Where Is the Proof? - A Review of Experiences from Applying MDE in Industry*, pages 432–443. Springer Berlin Heidelberg, Berlin, Heidelberg, 2008. ISBN 978-3-540-69100-6.
5. Parastoo Mohagheghi, Miguel A. Fernandez, Juan A. Martell, Mathias Fritzsche, and Wasif Gilani. Mde adoption in industry: Challenges and success criteria. In Michel R. V. Chaudron, editor, *Models in Software Engineering*, pages 54–59, Berlin, Heidelberg, 2009. Springer Berlin Heidelberg. ISBN 978-3-642-01648-6.
6. Parastoo Mohagheghi, Wasif Gilani, Alin Stefanescu, and Miguel A. Fernandez. An empirical study of the state of the practice and acceptance of model-driven engineering in four industrial cases. *Empirical Software Engineering*, 18(1):89–116, Feb 2013.
7. R. van Solingen and E. Berghout. *The Goal/Question/Metric Method: A Practical Guide for Quality Improvement of Software Development.* McGraw-Hill, 1999. ISBN 9780077095536.
8. J. Whittle, J. Hutchinson, and M. Rouncefield. The state of practice in model-driven engineering. *IEEE Software*, 31(3):79–85, May 2014.
9. Jon Whittle, John Hutchinson, Mark Rouncefield, Håkan Burden, and Rogardt Heldal. Industrial adoption of model-driven engineering: Are the tools really the problem? In Ana Moreira, Bernhard Schätz, Jeff Gray, Antonio Vallecillo, and Peter Clarke, editors, *Model-Driven Engineering Languages and Systems*, pages 1–17, Berlin, Heidelberg, 2013. Springer Berlin Heidelberg. ISBN 978-3-642-41533-3.
10. R.K. Yin. *Case Study Research: Design and Methods.* Applied Social Research Methods. SAGE Publications, 2003. ISBN 9780761925521. LCCN 93040567.

Towards the automation of a defect detection protocol for functional size measurements

Denisse Madrigal-Sánchez, Christian Quesada-López, Marcelo Jenkins

University of Costa Rica, San Pedro, Costa Rica
{denisse.madrigal, cristian.quesadalopez, marcelo.jenkins}@ucr.ac.cr

Abstract. There is a need to develop formal protocols to verify the accuracy of software functional size measurements and to calibrate the measurement processes. These protocols offer a mechanism for accomplishing such verification regardless of who performed the measurements (an expert or an automated tool). The detailed analysis of functional size measurement procedures results is necessary to understand the nature of the defects. The automation of these protocols decreases the effort and time required to verify the measurements accuracy and supports the calibration of procedures and tools for functional size measurement. This paper presents an empirical study for evaluating the results of a prototype tool that automates an accuracy verification protocol for IFPUG FPA measurements. Our tool uses a graph-based model to search for the causes of measurement mismatches detected in the verification process. The current prototype has reached an accuracy of 93.92%, a precision of 98.69% and a recall of 94.94%.

Keywords: Functional size measurement, defect detection tool, accuracy verification protocol automation, IFPUG FPA, empirical study

1 Introduction

Functional size measurement is one of the main factors influencing effort and cost estimations in a software development project [1]. There are five standardized methods for functional size measurement: COSMIC-FFP (ISO/IEC 19761), IFPUG FPA (ISO/IEC 20926), MkII (ISO/IEC 20968), NESMA (ISO/ IEC 24570) y FiSMA (ISO/IEC 29881). Historically, IFPUG FPA is the most popular one [2] and COSMIC-FFP is the one with the most increased adoption in the last years [3]. Both methods measure functionality delivered to final user by doing function points analysis.

Research related to procedures and tools for automated functional size measurement has increased in the last years [4]. With such increase, the need for research of empirical studies to verify measurement results obtained through these automated procedures has also been identified [4,5]. Symons [6] establishes that there are many functional size measurement procedures available in literature that should be carefully used by professionals. The author explains that an automated procedure is reliable when it has been calibrated and validated previously in the context of application measurement.

It is necessary to define mechanisms to verify the accuracy and reliability of results obtained by measurement procedures. Soubra, Abran & Ramdane-Cherif [4] state the need to define and use standardized accuracy verification protocols in order to proof the accuracy of functional size measurement procedures independently.

An accuracy verification protocol for functional size aims to evaluate the accuracy of functional size measurements by comparing control values (obtained by an expert) to results obtained by third parties as professionals applying measurement procedures or tools that automate such measurement. Accuracy verification protocols have been proposed and validated for measurement results following COSMIC-FFP and IFPUG FPA standards [4,7,5].

Manual execution of verification protocols is error prone, time and effort consuming. The prototype tool offers a mechanism to automate the execution of an accuracy verification protocol saving time and effort. The prototype tool could also provide support during the calibration of procedures and the identification and analysis of assignable causes for measurement errors.

We present a prototype tool that automates an accuracy verification protocol for functional size measurements based on method IFPUG FPA. We also present the results of an empirical evaluation to validate to prototype tool effectiveness. In the context of this study, our prototype reached an accuracy of 93.92%, a precision of 98.69% and a recall of 94.94%.

This paper is structured as follows: Section 2 presents the related work on accuracy verification protocols for functional size measurements. Section 3 describes the prototype tool implemented. Section 4 describes the empirical study conducted to validate the prototype tool effectiveness. Section 5 shows the results of the tool evaluation. Finally, Section 6 outlines conclusions and future work.

2 Related work

Protocols for accuracy verification report measurement results obtained through an specific procedure and compare them to the measurement results obtained by an expert [4,5]. In [8], a set of verification protocols were identified, in the following we briefly describe these protocols.

Soubra, Abran & Ramdane-Cherif [4] developed a protocol that allows the verification of accuracy in all steps of the measurement procedure of an automated tool implementing the standard COSMIC-ISO 19761. The protocol requires measurement results to be compared to measurement results manually obtained by a human expert so that the automated tool can be calibrated. Verification in every step allows to keep traceability between software input artifacts and functional measurement components. Bagriyanik & Karahoca [7] used Soubra et al. protocol [4] to verify the accuracy of measurements generated by an automated tool for COSMIC-FFP measurements. Authors keep the original 3 phases but also add two more steps for detailed verification in phase 2.

Yilmaz, Tunalilar & Demirors [9] developed a tool for automatic defect detection in COSMIC-FFP measurements. Authors also presented a methodology to validate the efficiency of their tool in terms of correctness and accuracy. Functional users trigger events to show function points and objects of interest verification. The tool takes such verification to conduct the analysis and generate a report of detected defects. In this study, error categories are associated to three error causes: Measurer Related, Measurement Process Related and Software Requirements Specification documented related. In order to evaluate the tool efficiency this study also required manual defect detection that was then compared to the results obtained by the tool.

The studies we presented so far refer to protocols for COSMIC-FFP measurements which is not the measurement method of our case of study. Nevertheless Soubra, Abran & Ramdane-Cherif and Bagriyanik & Karahoca studies provide the baseline for the accuracy verification protocol automated by our prototype tool. Quesada-López & Jenkins [5] adapted Soubra et al. protocol [4] to verify the accuracy of IFPUG FPA measurements. Measurements results are verified using a top-down evaluation to compare total unadjusted function points(UFP) and basic functional components (BFC). For every BFC, this protocol analyzes total number of data element types (DET), record element types(RET) and file types referenced (FTR). Such granular analysis allows to detect errors in the calculation of complexity of the BFCs. Same as [4], authors highlight the importance of keeping traceability between requirements and input artifacts and measurement results so that the protocol not only identifies measurement differences but their root cause.

Finally, Morris & Desharnais [10] described a verification method based on historic IFPUG FPA measurement data. The validation identifies errors based on variances to expected norms. Deviation from the norm happens when measurement results do not comply with measurement results specific for the context of the application. Based on historic data and application specific characteristics, ranges of variation for a specific BFC are determined. Measurements verification based on historic data and variances to expected norm is an approach different to the one proposed by Quesada-López & Jenkins so it can not be used as support for our prototype tool.

3 Prototype tool

Quesada-López & Jenkins [5] propose an accuracy verification that uses a top down evaluation of functional size measurement results in order to identify differences reported by applying one or more measurement processes. The protocol looks for consistency comparing measurement results differences against a true value reported by an expert. We selected this protocol as the one automated by our prototype tool because this protocol is designed to work with IFPUG FPA measurements and this standard is the subject of study of our research. Quesada-López & Jenkins [11] conducted a controlled experiment to compare functional size measurements for two different measurement procedures: IFPUG FPA and Automated Function Point (AFP). Two subsequent replications of this experiment were then conducted in [12] and they were analyzed using the verification protocol proposed by Quesada-López & Jenkins [5].

3.1 Protocol phases

The protocol has 3 phases: 1. Total UFP measurement results comparison 2. Detailed comparison of the accuracy of measurement results. 3. Identification and errors recovery. We analyzed the protocol phases in order to determine whether or not the level of detail of those was enough to accomplish the protocol automation and to determine which steps of the protocol procedure would required improvements. Here we discuss improvements applied:

- Delayed execution of phase 3: The protocol executes phase 3 whenever an error is identified in phase 2 so that errors in inputs (or procedures) are fixed and the measurement results are re-evaluated to verify the calibration success.The prototype delays the execution of phase 3 until a full scan of all measurement results is performed. Such delay allows to identify the status of all measurements before trying to find assignable causes for errors.
- Functional elements comparison: According to the protocol, measurement results have to be sorted by requirement, function and type. From automation point of view, it is necessary to come up with a mechanism to guarantee that the exact same elements are compared. We defined these requirements to perform numerical comparisons of measurement results: (1) Elements containing numerical attributes need an identification property. (2) Such property must be consistent between the *true value*[1] measurements and the subject[2] measurements.

To solve later requirements, we defined *pair measurement*. A measurement is a pair measurement of another one if they both have the exact same name. The prototype will only compare numerical data if it could previously pair two measurements.

Protocol coverage and prototype model The prototype implements phases 1 and 2 of the protocol. Phase 3 requires human intervention to inspect the quality of requirements, input artifacts and measurement procedure. The automation of this kind of inspection is out of the scope of this study, but a proposal to look for assignable causes based on the prototype data model and the measurement errors identified in phase 2 is described in Section 3. For phase 3 the prototype identifies and reports the measurement differences.

- Measurement results are represented with a graph data structure. Each set of measurements (subject and true value) are represented on its own graph.
- The prototype uses deep first algorithm to traverse the graphs and visit all nodes in both graphs simultaneously. In each node, measurements are compared and evaluated.

[1] *True value* measurement results refer to measurement results obtained by an expert and that will be considered true value when evaluating measurement results through the protocol

[2] Subject measurements results refer to measurement results that need to be evaluated, either obtained by a human being or a tool

- The graphs traversal to evaluate measurements and the search for assignable causes generate the results that are presented to the user.

The prototype was implemented using Java as programming language and *Spring-boot* framework. We selected *Neo4j*as graph database and we also used *Spring Data Neo4j* library for graphs processing.

Prototype process model The protocol execution requires input data loaded into the prototype. Such input data includes measurement results to be evaluated and measurement results that will be considered as true value. Once input data is loaded, it needs to be mapped to the prototype data model and then the prototype can start executing the protocol. Measurement differences and measurement errors are reported to the user and they are also used as input for the similarity analysis proposed in order to search assignable causes.

3.2 Measurement results modeling

Model design We used a graph to represent all measurements in a count of the same application performed by a single source, either the expert or the person or tool providing the measurement results that will be evaluated. The graph nodes represent characteristics of the measurement of a functional element: The count it belongs to, requirement, function type and basic functional components associated, data logical groups and data element types. Edges represent relations between these characteristics.

Model implementation Based on the design from previous section we implemented the model in Figure 1. Graph nodes are represented by a base class named Node that contains all attributes of a graph node. All other node types extend from Node. CountRoot node contains the number of data functions and transactional functions associated to a count. DFRoot node allows to group all data function requirements which are at the same time composed by data functions. TFRequirement nodes have the name of the artifact that presents the requirement. TransactionalFunction nodes show the type of the transactional function, the UFP size and the number of DETs and FTRs associated to the function. TransactionalFunction is similar to DataFunction, but the last one has different types and a attribute for RETs instead of FTRs. Graph edges allow us to keep traceability between a measurement and the elements it is associated to. More details of the prototype tool implementation can be found in [13].

3.3 Procedure modeling

Model design We defined some concepts as part of the procedure design phase. These need to be understood for a better understanding of the prototype procedure model:

- Subject node: Node currently analyzed in the subject graph.
- True value node: Node in the true value graph that corresponds to the subject node.

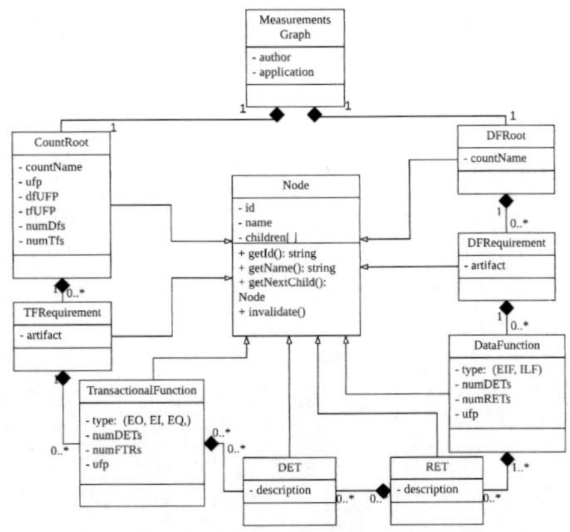

Fig. 1: Implemented Data Model

- Subject graph: Measurement results graph currently being evaluated.
- True value graph: True value measurement results.
- Pair node: Node that matches the name and path of a node in the counterpart graph.
- Invalidated node: Node that has no pair node in the counterpart graph.

As mentioned earlier, the prototype procedure takes advantage of deep first graph traversal. Such algorithm adapts naturally to the problem so that one measurement at a time is analyzed prioritizing nodes in deeper levels. Figure 2 shows the process flow followed by the prototype to implement protocol phases. Each sub-process tagged represents an algorithm implemented in the prototype.

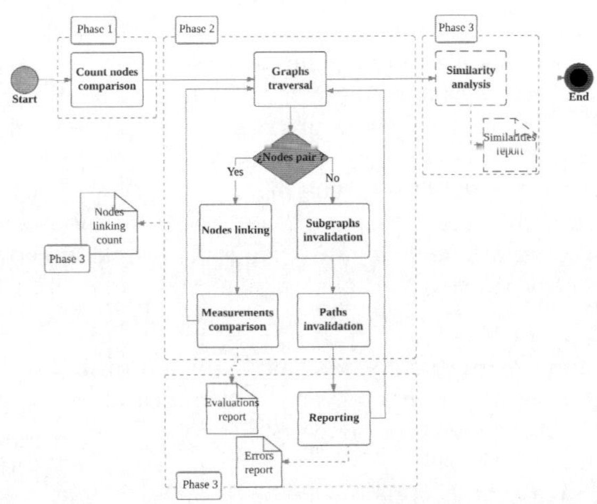

Fig. 2: Prototype execution process of protocol phases

The prototype first compares count nodes an register the evaluation results. Then the graphs traversal begins. Such traversal looks for pair nodes in order to allow the visit of a deeper level node. If the pairing between subject and true value nodes succeed, nodes are linked and the pairing is registered, then pair nodes measurements are evaluated. If the pairing fails, the algorithm has detected an invalidated path. This causes invalided nodes to be tagged and reported. This process continues until the entire top sub-graph is traversed. After this, a second traverse starts in the bottom sub-graph from the DF node. The proposal for sub-graphs similarities would be applied once both sub-graphs are traversed in both subject and true value graphs.

Model implementation The model design includes eight algorithms described now:

- Count nodes comparison: This algorithm implements phase 1 of the protocol by comparing total size measurement results. Total unadjusted function points and the total number of DFs and TFs are compared.
- Graphs traversal: This algorithm traverses both graphs using deep first algorithm. Detailed measurement results are compared if pairing succeeds. Otherwise, differences are reported.
- Nodes pair: This algorithm allows to determine if two given nodes, one from subject graph and another from true value graph, actually pair.
- Sub-graphs invalidation: This algorithm is triggered when it is possible to continue traversing a graph but its counterpart graph can no longer be traversed because a node was invalided or the total number of nodes between both graphs does not match. The algorithm invalidates an entire sub-graph with a root node that was just invalidated.
- Path invalidation: This algorithm is similar to the previous one but its goal is to invalidate a path. This algorithm is invoked by the previous one.
- Reporting: This algorithm is invoked every time a node is invalidated. It allows to keep track of the specific paths that generated an invalidated node.
- Node linking: This algorithm marks two nodes, one from subject graph and another from true value graph, as pairs.
- Measurements comparison: This algorithm generates metrics about the evaluation of two specific measurements, one from subject graph and another from true value graph. It uses magnitude of relative error (MRE), magnitude of error relative (MER) and balanced relative error (BRE).

Proposal for assignable causes search based on invalidated sub-graphs The execution of algorithms previously described allows to gather information about invalidated paths and paired nodes. When the execution of all these algorithms finishes, the search for assignable causes takes place. Such search has two characteristics:

- Search based on invalidated sub-graphs must be bi-directional. This means to look for subject invalidated sub-graphs in true value graph and to look for true value invalidated sub-graphs in subject graph.

- Sub-graphs search must be a similarity search. This means that if exact sub-graphs cannot be found in counterpart graph, then such sub-graph needs to be adjusted to run new searches. Adjustments need to continue until proofing no sub-graphs of the initial sub-graph are found in the counterpart graph.

The process to drive the similarity search based on invalidated sub-graphs is described now. Given a invalidated sub-graph:

- If the root is a requirement node, search through all requirement nodes in the counterpart graph, one with the same structure of BFC.
- If the root is a transactional function type (EI, EO, EQ) or a data function type (EIF, ILF), search through all function types in the requirement being analyzed in the counterpart graph, one with the same structure. If there is no match continue searching through remaining requirements.
- If the root is a RET node, search through all RET nodes in the requirement being analyzed in the counterpart graph, one with the same structure. If there is no match continue searching through remaining requirements.
- If the root is a DET node, this will be considered a lost node.

Previous process will report all similarities identified and will support the measurements analyst on the process of errors detection by reducing the amount of time and effort required to execute a verification protocol.

4 Tool evaluation

In order to evaluate the prototype tool we compared the measurement results obtained manually by one of the researchers using the protocol against the results obtained automatically by the tool. The evaluation reports the tool effectiveness to detect measurement errors. Based on the prototype results, we also reported results of measurement defect findings for measurement procedures applied to a small transactional application by two researchers with measurement expertise (true value measurement results) and a random selection of 7 measurement counts performed by 12 software engineering professionals. We selected 7 cases because it is the minimum number of measurements evaluated for one group in tests ran by [9]. Finally we analyzed the most common errors and we suggest assignable causes for those.

4.1 Case study design

This study aimed to answer two research questions:

1. Is the prototype tool effective to find measurement differences, report errors and suggest assignable causes? This research question allows to determine if the tool implements the protocol correctly and the tool effectiveness to detect defects and suggest assignable causes.
2. What are the assignable causes identified by the tool based on the measurement results evaluation? This research question allows to identify the most common type of errors and assignable causes identified by the tool for functional size measurement procedures.

We collected two groups of metrics in order two answer each research question. The first group represents metrics related to functional size measurements accuracy that have been used in previous studies [1,14,11]. These metrics allow the evaluation of measurements accuracy in regards to true value measurements: We collected MRE, MER and BRE to measure accuracy. We also collected total function points and size measurement for BFC components. To measure reproducibility we collected absolute value of difference between subject count and average count for the same sample. The second group of metrics allows to evaluate the tool effectiveness to detect defects based on the comparison against control values. We used confusion matrixes as described in [15,16]. We collected confusion matrix, accuracy, precision and recall.

4.2 Case study implementation

These steps describe how we implemented the case study:

1. Selection of software application to use as object of study and the elaboration of requirements specification following standard IEEE-830 [17]. The selected application has 144 UFP and the requirements document and the source code of the application are very similar to examples in a real management information system (MIS) in the industry.
2. Functional size measurement of the selected application. 2 researches with measurement experience measure the application. Results are considered true value.
3. Twelve professionals collect functional size measurement for the selected application using the IFPUG FPA method. The subjects were mainly developers and testers of a graduate metrics course, not the usual users of FSM measurement methods but familiar with software engineering practices. In order to accomplish leveling, first participants assist to four training sessions. Next, they measure the application using requirements specification as baseline and reporting all measurement results. After that, measurement results are reviewed to validate they are detailed enough to work as prototype tool inputs. Finally, seven cases are selected randomly to evaluate the prototype.
4. Accuracy verification protocol is applied manually to identify all differences and assignable causes between the true value measurements and the 7 cases selected. This step is executed by one of the researches and results are considered control values.
5. Prototype is designed and implemented to automate the accuracy verification protocol.
6. Measurement results are processed to generate inputs required by the prototype.
7. Verification protocol is applied with the prototype to identify measurement defects and assignable causes for such differences.
8. Prototype reports findings and accuracy verification results.
9. Prototype's results are compared against the control values using metrics mentioned early in this section.

4.3 Threats to validity

Internal Validity: Human factor could influence the results of manual procedures. Measurement differences between participants was reduced by selecting subjects with similar experience in the application of functional size measurement (FSM). Experiment artifacts could also influence results. The same requirements specification was used by all participants. The reduced number of participants in the sample also represents a thread, whereas the fact of all being industry practitioners is an advantage for this study. Prototype inputs were prepared in a semi-manual process that also represents a thread in the correctness of the Neo4j scripts. Control values used to evaluate the prototype results and the participants measurements were generated by one researcher who applied the accuracy verification protocol. This could influence the control values. Lastly, two researchers of this study, who have measurement experience, applied the FPA method to do the functional size measurement. They do not have a CFPS certification. *External Validity* Although the application analyzed is a small one (144 UFP), its requirements are similar to industry real cases. Participants were mainly analysts, developers or testers. It means they are not the ones who usually do functional size measurement but they do have understanding about software engineering practices. A similar performance is expected between all participants. *Construct Validity* Measurements reliability is an important consideration for the validity of conclusions about results. All measurements used in this study for the functional size evaluation and accuracy are based on known FSM methods proven in literature and standard ISO 14143-3 [18]. Confusion matrixes are also proven in literature as a way to evaluate results quality in a classification problem.

5 Results

Tool effectiveness was evaluated based on the results it generated when comparing participants results to true value results. Table 1 shows the results of measurements evaluation obtained by the prototype tool for total functional size and data functions (DFs) and transactional functions (TFs). Median Magnitude of error relative (MdMER), Median Magnitude of relative error (MdMRE) and Median Balanced relative error (MdBRE) are acceptable for TFs considering a variance of 10%. Standard deviation for such measures is around 10%. Results for DFs show MdMRE and MdBRE of 75% whereas MdMER is 42.86%. This means subjects' total size measurements for DF components are different to true value measurements. Standard deviation for DF components total size is 13.57%, this means results are closer to mean than TF components results even for the total size reported. Total size measurements show better results than DF components results. Total size results reproducibility is similar to total size results for TF components. DF components show reproducibility results almost 30% close to the mean value.

Table 2 shows measurement evaluation results for EI, EO and EQ components. EI and EQ show acceptable results with mean and median values for MRE, MER and BRE lower than 10%. EO components show results slightly higher

Table 1: Measurement evaluation results

	TF						DF						Total					
	UFP	MRE	MER	BRE	Diff	Rep	UFP	MRE	MER	BRE	Diff	Rep	UFP	MRE	MER	BRE	Diff	Rep
Mean	110.4	11.7%	13.2%	13.7%	13.6	14.5%	49.1	75.5%	38.5%	75.5%	21.1	28.3%	159.6	17.2%	15.7%	18.1%	24.7	14.5%
Median	110.0	10.3%	11.5%	11.5%	12.0	14.2%	49.0	75.0%	42.9%	75.0%	21.0	18.1%	161.0	18.8%	15.8%	18.8%	27.0	8.2%
Std Dv	17.2	9.3%	12.3%	12.5%	10.8	13.2%	13.6	48.5%	19.9%	48.5%	13.6	34.4%	24.6	9.3%	8.8%	10.1%	13.3	18.9%
Min	84.0	1.7%	1.8%	1.8%	2.0	1.9%	28.0	0.0%	0.0%	0.0%	0.0	0.9%	112.0	2.8%	2.7%	2.8%	4.0	1.6%
Max	139.0	27.6%	38.1%	38.1%	32.0	41.4%	70.0	150.0%	60.0%	150.0%	42.0	98.2%	188.0	30.6%	28.6%	30.6%	44.0	55.6%

Table 2: Measurement results for EI, EO and EQ

	EI						EO						EQ					
	UFP	MRE	MER	BRE	Diff	Rep	UFP	MRE	MER	BRE	Diff	Rep	UFP	MRE	MER	BRE	Diff	Rep
Mean	58.7	7.4%	7.9%	8.2%	4.4	8.8%	18.0	15.8%	18.1%	18.6%	3.0	0.0%	15.8	5.5%	6.2%	6.2%	1.0	9.8%
Median	61.0	4.8%	5.0%	5.0%	3.0	2.9%	18.0	15.8%	18.1%	18.6%	3.0	20.0%	17.0	3.9%	3.7%	3.9%	1.0	0.0%
Std Dv	6.2	7.0%	7.8%	8.0%	4.1	12.0%	3.5	6.1%	10.0%	9.3%	1.2	24.0%	10.3	6.1%	7.0%	7.0%	1.0	16.2%
Min	48.0	0.0%	0.0%	0.0%	0.0	0.4%	15.0	10.5%	9.5%	10.5%	2.0	0.0%	0.0	0.0%	0.0%	0.0%	0.0	0.0%
Max	64.0	17.2%	20.8%	20.8%	10.0	30.7%	21.0	21.1%	26.7%	26.7%	4.0	40.0%	27.0	13.3%	15.4%	15.4%	2.0	38.9%

than 10%. This means participants' results were close to true value results. A low UFP standard deviation for the three components also proofs mentioned closeness. Reproducibility has better results in EI and EO components.

None of the participants reported EIF components and all reported 28 UFP of ILF components. This matches with true value results. ILF components then have perfect accuracy and reproducibility for all participants.

Results show that the prototype can evaluate measurements automating the generation of accuracy metrics measurements for each evaluation executed by the prototype. Results also match with those shown in [12], according to the last one, for the group of 12 subjects, accuracy showed better results for TF components than DF components.

5.1 Tool effectiveness for error reporting and assignable causes suggestion

Measurement errors detected by the prototype were compared against control values obtained by one of the researchers. According to Figure 3, the prototype tool detected 901 errors correctly, it also reported 12 false positive cases. After analyzing this cases we determined those cases are nodes the prototype could not pair because of differences upper/lower case differences between subject and true value node name. The prototype tool reported 48 false negative cases. False negative cases are due to one of two reasons:

- Subject reported duplicated measurements.
- Subject reported measurements incompletely.

		Prediction			
		P	N	Accuracy	93.92%
Real	P	901	48	Precision	98.69%
	N	12	26	Recall	94.94%

Fig. 3: Tool effectiveness for error detection

These scenarios cannot be loaded into the graph database, the first one because nodes cannot have duplicated names and the second one because it represents missing information. Since data cannot be loaded into the database, it cannot be analyzed by the prototype tool. The prototype tool reported 26 true negative cases for nodes that matched the name and tag correctly. Based on

Table 3: Tool effectiveness for error detection by error category

Error Categories	Accuracy	Precision	Recall	Error Categories	Accuracy	Precision	Recall
Incorrect Classification	**100.0%**	**100.0%**	**100.0%**	**Unnecessary Report**	**100.0%**	**100.0%**	**100.0%**
Incorrect Association	100.0%	100.0%	100.0%	*Unnecessary BFC*	100.0%	100.0%	100.0%
Incorrect Type	100.0%	100.0%	100.0%	*Duplicated DET*	100.0%	100.0%	100.0%
Tagging Error	**96.4%**	**96.1%**	**100.0%**	*Unnecessary BFC*	100.0%	100.0%	100.0%
DET Tag does not match	96.4%	96.1%	100.0%	*Duplicated Logical Group*	100.0%	100.0%	100.0%
Missing Report	**100.0%**	**100.0%**	**100.0%**	*Duplicated Requirement*	100.0%	100.0%	100.0%
Missing DET	100.0%	100.0%	100.0%	*Unnecessary Requirement*	100.0%	100.0%	100.0%
Missing Message	100.0%	100.0%	100.0%				
Missing Requirement	100.0%	100.0%	100.0%				

Table 4: Error categories and types not detected by the tool

Missing Report	**14**	**Unnecessary Report**	**34**
Missing Association	14	*Duplicated Association*	34

previous results and for our case study scenario, the prototype tool detects defects correctly 93.92% of times. When the prototype tool detects a defect, it does it correctly 98.69% of times and when there are errors, the tool detects them 94.94% of times. Receiver operating characteristic curve (ROC) analysis to evaluate the tool effectiveness to detect defects show ROC equals to 0.82. This means the tool is classified as good on defect detection.

Besides reporting invalidated paths, the tool provides error categories. Such categories where defined by one researcher based on a proof of concept executed to validate the prototype tool. Table 3 shows prototype tool effectiveness for defect detection based on the error category. The prototype tool detects all errors categorized as incorrectly classified, unnecessary reports and missing reports. For tagging errors category, the tool can detect defects with 96.37% accuracy.

Regarding the errors not detected by the tool, Table 4 shows the number of cases present in the measurements analysis done by one researcher. As explained earlier, these cases correspond to scenarios in which the database does not have all the information, either because it is missing or because it is already reported.

5.2 Assignable causes identified by the tool based on the measurement results evaluation

These are the assignable causes identified by the tool after processing invalidated paths.

- Incorrect classification: The user identified a measurement correctly but classifies it incorrectly. Incorrect association refers the RETs reported by the user in incorrect BFCs. Incorrect type refers to BFCs reported with incorrect type.
- Tagging errors: Refers to DETs with names that do not match.
- Missing report: Refers to cases in which subject does not report a measurement but it does show in the true value measurement results. Missing DETs, missing button or messages reports and missing requirements.
- Unnecessary report: Refers to subjects reporting elements that do not show in the true value graph. BFCs reported by the subject but not by the true value, duplicated DETs with the same name but different tags, unnecessary DETs reported in BFCs, duplicated RETs, requirements with duplicated names but different tags and requirements reported by the subject but not by the true value.

5.3 Preliminary results for the similarity search

In order to validate the proposal for similarity search we conducted a proof of concept (PoC) based on the algorithm proposed for the similarity search. Our proof of concept is based on a subset of true value measurement results for Contoso application and a subject measurement created from seeded errors in the true value measurement. The prototype would report all invalidated paths and the sub-graphs with some similarity in the counterpart graph. The PoC showed the report of all invalidated paths for subject measurements. In this case, 13 paths were invalidated. 3 of them did not get a suggestion for similar sub-graphs.Two paths referred to paths that do not exist in the true value graph because they represent unnecessary reports. One path represented a data element reported by the true value but not by the subject.

6 Conclusions and future work

This study presents a prototype tool that automates an accuracy verification protocol for IFPUG FPA functional size measurements. The tool generates the report of detected defects and suggests assignable causes for such defects by categorizing them. To validate the tool we elaborated a case study to compare accuracy verification results obtained automatically by the prototype against control values obtained by three researchers manually. Such validation includes reporting the prototype tool effectiveness to find defects previously identified by researchers. Evaluation results show the effectiveness of the prototype tool to report measurement defects and suggest assignable causes for such defects. Results analysis determines that the prototype tool can detect four measurement error categories: Incorrect classification, tagging error, missing report and unnecessary report. These categories are associated to possible assignable causes by the error classification in each category. As future work, the accuracy verification protocol and the prototype tool can be used to verify functional size measurement of any procedure following a model (or a subset) with the same basic functional components of IFPUG FPA. A component to register measurement results in the prototype tool would not only reduce the time and effort required to load measurements results in the tool. It would allow to remove the risk of having a human being translating measurements to scripts that can then be imported into the database. Similarly the tool could be extended so that measurement results validation is also reported automatically by the tool. In regards to errors categorization, tags evaluation mechanism needs to be improved so that node names and tags are not an exact text match but a text similarity comparison. The component for assignable causes suggestions can be extended to include more scenarios. This require the execution of more cases and the evaluation of different algorithms for sub-graphs similarity detection.

References

1. S. M. Abrahao, "On the functional size measurement of object-oriented conceptual schemas: Design and evaluation issues," Ph.D. dissertation, 2004, aAI3154436.
2. S. Fingerman, *Practical software project estimation: a toolkit for estimating software development effort duration.* Boston, MA: McGraw Hill, 2011.

3. A. Abran and R. Dumke, "Cosmic function points: Theory and advanced practices," 2011.
4. H. Soubra, A. Abran, and A. Ramdane-Cherif, "Verifying the accuracy of automation tools for the measurement of software with cosmic – iso 19761 including an autosar-based example and a case study," in *2014 Joint Conference of the International Workshop on Software Measurement and the International Conference on Software Process and Product Measurement*, Oct 2014, pp. 23–31.
5. C. Quesada-López and M. Jenkins, "Applying a verification protocol to evaluate the accuracy of functional size measurement procedures: An empirical approach," in *Proceedings of the 16th International Conference on Product-Focused Software Process Improvement*, New York, 2015.
6. C. Symons, "Lies, damned lies and software metrics," in *2014 Joint Conference of the International Workshop on Software Measurement and the International Conference on Software Process and Product Measurement*, Oct 2014, pp. 174–175.
7. S. Bagriyanik and A. Karahoca, "Automated cosmic function point measurement using a requirements engineering ontology," *Information and Software Technology*, vol. 72, no. Supplement C, pp. 189 – 203, 2016.
8. C. Quesada-López and M. Jenkins, "Procedimientos de medicin del tamao funcional: un mapeo sistemtico de literatura," ser. CIBSE 2017, 2017.
9. G. Yilmaz, S. Tunalilar, and O. Demirors, "Towards the development of a defect detection tool for cosmic functional size measurement," in *2013 Joint Conference of the 23rd International Workshop on Software Measurement and the 8th International Conference on Software Process and Product Measurement*, Oct 2013, pp. 9–16.
10. P. Morris and J. Desharnais, "Function points analysis. validating the result." ser. TotalMetrics, 2001.
11. C. Quesada-López and M. Jenkins, "An evaluation of functional size measurement methods," in *Ibero-American Conference on Software Engineering*, Lima, Peru, 2015.
12. C. Quesada-López, D. Madrigal, and M. Jenkins, "An empirical evaluation of automated function points," in *Ibero-American Conference on Software Engineering*, Curran Associates, Inc. Quito,Ecuador: Curran Associates, Inc., 2016.
13. D. Madrigal, "Automatizacion de un protocolo de verificacion de la medicion del tamano funcional," Universidad de Costa Rica, San Pedro, Costa Rica, Tech. Rep., 2017. [Online]. Available: https://goo.gl/aAfy7f
14. S. Abrahao, G. Poels, and O. Pastor, "Evaluating a functional size measurement method for web applications: an empirical analysis," in *10th International Symposium on Software Metrics, 2004. Proceedings.*, Sept 2004, pp. 358–369.
15. N. V. Chawla, *Data Mining for Imbalanced Datasets: An Overview.* Boston, MA: Springer US, 2005, pp. 853–867.
16. in *Data Mining (Fourth Edition)*, fourth edition ed., I. H. Witten, E. Frank, M. A. Hall, and C. J. Pal, Eds. Morgan Kaufmann, 2017, pp. i – iii.
17. IEEE, "Ieee recommended practice for software requirements specifications," *IEEE Std 830-1998*, pp. 1–40, Oct 1998.
18. ISO/IEC, "Information technology - software measurement - functional size measurement. part 3: Verification of functional size measurement methods," International Organization for Standardization, Geneva, CH, Standard, 2007.

Mapeo entre la ISO/IEC 29110-5-1-2 y el MAAGTICSI dirigido a Organizaciones Pequeñas Desarrolladoras de Software en México

Miguel Morales-Trujillo[1], Orlando Becerra-Palma[2], Boris Escalante-Ramírez[1] y Pilar Ángeles[1]

[1] Facultad de Ingeniería, Universidad Nacional Autónoma de México
[2] Posgrado en Ciencias de la Administración, Universidad Nacional Autónoma de México
Av. Universidad 3000, Ciudad Universitaria, 04510, Ciudad de México, México

migmor@ciencias.unam.mx, felipeorlandobp@gmail.com, boris@servidor.unam.mx, pilarang@unam.mx

Resumen. En México, con la intención de homologar y simplificar procesos e impulsar el uso de mejores prácticas en el área de las TI, se implementó el Manual Administrativo de Aplicación General en Tecnologías de la Información y Comunicaciones, y en la Seguridad de la Información (MAAGTICSI). Este manual busca regular y hacer más eficientes los procesos gubernamentales relacionados con TI. En el caso de las pequeñas organizaciones mexicanas desarrolladoras de software, cuentan con MoProSoft, un modelo de procesos específico para ellas y que es una norma nacional mexicana y base de la norma ISO/IEC 29110. Con el objetivo de permitir un involucramiento más amplio de las pequeñas organizaciones en proyectos gubernamentales de TI, en este artículo se presenta un mapeo entre la norma ISO/IEC 29110-5-2-1 y el MAAGTICSI. Este mapeo permite a una organización que basa su forma de trabajo en la ISO/IEC 29110-5-1-2 conocer la brecha y las tareas necesarias para cumplir con el MAAGTICSI. Basados en los resultados del mapeo y en su aplicación en un caso práctico, se concluye que la norma cubre de manera total lo solicitado por el manual, sin que el esfuerzo requerido para ello se convierta en un obstáculo.

Palabras clave: ISO/IEC 29110, MAAGTICSI, mapeo, organización pequeña, VSE

1 Introducción

La creación de sistemas de información para automatizar procesos de negocio demanda la aplicación de prácticas de ingeniería de software. La incorporación de esta disciplina en el tratamiento y mantenimiento de procesos de negocio surge a finales del siglo XX ante la demanda de aplicar el desarrollo de software a sectores específicos como: la medicina, sistemas electromecánicos, financieros y estadísticos; sectores que constituyen un conglomerado industrial y empresarial relevante para el escalamiento económico y social. Aunado a esto, el surgimiento de tecnologías móviles ha ocasionado un aumento en la demanda de servicios y productos empresariales relativos a TI.

Ante la necesidad de proyectos de TI que cumplan con un alcance bien definido, un costo competitivo, tiempos bien establecidos y, desde luego, calidad en la manufactura, los sectores económicos demandan procedimientos transparentes y transferibles a distintos niveles. Para ello, en el contexto de las TI, se requieren estándares específicos para el desarrollo de software y administración de proyectos dirigidos a organizaciones pequeñas (OPs) [1][2].

La importancia de las OPs recae en su amplia participación en el mercado del desarrollo de software [1][2][3]. Esta presencia ha sido vista en México como una oportunidad para mejorar e incrementar la competitividad de este sector. Por tal razón, se introdujo el Modelo de Procesos para la industria del Software (MoProSoft) [4], que se convirtió en norma mexicana para los procesos de gestión e ingeniería de software en 2005 (NMX-059/01-NYCE-2005) [5] y que es la base de la norma internacional ISO/IEC 29110 [6]. Hasta 2016, en México había 481 centros de desarrollo certificados en la norma mexicana [7] y un amplio interés por el estándar ISO/IEC 29110.

Sin embargo, ni MoProSoft ni la ISO/IEC 29110 se encuentran alineadas con las normativas gubernamentales actuales del país, específicamente con el Manual Administrativo de Aplicación General en Tecnologías de la Información y Comunicaciones, y en la Seguridad de la Información (MAAGTICSI) [8].

Es a través de MAAGTICSI que las entidades gubernamentales gestionan los proyectos referentes a TI que se llevan a cabo de manera interna o externa, ya sea con otra dependencia gubernamental o a través de un proveedor. Siendo así, cualquier organización desarrolladora de software que esté interesada en atender proyectos con dependencias gubernamentales, deberá cumplir con lo establecido en el MAAGTICSI para ser tomada en cuenta.

Tanto MoProSoft como MAAGTICSI son el resultado de iniciativas del gobierno mexicano por mejorar la calidad de los servicios de TI que prestan sus organizaciones, por lo que resulta importante contar un mecanismo que permita compaginar la norma con el manual.

En este artículo se propone un mapeo para determinar la cobertura y la brecha entre la norma y el manual. El mapeo permitirá a las OPs, que basan sus procesos en MoProSoft o la ISO/IEC 29110, participar en proyectos de desarrollo de software gubernamentales sin que el esfuerzo requerido para ajustarse a lo solicitado por el MAAGTICSI se convierta en un obstáculo.

La decisión de utilizar la ISO/IEC 29110 y no MoProSoft radica en dos puntos: i) el alcance de la norma ISO/IEC 29110 es mayor que el de MoProSoft; y ii) la ISO/IEC 29110 está basada estrechamente en MoProSoft.

El mapeo de procesos presentado pretende apoyar y fortalecer a las OPs en su integración administrativa y base tecnológica. Para construirlo se analizaron los productos de trabajo definidos en la norma y el manual con el objetivo de establecer de manera tangible las evidencias que una OP deberá presentar ante las entidades gubernamentales para demostrar que está cumpliendo con el MAAGTICSI.

El resto de este artículo se desarrolla de la siguiente manera: la sección 2 presenta los antecedentes; la sección 3 detalla el mapeo realizado; la sección 4 muestra los resultados; y finalmente se presentan las conclusiones y el trabajo a futuro.

2 Antecedentes

En esta sección se describe la norma ISO/IEC 29110 y el MAAGTICSI, normativas base de este estudio.

2.1 ISO/IEC 29110

La norma ISO/IEC 29110 es el estándar internacional enfocado a los perfiles de ciclo de vida para OPs, representando una guía de administración e ingeniería [6]. Este estándar está compuesto por perfiles diseñados para utilizarse en conjunto con los procesos, técnicas y métodos que mejoran la satisfacción del cliente y la productividad de las OPs [6].

En particular, el Perfil Básico (ISO/IEC 29110-5-1-2) resulta relevante para este estudio ya que se enfoca en la parte operativa de una organización. El Perfil Básico está compuesto por dos procesos: Administración del Proyecto (AP) e Implementación de Software (IS).

Por una parte, el proceso de AP busca *establecer y realizar de modo sistemático las tareas del proyecto de implementación de software, las cuales permiten cumplir con los objetivos del proyecto dentro del marco de calidad, tiempo y costo esperados* [6], mientras que el proceso de IS permite *sistematizar la realización de las actividades de análisis, diseño, construcción, integración y pruebas para productos de software nuevos o modificados, de acuerdo a los requerimientos especificados* [6].

La ISO/IEC 29110-5-1-2 está constituida por 22 productos de trabajo relacionados con la AP, la IS y el Cliente; no obstante, para fines del presente mapeo, se consideran sólo 6 de los 9 productos involucrados con la AP. Esta decisión se tomó después de realizar un mapeo inicial entre la ISO/IEC 29110-5-1-2 y el MAAGTICSI, donde se descartaron aquellos productos cuya creación no es responsabilidad de la organización desarrolladora o no son solicitados por MAAGTICSI.

Por otra parte, para fines de MAAGTICSI, únicamente es relevante la parte administrativa, razón por la que el proceso de IS no fue incluido en el mapeo, contrariamente al de AP, que es la base para el mapeo.

2.2 MAAGTICSI

El Manual Administrativo de Aplicación General en Materia de Tecnologías de la Información y Comunicaciones, y en la Seguridad de la Información, representa la normativa mexicana aplicable a servicios para la correcta administración de proyectos relacionados a TIC.

MAAGTICSI tiene como predecesor a MAAGTIC [9]. MAAGTIC fue creado, a través de la Secretaria de la Función Pública [10], con el objetivo de establecer un control óptimo y sustancial dentro de la Administración Pública Federal [8] y entró en vigor el 20 de agosto del 2010 con orden de implementación obligatoria.

El objetivo de MAAGTIC era definir los procesos que en materia de TIC rigen hacia el interior de las Unidades de Tecnologías de la Información (UTIC) de la Administración Pública Federal. De manera que, independientemente de la estructura organizacional con que cuenten o que llegaran a adoptar las UTICs; los roles definidos puedan acoplarse a los procesos establecidos para lograr la cohesión total para una mejor gestión [8].

En la Figura 1 se presentan los principales marcos de referencia utilizados para la elaboración de MAAGTIC, entre los cuales se destacan la ISO 9001 [11], PMBOK [12], MoProSoft, CMMI [13], ISO/IEC 27001 [14] y TOGAF [15].

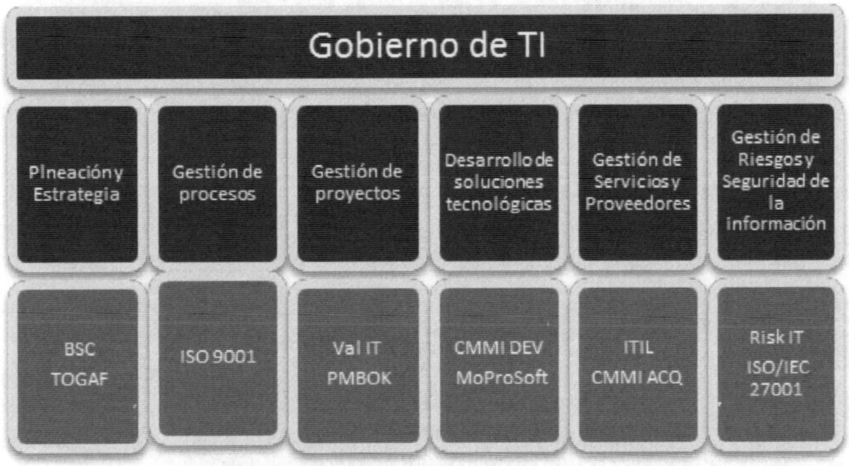

Fig. 1. Principales marcos de referencia para la definición de MAAGTIC.

En 2014, se presentó la reforma a MAAGTIC, hasta ahora definitiva y que respeta las directrices de la Estrategia Digital Nacional vigente, renombrándolo como MAAGTICSI, la "SI" en referencia a la Seguridad de la Información.

MAAGTICSI propone nueve procesos organizados en tres grupos (Ver Figura 2):

- **Gobernanza:** constituido por los procesos de Planeación Estratégica, y Administración del Presupuesto y Contrataciones.
- **Organización:** conformado por los procesos de Administración de Servicios, Administración de la Configuración y Administración de la Seguridad de la Información.
- **Entrega:** compuesto por los procesos de Administración de Proyectos, Administración de Proveedores, Administración de la Operación y Operación de los Controles de Seguridad de la Información.

De los procesos anteriores, para una OP resulta relevante el de Administración de Proyectos del grupo de Entrega, el cual cuenta con los siguientes productos de trabajo:

- **Acta de Constitución del Proyecto:** en este documento se describe la naturaleza del proyecto, la solución que se pretende obtener, los elementos que justifiquen su desarrollo y sus beneficios
- **Acta de Aceptación de Entregables:** registra los documentos entregados durante el proyecto, así como los responsables de generarlos, revisarlos y aprobarlos.
- **Acta de Cierre de Proyectos:** se asienta el cierre del proyecto así como la lista de entregables concluidos y los paquetes de código generado.

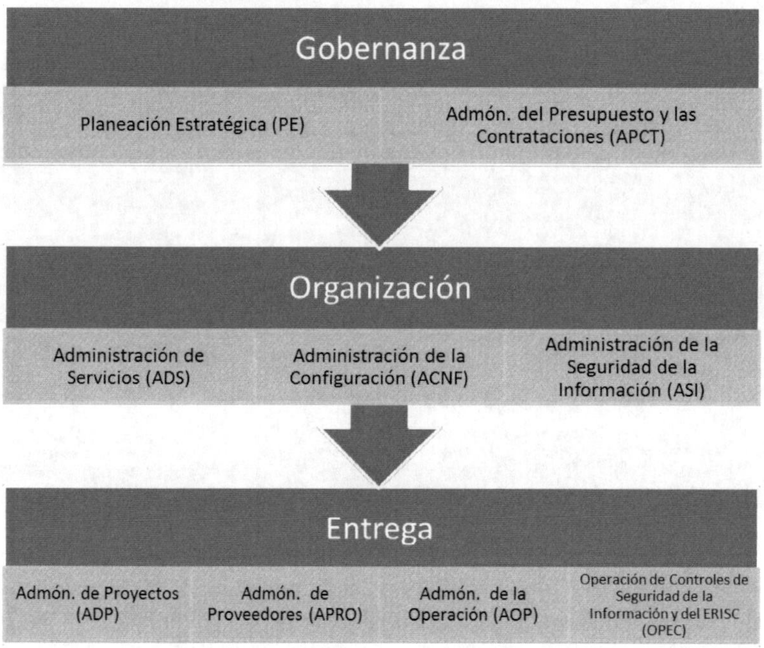

Fig. 2. Grupos de procesos de MAAGTICSI

Es de resaltar la naturaleza administrativa de los productos antes mencionados, dejando de lado lo referente a la calidad del producto que se genera en el proyecto. Es decir, MAAGTICSI centra sus regulaciones en las tareas administrativas del proyecto y no en el producto que se obtiene ni en las labores técnicas propias de un proyecto de TI.

3 Mapeo entre la ISO/IEC 29110-5-1-2 y MAAGTICSI

La metodología seguida para realizar el mapeo inició con la revisión de los puntos referentes al desarrollo, construcción o implementación de software incluidos en la

ISO/IEC 29110 y el MAAGTICSI. A partir de este primer análisis se identificaron las similitudes y diferencias contenidas en cada uno, en particular en los procesos de Organización y Entrega.

Como segunda etapa se definieron las relaciones, entre la norma y el manual, basadas en los elementos que conforman cada uno de los productos de trabajo que solicitan.

La tercera etapa consistió en verificar y validar el mapeo para, finalmente, establecer un nivel de cobertura entre ambos objetos de estudio, siguiendo lo establecido en [16].

De manera paralela, se generó una guía integradora con la finalidad de apoyar a las OPs con un procedimiento para la administración de proyectos en ingeniería de software que les permita optimizar procesos y alinear la estructura organizacional con la TI.

3.1 Identificación de similitudes y diferencias

Para dar apertura a la identificación de las similitudes y diferencias entre la ISO/IEC 29110-5-1-2 y el MAAGTICSI, se comenzó analizando la forma en que ambas normativas estructuran la descripción de sus procesos. Se encontró que ambos lo hacen en términos de 5 elementos principales (izquierda ISO/IEC 29110, derecha MAAGTICSI):

- Propósito – Objetivo general
- Objetivos – Objetivos específicos
- Roles involucrados – Roles
- Actividades y Tareas – Actividades del proceso
- Productos (entrada, salida e internos) – Productos del proceso

Las diferencias en estas parejas de apartados no son significativas salvo el nombrado de cada una, ya que cada rubro hace referencia a los mismos aspectos. Entre las similitudes resalta que, para ambas normativas, se tomaron en cuenta los fundamentos contenidos en el PMBOK, CMMI y MoProSoft.

No obstante, como ya se mencionó, la principal diferencia entre la ISO/IEC 29110-5-1-2 y el MAAGTICSI es la conceptualización de cada una. Mientras que MAAGTICSI se inclina a una orientación al control de procesos, la ISO/IEC 29110-5-1-2 se perfila para la administración y ejecución de los mismos desde una perspectiva operacional.

Derivado de la identificación de similitudes y diferencias, se descartó realizar un mapeo a nivel de actividades y/o tareas, debido a que el MAAGTICSI no está orientado a la manera de trabajo de la organización sino al cumplimiento de rubros específicos. Por ello, el mapeo se basó en los productos de trabajo especificados por la norma y por el manual. Lo anterior se soporta en que los productos de trabajo, ya que estos en la práctica son tomados como evidencia para determinar si se cumple o no con una normativa.

En seguida se muestran los productos de la ISO/IEC 29110-5-1-2 involucrados para el cumplimiento de los productos de trabajo, o actas, solicitados por MAGTICSI:

1. Documento de Aceptación
2. Lista de Verificación
3. Minuta
4. Plan del Proyecto
5. Reporte de Avance
6. Repositorio del Proyecto

3.2 Definición de relaciones para el mapeo

De acuerdo con la información expuesta en el apartado anterior, donde se muestra la estructura de cada norma así como la identificación de sus similitudes y diferencias, corresponde ahora definir a las relaciones existentes que constituirán el mapeo. Para ello se evaluó la cobertura entre los elementos que conforman a cada producto de trabajo, es decir, se analizó qué elementos son cubiertos y cuáles no para posteriormente establecer un nivel de cobertura global para cada producto de trabajo.

Por ejemplo, de acuerdo a lo requerido por el MAAGTICSI, el producto de trabajo *Acta de Constitución del proyecto* está constituido por 12 componentes. Los cuales son cubiertos por 4 componentes, todos ellos, pertenecientes al producto de trabajo *Plan de Proyecto* de la norma ISO/IEC 29110-5-1-2.

En la Tabla 1 se desglosan las relaciones entre estos productos. Dichas relaciones se pueden interpretar de la siguiente manera, La organización, que basa su manera de trabajo en la ISO/IEC 29110-5-1-2, al generar el *Plan del Proyecto*, estará cubriendo de manera total lo solicitado por MAAGTICSI en el *Acta de Constitución del Proyecto*. Para facilitar el mapeo, se decidió asignar acrónimos de tres caracteres a cada uno de los elementos.

Tabla 1. Mapeo entre la ISO/IEC 29110-5-1-2 y el Acta de Constitución del Proyecto del MAAGTICSI.

Producto MAAGTICSI	Sigla	Elemento MAAGTICSI	Sigla	Elemento ISO/IEC 29110-5-1-2	Producto ISO/IEC 29110-5-1-2
1. Acta de Constitución del Proyecto	CFR	1.0 - Código, fecha y revisión del proyecto	DDP	4.1 - Descripción de producto	4. Plan del Proyecto
	NYO	1.1 - Nombre y objetivo.	DDP	4.1 - Descripción de producto	4. Plan del Proyecto
			ODP	4.3 - Objetivos del proyecto	4. Plan del Proyecto
	JGR	1.2 - Justificación general.	DDP	4.1 - Descripción de producto	4. Plan del Proyecto
	DGP	1.3 - Datos generales del proyecto	DDP	4.1 - Descripción de producto	4. Plan del Proyecto
	IDP	1.3.1 - Identificación del proyecto	DDP	4.1 - Descripción de producto	4. Plan del Proyecto
	NDP	1.3.2 - Nombre del proyecto	DDP	4.1 - Descripción de producto	4. Plan del Proyecto
	UAS	1.3.3 - Unidad administrativa solicitante.	CET	4.8 - Composición del equipo de trabajo	4. Plan del Proyecto
	UAI	1.3.4 - Unidad administrativa impulsora.	CET	4.8 - Composición del equipo de trabajo	4. Plan del Proyecto
	NAD	1.4 - Necesidades del área al que va dirigido	DDP	4.1 - Descripción de producto	4. Plan del Proyecto
	OAD	1.5 - Objetivos del área al que va dirigido	DDP	4.1 - Descripción de producto	4. Plan del Proyecto
			ODP	4.3 - Objetivos del proyecto	4. Plan del Proyecto
	DEP	1.6 - Descripción del Proyecto	DDP	4.1 - Descripción de producto	4. Plan del Proyecto
			ODP	4.3 - Objetivos del proyecto	4. Plan del Proyecto
	ALC	1.7 - Alcance del proyecto.	DAL	4.2 - Descripción de alcance respecto a lo incluido y lo no incluido	4. Plan del Proyecto

De la misma forma, se realizó el mapeo para el *Acta de Aceptación de Entregables* y el *Acta de Cierre de Proyectos*, que son presentadas más adelante en la sección de Resultados.

Conforme se avanzó en el mapeo, fue notorio que los productos de trabajo de MAAGTICSI resultan ser demasiado generales al ser comparados con los productos que genera una OP disciplinada en la ISO/IEC 29110. Sin duda, esto resultaría en una ventaja para la OP en cuestión al momento de cumplir con MAAGTICSI. Sin embargo, desde otra perspectiva, resulta claro que mucha información documental básica de un proyecto de desarrollo de software no llegaría a la contraparte, en este caso el ente gubernamental, ya que no es considerada por el manual.

3.3 Verificación y validación del mapeo

El mapeo fue verificado a través de revisiones entre pares y las inconsistencias discutidas por los autores. En esta etapa, la principal inconsistencia surgió al discutir la reducción de la lista de productos de trabajo de la ISO/IEC 29110-5-1-2 necesarios para cubrir MAAGTICSI. Inicialmente, se detectó que eran necesarios 9 productos, que finalmente se redujeron a 6 al descartar al *Registro de Defectos*, *Respaldo del Repositorio del Proyecto* y *Solicitud de Cambio*.

Este descarte se fundamentó en que MAAGTICSI no establece la necesidad de contar con un respaldo del repositorio del proyecto en el que se almacenen los productos generados. En cuanto al Registro de Defectos y a las Solicitudes de Cambio, se descartaron del mapeo ya que ambos son responsabilidad del ente que recibe el producto y no de la organización que lo construye. Por lo que solicitar cambios o reportar defectos son actividades que inicia el cliente y no la organización desarrolladora de software. No obstante, MAAGTICSI dentro del acta de Aceptación de Entregables considera un apartado para este tipo de registros y solicitudes.

La validación consistió en dos etapas, una teórica y otra práctica. La validación teórica fue realizada por 4 expertos en el campo de la informática administrativa, quienes revisaron el mapeo. La principal observación tuvo que ver con la manera en que se presenta la información, dichas mejoras ya fueron tomadas en cuenta en lo mostrado en las Tablas 1, 3 y 4.

En cuanto a la validación práctica, ésta fue llevada a cabo en un proyecto de desarrollo de software real, en el que estuvieron involucradas una OP, que sigue la ISO/IEC 29110 como disciplina habitual de trabajo y compuesta por 18 personas, y una entidad gubernamental ligada al sector de la salud.

Las 18 personas que conforman a la organización tienen una formación académica relacionada con desarrollo de software: Ciencias de la Computación, Ingeniería en Computación o Ingeniería en Sistemas. Los roles de los participantes fueron: 1 administrador del proyecto, 1 coordinador, 1 administrador de servidores, 1 administrador de bases de datos, 1 líder técnico, 6 programadores y 7 analistas/probadores. Cabe mencionar que al ser una OP los roles no eran siempre exclusivos, por ejemplo, el administrador del proyecto fungió como líder en la especificación de requerimientos, actividad en la que los probadores y el coordinador tuvieron extensa participación como analistas. En el caso de los programadores, dos de ellos llevaron a cabo actividades de diseño bajo supervisión del líder técnico.

En cuanto a la experiencia dentro de proyectos de desarrollo de software en la Tabla 2 se muestra la distribución.

Tabla 2. Experiencia en proyectos de desarrollo de software de los integrantes de la organización.

Experiencia	Número de integrantes
Menos de 1 año	4
Entre 1 y 3 años	4
Entre 3 y 5 años	2
Entre 5 y 10 años	3
Más de 10 años	5

El proyecto tuvo una duración de 2 años y el software construido estuvo compuesto por 18 módulos. El proceso de desarrollo de software siguió un ciclo de vida iterativo incremental con entregas parciales en periodos no mayores a dos meses. Cada entrega consistió en un producto funcional listo para ser utilizado por los usuarios finales.

A la OP le fue requerido presentar la evidencia del cumplimiento del MAAGTICSI en cuatro puntos de control así como en la entrega final. Los puntos de control fueron establecidos por la entidad gubernamental y coincidieron con los meses 7, 13, 16 y 20 del proyecto.

Para ello, dos de los autores facilitaron el mapeo al administrador de proyectos de la OP, para que éste generara los productos de trabajo requeridos. El administrador de proyectos fue el encargado de generar los documentos, sin embargo, la coordinadora también tuvo participación como revisora entre pares. No fue necesario incluir a más integrantes de la organización ya que las dos personas involucradas contaban con los datos y la información requerida.

El esfuerzo requerido para ello fue de 3 horas la primera vez y menos de 2 horas las restantes cuatro, incluyendo la entrega final, totalizando 11 horas necesarias para transferir lo registrado en los productos generados durante el proyecto a las actas de MAAGTICSI.

4 Resultados

Como resultado general para este primer proceso de observación, se determinó que con 6 productos de la norma ISO/IEC 29110-5-1-2 se logra una cobertura total del MAAGTICSI en lo correspondiente a actividades relacionadas con desarrollo de software. A continuación, en las Tablas 3 y 4, se muestran los mapeos de los restantes dos productos solicitados por el MAAGTICSI.

Tabla 3. Mapeo entre la ISO/IEC 29110-5-1-2 y el Acta de Aceptación de Entregables del MAAGTICSI.

Producto MAAGTICSI	Sigla	Elemento MAAGTICSI	Sigla	Elemento ISO/IEC 29110-5-1-2	Producto ISO/IEC 29110-5-1-2
2. Acta de Aceptación de Entregables	INP	2.0 - Identificación y nombre del Proyecto.	IEE	1.3 - Identificación de los elementos entregados	1. Documento de Aceptación
	IDE	2.1 - Identificador del entregable (de acuerdo al documento de planeación del proyecto)	IEE	1.3 - Identificación de los elementos entregados	1. Documento de Aceptación
			ELP	4.4 - Entregables – lista de productos a entregar al cliente	4. Plan del Proyecto
	DEE	2.2 - Descripción del entregable.	DDP	4.1 - Descripción de producto	4. Plan del Proyecto
	FVE	2.4 - Fecha de Verificación del entregable.	FCH	2.2 - Fecha	2. Lista de Verificación
	2OS	2.7 - Observaciones	IAP	1.5 - Identificación de cualquier asunto pendiente (en caso de ser aplicable)	1. Documento de Aceptación
	IDB	2.8.1 - Identificador y descripción breve del entregable (de acuerdo al documento de planeación del proyecto)	IEE	1.3 - Identificación de los elementos entregados	1. Documento de Aceptación
			IDE	4.13 - Instrucciones de entrega	4. Plan del Proyecto
			RDE	4.13.2 - Requerimientos de entrega	4. Plan del Proyecto
	FER	2.8.3 - Fecha de Entrega/recepción	IFR	1.2 - Identificación de la fecha de recepción	1. Documento de Aceptación
	NCF	2.8.4 - Nombre, cargo y firma (de quien entrega y recibe)	RRE	1.1 - Registro de la recepción de la entrega	1. Documento de Aceptación
			FRC	1.6 - Firma de recibido por parte del cliente	1. Documento de Aceptación
	2OB	2.8.5 - Observaciones	RCA	1.4 - Registro de la verificación de los criterios de aceptación definidos por parte del cliente	1. Documento de Aceptación
	FFA	2.9 - Fechas y firmas de elaboración, revisión y aprobación	FRC	1.6 - Firma de recibido por parte del cliente	1. Documento de Aceptación

En muchos casos, la OP que se encuentra alineada, identificada y en función de la norma internacional, sólo debe trasladar la información recabada en sus productos de trabajo (6 en este caso) y ubicarlos en el apartado o elemento correspondiente de los formatos demandados por el MAAGTICSI. Una OP que sigue la norma ISO/IEC 29110-5-2-1 puede cubrir la totalidad de lo requerido por MAAGTICSI reutilizando los productos de trabajo que generó durante la ejecución del proyecto al 100%.

Otro punto importante, es que la OP no requiere cambiar su forma de trabajo ni su estructura organizacional para atender lo solicitado por MAAGTICSI.

Tabla 4. Mapeo entre la ISO/IEC 29110-5-1-2 y el Acta de Cierre de Proyectos del MAAGTICSI.

Producto MAAGTICSI	Sigla	Elemento MAAGTICSI	Sigla	Elemento ISO/IEC 29110-5-1-2	Producto ISO/IEC 29110-5-1-2
3. Acta de Cierre de Proyectos	DEC	3.4 - Descripción de los entregables concluidos.	ELA	2.6 - Elementos aprobados.	2. Lista de Verificación
			ERE	6.2 - Estado de los resultados reales contra los objetivos/metas establecidos.	5. Reporte de Avance
			ERR	6.3 - Estado de los recursos asignados reales contra los recursos planeados.	5. Reporte de Avance
			ECR	6.4 - Estado de los costos reales contra los presupuestos estimados.	5. Reporte de Avance
			RCT	7 - Registro de cualquier desviación de las tareas planeadas y su causa.	5. Reporte de Avance
			APP	7.1 - Almacena los productos del proyecto.	6. Repositorio del Proyecto
	RDP	3.5 - Relación documental de la administración del proyecto.	LGR	2.3 - Lugar	2. Lista de Verificación
			DUR	2.4 - Duración	2. Lista de Verificación
			PAR	2.1 - Participantes	2. Lista de Verificación
			ELA	2.6 - Elementos aprobados.	2. Lista de Verificación
			ENA	2.7 - Elementos no aprobados.	2. Lista de Verificación
			EPV	2.8 - Elementos pendientes de verificar	2. Lista de Verificación
			DIV	2.9 - Defectos identificados durante la verificación	2. Lista de Verificación
	3OB	3.6 - Observaciones.	CAA	3.7 - Cualquier asunto abierto	3. Minuta
			ACU	3.8 - Acuerdos	3. Minuta
			PXR	3.9 - Próxima reunión (en caso necesario)	3. Minuta
			RCT	7 - Registro de cualquier desviación de las tareas planeadas y su causa.	5. Reporte de Avance
	FAA	3.7 - Firmas de aceptación del cierre, elaboración, revisión y aprobación del Acta	RCA	1.4 - Registro de la verificación de los criterios de aceptación definidos por parte del cliente	1. Documento de Aceptación
			FRC	1.6 - Firma de recibido por parte del cliente	1. Documento de Aceptación

Existen oportunidades de mejora para el mapeo, entre ellas el validarlo en más proyectos de desarrollo que involucren OPs y entidades gubernamentales. Sin embargo, la principal limitante del estudio no es el mapeo, sino el alcance que tiene MAAGTICSI en el caso de proyectos de desarrollo de software. Lo solicitado por el manual resulta ser insuficiente para aquel departamento de TI que reciba el software para su operación y/o mantenimiento.

En consecuencia, el manual, que pretende gestionar de manera completa los procesos que en materia de TIC de sus entidades, se queda corto cuando se habla de sistemas de software. Es una carencia crítica si se considera la importancia y el gran número de sistemas de software necesarios para el contexto actual. A futuro, y como mejora fundamental al MAAGTICSI, éste debería tomar en cuenta aspectos relacionados con la calidad del producto de software que se construye, cubriendo así no sólo la parte administrativa del proceso sino también la técnica.

5 Conclusiones

Conocer y operar un marco técnico normativo alineado a estándares internacionales y locales involucra la comunión de distintos reglamentos y estilos de administración de activos y recursos. Al dominar sus procedimientos y las herramientas que proporcionan una mejor gestión y ejecución de algún producto o servicio, se induce a una homologación de actividades y roles dentro de una organización sin importar su escala. En el presente estudio se compagina la norma internacional ISO/IEC 29110 con el MAAGTICSI, para su integración y aplicación a procesos de OPs desarrolladoras de software en México.

Una vez realizado el mapeo, se concluye que la norma ISO/IEC 29110-5-1-2 cubre de manera total lo que respecta a desarrollo de software del MAAGTCSI. Basta con trasladar la información recabada en seis productos de trabajo de la ISO/IEC 29110-5-1-2 y ubicarlos en el apartado o elemento correspondiente de las actas definidas por el MAAGTICSI. Con este resultado, es posible afirmar que las OPs se encuentran en posibilidad de participar en proyectos de desarrollo de software gubernamentales, y de esta manera incrementar sus oportunidades de crecimiento sin afectar su forma de trabajo ni su estructura organizacional.

Es importante recalcar que MAAGTICSI no recopila en sus productos de trabajo la información suficiente y necesaria para que una UTIC sea capaz de administrar, operar y/o mantener de manera adecuada un sistema de software. Esta debilidad obligará a las UTICs a seguir un estándar o normativa de manera paralela a MAAGTICSI cuando se vea involucrada en proyectos o servicios que involucren sistemas de software.

Como trabajo futuro se espera que el mapeo sea utilizado por otras OPs que participen en proyectos gubernamentales con el fin de validar su utilidad en más casos prácticos. Por otra parte, una vez que existan un mayor número de validaciones y en consecuencia mejoras al mapeo, es deseable construir una herramienta de software que permita la creación automática de la documentación solicitada por MAAGTICSI a partir de los productos de trabajo generados en proyectos llevados a cabo bajo la ISO/IEC 29110-5-1-2.

Agradecimientos

Este trabajo fue posible gracias al apoyo del "Programa de Becas Posdoctorales en la UNAM" de la Dirección General de Asuntos del Personal Académico de la UNAM.

Referencias

1. Laporte, C., Alexandre, S. and O'Connor, R.: A software engineering lifecycle standard for very small enterprises. In: R. V. O'Connor et al. (Eds.). EuroSPI 2008, CCIS 16, pp.:129-141 (2008)
2. Oktaba, H. and Piattini, M.: Software Process Improvement for Small and Medium Enterprises: Techniques and Case Studies. Information Science Reference (2008)
3. Pino, F., Pardo, C., García, F. and Piattini, M.: Assessment methodology for software process improvement in small organizations. Inf. Sof., Vol. 52, No. 10, pp.:1044-1061(2010)
4. Modelo de Procesos para la Industria de Software: MoProSoft por Niveles de Capacidad de Procesos, Versión 1.3 (2005)

5. NMX-I-059-NYCE-2005 Tecnología de la información - Software - Modelos de procesos y evaluación para desarrollo y mantenimiento de software (2005)
6. ISO/IEC 29110 Software engineering – Lifecycle profiles for Very Small Entities (VSEs) (2011)
7. Centro de Desarrollo Certificados/Verificados Vigentes. Subsecretaría de Industria y Comercio Dirección General de Innovación, Servicios y Comercio Interior Dirección de Economía Digital (2016) https://prosoft.economia.gob.mx/doc/PADRON_CENTRO%20DE%20DESARROLLO%20VIGENTE_2016_abr-18.pdf (Consultado el 04/12/2017)
8. Manual Administrativo de Aplicación General en Tecnologías de la Información y Comunicación, y en la Seguridad de la Información. Secretaría de la Función Pública (2014)
9. Manual Administrativo de Aplicación General en Tecnologías de la Información y Comunicación. Secretaría de la Función Pública (2010)
10. Secretaría de la Función Pública. México, https://www.gob.mx/sfp (Consultado el 04/12/2017)
11. ISO 9001 Quality management systems, International Organization for Standardization (2008)
12. A Guide to the Project Management Body of Knowledge: PMBOK Guide, Project Management Institute, Fifth Edition, Project Management Institute, Newtown Square, Pennsylvania (2013)
13. Capability Maturity Model Integration (CMMI). Software Engineering Institute, Pittsburgh, PA, USA (2010)
14. ISO/IEC 27001 Information security management systems, International Organization for Standardization (2013)
15. The Open Group. The Open Group Architecture Framework (TOGAF) 9.1. Technical standard (2011)
16. Morales-Trujillo, M., Ventura, T., Torres, R. and Oktaba, H.: From MoProSoft Level 2 to ISO/IEC 29110 Basic Profile: Bridging the Gap. CLEIej, ISSN 0717-5000, Vol. 16 No. 1, pp: 28-41 (2013)

Linking Business and Information Need Goals with Functional and Non-functional Requirements

Luis Olsina and Pablo Becker

GIDIS_Web, Engineering School at Universidad Nacional de La Pampa, Argentina
[olsinal, beckerp]@ing.unlpam.edu.ar

Abstract. Organizations commonly establish and realize business goals for different types of purposes using strategies. Types of purposes and their associated strategies can aim basically at evaluating, developing, maintaining or changing some entity or situation. For instance, some specific evaluation purposes such as to understand, monitor and select alternative may be achieved by strategies embracing non-functional requirements definition, measurement, evaluation and analysis activities. But other specific evaluation purposes such as to improve and control also imply changing the entity, and therefore embracing functional requirements definition activities as well. Moreover, specific development and maintenance purposes always involve functional requirements. This paper discusses the linking of business and information need goals with functional and non-functional requirements concepts, which are paramount for more comprehensive, well-established strategies. To do this, we specify conceptual bases for them, and show their applicability by means of a proof of concept. Having well-structured conceptual bases serving as a ground for different strategies may foster a more effective operationalization of development, maintenance and evaluation goal purposes.

Keywords: Functional and Non-functional Requirements, Ontology, Goal, Purpose, Strategy.

1 Introduction

In any organization, project goals should not be established in a fuzzy and isolated manner. Gilb *et al.* state as the principle of fuzzy targets that "*projects without clear goals will not achieve their goals clearly*" [5]. Organizations commonly establish and carry out business goals for different types of purposes using strategies. Types of purposes can be classified into evaluation, development, maintenance or change categories.

Business goals are the main or primary goals that an organization intends to achieve setting them at different organizational levels. Commonly, projects in conjunction with strategies operationalize specific purposes of business goals for evaluation, development, maintenance or change categories. The purpose of a goal is the rationale for achieving it. For example, to realize specific development and maintenance purposes such as create, add, delete or modify concrete features and capabilities of an entity, the statement of functional requirements (FRs) is always involved. Moreover, being aware that usually FRs may require to be satisfied by non-functional requirements (NFRs) constraints, specific evaluation purposes play also a central role in this endeavor. Different specific evaluation purposes are for instance to understand, monitor, control, improve, compare, select, among others.

On the other hand, information need goals are support goals for business goals. Usually, they provide useful information in order to know the degree of achievement of business goals as well as to give the necessary information to reach them. An information need goal may also require measurement and evaluation (ME) information need goals, which are always stated by NFRs specifications.

As commented above, the different goals established in an organization are operationalized through projects. So various strategies can be used for helping to achieve the project goal purposes. A strategy defines a specific course of action to be followed, i.e., it specifies what should be done and how should be performed. Also, we have conceived a strategy as having three integrated capabilities, namely: process specifications, method specifications, and well-established domain conceptual bases.

In [12], a family of strategies for different evaluation purposes was discussed. For instance, some specific evaluation purposes such as to understand, monitor and select alternative may be achieved by strategies embracing NFRs definition, measurement, evaluation and analysis activities. But other specific evaluation purposes such as to improve and control usually imply changing the entity. Hence, FRs definition activities are implied as well.

At this point, it is important to remark that in [12] and previous works [2, 16], the FRs conceptual base for the family of evaluation strategies was not specified. Looking at the shaded part of Fig. 1, we had specified subontologies for the business goal, project, context, non-functional requirements, measurement and evaluation components. But the rest of conceptual components viz. the functional requirements, development and maintenance ones remained unspecified.

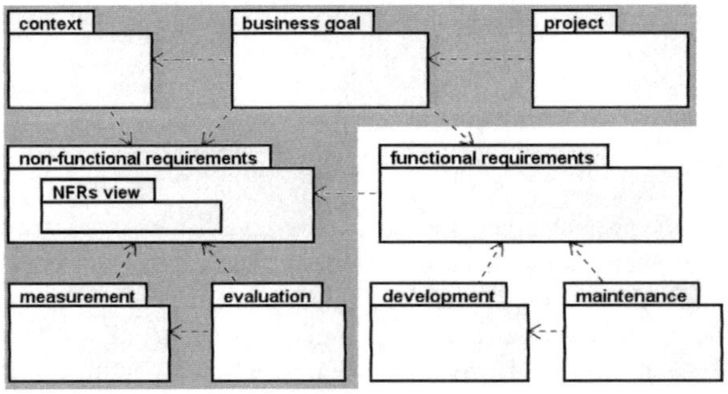

Fig. 1. Relationships between the *business goal* component with the *project*, *context*, *functional* and *non-functional requirements* components (packages).

Thus, the contribution of this paper is twofold: Firstly, to specify the terms, attributes and relationships included into the new *functional requirements* component, and the linking of the business goal concept with the remainder components' terms. Particularly, we focus on the linking of business and information need goal terms with FRs and NFRs terms. Secondly, to run a proof of concept addressing a specific business goal that requires both functional and non-functional concepts. Particularly, we use the Facebook mobileapp case for the improvement purpose. This will permit to gauge the applicability of the extended conceptual base for more comprehensive, multipurpose-oriented strategies. Ultimately, having well-structured conceptual bases serving as a ground for different strategies may benefit a more effective operationalization of development, maintenance and evaluation goal purposes.

The rest of the paper is organized as follows: Section 2 analyzes related work. Section 3 specifies the FRs conceptual component and relates business goals with the remainder components' terms. Section 4 shows the approach applicability through a proof of concept. Finally, Section 5 summarizes conclusions and outlines future work.

2 Related Work

In [12], we have documented a family of strategies for various evaluation goal purposes. These strategies are made up of three integrated capabilities, namely: i) process specifications, ii) method specifications, and iii) well-established domain conceptual bases. Regarding the third capability, in the present work, we are adding the FRs conceptual base and relating it to the previously developed NFRs and goal conceptual bases. Hence, strategies have now a wider ground for supporting not only evaluation goal purposes that include non-functional and functional requirements but also for development and maintenance goal purposes.

Considering that a strategy is an important resource in helping to achieve project goal purposes, it should be noted that there exist few strategies that integrate these three capabilities at once, as discussed in [2]. An approach related to integrated strategies is *GQM⁺Strategies* [1], which includes a goal-oriented framework for the design and implementation of measurement software projects at different organizational levels. In this approach, business goals are linked to measurement goals using the Goal Question Metrics method. *GQM⁺Strategies* has a conceptual base structured as a glossary. But it neither makes explicit the FR and NFR terms and their relationships with business goals, nor has the semantic richness that an ontology provides.

Regarding conceptual bases for NFRs and FRs linked to organizational goals we can consider [14], in which the goals are classified into business, enterprise architecture, or IT goals. The scope of the proposed conceptual base aims at designing decision-making strategies. But the approach does not consider integrated strategies for evaluation goal purposes, as documented in [12]. Another related work worth mentioning is [9], where authors state that NFRs are not stand-alone goals, as their existence is always dependent on other concepts in the project context. Also, considering ISO 9126 standard (the former one to [7]), they state that NFRs, namely quality requirements, are defined with an existential restriction to have at least one association point with FRs as they represent a set of attributes that bear on the existence of a set of functions and their specified properties. Moreover, they relate NFRs with ME concepts. However, the [9] terminology is not exploited as one capability by ME integrated strategies.

Additionally, some research considers only NFRs and FRs terminologies without explicitly linking them with business and information need goal concepts. For example, [18] presents the Softgoal UML profile for seamlessly representing NFRs and FRs using the goal-oriented NFR Framework [11]. This profile defines the visual syntax and semantics of the modeling concepts, relationships, and constraints. On the other hand, authors in [3] present an evolution of a Software Requirements Ontology (SRO) that was reengineered by mapping the concepts of its previous version to the Unified Foundational Ontology (UFO). They say that "*SRO also covers requirements quality evaluation that was not discussed in this paper. However, there are other aspects of the requirements domain that are not addressed by the SRO and that should be incorporated to it in future works, such as traceability of requirements to business goals*". However, to our knowledge the referred future work has not been issued so far.

Lastly in [6], authors claim that the definitions of NFR/FR and hardgoal/softgoal are, in fact, orthogonal, allowing them to identify NFRs that are in fact hardgoals as well as FRs that are softgoals. Moreover, they state that categories of NFRs and FRs are not disjoint, indicating that a requirement can fall into both categories. We can observe, however, that the NFR and FR terms are not related between them as we discuss in the next Section.

3 Relating Goals with Functional and Non-functional Concepts

In this Section, we are addressing the first contribution stated in the Introduction Section. In Fig. 1, we have highlighted the previously developed conceptual components, pointing out that the FRs component had remained unspecified. It is important to remark that our proposed Quality Evaluation Approach [16], particularly its conceptual components, relies on ontologies as a way to formally structure and define the terms, attributes and relationships involved in measurement, evaluation and improvement activities.

In the current research, as a consequence of adding the new FRs conceptual component, some previously developed components such as the NFRs subontology undertook some slight changes due to the harmonization of the conceptual framework as a whole. Also, for the business goal component, some new relationships were added, such as the relations between the Goal term and the Context term, and between the Business Goal term and the Functional Requirement term. Fig. 2 depicts the main terms, attributes and relationships for the *project*, *business goal*, *context*, *NFRs* and *FRs* conceptual components. Additionally, Table 1 shows just the definition of terms for these subontologies. On the other side, the measurement and evaluation components were documented in [2], which are not the main focus of the present work. In the sequel, we describe the abovementioned components, highlighting some terms, attributes and relationships in *italic* the first time they appear in the text below.

An *Organization establishes Goals* which contain an explicit declaration (*statement*) about the major *purpose* that should be achieved in a period of time (*timeframe*), which *is characterized by* a given *Context*. The purpose of a goal is the rationale for achieving it (e.g., to understand, improve, modify, create, among many others). Also, goals can be classified into *Business* and *Information Need Goals.*

Business goals are the main or primary goals that an organization intends to achieve by setting them at different *Organizational Levels*. In turn, a business goal can *have* business *subgoals*. On the other hand, information need goals *support* business goals. Usually, they provide useful information in order to know the degree of achievement of business goals. An information need goal can also *require ME Information Need* goals. The latter is a more specific type of information need goal which is driven by NFRs definition and ME activities.

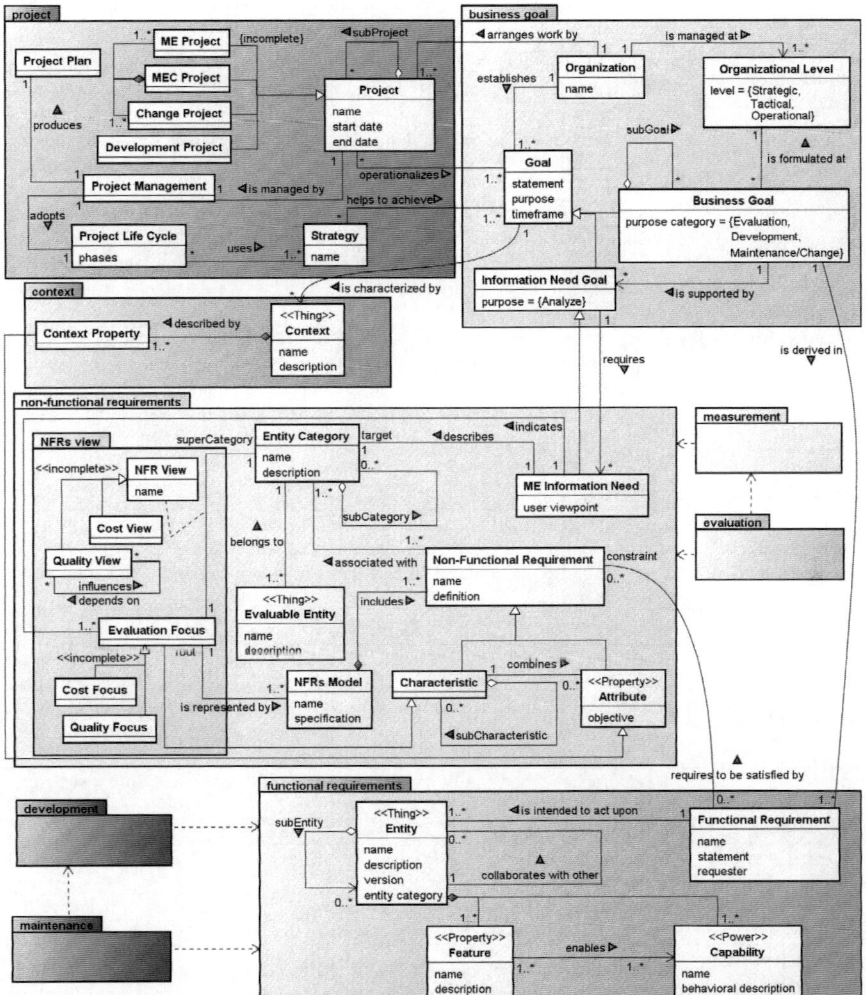

Fig. 2. Key concepts from the business goal domain (*business goal* package) linked with some concepts for the project, context, functional and non-functional requirements domains (*project*, *context*, *functional* and *non-functional requirements* packages). Note that NFRs stands for *Non-Functional Requirements*, ME for *Measurement* and *Evaluation*, and MEC for *Measurement*, *Evaluation* and *Change*.

Table 1. Term definitions for the *business goal, project, context, functional requirements* and *non-functional requirements* subontologies. Note that subontologies are represented as UML packages in Fig. 2.

Term	Definition
Business Goal Subontology	
Business Goal	It is a main or primary Goal that the Organization intends to achieve.
Goal (synonym: Organizational Goal, Objective)	The statement of the aim to be achieved by the Organization which considers the propositional content of a purpose in a given time frame and context.
Information Need Goal	It is a Goal intended to get insight for a given Business Goal. Note: Information Need, as per [8], is defined as "Insight necessary to manage objectives, goals, risks, and problems".
Organization	An Entity comprising people that is structured and managed to establish and pursue organizational Goals and is affected by and affects to its environment or Context.
Organizational Level	It represents a management and decision-making level in which Organization's Business Goals are formulated and Information Need Goals are taken into account. Note: Usually, long-term Business Goals are formulated at strategic Organizational Level, while short-term Business Goals are formulated at operational Organizational Level.
Context Subontology	
Context	It represents the state of the situation of a target entity, which is relevant for a particular organizational Goal. Note 1: Context has semantic of thing [4]. Note 2: In the above definition the target entity can refer to both the Evaluable Entity (in the NFRs component) and the Entity (in the FRs component).
Context Property	It is an Attribute that describe the Context.
Functional Requirements Subontology	
Functional Requirement(FR)	It states what the new or existing Entity (or subEntity) does, or shall do by referring to its Features and/or Capabilities considering a given requester need. Note: To be operationalized, it can state the action to be performed upon the Entity.
Capability	It is a power of an Entity which refers to what it is supposed to do and behave.
Entity (synonym: Concrete Object)	A concrete object to be developed or modified considering its Features and Capabilities. Note 1: Entity has semantic of thing [4]. Note 2: Things (Entities), properties (Features) and powers (Capabilities) do not exist in spatiotemporal isolation from one another, so they all emerge simultaneously to form a unity [4].
Feature	It is a property of an Entity which refers to the intrinsic constitution, structure, or parts of it.
Non-Functional Requirements Subontology	
ME Information Need	It is an Information Need Goal driven by measurement and evaluation activities.
Attribute	It is a measurable physical or abstract property associated with an Entity Category. Note: An Attribute represents an elementary NFR.
Characteristic (synonym: Dimension, Factor, Calculable Concept)	It represents a non-elementary NFR, which combines measurable Attributes. Note 1: Characteristics can be evaluated but cannot be measured as an Attribute -at least in a non-very trivial way such as "good" or "bad". Note 2: A Characteristic can have subcharacteristics.
NFRs Model (synonym: Calculable-Concept Model)	A set of Characteristics, and eventually subcharacteristics, and the relationships between them, which provide the basis for specifying the NFRs and their further evaluation. Note: A possible instance of a NFRs Model is the ISO 25010 quality-in-use model [7].

Evaluable Entity (synonym: Concrete Object)	A concrete object to be evaluated. Note: Evaluable Entity has semantic of thing [4].
Non-Functional Requirement (NFR)	It represents a constraint by means of a Characteristic or Attribute to be evaluated on how or how well an Evaluable Entity performs or shall perform. Note: FRs should require to be satisfied by constraints or 'ilities', which are represented by NFRs.
Entity Category (synonym: Object Category)	Object category to be evaluated by associating its Characteristics and Attributes.
NFRs View Subontology (which is included the Non-Functional Requirements package)	
Evaluation Focus (synonym: Calculable-Concept Focus)	It is a Characteristic which represents the root of a NFRs Model.
NFR View (synonym: Calculable-Concept View)	Association relationship between one Evaluation Focus and one Entity Category. Note 1: The Entity Category must be the super-category, i.e., the highest abstraction level of an Entity Category of value to be evaluated in a given Organization. Note 2: Names of entity super-categories are *Resource*, *Process*, *Software Product*, *System*, *System in use*, among others. Note 3: Names of NFR views are: Quality, Cost Views, etc. [17].
Cost Focus	It is an Evaluation Focus for cost.
Cost View	It is a NFR view for cost.
Quality Focus	It is an Evaluation Focus for quality.
Quality View	It is a NFR view for quality.
Project Subontology	
Change Project (synonym: Maintenance Project)	It is a Project for operationalizing a Business Goal with the purpose of changing the current state of an Entity. Note: Different kinds of changes (e.g., adaptive, perfective, corrective changes) can be made in the maintenance phase.
Development Project	It is a Project for operationalizing a Business Goal with the purpose of developing a new Entity.
ME Project	It is a Project for operationalizing a Business Goal with the purpose of measuring and evaluating an Evaluable Entity that requires a ME Information Need.
MEC Project	It is a Project for operationalizing a Business Goal with the purpose of evaluating and changing a concrete object by performing ME-driven changes. Note: A MEC Project comprises both Change and ME Projects.
Project	An Entity representing a temporary and goal-oriented endeavor with definite start and finish dates, which considers a managed set of interrelated activities, tasks and resources aimed at producing and modifying unique work products (i.e., artifacts, services or results) for satisfying a given requester need.
Project Life Cycle	The series of phases that a Project passes through from its initiation to its closure [15]. Note: Examples of phases to be managed in any Project are planning, scheduling, monitoring, among others.
Project Management	The set of managerial processes and activities intended to achieve the Goal operationalized by a Project. Note: The application of knowledge, skills, tools, and techniques to project activities to meet the project requirements, as per [15].
Project Plan	The document that describes how the Project will be executed, monitored, and controlled [15].
Strategy	Principles, patterns, and particular domain concepts and framework that can be specified by a set of core processes, in addition to a set of appropriated methods and tools, as core resources, for helping to achieve the Project's Goal purpose.

Note that a ME information need *describes* the target object to be evaluated (*Entity Category*) *indicating* also an *Evaluation Focus*, which can be for instance the *Quality Focus*, *Cost Focus*, among others. A key concept is the *Non-Functional Requirement* term which is specialized by means of *Characteristics* and *Attributes* to be evaluated on how or how well an *Evaluable Entity* performs or shall perform. From other perspective, a *Functional Requirement* should *require to be satisfied by* constraints or 'ilities', which can be represented by NFRs, particularly, by a *NFRs Model*.

Coming back to the Business Goal term, we have recently added to it the *purpose category* attribute. We have identified three categories of purposes, namely: *"Evaluation"*, *"Development"*, and *"Maintenance/Change"*. For the Evaluation category, we have discussed in [12] three specific subcategories which include specific purposes and a family of evaluation *Strategies*. A business goal dealing with some specific evaluation purpose such as to 'understand', or 'monitor' may be achieved by strategies embracing NFRs definition, measurement, evaluation and analysis activities. But other specific evaluation purposes such as to 'improve' or 'monitor and control' usually imply changing the *Entity* and therefore embrace FRs definition activities as well. Likewise, specific Development and Maintenance/Change purposes such as 'create', 'modify', 'delete' or 'add' always involve FRs. As a consequence, a given business goal *is derived in* one or more Functional Requirements.

Looking at the *functional requirements* component in Fig. 2, we can say that a particular Functional Requirement *is intended to act upon* an *Entity*. Entity is the concrete object to be developed or modified considering its *Features* and *Capabilities*. An Entity *has* both Features and Capabilities. The former has semantic of property of an Entity, which refers to the intrinsic constitution, structure, or parts of the Entity. While the latter has semantic of power of an Entity, which refers to what it is supposed to do and behave. Analyzing the discussion raised in the article named "*The Ontology of Things, Properties and Powers*" [4], we adopt its three terms. So, Entity in our proposed ontology has semantic of Thing, Feature has semantic of Property, and Capability has semantic of Power. The author argues that things (Entities), properties (Features) and powers (Capabilities) do not exist in spatiotemporal isolation from one another, so they all emerge simultaneously to form a unity.

Note that in Fig. 2, for instance, the «Thing» stereotype enriches semantically to three terms, namely: Entity (in the FRs component), Context (in the Context component), and Evaluable Entity (in the NFRs component). The reasons of using stereotypes are the same that those exposed in [2]. On the other hand, it is also worth mentioning that the terms, attributes and relationships included in the *functional requirements* component are the minimum and necessary ones for describing functional requirements. Specific conceptual domain components for *requirements development*, *testing*, among others will be related to or included in the *development* and *maintenance* packages.

Lastly, aimed at having the general description of components, we can say that an Organization *arranges work by* means of *Projects*, which allow *operationalizing* the established organizational Goals. There exist different types of projects such as development, maintenance, among others. For example, a *Development Project* operationalizes a business goal that has a development purpose category, e.g., to create a new software product or system. A *ME Project* operationalizes a business goal that has an evaluation purpose category, which is always supported by ME information need goals. Additionally, a MEC Project operationalizes both a business goal and its related ME information need goals with the purpose of improvement. Fig. 2 shows that a *MEC project* is composed by a ME subproject and by a change subproject in which changes are driven by ME. A *Change Project* operationalizes a business goal with the purpose of changing or improving the current state of an entity. Finally, a project uses as resource a Strategy, which *helps to achieve* a business goal for any purpose category.

4 Approach Applicability by means of a Proof of Concept

In this Section, we are addressing the second contribution stated in the Introduction Section. That is, we are running a proof of concept which deals with the linking of business and information need goals with functional and non-functional requirements concepts. In [16], we have shown the step by step of our Quality Evaluation Approach which defines the necessary activities to establish goals, projects and evaluation strategies at different organizational levels. Instead, in the present work, we just concentrate on a business goal for the *evaluation purpose category* at operational level of an organization. Particularly, we exemplify the *improve* purpose which implies both evaluation and change activities. Therefore, it requires instantiating both non-functional and functional requirements concepts. It is important to remark that the used strategy should support at least the following four aspects: i) to understand the current quality state for the evaluable entity; ii) to recommend changes mainly for the weakly benchmarked indicators; iii) to make changes on the concrete entity or its subentities; and iv) to understand the ulterior quality state (the improvement) after changes.

Let's suppose that the "*Facebook Inc.*" organization establishes the following business goal at operational level: "*Improve 10% the Facebook mobileapp usability in 1 month*", as depicted in Fig. 3. In order to give supporting information to this evaluation business goal an information need goal should be established such as "*Analyze if usability has improved 10% after changes*" across the 1-month time frame.

The above information need goal will allow to understand the extent to which the established business goal has been achieved after making MEC activities. For our case, this business goal is operationalized by a MEC project using the GOCAMEC (*Goal-Oriented Context-Aware Measurement, Evaluation and Change*) strategy (see e.g. [17] for the application of its activities and methods). Fig. 3 shows that for the above business/information need goals, two ME information need goals are instantiated as well as one business subgoal, labelled accordingly such as:

(a) "*Understand the Facebook mobileapp usability weaknesses*";
(b) "*Apply changes on the current Facebook mobileapp version (v.14) in 7 days*";
(c) "*Understand the Facebook mobileapp usability after changes (v.14.1)*".

So if we analyse these aspects in Fig. 3, we see that (a) and (c) are ME information need goals, which are operationalized by ME projects. Hence, the GOCAMEC's activities and methods require to instantiate non-functional requirements concepts. Conversely, (b) is a business subgoal, which is operationalized by a change project, so GOCAMEC's activities and methods require to instantiate functional requirements concepts as well.

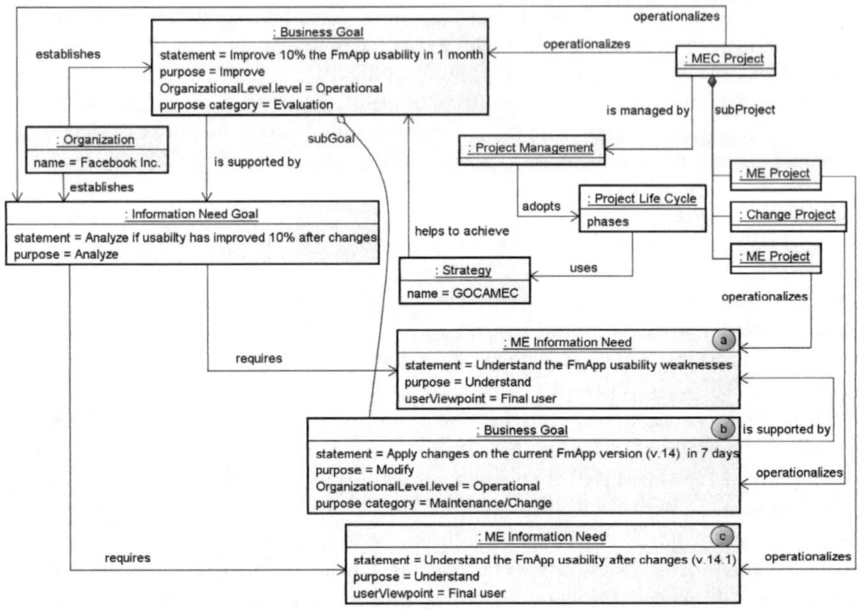

Fig. 3. Scenario instantiation where a *Business Goal* from the operational level is supported by an *Information Need Goal*. Regarding the GOCAMEC strategy, these goals are decomposed in two *ME Information Need Goals*, and in one *Business subGoal*. Note that FmApp stands for *Facebook mobile Application*, and ME for *Measurement and Evaluation.*

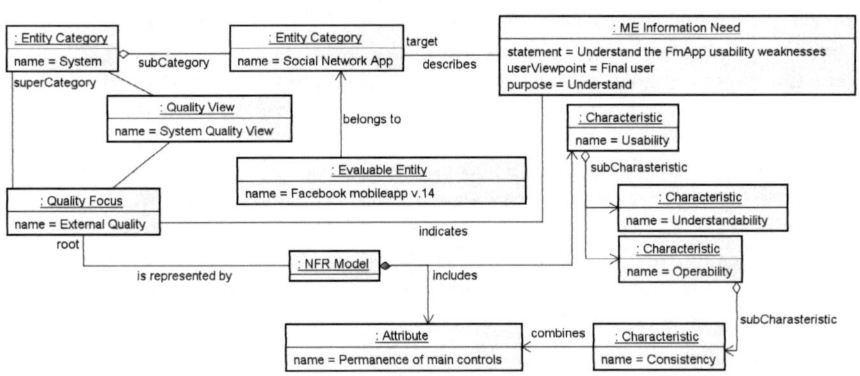

Fig. 4. Instantiation of terms for the *non-functional requirements* and *NFRs View* components for the given *ME Information Need Goal* (see Fig. 3, label a). Note that FmApp stands for *Facebook mobile Application*, and ME for *Measurement and Evaluation*.

First, to illustrate (a), Fig. 4 instantiates terms of the *non-functional requirements* component (recall Fig. 2), which includes also the *NFRs view* component. For the "*Understand the Facebook mobileapp usability weaknesses*" goal, the quality focus is "*External Quality*". This focus is represented by a NFRs (quality) model which includes the "*Usability*" characteristic as well as the "*Understandability*" and

"*Operability*" subcharacteristics. In turn, for "*Operability*", a sub-subcharacteristic like "*Consistency*" combines attributes such as "*Permanence of main controls*". (Note that Fig. 4 just includes one attribute in order not to clutter the diagram. The complete requirements tree for this case study can be found in [13, 17]).

The definition of "*Permanence of main controls*" attribute is "*degree to which main controls (or buttons) are consistently available for users in all appropriate screens or pages*". Therefore, the objective for measuring this attribute is "*to determine the degree to which the main controls are present in all appropriate screens*". The quantification of each attribute is made by means of *metrics* and their interpretation by means of *indicators* (both terms are included in the *measurement* and *evaluation* components).

Finally, the (a) ME information need also describes the "*Facebook mobileapp v.14*" evaluable entity, which belongs to the "*Social network application*" entity category. In turn, its super category pertains to "*System*". Also, note that the association between the quality focus and the entity super category determines the quality view; in our case, the "*System Quality View*".

In order to help to achieve (a), the GOCAMEC activities in short are: Define NFRs for the System Quality View; Design the Measurement, Evaluation and Analysis; and Implement the Measurement, Evaluation and Analysis for Recommendation. In [13], the indicator value for the "*Permanence of main controls*" attribute gave 54.9%, representing thus a weakness. So, a recommendation for change actions aimed at fixing and improving not only this weakness but also other detected weaknesses were issued. For this attribute, the recommendation was "*to ensure that in the set of selected screens, the main controls bar has always the same main buttons*".

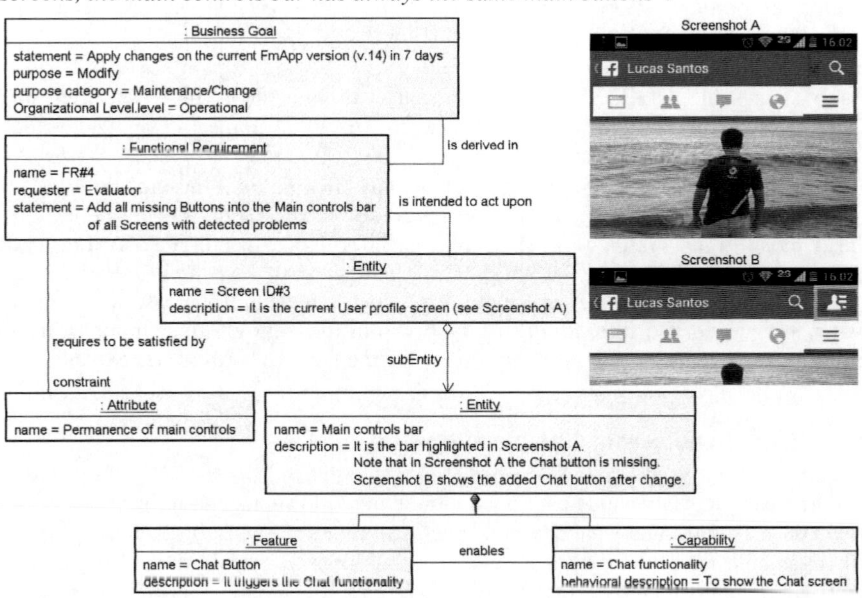

Fig. 5. Instantiation of the terms for the *functional requirements* component for the given *Business subGoal* (see Fig. 3, label b).

Going a step forward, in order to illustrate the (b) business subgoal for the change purpose category, Fig. 5 instantiates the terms of the *functional requirements* component. For the statement "*Apply changes on the current Facebook mobileapp version (v.14) in 7 days*", one or many specific FRs are derived in. In principle, it can be derived as many FRs as recommendations for change actions were issued in the GOCAMEC analysis activity. This figure instantiates just one FR, namely: "*Add all missing Buttons in the Main controls bar of all Screens with detected problems*". This FR is intended to act upon a concrete entity (the "*Screen*") and its subentity (the "*Main controls bar*"). Again, Fig. 5 shows just one screen with the detected problem. That is, the screen "*ID#3*" has the "*Chat Button*" missing from its main controls bar. In other words, the main controls bar subentity has buttons (features) as constituent parts of it, each one enabling accordingly the expected behaviour (capability).

In order to help to achieve the (b) subgoal, the GOCAMEC includes two activities which are Design and Implement Change Actions. GOCAMEC is a strategy in which the changes are driven by evaluation. This means that for instance a good metric specification can help taking better decisions in planning and performing change actions. For example, using the appropriate metric specification for quantifying the "*Permanence of main controls*" attribute (see specification in [17]) allows to record, at measurement time, the availability of each main button of the main controls bar per each Facebook screen in which the button must remain permanent. Therefore, evaluators have each button ID# that is absent in the corresponding screen ID#, at change time. In our case, Fig. 5 shows screen "*ID#3*" before and after the change (in Screenshots A and B respectively).

Once all problems were fixed and the new application version was produced, the improvement gain can be analyzed be achieving the (c) ME information need goal, namely "*Understand the Facebook mobileapp usability after changes (v.14.1)*". To reach this, some GOCAMEC activities such as Implement the Measurement, Evaluation and Analysis are performed again. To our example, if we would add accordingly all missing buttons to screens, the "*Permanence of main controls*" attribute –as an elementary NFR that requires to be satisfied- will raise to 100%.

Ultimately, we can "*Analyze if usability has improved 10% after changes*" across the 1-month time frame (as stated in the information need goal in Fig. 3). Consequently, we can gauge if the linked business goal, i.e., "*Improve 10% the Facebook mobileapp usability in 1 month*" has been achieved. If the case were that it was not achieved and there would be time within the 1-month time frame, a new change and evaluation cycle can be performed using the GOCAMEC strategy again.

5 Conclusions and Future Work

In this paper, we have mainly addressed the linking of business and information need goal concepts with functional and non-functional requirements subontologies, which are paramount for envisioning and developing multipurpose goal-oriented strategies. The underlying hypothesis is that having robust conceptual bases serving as a ground for different strategies may foster a more effective operationalization of evaluation, development and maintenance/change project goal purposes.

Regarding the first contribution listed in the Introduction Section, we have enhanced the conceptual framework of our Quality Evaluation Approach [16] by building the FRs conceptual component structured on the basis of ontological grounds. As a consequence of adding the new FRs component, some previously developed components such as for example the NFRs component undertook some slight updates in order to harmonize the conceptual framework as a whole, as described in Section 3. Considering the scope of the FRs subontology, the terms, attributes and relationships included in the new component are the minimum and necessary for describing this subdomain. It is important to remark that more specific ontologies for the development and maintenance subdomains can be built and related to the FRs conceptual domain. For example, components for requirements development, among others, will be included in the development package (recall Fig. 1).

The construction of both development and maintenance components are part of our future line of research. So we would like to draw the reader attention on the benefits for envisioning various strategies regarding the purpose category of business goals. A family of strategies for evaluation business goal purposes was presented in [12]. However, we can augment the family with new strategies for development and maintenance business goal purposes. For example, if the purpose category of the business goal is 'development', and the specific purpose is 'testing', we can envision a strategy with specific process and method specifications for the testing subdomain. Since this business goal could require supporting ME information needs, e.g., to evaluate the level of efficiency and effectiveness of the testing endeavour, or to analyse the amount of types of errors and faults by severity detected in the testing process, then the former ME strategies can be integrated into the new development (testing) strategy. Similarly, new strategies can be conceived if the purpose category of the primary business goal is 'maintenance' for various specific purposes.

Regarding the second contribution, in Section 4, we have employed the proof of concept approach in order to demonstrate the linking of business and information need goal terms with functional and non-functional requirements terms, attributes and relationships. We have used a proof of concept in principle with the aim to verify that the proposed conceptual bases have practical potential. Hence, in the present paper, we have concentrated on a business goal for the evaluation purpose category at operational level of an organization. Particularly, we have exemplified the 'improve' purpose which implies measurement, evaluation and change activities and methods; therefore, they require instantiating both non-functional and functional requirements concepts.

Lastly, it is worthy to point out that a limitation of the current research is the lack of a broader evidence which does corroborate that the different strategies (the already developed and the forthcoming ones) fit well to the corresponding purpose and category. Thus, we will design surveys in order to gain empirical evidence on their appropriateness with domain experts from both the academy and industry.

Acknowledgments. This work and line of research are supported by Science and Technology Agency of Argentina, in the PICT 2014-1224 project at Universidad Nacional de La Pampa.

References

1. Basili V., Lindvall M., Regardie M., Seaman C., Heidrich J., Jurgen M., Rombach D.,Trendowicz A.: Linking Software Development and Business Strategy through Measurement. IEEE Computer, 43:(4), pp. 57–65, (2010)
2. Becker P., Papa F., Olsina L.: Process Ontology Specification for Enhancing the Process Compliance of a Measurement and Evaluation Strategy. CLEIej.18:(1), pp. 1-26, (2015)
3. Falbo R., Nardi J.: Evolving a Software Requeriments Ontology. In: Proc. of the XXXIV Conferencia Latinoamericana de Informática (CLEI), Santa Fe, Argentina, 10 pp., (2008)
4. Fleetwood S.: The ontology of things, properties and powers. Journal of Critical Realism, 8:(3), pp. 343-366, Available from: http://eprints.uwe.ac.uk/15967, (2009)
5. Gilb T., Finzi S.: Principles of Software Engineering Management, Addison-Wesley, (1988)
6. Guizzardi R., Li F-L., Borgida A., Guizzardi G., Horkoff J., Mylopoulos J.: An Ontological Interpretation of Non-Functional Requirements. In: Proc. 8th Int'l Conf. on Formal Ontology in Information Systems (FOIS), Rio de Janeiro, Brazil, Vol 267, pp. 344-357, (2014)
7. ISO/IEC 25010: Systems and software engineering - Systems and software Quality Requirements and Evaluation (SQuaRE) - System and software quality models, (2011)
8. ISO/IEC/IEEE 15939: Software Engineering - Software Measurement Process, 1st Ed., (2017)
9. Kassab M., Ormandieva, O., Daneva, M.: An Ontology Based Approach to Non-Functional Requirements Conceptualization. In: 4th Int'l Conf. on Software Engineering Advances (ICSEA), Porto, Portugal, pp. 299- 308, (2009)
10. Li F-L., Horkoff J., Mylopoulos J., Guizzardi R., Guizzardi G., Borgida A., Liu L.: Non-functional Requirements as Qualities, with a Spice of Ontology. In: IEEE 22nd Int'l Requirements Engineering Conference (RE), Karlskrona, Sweden, pp. 293-302, (2014)
11. Mylopoulos J., Chung L., and Nixon B. A.: Representing and using nonfunctional requirements: A process-oriented approach. In: IEEE Transactions on Software Engineering, 18(6), pp. 483-497, (1992)
12. Olsina L., Becker, P.: Family of Strategies for different Evaluation Purposes. In: Proc. of the XX Conferencia Iberoamericana en Software Engineering (CIbSE'17) held in the framework of ICSE, CABA, Argentina, pgs 14, (2017)
13. Olsina L., Santos L., Lew P.: Evaluating Mobileapp Usability: A Holistic Quality Approach. In: 14th Int'l Conference on Web Engineering, ICWE 2014, Casteleyn S., Rossi G., and Winckler M. (Eds.): Springer, LNCS 8541, pp. 111-129, (2014)
14. Plataniotis G., Kinderen S., Qin M., Proper E.: A Conceptual Model for Compliance Checking Support of Enterprise Architecture Decisions. In: Proc. of IEEE, 17th Conference on Business Informatics, Lisbon, Portugal, pp. 191-198, (2015)
15. PMBOK: A Guide to the Project Management Body of Knowledge. 5th Edition, (2013)
16. Rivera M.B., Becker, P., Papa, M.F., Olsina L.: A Holistic Quality Evaluation, Selection and Improvement Approach driven by Multilevel Goals and Strategies. In CLEIej.19:(3), Paper 3, pp. 1-28. ISSN 0717-5000, (2016)
17. Rivera M.B., Becker, P., Olsina L.: Quality Views and Strategy Patterns for Evaluating and Improving Quality: Usability and User Experience Case Studies. Journal of Web Engineering, Rinton Press, USA, 15:(5&6), pp. 433-464, (2016)
18. Supakkul S., Chung L.: A UML profile for goal-oriented and use case-driven representation of NFRs and FRs. In: Proc. 3rd ACIS Int'l Conf. on Software Engineering Research, Management and Applications (SERA), Mount Pleasant, USA, pp. 112- 119, (2005)

Indicadores de Medição de Testes em um Contexto Ágil Usando o Template ASM.br

Douglas Silva Lima, Cristina Cerdeiral, Gleison Santos

Programa de Pós-Graduação em Informática – PPGI
UNIRIO – Universidade Federal do Estado do Rio de Janeiro
Av. Pasteur 458, Urca – CEP 22290-240 – Rio de Janeiro – RJ – Brasil
{douglas.silvalima, cristina.cerdeiral, gleison.santos}@uniriotec.br

Abstract. Testes apoiam a verificação e validação dos requisitos, confirmando a qualidade dos produtos de software e favorecendo a aceitação pelo cliente. Em geral, as abordagens ágeis valorizam os testes como um dos caminhos para equilibrar a leveza do processo e oferecer compensação para se alcançar um pouco mais de confiança no desenvolvimento ágil. O objetivo deste trabalho é apresentar um conjunto de indicadores relacionados a testes em projetos ágeis que favoreça a detecção de problemas e a melhoria do gerenciamento das atividades executadas. Foram identificados 15 indicadores aplicáveis a esse contexto a partir de um mapeamento sistemático da literatura. Os indicadores foram descritos em fichas usando o template ASM.br (*Assistance for Software Measurement based on relationships*) visando à padronização dos procedimentos de coleta e análise e explicitação dos relacionamentos dos indicadores entre si e aos objetivos de negócio, além de favorecer a reutilização em diferentes projetos. Por meio de um estudo de caso, as fichas dos 15 indicadores criadas foram avaliadas em relação ao conteúdo e à capacidade de os procedimentos descritos apoiarem atividades de gerência. Foram obtidas evidências de facilidade de entendimento das fichas e dos procedimentos descritos, e também percepção de que as fichas podem ser úteis na gestão de projetos de teste.

Keywords: Medição de Software, Métodos Ágeis, Testes de Software.

1 Introdução

Um dos grandes desafios enfrentados pelas organizações que desenvolvem software é encontrar formas de fornecer mais funcionalidades aos seus clientes, desenvolver os produtos e manter a qualidade do software [17]. A presença de defeitos, indicativo de falta de qualidade, é um fenômeno comum que ocorre durante o processo de desenvolvimento de software. Defeitos levam a várias consequências afetando a entrega do produto, podendo causar ainda falha total no produto devido à utilização de técnicas de remoção de defeitos não apropriadas [16]. Teste de software visa encontrar falhas e possibilitar que sejam corrigidas, de forma a aumentar a confiabilidade do software [8]. Em geral as abordagens ágeis valorizam os testes de software como um dos caminhos para equilibrar a leveza dos respectivos processos e oferecer uma compensação para se alcançar um pouco mais de confiança no desenvolvimento ágil [1].

Uma das formas de alcançar a visibilidade do andamento ou dos resultados de um projeto de software é por meio da medição de software, que pode ser definida como uma avaliação quantitativa de qualquer aspecto dos processos e produtos da Engenharia de Software [5]. Grande parte das pesquisas e relatos sobre medição relacionada a teste de software em contexto ágil não detalha aspectos de coleta e análise dos indicadores que permitam sua reutilização, muitas vezes apenas citando seus nomes. Esta lacuna cria uma necessidade para líderes de teste e gerentes de projeto de possuir indicadores mais apropriados ao gerenciamento dos testes e que apoiem na análise do progresso das atividades de testes executadas.

Este trabalho descreve indicadores que apoiam a gerência de testes em projetos que utilizam metodologia ágil provendo informações que possibilitam a coleta, geração e análise dos indicadores. Líderes de teste e gerentes de projeto podem utilizar tais informações no apoio à gestão do ciclo de testes e análise de possíveis problemas.

Para atender a esse objetivo, os seguintes passos foram executados: (i) identificação de medidas relacionadas a testes em projetos ágeis de desenvolvimento; (ii) consolidação de uma lista de indicadores relacionados a testes e criação das fichas baseadas no *template* ASM.br [6] com informações de coleta e análise levando em consideração a natureza do próprio indicador e do seu relacionamento com outros indicadores; (iii) avaliação das fichas em um estudo de caso em uma organização que executa testes de software em projetos de desenvolvimento de software com metodologia ágil.

Além desta introdução, este artigo está estruturado assim: a Seção 2 apresenta a revisão da literatura sobre medição de software e testes em projetos ágeis, a Seção 3 apresenta o template ASM.br, a Seção 4 apresenta os indicadores de testes para projetos ágeis, a Seção 5 contém as discussões dos resultados da avaliação realizada para avaliar o conteúdo dos indicadores, por fim, a Seção 6 apresenta as considerações finais.

2 Medição de Software e Testes em Projetos Ágeis

Teste de software é o processo de execução de um programa com a finalidade de encontrar falhas, que possibilita aumentar a confiabilidade do software ao corrigir suas causas [8]. De forma geral, os testes visam assegurar um nível de qualidade de produto superior ao antecipar a descoberta de falhas e incompatibilidades, reduzindo o custo do projeto. Em projetos ágeis também há uma preocupação em testar sob o ponto de vista do cliente por meio de testes de aceitação. Para criação de testes de aceitação, há um esforço colaborativo entre um especialista do negócio ou domínio e o desenvolvedor, analista ou qualquer outro membro do time de desenvolvimento. Cada história de usuário deve ter um ou mais casos de teste de aceitação associados, que idealmente são baseados em exemplos fornecidos pelo cliente e além de ajudar na compreensão das histórias, validam o software desenvolvido [11].

A análise dos resultados dos testes tem um importante papel no ciclo de desenvolvimento de software. Para o negócio que envolve software não há espaços para desculpas por falta de qualidade [17]. Para a análise dos testes, os desenvolvedores precisam de relatórios de análise dos resultados e testes, que podem conter gráficos e relatórios mostrando as causas raízes dos problemas de desempenho ou qualidade [17]. Segundo [9], em projetos que utilizam metodologias ágeis, a medição de software aponta para os principais focos do desenvolvimento ágil, como testes e integração contínua, e assim possibilitam a monitoração dos projetos. Como exemplo de indicadores relacionados pode-se citar quantidade de casos de testes, grau de cobertura de teste, taxa de crescimento de teste e implementações falhadas [9].

Um conjunto de medidas bem projetado pode ser utilizado para medir a qualidade de produtos de trabalho, dar apoio à tomada de decisão dos gerentes de projeto e aumentar o retorno de investimento do produto [11]. Medições devem ser planejadas e coletadas de forma organizada, para que possam ser monitoradas e ajustadas de acordo com os objetivos e necessidades da organização [14]. Quando uma medida é utilizada para indicar o alcance a objetivos, ela desempenha o papel de indicador [2]. Os indicadores representam produtos de informação que atendem as necessidades de informação inicialmente identificadas e são registrados em um plano de medição [13].

O número de indicadores descritos na literatura é extenso e isso expõe as organizações ao risco de ter planos de medição com indicadores sem sinergia com seus objetivos ou com os demais projetos da organização. Isto pode gerar problemas de entendimento e a impossibilidade de acompanhar os resultados de todos os projetos de forma consistente. Por esse motivo, as organizações devem definir um conjunto predeterminado de indicadores para ajudar no planejamento e acompanhamento de suas medições [6].

Foram identificados trabalhos como [8] que analisa métodos ágeis, abordagens de teste e medidas de teste mais utilizados através de um *survey* aplicado a desenvolvedores e testadores em projetos ágeis de desenvolvimento de software. Foram identificadas 6 medidas relacionadas a testes: quantidade de defeitos encontrados, tempo de execução de testes, funcionalidade testadas e entregues, quantidade de casos de teste e assertivas, fator de teste e cobertura de código (no trabalho o foco é na cobertura para testes unitários realizados pelos desenvolvedores). No *survey* foram observadas quais medidas são mais utilizadas, mas os autores não descrevem como coletá-las e calculá-las. Também não era objetivo do trabalho explorar a utilização das medidas em projetos.

Mota e Dias-Neto [14] identificaram, por meio de um mapeamento sistemático da literatura, 24 medidas utilizadas em projetos de desenvolvimento de software com métodos ágeis e que podem ser aplicadas no processo de teste. Apesar de o trabalho listar medidas, não foram apresentados os detalhamentos referentes à coleta ou análise, nem foram identificadas medidas que apoiem a gestão de testes de software.

3. Template ASM.br

O ASM.br (*Assistance for Software Measurement based on relationships*, ou Apoio a Medição de Projetos de Software baseado em relacionamentos) [6] foi criado devido à falta de padronização de registro de especificações de indicadores e à ausência de informações importantes em indicadores registrados na literatura. O ASM.br é dividido em três partes, descritas a seguir.

Componente Perfil Organizacional – Utilizado para indicar as características da organização que utilizará o ASM.br na representação de seus indicadores e informa: nome da organização, repositório de arquivos e versão do documento.

Componente Mapeamento de Indicadores – É composto de três mapas. O Mapa de Objetivos e Indicadores fornece visibilidade ao gerente de projeto sobre quais indicadores são importantes a fim de alcançar os objetivos da organização. É composto por objetivos estratégicos da organização, que por sua vez são a base da formação dos objetivos de medição. A partir desses últimos são identificadas as necessidades de informação e, por fim, os indicadores são formados a partir dessas necessidades. O Mapa de Indicadores apresenta o relacionamento entre os indicadores considerando algumas categorias preenchidas: Esforço, Escopo, Tempo, Custo, Qualidade e Produtividade. Por fim, o Mapa para o MR-MPS-SW (ou CMMI) relaciona os níveis do MR-MPS-SW apoiados pelos indicadores contemplados.

Componente Fichas – Apresenta descrição detalhada dos indicadores em uma única página (chamada de Ficha de Registro de Indicador), visando simplificar o acesso às informações de cada indicador. A Fig. 1 mostra um exemplo de ficha de registro de Indicadores. Cada ficha é dividida em áreas específicas (identificada por letras):

- *Informações Gerais* (a) – Apresenta nome e descrição do indicador, além de informações sobre objetivos de medição e necessidade de informação, tipo (controle, qualidade, desempenho), categoria (esforço, escopo, tempo, custo, qualidade, produtividade) e processo do MR-MPS-SW associados ao indicador.

- *Representação gráfica do indicador* (b) – Exibe gráfico gerado através de planilhas de coleta de medidas e possibilita a análise de evolução do indicador.

- *Procedimento de medição e análise* (c) – Detalha os artefatos e medidas necessárias para coleta e fórmula de geração do indicador, assim como informações básicas de como analisar o indicador gerado.

- *Procedimento de análise baseado em critérios* (d) – Aponta premissas definidas com base nos possíveis valores e resultados para os indicadores e, para cada premissa uma possível conclusão para a razão do indicador apurado e possíveis ações de apoio à resolução ou mitigação do problema são sugeridas. Algumas das premissas possuem valores que devem ser definidos de acordo com a organização ou projeto, como, por exemplo, valores qualitativos (como "médio", "alta" ou "muito baixo") ou faixas de valores numéricos. No caso das faixas, em geral, as ações de um nível inferior são aplicáveis aos níveis superiores tendo em vista que o indicador poderá atingir o nível anterior em algum momento do monitoramento e a ação também ser recomendada para apoio na análise.

- *Procedimento de análise baseado em relacionamento* (e) – Apresenta o relacionamento do indicador detalhado na ficha com outros, e possíveis influências positivas ou negativas destes relacionamentos, com possíveis ações para cada indicador relacionado. Este procedimento foi incluído no template com o objetivo de complementar os procedimentos de análise considerados na Ontologia de Referência para Medição de Software [2] e no PSM [4]. As linhas registram as sugestões de análise para que o possível impacto dos relacionamentos em outros indicadores seja avaliado. Os sinais (-) e (+) representam o comportamento esperado entre os indicadores devido às relações existentes. No exemplo da Fig. 1, um aumento da Densidade de Defeitos (DD) pode gerar aumento no Esforço Gasto nos Testes (EGT).

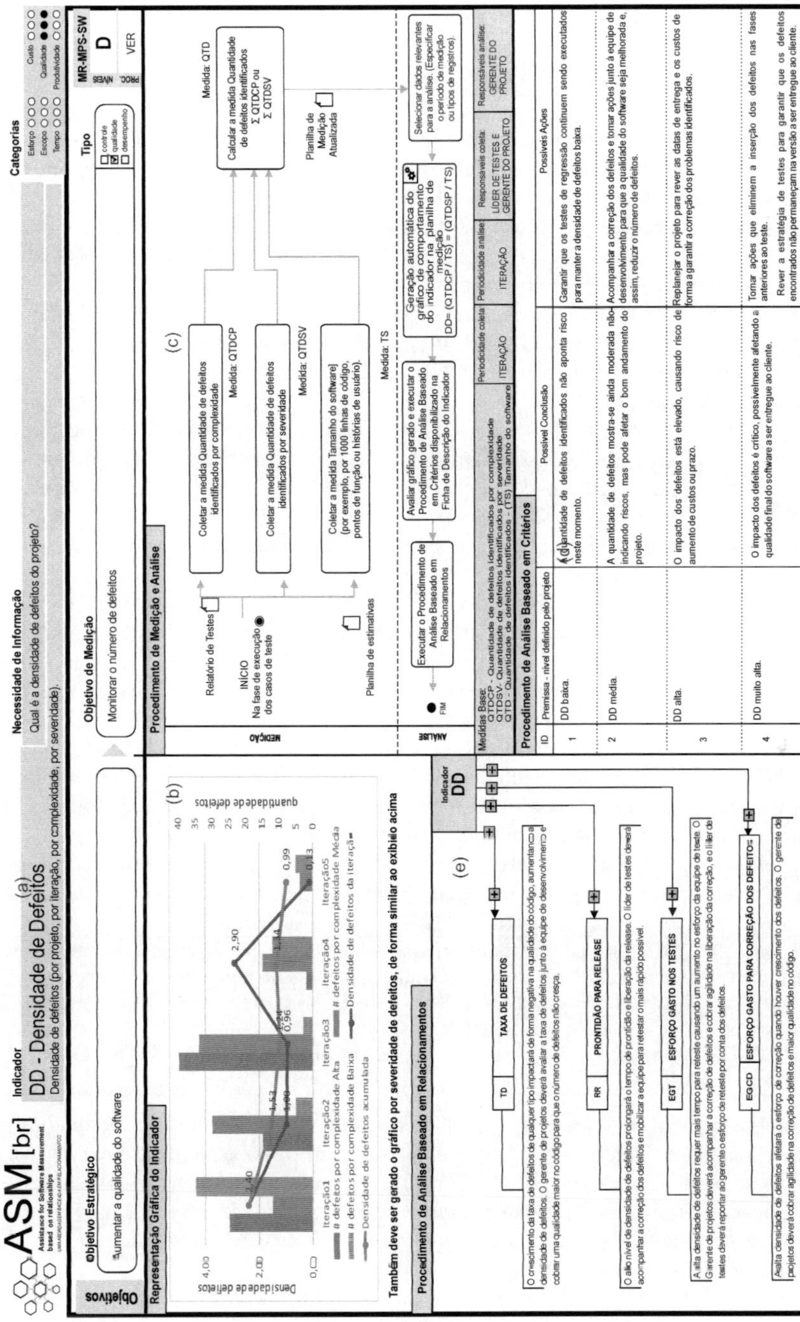

Fig. 1 Ficha baseada no ASM.br para o Indicador Densidade de Defeitos.

4. Indicadores de Teste em Projetos Ágeis

Durante uma busca informal da literatura sobre medidas ou indicadores de apoio a atividades de teste em projetos ágeis, identificou-se que a maioria dos trabalhos citavam indicadores relacionados a outras atividades de gerenciamento de projeto de desenvolvimento ou citavam apenas as medidas relacionadas a teste, sem detalhamento de coleta e análise de indicadores. Dessa forma, resolveu-se realizar um mapeamento sistemático da literatura com o objetivo de consolidar um conjunto de indicadores aplicáveis à gerência de atividades relacionadas a testes em contextos ágeis. Durante a revisão da literatura, foi identificado o trabalho de Mota e Dias-Neto [14] citado na Seção 2.1. Como o trabalho não apresentava em detalhes o protocolo utilizado e a busca não estava atualizada, resolveu-se aproveitar as informações descritas no trabalho para criar um protocolo (cujos detalhes podem ser vistos em [12]) baseado nas diretrizes propostas por [10] e [15] e executá-lo.

Seguindo o GQM [3], o objetivo do estudo foi: *analisar* relatos de experiência e publicações científicas sobre projetos ágeis de desenvolvimento de software *com o propósito* de identificar medidas e indicadores *com relação* às atividades relacionadas a testes *do ponto de vista* de pesquisadores no contexto acadêmico e industrial. A questão de pesquisa (QP) definida foi: *Que indicadores relacionados a teste durante o desenvolvimento ágil de software podem ser derivados das medidas citadas na literatura?*

Foram utilizadas as bases Scopus e IEEE eXplore, as mesmas do mapeamento original, considerando publicações de Computação. Não foram feitas buscas manuais. Foram aplicados critérios de inclusão e exclusão em dois filtros. Tais critérios não haviam sido definidos em [14]. No primeiro filtro, aplicados a partir da análise de título e resumo das publicações identificadas a partir da string de busca (Tabela 1), garantiu-se que as fontes consideradas propusessem ou descrevessem medidas/indicadores (gerais ou relacionadas a teste) em projetos ágeis de desenvolvimento de software. Utilizou-se a string de busca original, sem modificações. No segundo filtro, aplicado a partir da leitura completa dos trabalhos, garantiu-se as medidas/indicadores identificados estavam relacionados a testes de software em projetos ágeis. Foram considerados apenas artigos de conferência ou periódicos que tenham passado por revisão por pares.

Tabela 1. String de busca utilizada

“(("agile" OR "SCRUM" OR "extreme programming" OR "lean development" OR "feature driven development" OR "dynamic system development" OR "agile unified process") AND ("metric" OR "metrics" OR "measure" OR "measures" OR "measured" OR "measurement" OR "measurements" OR "indicator" OR "indicators" OR "evaluation") AND ("software project" OR "software projects" OR "software process" OR "software processes" OR "software product" OR "software products" OR "software production”)

Em um primeiro momento (Ciclo 1), foram lidos todos os artigos selecionados pelo mapeamento sistemático original, aplicando-se os critérios de inclusão e exclusão e extraindo-se os dados relevantes. Neste ciclo, 15 medidas listadas em [14] não foram identificadas durante a replicação e revisão dos artigos, sendo descartadas. Em contrapartida, 13 novas medidas foram mapeadas e adicionadas à lista de medidas do Ciclo 1, gerando um total de 22 medidas.

No Ciclo 2, foi realizada a extensão do mapeamento para o período de 2014 até 2016. Neste ciclo, a mesma string de busca utilizada no Ciclo 1 foi executada nas mesmas bases. Foram retornadas 139 publicações, que tiveram títulos e resumos lidos para aplicação dos critérios de inclusão e exclusão. Dos 22 artigos selecionados para leitura completa, 9 foram considerados válidos e, assim, 58 medidas foram mapeadas. Após exclusão de medidas duplicadas ou já mapeadas, restaram 17 novas medidas. Ambas as análises da replicação foram auditadas por um pesquisador que validou as medidas novas e/ou excluídas. A Tabela 2 apresenta os artigos no escopo do mapeamento. Os artigos identificados por P1 são oriundos do Ciclo 1, os por P2, do Ciclo 2.

Tabela 2. Artigos utilizados no mapeamento sistemático

Referência Completa
P1_01 - Ilieva, S., Ivanov, P. and Stefanova, E. (2004) "Analyses of an agile methodology Implementation", Proceedings of the 30th EUROMICRO conference. Pp. 326-333.
P1_02 - Schooenderwoert, N. V. (2006) "Embedded Agile Project by the Numbers with Newbies", Agile Confere 2006, Minneapolis - EUA. DOI: 10.1109/AGILE.2006.24.
P1_03 - Ayed, H., Habra, N. and Vanderose, B. (2013) "AM-QuICk: A Measurement-Based Framework for Agile Methods Customisation", In Proc. IWSM/Mensura 2013:71-80.
P1_04 - Green, P. (2011) "Measuring the Impact of Scrum on Product Development at Adobe Systems", In: 44th Hawaii International Conference on System Sciences, p.1-10.
P1_05 - Ruiz, J.C., Osorio, Z.B., Mejia, J., Munoz, M., Chavez, A.M. and Olivares, B.A., (2011) "Definition of a hybrid measurement process for the models ISO/IEC 15504-ISO/IEC 12207:2008 AND CMMI-DEV1.3, SMEs" Electronic, Robotics and Automotive Mechanics Conference (CERMA), 2011 IEEE, 421-426.
P1_06 - Heidenberg, J. and Porres, I., (2010), "Metrics Functions for Kanban Guards", In: IEEE International Conference and Workshops on Engineering of Computer-Based Systems. Oxford, UK. DOI: 10.1109/ECBS.2010.43.
P1_07 - Atiwithayaporn, S. and Rivepiboon, W., (2013), "A development of the effectiveness evaluation model for agile software development using the balanced scorecard", International MultiConference of Engineers and Computer Scientists 2013 Vol I, IMECS 2013, Hong Kong.
P1_08 - Ayed, H., Vanderose, B. and Habra, N., (2012), "A metamodel-based approach for customizing and assessing agile methods", In: The International Conference on the Quality of Information and Communications Techonology (QUATIC), Lisbon - Portugal. DOI: 10.1109/QUATIC.2012.11
P1_09 - Mahnic, V. and Vrana, I., (2007), "Using stakeholder driven process performance measurement for monitoring the performance of a Scrum based software development process", Electrotechnical Review, 74(5): 241-247, 2007.
P1_11 - Brown A., Ambler S. and Royce W., (2013), 'Agility in Scale: Economic Governance, Measured Improvement, and Disciplined Delivery", Proceedings of the 2013 International Conference on Software Engineering (ICSE '13), San Francisco – USA, pp 873-881.
P1_13 - Hodgetts, P., (2004), "Refactoring the development process: experiences with the incremental adoption of agile practices", Agile Development Conference, Salt Lake City, USA. DOI: 10.1109/ADEVC.2004.17.
P1_14 - Racheva, Z., Daneva, M. and Buglione, L., (2008), "Complementing Measurements and Real Options Concepts to Support Inter-iteration Decision-Making in Agile Projects", Proc. 34th Euromicro Conf. Software Engineering and Advanced Applications, pp-457-464.
P1_16 - Ktata, O. and Levesque, G., (2010), "Designing and implementing a measurement program for Scrum teams: what do agile developers really need and want?", Proceedings of the Third Conference on Computer Science and Software Engineering, p.101-107.
P2_01 - Kayes I., Sarker M., Chakareski J., (2016), "Product backlog rating: a case study on measuring test quality in scrum", Innovations Syst Softw Eng (2016) 12: 303. https://doi.org/10.1007/s11334-016-0271-0.

Referência Completa
P2_02 - Yamada S., Kii R., (2015), "Software quality analysis for agile development", 4th International Conference on Reliability, Infocom Technologies and Optimization: Trends and Future Directions, ICRITO 2015, Noida, India. DOI: 10.1109/ICRITO.2015.7359201.
P2_03 – Kupiainen E., Mäntylä M.V., Itkonen J. (2015), "Using metrics in Agile and Lean software development – A systematic literature review of industrial studies", Information and Software Technology, Volume 62, June 2015, pp. 143-163. DOI: 10.1016/j.infsof.2015.02.005.
P2_04 - Staron M., Meding W., Palm K., (2012), "Release readiness indicator for mature agile and lean software development projects", In: Wohlin C. (eds) Agile Processes in Software Engineering and Extreme Programming. XP 2012. Lecture Notes in Business Information Processing, vol 111. Springer, Berlin, Heidelberg.
P2_05 – Staron, M., Meding, W., Hansson, J., Höglund, C., Niesel, K., Bergmann, V., (2014), "Dashboards for Continuous Monitoring of Quality for Software Product under Development", Relating System Quality and Software Architecture, pp 209-229. DOI: B978-0-12-417009-4.00008-9.
P2_06 - Willamy R., Nunesy J., Perkusichz M., Freirex A., Saraiva R., Almeidak H., Perkusich A., (2016), "A method to build Bayesian networks based on artifacts and metrics to assess agile projects", Proceedings of the International Conference on Software Engineering and Knowledge Engineering, SEKE. DOI: 10.18293/SEKE2016-213.
P2_07 - Gupta R.K., Manikreddy P., Gv A., (2016), "Challenges in adapting agile testing in a legacy product", 2016 IEEE 11th Int'l Conference on Global Software Engineering (ICGSE). Irvine, CA, USA. DOI: 10.1109/ICGSE.2016.21.
P2_08 - Malhotra R., Chug A., (2016), "Comparative analysis of agile methods and iterative enhancement model in assessment of software maintenance", INDIACom; 2016 3rd International Conference on Computing for Sustainable Global Development, New Delhi, India.
P2_09 - X. Zhao; X. Xuan; A. Wang; D. Liu; L. Zheng, (2014), "Software Quality Control via Exit Criteria Methodology: An Industrial Experience Report", 2014 21st Asia-Pacific Software Engineering Conference. Jeju, South Korea. DOI: 10.1109/APSEC.2014.86.

Como resultado desta etapa inicial, foi possível mapear 39 medidas relacionadas a testes durante o desenvolvimento ágil de software citadas na literatura. O conjunto de medidas foi revisado por 2 especialistas em engenharia de software com alto grau de conhecimento para avaliar possíveis medidas duplicadas em razão de utilizarem nomes semelhantes na língua inglesa ou nomes diferentes executando medições semelhantes. Também foram removidas medidas cujo cálculo era definido de forma subjetiva, não sendo apresentado qualquer tipo de fórmula que deixasse claro como calculá-las.

Desta forma, as 39 medidas foram analisadas visando consolidar indicadores que pudessem estar alinhados com necessidades de informação e/ou objetivos de negócio das organizações e que pudessem ser utilizados para tomada de decisão nos projetos. Assim, 15 indicadores foram propostos, respondendo à questão de pesquisa formulada. Foram levados em consideração a análise do contexto dos artigos em que os indicadores são citados e das informações de como coletá-los ou calculá-los. Além disso, houve medidas agrupadas em um único indicador por serem medidas semelhantes com nomes diferentes. Por exemplo, Cobertura de Teste e Percentual de Cobertura de Testes foram agrupadas em Índice de Cobertura de Testes. A Tabela 3 apresenta os indicadores propostos e indica, entre colchetes, os artigos que contribuíram para sua definição.

Para cada indicador foram criadas fichas de registro com o conteúdo definido no template do ASM.br, além das outras fichas previstas pelo ASM.br. A Fig. 1 apresenta a ficha criada para o indicador *DD – Densidade de defeitos*, conforme descrito na Seção 3. Todas as demais fichas podem ser vistas em [12].

Tabela 3. Indicadores definidos com base na análise das medidas mapeadas

Indicadores
Índice de Cobertura de Teste (ICT) - Índice de cobertura de teste, considerando total e por tipo de teste (unidade, integração, funcional e aceitação). Total de requisitos já desenvolvidos que tenham ao menos um caso de teste associado sobre o total de requisitos do projeto já desenvolvidos do projeto/iteração. *[P1_03, P1_06, P1_16, P2_03, P2_07, P2_08, P2_10]*
Taxa de Defeitos (TD) - Taxa de defeitos (abertos, analisados e não resolvidos, removidos) por iteração e por projeto em relação ao total de defeitos identificados no projeto/iteração. *[P1_01, P1_02, P1_04, P1_06, P1_07, P1_11, P2_03, P2_04, P2_07, P2_08]*
Quantidade de defeitos reportados pelo cliente (QDRC) - Quantidade de defeitos reportados pelo cliente (por severidade). Calculado pelo somatório de defeitos acumulado por severidade por mês/período definido pelo projeto/iteração. *[P1_02, P2_03]*
Densidade de Defeitos (DD) - Densidade de defeitos (por projeto, iteração, complexidade e severidade). Calculado pela quantidade de defeitos por severidade ou complexidade acumulado por iteração sobre o tamanho do projeto conforme definição (linhas de código, pontos de função, histórias de usuários). *[P1_01, P1_02, P1_03, P1_04, P1_05, P1_08, P1_09, P1_13, P2_01, P2_02, P2_03, P2_04, P2_05, P2_07, P2_08, P2_09]*
Taxa de funcionalidades que passam nos testes de aceitação automatizados (TFTA) - Taxa de funcionalidades que foram implementadas e automatizadas. Calculado pela quantidade de funcionalidades aceitas nos testes automatizados sobre o total de funcionalidades implementadas no projeto. *[P1_14, P1_16, P2_03, P2_04]*
Tempo entre detecção de defeitos (TDD) - Tempo decorrido entre detecções consecutivas de defeitos por parte do cliente. Calculado pelo número de dias em espera, até a correção do defeito para cada dia da iteração. *[P2_09]*
Taxa de aumento de casos de testes entre releases (TACT) - Indica o percentual de aumento de casos de testes entre releases. *[P2_03]*
Taxa de casos de testes automatizados (TCTA) - Número de casos de testes automatizados sobre o total de casos de testes existentes em cada iteração. *[P1_03, P2_03]*
Prontidão para release (RR) - Número de semanas previstas para disponibilização da release com base no número de defeitos identificados. O indicador sinaliza em quantas semanas a release estará liberada para implementação. [P2_04, P2_05]
Tempo médio para correção de um defeito (TMCD) - Tempo médio de correção de defeitos por cada nível de severidade, considerando também o SLA definido pelo projeto. *[P1_06]*
Tempo para correção dos testes (TCT) - Tempo para correção dos defeitos identificados nos testes em cada rodada de testes ou iteração. *[P1_03]*
Taxa de casos de testes executados em relação ao planejado (TCEX) - Taxa de casos de testes (não executados, executados com sucesso, executados com falha) em relação ao planejado. Calculado em relação ao total de caso de teste planejados para a iteração/projeto. *[P1_07, P2_02, P2_03, P2_04, P2_05]*
Esforço gasto nos testes (EGT) – Percentual de esforço gasto por nível de teste (unidade, integração, funcional e aceitação) em relação ao total de horas da iteração. *[P1_01]*
Quantidade de defeitos não cobertos por casos de testes (QDNC) - Quantidade de defeitos identificados no software pela equipe não capturados pelos casos de teste. *[P2_01]*
Esforço gasto para correção de defeitos (EGCD) - Esforço gasto para correção de defeitos por tipo de teste (unidade, integração, funcional e aceitação). Calculado pela porcentagem de horas gastas na correção dos defeitos sobre total de horas gastas na iteração. *[P1_01]*

Para identificação dos objetivos estratégicos, foram utilizados por base os definidos em [6] e também a definição de cada indicador a partir do resultado do mapeamento. Foram também definidos objetivos de medição e necessidade de informação associados a cada indicador. A experiência do pesquisador (primeiro autor deste artigo) como líder de testes e atuação na área por vários anos ajudou na definição dos indicadores, além do conteúdo de medidas e indicadores mapeados. Os objetivos estratégicos e de medição foram propostos com base na literatura e experiência dos autores com o objetivo de apresentar as fichas completas, como previstas pelo template ASM.br. Porém, vale ressaltar que as fichas devem ser adaptadas para a realidade de cada organização e assim os indicadores serem escolhidos de acordo com suas características.

O conjunto de indicadores criados não é, no entanto, completo, capaz de atender as necessidades de todas as organizações e projetos de desenvolvimento ágil no gerenciamento dos testes. Deve ser visto como um conjunto inicial, aderente à realidade de projetos de desenvolvimento ágil de software, definido com base nas medidas identificadas no mapeamento sistemático e revisado por especialistas em engenharia de software. Antes de seu uso, deve ser revisto pelas organizações. A adaptação envolve o entendimento de medição de software e dos objetivos estratégicos e de medição da organização de forma a defini-los usando o mapa de objetivos e selecionar os indicadores a serem criados a partir dos objetivos definidos. É necessária também a revisão das seções de coleta, medição e análise baseado nas particularidades dos projetos e da organização em questão.

Dentre as limitações do mapeamento sistemático realizado, pode-se destacar:

- Não ter o resultado de retorno da string e análise dos critérios de inclusão e exclusão no subconjunto de artigos do mapeamento original. Por este motivo foi decidido aplicar os critérios de inclusão e exclusão nos 24 artigos selecionados e confirmar as medidas a partir dos artigos citados pelos autores.
- Não considerar outras bases bibliográficas. No entanto, a Scopus é uma metabase, indexando artigos disponíveis em outras, reduzindo-se assim o risco de não obter mais trabalhos relevantes. Também não foram executadas buscas manuais ou snowballing para complementar os resultados obtidos.
- A possibilidade de ter-se catalogado medidas utilizadas em projetos tradicionais que sejam aplicáveis em projetos ágeis (e vice-versa). Porém, observa-se que foi identificado um conjunto extenso de medidas aplicáveis a projetos "tradicionais" e "ágeis", minimizando este risco.
- Grande parte dos artigos não detalham as medidas, por isso, muitas vezes, a interpretação dependeu dos pesquisadores. Como tratamento, a lista final das medidas foi revista por outro pesquisador e a definição dos indicadores foi revista por dois pesquisadores com conhecimento em Engenharia de Software.

5. Avaliação dos Indicadores de Testes para Projetos Ágeis

Foi executado um estudo de caso visando avaliar o conteúdo das fichas de registro dos indicadores em uma organização de desenvolvimento de software ágil.

Definição dos objetivos: Com base no GQM [3], definiu-se o objetivo da avaliação como *analisar* o conteúdo das fichas de indicadores de testes para projetos ágeis *com o propósito de* avaliar sua utilidade, facilidade de uso e aplicabilidade *do ponto de vista* de líderes de teste e gerentes de projeto *no contexto de* projetos de desenvolvimento de software utilizando metodologias ágeis.

Método de Avaliação: Utilizou-se o modelo *Technology Acceptance Model* – TAM [7], que procura determinar os aspectos de utilidade e facilidade de uso de uma tecnologia segundo a percepção de seus usuários. Também procurou-se identificar se o participante do estudo de caso demonstra interesse em utilizar ou não os indicadores no futuro. Os participantes avaliaram o conteúdo das fichas e simularam o seu uso em um contexto real. As perguntas feitas indicavam ao participante a percepção de facilidade no entendimento das informações e formato da ficha, além de confirmar utilidade de implementação delas, melhorias no desempenho e apoio no gerenciamento dos testes e interesse em utilizá-las na organização do participante.

Caracterização da Organização: A pesquisa foi realizada em uma organização da área de telecomunicações no Rio de Janeiro, em projetos de teste de software sob a gerência de qualidade ligada à diretoria de TI. Este departamento possui um grupo de líderes de testes que atuam sob demanda nos projetos na fase de teste. Os líderes participam das fases de planejamento e execução de testes por projeto, assim como alinhamento e discussão de defeitos com as fábricas de desenvolvimento e com os líderes técnicos durante a fase de execução dos testes. As fábricas de desenvolvimento são demandadas pelos contratos em utilizar metodologia ágil, porém o time de testes não possui visibilidade de quais métodos são aplicados, participam efetivamente dentro das releases com duração bimestrais e sprints de 15 dias cada. A organização onde foi realizado o estudo de caso, apesar de pregar a utilização de práticas ágeis, possuei um modelo adaptado onde as equipes possem papeis específicos, e não autoatribuídos como previsto em times ágeis, além de possuir um líder de testes focado nas atividades de teste. Este fato se deve ao fato da indústria de telecomunicações possuir alta demanda de mudanças em sistemas e ao fato de possuir múltiplos fornecedores. Apesar disso, a essência de entregas em releases periódicas e sprints quinzenais e consideração de outras práticas ágeis corroboram para a aplicação do estudo na avaliação dos indicadores.

Caracterização dos Participantes: 5 participantes atuaram na avaliação, todos graduados e um com pós-graduação. Todos já haviam executado atividades de medição antes. Todos os participantes possuem dez anos ou mais de experiência em TI, mais de um ano atuando dentro da organização do estudo e no mínimo dois anos na área de testes (sendo que dois possuíam mais de cinco anos). Foi realizada uma capacitação, com duração de 45 minutos, para explicar o conteúdo as fichas, as planilhas de apoio a medição e como reportar os resultados no formulário com as perguntas do TAM.

Avaliação do conteúdo das fichas de registro de indicadores: Após uma capacitação para utilização das fichas de indicadores, foram distribuídas aleatoriamente três fichas diferentes para cada participante, devido a questões de disponibilidade de tempo apontadas pelos próprios participantes. Cada participante foi responsável por simular a utilização das fichas sendo responsáveis por coletarem as medidas, gerarem os gráficos e analisar os resultados com base nas premissas e ações recomendadas pelas fichas. Para coleta das medidas cada participante atuou dentro do seu próprio projeto de testes com apoio das planilhas fornecidas para coleta, geração e análise dos resultados.

Análise dos resultados: Dados quantitativos coletados podem ser vistos na Fig. 2. A avaliação indica uma grande aceitação pelos participantes. Das 65 respostas, 44 indicaram "Concordo totalmente" com as afirmações, 18 indicaram "Concordo parcialmente” e 3 respostas indicaram “Indiferente”. Não houve respostas indicando discordância. Para as 3 respostas “Indiferente”, não é possível afirmar que haja risco aos resultados de forma geral, uma vez que foram concentrados em apenas 2 questões.

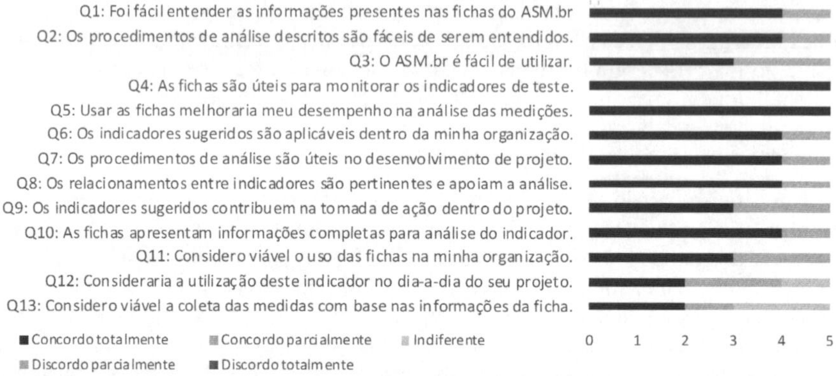

Fig. 2 – Resultado da avaliação

Assim, foi identificada a percepção de facilidade de entendimento das fichas e de seus conteúdos. Também se percebeu a utilidade dos indicadores dentro da organização no dia-a-dia dos participantes e de suas tarefas. Para o objetivo de interesse em usar as fichas é percebida uma pequena dificuldade de se viabilizar a utilização dos indicadores nos projetos da organização, talvez por alguma resistência de mudança nos procedimentos de coleta e análise de medidas dentro da organização ou por falta de um apoio gerencial de nível superior para adoção deste novo processo de coleta e análise.

Duas questões adicionais e subjetivas avaliaram o conjunto de indicadores que cada participante recebeu para análise: “Quais indicadores são mais interessantes na sua opinião para uma melhor gestão dos testes considerando o esforço para coleta e análise dos dados?” e “Você teria sugestões de melhoria para as fichas?”. Para a primeira, foi possível notar interesse dos participantes na melhoria dos indicadores e também a percepção de preferência por alguns indicadores possivelmente ligados ao cotidiano dos participantes, como o monitoramento de defeitos. Como ponto fraco, pode-se indicar uma pequena dificuldade de alguns participantes, pois as sugestões revelaram alguma confusão na análise dos procedimentos de relacionamentos. Uma possível explicação para isso pode ser a tentativa de comparação com os procedimentos usados atualmente pelos participantes ou pela falta deles. Em relação à segunda, as respostas recebidas citaram algumas poucas melhorias e sugestões, na sua maioria sugerindo adição de mais informações nas fichas. Algumas foram consideradas e podem ser vistas em [12].

Notou-se também que o tempo de análise da ficha não é longo (variando de 8 a 21 minutos, com média de 14 minutos), e não deve representar esforço adicional para o líder de testes ou gerente de projetos. Um dos participantes comentou que acredita que com maior utilização das fichas e dos indicadores, os tempos tendem a ser menores devido ao maior conhecimento dos procedimentos das fichas. Para a adoção das fichas de indicadores sugeridas nesta pesquisa, não se faz necessário um processo complexo de operacionalização. Entende-se que basta os responsáveis pelos projetos indicarem a utilização das planilhas de apoio a coleta e geração dos indicadores e utilizarem as fichas como de apoio para análise e ações a serem tomadas. Caso haja necessidade de alterações, as fichas podem ser customizadas para atender as premissas da organização.

Limitações e Ameaças à Validade: Havia o risco de dificuldade de avaliação pelos participantes pelo fato de não executarem ou utilizarem alguns indicadores propostos. Para minimizar este risco, durante a sessão de capacitação para avaliação das fichas dos indicadores, foi reforçado aos participantes o objetivo de analisar o indicador com foco nas ações, recomendações, fórmula de coleta e cálculo da medição e relacionamentos propostos. Cada ficha foi analisada apenas uma única vez. Com isso, não se pode afirmar que as avaliações realizadas são suficientes para confirmação de utilidade das fichas, sendo necessárias outras rodadas de avaliação.

A análise dos relacionamentos não foi realizada por completo, devido à limitação de apenas 3 fichas terem sido analisadas por cada participante. Os comentários relativos a esta parte da ficha foram baseados apenas nas informações descritas na parte de relacionamento da ficha principal. Assim, não se pode afirmar que os relacionamentos são pertinentes ou necessitam de ajustes quanto as sugestões de ações. A impossibilidade de coleta de todas as medidas não permitiu avaliar as planilhas de apoio para todos os indicadores nem avaliar se as premissas e conclusões na análise baseada em critérios são realmente pertinentes quando analisados dados reais de projeto, durante a monitoração dos testes. A coelta aconteceu em sua maioria em projetos já finalizados. Assim, apesar do *feedback* apresentado, as ações sugeridas não foram sido executadas.

O estudo envolveu apenas uma única organização. Desta forma seu resultado não é conclusivo, uma vez que pode significar adequação ao cenário desta organização e não à realidade de outras organizações ágeis que realizam testes de software.

6. Considerações Finais

Medição de software é importante para prover informações necessárias para tomar decisões no contexto organizacional e dos projetos. No entanto, medir também é considerada uma atividade não trivial e custosa. Contribuem para isso a falta de padronização dos termos utilizados, a existência de muitas fontes sobre indicadores que podem ser utilizados e a pouca profundidade das informações sobre os relacionamentos existentes entre os indicadores, assim como detalhamento de coleta e análise.

Este trabalho propôs um conjunto de fichas de indicadores de medição para testes em contexto ágil utilizando o template ASM.br para registro dos indicadores, informações de coleta e medição, e análise baseada em critérios e relacionamentos. Realizou-se um estudo de caso com profissionais que atuam na gestão de projetos de teste. Constatou-se evidências de que as fichas são fáceis de serem entendidas, demonstram ser úteis para apoio no gerenciamento e os participantes mostram interesse em seu uso. As fichas podem ser adaptadas a outras organizações com base em suas necessidades, e podem ser consideradas como ponto inicial para implementação de um plano de medição. As planilhas de coleta de medidas também auxiliam o cálculo automático dos indicadores e dos gráficos após inserção das medidas necessárias.

Trabalhos futuros incluem a extensão do conjunto de indicadores pela replicação do mapeamento sistemático em outras bibliotecas de busca, a avaliação das fichas em novos estudos de caso e o uso das fichas durante a execução de projetos reais. Além disso, pode-se citar a automatização da geração das fichas baseadas no template ASM.br e o apoio à coleta automática dos indicadores e geração dos gráficos para análise.

Agradecimentos. Os autores agradecem à FAPERJ (projetos E-26/010.000883/2016, E-26/010.001644/2016) e à UNIRIO (PQ-UNIRIO 01/2017) pelo auxílio financeiro.

Referências

1.ABRANTES, J., F.: "Estudos Experimentais sobre Agilidade no Desenvolvimento de Software e sua Utilização no Processo de Teste", Tese de Doutorado, UFRJ, COPPE, Rio de Janeiro – Brasil (2012)

2. BARCELLOS, M. P., FALBO, R., A., DALMORO, R.: "A Well-Founded Software Measurement Ontology." In: 6th International Conference on Formal Ontology in Information Systems (FOIS 2010), Toronto - Canada. Frontiers in Artificial Intelligence and Applications. Amsterdam: IOS Press, v. 209, pp. 213-226 (2010)

3. Basili, V.R., Rombach, H.D. And Caldiera, G.: "Goal Question Metric Paradigm". Encyclopedia of Software Engineering, 2 Volume Set, John Wiley & Sons, Inc (1994)

4. McGARRY, J., CARD, D., LAYMAN, B., CLARCK, E., DEAN, J., HALL, F.: "Practical Software Measurement: objective information for decision makers. Prentice Hall (2012)

5.BASS, L.: "Constructing Superior Software; Applying Proven Practices", New Riders Publishing, Thousand Oaks, CA, USA (1999)

6.BONELLI, S., SANTOS, G., BARCELLOS, M.: "ASM.br: A Template for Specifying Indicators", Proceedings of the 21st International Conference on Evaluation and Assessment in Software Engineering (EASE'17), Karlskrona, Sweden, pp 208-213 (2017). DOI: 10.1145/3084226.3084280.

7. DAVIS, F. D.; BAGOZZI, R. P.; WARSHAW, P. R.: User acceptance of computer technology: A comparison of two theoretical models, Management Science 35: 982– 1003 (1989)

8.BORTOLUCI, R., DUDUCHI, M.: "Indicadores para teste de software em desenvolvimento ágil",X Workshop de Pós-graduação e Pesquisa Centro Paula Souza, São Paulo, Brazil (2015)

9.JANUS, A., SCHMIETENDORF, A., DUMKE, R., JAGER, J.: "The 3C approach for Agile Quality Assurance". 3rd International Workshop on Emerging Trends in Software Metrics (WETSoM), Zurique, Suiça (2012). DOI: 10.1109/WETSoM.2012.6226998

10.KITCHENHAM, B., CHARTERS, S.: "Guidelines for Performing Systematic Literature Reviews in Software Engineering", EBSE Technical Report EBSE-2007-01 (2007)

11. VICENTE, A. A: "Definição e gerenciamento de métricas de teste no contexto de métodos ágeis, Dissertação de Mestrado, Instituto de Ciências Matemáticas e de Computação – ICMC/USP, São Carlos, Brazil (2010)

12.LIMA, D. S. "Indicadores de Medição de Testes em Projetos Ágeis, Dissertação de Mestrado, Universidade Federal do Estado do Rio de Janeiro – UNIRIO, Brasil (2017). Disponível em: https://goo.gl/Hvcj9a. Último acesso: 18/12/2017.

13. ROCHA, A. R., BARCELLOS, M. P. e SANTOS, G.: "Medição de Software e Controle Estatístico de Processos", Ministério da Ciência, Tecnologia e Inovação - SEPIN - PBQP Software (2012)

14.MOTA, T., DIAS-NETO, A.: "Mapeamento Sistemático sobre métricas no Contexto de Métodos Ágeis aplicadas a testes de software", Workshop Anual do MPS (WAMPS), Campinas, Brasil (2014)

15. PETERSEN K., VAKKALANKA S., KUZNIARZ L.: Guidelines for conducting systematic mapping studies in software engineering: An update. In: Information and Software Technology. Vol. 64, pp 1–18 (2015). DOI 10.1016/j.infsof.2015.03.007

16.POOJA, J., PATNAIK, K.S: "Applicability of Process Capability Analysis in Metrifying Quality of Software", Department of CSE, BIT, Mesra, Ranchi, India (2016)

17.RATHOD, N.: "Test Orchestration, A framerwork for Continuos Integration and Continuos Deployment", 2015 International Conference on Pervasive Computing (ICPC) (2015)

Um Estudo sobre a Percepção do Uso de Métodos Ágeis por Equipes de Infraestrutura de TI durante a Transformação Ágil

Gian Biolchini Abi-Saber[1], Gleison Santos[2]

[1] Departamento de Informática Aplicada – DIA/CCET
[2] Programa de Pós-Graduação em Informática – PPGI
UNIRIO – Universidade Federal do Estado do Rio de Janeiro
Av. Pasteur 458, Urca – CEP 22290-240 – Rio de Janeiro – RJ – Brasil
{gian.saber, gleison.santos}@uniriotec.br

Abstract. *Contexto*: É cada vez mais comum que organizações de diferentes indústrias se afastem dos métodos tradicionais e adotem práticas e metodologias ágeis visando melhorar a produtividade e o atendimento da demanda dos clientes. Apesar disso, não são tão comuns relatos dessa adoção em organizações ou equipes fora do desenvolvimento de software. *Objetivo*: Esse trabalho investiga uma organização passando por uma transformação ágil e visa analisar se o uso das metodologias ágeis por áreas fora do escopo de desenvolvimento de software geram benefícios de acordo com a percepção e experiência dos envolvidos. *Método*: Foi executado um survey em três equipes de infraestrutura de uma mesma empresa multinacional de TI (Tecnologia de Informação) que, há aproximadamente 1 ano, decidiu implementar os princípios e valores ágeis em sua cultura organizacional. *Resultados:* Os fatores de influência positiva no sucesso mais citados foram coaching e treinamento, suporte da gerência e engajamento com as metodologias. Os de influência negativa foram resistência a mudança, falta de experiência com métodos ágeis e perseverança da forma antiga de trabalho. A prática ágil identificada como mais benéfica foi a definição de histórias e divisão de tarefas. *Conclusões*: De forma geral, a maioria dos respondentes acredita que as metodologias ágeis são benéficas e podem ser usadas em diferentes tipos de equipes e áreas.

Keywords: Métodos Ágeis, Transformação Ágil, Mudança Organizacional.

1 Introdução

Tem sido cada vez mais comum a adoção de métodos ágeis de desenvolvimento em detrimento dos métodos ditos tracionais. Desde a criação do Manifesto Ágil, a comunidade acadêmica vem tendo crescente interesse nos problemas que envolvem desenvolvimento de software e áreas relacionadas, isso se comprova pelo aumento do número de países engajados em pesquisas acerca do tópico e pelo aumento de artigos acadêmicos publicados [5]. Nos métodos tradicionais, os requisitos do projeto devem ser antecipados e planejados a fim de evitar custos adicionais e retrabalho com mudanças que possam vir a ocorrer. Porém, tentar evitar essas mudanças de forma antecipada significa não ser responsivo frente às constantes demandas do mercado. Diferentes ações, como medição contínua, identificação de erros e refinamento do processo, tentam eliminar essas variações do processo, pois assumem que são consequências da falta de planejamento ou de erros, mas o que esses métodos não consideram é o fato de que imprevistos e mudanças, além de serem inevitáveis, são um fator crítico para a estratégia do negócio [2]. As metodologias ágeis vêm sendo adotadas crescentemente por diferentes organizações para reduzir o custo de resposta a essas mudanças [5].

Conboy [3] afirma que as pesquisas acerca de métodos ágeis têm ganhado impulso, mas ressalta o fato de que a maioria desses estudos são relativos aos métodos práticos definidos pela indústria e que não abordam outros temas conceituais. Apesar de as metodologias ágeis e suas propostas de engajamento serem comumente usadas no escopo de software, os seus princípios e artefatos também podem ser aplicados a outras organizações que não desenvolvem software. O "*11th annual State of Agile*" [14] colheu informações de diversas empresas e concluiu que a aplicação do ágil entre organizações de todas as indústrias está crescendo de forma acelerada. Isso se torna evidente pelo fato de 77% dos participantes que responderam a pesquisa não trabalhavam para empresas de software, um número significativamente maior quando comparado ao ano anterior. No entanto, mesmo com esse crescente aumento, ainda são poucos os relatos de uso de práticas e metodologias ágeis em organizações ou equipes que não são de desenvolvimento de software.

Esse trabalho tem por objetivo investigar uma organização que está passando por um processo de transformação ágil e analisar se o uso das metodologias ágeis por áreas fora do escopo de desenvolvimento de software geram benefícios de acordo com a percepção e experiência de diferentes equipes. O resultado da pesquisa evidenciou que os integrantes das equipes de infraestrutura, em geral, acreditam que as metodologias ágeis são benéficas e podem ser usadas em diferentes tipos de equipes e áreas.

O estudo foi realizado por meio de um *survey* tendo em foco três equipes de uma mesma empresa multinacional de TI (Tecnologia da Informação) que aproximadamente um ano decidiu implementar os princípios e valores ágeis em sua cultura organizacional. Essas equipes foram formadas especialmente para essa mudança organizacional, ainda estão em processo de aprendizagem e ganho de maturidade ágil no novo modelo de trabalho. A pesquisa também foi enviada a profissionais da mesma empresa que trabalham na área de desenvolvimento de software para comparação e análise da percepção deles acerca do tema.

Além desta introdução, este artigo está estruturado da seguinte forma: a Seção 2 apresenta uma revisão da literatura sobre a Transformação Ágil, a Seção 3 apresenta a metodologia da pesquisa utilizada, a Seção 4 contém as discussões dos resultados do *survey*, por fim, a Seção 5 apresenta as considerações finais.

2 Métodos Ágeis e Transformação Ágil

Agilidade não é um conceito único de desenvolvimento de software, sua primeira aparição se deu na literatura tradicional do campo de negócios em 1991 e desde então o termo vem sendo amplamente utilizado em diversos temas e disciplinas desse domínio [3]. Highsmith e Cockburn [8] discutem que agilidade está relacionada diretamente à criação e resposta a mudanças, afirmando que a característica mais inovadora da agilidade não são os métodos e as práticas em si, mas o reconhecimento de que as pessoas são o fator primordial para o sucesso do projeto.

Definições de agilidade inspiradas principalmente da indústria manufatureira e da área de negócios vêm sendo criadas de forma crescente [5]. Conboy [3] analisou as várias definições de agilidade de diferentes disciplinas, fazendo uma distinção entre agilidade, flexibilidade e simplicidade (*leanness*). Com essas análises, ele chega a uma das definições mais abrangentes de desenvolvimento ágil: "*A contínua disponibilidade de um método de desenvolvimento de sistemas de informação de criar mudanças de maneira rápida e intrínseca, abraçar a mudança pró-ativamente ou re-ativamente, e aprender com a mudança enquanto contribui com valor percebido ao cliente (economia, qualidade e simplicidade), através de seus componentes coletivos e relacionamentos com seu ambiente*" [3].

A adoção de métodos ágeis é algo relativamente novo para algumas organizações de TI (Tecnologia da Informação). Realizar uma transformação ágil em toda uma organização é algo desafiador e complexo, principalmente para aquelas que possuem estrutura e normas organizacionais voltadas à criação de um único plano (métodos tradicionais) para desenvolvimento de seus projetos [11]. Com o objetivo de definir agilidade de um ponto de vista de gerenciamento de projeto e desenvolvimento de produtos fora do escopo de desenvolvimento de software foi definida a Declaração de Interdependência (DOI) que conecta pessoas, projetos e valor a abordagem ágil [9]. Para Cockburn [2] essa declaração corresponde à versão não-software do manifesto ágil. Os seis pontos da Declaração de Interdependência são [10]:

- Aumentamos o retorno do investimento, tornando o fluxo contínuo de valor o nosso foco;
- Entregamos resultados confiáveis, engajando os clientes em iterações frequentes e propriedade compartilhada;
- Gerenciamos incertezas através de iterações, antecipação e adaptação;
- Promovemos criatividade e inovação reconhecendo que indivíduos são a fonte definitiva de valor e criando um ambiente em que eles possam fazer a diferença;
- Impulsionamos o desempenho por meio do compromisso do grupo em obter resultados e da responsabilidade compartilhada pela eficácia do time;
- Melhoramos a eficácia e a confiabilidade por meio de estratégias situacionais específicas, processo e práticas".

Uma organização precisa saber quando efetivamente se tornou ágil. A literatura não define o ponto exato em que uma organização é considerada ágil, em geral, a agilidade está mais relacionada com a forma com que se responde a diferentes cenários do que a práticas predefinidas em si [9]. Mas a agilidade no escopo organizacional precisa de algo que possa ser desenvolvido, entregue e medido [9], pois organizações são sistemas de adaptação complexos. Isso significa que indivíduos independentes e descentralizados interagem de maneira auto-organizada guiados por um conjunto de regras simples e generalistas, tendo como objetivo gerar inovação e resultados [8].

As mudanças necessárias para uma transformação ágil envolvem toda a estrutura da organização, desde papéis e responsabilidades das pessoas a cultura da organização em si. Gandomani e Nafchi [7] chegam a definir essa transformação como uma "mutação organizacional". Eles afirmam que essa mutação não é algo simples, pois além de necessitar de tempo e esforço, diversos desafios e impedimentos relacionados a fatores humanos são encontrados durante o processo. Dikert *et al.* [6], Gandomani e Nafchi [7], Waardenburg e Vliet [15] destacam e analisam diversos impedimentos relacionados ao comportamento humano que representam pontos críticos durante a transição ágil de uma organização, esses pontos foram: falta de conhecimento, problemas culturais, resistência à mudança, mentalidade errada (*wrong mindset*) e falta de colaboração efetiva do time e de diferentes áreas da organização.

Dikert *et al.* [6] também analisaram os principais fatores que levam ao sucesso de uma transformação ágil de larga escala em uma organização, os 29 pontos foram identificados e distribuídos em 11 fatores: apoio da gerência, comprometimento com a mudança, liderança, escolha e adaptação da abordagem ágil, criação de um piloto, *coaching* e treinamento, pessoas engajadas, transparência e comunicação, mentalidade (*mindset*), autonomia do time, gerência de requisitos.

Todos esses 11 fatores mostram que a transformação ágil em larga escala não pode ser feita apenas seguindo um processo predeterminado, é necessária uma customização da metodologia para se adequar às necessidades da organização. A transformação não só inclui a aplicação da metodologia em si, mas do entendimento dos valores e princípios por trás das práticas pelas pessoas da organização [6]. Uma organização que quer se adequar ao modelo ágil precisa fazer ajustes em seu negócio como um todo [2].

Não são comuns os relatos de uso de práticas e metodologias ágeis em organizações ou equipes que não são de desenvolvimento de software. Um dos exemplos é o da empresa Salesforce.com [4] que passou por uma profunda transformação ágil em todas as áreas da organização e decidiu adotar o Scrum, gerando bons resultados. Salengue [12] apresenta um relato sobre uma empresa de TI de médio porte que aplicou o Scrum em uma equipe de infraestrutura cujas atividades envolvem atividades operacionais e de gestão. Segundo o autor, o time foi bastante receptivo frente à nova forma de trabalho e o consenso foi que após 7 meses de constante aprimoramento o time passou a ter uma melhor comunicação e a atender as demandas de cada sprint. Após 14 sprints, a taxa de conclusão das demandas se tornou significativamente melhor, visto que a pontuação de demanda era cerca de 40% maior do que na sprint 1 e, mesmo assim, nenhum integrante deixou de concluir suas demandas.

Waldron [13] mostra como a empresa LexisNexis implementou metodologias ágeis e seus valores em toda sua organização, na expectativa de descobrir novas formas de entregar seus produtos e aprimorá-los. A mudança afetou múltiplos departamentos da empresa no Reino Unido e em outros países, gerando benefícios que vão além do desenvolvimento de software, por exemplo: divisão de prioridades, aumento da visão de progresso e de resultados, implementações mais rápidas de melhorias no produto e um melhor planejamento com os times. As práticas ágeis adotadas foram: quadros kanban, reuniões diárias (*daily standups*), retrospectivas e reuniões de planejamento. A empresa também teve desafios durante a transformação: devido à resistência à mudança, um período de adaptação foi necessário. Segundo o autor, o fator chave na implementação da agilidade foi adaptar de forma precisa as metodologias ágeis atendendo às características únicas da organização. Apesar de todos os desafios, a transformação gerou benefícios reais (melhores serviços e produtos) e permitiu com que ela se tornasse mais flexível frente às mudanças da sua área de negócios [13].

3. Metodologia de Pesquisa

Definição do Objetivo da Pesquisa e Método Utilizado – O objetivo da pesquisa é analisar por meio de um *survey* se o uso das metodologias ágeis por áreas fora do escopo de desenvolvimento de software geram benefícios de acordo com a percepção e experiência de diferentes equipes. Considerando as vantagens e limitações expostas e outras questões como tamanho da amostra, tempo disponível para sua aplicação e objetivo da pesquisa, preferiu-se a adoção do modelo survey descritivo interseccional [1]. Neste tipo de *survey*, os dados são coletados em um curto espaço de tempo por meio de uma amostra selecionada do mesmo período de tempo e possibilita determinar relações entre variáveis [1]. Deve-se notar, também, que, no escopo dessa pesquisa, não se pretende generalizar os resultados fora da população estudada.

Elaboração e Estruturação do Questionário – Durante a criação do questionário, o número de perguntas foi otimizado para poupar esforço dos respondentes (por exemplo, lista de práticas, fatores de impacto e beneficio foram consolidados) e evitar possíveis problemas em seu comprometimento com as respostas. A disposição das perguntas foi organizada de forma consistente e otimizada em 5 partes, descritas a seguir, a fim de facilitar o entendimento dos respondentes e a análise de seus resultados.

- *Parte 1: Identificação e caracterização do pesquisado.* Visa caracterizar o perfil do respondente.
- *Parte 2: Percepção sobre as metodologias utilizadas atualmente e maturidade organizacional.* Nessa parte identifica-se quais metodologias o respondente utilizava no momento da execução da pesquisa e seu grau de satisfação acerca de seu uso. Também se pergunta a percepção do profissional sobre o nível de maturidade de sua organização em relação aos métodos ágeis. Esses dados são úteis para entender melhor qual a visão dos profissionais de uma mesma organização acerca do uso das metodologias e da própria organização.
- *Parte 3: Influência de fatores positivos e negativos no sucesso das equipes ágeis.* Nessa parte, deseja-se identificar qual o grau de benefício percebido pelos respondentes em relação aos principais fatores de sucesso das equipes ágeis. Também deseja-se identificar o grau de impacto percebido pelos respondentes em relação aos principais fatores de impedimento no sucesso das equipes ágeis. A lista de fatores apresentadas foi baseada em [6].
- *Parte 4: Utilização dos métodos ágeis seus benefícios.* Nessa parte, as perguntas são relacionadas ao uso das principais práticas ágeis pelos respondentes e seus benefícios percebidos. As perguntas também questionam se são feitas alterações nas práticas para melhor adaptação ao cenário de sua equipe.
- *Parte 5: Percepção do respondente acerca do uso de métodos ágeis para áreas dentro e fora de desenvolvimento de software.* Visa identificar a opinião e o grau de benefício percebido pelo respondente acerca do uso de metodologias ágeis dentro e fora do escopo de software. Essa parte representa o tema central de estudo deste trabalho, sendo essencial que as informações obtidas sejam correlacionadas durante a fase de análise dos dados.

Foi realizado um piloto com a intenção de identificar problemas e melhorias no questionário. O piloto foi respondido por um profissional fora da organização com 3 anos de experiência com metodologias ágeis e que trabalha em uma empresa considerada referência acerca do tema. Como resultado desse piloto, algumas questões forem revistas, por não serem consideradas claras o suficiente, e alguns campos obrigatórios foram definidos como opcionais, para reduzir o tempo mínimo de resposta.

Instrumento de Distribuição do Questionário – O Google Forms foi o meio de distribuição escolhido para realização desse *survey*. Foi incluída uma apresentação inicial, com o objetivo e tema do trabalho, a garantia de anonimato dos respondentes e informações para contato em caso de dúvidas. Com exceção de alguns dos textos de campo livre que são opcionais, a ferramenta foi configurada de maneira que todas as perguntas devessem ser respondidas, ou seja, respostas em branco não eram possíveis.

Amostra – A limitação que o próprio escopo do trabalho cria foi um dos principais motivos para adoção de uma amostra não probabilística, pois os membros escolhidos para responder o questionário devem pertencer à mesma organização, ter experiência com métodos ágeis e uma parcela deles deve trabalhar em áreas fora do escopo de desenvolvimento de software, tornando a escalabilidade dessa amostra extremamente difícil. O tempo disponível para a distribuição, análise da pesquisa e a ausência de recursos financeiros também foram fatores que influenciaram nessa decisão. Dado esses fatos e critérios, o tipo de amostra que mais se adequou às características desse trabalho foi a amostragem por julgamento.

Uma requisição de participação, juntamente com a URL para a pesquisa, foi enviada por e-mail através de uma lista de contatos composta pelos integrantes das três equipes de infraestrutura de uma mesma organização que está passando por um processo de transformação ágil. Os integrantes possuem uma faixa etária entre 29 e 60 anos e já possuem experiência prévia nos setores que atuam. Os participantes (previamente conhecidos) se adequam aos critérios de seleção citados. Adicionalmente, as perguntas abordadas na Parte 1 do questionário serviram como mais uma forma de filtrar e selecionar os elementos da amostra, assegurando dessa forma a amostragem por julgamento. A amostra é composta pelos integrantes das equipes a seguir:

- *Equipe A*: É composta por 6 integrantes e trata da parte operacional de redes ("*network*") da própria empresa (nível Brasil) e projetos de infraestrutura que tangem a mesma área.
- *Equipe B*: É composta por 6 integrantes e é responsável pela distribuição de computadores e celulares aos funcionários, pela coordenação de todo suporte ao executivo e também é responsável por toda a estratégia e gerenciamento da área de multimídia (webconferências, salas de telepresença, softwares de streaming) e impressoras no Brasil.
- *Equipe C*: É composta por 8 integrantes e tem as mesmas atividades dos times A e B, atua para a América Latina (México, Argentina, Colômbia, Peru, Uruguai, Chile, Venezuela e Equador).

Uma amostra paralela composta por 5 desenvolvedores de software da mesma organização também foi analisada para comparação e análise da percepção deles acerca do uso de metodologias ágeis fora do escopo de software.

4. Análise dos Resultados

A análise dos resultados foi feita utilizando principalmente o cálculo da distribuição de frequências absoluta: quantidade de vezes que um valor aparece na amostra, e relativa, razão entre a frequência absoluta e o tamanho da amostra. Apesar de o questionário ter sido enviado a 20 pessoas (sem contar a amostra paralela), a amostra é composta por 17 respondentes, sendo que 6 deles pertecem a equipe A, 4 são da equipe B, 7 da equipe C. Como o escopo do trabalho e a composição das equipes é similar, decidiu-se por apresentar as respostas de forma consolidada. Além disso, não se observou nenhum padrão de respostas que diferenciasse as 3 equipes de infraestrutura, No caso da amostra paralela de desenvolvedores, obteve-se 5 respostas.

Perfil da Amostra - A maioria dos participantes da pesquisa declarou ter entre 1 e 3 anos de experiência com práticas e metodologias ágeis (52%) e ocupar cargos Sênior ou de Gerente (64%). Apesar do alto nível de experiência na área por parte dos pesquisados (ver Fig. 1(a)), apenas 18% da amostra declararam ter mais de cinco anos de experiência com métodos ágeis, como visto na Fig. 1(b).

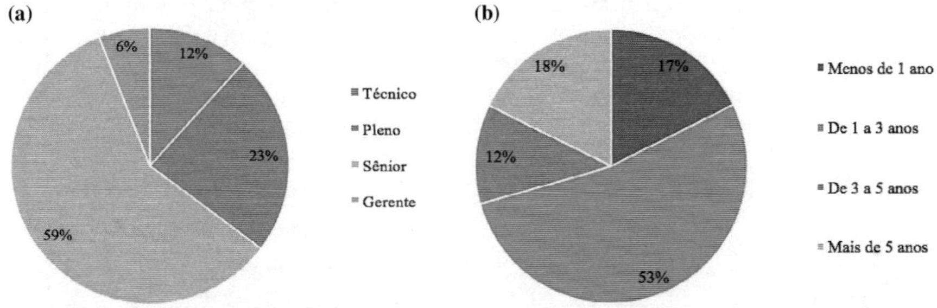

Fig. 1. **(a)** Grau Hierárquico na Empresa e **(b)** Tempo de experiência com métodos ágeis

Percepção sobre as metodologias e a organização – Os profissionais foram indagados sobre quais metodologias ágeis eles utilizam em seus projetos. Os dados obtidos mostraram que a metodologia mais utilizada foi o Scrum, sendo identificado por 81% dos respondentes. Atenta-se ao fato de que o questionário permitiu a seleção de múltiplas respostas nessa pergunta, ou seja, os profissionais podem responder que utilizam múltiplas metodologias ágeis. Dada essa informação, ao se analisar os resultados apresentados na Fig. 2(a), verifica-se que 76% dos respondentes das equipes A, B e C relatam adotar múltiplas metodologias, ou seja, apesar de o Scrum ser o método mais utilizado, as equipes também utilizam práticas de outros métodos ágeis, por exemplo, o Kanban.

Em relação ao grau de satisfação das equipes A, B e C com a(s) metodologia(s) adotada(s), ao se analisar a Fig. 2(b), percebe-se claramente que a maioria (53%) dos respondentes estão satisfeitos com o uso dessas metodologias. Apesar disso, 41% dos respondentes ainda não se sentem totalmente satisfeitos, sendo que somente 1 profissional se mostrou levemente insatisfeito com a adoção dos métodos ágeis.

Um campo de texto livre para que os respondentes justificassem sua resposta e expressassem suas opiniões foi incluído no questionário. Após a análise e consolidação de suas justificativas, identificou-se que existem pontos positivos e negativos independentes do grau de satisfação do profissional. Devido à semelhança das respostas de todas as equipes, as respostas foram consolidadas e destacadas de acordo com sua frequência. Sendo assim, os pontos positivos mais citados acerca da adoção da metodologia ágil, foram: (i) Gera valor agregado ao negócio; (ii) Melhoria contínua a cada ciclo; (ii) Representa uma forma eficiente de se trabalhar; e (iv) Melhoria visível do relacionamento com o cliente e o time.

Quanto aos benefícios gerados pela metodologia utilizada, um profissional respondeu:

> "*As entregas parciais entregam valor mais rápido aos clientes, as dúvidas (blockers) são rapidamente sanadas, as reuniões de acompanhamento permitem que observemos os pontos negativos da sprint e possamos melhorá-los no futuro, e nos faz ficar mais próximos dos clientes.*" (Estagiário, 1 a 3 anos de experiência com métodos ágeis)

Os pontos negativos mais comumente encontrados nas respostas de menor grau de satisfação foram: (i) Área de atuação não favorece a adoção da metodologia; (ii) Período de muitas mudanças organizacionais e necessidade constante de se adaptar a nova forma de trabalho geram resistência dos times; (iii) Falta de conhecimento tanto teórico como prático impacta na execução das metodologias; e (iv) Medição e documentação geram preocupação. Uma possível explicação para o último item é o fato de o uso das metodologias evidenciarem onde está o gargalo da execução das tarefas e essa informação ser utilizada para prejudicar algum membro do time.

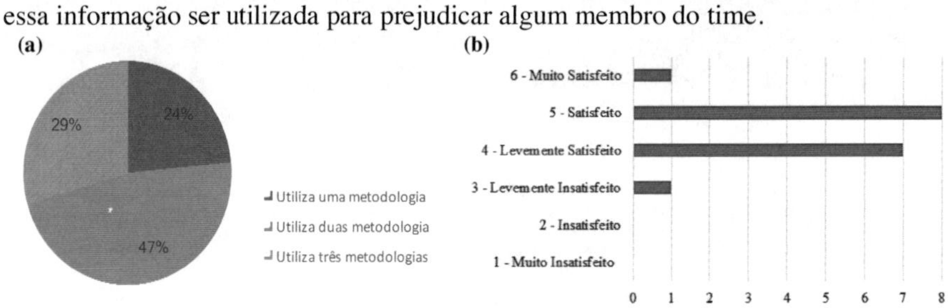

Fig. 2. **(a)** Adoção de Múltiplas Metodologias Ágeis e **(b)** Grau de Satisfação com as Métodologias.

A pergunta seguinte do questionário abordou a percepção dos profissionais da amostra sobre a percepcção de maturidade da organização em relação ao uso de metodologias ágeis. Na Fig. 3, pode se observar que 86% dos respondentes acreditam que a organização ainda está em processo de amadurecimento no que tange às metodologias ágeis. Apenas uma pequena parcela (14%) crê que a organização tem um alto nível de competência ágil ou é referência no uso de metodologias ágeis no contexto pesquisado. Nenhum dos profissionais respondeu que a organização não possui iniciativas ágeis ou que ela seja referência no que tange métodos ágeis no mercado.

Um campo de texto livre para que os participantes justificassem as respostas. Apesar de identificadas duas respostas diferentes acerca da percepção de maturidade ágil da organização, ao se analisar as justificativas dos respondentes, praticamente ambas chegam a um consenso: que a organização já adota em diversas áreas as práticas e técnicas ágeis, mas seu processo de transformação e adaptação ainda está ocorrendo.

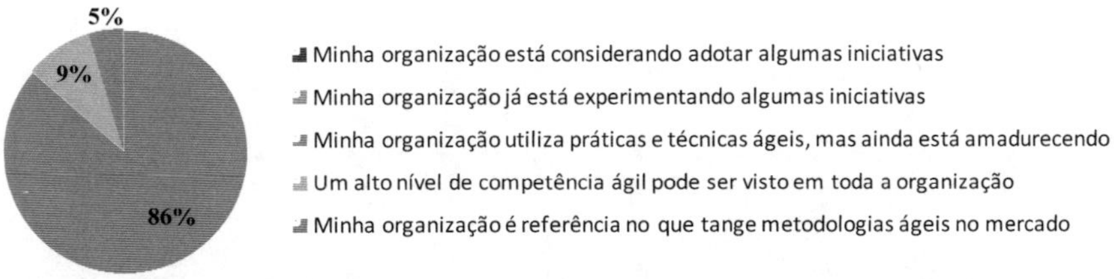

Fig. 3. Nivel de maturidade da organização de acordo com a percepção de múltiplos respondentes.

Pontos positivos e negativos no sucesso de equipes ágeis – Correspondendo à Parte 3 do questionário, desejou-se identificar qual o grau de benefício percebido pelos respondentes em relação aos principais fatores de sucesso das equipes ágeis. Ao se analisar a Fig. 4, identifica-se que aproximadamente 70% dos respondentes das equipes A, B e C creem que os 10 fatores expostos possuem influência alta ou muito alta para o sucesso de equipes ágeis. As 5 variáveis avaliadas com maior grau de influência pelos respondentes das equipes foram: *coaching* e treinamento, suporte da gerência, pessoas engajadas com as metodologias, mentalidade alinhada aos princípios e valores ágeis e pessoas abertas a mudanças.

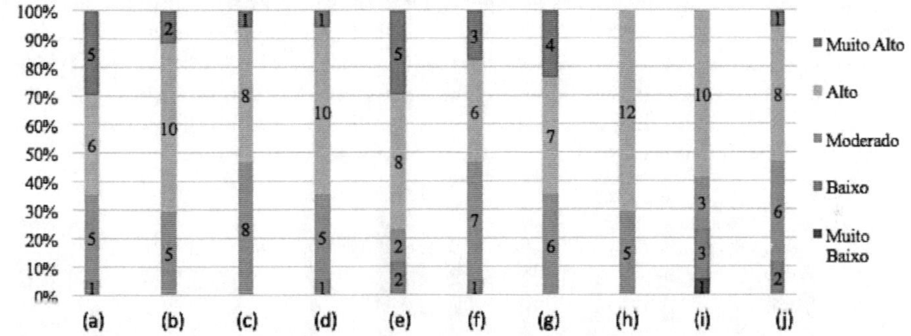

Fig. 4. Fatores de Influência no Sucesso de Equipes Ágeis: (a) Apoio da gerência; (b) Pessoas abertas a mudanças; (c) Liderança; (d) Escolha e adaptação da abordagem ágil; (e) *Coaching* e treinamento; (f) Mentalidade (*mindset*) alinhada aos valores e princípios ágeis; (g) Pessoas engajadas com a metodologia; (h) Transparência e comunicação; (i) Tipo possui autonomia para tomar decisões; (j) Requisitos do negócio bem definidos e entendidos.

Também desejou-se identificar o grau de impacto percebido pelos respondentes em relação aos principais fatores que podem ocasionar problemas nas equipes ágeis, como pode ser visto na Fig. 5.As 5 variáveis avaliadas com maior grau de impacto negativo pelos respondentes, considerando respostas Alto e Muito Alto, foram: resistência a mudança, falta de experiência com métodos ágeis, perseverança da forma antiga de trabalho, práticas e processos inconsistentes, preocupação acerca de papéis e responsabilidades na nova estrutura da organização.

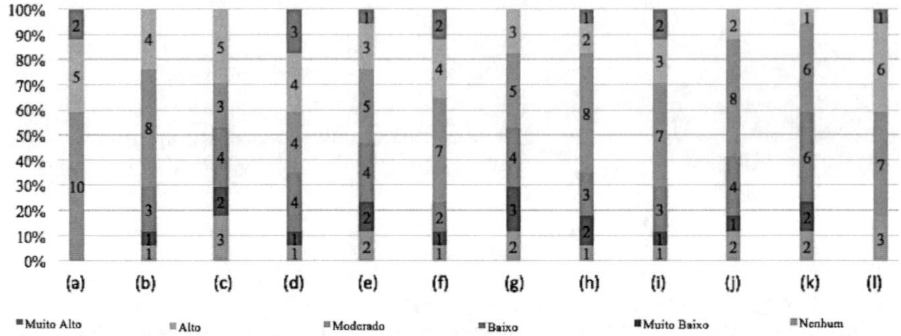

Fig. 5. Fatores de Impacto Negativo nas Equipes Ágeis: (a) Falta de experiência com métodos ágeis; (b) Cultura da organização não está alinhada com a filosofia ágil; (c) Falta do suporte gerencial; (d) Resistência a mudança; (e) Treinamento insuficiente; (f) Perseverança da forma antiga de trabalho; (g) Falta de colaboração efetiva do time; (h) Falta de colaboração de outras áreas da organização; (i) Práticas e processos inconsistentes; (j) Mentalidade Errada (*Wrong Mindset*); (k) Integrantes da equipe distribuídos geograficamente; (l) Preocupação acerca de papéis e responsabilidades na nova estrutura da organização.

Experiência acerca das práticas ágeis: Desejou-se identificar quais práticas os respondentes utilizam, se fazem algum tipo de adaptação e sua percepção acerca delas. Na Figura 6 percebe-se que 66% dos respondentes das equipes A, B e C acreditam que as 12 práticas utilizadas são benéficas para seus projetos e que apenas 21% deles utilizam essas práticas de forma adaptada. Esse resultado é esperado, visto que elas não exigem conhecimentos específicos de desenvolvimento de software.

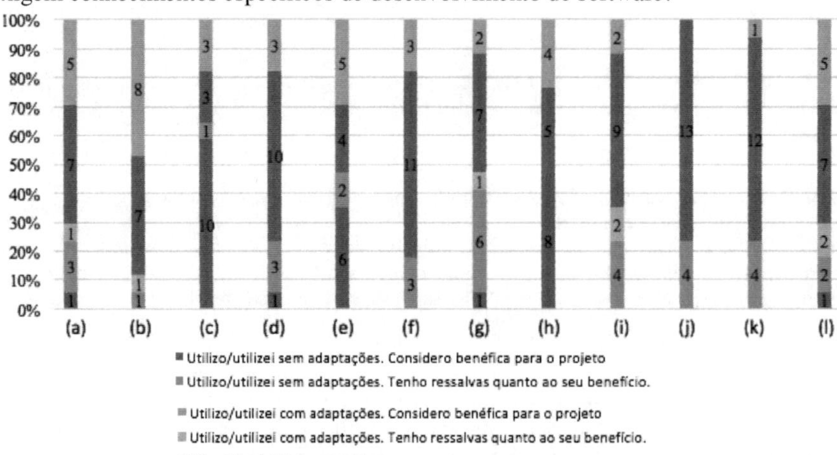

Fig. 6 – Experiência dos respondentes no uso de metodologias ágeis: (a) Duração preestabelecida das sprints; (b) Definição das historias e divisão de tarefas; (c) Gráfico Burndown; (d) Planning Poker; (e) Scrum of Scrums; (f) Backlog do Produto; (g) Mapeamento do Sentimento da Equipe; (h) Quadro Kanban; (i) Reuniões Diárias; (j) Reuniões de Planejamento; (k) Reuniões de retrospectiva; (l) Entregas curtas e frequentes.

A Tabela 1 foi criada consolidando as respostas das equipes A, B e C e estruturada de acordo com critérios relativos às práticas mais votadas.

Tabela 1. Práticas mais votadas

Critério	**Equipe A, B e C**
Prática mais benéfica	Definição de histórias e divisão de tarefas
Prática menos benéfica	Mapeamento do sentimento da equipe
Prática mais adaptada	Definição de histórias e divisão de tarefas
Prática menos utilizada	Gráfico *Burndown*

Percepção do uso de métodos ágeis em diferentes áreas: Essa parte representa o tema central de estudo deste trabalho, identificando a opinião e o grau de benefício percebido dos respondentes acerca do uso de metodologias ágeis fora do escopo de software. A Fig. 7 mostra que 18% (3 pessoas) dos participantes acreditam que o benefício seja baixo, mas 82% (14) dos respondentes acreditam que as metodologias proporcionam um bom grau de benefício ao serem usadas por equipes fora do escopo de software. Em geral, os participantes com percepção negativa mencionam a necessidade de adaptação da metodologia para funcionar no escopo de infraestrutura. Apesar de as afirmações corroborarem com a literatura que as metodologias ágeis precisam ser adaptadas para atender as necessidades das equipes, isto pode indicar uma percepção da dificuldade de se fazer essa adaptação ou a não adequação da das adaptações realizadas no contexto da organização pesquisada. Em relação a percepção de alto benefício, destaca-se a resposta de um dos profissionais:

> *"A adaptação pode ser mais lenta, o sentimento de efetividade menor no início, mas o ganho com o mindset de equipe é praticamente imensurável. Os times têm por padrão se isolarem em nichos de atuação e as interações são sempre em problemas de grande impacto, deteriorando os relacionamentos e não proporcionando ambientes saudáveis. Com as metodologias ágeis, as equipes interagem diariamente e são "forçadas" a trabalharem unidas em função do melhor coletivo. É como um mantra, O sucesso não é meu, é coletivo, assim como o fracasso, mas se todos se ajudarem, mesmo o fracasso coletivo levará a aprendizados importantes, ajustes necessários em busca da melhoria contínua para o time. Este, para mim, é o maior legado do ágil para infraestrutura."* (Pleno da área de infraestrutura, possui de 3 a 5 anos de experiência com metodologias ágeis)

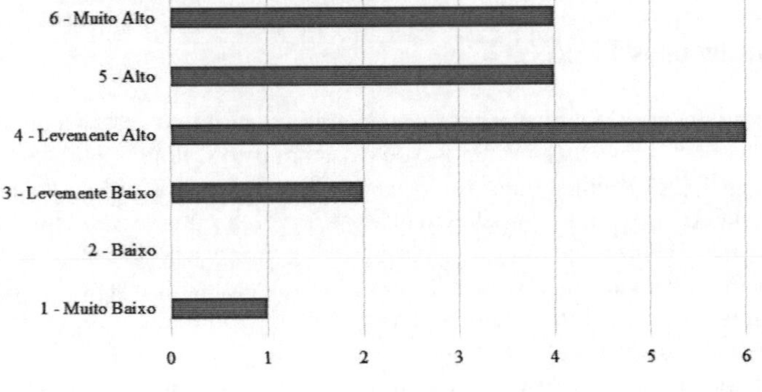

Fig. 7 - Grau de benefício do uso de metodologias ágeis fora do escopo de software.

Apesar de existirem fatores de impedimento específicos que dificultam a adoção de metodologias ágeis, o mais citado nas respostas de campo livre foi a necessidade de adaptação do time frente ao novo modelo de trabalho. Esse desafio se mostra um dos mais comuns em qualquer equipe (independente do escopo de trabalho) de uma organização que está em processo de transformação ágil, corroborando com os pontos abordados neste trabalho.

Na Fig. 8, a mesma análise foi feita através das respostas dos integrantes da amostra paralela. Apesar do baixo valor da amostra (somente 5 pessoas), 60% dos respondentes creem que a metodologia gera um alto benefício em equipes fora do escopo de software, eles alegam que as metodologias podem ser aplicadas e gerar valor em qualquer time. Em contrapartida, os 40% restantes afirmaram que o uso das metodologias gera baixo benefício.

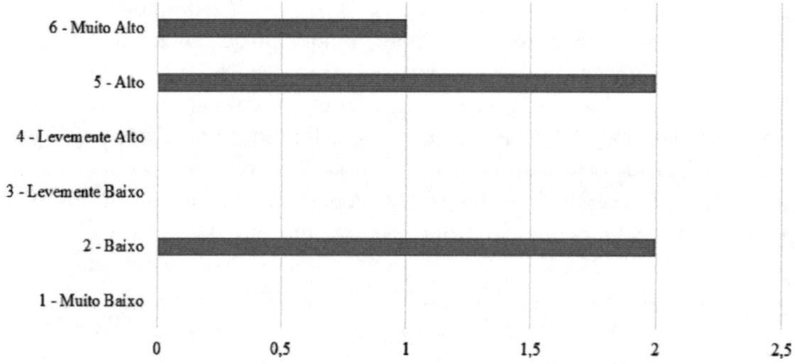

Fig. 8 - Grau de benefício do uso de metodologias ágeis fora do escopo de software pelos desenvolvedores.

Com base nos relatos dos respondentes e na análise das respostas, tanto os profissionais da área de infraestrutura quanto os de desenvolvimento de software corroboram em diversos pontos, por exemplo: nos fatores que influenciam o sucesso de times ágeis, nas práticas menos benéficas e menos utilizadas de acordo com suas experiências e no uso do Scrum que foi a metodologia de trabalho mais adotada. O resultado da pesquisa também evidencia que os respondentes em geral acreditam que as metodologias ágeis são benéficas e podem ser usadas em diferentes tipos de equipes e áreas, atendendo dessa forma o objetivo deste trabalho.

5. Considerações Finais

O objetivo desse trabalho foi investigar uma organização que está passando por um processo de transformação ágil e analisar se o uso das metodologias ágeis por áreas fora do escopo de desenvolvimento de software gera benefícios de acordo com a percepção e experiência de diferentes equipes. Optou-se por realizar um *survey* entre as equipes de uma mesma organização, com perguntas que abordaram: a percepção dos integrantes acerca das metodologias, os pontos positivos e negativos que impactam o sucesso das equipes ágeis, as suas experiências e a percepção deles sobre o seu uso em outras áreas que não são de desenvolvimento de software.

O resultado final coletado após a análise das respostas indica que a maioria dos profissionais da amostra acreditam que as metodologias ágeis são benéficas e podem ser usadas em diferentes tipos de equipes e áreas. Entende-se que o objetivo do trabalho foi alcançado, uma vez que foi possível identificar, no contexto da amostra, a percepção dos profissionais acerca do uso das metodologias ágeis em equipes fora da área de desenvolvimento de software. Também foi possível avaliar a percepção acerca das práticas ágeis e os pontos positivos e negativos que impactam as metodologias. Percebe-se pelas respostas obtidas que as equipes envolvidas ainda estão amadurecimento o uso das práticas ágeis. Deve-se destacar que a organização em questão apoia a adoção das práticas e continua a fomentar o seu uso e adequação às necessidades das equipes envolvidas.

As informações coletadas neste trabalho contribuem para evidenciar a possibilidade do uso das metodologias ágeis em um escopo fora da área de desenvolvimento de software e como os profissionais percebem essa mudança. Os relatos de experiência dos profissionais trouxeram diversos obstáculos específicos da área de infraestrutura ao adotar metodologias ágeis. Isso pode contribuir para o preparo de times que pretendem adotar metodologias ágeis e se encontram sob as mesmas condições.

A principal limitação do trabalho é derivada do próprio escopo do trabalho que o limita à adoção de uma amostra não probabilística. A amostra disponível também limitou o estudo somente a equipes da área de infraestrutura e desenvolvimento (amostra paralela).

Durante a execução desse trabalho, foi possível detectar algumas propostas para trabalhos futuros, como: reaplicação da pesquisa em contexto de amostras probabilísticas, e de maior tamanho para que ele possa ser generalizado; realização da pesquisa em diferentes organizações e correlacionar os seus níveis de maturidade aos resultados obtidos; estudo mais aprofundado das questões organizacionais que podem impactar as equipes que não desenvolvem software.

Agradecimentos. Os autores agradecem à FAPERJ (projetos E-26/010.000883/2016, E-26/010.001644/2016) e à UNIRIO (PQ-UNIRIO 01/2017) pelo auxílio financeiro.

Referências

1. BABBIE, E. Métodos de Pesquisas de Survey. Tradução Guilherme Cezarino. Belo Horizonte: Ed. UFMG, 519 p (1999)
2. COCKBURN, A. Agile Software Development: The Cooperative Game. 2nd Edition. Pearson Education, Boston, USA, ISBN 978-0321482754 (2007)
3. CONBOY, K. Agility from First Principles: Reconstructing the Concept of Agility in Information Systems Development. Information Systems Research, Vol. 20, No. 3, pp. 329-354 (2009). DOI: 10.1287/isre.1090.0236
4. DENNING, Steve. Scrum Is A Major Management Discovery (2017). Disponível em: https://www.forbes.com/sites/stevedenning/2011/04/29/scrum-is-a-major-management-discovery/#7b6e397c7782. Acesso em: 02/03/2018.
5. DINGSØYR, T.; NERUR, S.; BALIJEPALLY, V.; NILS, B. M. A decade of agile methodologies: Towards explaining agile software development. Journal of Systems and Software, Volume 85, Issue 6, pp. 1213-1221 (2012). DOI: 10.1016/j.jss.2012.02.033
6. DIKERT, K.; PAASIVAARA, M.; LASSENIUS, C. Challenges and success factors for large-scale agile transformations: A systematic literature review. Journal of Systems and Software, Volume 119, pp. 87-108 (2016). DOI: 10.1016/j.jss.2016.06.013

7. GANDOMANI, J. T.; NAFCHI, Z. M.; Agile transition and adoption human-related challenges and issues: A Grounded Theory approach. Computers in Human Behavior, Volume 62, pp. 257-266 (2016). DOI: 10.1016/j.chb.2016.04.009
8. HIGHSMITH, J.; COCKBURN, A. Agile software development: the business of innovation. IEEE Computer, Vol. 24, n. 9, IEEE, pp. 120-122 (2001). DOI: 10.1109/2.947100
9. LAANTI, M. Agile methods in large-scale software development organizations: Applicability and model for adoption. PhD Dissertation, University of Oulu, Department of Information Processing Science, Oulu, Finlândia (2012)
10. ANDERSON, D.; AUGUSTINE, S.; AVERY, C.; COCKBURN, A.; COHN, M.; DECARLO, D.; FITZGERALD, D.; HIGHSMITH, J.; JEPSEN, O.; LINDSTROM, L.; LITTLE, T.; MCDONALD, K.; PIXTON, P.; SMITH, P.; WYSOCKI, R. "*Declaration of Interdependence*" (2005). Disponível em: http://pmdoi.org/. Acesso em: 02/03/2018.
11. ROSE, D. Symbolic Innovation in Agile Transformations. Agile Conference, Washington, USA (2015). DOI: 10.1109/Agile.2015.17
12. SALENGUE, J. Scrum em equipes de infraestrutura: Relatos práticos do consultor de TI. Auto Publicação, 96 p. (2016)
13. WALDRON, K. Implementing a Collaborative Working Environment Using Agile: the LexisNexis Experience. Legal Information Management, vol. 17, n. Issue 1, pp. 16-19 (2017). DOI 10.1017/S147266961700007X
14. VERSIONONE. The 11th annual State of Agile Report (2017). Disponível em: https://explore.versionone.com/state-of-agile/versionone-11th-annual-state-of-agile-report-2. Acesso em: 02/03/2018.
15. WAARDENBURG, G.; VLIET, H. When agile meets the enterprise. Information and Software Technology, Vol. 55, Issue 12, pp. 2154-2171 (2013). DOI 10.1016/j.infsof.2013.07.012

Usability Evaluation Methods Adopted in Agile Development Processes

Daniel A. Magües[1], Efraín R. Fonseca C.[2], John W. Castro[3], and Silvia T. Acuña[1]

[1]Escuela Politécnica Superior, Universidad Autónoma de Madrid, Madrid, España
[2]Departamento de Ciencias de la Computación, Universidad de las Fuerzas Armadas ESPE, Sangolquí, Ecuador
[3]Departamento de Ingeniería Informática y Ciencias de la Computación, Universidad de Atacama, Copiapó, Chile
daniel.magues@estudiante.uam.es
erfonseca@espe.edu.ec
john.castro@uda.cl
silvia.acunna@uam.es

Abstract. Integration of agile software development process (ASDP) with user-centred design (UCD) has awakened the interest of researchers during the last decade. However, to the best of our knowledge there is no clarity about what techniques or methods are being applied and how to apply them. Our purpose is to identify Usability Evaluation Methods (UEM) which are being incorporated into ASDP and practicalities of its use. Based on primary studies of a previous systematic mapping study about application of usability methods in ASDP, we conducted an analysis of such methods through a compiled catalog of usability methods made by researchers of Software Engineering. Finally, we determine the form or type of application of each method into ASDP. The agile community show great interest in the incorporation of usability evaluation methods. However, there is no consensus on how to apply these techniques within the agile community. We identify four UEMs within the literature that are the most used in ASDP: Usability Test, Heuristic Evaluation, Thinking Aloud and Focus Group. The analysis of usability evaluation methods and its use provided us specific methods that are being incorporated and an overview of activities performed to incorporate such methods into ASDP, which will be an input to define a unified framework of usability evaluating methods in ASDP.

Keywords: Agile Software Development, Usability, Usability Techniques, Usability Evaluation, User-centred Design

1 Introducción

La integración de los procesos de desarrollo de software ágiles (PDSA) (por ejemplo XP [5] y SCRUM [13]) con el proceso de Desarrollo Centrado en el Usuario (DCU) ha sido objeto de investigación en los últimos años [30,49,55]. Hemos percibido que este creciente interés se debe a que el DCU permite entender las necesidades reales de los usuarios del sistema, y cómo sus objetivos y actividades pueden ser soportados por el software para mejorar la usabilidad y la satisfacción de los usuarios que interactúan con el sistema. Sin embargo, dichas características no son tomadas en cuenta en los PDSA durante el diseño de la interacción del usuario con el sistema software [1]. Los desarrolladores ágiles experimentan frustración realizando las tareas relacionadas con la evaluación de la usabilidad debido a la brecha de integración existente entre los PDSA y el DCU [56]. La usabilidad es un atributo de calidad en el uso de los sistemas software y no solo radica en la apariencia de la interfaz de usuario, sino en cómo el usuario interactúa con el sistema [37].

Por un lado, en los PDSA la evaluación de las funcionalidades se hace en cada historia de usuario y en cada iteración. Según Cohn [13], esta estrategia permite asegurar la calidad en cada historia de usuario ya que el equipo incluye tareas de evaluación como test funcionales y control de calidad realizadas por los miembros del equipo y test de aceptación de usuario o *sprint reviews* en SCRUM, cuyo objetivo es validar el cumplimiento de los requisitos desarrollados en las historias de usuario. Por otro lado, el DCU nos permite poner al usuario en el centro de las actividades de análisis de requisitos, diseño y evaluación para mejorar la usabilidad del producto final [30]. Los profesionales de DCU buscan involucrar al usuario aplicando métodos de DCU en un proceso colaborativo e iterativo que permita validar y evolucionar el producto con los usuarios en un contexto real [12,26,3]. Por lo tanto, los profesionales de DCU y los equipos que utilizan los PDSA podrían ser compatibles, permitiendo así mejores experiencias de usuario. Sin embargo, la evaluación en los PDSA no prioriza la usabilidad desde el punto de vista de la disciplina de DCU. Esto ocurre cuando, por ejemplo, los requisitos de usabilidad se postergan por las necesidades de los clientes con mayor valor de negocio y no se consideran los distintos tipos de usuarios finales del sistema, dificultando la identificación de los problemas de usabilidad que puedan tener los usuarios finales con menor experiencia [38,52]. El DCU, en cambio, tiene como uno de sus principios entender a todos los perfiles de los usuarios [52]. Muchos autores de la disciplina de la Interacción Persona-Ordenador (IPO) afirman que los profesionales de DCU deben acoplar su mentalidad al proceso ágil [4,10,50]. Sin embargo, dicho acoplamiento no resulta del todo sencillo por dos razones. En primer lugar, muchos profesionales de DCU trabajan en equipos separados del equipo de desarrollo ágil, lo que hace que la cultura sea diferente entre ellos. En segundo lugar, muchos profesionales han tenido que desarrollar sus propias estrategias para mantener las prácticas de DCU en sintonía con la organización, mientras ésta adopta los PDSA [6]. Así, los profesionales de DCU deben adaptar métodos de usabilidad siguiendo su experiencia, y muchas de estos métodos de usabilidad requieren de tiempos y recursos que un proceso ágil no permite. Además, los procesos ágiles no proveen guías para este tipo de adaptaciones.

El presente trabajo de investigación realiza un primer acercamiento en la identificación de como otros proyectos ágiles han incorporado Métodos de Evaluación de la Usabilidad (UEM por sus siglas en inglés). Este artículo analiza los resultados de una revisión de la literatura previa [46] que busca identificar los métodos de usabilidad que están siendo incorporadas en los PDSA y cómo se están incorporando. El análisis detallado de cómo se están adaptando las UEM en los PDSA será realizado como trabajo futuro. Posteriormente, con base en este análisis se realizará la propuesta de un marco de trabajo formalizado y sistematizado para que los practicantes de desarrollo ágil tengan una guía para el uso de estos métodos. Las contribuciones de nuestro trabajo son las siguientes:

- Identificamos métodos de usabilidad relacionadas con actividades de Evaluación que algunos autores han incorporado en los PDSA y analizamos si estas métodos han sido utilizadas tal como lo prescribe la IPO o si han requerido adaptaciones al contexto del desarrollo ágil para poder ser aplicadas.
- Determinamos los impedimentos que motivaron las adaptaciones para los UEMs relacionados con las actividades de Evaluación.

Lo que resta del artículo está organizado de la siguiente manera. En la Sección 2 presentamos brevemente el catálogo de métodos de la IPO que hemos usado como base para determinar que UEMs relacionadas con la Evaluación están siendo usadas por la comunidad ágil. La Sección 3 describe el método de investigación. La Sección 4 reporta el uso de UEMs relacionados con las actividades de evaluación en los PDSA. La Sección 5 presenta la discusión de cómo han sido incorporadas estos métodos por los PDSA. Finalmente, la Sección 6 reporta nuestras conclusiones y trabajos futuros.

2 Trabajos Relacionados

Para investigar de manera general, entre otros aspectos, los métodos de usabilidad que pueden ser incorporadas en los PDSA, algunos investigadores han realizado estudios empíricos [9,27,28], mientras que otros pocos han estudiado la literatura [49,8]. El objetivo de nuestra investigación es conocer el estado actual de la usabilidad en los PDSA desde una perspectiva más amplia. Para analizar los beneficios de la usabilidad en los PDSA e identificar qué métodos de usabilidad relacionadas con la actividad de Evaluación están siendo adoptadas y cómo están siendo adoptadas, hemos llevado a cabo un *Systematic Mapping Study* (SMS) sobre la usabilidad y los PDSA.

Encontramos cinco trabajos [8,52,49,15,36] que son revisiones sistemáticas relacionadas con nuestra pregunta de investigación. En el primero, Brhel y colegas [8] revisan la literatura dividiendola en cuatro dimensiones de integración (procesos, prácticas, tecnología y gente/social), y aunque logra identificar las practicas más usadas, concluye que la traducción de las prácticas de desarrollo ágil centrado en el usuario de la academia a la práctica sigue siendo un desafío. En el segundo, Sohaib y Khan [52] realizan una revisión de literatura e identifican que los proyectos ágiles deben adoptar aspectos de ingeniería de usabilidad incorporando escenarios de usuario e incluyendo especialistas en usabilidad en el equipo. El tercer trabajo por Salah y colegas [49] tiene como objetivo identificar y clasificar varios factores desafiantes que restringen la integración PDSA-DCU y explorar las prácticas propuestas y los factores de éxito para enfrentar estos desafíos. El cuarto trabajo de Da Silva y colegas [15] reportan una revisión de literatura que ha identificado temas recurrentes y patrones de las actividades y artefactos más comunes utilizados por equipos de diseñadores DCU para la integración con equipos de desarrolladores en PDSA. Por último, Jurca [36] realiza un SMS que permite evaluar la integración PDAS-DCU desde varias tendencias como el uso de sprints 0 o LDUF, problemas organizacionales y recomendaciones para la integración, artefatos y practicas mas comunes (Workshops, Lo-Fi Prototyping, Interviews, Meetings with Users and Scenarios) y marcos de integración. Aunque, estos trabajos [8,52,49,15,36] describen el estado de la integación entre el DCU y los PDSA desde diferentes puntos de vista, sin embargo no precisan cómo estan siendo adoptados los UEM por los propios practicantes de los PDSA, siendo que los UEM no son los más complejos de aplicar por las restricciones que imponen los PDSA [49].

La literatura sobre la integración de métodos de usabilidad en los PDSA está compuesta por un conjunto de publicaciones desacopladas que estudian diferentes aspectos del tema. En este conjunto, se identifican dos problemas. En primer lugar, existen pocos trabajos que estudian como un todo el tema y reportan cuál es el estado actual de la integración de los PDSA con el DCU [8,15,52,49,36]. En segundo lugar, no existen propuestas formalizadas de incorporación de los métodos de usabilidad en los PDSA [22,28,31] que establezcan, para cada método, guías sobre como incorporarlas.

Con el fin de investigar qué métodos de usabilidad se están utilizando en los PDSA para producir sistemas usables, es preciso identificar primero el universo de los métodos de la IPO. Esto no es una labor sencilla, porque existe una amplia gama de métodos de usabilidad de la IPO, donde el misma método puede ser referida de manera diferente dependiendo del autor y puede existir más de una variante para el misma método. Afortunadamente, otros investigadores de la ingeniería de software (IS) ya han realizado el trabajo de compilar un catálogo de métodos de la IPO, como es el caso de Ferré [24][25], quien compiló una lista de métodos de las fuentes más reconocidas en el área de la IPO. Si bien existe el catalogo de Fernandez y colegas [20], este solo considera los métodos de evaluación de usabilidad para aplicaciones Web. Además, el catalogo que hemos seleccionado es mas genérico y es el que hemos utilizado a lo largo de nuestra investigación. A continuación, se presenta un breve resumen del catálogo de Ferré [24][25] que debería ayudar a los lectores a seguir el resto del documento y a comprender qué métodos de usabilidad se están aplicando actualmente en los PDSA y cómo se están adoptando.

Según Ferré [21,24,25], las actividades más representativas del proceso de la IPO son la especificación de contexto de uso, especificaciones de usabilidad, desarrollo de concepto del producto, prototipado, diseño de la interacción y evaluación de la usabilidad. Ferré [21,24,25] traza estas actividades (y sus respectivos métodos asociadas) a las principales etapas de desarrollo de la IS. En algunos casos, las actividades de la IPO se integran en las actividades existentes de la IS. Por ejemplo, la actividad de especificaciones de usabilidad se puede integrar en la especificación de requisitos. En otros casos, sin embargo, otras actividades que normalmente no se llevan a cabo en un proceso de desarrollo no centrado en el usuario, como el diseño de la interacción, tienen que ser agregadas. Estas actividades adicionales serán referidas como se acostumbra en la comunidad de la IPO. Las actividades de la IPO han sido mapeadas teniendo en cuenta las etapas de desarrollo de la IS: Ingeniería de requisitos, diseño y evaluación. La actividad de la IPO diseño de la interacción se ha asignado a la actividad de diseño de la IS. Es importante mencionar, que los métodos de la IPO en el catálogo están clasificadas en tres grandes grupos: métodos relacionadas con las actividades de la ingeniería de requisitos, métodos relacionadas con las actividades de diseño y métodos relacionados con las actividades de evaluación. El análisis de los métodos de usabilidad relacionadas con las actividades de la Ingeniería de Requisitos han sido reportadas en [45]. En este trabajo nos centramos en las actividades de Evaluación, es decir, en el estudio de cómo están siendo incorporadas por los PDSA los métodos de evaluación de la usabilidad.

3 Método de Investigación

A partir de los estudios primarios obtenidos en un SMS previo, hemos identificado las UEMs que se están utilizando en los PDSA. Posteriormente, hemos comparado lo reportado en los estudios primarios con lo prescrito por la IPO, para cada método identificado con el objetivo de identificar como se están incorporando en los PDSA. En la sección 4 describimos el proceso seguido para realizar tal identificación. En esta sección presentamos un resumen del SMS realizado y los detalles del mismo pueden ser consultados en [46]. Las bases de datos electrónicas (BBDD) utilizadas en el SMS fueron *Scopus*, *ACM Digital Library* e *IEEE Xplore*. La revisión abarca los trabajos publicados hasta el 15 de octubre del 2015. Inicialmente, al menos dos de los investigadores que participa en el SMS realiza una revisión inicial individual de literatura y propone un grupo de estudios que responden al objetivo planteado en el SMS, sin descuidar la fiabilidad del origen de dichos estudios. Esta revisión tiene como propósito identificar términos generales o comunes entre los estudios (y sus sinónimos), para conformar la cadena de búsqueda (ver Tabla 1).

Los criterios de inclusión de la revisión de la literatura indican que los trabajos de investigación deben mencionar algún tema relacionado con la usabilidad y el desarrollo ágil. La búsqueda se dividió en dos etapas. Durante la primera etapa, examinamos el título, las palabras clave y el resumen para inspeccionar los 409 documentos recuperados de las tres BBDD, de los cuales seleccionamos 172 como documentos posiblemente relevantes. Sólo se seleccionaron los trabajos escritos en inglés y cuyo resumen o título mencionaba algún tema relacionado con la integración de procesos ágiles y usabilidad, algún tema relacionado con la ingeniería de usabilidad o métodos de la IPO, o relacionado con el proceso de DCU. Los trabajos fueron rechazados si no hacían mención alguna a la integración de procesos ágiles y usabilidad o al proceso de DCU. Durante la segunda etapa, leímos el resumen, la introducción y las conclusiones para determinar si el documento describía cualquier tipo de integración entre procesos ágiles y usabilidad. Finalmente, como resultado de la segunda etapa, se recuperaron un total de 31 artículos relevantes (estudios primarios).

Tabla 1. Palabras clave utilizadas para la cadena de búsqueda

Palabras Clave		
"usability" **OR**		"agile development" **OR**
"usability method" **OR**		"agile software development" **OR**
"usability technique" **OR**		"agile method" **OR**
"usability engineering" **OR**		"agile process" **OR**
"usability practice" **OR**	**AND**	"agile project" **OR**
"user centered design" **OR**		"agile practice" **OR**
"user-centered design" **OR**		"extreme programming" **OR**
"user interaction" **OR**		"scrum"
"user experience"		

Todos los miembros del equipo de investigación ayudaron a definir la estrategia de búsqueda. Dos investigadores diseñaron y realizaron las búsquedas y extrajeron los datos. Posteriormente, los resultados fueron discutidos en reuniones a las que asistieron todos los miembros del equipo. Luego de analizar los estudios primarios, los clasificamos por tipo de integración en 4 grupos: Integración de procesos, integración de prácticas, integración de equipos e integración con apoyo de la tecnología. En este trabajo de investigación, realizamos el análisis de los trabajos del grupo Integración de Prácticas, que identifica la adopción de métodos de usabilidad en los PDSA y viceversa.

Los estudios primarios que estudiamos para analizar los métodos de usabilidad adoptadas en los PDSA se refieren a la integración de prácticas (31 publicaciones). La razón por la que seleccionamos este tipo de integración radica en que, como no se requieren cambios profundos en los procesos, sería más factible integrar los métodos de usabilidad en los PDSA, ya que no se requeriría de un gran esfuerzo para capacitar a los equipos de los PDSA, ni sería necesario realizar una inversión adicional para incluir nuevos roles en el equipo. Después de discutir cada artículo en las reuniones a las que asistieron todos los miembros del equipo de investigación, determinamos qué UEMs se han adoptado en los PDSA, proporcionando la descripción dada por el autor a cada método. Estos métodos se analizaron comparando la forma en que se aplicó el método en los PDSA con la recomendación original establecida por el área de la IPO. Se necesitaron varias iteraciones para identificar estos métodos. El proceso se complicó por el hecho de que los autores de los estudios primarios no utilizaron los nombres habituales del método utilizados comúnmente en la literatura de la IPO. Por lo tanto, fue necesario leer el documento más a fondo con el fin de identificar el método a la que los autores se refieren. A través de la descripción de los métodos adoptados en los PDSA, el uso de un catálogo de métodos de la IPO [24][25] y la consulta con expertos, se identificaron los métodos de usabilidad reportadas en la literatura que han sido adoptadas en los PDSA. Dos expertos en métodos de usabilidad participaron en este proceso de identificación. El resultado de este proceso dio lugar a una clasificación preliminar de los diferentes métodos de usabilidad relacionadas con las actividades de evaluación adoptadas en los PDSA.

A continuación, analizamos cómo se adoptaron los UEM en las actividades de evaluación de los PDSA. Como resultado de este análisis, encontramos que algunos métodos fueron adoptados según las recomendaciones de la IPO, mientras que otros necesitaron adaptaciones para poder ser incorporados. Para cada uno de los métodos adoptados, identificamos las adaptaciones realizadas (discutidas en la Sección 5). Esta identificación resultó ser uno de los procesos más complejos, debido al hecho de que los autores de los estudios primarios solo describen el método de usabilidad adoptada, es decir estos autores no compararon el método de usabilidad con lo prescrito por la IPO. Esta comparación fue necesaria para poder identificar las adaptaciones realizadas a los métodos.

4 Uso de Métodos de la IPO Relacionadas con la Evaluación en los Desarrollos Ágiles

Hemos encontrado que la comunidad ágil ha adoptado una serie de métodos de usabilidad en sus proyectos de desarrollo. Hemos clasificado los métodos de usabilidad adoptadas en dos grupos. El primer grupo incluye todos los métodos que se han adoptado tal cual, es decir, se han aplicado según lo recomendado por la IPO. El segundo grupo incluye los métodos que han tenido que ser adaptadas para poder su adopción. Con el fin de identificar los métodos adoptadas en los PDSA, hemos examinado los estudios primarios pertenecientes al grupo de Integración de Prácticas. Luego, leímos cada documento cuidadosamente para identificar los nombres de todas los métodos reportados por el autor y su respectiva descripción. Es importante mencionar que algunos autores reportan la adopción de más de un método de usabilidad. Luego de leer sus respectivas descripciones, clasificamos cada método adoptada en los PDSA de acuerdo con el catálogo de métodos de la IPO [24][25]. Esta tarea se llevó a cabo conjuntamente con expertos en el área como parte de las sesiones de trabajo destinadas a identificar qué métodos del catálogo habían sido adoptadas por los PDSA. Para identificar estos métodos, no consideramos los nombres dados por los autores de los estudios primarios, por dos razones. En primer lugar, porque estos autores no usan los nombres de los métodos comúnmente aceptados por el área de la IPO para cada método. En segundo lugar, porque los autores de los estudios primarios al no ser expertos en usabilidad, ni en el catalogo de métodos, podían asignar de manera errónea los nombres a las mismas. Por tanto, solo consideramos la descripción dada por el autor que adoptó el método. Obsérvese que algunas de los métodos y su respectiva descripción requerían de un análisis más profundo para identificar el método de la IPO en el catálogo. Encontramos que los PDSA han adoptado 13 de las 39 (33.33%) UEMs. Los 39 métodos se encuentran agrupadas en tres grandes grupos: Evaluación por expertos, Test de Usabilidad y

Tabla 2. Métodos de Usabilidad de la IPO Relacionadas con la Evaluación Adoptadas por los PDSA.

Tipo de Actividad	Método de la IPO	Nombre según Autores IPO	Nombre según Autores PDSA	Ref.	Tipo de Aplicación
Evaluación por Expertos	Evaluación Heurística	Evaluación Heurística	Heuristic Evaluation	[3][19][42][56]	Pura
			Heuristic Evaluation	[38][53]	Adaptada
	Inspecciones	Inspecciones	Inspection Evaluation	[43]	Adaptada
			Usability Inspections	[16]	Adaptada
	Recorridos Cognitivos	Recorridos Cognitivos	Cognitive Walkthrough	[19][42]	Pura
			Informal Cognitive Walkthrough	[27]	Adaptada
	Evaluación por Expertos	Evaluación por Expertos	Expert Evaluations	[18]	Adaptada
			Usability Expert Evaluations	[32]	Pura
Test de usabilidad	Pensar en Voz Alta	Pensar en Voz Alta	Simplified Thinking Aloud	[38]	Adaptada
			Thinking Aloud	[42][41]	Pura
			Thinking Aloud	[53]	Adaptada
	Medición del Rendimiento	Métricas de Rendimiento	Measuring User Performance	[43]	Adaptada
			Performance Measurement	[42]	Pura
	Test Usabilidad en Laboratorio	Laboratorios de Usabilidad	Laboratory Usability Testing	[32]	Pura
	Eval. por Control Remoto	Eval. por Control Remoto	Remote Synchronous User Testing	[40]	Adaptada
	Test de Usabilidad	Test de Usabilidad	Usability Testing	[2][56][54][57]	Adaptada
			Usability Testing	[3][23][29][44][58][31]	Pura
			Test UIs with Users in Paper with Mock-up Interviews	[7]	Adaptada
			Informal Usability Testing	[17]	Adaptada
			Automated Usability Evaluations	[31]	Adaptada
			Rapid Iterative Testing	[32]	Adaptada
			Low and High Fidelity Prototypes Based Usability Tests	[33]	Adaptada
			Usability Sessions	[34]	Adaptada
			Low-cost Rapid Usability Testing	[39]	Adaptada
			Rapid Iterative Test and Evaluation Method	[47]	Adaptada
			Micro Tests	[48]	Adaptada
			Extended Unit tests for Automated Usability Evaluation	[57]	Adaptada
Estudio de Seguimiento de Sistemas	Cuestionario y Encuestas	Cuestionarios	Questionnaires	[18]	Pura
		Encuestas	Surveys	[43]	Pura
	Focus Groups	Focus Groups	Focus Groups	[3][42][41]	Pura
			Workshops	[35][58][11]	Pura
	Retroalimentación del Usuario	Retroalimentación del Usuario	Feedback from User Surrogates	[43]	Adaptada
			Asking User Their Opinions	[43]	Adaptada

Estudio de seguimiento de sistemas instalados. En el grupo de Evaluación por expertos, la técnica más adoptada por los autores es la Evaluació Heurística. En los métodos del grupo Test de Usabilidad, la que lleva el mismo nombre, Test de Usabilidad, ha sido la más adoptada. En el grupo de Estudio de seguimiento encontramos que el método de Cuestionarios es la más adoptada. La Tabla 2 resume los métodos de la IPO relacionadas con las actividades de Evaluación que identificamos están siendo adoptadas por los PDSA. Para cada método, se especifica el tipo de actividad de Evaluación con la que se relaciona, el nombre genérico del método, el nombre dado por los diferentes autores de la IPO, el nombre utilizado por los autores de los PDSA, las referencias correspondientes y el nivel de adopción (pura o con adaptaciones).

5 Resultados y Discusión

En esta sección, discutiremos cómo los PDSA han adoptado las técnicas de usabilidad relacionadas con las actividades de Evaluación. Es importante mencionar que todas las técnicas de usabilidad identificadas y que han sido adoptadas en proyectos de desarrollo ágil, corresponden a las técnicas reportadas en la literatura y obtenidas a partir de nuestro SMS. Hemos clasificado todas y cada una de las técnicas de usabilidad que han sido adoptadas por los desarrollos de los PDSA. Esta clasificación la hemos realizado según un catálogo de métodos de la IPO [24][25], comparando cómo se aplicó el método con lo prescrito por la IPO. Como resultado de esta clasificación hemos encontrado que los métodos se están adoptando de dos maneras. En primer lugar, los métodos de usabilidad que han sido aplicadas puras, es decir, el método ha sido aplicado según lo recomendado por la IPO. En segundo lugar, los métodos que han sido adaptadas para poder ser aplicadas en los desarrollos ágiles. Hemos identificado en la literatura que los métodos de usabilidad más adoptadas en las actividades de Evaluación de los PDSA son: Evaluación Heurística [3,19,42,56,38,53], Pensar en Voz Alta [38,42,41,53], Test de Usabilidad [2,56,54,57,3,23,29,44,58] [31,7,17,32,33,34,39,47,48,57] y Focus Groups [3,42,41,35,58,11].

Encontramos métodos que se han adoptado en los desarrollos ágiles de las dos maneras, es decir, pura y con adaptaciones. El tipo de adopción (pura o adaptada) depende de las características y recursos particulares de cada proyecto. El método de Test de Usabilidad se ha adoptado con adaptaciones en la mayoría de los casos, según los estudios primarios. Muchos practicantes de equipos ágiles indican que es muy difícil realizar tests de usabilidad de la forma tradicional debido a los cronogramas ajustados de los *sprints* [16]. Por lo tanto, hemos identificado adaptaciones que proponen realizar tests de usabilidad sobre maquetas de papel o prototipos de baja fidelidad [33][7], las cuales son menos formales y permiten tener retroalimentación de los usuarios durante el desarrollo de un *sprint* o iteración. Nos llama la atención el método Test de Usabilidad porque en la gran mayoría ha sido adaptada (70%). Hemos identificado que los autores adoptan tests de usabilidad más informales para cumplir con las condiciones de los PDSA. El 30% restante, el método Test de Usabilidad se ha adoptado pura.

Son tres las estrategias que identificamos permiten adoptar este método con adaptaciones. En primer lugar, realizar Test de Usabilidad con los usuarios para evaluar cambios cada 2 o 3 *sprints* con la ayuda de un equipo externo dedicado a temas de usabilidad [54][56]. En segundo lugar, definir Test de Usabilidad de bajo costo o micro tests. Un micro test [48] es una prueba de usabilidad en línea, a menudo sin moderador. Esto implica realizar un número limitado de pruebas, de 3 a 5 pruebas para un determinado conjunto de tareas que se ha desarrollado durante una iteración en particular. Además, el test de usabilidad de bajo costo [39] es un método donde las pruebas se pueden llevar a cabo rápidamente, a bajo costo y en cualquier lugar, lo que permite realizar tests en cualquier etapa del ciclo de desarrollo ágil. En tercer lugar, evaluar la usabilidad por medio de Tests sobre prototipos de baja y alta fidelidad [7][33]. Esta estrategia permite evaluar una funcionalidad con el usuario sin necesidad de tener software funcional y permite realizar ciclos de revisión más cortos de manera más informal. Las formas de los prototipos pueden incluir prototipos de papel, *screenshots*, transparencias de *PowerPoint* o maquetas en *html*.

La disciplina de la IPO estipula que la Evaluación Heurística es una inspección del diseño de la interfaz, realizada por especialistas de usabilidad, que verifica el cumplimiento de principios de usabilidad reconocidos [51]. Sin embargo, no es común que existan especialistas de usabilidad en el equipo ágil, por tanto se requiere trabajar con equipos de diseñadores para suplir estas carencias [3]. Una heurística es un conjunto de directrices dadas a los evaluadores para identificar muchos problemas de usabilidad. Es mejor utilizarlas temprano en la fase de diseño porque es más fácil solucionar muchos de los problemas de usabilidad que surgen. Sohaib y Kahn [53] identificaron, por medio de entrevistas, que los equipos ágiles utilizan las heurísticas como una lista de chequeo a evaluar durante las pruebas de aceptación que se deben realizar en XP.

En el método de Pensar en Voz Alta, los usuarios son alentados a "pensar en voz alta", manteniendo un monólogo sobre lo que están haciendo mientras lo hacen. El propósito de esto es acceder a lo que los usuarios están pensando y cuáles son sus intenciones cuando usan el sistema [14]. Losada y colegas [42][41] proponen aplicar el método tal cual lo prescribe la IPO en su método ágil llamado *InterMod*. Kane [38] propone una versión "simplificada" de pensar en voz alta con la modificación que se puede utilizar para evaluar prototipos de papel en lugar de evaluar el sistema software ya terminado. Por último, Focus Groups ha sido considerada como el método más utilizado por equipos ágiles que aplican el proceso *Scrum* según reportan los trabajos de Jia y colegas [35] y Ovad y Larsen [58]. Este método tal cual lo prescribe la IPO se utiliza en los PDSA para validar las funcionalidades liberadas en cada *sprint*.

Resumiendo, hemos identificado dos principales condiciones desfavorables para aplicar los UEMs en los PDSA. En primer lugar, estos métodos requieren de especialistas de usabilidad o DCU que permitan aplicar el método, es por ello que se proponen el trabajo colaborativo entre equipos ágiles y equipos de DCU. En segundo lugar, los UEMs requieren de planeación de tiempo y recursos para poder aplicar el método, lo que conlleva a que están muy limitadas a los tiempos cortos de los PDSA, en estos casos se plantean métodos más informales que puedan ser aplicadas en ciclos más cortos.

6 Conclusiones

En esta investigación determinamos qué UEMs se están adoptando en los proyectos de desarrollo ágil y analizamos cómo se están adoptando. Además, identificamos cómo algunos de los PDSA están adaptando las UEMs para poder ser adoptadas. Identificamos que la mayoría (66%) de adopciones de UEM reportadas en la literatura son propuestas adaptadas es decir, requieren de modificaciones para poder ser utilizadas dentro de un ambiente ágil. Las UEMs más utilizadas son Test de Usabilidad, Evaluación Heurística, Pensar en Voz Alta y Focus Groups. Por un lado, muchas UEMs pueden ser adoptadas tal cual lo prescribe la IPO (por ejemplo, Focus Groups), mientras que otras requieren de adaptaciones para poder ser adoptadas en algunos proyectos ágiles (por ejemplo, Evaluación Heurística y Test de Usabilidad). Sin embargo, estas adaptaciones no son generalizadas ni prescriptivas. Además estas adaptaciones son realizadas generalmente por practicantes de DCU que trabajan en conjunto con equipos ágiles, lo que hace necesario un mayor esfuerzo de investigación al respecto y determinar que UEMs pueden ser incorporadas en las actividades de Evaluación de los PDSA. Según los resultados de nuestro SMS, parece que no existen propuestas formalizadas de incorporación de las UEMs en los PDSA que establezcan guías de cómo incorporar cada método. Nuestra investigación busca realizar un aporte para intentar resolver este problema. Nuestros resultados sugieren que la comunidad de desarrollo ágil está adoptando métodos de usabilidad en sus proyectos de desarrollo, con especial interés en las UEMs. Existen propuestas para aplicarlas tanto puras como con modificaciones, pero no hay un consenso de como será la mejor manera de adaptarlas. Esto puede deberse a la falta de una propuesta general, prescriptiva y sistemática que permita a los equipos de desarrollo ágiles adoptar métodos de usabilidad en sus proyectos de desarrollo.

Como trabajos futuros, consideramos ampliar las búsquedas de artículos para cubrir otras BBDD (por ejemplo, SpringerLink). El objetivo es aumentar el número de trabajos relevantes recuperados, para poder encontrar otras propuestas de aplicación de UEMs, ya que hemos identificado que hay un gran interés en este tema dentro de la comunidad científica. Además, como trabajos futuros, vamos a adaptar UEMs para su incorporación en un proyecto de desarrollo ágil real. A largo plazo, consideramos la creación de un marco de integración de métodos de usabilidad que guíe a los practicantes ágiles en cómo adaptar sistemáticamente estos métodos y poder reducir los tiempos de evaluación a fin de cumplir con los tiempos reducidos de las iteraciones ágiles.

Agradecimientos

La presente investigación ha sido financiada por los proyectos del Ministerio de Educación, Cultura y Deporte de España FLEXOR (TIN2014-52129-R) y

TIN2014-60490-P, el proyecto eMadrid-CM (S2013 / ICE-2715), el "Proyecto DIUDA 22316 "de la Universidad de Atacama, y el proyecto de investigación "Laboratorio Industrial en Ingeniería del Software Empírica (LI2SE) "de la ESPE.

Referencias

1. Adikari, S., McDonald, C., Campbell, J.: Reframed contexts: Design thinking for agile user experience design. Lecture Notes in Computer Science 8012 LNCS(1), 3–12 (2013)
2. Ambler, S.: Bridging the gap. Dr. Dobb's Journal 31(8), 64–67 (2006)
3. Anwar, S., Motla, Y., Siddiq, Y., Asghar, S., Shabbir Hassan, M., Khan, Z.: User-centered design practices in scrum development process: A distinctive advantage? In: IEEE 17th Intern. Multi-Topic Conference (INMIC). pp. 161–166 (Dec 2014)
4. Barksdale, J., Ragan, E., McCrickard, D.: Easing team politics in agile usability: A concept mapping approach. In: Agile Conference. pp. 19–25 (2009)
5. Beck, K.: Embracing change with extreme programming. Computer 32(10), 70–77 (1999)
6. Bertholdo, A., Da Silva, T., De O. Melo, C., Kon, F., Silveira, M.: Agile usability patterns for ucd early stages. Lecture Notes in Computer Science 8517 LNCS(1), 33–44 (2014)
7. Beyer, H., Holtzblatt, K., Baker, L.: An agile customer-centered method: Rapid contextual design. Lecture Notes in Computer Science 3134, 50–59 (2004)
8. Brhel, M., Meth, H., Maedche, A., Werder, K.: Exploring principles of user-centered agile software development: A literature review. IST 61, 163–181 (2015)
9. Broschinsky, D., Baker, L.: Using personas with xp at landesk software, an avocent company. In: Agile Conference. pp. 543–548 (ago 2008)
10. Brown, D.: Agile User Experience Design. Newnes (2013)
11. Cajander, A., Lárusdóttir, M., Gulliksen, J.: Existing but not explicit - the user perspective in scrum projects in practice. Lecture Notes in Computer Science 8119 LNCS(3), 762–779 (2013)
12. Chamberlain, S., Sharp, H., Maiden, N.: Towards a framework for integrating agile development and user-centred design. Lecture Notes in Computer Science 4044 LNCS, 143–153 (2006)
13. Cohn, M.: Succeeding with Agile: Software Development Using Scrum. Pearson Education (2009)
14. Constantine, L.L., Lockwood, L.A.: Software for Use: A practical Guide to the Models and Methods of Usage-centered Design. Pearson Education (1999)
15. Da Silva, T., Martin, A., Maurer, F., Silveira, M.: User-centered design and agile methods: A systematic review. In: Agile Conference. pp. 77–86 (2011)
16. Da Silva, T., Silveira, M., Maurer, F.: Usability evaluation practices within agile development. In: Hawaii Intern. Conf. on System Sciences. pp. 5133–5142 (2015)
17. Dayton, D., Barnum, C.: The impact of agile on user-centered design: Two surveys tell the story. Technical Communication 56(3), 219–234 (2009)
18. Düchting, M., Zimmermann, D., Nebe, K.: Incorporating user centered requirement engineering into agile software development. Lecture Notes in Computer Science 4550 LNCS(1), 58–67 (2007)
19. Faulring, A., Myers, B., Oren, Y., Rotenberg, K.: A case study of using hci methods to improve tools for programmers. In: 5th International Workshop on Co-operative and Human Aspects of Software Engineering. pp. 37–39 (2012)

20. Fernandez, A., Insfran, E., Abrahão, S.: Usability evaluation methods for the web: A systematic mapping study. Inf. Softw. Technol. 53(8), 789–817 (Aug 2011)
21. Ferré, X.: Integration of usability techniques into the software development process. In: ICSE Workshop on SE-HCI (2003)
22. Ferreira, J.: Agile development and ux design: Towards understanding work cultures to support integration. Lecture Notes in Business Information Processing 112 LNBIP, 608–615 (2012)
23. Ferreira, J., Noble, J., Biddle, R.: Agile development iterations and ui design. In: Agile Conference. pp. 50–58 (2007)
24. Ferré, X.: Marco de integración de la usabilidad en el proceso de desarrollo software. Ph.D. thesis, Universidad Politécnica de Madrid (2005)
25. Ferré, X., Juristo, N., Moreno, A.M.: Framework for integrating usability practices into the software process. In: Bomarius, F., Komi-Sirviö, S. (eds.) Product Focused Software Process Improvement. pp. 202–215. Berlin, Heidelberg (2005)
26. Fox, D., Sillito, J., Maurer, F.: Agile methods and user-centered design: How these two methodologies are being successfully integrated in industry. In: Agile Conference. pp. 63–72 (2008)
27. Grigoreanu, V., Mohanna, M.: Informal cognitive walkthrough (icw): Paring down and pairing up for an agile world. pp. 3093–3096 (2013)
28. Hodgetts, P.: Experiences integrating sophisticated user experience design practices into agile processes. In: Agile Conference. pp. 235–242 (2005)
29. Hudson, W.: Adopting user-centered design within an agile process: A conversation. Cutter IT Journal 16(10), 5–12 (2003)
30. Humayoun, S., Dubinsky, Y., Catarci, T.: A three-fold integration framework to incorporate user-centered design into agile software development. Lecture Notes in Computer Science 6776 LNCS, 55–64 (2011)
31. Hussain, Z., Milchrahm, H., Shahzad, S., Slany, W., Tscheligi, M., Wolkerstorfer, P.: Integration of extreme programming and user-centered design: Lessons learned. Lecture Notes in Business Information Processing 31 LNBIP, 174–179 (2009)
32. Hussain, Z., Slany, W., Holzinger, A.: Current state of agile user-centered design: A survey. Lecture Notes in Computer Science 5889 LNCS, 416–427 (2009)
33. Hussain, Z., Slany, W., Holzinger, A.: Investigating agile user-centered design in practice: A grounded theory perspective. Lecture Notes in Computer Science 5889 LNCS, 279–289 (2009)
34. Illmensee, T., Muff, A.: 5 users every friday: A case study in applied research. pp. 404–409 (2009)
35. Jia, Y., Lárusdóttir, M., Cajander, A.: The usage of usability techniques in scrum projects. Lecture Notes in Computer Science 7623 LNCS, 331–341 (2012)
36. Jurca, G., Hellmann, T.D., Maurer, F.: Integrating agile and user-centered design: A systematic mapping and review of evaluation and validation studies of agile-ux. In: 2014 Agile Conference. pp. 24–32 (July 2014)
37. Juristo, N., Moreno, A., Sanchez-Segura, M.I.: Guidelines for eliciting usability functionalities. IEEE Transactions on Software Engineering 33(11), 744–758 (2007)
38. Kane, D.: Finding a place for discount usability engineering in agile development: throwing down the gauntlet. In: Agile Development Conference. pp. 40–46 (2003)
39. Kushniruk, A., Borycki, E.: Integrating low-cost rapid usability testing into agile system development of healthcare it: A methodological perspective. vol. 210, pp. 200–204 (2015)
40. Lizano, F., Sandoval, M., Stage, J.: Integrating usability evaluations into scrum: A case study based on remote synchronous user testing. Lecture Notes in Computer Science 8510 LNCS(1), 500–509 (2014)

41. Losada, B., Urretavizcaya, M., López, J., Fernández-Castro, I.: Applying usability engineering in intermod agile development methodology. a case study in a mobile application. Journal of Universal Computer Science 19(8), 1046–1065 (2013)
42. Losada, B., Urretavizcaya, M., López-Gil, J., Fernández-Castro, I.: Combining intermod agile methodology with usability engineering in a mobile application development. In: ACM International Conference. pp. 39:1 – 39:8 (2012)
43. Lárusdóttir, M., Cajander, A., Gulliksen, J.: Informal feedback rather than performance measurements - user-centred evaluation in scrum projects. Behaviour and Information Technology 33(11), 1118–1135 (2014)
44. Lárusdóttir, M., Bjarnadottir, E., Gulliksen, J.: The focus on usability in testing practices in industry. IFIP Advances in Information and Communication Technology 332, 98–109 (2010)
45. Magües, D.A., Castro, J.W., Acuña, S.T.: Requirements engineering related usability techniques adopted in agile development processes. In: International Conference on Software Engineering and Knowledge Engineering, SEKE. pp. 537–542 (2016)
46. Magües, D.A., Castro, J.W., Acuña, S.T.: Usability in agile development: A systematic mapping study. In: Latin American Computing Conference (CLEI). pp. 1–8 (2016)
47. McGinn, J.J., Chang, A.R.: Rite+krug: A combination of usability test methods for agile design. J. Usability Studies 8(3), 61–68 (May 2013)
48. Nielsen, L., Madsen, S.: The usability expert's fear of agility - an empirical study of global trends and emerging practices. pp. 261–264 (2012)
49. Salah, D., Paige, R., Cairns, P.: A systematic literature review for agile development processes and user centred design integration. In: ACM International Conference. pp. 5–14 (2014)
50. Seyam, M.: Enhancing usability through agility: Pair programming for a practice-oriented integration approach. In: 2015 International Conference on Collaboration Technologies and Systems (CTS). pp. 460–463 (June 2015)
51. Shneiderman, B.: Designing the User Interface: Strategies for Effective Human-Computer Interaction. Addison-Wesley Longman Publishing, 3 edn. (1997)
52. Sohaib, O., Khan, K.: Integrating usability engineering and agile software development: A literature review. In: Intern. Conference on Computer Design and Applications. pp. 232–238 (2010)
53. Sohaib, O., Khan, K.: Incorporating discount usability in extreme programming. Intern. Journal of Software Engineering and its Applications 5(1), 51–62 (2011)
54. Sy, D.: Adapting usability investigations for agile user-centered design. J. Usability Studies 2(3), 112–132 (May 2007)
55. Wale-Kolade, A.: Integrating usability work into a large inter-organisational agile development project: Tactics developed by usability designers. JSS 100, 54–66 (2015)
56. Wale-Kolade, A., Nielsen, P., Paivarinta, T.: Integrating usability practices into agile development: A case study. pp. 337–347 (2014)
57. Wolkerstorfer, P., Tscheligi, M., Sefelin, R., Milchrahm, H., Hussain, Z., Lechner, M., Shahzad, S.: Probing an agile usability process. pp. 2151–2157 (2008)
58. Øvad, T., Larsen, L.B.: The prevalence of ux design in agile development processes in industry. In: Agile Conference. pp. 40–49 (Aug 2015)

CollabIDE

A collaborative IDE for dynamic multi-versioning and variant management

Santiago Beltrán and Nicolás Cardozo

Systems and Computing Engineering Department
Universidad de los Andes - Bogotá, Colombia
{s.beltran10, n.cardozo}@uniandes.edu.co

Abstract. Current practices in software development are anchored in the use of version control systems to manage the development progress of software projects. Additionally, version control systems can be used to drive the release process of software products, by managing different variants of the main product in a repository. Despite the benefits of versioning systems, using such systems requires developers to interrupt their development work in order to interact with them, affecting their productivity. This paper presents CollabIDE, a collaborative environment for distributed development designed for automated versioning and product variant generation. The goal of CollabIDE is to increase developers' productivity, therefore, we conducted a small empirical study with users working in distributed teams, measuring the time to complete different tasks using versioning, and the ease to release different products' functionality based on recorded versions.

Keywords: Collaborative development, Version control, Software variability, Context-oriented programming

1 Introduction

The current practice of software development is strongly supported by Version Control Systems (VCSs) like subversion[1] and Git,[2] as they enable software developers to reduce the risk of losing progress of their activities, and offer the possibility of maintaining different variants of the code-base to serve different costumers. The main characteristics of using VCSs in software development processes are: (1) traceability over each file's change history, (2) concurrent editing, and (3) branching and merging of code extracts on independent streams of changes. These characteristics, enable to manage progress, backups, and variations of a software system as part of the development and maintenance activities of a software project [13].

[1] http://subversion.apache.org/
[2] http://git-scm.com

Taking advantage of VCSs, it is possible for software developers to embrace a Distributed Software Development (DSD) model, in which development teams are distributed in both, location and time. This model is beneficial in reducing costs, and finding human talent in different locations; which are aimed to increase the productivity of a development team. Similar to the DSD model, a Software Product Line (SPL) model can be supported by VCSs. Different variants of a product can be maintained independently, as part of a single development project, to provide personalized alternatives to different customers. This reduces development costs, due to resource reutilization, and provides a faster go to market cycle [10].

VCSs offer mechanisms like commit, push, and merge to manage versions and variants in a software project. With these mechanisms it is possible to solve synchronization and coordination problems as they arise. Notwithstanding, these mechanisms introduce an overhead for the development workflow. Users must interrupt their development tasks to interact with the VCS. For example, 70% of developers spend between 5 and 20 minutes solving synchronization and merging issues, significantly harming developer's productivity [3]. Additionally, in some cases, developers are unaware of the work produced by other team members, having a negative impact on productivity when working with existing code (*e.g.,* in maintenance tasks) [2].

Using VCSs for variant management also presents overhead in the productivity of software development teams, as the initial configuration is created [8]. Moreover, frequent interaction with the VCS increases the development time due to the context switch in the developer's mindset, taking longer to focus back on the development activity. Sporadic interaction with the VCS can lead to synchronization issues, and in turn, to longer development cycles [12].

To address the aforementioned problems when using VCSs to track program versions or manage SPLs, we propose an integrated development environment, CollabIDE, focused on the distributed collaboration in software product development (Section 2). CollabIDE integrates an automated VCS, and a lightweight SPL model for the generation of multiple variants from a single code base. CollabIDE is built on top of the dynamic behavior adaptation model proposed by Context-oriented Programming (COP) [11]. To use this model, we define versions as context objects (based on available information *e.g.,* the logged in user). Product variants are managed based on the defined versions, where a variant is generated using a subset of all defined versions.

To validate CollabIDE, we conducted a small empirical study with users working in distributed teams (Section 3). Each team had to develop different programming tasks following a sequence of commands to share code with their development team, and release different product variants. For each team we gathered information about the time spent performing actions related to version control and the percentage of tasks they could complete in the time limit. This information shows an improvement in productivity of about 11%, and a general acceptance towards the tool (gathered from a survey after the experiment).

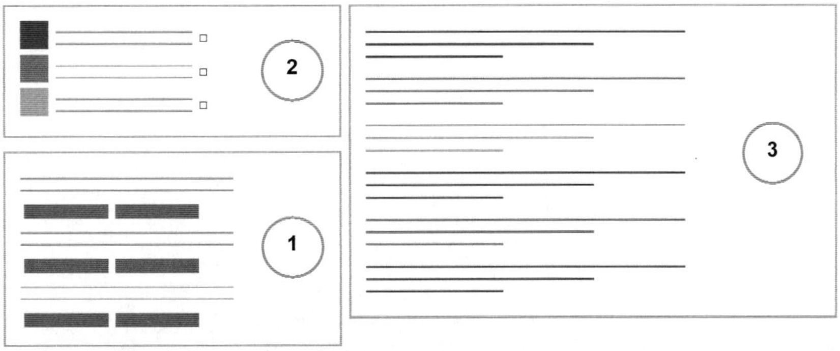

Fig. 1: General view of CollabIDE

2 CollabIDE

CollabIDE[3] is a cloud-based integrated development environment presenting collaboration facilities for distributed development teams working on a software project. CollabIDE has three key features which help to reduce the overhead of managing versions or product variants. These features are: (1) version management, (2) product variant management, and (3) collaborative development. Fig. 1 shows the distribution of the IDE's features in the user interface.

2.1 Version Management

Software products evolve over time [6]. Rather than releasing a fully working product at once, developers implement products incrementally. Each product increment focuses on a single feature or part of the functionality at a time. Each of these features marks a new *version* of the system, moving forward linearly in time. Defining and synchronizing between these pieces of functionality must be carried out multiple times in a project's lifespan. In the long-term, this process has a lasting impact in the productivity.

CollabIDE takes the association between a feature's development, and program versions to an extreme. In CollabIDE, every code modification (regardless of its size) is marked as a new product increment, meaning every character entered or modified is versioned. Furthermore, instead of asking developers to continuously create and manage product versions, CollabIDE automatically generates versions for each code increment. These increments are identified by a set of variables relevant to the project development. For example, relevant information to generate versions may include the developer's name, or the time of the day. Additionally, if developers want to create their own versions, it is possible to do so simply by giving them a name in the versions pane of the interface. Fig. 2 shows the way product versions are managed in CollabIDE.

A differentiating feature of CollabIDE is that versions are live. That is, every time a new version is created by any of the developers, it is made available to all developers. For a user this means being able to view all of the code written

[3] `https://collabide.herokuapp.com/`

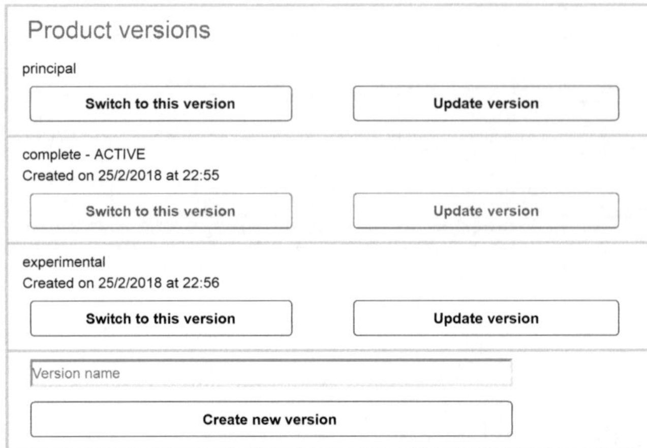

Fig. 2: Version visualization and management in CollabIDE

by the participants of a project the moment they type it. As a consequence, this synchronic approach at collaboration lets versioning conflicts become nonexistent since developers see the latest version of the code at all times and any change they make, be it insertion or edition (theirs or someone's else code) is also immediately reflected for all other developers. Moreover, when switching between versions, developers have an immediate view of the complete state of the code at the moment the version was created or edited.

The facilities for version management in CollabIDE help reduce the long-term impact of creating, updating, and synchronizing product versions, as these processes occur autonomously upon simple interactions.

2.2 Product Variant Management

In SPL development, product variants are managed through variability models, describing the different components of the product, and the different options for each of these components [10]. A product variant consists of the composition of a base product with different features, usually specialized for each costumer or purpose. This process requires developers to define beforehand both, the base product, and the variation points (*i.e.,* those features that can be interchanged with other features). This process is time consuming for the project setup, and fixed in the points where variations may take place.

CollabIDE takes advantage of its VCS to enable a more flexible product variation model. Product variants are defined by the composition of the different versions available in the system. These versions may be chosen based on the time of their creation (as explained in the previous section), or taking into account the contributions made by specific developers. The composition takes place behind the scene using COP facilities for dynamic software composition (*cf.* Section 2.4).

Fig. 3 shows the panel in the CollabIDE interface to select the different variants, in this case according to developers' contributions. Selecting one of the contributions renders the associated code as part of the interface, and composes the variant with the currently working code. From a product variant point of view, this feature eases the process of building new variants from existing fragments of code, effectively reducing the overhead derived from executing initial configuration processes.

Fig. 3: Product composition through contribution selection

2.3 Collaborative Development

CollabIDE offers a feature for collaborative development. Taking advantage of the VCS, developers are able to work concurrently on the same code base, having immediate feedback about the contributions of other developers. Developers' code is differentiated by highlighting, in a unique color, the code contributed by each developer, as shown in Fig. 4. First, colored code, offers a first-hand view about the contributions of each team member, increasing awareness about code owners, and coordination to develop or fix code increments. Second, code highlighting is used as a means to identify features a developer has worked on, enabling the composition of specific product variants by selecting the work of developers associated to specific features. When a specific developer is selected for a composition, every contribution the developer has made is included in the product variant resulting from said composition.

2.4 Implementation

The implementation of CollabIDE is based on the Context-oriented Programming (COP) paradigm, incorporated in Firepad.[4]

COP in a Nutshell COP is a programming paradigm designed for the dynamic adaptation of software systems based on context information gathered from the system's surrounding execution environment [11]. COP consists of three main abstractions: *Contexts*, *Behavioral adaptations*, and *Context activations*.

[4] `https://firepad.io/#1`

```
var config = {
        apiKey: "",
        authDomain: "collabide-c9fb9.firebaseapp.com",
        databaseURL: ""
    };
    firebase.initializeApp(config);

var userRef = firebase.database().ref(proID + "/users");
    userRef.on('child_added', function (snapshot) {
        updateRulesContext(snapshot);
    });

var userconnectedRef = firebase.database().ref(proID + "/users/" + loggedUser.username);
    userconnectedRef.onDisconnect().update({
        online: false,
    });



var actualVersionRef = firebase.database().ref(proID + "/activeVersion");
    actualVersionRef.on('value', function (snapshot) {
        console.log(snapshot.val());
        restoreVersion(snapshot.val());
    })



    function firepadInitialization(firepadNewRef) {
    //// Create CodeMirror (with lineWrapping on).
    codeMirror = CodeMirror(document.getElementById('firepad'), {
        lineNumbers: true,
        mode: 'javascript',
        matchBrackets: true,
        autoCloseBrackets: true,
    });
```

Fig. 4: First-hand view of developers' contributions

Contexts represent semantically meaningful situations gathered from a system's surrounding environment [1]. Contexts are defined as first-class entities of the system that are manipulated in reaction to external stimulus (*e.g.,* changes in sensed information, actions executed by users). A context can be in an active state, stating that the situation it represents is taking place in the surrounding environment. Otherwise, the context is said to be inactive.

Behavioral adaptations are fine-grained behavior definitions associated to one or several context entities. Behavioral adaptations dictate the observable behavior of a system under a particular situation sensed from the surrounding environment. The combination of behavioral adaptations and contexts constitute what we call an *adaptation.*

Context activations correspond to the systems' reaction to the surrounding environment. Whenever a context is sensed to be active (the information associated with the contexts satisfies a given activation condition), an activation message is sent to the system. Upon the message's evaluation, the system is dynamically recomposed taking into account all behavioral adaptations associated with the context. This process may overwrite previous behavior definitions already composed in the system. Whenever the activation conditions of a context are unsatisfied, a deactivation message is sent, effectively withdrawing the behavioral adaptations associated with the context. That is, the system is dynamically recomposed, not taking into account the context's behavioral adaptations. Note that, different combinations of contexts may compose the system at a time.

CollabIDE Internals To implement the features described in Section 2, we create a one to one association between adaptations and versions. Versions consist of the code introduced by developers and the conditions of the surrounding environment in which these take place.

As a cloud-based platform, CollabIDE is implemented in ECMAScript, using node.js[5] for the backend, and Firepad, an open source collaborative text editor, for the frontend. To define and manage contexts we use Context Traits [5].

As mentioned before, versions and product variants are defined dynamically based on the time in which a code increment is defined, and the user defining such increment, respectively. Each of these situations defines a condition in which the code is created; therefore, they constitute contexts. First, whenever users log into the system, a context is automatically defined using the timestamp as its identifier. The following snippet show the example of a context created for a contribution made on 19/05/2017 at 14 : 28

```
var 190520171428 = new cop.Context{
  name: "190520171428"
}
```

Additionally, the system defines a context per user, associating all code increments to this context too. The purpose of this additional association is twofold. On the one hand, we use it to select product variants per user. On the other hand, it is used to adapt the behavior of the text rendering in Firebase, in order to display the colored layer indicating the contributions for each developer.

All code increments are recorded as part of a behavioral adaptation associated to a context. The following code snippet defines the behavioral adaptation (Lines 1-6) to modify the text highlighting feature for a particular developer. Behavioral adaptations are then associated to contexts (Line 7) to be used in the system, in this case adapting the `defineVisibility` function of the `highlighter` Firebase object. In this example, as a particular developer is selected (as in Fig. 3), this activates the DevContext, coloring the text with the color associated to the developer. The **proceed** call in Line 4 works as a super-call, to invoke the original behavior of the system (*i.e.,* without adaptation)

```
1 HighlightTrait = Trait = ({
2   defineVisibility : function() {
3     developerRule.style.display = "inline";
4     this.proceed();
5   }
6 })
7 DevContext.adapt(highlighter, HighlightTrait);
```

Once all contexts and their associated behavioral adaptations are defined, these can be combined dynamically to compose different variants of the system

[5] http://nodejs.org/

under development. Moreover, while the system is running, is possible to switch between its versions, for example, to test/rollback new features seamlessly.

3 Validation

To validate the appropriateness of CollabIDE, we define two research questions: (1) Does an automated VCS improve productivity in software development?, and (2) Is it possible to use software versions to generate multiple software variants from a product? To answer these questions, we conducted an empirical evaluation to measure how effective CollabIDE was at reducing overhead problems in both Distributed Software Development and Software Product Lines.

3.1 Experiment Design

To help answer each question, we designed two isolated experiments. Each experiment asks a group of developers to solve a programming task using either CollabIDE or a conventional IDE, following a set of instructions aimed to emulate the workflow of each development model. The experiments differed in team sizes, the required tasks to complete and the instructions assigned to each group. The programming tasks in conjunction with the set of instructions were designed to force participants into situations that are commonplace in real life projects. In the collaborative experiment, participants would eventually need to work on the same piece of functionality at the same time, bringing about a number of conflicts. In the second experiment, participants would need to build multiple"products" that shared the same basic functionality but differ in specific features. Two measures are taken in each experiment: (1) the completion percentage of the total tasks assigned, and (2) the amount of time in minutes spent performing actions related to version control.

Experiment 1: Software development in a distributed set-up The objective of this experiment was to quantify the overhead reduction that can be achieved when using CollabIDE versus using other IDEs in a distributed set-up. This experiment targets to answer the first research question. For the experiment, groups of two developers had to implement a set of common graph algorithms using only JavaScript. The specific instruction they had to follow was that they needed to use version control periodically (at set moments during the experiment) so that both team members code remained up to date with their partner's changes through the experiment.

Experiment 2: Product variants development and deployment In this second experiment the objective was to quantify the overhead reduction that can be achieved with CollabIDE in a product line generation set-up. This experiment targets to answer both research questions. In this case, the programming task was to implement (individually) a set of data structures with basic functionality using JavaScript or Java. Each data structure also had to be a variant of a given base data structure. Participants had to use version control to manage the different product variants that were involved in the programming tasks.

3.2 Experiment Setup

Six developers were gathered for the first experiment and split into three groups of two developers. Two groups used CollabIDE and the remaining group used the Sublime Text IDE[6] in conjunction with git and github. The participants were given a total of 90 minutes to accomplish the tasks in Experiment 1. Each group was required to obtain their partners changes every 15 minutes using the tools at hand. For experiment 2, a different group of four developers working individually was gathered. Two of them using CollabIDE and the other two using Eclipse in conjunction with git and github. These participants were also given 90 minutes to complete their task. For experiment 2, there was no constraint in how often participants needed to use version control. On both experiments we made sure the participants that weren't employing CollabIDE had prior experience with their respective IDEs. The participants that used CollabIDE were presented with a small explanation of how to use its features. We avoided giving a detailed explanation with the intent of knowing how intuitive the participants would think the IDE felt.

3.3 Results

In this section we analyze the results of each experiment, specifically how each measure provides evidence of CollabIDE's strengths over the other IDEs. We also use theses results to answer the research questions proposed initially.

Experiment 1 Results Fig. 5 shows the results for each group of participants and their backgrounds. The two groups using CollabIDE achieved a higher completion rate, on average 11% more tasks completed than the control group. On top of that, they also spent significantly less time performing actions related to version control, an average of 33.2 minutes less. The higher completion rate achieved by the groups that used CollabIDE can be attributed to the fact that the developers could spend more time coding as they did not have to invest much in version control. It is clear why there is such a significant difference in time for both IDEs results. While the control group had to follow the common git workflow of committing, pushing, pulling changes and solving the possible conflicts that could arise, the CollabIDE groups could avoid this process altogether as CollabIDEs features ensured that both team members always had each other's latest changes without conflicts. Thus, the only action they needed to perform was creating a new version using the version management feature.

When analyzing the developers' background, one factor that could have influenced the results is the fact that all of the participants that used CollabIDE had more experience in Javascript. Nevertheless, the experiment was designed in a way that only a basic knowledge of Javascript and data structures was required so the results were most likely not influenced by this.

These first results relate to our first research question. We can state that an automated VCS can indeed increase productivity in software development.

[6] `https://www.sublimetext.com`

Participant	Participant's Background				Experiment Results		
	Language experience	Versioning tools experience	Collaborative development experience	Group	IDE	Completion	Minutes spent in VSC
Developer 1	Less than 1 year	2 to 3 years	2 to 3 years	Group 1	CollabIDE	73%	0.51
Developer 2	2 to 3 years	More than 3 years	2 to 3 years				
Developer 3	1 to 2 years	2 to 3 years	2 to 3 years	Group 2	CollabIDE	69%	0.51
Developer 4	Less than 1 year	1 to 2 years	Less than 1 year				
Developer 5	Less than 1 year	Less than 1 year	Less than 1 year	Group 3	Sublime	60%	33.71
Developer 6	Less than 1 year	1 to 2 years	1 to 2 years				

Fig. 5: Results for Experiment 1

Experiment 2 Results Fig. 6 shows the results for each developer. Similar to the first experiment, the developers that employed CollabIDE obtained better results, but in this case, the difference between using an IDE versus using the other was not very significative. With CollabIDE, the developers finished an average of 4% more tasks and spent 2.83 minutes less in version control than the developers using Eclipse. The process of creating new product variants and their respective functionalities varied significantly in each IDE. With Eclipse and git, participants had to create a branch for each variant and then checkout between branches when they needed to work on a variants specific code. Using CollabIDE, participants needed to first create a product version for each variant, then, for each variant create a new developer. This way the participants could take advantage of code highlighting and hiding to easily distinguish which code fragments belonged to which variant. Thus, while Eclipse and Git make variant creation straightforward, the process of switching between them is not as smooth. The contrary happens with CollabIDE, where creating a variant is a longer process but switching between them is faster. According to this, it makes sense that in the results were close together, as there is a tradeoff when using one IDE over the other. However, in real life contexts, projects usually take longer to complete and variant switching operations are more frequent than variant creating ones. Therefore, in a real life context CollabIDE could provide better productivity.

When analyzing other factors that could have influenced the experiment, we found one with a potential impact on the results. As the tasks needed to be implemented in different languages, the differences between these could have led to some developers being more familiar with one of the languages. Nevertheless, when we assigned the tasks to each developer we took into account their prior experience with the language, so the impact of languages differences may have not been significative

One situation worth mentioning is that one of the developers had problems pushing his changes to github, and at the end of the experiment he only had one branch, meaning he lost the changes he made to all the other product variants. This occurrence helps reinforce our claim that the use of VCS can in some cases be detrimental to productivity.

While the results show that CollabIDE does not outperform the other development set-up by a wide margin, they do support our second research question up to certain extend. Through the experiment the participants were able to effectively generate multiple product variants and switch between them with relatively ease, proving that CollabIDE's features are robust enough to enable this type of development model.

Participant	Participant's Background		Experiment Results		
	Language experience	Versioning tools experience	IDE	Completion	Minutes spent in VSC
Developer 1	Less than 1 year	Less than 1 year	CollabIDE	60%	2.10
Developer 2	Less than 1 year	1 to 2 years	CollabIDE	44%	1.57
Developer 3	More than 3 years	1 to 2 years	Eclipse	45%	3.66
Developer 4	1 to 2 years	Less than 1 year	Eclipse	55%	2.84

Fig. 6: Experiment 2 results

Survey At the end of the experiment, we asked the participants that used CollabIDE their opinion on the tool's main features. All of them agreed that collaborative programming was easy to understand, and of great help in completing their tasks. Version management received mixed results as participants thought it was not too complex, but not all of them felt this feature helped them during development. Finally, most participants found the product variant management feature useful and easy to use. Overall, participants perceived CollabIDE as an intuitive IDE, which let them solve the programming tasks in an efficient manner.

3.4 Threats to Validity

In this section we discuss some aspects of the experiments that can put at risk the validity of the results discussed previously. First, the subject sample size used is small, having only one control group in Experiment 1, and two in Experiment 2. Small sample sizes can easily lead to bias [9]; in this case, the bias would be towards CollabIDE performing better. Another aspect that can be considered a threat is the low duration of each experiment. In real life contexts, software projects where version control systems are employed usually take weeks to months to complete. Additionally, the time intervals between each version control operation are longer, whereas in the experiment they needed to be performed each 15 minutes. These lower times could also lead to bias towards one of the IDEs, as the development workflow was unfaithful in comparison to those carried out in a real life context.

4 Related Work

Different tools exist for collaborative writing or coding. In this section we discuss the features available in such tools and put them in perspective to CollabIDE.

Collaborative writing platforms like Google Docs and meetingwords[7] are not designed for code editing, however, they employ mechanics similar to those of CollabIDEs. In Google Docs, changes made to a document are asynchronous and saved automatically. Contributions by collaborators are visible in real time by following user-specific markers. However, changes are all merged into a single document as users edit. Nonetheless, color highlighting is used to highlight changes made by individual collaborators when reviewing a documents history. Meetingwords provides similar features to those in Google Docs, with the additional feature of color highlighting for the editions each user contributes to the document. Such color highlighting served as inspiration for the same feature in CollabIDE. However, this is just a visual aid to see who contributed each part of the text, and cannot be manipulated as versions in CollabIDE.

Distributed tools for code editing targeting development productivity have also been explored. Ghorashi and Jensen [4] present Jimbo, an IDE that allows developers to collaborate on a common project. Jimbo's most relevant features are synchronic and asynchronic collaboration, and user identification. The first one lets developers make changes without worrying about conflicts. The second one provides version management by allowing developers to follow specific fragments of code in a project to later receive notifications if said fragment received any modifications. This second feature may not be optimal on big projects where there are thousands of lines of code as it requires continuous user intervention, effectively creating an overhead that harms productivity. CodeBunk[8]. is a cloud-based tool enabling playback. Playback saves the history of all changes made in an instance of the code editor. Users can playback these changes, showing each one in the order they were made. This feature reduces conflicts and improve awareness in a project. Similar to Jimbo, an overhead is introduced as developers need to interrupt their workflow and sit through a historys playback to identify possible conflicts and changes made by others. If an history gets long enough, the interruption times also get longer, and more time is needed to get back into the coding workflow.

In CollabIDE, both of these overhead problems are avoided by providing passive aids to developers for (automatic) code versioning, and identifying distinct users contributions (code highlighting). This way developers can focus on writing code rather than on performing additional actions.

---

[7] `http://meetingwords.com`
[8] `https://codebunk.com`

5 Conclusion

CollabIDE is a development environment prototype for distributed teams, incorporating automated versioning and enabling the generation of multiple software products according to the code's version base.

CollabIDE is developed with the goal of increasing the productivity of software development teams by reducing the time developers must dedicate to tasks other than coding; specifically targeting the versioning and product variant deployment tasks of the software development process. CollabIDE is based on COP to tackle both tasks. Situations in which the development task take place (*e.g.,* user, time, code extract of the modification) are defined as contexts, which can be use directly to represent and define the versions of the system. Extraction, definition, and usage of such contexts/versions takes place autonomously, so developers need not to be distracted by these activities. COP enables flexible composition of software systems while they execute. Using this feature it is possible to compose different versions as part of a fully working program variant. Composition of such variants requires developers to select which of the contexts they want to use. Available contexts in the project are accessible to developers within the tool itself, in order to minimize the disruption and time spent in generating the variants.

The validation of CollabIDE evidences its effectiveness in reducing the overhead of dealing with version control or product variant generation systems, when working in a distributed software development team or when employing the product lines development model. Although the scale of the experiment is small, it already shows the potential that an approach like CollabIDE has. Thanks to the flexibility of the technology used to create CollabIDE, it can easily be extended with features that are common in other IDEs like code linting, auto-completion, support for other programming languages and debugging among others. One important extension that could be made is the possibility of managing various files and folders as a software development project rarely relies on only one file. Furthermore, there are many ways the existing features can be tweaked to make them better at approaching the problem they intend to solve. Some examples would be introducing additional code highlighting, a code history feature that lets users navigate to a specific change made or even letting different product variants be merged in a similar fashion of how its done on git. Another limitation of CollabIDE that is worth discussing is the maximum amount of developers in a project. Currently CollabIDE supports up to 8 developers. This is due to the need to identify each one with an easily distinguishable color. If the number of developers was higher it would get increasingly difficult to choose colors that can be distinguished from one another. This limitation is worth approaching for the case of open-source projects where there can be a high number of developers lending their contributions in single or multiple files. As future work, we plan to conduct a more extensive case study to evaluate the relevance of CollabIDE in larger development teams. Additionally, we see the value of the tool for code reviews, therefore we want to extend CollabIDE with code productivity metrics (*e.g.,* Lines of Code, code clones) and analysis facilities [7]. Such extension would enable code reviewers to better evaluate the productivity of particular developers. CollabIDE, can be particularly useful in academic/teaching environments to quickly differentiate how much a particular student participated in an assignment, or when the majority of work took place.

Bibliography

[1] A. K. Dey. Understanding and using context. *Personal Ubiquitous Computing*, 5(1):4–7, Jan. 2001.

[2] P. Dourish and V. Bellotti. Awareness and coordination in shared workspaces. In *Proceedings of the 1992 ACM Conference on Computer-supported Cooperative Work*, CSCW '92, pages 107–114, New York, NY, USA, 1992. ACM. ISBN 0-89791-542-9. doi: 10.1145/143457.143468. URL `http://doi.acm.org/10.1145/143457.143468`.

[3] H. C. Estler, M. Nordio, C. A. Furia, and B. Meyer. Awareness and merge conflicts in distributed software development. In *2014 IEEE 9th International Conference on Global Software Engineering*, pages 26–35, Aug 2014. doi: 10.1109/ICGSE.2014.17.

[4] S. Ghorashi and C. Jensen. Jimbo: A collaborative ide with live preview. In *2016 IEEE/ACM Cooperative and Human Aspects of Software Engineering (CHASE)*, pages 104–107, May 2016. doi: 10.1109/CHASE.2016.029.

[5] S. González, K. Mens, M. Colacioiu, and W. Cazzola. Context Traits: Dynamic behaviour adaptation through run-time trait recomposition. In *Proc. of the Conf. on Aspect-oriented Software Development*, AOSD'13, pages 209–220. ACM, 2013. ISBN 978-1-4503-1766-5.

[6] M. M. Lehman and J. F. Ramil. Software evolution and software evolution processes. *Annals of Software Engineering*, 14:275–309, 2002.

[7] A. Lienhard, T. Girba, and O. Nierstrasz. Specifying dynamic analyses by extending language semantics. *IEEE Transactions on Software Engineering*, 38(3):694–706, May 2012. ISSN 0098-5589. doi: 10.1109/TSE.2011.38.

[8] N. Niu, J. Savolainen, Z. Niu, M. Jin, and J. R. C. Cheng. A systems approach to product line requirements reuse. *IEEE Systems Journal*, 8(3): 827–836, Sept 2014. ISSN 1932-8184. doi: 10.1109/JSYST.2013.2260092.

[9] Ohlund and C. h. Yu. Threats to validity of research design. URL `http://web.pdx.edu/~stipakb/download/PA555/ResearchDesign.html`.

[10] K. Pohl, G. Böckle, and F. van der Linden. *Software Product Line Engineering: Foundations, Principles and Techniques.* Springer-Verlag Berlin Heidelberg, 2005. ISBN 978-3-540-24372-4.

[11] G. Salvaneschi, C. Ghezzi, and M. Pradella. Context-oriented programming: A software engineering perspective. 85(8):1801–1817, Aug. 2012.

[12] F. Schwgerl, T. Buchmann, and B. Westfechtel. Supermod: A model-driven tool that combines version control and software product line engineering. In *International Conference on Software Technologies*, volume 2 of *ICSOFT'15*, pages 1–14, July 2015.

[13] D. Spinellis. Version control systems. *IEEE Software*, 22(5):108–109, Sept 2005. ISSN 0740-7459. doi: 10.1109/MS.2005.140.

Un algoritmo genético para generar casos de prueba funcionales con oráculo

Macario Polo[1], Óscar Pedreira[2], Ignacio García-Rodríguez[1], Nieves R. Brisaboa[2] y Mario Piattini[1]
[1] Escuela Superior de Informática, Universidad de Castilla-La Mancha, Ciudad Real, España
[2] Facultade de Informática, Universidad de A Coruña, A Coruña, España
macario.polo@uclm.es, oscar.pedreira@udc.es, ignacio.grodriguez@uclm.es, brisaboa@udc.es, mario.piattini@uclm.es

Abstract. Muchos autores han utilizado algoritmos genéticos para la generación automática de casos de prueba. En este contexto, la función de fitness se describe dependiendo del objetivo del test suite que se desea obtener, que suele corresponder con algún criterio de cobertura, como cubrir todas las decisiones con MC/DC o cubrir todos los usos de una variable. Uno de los principales problemas de los casos de prueba generados automáticamente es la ausencia del oráculo, que es el mecanismo del que se dota al caso de prueba para que éste determine si ha encontrado o no error en el sistema bajo prueba: en efecto, un caso de prueba obtenido del cruce de dos progenitores estará describiendo un escenario de ejecución no previsto y del que se desconoce su resultado esperado. Por ello, tras la convergencia del algoritmo genético mediante la producción de un test suite que alcanza el requisito de prueba deseado, el tester debe añadir manualmente el oráculo a cada uno de los casos de prueba obtenidos.
En este artículo se presenta un método que permite describir de manera genérica multitud de situaciones de ejecución, así como una estrategia para generar casos que combina expresiones regulares y técnicas combinatorias. Los casos de prueba que se obtienen con esta estrategia conforman la población inicial de un algoritmo genético, que en cada iteración produce una nueva población de casos. Cada uno de estos casos ejercita una de esas situaciones de ejecución genéricas. Como estas situaciones tienen su oráculo descrito también de forma genérica, el test suite que se obtiene está formado por casos de prueba con oráculo. La función de fitness está basada en el Mutation Score que se alcanza al matar mutantes producidos mediante operadores que utilizan programación orientada a aspectos.

Keywords: Generación de casos de prueba, Algoritmos genéticos, Mutación, Oráculo.

1 Introducción

El objetivo principal del testing de software es encontrar errores en el SUT (el *system under test* o sistema bajo prueba). Para ello, el tester escribe casos de prueba que ejercitan tantos escenarios diferentes del SUT como sea posible, teniendo en cuenta las restricciones de coste y tiempo del proyecto. Una propiedad importante de los casos de prueba es que sean reproducibles: es decir, que ofrezcan siempre el mismo resultado (denominado *veredicto* en este contexto) independientemente del momento en que se ejecuten. La reproducibilidad es importante, sobre todo, en metodologías ágiles o iterativas (pues tras cada iteración o *sprint* se reejecutan los casos de prueba procedentes de iteraciones anteriores) y durante las pruebas de regresión en el proceso de mantenimiento (se ejecutan los casos de prueba de versiones anteriores para comprobar que no se han introducido en la nueva *release* errores que antes no existían). En este sentido, un caso de prueba consta en general de tres partes [1][2]: (1) **Especificación de la situación inicial**, que pone al SUT en el estado requerido para ejecutar el caso. Puede incluir, por ejemplo, la creación de una base de datos, el levantamiento de un servidor, etcétera; (2) **Ejecución de las operaciones del SUT** que se desean reproducir, con los datos que correspondan; y (3) **Comparación del resultado** obtenido con el esperado para emitir el veredicto, normalmente un resultado de paso o fallo en función de que, respectivamente, el caso de prueba haya o no encontrado error en el SUT. A este mecanismo de comparación se lo llama *oráculo.*

La automatización de las tareas de testing pretende la ejecución, tan desatendida como sea posible, de sus diferentes fases. De éstas, las más dependientes de la tecnología y del entorno en que se ejecuta el SUT son las siguientes:

1. **Generación de datos y casos de prueba**. Una vez identificados los escenarios que se desean probar, el tester debe identificar las operaciones necesarias para ejecutarlos, así como los datos que se deben pasar a dichas operaciones como parámetros.
2. **Ejecución de casos de prueba**. Los casos de prueba se lanzan contra el SUT. Dependiendo de la plataforma en que corre el SUT, se necesitarán entornos de ejecución de diferentes tipos.
3. **Análisis de resultados**. Además de revisarse los veredictos que hayan arrojado los casos de prueba (y con los cuales se reportan los errores encontrados para que sean corregidos), se realiza también un análisis de cobertura, con el que se conocen las áreas del sistema que han sido recorridas y las que no.

Así pues, en la fase de análisis de resultados se hace tanto una comprobación de los veredictos como de las zonas del código que se han recorrido. De acuerdo con Polo y Reales [3], en un proceso de pruebas en el que se combinan pruebas de caja negra y de caja blanca: (1) se determina inicialmente el nivel de cobertura que se desea alcanzar en el SUT; (2) se construye un test suite para encontrar errores y se analizan los veredictos; (3) si hay errores, el SUT se corrige; (4) si no los hay, se evalúa la cobertura alcanzada: si es igual o superior al umbral preestablecido, se detiene el proceso porque el SUT se está recorriendo suficientemente sin haber encontrado errores; si es inferior, se añaden nuevos casos de prueba para subir la cobertura. Estos nuevos casos de prueba pueden encontrar errores en esas áreas que habían permanecido inexploradas.

Mientras que la generación de datos y casos de prueba para alimentar el test suite inicial son tareas relativamente resueltas, la inclusión automática del oráculo en los casos de prueba, incluso para el test suite inicial, es una tarea complicada que es aún objeto de investigación. En un proceso de generación, ejecución y análisis automáticos, la situación se complica mucho.

Este artículo describe un proceso automático para generar casos de prueba con oráculos basado en un algoritmo genético, así como una herramienta de soporte. El trabajo está organizado como sigue: en la Sección 2 se presenta un ejemplo ilustrativo que describe el problema objeto de estudio. En la Sección 3 hacemos un breve repaso a algunos trabajos relacionados. La Sección 4 es la principal contribución de este trabajo, presentando el algoritmo genético. Finalmente, la Sección 5 incluye nuestras conclusiones y las líneas de trabajo futuro.

2 Descripción del problema

Supongamos, con fines ilustrativos, la clase *Account* de la Figura 1, que representa una posible cuenta bancaria que, además de un constructor y una operación para conocer el saldo (*getBalance)*, incluye tres operaciones para ingresar (*deposit),* retirar (*withdraw)* y transferir (*transfer).*

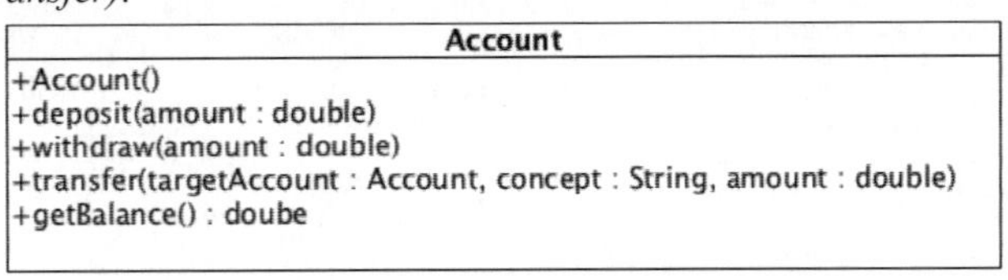

Fig. 1. Una cuenta bancaria

Asumamos que las tres operaciones pueden lanzar las siguientes excepciones: (1) *NegativeAmountException,* si se intenta ingresar, retirar o transferir un importe cero o negativo; (2) *InsufficientBalanceException,* si se intenta retirar o transferir un importe superior al saldo de la cuenta; y (3) *NullTargetAccountException,* si la cuenta de destino de una transferencia (parámetro *targetAccount)* no se ha establecido.

En la Tabla 1 se muestran tres posibles casos de prueba para esta clase: el del lado izquierdo, arriba (*testNormal_700)* ejercita un escenario "normal", en el que no se espera que se lance ninguna excepción; en el de la izquierda, arriba (*testNoBalanceTransfer)*, se intenta transferir más dinero del que se dispone en la cuenta; en el tercero (*testNegativeTransfer)*, se intenta transferir una cantidad negativa:

1. En el primer caso, el oráculo consta de una instrucción *assertTrue* (que comprueba si el saldo obtenido es igual al esperado, emitiendo el veredicto de paso o de fallo que corresponda) y de una instrucción *fail* (que, en caso de alcanzarse, emite veredicto de fallo).
2. En el segundo y tercer casos, y puesto que lo que se espera es que respectivamente se lance una *InsufficientBalanceException* o una *NegativeAmountException,* el oráculo consta de dos instrucciones *fail* (una en el bloque *try,* que emite veredicto de fallo si no se lanza excepción; otra en el segundo bloque *catch,* que emite veredicto de fallo si la excepción que se lanza no es la esperada) y un bloque *catch* vacío (si se captura la excepción que se esperaba, caso en el que el SUT se ha comportado

correctamente y se emite veredicto de paso).

Tabla 1. Tres casos de prueba para la clase *Account*

```
@Test
public void testNormal_700() {
  Account c=new Account();
  try {
    c.deposit(1000);
    c.withdraw(200);
    c.transfer(new Account(),
        "Telephone", 100);
    assertTrue(c.getBalance()==700);
  }
  catch (Exception e) {
    fail("No exception expected");
  }
}
@Test
public void testNoBalanceTransfer() {
  Account c=new Account();
  try {
   c.deposit(1000);
   c.withdraw(200);
   c.transfer(new Account(),
        " Telephone ", 5000);
   fail("InsufficientBalanceException "
        + "expected");
  }
  catch (InsufficientBalanceException e)
  {}
  catch (Exception e) {
    fail("InsufficientBalanceException "
        + expected");
  }
}
```

```
@Test
public void testNegativeTransfer() {
  Account c=new Account();
  try {
    c.deposit(1000);
    c.withdraw(200);
    c.transfer(new Account(),
      " Telephone ", -100);
    fail("NegativeAmountException " +
          expected");
  }
  catch (NegativeAmountException e) {}
  catch (Exception e) {
    fail("NegativeAmountException " +
          expected");
  }
}
```

Como se ve, los tres casos de prueba tienen prácticamente la misma estructura: se construye la instancia y se llama a *deposit, withdraw* y *transfer.* Pero, sin embargo, el oráculo es muy distinto en los tres casos.

En un generador automático de datos y casos de prueba, el tester puede asignar diferentes valores a los parámetros de las operaciones involucradas en los casos. Por ejemplo, si se asignan los valores {1000, 500} a *deposit,* {200, 50} a *withdraw* y {5000, 100, -100} al tercer parámetro de *transfer,* aplicando un algoritmo de generación de todas las combinaciones se podrían obtener los 2x2x3=12 casos de prueba de la Tabla 2. Entre ellos, se encuentran los tres que hemos especificado arriba.

Tabla 2. Posibles combinaciones

#	*deposit*	*withdraw*	*transfer*	#	*deposit*	*withdraw*	*transfer*
	{1000, 500}	*{200, 50}*	*{5000, 100, -100}*		*{1000, 500}*	*{200, 50}*	*{5000, 100, -100}*
1	1000	200	5000	7	500	200	5000
2	1000	200	100	8	500	200	100
3	1000	200	-100	9	500	200	-100
4	1000	50	5000	10	500	50	5000
5	1000	50	100	11	500	50	100
6	1000	50	-100	12	500	50	-100

Una vez generadas estas combinaciones y traducidas a casos de prueba, es el tester quien debe decidir, para cada una, cuál es el oráculo que le corresponde. En la Tabla 2 mostramos tres parámetros numéricos, con lo que la determinación del oráculo es casi trivial. En situaciones reales, la variedad de escenarios, operaciones y parámetros hace ya compleja la asignación manual del oráculo, y mucho más difícil aún su determinación e inclusión automáticas.

Por otro lado, y aunque la cobertura que alcanza un test suite obtenido generando todas las combinaciones es la máxima que, con esos datos de prueba, se puede obtener, aplicar todas las combinaciones produce una cantidad enorme de casos de prueba, muchos de los cuales serán además redundantes (es decir, ejercitan exactamente las mismas áreas del código) [4]: los casos números 2, 5, 8 y 11 de la Tabla 2 corresponden a un escenario "normal", en el que se retiran y transfieren importes teniendo para ambas operaciones saldo suficiente: probablemente con utilizar uno de esos cuatro casos sería suficiente.

Por estos motivos se utilizan otras estrategias para generar casos de prueba, como algoritmos de *pairwise* [5, 6], que producen menos casos de prueba que *all combinations* pero que, si los datos de prueba están bien elegidos, alcanzan por lo general una cobertura bastante alta.

El problema viene cuando esta cobertura "bastante alta" no alcanza el umbral deseado: de acuerdo con el proceso descrito en la Figura 1, se deben crear nuevos casos de prueba que recorran las zonas inexploradas del SUT, y a estos casos de prueba hay que dotarlos de un oráculo adecuado. Este es precisamente el problema cuya solución abordamos en este trabajo.

3 Trabajos relacionados

3.1 Generación de casos de prueba

La generación automatizada de casos de prueba es una línea de investigación prolífica en ingeniería de software: como ejemplo, una búsqueda simple en Scopus para publicaciones con los términos "generación de casos de prueba" en el título arroja 170 documentos de conferencia y 61 artículos, solo de 2011 a octubre de 2015. Nueve reconocidos especialistas, dirigidos por Bertolino, Li y Zhu, han coordinado el artículo *An orchestrated survey on automated software test case generation* [7], que clasifica las técnicas para la generación de casos de prueba en cinco categorías: (1) ejecución simbólica y cobertura estructural del programa ; (2) generación basada en modelos (MBT); (3) pruebas combinatorias; (4) prueba aleatoria adaptativa (ART); y (5) pruebas de software basadas en búsqueda (SBST). A continuación se describen algunas conclusiones de esta survey:

- En cuanto a la ejecución simbólica, Anand y Harrold destacan algunos problemas importantes de esta categoría: un número extremadamente grande de caminos en el software del mundo real, variedad de lenguajes de programación, imposibilidad o dificultad para recuperar la estructura de los módulos binarios e indecibilidad de las restricciones de ruta. En sus conclusiones, los autores explican que "se necesita más investigación para mejorar la utilidad de la técnica en los programas del mundo real".

Desafortunadamente, la mayoría de los problemas de ejecución simbólica aplicados a testing están abiertos desde hace muchos años.

- En la citada survey, Grieskamp revisa las técnicas de generación de MBT. Los desafíos pendientes de esta categoría se resumen en un informe externo, escrito por el propio Grieskamp y colaboradores [8]. Los autores destacan mejoras significativas desde 2004 (año del informe anterior) hasta 2011, sobre todo en la disponibilidad de herramientas para MBT. Sin embargo, varios de los desafíos de investigación de 2004 siguen abiertos; en particular: el tratamiento del no determinismo en los modelos; la brecha entre el nivel de abstracción de los modelos y el código; repetibilidad de casos de prueba (sobre todo en entornos distribuidos y en la nube); dificultades para la trazabilidad desde los requisitos hasta los modelos; y la falta de uso de ingeniería dirigida por modelos en la industria.
- Cohen está a cargo de la revisión de los métodos de prueba combinatoria. Esta autora resalta que ésta es "una prometedora área de investigación [...] con oportunidades para mejorar nuevos dominios de aplicación". Algunas direcciones futuras fructíferas en el campo de las pruebas combinatorias incluyen "la extracción automática del modelo, la adaptación a la evolución del modelo y el desarrollo de técnicas que reutilicen o compartan información entre diferentes pruebas".
- La prueba aleatoria adaptativa (ARV) es una mejora de las pruebas aleatorias de cuya revisión, en la citada survey, se encarga Chen. La efectividad de ART con respecto a las pruebas aleatorias es significativamente mayor, pero presenta problemas de eficiencia con respecto al tiempo y los recursos computacionales. Por lo tanto, la investigación en esta línea debe centrarse en la mejora de la eficiencia de los algoritmos.
- Harman, McMinn, Clark y Burke redactan la sección sobre SBST, que se considera una rama de la ingeniería de software basada en la búsqueda. SBST utiliza algoritmos de optimización para automatizar la búsqueda de datos de prueba que maximiza el logro de los objetivos de prueba, mientras que minimiza sus costos. Según estos autores, "el principal objetivo [de estas técnicas] es la definición de una función objetivo que capture adecuadamente los requisitos de la prueba y que guíe correctamente al algoritmo de optimización basado en la búsqueda". Los algoritmos genéticos o de colonias de hormigas son técnicas que entran en esta categoría. La posibilidad de modelar con funciones de acondicionamiento físico cualquier requisito de prueba da a las técnicas de SBST "muchos objetivos de prueba emocionantes, importantes y productivos que aún no se han atacado [...], proporcionando así muchas vías fructíferas para el trabajo futuro".

3.2 El problema del oráculo

En una survey reciente, Barr et al. revisan casi cuarenta años de investigación sobre el problema del oráculo [9]. Clasifican las técnicas propuestas en 694 publicaciones de 1978 a 2012 en cuatro categorías: (1) oráculos de prueba especificados, que requieren algún tipo de especificación formal; (2) oráculos de prueba derivados, que involucran artefactos de los cuales se puede derivar un oráculo de prueba (como una versión anterior del sistema, por ejemplo); (3) oráculos implícitos, que están relacionados con la

detección de errores obvios (bloqueos del programa, excepciones de puntero nulo, etc.); y (4) falta de oráculo de prueba automatizado (oráculo humano, por ejemplo).
Según estos autores, el oráculo es un "problema abierto actual que representa un importante cuello de botella que requiere una mayor automatización de las pruebas y la adopción de métodos y herramientas de pruebas automatizadas de manera más amplia". De hecho, así como la generación de casos de prueba puede ser un problema relativamente resuelto, la adición de oráculos a cada caso de prueba permanece prácticamente sin resolver.
Bertolino [10] también enfatizó la automatización de la generación de Oracle como uno de los principales desafíos de la investigación de pruebas de software. Para ella, un "oráculo ideal" debería proporcionar "los resultados esperados para cada caso de prueba dado". Tal oráculo ideal sería un "motor o heurística que emita un veredicto de paso/fallo sobre las salidas de prueba observadas". Baresi y Young [11] también mencionaron el concepto de "oráculo ideal", que "satisfaría las propiedades deseables de las especificaciones del programa, como ser completo, evitando la sobreespecificación y permitiendo al mismo tiempo la eficiencia en las comprobaciones". Los métodos formales o los modelos completos del sistema son actualmente el método más adecuado para el desarrollo automático de oráculos, pero necesitan esa sobreespecificación mencionada por Baresi y Young. Pérez et al., por ejemplo, obtienen casos de prueba extraídos de modelos de secuencia UML en líneas de productos de software [12]. Su enfoque requiere, de hecho, una especificación bastante compleja de los escenarios de prueba con sus pre y poscondiciones, mensajes, parámetros, etc. La propuesta es económicamente viable porque es altamente reutilizable en el contexto de SPL, pero es demasiado costosa para el desarrollo de desarrollos aislados.
Pero, como Barr et al. señalan, "en la industrial, para probar la mayoría de los sistemas, el tester no dispone de las especificaciones formales, aserciones u oráculos parciales. [...] El tester se enfrenta a la abrumadora tarea de verificar manualmente el comportamiento del sistema para cada uno de los casos de prueba ".
El problema oráculo sigue siendo un importante desafío (quizá el que más) para la generación automatizada de casos de prueba. Con respecto a este problema, Annand et al. afirman que "la mayoría de los trabajos sobre automatización del testing se centran en la búsqueda de buenas entradas de prueba, pero no abordan el problema igualmente importante de reducir el costo de verificar el producto producido en respuesta a esas entradas" [7].

4 Generación de casos de prueba con oráculo

El proceso que aquí presentamos está soportado por SMACTesting, una herramienta web específicamente diseñada para la automatización de pruebas de sistemas *Social*, *Mobile*, *Analytics*, *Internet of Things* y *GIS* que se encuentren implementados en Java. Inicialmente, el tester crea en la herramienta un proyecto en el cual carga el código del SUT, incluyendo el código compilado.

Mediante un motor que, respectivamente, hace uso de la *Reflection API* de Java y de la librería Jsoup [13], la herramienta muestra al tester el conjunto de ficheros *.class* y de páginas *html* y *jsp* contenidas en el proyecto, así como las operaciones (en los *.class)* y controles (botones, cajas de texto, etcétera) de cada uno. El tester puede seleccionar las operaciones que desee y, con ellas, escribir una expresión regular que describe un conjunto genérico de escenarios de prueba. Volviendo al ejemplo de la clase *Account,* una expresión regular como *new Account·deposit·[deposit|withdraw|transfer]** puede ser expandida para obtener, entre otras, las siguientes secuencias de operaciones (en las que, por brevedad, obviamos los dos primeros parámetros de *transfer*):

1. *a=new Account(); a.deposit(amount);*
2. *a=new Account(); a.deposit(amount); a.deposit(amount);*
3. *a=new Account(); a.deposit(amount); a.withdraw(amount);*
4. *a=new Account(); a.deposit(amount); a.transfer(amount);*
5. *a=new Account(); a.deposit(amount); a.withdraw(amount); a.transfer(amount);*

Los tres casos de prueba que pusimos como ejemplo en la Tabla 1 proceden de la secuencia número 5 pero, obviamente, los parámetros de las operaciones involucradas deben anotarse con valores de prueba para obtener casos efectivamente ejecutables. De este modo, con los valores que dábamos como ejemplo en la Tabla 2 para generar todas las combinaciones, de la secuencia número uno obtendríamos 2 casos de prueba, 4 de la segunda y tercera, 6 de la cuarta y los 12 que mostrábamos en la Tabla 2 en el caso de la quinta. SMACTesting incluye el mecanismo necesario para asignar los valores a los parámetros de las operaciones seleccionadas.

4.1 Creación de oráculos y plantillas de prueba

Un caso de prueba debe comprobar (1) que el sistema hace lo que debe hacer y (2) que no hace lo que no debe hacer. En general:

- Los casos del primer tipo incluyen un bloque *try* en el que se ejercita el escenario y se realiza una comprobación (mediante un *assert).* Después se incluye un *catch* en el que se emite con *fail* un veredicto de fallo, pues si se ha llegado a este *catch* es porque se ha lanzado una excepción que no se esperaba. Así pues, los casos de prueba de este estilo siguen el modelo del caso *testNormal_700* de la Tabla 1.
  En efecto, la plantilla básica con la que SMACTesting genera estos casos es la de la Figura 2. El token *TCNUMBER* se sustituirá más adelante por un número de caso de prueba. El token *<sequence/>* se sustituye por la secuencia de operaciones que procedan de la secuencia que se esté tratando.

```
@Test
public void testDefaultTCNUMBER() {
  try {
    <sequence/>
  }
  catch (Exception e) {
    fail("No exception expected");
  }
}
```

Fig. 2. Plantilla *testDefault,* para casos que prueban que *el sistema hace lo que debe hacer*

- Los casos del segundo tipo incluyen un bloque *try* con un *fail* al final (pues si se ha llegado a ese punto es porque no se ha lanzado una excepción que se esperaba), un *catch* que recoge la excepción esperada (y que emite veredicto de paso) y otro *catch* que captura cualquier otro tipo de excepción (y que lanza veredicto de fallo, pues la excepción es diferente de la esperada). De este modo, los casos de prueba de esta categoría siguen el modelo de los casos *testNoBalanceTransfer* y *testNegativeTransfer* de la Tabla 1.

  La plantilla básica para estos casos es la de la Figura 3. Igual que antes, los tokens *TCNUMBER y <sequence/>* se sustituirán más tarde por el número de caso de prueba que corresponda y por la secuencia de operaciones que procedan de la secuencia que se esté tratando. El token *EXPECTED_EXCEPTION* se sustituye por la excepción esperada.

```
@Test
public void testExceptionTCNUMBER() {
    try {
    <sequence/>
    fail("EXPECTED_EXCEPTION expected");
  }
  catch (EXPECTED_EXCEPTION e) {}
  catch (Exception e) {
    fail("EXPECTED_EXCEPTION expected");
  }
}
```

Fig. 3. Plantilla *testException,* para casos que prueban que *el sistema no hace lo que no debe hacer*

Una vez que el tester ha seleccionado las operaciones, asignado valores a sus parámetros y escrito la expresión regular, un motor de generación expande la expresión regular obteniendo las secuencias de operaciones. A continuación, el tester debe describir oráculos genéricos que asignará a la expresión regular. Cuando, más adelante, se generen los casos de prueba, SMACTesting irá comprobando, para cada uno, qué oráculo le corresponde, y generará su código conforme a la plantilla.

Los oráculos se describen mediante *cláusulas when,* que determinan, en términos de los valores de los parámetros, con qué plantilla de caso de prueba (figuras 2 y 3) debe generarse el código.

Así, una cláusula *when* para el ejemplo de la cuenta corriente y los valores de la Tabla 2 es el siguiente:

when transfer.amount = 5000, usar plantilla testException, siendo EXPECTED_EXCEPTION = InsufficientBalanceException

Lo que este *when* especifica es que cuando valor del parámetro *amount* de la operación *transfer* sea 5000 (que es uno de los valores de prueba que el tester seleccionó para este parámetro), el caso de prueba debe generarse usando la plantilla *testException,* y sustituyendo el token *EXPECTED_EXCEPTION* por *InsufficientBalanceException.*

En SMACTesting pueden definirse tres tipos de cláusulas *when.* Si bien en la herramienta se describen visualmente mediante su interfaz gráfica, los presentamos a continuación de manera textual:

1. Los *when* de tipo *OR* se verifican cuando cualquiera de las condiciones que contienen es cierta. Suponiendo que hubiéramos asignado el valor -100 a los tres parámetros numéricos de las tres operaciones, podríamos especificar lo siguiente:

```
when deposit.amount = -100 OR
        withdraw.amount = -100 OR
        transfer.amount = -100,
        usar plantilla testException, siendo
                EXPECTED_EXCEPTION = NegativeAmountException
```

2. Los *when* de tipo *AND* se verifican cuando todas las condiciones incluidas en la cláusula son ciertas. La siguiente cláusula *when* indica que el caso de prueba en el que se ingresan 1000, se retiran 200 y se transfieren 100 debe generarse con la plantilla *testNormal.*

```
when deposit.amount = 1000 AND  withdraw.amount = 200
AND transfer.amount = 100,  usar plantilla testDefault
```

   Tanto las cláusulas *OR* como las *AND* admiten paréntesis. Así, suponiendo que los valores utilizados hubieran sido asignados a los parámetros, la siguiente cláusula indica que los caos en los que se ingresen 1000 o 2000, se retiren 200 o 100, y se transfieran 100, deben generarse con la plantilla *testNormal.*:

```
when (deposit.amount = 1000 OR deposit.amount = 2000) AND
        (withdraw.amount = 200 OR withdraw.amount = 100) AND
        transfer.amount = 100,
        usar plantilla testDefault
```

3. Los *when* de tipo *ELSE* se utilizan para generar el código de todos los casos de prueba que no correspondan con ninguna de las cláusula *when* de tipo *OR* o *AND* que se hayan descrito. La plantilla para estos casos de prueba (la básica se muestra en la Figura 4) emite siempre un veredicto de fallo, pues ha ejercitado un escenario del SUT que el tester no había previsto.

```
@Test
public void testElseTCNUMBER() {
    try {
        <sequence/>
        fail("Unexpected situation");
    }
    catch (Exception e) {
        fail("Unexpected situation");
    }
}
```

Fig. 4. Plantilla *testElse,* para casos que prueban que ejercitan escenarios imprevistos

4.2 Algoritmo genético

Cuando el motor de combinación ha generado los casos de prueba, cada uno a partir de la plantilla de caso de prueba que corresponda según su cláusula *when,* el tester puede pasar a ejecutar los casos. Si opta por ejecutarlos con un algoritmo genético, el motor de ejecución irá pasando los resultados a un motor de enriquecimiento, que toma los casos de prueba originales, los combina genéticamente y produce una nueva población (es decir, un nuevo test suite), que envía al motor de ejecución. El proceso se detiene cuando se alcanza el mutation score que se haya preestablecido o cuando se haya alcanzado el número de iteraciones que el tester haya prefijado. Es importante notar que los operadores de mutación se introducen mediante programación orientada a aspectos, evolucionado a partir del que ya presentamos hace unos años en este mismo foro [14].

Codificación de individuos. Siendo el test suite la población del algoritmo genético, cada caso de prueba es un individuo de esa población. Desde el punto de vista de su codificación genética, el caso de prueba tiene su secuencia de operaciones y, para cada una, los valores de sus parámetros. Además, cada parámetro mantiene un puntero a los valores que el tester estableció para ese parámetro. La Figura 5 ilustra dos casos de prueba codificados: el primero corresponde a una situación normal (y su código se habrá generado con la plantilla *testDefault),* y el segundo a una situación de excepción.

Valores de prueba que estableció el tester		
deposit: {1000, 500, 100}	**withdraw:** {200, 50}	**transfer:** {5000, 100, -100}

testDefault1				
Operación	*new Account*	*deposit*	*withdraw*	*transfer*
Valor		*1000*	*200*	*100*

testException2				
Operación	*new Account*	*deposit*	*withdraw*	*transfer*
Valor		*500*	*50*	*-100*

Fig. 5. Ejemplo de codificación de dos individuos

Función de cruce. La función de cruce produce dos casos de prueba hijos a partir de dos progenitores. Se genera un punto de corte aleatorio por el que se parten los dos individuos. El primer hijo se forma con la porción izquierda (respecto del punto de corte) del primer progenitor y la porción derecha del segundo. El segundo hijo se forma con la porción izquierda del segundo progenitor y la porción derecha del segundo. Suponiendo que, siendo los progenitores los dos casos de prueba de la Figura 5, y asumiendo que el punto de corte aleatorio está justo en la mitad, la Figura 6 muestra los dos descendientes que se obtendrían.

testHijo1_1				
Operación	*new Account*	*deposit*	*withdraw*	*transfer*
Valor		*1000*	*50*	*-100*

testHijo2_1				
Operación	*new Account*	*deposit*	*withdraw*	*transfer*
Valor		*500*	*200*	*100*

Fig. 6. Cruce de los dos individuos de la Figura 6

Función de mutación genética. Los nuevos descendientes se van mutando con una pequeña probabilidad. Si a un individuo le toca mutarse, se selecciona al azar uno cualquiera de sus parámetros, y se sustituye por otro valor al azar de entre los que suministró el tester. En la Figura 7, el valor inicial pasado a *deposit* (1000) se ha sustituido por 100.

Valores de prueba que estableció el tester		
deposit: {1000, 500, 100}	**withdraw:** {200, 50}	**transfer:** {5000, 100, -100}

testHijo1_1				
Operación	*new Account*	*deposit*	*withdraw*	*transfer*
Valor		*1000*	*50*	*-100*

testHijo1_1 (mutado)				
Operación	*new Account*	*deposit*	*withdraw*	*transfer*
Valor		*100*	*200*	*100*

Fig. 7. Mutación del primer hijo

Función de fitness. La función de fitness se calcula en función del número de mutantes que mata el caso de prueba. Como se comenta en la sección 5 (conclusiones y trabajo futuro), es un elemento de estudio y *tunning* muy interesante.

Algoritmos de cruce. Se han implementado tres algoritmos de cruce en SMACTesting:

1. *BestToWorst:* partiendo de los casos de prueba ordenados por fitness, elige como pareja de progenitores al primer individuo (el mejor) y al último (el peor); luego, al segundo con el penúltimo; al tercero con el antepenúltimo, etcétera.
2. *BestWithBest:* partiendo de los casos de prueba ordenados por fitness, cruza al primero con el segundo, al tercero con el cuarto, etcétera.
3. *RandomCrosser:* cruza a los individuos aleatoriamente.

Proceso genético. Independientemente del algoritmo de cruce seleccionado, el algoritmo genético procede siempre de la misma manera (Figura 9): se comienza ejecutando el test suite y construyendo la matriz de muertos (*killingMatrix).* Si no se alcanza la condición de parada, la matriz se ordena por *fitness* y se selecciona un porcentaje de los mejores individuos (*elite)*, que son los que se cruzan para pasar a la nueva población. Estos individuos se mutan genéticamente conforme al procedimiento descrito con una probabilidad baja (en la figura, el 5%). Cuando un individuo es mutado, es necesario proporcionarle una plantilla para generar su código, que se le busca y asigna mediante la función *buscarPlantillaPara*. La nueva población se construye con la élite de la generación anterior y los descendientes de ésta, contenidos en la *nuevaPoblación*.

```
Sean: TS el test suite, t un caso de prueba, template una plantilla de caso
de prueba

iteraciones=1;
do {
   killingMatrix = execute(TS)
   if (mutationScore(killingMatrix)>=umbral || iteraciones>I)
      break;
   ordenarPorFitness(killingMatrix)
   elite = seleccionarElite(%)
   nuevaPoblación = cruzar(elite)
   for i=0 to |nuevaPoblación|
      t = nuevaPoblación [i]
      if random()<0.05 {
         mutate(t)
         template = buscarPlantillaPara(t)
      }
   }
   TS = elite ∪ nuevaPoblación
   iteraciones = iteraciones + 1
} while (true)
```

Fig. 8. Pseudocódigo del algoritmo genético

Como puede apreciarse, la aplicación de este algoritmo nunca generará casos de prueba que no hubieran podido ser generados mediante todas las combinaciones. No obstante, en los primeros experimentos hemos comprobado que, incluso a partir de un test suite inicial muy pequeño (generado incluso con el algoritmo de combinación *Each choice* [4], el tiempo total de ejecución para conseguir un test suite que alcance el umbral de mutación preestablecido es mucho menor que ejecutando absolutamente todos los casos de prueba posibles.

5 Conclusiones y trabajo futuro

En este artículo se ha descrito un algoritmo genético que, junto a otras técnicas de prueba, se encuentra implementado en SMACTesting, una herramienta que se encuentra en estos momentos en su última etapa de desarrollo, casi lista para pasar a producción. Es por ello por lo que aún no podemos ofrecer datos concretos de validación experimental, si bien los primeros resultados, obtenidos informalmente, son muy prometedores.

Con respecto del algoritmo genético, en la próxima fase experimental deseamos:

1. Estudiar diferentes métodos de cálculo del *fitness*: con el criterio actual, no se seleccionan los casos de prueba que, aún matando pocos mutantes, matan a mutantes que no matan a otros. Así, por ejemplo, sería conveniente pasar a la siguiente generación a un caso de prueba que es el único que mata un determinado mutante.
2. Estudiar el porcentaje de elite (mejores individuos), así como la conveniencia o no de pasar a toda la elite a la siguiente generación.
3. Como se ha comentado, nuestro algoritmo genético nunca producirá un test suite que alcance un mutation score mayor que el obtenido con todas las combinaciones. ¿no

obstante, como el tiempo de ejecución sí es menor, es necesario extender la potencia de las cláusulas *when* permitiendo la descripción de más situaciones con operadores como <, >, <=, <>, etcétera, de manera que la mutación genética pueda insertar valores diferentes del conjunto de valores iniciales.

Agradecimientos

Este trabajo es parte de los proyectos GINSENG (TIN2015-70259-C2-1) y SMACTesting (programa Innterconecta, EXP-00082064 / ITC-20151305), financiados por el Ministerio de Economía, Industria y Competitividad y fondos FEDER.

Referencias

1. IEEE Computer Society: IEEE Standard 829 for Software and System Test Documentation. (2008).
2. Beck, K., Gamma, E.: Test-infected: programmers love writing tests. In: More Java Gems. Cambridge University Press (2000).
3. Polo, M., Reales, P.: Mutation Testing Cost Reduction Techniques: A Survey. IEEE Softw. 27, 80–86 (2010).
4. Grindal, M., Offutt, J., Andler, S.F.: Combination testing strategies: A survey. Software Testing, Verification, and Reliability. 15, 167–199 (2005).
5. Cohen, D., Society, I.C., Dalal, S.R., Fredman, M.L., Patton, G.C.: The AETG System: An Approach to Testing Based on Combinatorial Design. IEEE Transactions on Software Engineering. 23, 437–444 (1997).
6. Pérez Lamancha, B., Polo, M., Piattini, M.: PROW: A Pairwise algorithm with constRaints, Order and Weight. Journal of Systems and Software.
7. Anand, S., Burke, E.K., Chen, T.Y., Clark, J., Cohen, M.B., Grieskamp, W., Harman, M., Harrold, M.J., McMinn, P., Bertolino, A., Jenny Li, J., Zhu, H.: An orchestrated survey of methodologies for automated software test case generation. Journal of Systems and Software. 86, 1978–2001 (2013).
8. Grieskamp, W., Hierons, R.M., Pretschner, A.: 10421 Summary -- Model-Based Testing in Practice. Dagstuhl Seminar Proceedings. (2011).
9. Barr, E.T., Harman, M., McMinn, P., Shahbaz, M., Yoo, S.: The Oracle Problem in Software Testing: A Survey. IEEE Transactions on Software Engineering. 41, 507–525 (2015).
10. Bertolino, A.: Software Testing Research: Achievements, Challenges, Dreams. In: Future of Software Engineering, 2007. FOSE '07. pp. 85–103 (2007).
11. Luciano Baresi, Michal Young: Test oracles, Technical Report CIS-TR-01-02, http://ix.cs.uoregon.edu/~michal/pubs/oracles.pdf, (2001).
12. Pérez Lamancha, B., Polo, M., Caivano, D., Piattini, M., Visaggio, G.: Automated generation of test oracles using a model-driven approach. Information and Software Technology. 55, 301–319 (2013).
13. jsoup Java HTML Parser, with best of DOM, CSS, and jquery, https://jsoup.org/.
14. Polo Usaola, M.: Using Aspect-Oriented Programming for mutation testing of third party components. In: Proc. of the 17th CIBSE. pp. 247–261. , Pucón, Chile (2014).

CodeForest: Uma ferramenta visual de depuração

Fabio Pereira da Silva, Danilo Mutti, Higor Amario de Souza e Marcos Lordello Chaim

Universidade de São Paulo,
São Paulo, Brasil
{fabio.dasilva}@usp.br,{dmutti}@usp.br},{hamario}@ime.usp.br,{chaim}@usp.br

Abstract Testing and debugging are important tasks during the development cycle. Spectrum-Based Fault Localization (SFL) is a promising debugging technique due to it is relative low execution cost. SFL pinpoints the most suspicious program elements ranking excerpts more likely to contain faults. Recently, visualization tools that use SFL techniques have been proposed. This article presents the main features of a visual debugging tool, called CodeForest. The metaphor receives lists of suspicious classes, methods and blocks (set of statements executed in sequence) to build a three-dimensional cacti forest representing the program inspected. CodeForest was assessed with graduation students about the effectiveness and efficiency during fault localization and presented promising results. A video containing the main CodeForest features can be viewed in: https://www.youtube.com/watch?v=WsSoydFXYMw

Keywords: Visualization of Debugging Information; Visual Metaphor; Debugging Tools.

1 Introdução

Segundo Araki, Furukawa e Cheng [1], depuração é o processo que consiste na coleta e análise de informações em uma ou mais execuções que auxiliem na identificação das causas de comportamentos errôneos no sistema.

A localização de defeitos é uma tarefa custosa no processo de desenvolvimento de software. As atividades de teste de software e depuração são responsáveis por mais de 50% dos custos totais de um projeto [8]. Diversas ferramentas que apoiam os desenvolvedores em atividades do processo de desenvolvimento de software foram propostas nas últimas décadas; entretanto não houve mudanças significativas na forma como a atividade de depuração é executada e na prática ela ainda é realizada da mesma forma desde a década de 1960 [8]. Os desenvolvedores geralmente utilizam depuradores simbólicos para acompanhar a execução do programa e observar as alterações nas variáveis durante a depuração [4].

Com o objetivo de minimizar as dificuldades existentes na forma como a atividade de depuração é executada, foi proposta a técnica de localização de defeitos baseada em cobertura de código (LDC), em inglês *Spectrum-based fault localization*, também conhecida como *SFL*. Para Renieris e Reiss [10], LDC é definida por um conjunto de componentes (e.g., comandos, blocos, predicados, associações definição-uso ou subprogramas) cobertos durante a execução de um teste. LDC baseia-se nos dados de cobertura, em heurísticas e nos resultados dos testes (sucesso ou falha) para atribuir valores de suspeição para cada componente do programa.

As heurísticas utilizam as informações de cobertura para realizar o mapeamento dos valores de suspeição do programa avaliado [4]. Elas são baseadas em coeficientes que levam em consideração os componentes que foram, ou não foram, executados pelos casos de testes. Os trechos do programa que ocorrem mais frequentemente em casos de testes que falharam são classificados com maior grau de suspeição [10].

A utilização de técnicas LDC têm apresentado resultados promissores devido ao seu baixo custo de execução; entretanto ainda é necessário comprovar a sua escalabilidade quando combinada com ferramentas visuais de depuração [10].

Nas últimas décadas, foram desenvolvidas ferramentas que utilizam técnicas LDC em metáforas visuais [4, 7, 9, 11]. As ferramentas Jaguar [11], GZoltar [9] e CodeForest [7] utilizam diferentes metáforas visuais para representar as informações de suspeição associadas ao código do programa.

Este artigo apresenta uma ferramenta visual de depuração chamada CodeForest[1]. A principal contribuição do trabalho é a apresentação de uma nova ferramenta de depuração, juntamente com resultados preliminares de estudos realizados.

O restante deste artigo está organizado da seguinte forma. Na Seção 2 são detalhadas as principais características da CodeForest, descrevendo suas vantagens e desvantagens. A Seção 3 dedica-se as evidências experimentais de avaliações já realizadas com a ferramenta. A Seção 4 dedica-se há uma visão geral de ferramentas similares existentes na literatura. Na Seção 5 são apresentadas as ameaças à validade. Por último são apresentadas as considerações finais.

2 CodeForest

A CodeForest proposta por Mutti [7] tem como objetivo auxiliar os desenvolvedores na atividade de depuração através de representações visuais tridimensionais em uma floresta de cactus que demonstra os elementos de um programa.

A CodeForest recebe listas de classes, métodos e blocos suspeitos (conjunto de instruções executadas em sequência) para construir uma floresta de cactus tridimensional representando o programa inspecionado. Na CodeForest, as classes são representadas como cactus, os métodos como galhos e as linhas do programa avaliado são representadas como espinhos de um galho. Os elementos mais suspeitos da floresta são pintados de vermelho. Quanto mais um elemento (classe, método ou declaração) for executado por um caso de teste que falhou mais suspeito ele é.

[1] https://github.com/fabiodasilva500/CodeForest-Plugin

Os elementos da floresta são coloridos de acordo com o seu valor de suspeição, considerados no intervalo entre 0 e 1. A cor verde representa a menor probabilidade dele apresentar defeitos. A cor amarela representa um estado intermediário. A cor laranja indica uma alta probabilidade. Por último, a cor vermelha representa os elementos com maior valor de suspeição.

A instrumentação dos dados do programa ocorre com a utilização da ferramenta Jaguar [11]. A Jaguar coleta informações dos testes realizados e gera um arquivo XML com o valor de suspeição de cada linha do programa coberta pelos testes. Ela coleta informações da cobertura do código invocando testes de unidade do programa e recolhe estas informações para cada elemento avaliado. A suspeição de cada linha pode ser definida por dez heurísticas diferentes (DRT, Jaccard, Kulczynski2, McCon, Minus, Ochiai, Op, Tarantula, Wong3, Zoltar).

A CodeForest funciona de maneira integrada com a Jaguar. Primeiramente a Jaguar é executada e coleta as informações de suspeição dos elementos do programa. A CodeForest realiza a interpretação dos relatórios gerados pelas dez heurísticas implementadas pela Jaguar. Os relatórios possuem as informações do valor de suspeição de cada elemento do programa avaliado. As informações do arquivo são armazenadas e recuperadas no momento em que for solicitada a visualização com a ferramenta. Quando ela for requisitada o arquivo é interpretado com o uso do *plugin* da Jaguar e suas informações são apresentadas na CodeForest.

O posicionamento, a coloração e a espessura de cada cactu da floresta são determinados com base em seu valor de suspeição. Os cactus são posicionados de maneira ordenada da esquerda para a direita da base onde encontram-se os elementos mais suspeitos do programa. A Figura 1 ilustra o processo descrito. Primeiramente, o cactu com menor valor pintado de verde está posicionado no canto superior esquerdo. Outro com probabilidade média está localizado no centro. O cactu com maior probabilidade de apresentar defeitos está posicionado no canto inferior à direita da base.

Figura 1. Posicionamento dos cactus na CodeForest

A CodeForest permite que o desenvolvedor aumente ou diminua o valor de suspeição que ele deseja avaliar. O desenvolvedor tem a opção de interagir clicando nos galhos da floresta. Ao clicar a janela, será exibida, como na Figura 2, o código fonte, com todas as suas linhas coloridas de acordo com o valor de suspeição calculado para cada uma delas com a floresta de cactus minimizada.

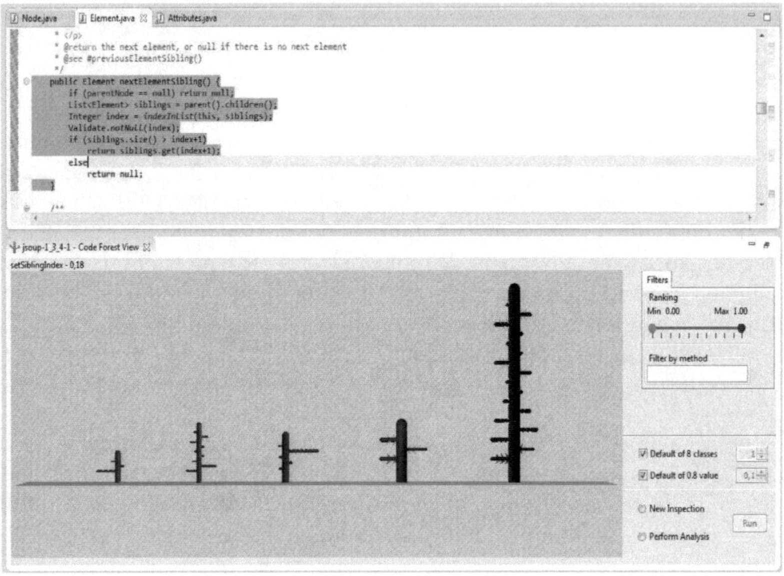

Figura 2. Interação com o código do programa

2.1 Vantagens e desvantagens

Em estudos preliminares descritos na Seção 3, a CodeForest apresentou potencial de utilização em situações reais de desenvolvimento. Além disso, a Seção 3 apresenta o único experimento existente na literatura sobre o uso de ferramentas visuais e textuais de depuração que utilizam técnicas LDC para a localização de defeitos. Anteriormente a este trabalho, apenas o estudo de Gouveia, Campos e Abreu [3] avaliou a eficácia e eficiência da ferramenta GZoltar para a localização de defeitos. Entretanto, não foi realizada nenhuma comparação entre ferramentas visuais e textuais. Outras vantagens da CodeForest são:

– A instalação completa da CodeForest, incluindo a obtenção do código fonte da ferramenta é simples e não requer a instalação de várias aplicações para que ela seja utilizada.
– Facilidade de manuseio, por não agrupar uma quantidade significativa de informações na metáfora visual.

- A CodeForest é uma ferramenta de código aberto para a comunidade de desenvolvedores.

Entretanto, ela é voltada apenas para a depuração de programas desenvolvidos na linguagem Java, impossibilitando a sua utilização em outras plataformas de desenvolvimento. Além disso, o *plugin* da ferramenta funciona integrado apenas para a IDE Eclipse. Embora com base nas avaliações realizadas muitas melhorias tenham sido implementadas, outra desvantagem foi a dificuldade de entendimento que alguns participantes mencionaram durante a realização do experimento.

3 Evidências experimentais

3.1 Experimento exploratório

Em um experimento exploratório realizado por Mutti [7] em 2014, os resultados indicam que a ferramenta apoia a tarefa de depuração tanto de desenvolvedores experientes quanto inexperientes. Usuários com nenhuma experiência utilizam o roteiro e o ambiente virtual 3D proposto pela CodeForest para investigar o defeito. Usuários com maior experiência preferiram utilizar o roteiro como um guia para restringir quais partes do código fonte da aplicação devem ser exploradas.

3.2 Avaliação da metáfora visual

A CodeForest foi apresentada a desenvolvedores e estudantes de cursos de graduação por meio de avaliações presenciais ou conferências pelo Skype e Hangout. Elas envolveram ao todo 10 pessoas. As entrevistas foram realizadas com duração em torno de 40 a 60 minutos e todos os participantes tiveram contato com a ferramenta. Com o objetivo de tornar as avaliações dinâmicas não foi definido um roteiro específico de questões.

O principal ponto positivo mencionado foi a capacidade de apresentação dos elementos mais suspeitos. Entretanto, os participantes apontaram como principal dificuldade a necessidade de muitas configurações para uso da CodeForest. A partir das considerações foram realizadas várias melhorias na metáfora visual da ferramenta. As melhorias implementadas podem ser visualizadas na Tabela 1

Tabela 1. Melhorias implementadas

Funcionalidade	Descrição
Site da CodeForest	Contém informações como exemplo de uso, questionários de satisfação, avaliações de usabilidade e report de erros
Integração com a Jaguar	A CodeForest se tornou capaz de interpretar todos os relatórios com valores de suspeição gerados pela ferramenta Jaguar.
Representação da floresta	Melhor organização dos cactus na floresta facilitando a visualização e inspeção pelo desenvolvedor.

3.3 Avaliação experimental

Em 2017, a CodeForest passou por um experimento com 119 estudantes do curso de graduação em Análise e Desenvolvimento de Sistemas da *Faculdade de Tecnologia da Zona Leste da cidade de São Paulo* para avaliar a eficácia e eficiência para a localização de defeitos em relação a ferramenta Jaguar que oferece representações textuais. A eficácia e a eficiência foram avaliadas, respectivamente, se a ferramenta foi capaz de direcionar ou não o desenvolvedor a linha do defeito e o tempo necessário para localizá-la.

O experimento foi realizado no contexto de disciplinas do curso de graduação. Os estudantes deveriam realizar a localização e correção de dois defeito em dois programas de código aberto chamados JSoup e XStream, um defeito em cada programa. Os participantes foram alocados no experimento de maneira aleatória por meio do delineamento em quadrados latinos [2].

Para a avaliação foram considerados os arquivos de *log* gerados durante o experimento. Foi implementado um programa de extração de informações com o objetivo de verificar para a eficácia e a eficiência, respectivamente, se o participante conseguiu interagir com a linha do defeito e o consumo de tempo gasto para que ocorresse a primeira interação com a linha do defeito.

Com base nas informações extraídas, a avaliação foi realizada por meio do teste de *Wilcoxon* [6]. Primeiramente foi validada se há igualdade entre as ferramentas considerando um intervalo de confiança de 95%. As hipóteses consideradas são listadas abaixo. A Tabela 2 apresenta os resultados obtidos.

– H_0: há igualdade para a eficácia e eficiência entre CodeForest e Jaguar.
– H_1: há diferenças para a eficácia e eficiência entre CodeForest e Jaguar.

Tabela 2. Teste de *Wilcoxon* para a igualdade

Variável avaliada	Descrição do teste	Resultado do teste (p-valor)
Eficácia	Quantidade de interações com a linha do defeito	0,003075
Eficiência	Tempo gasto para que ocorresse a primeira interação com a linha do defeito	0,01696

Como em todos os casos rejeitou-se a hipótese nula de igualdade entre as ferramentas foi avaliada qual delas foi melhor para as variáveis de interesse. As hipóteses consideradas são listadas abaixo. A Tabela 3 apresenta os resultados obtidos.

– H_0: a CodeForest foi mais eficaz e eficiente do que a Jaguar.
– H_1: a Jaguar foi mais eficaz e eficiente do que a CodeForest.

Os resultados preliminares do estudo indicam que a Jaguar foi mais eficaz e eficiente do que a CodeForest para a localização de defeitos.

Tabela 3. Teste de *Wilcoxon* para as diferenças

Variável avaliada	Descrição do teste	Resultado do teste (p-valor)
Eficácia	Quantidade de interações com a linha do defeito	0,001538
Eficiência	Tempo gasto para que ocorresse a primeira interação com a linha do defeito	0,00848

4 Visão geral de ferramentas similares

Apenas duas ferramentas visuais de depuração que utilizam técnicas LDC foram encontradas na literatura. A ferramenta Tarantula proposta por Jones, Harrold e Stasko [5] utiliza cores para mapear de maneira visual os elementos mais suspeitos de um programa. Ela identifica os casos de testes que foram executados com sucesso ou com falha e representa as informações a partir de um esquema de coloração.

A GZoltar proposta por Gouveia, Campos e Abreu [3] exibe os elementos mais suspeitos de um programa em uma metáfora bidimensional. As informações da aplicação podem ser visualizadas em uma representação em anel, particionamento vertical ou ordenação hierárquica. A GZoltar é o único trabalho encontrado na literatura em que a ferramenta proposta foi avaliada com desenvolvedores em comparação com depuradores simbólicos.

5 Ameaças à validade

Os resultados de um projeto de pesquisa são influenciados por fatores que afetam a validade externa, interna e de construto.

A validade externa indica a capacidade dos resultados serem generalizados para outros trabalhos. Dentre as ferramentas visuais de depuração existentes, apenas a CodeForest foi considerada em todas as avaliações descritas.

A validade interna avalia as condições básicas aplicáveis ao estudo. A condução da avaliação experimental ocorreu apenas com alunos de cursos de graduação, que possuem pouca experiência na área de desenvolvimento de software.

A validade de construto verifica o quanto uma medida está correlacionada com o grupo de variáveis de interesse. No primeiro e no segundo experimento não foi realizada nenhuma análise estatística. Entretanto no terceiro experimento, as variáveis foram avaliadas com o teste de *Wilcoxon*.

6 Conclusões

Neste artigo foram apresentadas as principais características da CodeForest. Uma ferramenta visual de depuração que utiliza técnicas LDC para a localização de defeitos. O tema central envolvido em sua utilização é avaliar se ferramentas visuais de depuração agregam valor em relação a técnicas puramente textuais.

Foram descritos estudos com a CodeForest que apresentou resultados promissores em relação a sua capacidade de auxiliar os desenvolvedores na atividade de depuração. Embora os resultados obtidos indiquem que a Jaguar seja mais eficaz e eficiente do que a CodeForest, será avaliado o tamanho do efeito estatístico que a diferença representa em relação a amostra, ou seja, para a quantidade total de participantes do experimento.

Trabalhos futuros apresentarão os resultados completos da avaliação experimental. A análise de dados será concluída, em que serão avaliadas também outras medidas. Serão detalhados, o tempo de execução da tarefa, experiência profissional, observações dos estudantes sobre as ferramentas e percepção de usabilidade para a localização de defeitos.

A CodeForest será melhorada com base nos comentários dos participantes e pretende-se conduzir um novo experimento com pessoas que tenham maior experiência profissional na área de desenvolvimento de software, conciliando também outras ferramentas visuais de depuração.

Referências

1. ARAKI, K., FURUKAWA, Z., CHENG, J.: A general framework for debugging. IEE Software Magazine v.8(3) (1991)
2. Calinger, R.S.: Leonhard Euler: Mathematical Genius in the Enlightenment. Princeton University Press, Princeton, NJ, USA (2015)
3. Golveia, C., Campos, J., Abreu, R.: Using html5 visualizations in software fault localization. 1st IEEE Working Conference on Software Visualization (2013), https://www.computer.org/csdl/proceedings/vissoft/2013/9999/00/06650539.pdf
4. Jones, J.A., Harrold, M.J., Stasko, J.: Visualization of test information to assist fault localization. In: Proceedings of the 24th International Conference on Software Engineering. pp. 467–477 (2002)
5. Jones, J.A., Harrold, M.J., Stasko, J.: Visualization of test information to assist fault localization. Proceedings of the 24th ACM/IEEE International Conference on Software Engineering (2002), http://dl.acm.org/citation.cfm?id=1273468
6. Kazmier, L.J.: Estatística aplicada a administração e economia. Bookman, Porto Alegre, 4a edn. (2007)
7. Mutti, D.: Coverage Based Debugging Visualization. Master's thesis, Universidade de São Paulo (2014), http://www.teses.usp.br/teses/disponiveis/100/100131/tde-15122014-230109/en.php
8. Myers, G.J., Badgett, T., Sandler, C.: The Art of Software Testing. John Wiley & Sons, Inc., New Jersey, 3a edn. (2012)
9. Perez, A., Abreu, R.: Cues for scent intensification in debugging. IEEE International Symposium on Software Reliability Engineering Workshops (ISSREW) (2013), http://haslab.uminho.pt/ruimaranhao/files/alexandreperez-iwpd-2013.pdf
10. Renieris, M., Reiss, S.P.: Fault localization with nearest neighbor queries. In: ASE. pp. 30–39. IEEE Computer Society (2003)
11. Ribeiro, H.L.: On the use of control- and data-flow in fault localization. Master's thesis, Universidade de São Paulo (2016), http://ppgsi.each.usp.br/dissertacoes-defendidas/

Goal and Risk Analysis in the Development of Information Systems for the Web of Data

Marcio Louzada de Freitas, Allan Araujo Silva, Renata S. S. Guizzardi, and Vítor E. Silva Souza

Ontology and Conceptual Modeling Research Group (NEMO)
Department of Computer Science, Federal University of Espírito Santo (UFES), Brazil
marciolfreitas@outlook.com, allan.lp001@gmail.com,
{rguizzardi,vitorsouza}@inf.ufes.br

Abstract. The publication of Linked Data on the World Wide Web, regarding several application domains, leads to new problems related to requirements engineering, which needs to take into account aspects related to new ways of developing systems and delivering information integrated with the Web of Data. The use of vocabularies is an intrinsic activity when publishing or consuming Linked Data and their choice can be supported by the elicited requirements and domain ontology. In this context, we propose the Goals and Risks Analysis for Linked Data (GRALD), an approach for modeling goals and risks for information systems for the Web of Data.

Keywords: Goal Modeling, Risk Modeling, Linked Data, Vocabularies

1 Introduction

The Semantic Web was presented by Berners-Lee et al. [2] as the Web version that seeks to make content understandable by both humans and machines, improve search engines by giving meaning to published content and take into account contextual information of time, space and states of things. A challenge of the Semantic Web is to ensure the expressiveness and generate inference of the published content, without losing performance in the representation of data on the Web [2].

At the core of the Semantic Web idea is the concept of *Linked Data*. Bizer et al. [3] define Linked Data as a set of data interconnected by *Uniform Resource Identifiers* (URIs) whose contents can be processed by machines, forming a Web of Data. The published content is based on the *Resource Description Framework* (RDF, https://www.w3.org/RDF/) and data can be extracted using *SPARQL* queries (https://www.w3.org/TR/rdf-sparql-query/). Metadata (e.g., Microformats, RDFa) can be used to annotate Web pages with semantic content [17].

According to Heath & Bizer [9], data published in Linked Data refer to several domains, such as Geographic, Media, Social Media, Governmental, Libraries and Education, Life Sciences and so on. With the adoption and implementation of Linked Data in several areas of knowledge by companies, institutions and governments, it becomes necessary to analyze goals and requirements, as well as to identify and analyze the risks of adopting Linked Data in Web-based Information Systems. Given that the Web follows an open and decentralized architecture, connecting an information system with external data sources can lead to potential risks, thus the need to understand their impact on stakeholder goals.

This paper proposes *Goal and Risk Analysis for Linked Data* (*GRALD*), an approach that applies Goal-Oriented Requirements Engineering (GORE) and risk analysis techniques for the development of Information Systems for the Web of Data. *GRALD* is based on the *RISCOSS* approach [6] which seeks to align business goals and risks in the adoption of open source software, modeling risks with the *RiskML* language. The modeling of goals is done with *iStar* [7], aiming to understand the social domain to enable requirements engineering, defining social concepts. GRALD is integrated with our previous work, *FrameWeb-LD* [5], a method for building Web-based Information Systems that publish Linked Data.

GRALD is motivated by the growing publication of Linked Data in various domains, in which goal modeling and risks analysis can be applied. Tasks such as requirements elicitation, creation of a domain ontology, and modeling of system goals can also help in the choice of vocabulary for Linked Data publication. The objective of this paper is to demonstrate the applicability of goal and risk analysis in the development of linked data systems, and to assist in the process of choosing vocabularies.

The remainder of the paper is divided as follows: Section 2 summarizes the baseline of our work; Section 3 presents GRALD; Section 4 describes its evaluation; Section 5 discusses related work; and Section 6 concludes.

2 Baseline

Goal and Risk Analysis for Linked Data (*GRALD*) is based on two existing approaches: RISCOSS and FrameWeb-LD. We chose RISCOSS because it uses two different languages for modeling goals (iStar) and risks (RiskML), which allows one to study how the same risks may affect different strategies or ecosystems [6]. RISCOSS extends the goal analysis support in iStar, allowing us to analyze how risks are propagated in the goal graph. Frameweb-LD was chosen because it is focused on the publication of Linked Data in Web-based Information Systems. Through GRALD, we seek synergy between these two approaches.

With some effort, other approaches related to risks and goals could be adapted to use in GRALD, e.g., the GR Framework [1] for modeling and reasoning about risks during requirements analysis or the KAOS language [12] for goal modeling and obstacle analysis. This is, however, out of the scope of this paper.

2.1 The RISCOSS Approach

The *RISCOSS* project [6] (http://www.riscoss.eu) aims at analyzing risks in the adoption of *Open Source Software* (*OSS*) by organizations, modeling their goals using iStar [15].

iStar modeling seeks to understand social concepts and applies them in systems engineering processes. The central concept is the *actor*, which can be human beings, organizations, hardware, software or a combination thereof. The actor is able to act independently, has autonomy, intention to perform an action and her behavior is not totally controllable. Other concepts such as *tasks*, *resources*, *goal*, *softgoal*, *agent*, *roles*, etc. are part of this approach [7].

In RISCOSS, the modeling of risks is done using *RiskML* [6], a language that uses primitive concepts like *Goal* (something of interest for a stakeholder to obtain or maintain), *Event* (the occurrence of something that may undermine the objectives), *Situation* (circumstances where risks are likely to occur), and *Indicators* of risks (existing data measurements approved by experts [14], which can be simple or composite). The impact relationship between an event E and a goal G indicates how the occurrence of E impacts the satisfaction of G.

The attributes of RiskML's primitive constructs are *Likelihood* (Event), *Significance* (Event), *Exposure* (Event), *Satisfaction* (Situation) and *Satisfiability* (Goal); and relationships are *indicate* (between Indicator and Situation); *expose*, *protect*, *increase*, *reduce* (between Situation and Event); *expose* and *protect* (between Events); and *impact* (between Event and Goal). For more detail, see the integrated Goal and *RiskML* metamodel available in [14].

2.2 The FrameWeb-LD Approach

FrameWeb-LD [5] is an approach for building Web-based Information Systems (WIS) that publish Linked Data. It proposes a process divided in five stages: Analysis, Design, Implementation, Testing and Deployment. The main contributions of this approach are an extension of *FrameWeb*'s metamodel [16] allowing Linked Data mappings to be represented in its design models and a tool for code generation to assist developers in publishing Linked Data.

FrameWeb proposes the creation of an *Entity Model* at the architectural design phase, based on the conceptual models/ontologies built in the preceding Requirement Engineering phases, in order to represent domain classes and their integration to frameworks that are commonly used in the development of WISs [16]. *FrameWeb-LD* adds annotations on top of the basic *FrameWeb Entity Model* to specify Linked Data vocabulary mappings [5].

We illustrate this with a running example that will be used throughout the paper: an academic WIS called Marvin (http://dev.nemo.inf.ufes.br:8180/Marvin/) under development in our department at the university. In particular, we focus on a module of Marvin called C2D, which keeps track of members of our postgraduate program and their respective publications for evaluation purposes. Researchers and their publications are registered in the system, venues are then matched to a list of qualified conferences and journals provided by the federal government and, based on this list, each publication is then assigned a score, which is then used to calculate the score of each researcher.

Figure 1 shows the *Entity Model* for C2D, in which UML Classes about researchers, publications, etc. are linked to popular vocabularies, such as FOAF (http://xmlns.com/foaf/spec/) and DBLP (http://dblp.uni-trier.de/). For instance, `Researcher` is equivalent to `dblp:Person`, given that the scope of the DBLP vocabulary is to represent researchers and their publications. *Subclass* relations between vocabulary classes and domain classes can be represented by inheritance, e.g., `Researcher` is subclass of `foaf:Person` (FOAF has a broader scope and represents not only researchers). In the `User` class, the `ld-ignore` stereotype represents that user data will not be published in Linked Data. Note that, due to space constraints, the figure also displays vocabularies which were added to the model during the GRALD process, explained in Section 3.

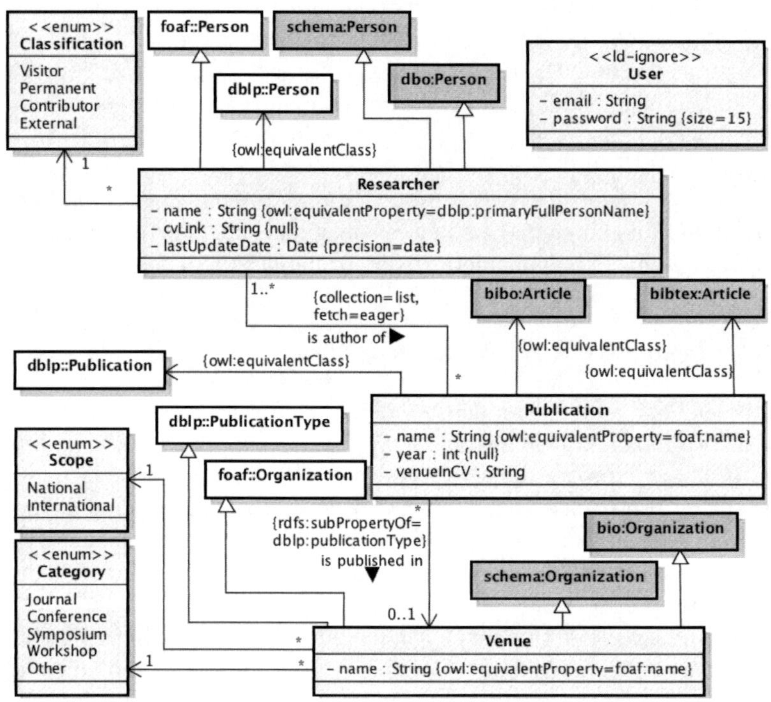

Fig. 1. A FrameWeb-LD Entity Model for C2D [5] with newly added vocabularies using GRALD (dark/blue background).

It is important to note that while FrameWeb-LD allows us to link to external vocabularies, it does not aid developers in finding the most appropriate vocabularies to link. This is very important in the publication of Linked Data, as the objective is to make our data understandable by third party software which has already been programmed to understand some of these popular vocabularies [9]. Linking to unknown vocabularies or to terms that do not properly represent your data can compromise this objective.

In [5], the implementation phase contains three activities: *Encode Operational Ontology in OWL* (which can be automated by tools), *Encode Web Information*

System and *Build Databases*. For the latter, a relational database is created and a Linked Data layer above it is added with the use of D2RQ (http://d2rq.org/) which provides triplestore (a database of RDF triples) features such as a SPARQL endpoint. After Implementation, Test and Deployment phases are carried on, with the deployment of Linked Data done by D2RQ.

3 Proposal

In this section, we present our proposal, named *Goal and Risk Analysis for Linked Data* (*GRALD*). The main contributions of the approach are: (a) modeling of system requirements using a goal-oriented language, with a particular focus on the publication of Linked Data; (b) creation of risks models to support the analysis of risks in the publication of Linked Data; and (c) searching of vocabularies according to the elicited goals and conceptual models of the domain.

An overview of the development process proposed by *GRALD* is presented in Figure 2. The process is divided in three stages (the names of the roles defined in each swimlane). Blue rectangles (light background) represent activities proposed in FrameWeb-LD [5], presented in Section 2.2, whereas gray rectangles (dark background) represent activities proposed by *GRALD* to meet the above contributions. Arrows represent the sequences of activities. The phases of the process are detailed in the following subsections.

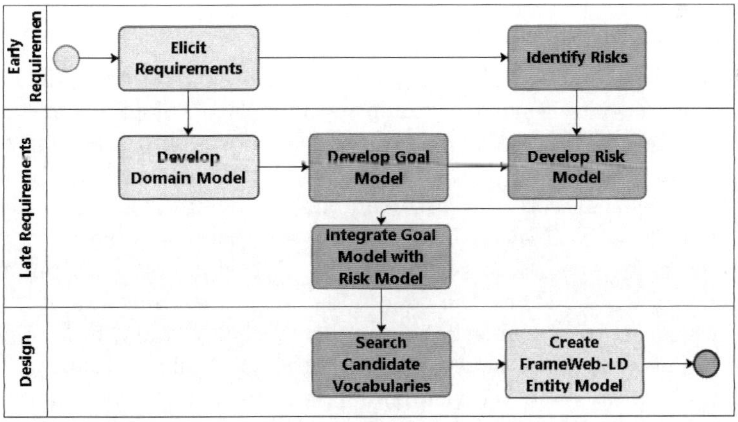

Fig. 2. Overview of the GRALD process.

In our proposal we apply these approaches in a unified way, performing goal and risk modeling with iStar and RiskML (RISCOSS), respectively, for the publication of Linked Data with FrameWeb-LD. Thus, we seek synergy between these approaches to aid in the choice of Linked Data vocabulary to be used by a Web-based Information System, understanding the risks involved in the publication and integration of Linked Data.

3.1 Early Requirements

The first phase starts with the *Elicit Requirements* activity, in which functional and non-functional requirements are captured. These requirements are used to elaborate iStar and related models in the next phase.

Next, the activity *Identify Risks* follows. In RISCOSS [13], risk management is based on a three-layered strategy, the layers cover the gathering of data. In layer I, data about risks is collected from OSS communities, projects and experts that determine the risks drivers; in layer II, risk indicators and models are defined; and in layer III, the risk model is linked with the goal models to represent the impact that the possible risk events have on strategic and business goals. We adapt this strategy to the case of Linked Data publication, collecting data about risks from the bibliography and Linked Data community websites.

According to the W3C [10], best practices for publishing Linked Data should be considered, such as choice of dataset; URI creation; choice and creation of vocabulary; choice of an appropriate license for the publication of content; among others. The adoption of these best practices helps prevent risks and, besides, starting from them we can identify possible risks related to the publication of Linked Data in our projects.

According to [4], traditional Web risks are extended to the Semantic Web, such as *SPARQL* and *SPARUL* injections, etc. Risks related to the creation and maintenance of ontologies and trust and proof of information are also addressed. In our case, we try to consider these risks for systems publishing Linked Data.

3.2 Late Requirements

The second phase of *GRALD* starts with the *Develop Domain Model* activity. Based on elicited requirements, conceptual models/ontologies representing elements from the domain of discourse of our system are built following the guidelines of FrameWeb-LD [5]. In our running example, for instance, researchers, publications, venues, score, etc. are examples of domain elements.

Next, we *Develop Goal Model.* The purpose of this activity is to model the goals (requirements) of the system, with a particular focus on publication of Linked Data. Figure 3 shows the goal model for our running example, C2D.

The actor *C2D* represents the system itself, deployed and maintained in our university. The actor Community represents the academic community, composed by students, professors (researchers), staff, etc. As such, the community has the goals *Data obtained for E-learning*, *Data obtained for academic research* and *Data obtained for curriculum databases*, accomplished by the task *Search information in linked data* and depends on C2D for its publication and availability.

The central goal for C2D, therefore, is *Data Published in Linked Data*, divided in subgoals, according to the data that will be published: *Scores*, *Venues*, *Publications* and *Researchers*; and the goal *Use W3C standards to encode data.* The goal *Users not published in linked data* represents the fact that user data should not be published. The data is registered in the system by the tasks *Calculate researcher score*, *Manage venues*, *Manage publications*, *Manage researchers* and *Manage and authenticate users.*

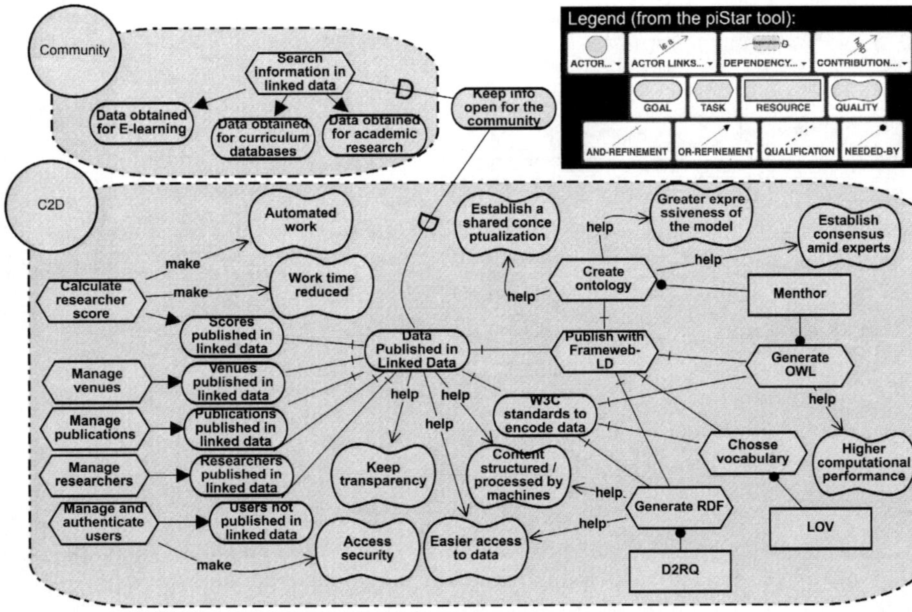

Fig. 3. iStar goal model for C2D, built with http://www.cin.ufpe.br/~jhcp/pistar/.

About the *qualities* of the system, the main goal *Data Published in Linked Data* helps C2D to *Keep transparency* because the data on researcher accreditation are open for the community to search; *Content structured and processed by machines* and *Easier access to data* are helped because the data is published in RDF format, allowing the possibility of a computational agent to process it. The task *Calculate researcher score* makes the *Automated work* and *Work time reduced* sofgoals, as it replaces the manual calculation of the scores. The qualities *Establish a shared conceptualization*, *Greater expressiveness of the model* and *Establish consensus amid experts* are helped by the task *Create ontology.* The task *Generate OWL* helps the quality *Higher computational performance.* Finally, the task *Manage and authenticate users* makes *Access security.*

Implementation is performed according to the FrameWeb-LD approach and the tasks that are necessary are: *Create ontology*, *Generate OWL*, *Chosse vocabulary* and *Generate RDF.* Resources being used, in this case, are: the *Menthor* editor (http://www.menthor.net/), *LOV (Linked Open Vocabularies)* (http://lov.okfn.org) and *D2RQ* respectively. Although these tasks are about the same in different projects (that use FrameWeb-LD), the resources used to accomplish them can vary from one project to another.

Once the goal model is produced, we move on to the activity *Develop Risk Model.* Based on the risk situations captured during *Early Requirements*, a risk model is created with the RiskML language, in order to capture the impact of the occurrence of risk events on goals. Figure 4 shows the risk model produced for C2D, related to the choice of Linked Data vocabulary.

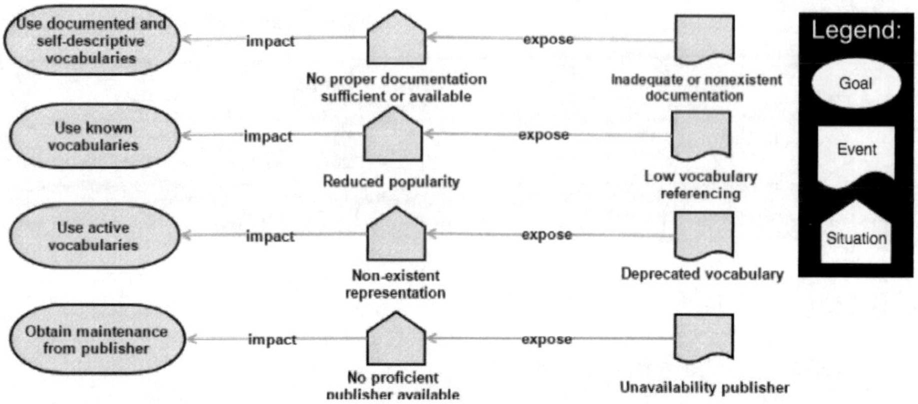

Fig. 4. RiskML model for C2D w.r.t. vocabulary adoption.

In this model, we can capture new goals related to the choice of vocabulary that are impacted by risk events. For instance, the goal *Use documented and self-descriptive vocabularies* is impacted by risk event *No proper documentation sufficient or available* exposed by risk situation *Inadequate or nonexistent documentation*. Other risks related to the creation and maintenance of vocabulary and ontology, dataset selection, trust and proof of information, publishing data and traditional Web risks can be modeled in separate models, not shown here.

Again based on RISCOSS, the last activity of this phase is *Integrate Goal Model with Risk Model*, aligning goals and risks. To this end, goals that were elicited during the construction of the RiskML model are added to the iStar model and are associated with existing goal model elements. At this point, elements from both models can be maintained, added or discarded in order to produce an integrated model.

Once the models are integrated, risk analysis can be performed as per [6]. The impact relation between a risk and a goal represents a negative effect when the event is likely and significant, increasing the evidence that the goal is not achieved. Such evidence is then propagated through the goal graph calculating, for each intentional element, if it is totally/partially satisfied/denied. We are then able to see how risks affect the strategic/high-level goals of each of the involved actors and prioritize our risk mitigation efforts based on this analysis.

In the case of C2D, elements from Figure 3 (goal model) and Figure 4 (risk model) were aligned, producing the integrated model shown in Figure 5. Due to space constraints, the figure concentrates on goals related to the publication of Linked Data only. We can thus see how risk propagation can impact the main goal *Data Published in Linked Data*, which interests the actors C2D and Community. The risk event *Non-existent representation* can impact the goal *Active Vocabularies Used* and, in this case, other vocabularies will have to be chosen, incurring in system maintenance. Further, the risk event *Reduced Popularity* impacts the goal *Know vocabularies used* if the adopted vocabulary is not well

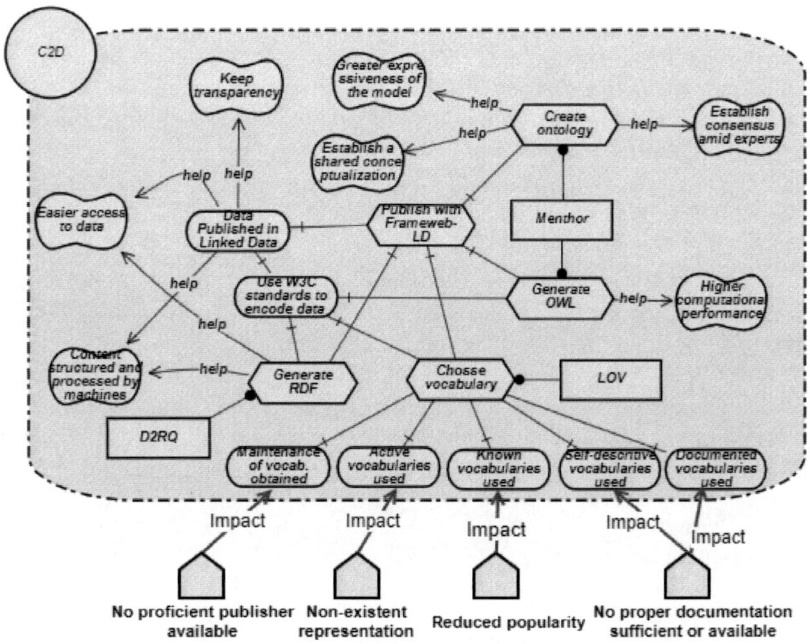

Fig. 5. Goal model for Linked Data implementation connected to RiskML risk events.

referenced by other datasets in the Linked Data community. The total or partial dissatisfaction of the goals *Use documented and self-descriptive vocabularies* and *Obtain maintenance from publisher* can hinder the process of vocabulary adoption and maintenance. In these cases, a benefit of risk analysis is to help in the choice of vocabularies.

3.3 Design

Based on tasks *Elicit Requirements*, *Develop Domain Model* and *Develop Goal Model*, design begins with the *Search for Candidate Vocabularies* for Linked Data publication. The activities in the previous phases help identify existing classes and relations and, based on them, we can search for vocabularies. For this activity, Hyland et al. [10] suggest Linked Data search engines such as Linked Open Vocabularies (LOV), Watson (http://watson.kmi.open.ac.uk/WatsonWUI/), Prefix.cc (http://prefix.cc/), Swoogle (http://swoogle.umbc.edu/2006/), Bioportal (biological domain, http://bioportal.bioontology.org/), etc.

According to [10], in the process of choosing a vocabulary we must take into account if the vocabularies are published by a trusted group or organization, if the vocabularies have permanent URIs, confirm a version control policy, choose documented vocabularies, choose self descriptive vocabularies, choose vocabularies described in more than one language, choose vocabularies used by other data sets and choose vocabularies that are available for access for a long or infinite time. These recommendation form a checklist developers should go through in order to determine the quality of each candidate vocabulary.

Regarding the choice of vocabularies, for our running example, we used with more emphasis the LOV search engine. To search for vocabulary classes for the *Researcher*, *Publication* and *Venue* domain classes, we searched the categories (tags) *People*, *Catalogs* and *Academy*. Analyzing results using the aforementioned recommendation checklist resulted in the choice of new vocabularies for C2D, namely *Schema.org*, *DBPedia*, *Bio*, *Bibtex* and *Bibo*. Analyzing links between vocabularies also helped in the discovery of new vocabularies to consider.

The checklist used in this process is shown in Table 1. Vocabulary attributes are presented in different rows, whereas the columns indicate if the vocabularies being checked meet the criteria (represented by a checkmark: ✓), do not meet the criteria (represented by an ×), or partially meet the criteria (represented by a plus/minus sign: ±). For each attribute, the data presented by LOV was analyzed, as well as the vocabularies' own documentation and their OWL schema.

Table 1. Vocabulary checklist for C2D.

#	**Attributes**	**Dbo**	**Schema**	**Bibo**	**Bio**	**Bibtex**
1	Published by a trusted organization	✓	✓	✓	✓	✓
2	Have permanent URIs	✓	✓	✓	✓	✓
3	Version control policy	✓	✓	✓	✓	✓
4	Documented vocabularies	✓	✓	✓	✓	✓
5	Self descriptive vocabularies	✓	✓	✓	✓	✓
6	Described in more than one language	✓	×	×	×	×
7	Used by other data sets	✓	✓	✓	✓	±
8	Available for access for a long time	✓	✓	✓	✓	✓

Linked Data search engines provide vocabulary information such as label, URI, namespace, description, creator, publisher, comment and language. Also, information such as vocabulary version history is important to measure the reliability of vocabulary regarding the level of updates that may represent the addition of new classes, properties and deprecated classes. Incoming links represents the popularity of vocabulary because it means that other projects are referencing it. Below, we further describe how each item of the checklist can be verified:

- Item 1: check if there is at least one creator, URI and namespace;
- Item 2: check if the URI is fixed and stable;
- Item 3: check if the vocabulary uses any sort of versioning system, e.g., are there previous versions with different numbering?
- Item 4: check if there is a website with documentation;
- Item 5: check the vocabulary OWL schema for triples that describe its classes and properties (e.g., comments or labels);
- Item 6: check the vocabulary OWL schema for strings in more than one language (in our example, Dbo was the only vocabulary that met this criterion);

- Item 7: check if the vocabulary has a substantial amount of incoming links (in our example, LOV indicated Bibtex had only a single incoming link, therefore we consider that it partially met this criterion);
- Item 8: check for how long the vocabulary has been maintained and if they are published in a stable domain.

The above checklist is, of course, not exhaustive and could be improved with further vocabularies and/or desired attributes to check, depending on the availability of resources involved in the software development project.

Once the vocabularies are chosen, we move on to *Create FrameWeb-LD Entity Model*. In this activity, we build an Entity Model as proposed by [5], by adding Linked Data mapping annotations to the domain model, based on FrameWeb-LD meta-model, to the vocabulary chosen in the previous activity. Figure 1, shown earlier, represents the model built for C2D, which is based on the model exemplified in [5], with new vocabulary classes added by the process suggested by *GRALD*, which are filled in blue (darker background).

For instance, for the domain class `Researcher` vocabularies `schema:Person` and `dbo:Person` were added; for `Publication`: `bibo:Article` and `bibtex:Article`; and for `Venue`: `schema:Organization` and `bio:Organization`.

4 Evaluation

The evaluation of this proposal was conducted by the first and second authors of this paper using Web-based Information Systems developed by students of the *Web Development & Semantic Web* course of our Postgraduate Program in Computer Science, all of which aim to publish Linked Data. We evaluated our proposal by creating goal and risk models for these systems and searching for vocabularies based on these models. Artifacts are available in a public source code repository: https://github.com/nemo-ufes/FrameWeb-GRALD.

Regarding tools, we used piStar (cf. Figure 3) to create goal models, we built a simple RiskML editor based on their metamodel (c.f. *Tool* folder in the repository) and we used the generic draw.io tool to produce the integrated models. Future work includes expanding the RiskML editor to support all models.

During evaluation, we particularly focused on three research questions about GRALD: **RQ1**: can it be applied to different systems and domains? **RQ2**: can it be applied to identify risks and new related GORE elements? **RQ3**: can it aid in the identification of vocabularies?

We applied GRALD to five different systems: RightPlace (a system that helps people find a place to live according to their preferences), Rural (management of rural properties), Semed (information system for a medical practice), TransparencyPortal (display government data for citizens) and TravelNM (storefront for a travel agency). By applying GRALD on these existing systems, we were able to identify their goals, tasks, resources and actors, and build their goal models. Moreover, we were able to identify risks related to linked data and other risks, producing their risk models.

For instance, in the case of TravelNM (whose goal model can be found under *goal-models/TravelNM/* in the repository), publication of Linked Data about cities and tour packages being offered is represented by the goal *Data published in linked data*. The data is stored in a triplestore using the resource *Stardog*, which is the triplestore chosen for this project. There is an *Agent* that represents websites that provide unified search engines for traveling services, such as Trivago or Expedia, with a goal *Process data published in LD*, processing the Linked Data published by *TravelNM*. Different from the goal model of C2D, the task *Generate RDF* is performed by the resource *DotNet RDF* (http://www.dotnetrdf.org/), the tasks *Create ontology and Generate OWL* can be performed by the resource *Protégé* (http://protege.stanford.edu/) and so on.

TravelNM's risk model is also available at the repository (under *risk-models/TravelNM/*), presenting four new goals and risk events, for example a goal related to the creation of vocabulary *Use cool URI*, that is impacted by a risk event *URI not provided in accordance to best practices* exposed by a risk situation *URI non-compliant with best practices*. The integrated model of risks and goals was also created (see *impact-models (Goals and Risks)* in the repository) according to the guidelines of our proposal, having new goals added to the model with their respective risks events. Regarding vocabulary search, for the class *City*, for instance, we found vocabularies such as `schema:City` and `dbo:City`, which were not originally found by the students when their assignment was produced.

Finally, we analyze the proposed research questions:

RQ1: Can GRALD be applied to different systems and domains? The systems in which GRALD was successfully applied during this evaluation involved many different domains, such as education, geographical, government, medical, etc., which indicates a positive answer to this RQ.

RQ2: Can GRALD be applied to identify risks and new related GORE elements? Applying GRALD to the aforementioned systems, although very simple and small, we were able to elicit and model risk elements, then augment the goal model with new elements (goals) related to these risks. Further risks could be found with the use of risk identification techniques that are out of the scope of this paper.

RQ3: Can GRALD aid in the identification of vocabularies? GRALD activities *Elicit Requirements*, *Develop Domain Model* and *Develop Goal Model* allowed us to model the classes of the system and clearly specify those that will have the published objects in Linked Data. The checklist used during *Design* aided us in the definition of at least two new (i.e., not previously found by the students) links to external vocabularies per class.

5 Related Work

There are many works published on Linked Data, but in our case we are particularly interested in publications that involve requirements elicitation, risks identification, risk modeling and goal modeling for the development of systems that publish or consume Linked Data. In our search, we had difficulty to find specific references related to above subjects, which seems to imply that this is an open area of research. In this context, this section refers to proposals on risk/goal modeling for software in general.

In [8], requirements analysis is performed with the iStar-based Tropos methodology in two phases: *Early Requirements*, which seeks to understand the organizational context where the system can work, and *Late Requirements*, which seeks to define functional (goals) and non-functional (softgoals) requirements for the system-to-be. The authors also propose reasoning with goal models using forward and backward reasoning. In our proposal we have requirements elicitation and risk identification performed in *Early Requirements* and the creation of the models for WIS that use Linked Data in *Late Requirements*.

Kenett et al. [11] propose capturing, filtering, analyzing and reasoning about risks, based on RISCOSS, using a three layered approach to risk management in FLOSS (*Free Libre Open Source Software*) projects. In the first layer, raw data is collected from FLOSS communities and projects; in the second layer risk indicators are defined and models are produced, in which the risks can be linked to the objectives; finally, in the third layer the risks indicators are converted in Business Risks and, linked with iStar, model business goals to see how risks impact them. In our case we are seeking to apply the RISCOSS approach with the focus on Linked Data.

In [18], the software risk management process is performed with steps Risk Identification, Risk Analysis, Plan and Tracking. In our work, we propose risk identification and modeling related to the development of information systems for the Web of Data.

6 Conclusions

In this paper, we presented GRALD, *Goal and Risk Analysis for Linked Data*, an approach based on RISCOSS, which applies Goal-Oriented Requirements Engineering (GORE) for the development of Web-based Information Systems that publish Linked Data, integrating goal models with risk models in order to perform risk analysis.

GORE is applied in order to help developers to analyze their system objectives, as well as the goals and actors related to the implementation of Linked Data, mapping the necessary resources and tasks to accomplish it. Moreover, performing risk analysis helps to analyze the impact of the occurrence of risk events on system/business goals, as well as to carry out the prevention/mitigation of these risks. Finally, GRALD assists developers in the choice of vocabularies based on the tasks performed in the phases of early and late requirements, having the search of such vocabularies accomplished using Linked Data search engines following guidelines from a checklist.

Our research proposal is a work in progress and with some limitations, which we intend to address in future work, such as (i) evaluate the proposal with more systems and practitioners, going through goal-oriented modeling and risk analysis; (ii) evaluate the scalability of our models; (iii) create a repository of risk indicators related to Linked Data; and (iv) develop a tool integrated with Linked Data search engines (e.g., LOV) to assist developers in the task of choosing vocabulary.

References

1. Asnar, Y., Giorgini, P., Mylopoulos, J.: Goal-driven risk assessment in requirements engineering. Requir. Eng. 16(2), 101–116 (Jun 2011)
2. Berners-Lee, T., Hendler, J., Lassila, O.: The Semantic Web. Scientific American 284(5), 34–43 (2001)
3. Bizer, C., Heath, T., Berners-Lee, T.: Linked data-the story so far. Int. J. Semant. Web Inf. Syst. 5(3), 1–22 (2009)
4. Bruwer, R., Rudman, R.: Web 3.0: governance, risks and safeguards. Journal of Applied Business Research 31(3), 1037 (2015)
5. Celino, D.R., Reis, L.V., Martins, B.F., Souza, V.E.S.: A Framework-based Approach for the Integration of Web-based Information Systems on the Semantic Web. In: Proc. of the 22nd Brazilian Symposium on Multimedia and the Web. pp. 231–238. ACM (nov 2016)
6. Costal, D., López, L., Morandini, M., Siena, A., Annosi, M.C., Gross, D., Méndez, L., Franch, X., Susi, A.: Aligning business goals and risks in oss adoption. In: International Conference on Conceptual Modeling. pp. 35–49. Springer (2015)
7. Eric, S.Y.: Social Modeling and i*. In: Conceptual Modeling: Foundations and Applications, pp. 99–121. Springer (2009)
8. Giorgini, P., Mylopoulos, J., Sebastiani, R.: Goal-oriented requirements analysis and reasoning in the tropos methodology. Eng. Appl. Artif. Intell. 18(2), 159–171 (2005)
9. Heath, T., Bizer, C.: Linked Data: Evolving the Web into a Global Data Space. Synthesis Lectures on the Semantic Web: Theory and Technology, Morgan & Claypool Publishers (2011)
10. Hyland, B., Atemezing, G., Villazón-Terrazas, B.: Best Practices for Publishing Linked Data, https://www.w3.org/TR/ld-bp/ (last access: May 26th, 2017) (2014)
11. Kenett, R.S., Franch, X., Susi, A., Galanis, N.: Adoption of free libre open source software (floss): A risk management perspective. In: 2014 IEEE 38th Annual Computer Software and Applications Conference. pp. 171–180 (July 2014)
12. van Lamsweerde, A., Letier, E.: Handling obstacles in goal-oriented requirements engineering. IEEE Trans. Softw. Eng. 26(10), 978–1005 (Oct 2000)
13. López, L.: Welcome to the RISCOSS Risk Modeling repository, https://github.com/RISCOSS/riscoss-risk-modeling/wiki (last access: May 26th, 2017) (2015)
14. López, L., Siena, A.: How to create a Risk Model, https://github.com/RISCOSS/riscoss-risk-modeling/wiki/How-to-create-a-Risk-Model (last access: May 25th, 2017) (2015)
15. López Cuesta, L., Franch Gutiérrez, J.: Applying business strategy models in organizations. In: Proceedings of the 7th International i* Workshop (2014)
16. Martins, B.F., Souza, V.E.S.: A Model-Driven Approach for the Design of Web Information Systems based on Frameworks. In: Proc. of the 21st Brazilian Symposium on Multimedia and the Web. pp. 41–48. ACM (2015)
17. Pohorec, S., Zorman, M., Kokol, P.: Analysis of approaches to structured data on the web. Comput. Stand. Interfaces 36(1), 256–262 (2013)
18. Westfall, L., Road, C.: Software Risk Management. Risk Manag. pp. 1–8 (2001)

As Técnicas de Elicitação e de Documentação de Requisitos nos Métodos Ágeis

Angélica Toffano Seidel Calazans[1], Roberto Avila Paldês[1], Fernando de Albuquerque Guimarães[1], Eloisa Toffano Seidel Masson[1]

[1] Centro Universitário de Brasília, Distrito Federal, Brazil
{angelica.calazans, roberto.paldes, fernando.guimaraes, eloisa.masson}@ceub.edu.br

Resumo. A popularidade do desenvolvimento ágil não tem sido acompanhada na mesma extensão pela engenharia de requisitos. O objetivo do estudo foi identificar as técnicas de elicitação e documentação de requisitos para os métodos ágeis. A partir da revisão da literatura, foi realizado um estudo de caso no setor de desenvolvimento de software de uma Instituição de Ensino Superior (IES) com uso do método Delphi com Q-sort. O caso analisado foi o do setor de desenvolvimento de uma instituição de ensino, onde trabalham 20 indivíduos com experiência em métodos ágeis. Para análise dos dados utilizou-se o software Minitab e o coeficiente Kendall's W. Como grau de concordância dos investigados, foi obtido 0,579 para as técnicas de elicitação e 0,437 para a documentação. As técnicas de elicitação de maior aplicabilidade identificadas foram entrevistas, brainstorming e user stories. Com relação à documentação, destacaram-se as técnicas tasks, user stories e protótipos. Os resultados servem de referência para pesquisadores e para equipes que buscam maior produtividade.

Palavras chave: Aspectos sociais. Aspectos culturais. Perfil profissional. Conformidade. Analista de requisitos.

1 Introdução

O relacionamento entre a Engenharia de Requisitos (ER) e os Métodos Ágeis tem atraído bastante atenção pelos pesquisadores [1,2,3,4]. A ER desempenha um papel fundamental em todos os tipos de processos de desenvolvimento de software. O desenvolvimento ágil de software vem crescendo em popularidade e, em contraste com a extensa pesquisa de ER focada no desenvolvimento de software tradicional, o papel da ER no desenvolvimento ágil ainda não foi estudado em profundidade [4]. A ER é utilizada de forma diferente no desenvolvimento ágil quando comparada aos processos de desenvolvimento mais tradicionais [3].

O manifesto de desenvolvimento ágil de software é apontado como sendo o guia para todos os métodos de desenvolvimento considerados ágeis [5]. Esse manifesto foi lançado em 2001 com o intuito de discutir ideias e procurar alternativas aos processos burocráticos e às práticas adotadas nas abordagens tradicionais de Engenharia de Software e Gerência de Projetos. O manifesto define os seguintes valores a serem utilizados por todos os Métodos Ágeis [6,7]:

- Indivíduos e interações são mais importantes que processos e ferramentas;
- Software funcionando é mais importante que documentação completa e detalhada;
- Colaboração com o cliente é mais importante que negociação de contratos;
- Adaptação às mudanças é mais importante que seguir um plano.

A ER é dividida em dois grupos de atividades relacionadas: o Desenvolvimento de Requisitos (DRE), que inclui as atividades de elicitação, análise, especificação e validação; e a Gerência de Requisitos (GRE), incluindo as atividades de rastreabilidade e gerência de mudanças nos requisitos [8].

Na literatura, encontram-se várias revisões sistemáticas abrangendo a Engenharia de Requisitos e os Métodos Ágeis [2, 4, 9,10]. Grande parte desses estudos identificam as principais técnicas, métodos e práticas aplicadas no contexto da Engenharia de Requisitos considerando o quantitativo de publicações acadêmicas. Estudos que relacionam quais dessas técnicas, métodos e práticas são efetivamente utilizadas pela indústria para elicitar e documentar os requisitos possuem um quantitativo menor de pesquisa, principalmente no Brasil.

Um *survey* [3] com 92 organizações sobre as práticas da Engenharia de Requisitos e seus problemas quando utilizadas pelos Métodos Ágeis identificaram algumas práticas tais como entrevistas, prototipagem, reuniões como as técnicas de elicitação mais utilizadas pelos participantes. Outro estudo empírico sobre o papel da Engenharia de Requisitos frente aos Métodos Ágeis [4] identifica que para 90% dos 108 participantes (8 equipes de 4 organizações) que participaram do *survey*, a Engenharia de Requisitos é considerada importante. Para 75% dos participantes os requisitos funcionais são mais importantes que os não funcionais. O estudo também identifica as técnicas de elicitação mais utilizadas: entrevista, *survey* (*business process modeling e goal modeling*) e documentação utilizada, *brainstorm*, prototipação e outras.

Considerando o contexto abordado, e a necessidade de aprofundar esses estudos identificando quais técnicas citadas pela literatura tem maior aplicabilidade na indústria e quais a formas utilizadas pela indústria para documentar os requisitos nos modelos ágeis, o foco deste estudo está nas atividades de elicitação e na documentação do DRE. Ou seja, investigar como as práticas, princípios e valores dos Métodos Ágeis são utilizados para as atividades de elicitação e documentação de requisitos. Como os requisitos estão sendo elicitados de forma mais dinâmica, adaptativa e colaborativa, atendendo os princípios do desenvolvimento ágil? Quais as técnicas mais utilizadas para a elicitação e documentação de requisitos?

Considerando essas questões, pode-se levantar os seguintes questionamentos, os quais serão respondidos por esta pesquisa: Quais as técnicas e práticas utilizadas para e elicitação de requisitos pela indústria considerando os Métodos Ágeis? Quais as técnicas mais utilizadas para documentar ou especificar os requisitos, no contexto ágil de desenvolvimento (SCRUM), na indústria?

Assim, o objetivo geral desta pesquisa é identificar e analisar as técnicas e práticas de elicitação e documentação para os Métodos Ágeis e contextualizar sua atuação no processo ágil de desenvolvimento, especificamente no processo SCRUM. São objetivos específicos deste trabalho: identificar as técnicas e práticas de elicitação de requisitos utilizados pelos Métodos Ágeis; identificar as técnicas e práticas de especificação/documentação de requisitos utilizados pelos Métodos Ágeis; identificar as técnicas e práticas de elicitação e especificação mais utilizadas no ambiente de uma indústria que utiliza o SCRUM.

A seguir, na seção 2, apresentam-se alguns Métodos Ágeis. A seção 3 apresenta a metodologia da pesquisa. A seção 4 demonstra a análise dos resultados e, na seção 5 as conclusões obtidas.

2 Métodos Ágeis

Para a criação de um produto de software é necessário a interação dos vários fatores, como processos e pessoas. A dinâmica de mercado atual impõe agilidade na entrega de produtos e atendimento, cada vez mais satisfatório, ao que foi demandado pelo cliente. Os Métodos Ágeis representam uma evolução diante das metodologias tradicionais porque valorizam a interação entre pessoas, a comunicação com o cliente e priorizam as atividades que efetivamente agregam valor. Encontram-se na literatura, várias propostas de métodos ágeis de desenvolvimento de sistemas, alguns descritos sucintamente, a seguir.

O propósito da Programação Extrema (Extreme Programming - XP) é garantir o sucesso no desenvolvimento de softwares, especialmente para equipes pequenas e médias envolvidas com projeto, nos quais os requisitos são desconhecidos e voláteis. O XP foi formalizado por meio de quatro princípios que são: Comunicação, Simplicidade, *Feedback* e a Coragem. É composto de doze práticas [11,12]: planejamento das iterações, incrementos curtos e pequenos, uso da metáfora para facilitar a comunicação, projeto simples ou incremental, desenvolvimento orientado a testes, reestruturação constante do código, programação em pares, propriedade coletiva, integração contínua, ritmo sustentável, cliente no local e padrão de codificação.

Já o Scrum se baseia em algumas características [13]: flexibilidade dos resultados e dos prazos, times pequenos, revisões frequentes e colaboração. Sua equipe é composta por três principais papéis: *Product Owner* (PO), *Scrum Master* e time Scrum. Outra característica da metodologia Scrum [14] é a existência de três principais artefatos produzidos e acessíveis por toda a equipe: *Product Backlog* (uma lista, ordenada por prioridades, com todas as necessidades e funcionalidades a serem desenvolvidas, custos estimados e as datas de entrega); *Sprint Backlog* (subconjunto do *Product Backlog*, o qual divide as atividades por períodos de desenvolvimento chamados *Sprint's*; Gráfico *Sprint Burndown* (representação gráfica do trabalho já realizado e o que resta a ser realizado.

O método Scrum tem as seguintes fases: reunião de planejamento (seleção do *Backlog* e definição das estimativas), planejamento da *sprint* (*backlog* da *sprint* com atividades ou tarefas), *sprint* de desenvolvimento (análise, projeto, evolução teste, entrega) e reunião de revisão do *sprint* e retrospectiva.

A literatura apresenta outros métodos, tais como: Crystal, ASD (Desenvolvimento ágil de software), DSDM (Metodologia de Desenvolvimento de Sistemas Dinâmicos), FDD (Desenvolvimento Guiado por Funcionalidades) etc.

3 Metodologia

Assim, essa investigação utilizou a abordagem qualitativa. No que tange ao alcance temporal, a pesquisa caracterizou-se como uma pesquisa interseccional, uma vez que investiga os Métodos Ágeis e as abordagens de Engenharia de Requisitos, em determinado período de 2012 a 2017.

O método adotado foi o estudo de caso e os instrumentos de coleta de dados -aplicados foram a revisão de literatura e o método Delphi.

O estudo baseado na revisão de literatura abrangeu os Métodos Ágeis, suas métricas e aplicações. Foram pesquisados no Portal da Capes (somente os artigos acessíveis) no período de janeiro/2012 e Outubro/2017. É interessante ressaltar que o Portal da CAPES é uma biblioteca virtual que disponibiliza a instituições no Brasil o melhor da produção científica internacional, Esse portal conta com um acervo de mais de 38 mil títulos com texto completo, 134 bases referenciais, etc [15].

Foram pesquisados os *strings* nos títulos: *"agile model"*, "requirements", "modelo ágil" e "requisitos". Foram selecionados os títulos relacionados ao assunto e posteriormente, lidos os resumos e selecionadas as publicações pertinentes. Estas foram lidas integralmente.

Esse levantamento permitiu identificar as técnicas de elicitação e algumas referências apresentadas na Tabela 1. Da mesma forma, as técnicas de documentação e algumas referências foram identificadas e relacionadas na Tabela 2.

O estudo de caso foi escolhido pela relação observada entre o objeto e as características básicas do estudo de caso [16]: fenômeno observado em seu ambiente natural; estudo exploratório, descritivo ou explanatório uma ou mais entidades (pessoa, grupo, organização) são examinadas, a complexidade da unidade é estudada intensamente, não são utilizados controles experimentais ou manipulações.

Considerando o caráter exploratório e descritivo da pesquisa e a aplicação (acadêmica e comercial) das abordagens identificadas na revisão da literatura, optou-se pelo método Delphi com Q-Sort para obter a percepção e consenso de técnicos sobre as abordagens mais aplicáveis para o ambiente de desenvolvimento que utilize a metodologia ágil. A realização de uma pesquisa utilizando o Delphi ocorre mediante sucessivos questionamentos a um grupo de especialistas. As respostas são cumulativamente analisadas para verificar a obtenção ou não de consenso. O consenso no Método Delphi representa uma consolidação do julgamento intuitivo do grupo participante [17].

O método Delphi com Q-sort é um método de pesquisa utilizado em diversas áreas de conhecimento, como técnica de comunicação em grupo, particularmente, em situações onde se pretende alcançar consenso de opinião [18]. Neste tipo de estudo, os peritos são postos perante um conjunto de cartões contendo declarações sobre um determinado assunto. São, então, solicitados a ordenar estes cartões segundo uma escala contínua de "pouco importante" a "muito importante", conforme a sua opinião. Encontram-se trabalhos na literatura [19,20] em que o Q-sort tem sido utilizado sem os cartões, mas solicitando que os peritos identifiquem em uma lista de declarações a ordem de importância, valor etc.

O Q-Sort [21] apresenta alguns benefícios, tais como: oferecer um meio para um estudo em profundidade para pequenas amostras; poder ajudar a investigação exploratória; capturar a subjetividade com a mínima interferência do investigador; os participantes não precisam ser selecionados aleatoriamente; as suas técnicas de análise ajudam a proteger os respondentes da influência do investigador.

Tabela 1. Relação de técnicas de elicitação

Técnica/Referências	Descrição
Análise de domínio [2], [3]	O processo de identificação, coleta, organização e representação das informações relevantes é baseada em um domínio. Por exemplo, baseado no estudo de sistemas existentes ou em suas histórias de desenvolvimento.
Análise documental [4]	Estudo e reutilização de documentação de diferentes naturezas (leis, manuais de usuário, relatório de pesquisas de mercado, glossário de termos de negócio) para a identificação de requisitos a serem implementados no sistema.
Brainstorming [2],[4],[10],[24]	Técnica usada para gerar novas ideias e encontrar a solução para uma questão específica, além de promover o pensamento criativo
Brainwriting [19]	É a técnica onde um grupo de pessoas registram por escrito possíveis formas de como resolver um problema, desenvolver um projeto ou melhorar uma situação existente.Também conhecida como Método 6-3-5.
Cenários (*Scenários*) [2],[3],[23]	Trata-se de uma abordagem informal, prática e aplicável a qualquer tipo de sistema. Scenarios são exemplos reais de como um sistema pode ser usado, o que geralmente proporciona uma melhor compreensão dos *stakeholders*.
Entrevistas [2],[3],[4],[10],[22]	Colóquio entre pessoas em local combinado, para obtenção de esclarecimentos, avaliações ou opiniões.
Features [2]	São declarações de alto nível, uma vez que não possuem detalhes necessários para a implementação, derivadas das necessidades dos *stakeholders*. Para cada *feature* identificada, temos um ou mais requisitos de software.
Grupo focal [10],[24]	São debates ou entrevistas com um pequeno grupo selecionado de indivíduos, que discute um tópico específico, pré-definido e limitado, sob a orientação de um facilitador ou moderador.
Mapa mental [2],[23]	É uma técnica usada para acelerar a aquisição de conhecimentos, baseado em imagens e textos e seus relacionamentos.
Observações [3]	É uma técnica que acompanha e relata as coisas, os seres, os eventos a serem analisados.
Personas [2],[23]	É uma técnica que consiste na criação de perfis e personificação de grupo de usuários. Representa uma caracterização de um personagem que, embora seja fictício, expõe as características importantes da população de usuários .

Técnica/Referências	Descrição
Prototipação [2],[3],[4],[23]	Representa o produto real tanto no sentido funcional quanto no sentido gráfico. Trata-se de uma versão inicial do sistema, baseada em requisitos ainda pouco definidos.
Questionários [10],[24]	São utilizados quando há a necessidade de coletar as mesmas informações de muitos usuários e ao mesmo tempo.
Refining meetings [3]	Prática que permite o refinamento dos requisitos ou *user stories* em uma reunião estruturada.
Reuniões [2],[3], [24]	Trata-se de uma técnica de elicitação em grupo usada em uma reunião estruturada. Devem fazer parte do grupo uma equipe de analistas e os *stakeholders*.
Sessões de JAD [2],[10],[24]	Entrevista de grupo com líder imparcial. É uma técnica que visa reunir autoridades representativas e gerenciais em um *workshop* organizado para a elicitação de requisitos ou para promover decisões.
UI mockups [2]	É uma representação estática de média a alta fidelidade de um design. Muitas vezes um *mockup* é um rascunho bem próximo do *design* final do produto, ou até o próprio *design* visual do produto final
User story [4],[10],[22],[23],[24]	É um requisito de sistema de software formulado como uma ou duas frases na linguagem cotidiana do usuário.
W*orkshops* [2],[3],[10],[24]	Técnica de elicitação em grupo realizada em uma reunião estruturada com apresentação por parte de uma ou mais equipes.

Assim, foi elaborada uma lista com 19 técnicas de elicitação utilizadas no contexto ágil e uma lista com 15 técnicas para documentação de requisitos que foram apresentadas aos técnicos/peritos. Para direcionar as questões do Delphi, foram identificadas e analisadas as técnicas de elicitação e documentação mais citadas e aplicadas no universo acadêmico e/ou comercial, considerando o material pesquisado. O Delphi com Q-Sort foi aplicado em 02 e 03 rodadas. Foi utilizado o software Minitab para análise dos resultados.

Tabela 2. Relação de técnicas de documentação

Técnica	Descrição
Cenários (*Scenários*) [2],[10],[23],[24]	Trata-se de uma abordagem informal, prática e aplicável a qualquer tipo de sistema. Scenarios são exemplos reais de como um sistema pode ser usado, o que geralmente proporciona uma melhor compreensão dos *stakeholders*.
Data models [3]	É um subconjunto do modelo de implementação que descreve a representação lógica e física dos dados persistentes no sistema. Pode se valer da Linguagem Natural (técnica extremamente flexível e expressiva, não adota nenhuma estrutura e semântica pré-definida), de uma Notação Semiformal (possui alguma estrutura e semântica) ou de uma Notação Formal (que utiliza semântica precisa e detalhamento completo de modelos).
Features [2],[10],[24]	São declarações de alto nível, uma vez que não possuem detalhes necessários para a implementação, derivadas das necessidades dos *stakeholders*. Para cada *feature* identificada, temos um ou mais requisitos de *software*.

Técnica	Descrição
Goal Preference Model [3],[24]	Técnica onde os *stakeholders* atribuem um valor inteiro para cada meta descrita em uma lista, denominada de lista inicial de metas. Esse valor representa o grau preferencia de prioridade de cada meta.
Modelos de Casos de Uso [2],[3],[4],[10],[23],[24]	É uma técnica que especifica uma sequência de interação entre um sistema e um ator externo incluindo variantes e extensões que o sistema pode executar.
Ontologias [26]	Ontologias permitem uma representação de tais abstrações de forma fidedigna e não ambígua. Dessa forma, podem atuar na complementação a modelos, facilitando o entendimento do domínio.
Personas [2],[10],[23],[24]	É uma técnica de usabilidade, que consiste na criação de perfis e personificação de grupo de usuários, ou seja, representa uma caracterização de um personagem que, embora seja fictício, expõe as características importantes da população de usuários para a qual se destina o produto o projeto.
Protótipos [2],[10],[23],[24]	Representa o produto real tanto no sentido funcional, quanto no sentido gráfico. Trata-se de uma versão inicial do sistema, baseada em requisitos ainda pouco definidos.
Story card [2], [10],[23],[24]	Tem o objetivo de capturar os requisitos macros, e se concentram em "quem, o quê e porquê de um recurso, e não como". *Story Card* deve ser escrito a partir de uma perspectiva do usuário e deve ser utilizada linguagem do negócio, para que seja compreendido por todos.
Structured requirements list [3],[10],[22],[23],[24]	E a declaração oficial do que é exigido para os desenvolvedores do sistema. Ela deve incluir uma definição das necessidades dos utilizadores e uma especificação dos requisitos do sistema.
Tasks [10],[24]	São unidades menores das histórias de usuário. Durante a o *sprint planning*, os itens do *backlog* que serão desenvolvidos na *sprint* são escolhidos. Em seguida, esses itens são quebrados em unidades menores, o que é denominado de *tasks*
User stories [4],[10],[22],[23],[24]	É um requisito de sistema de software formulado como uma ou duas frases na linguagem cotidiana do usuário.
Wall [10],[24],	A ideia básica da parede de cartões é de ter o fluxo de trabalho visível na própria parede.
XSBD [2],[10],[24]	O objetivo principal do processo XSBD é que o engenheiro de usabilidade possa desenvolver eficientemente um sistema de software que atenda a usabilidade do projeto e metas de desenvolvimento
XXM *(Extreme X-Machine)* [2],[10],[24]	São utilizados para mostrar um modelo de alto nível da totalidade sistema. Uma *Extreme X-Machine* permite modelar as estruturas de controle de uma história e, finalmente, de todo o sistema.

Para pesquisar sobre a aplicabilidade das técnicas, foi escolhido o setor de desenvolvimento de uma Instituição de Ensino Superior (IES) responsável por diversos projetos relacionados ao seu portal institucional. A escolha justifica-se por ser uma empresa de Brasília (escopo da pesquisa), com grande credibilidade na região e por sua experiência prática com métodos ágeis (Scrum) há mais de cinco anos. A empresa trabalha desenvolvendo software tanto para uso interno, como para clientes externos. Na sua área de

TI, trabalham 20 técnicos e gerente com Métodos Ágeis, definindo assim a população da pesquisa.

4 Resultados e discussão

A análise inicial do perfil dos respondentes correspondeu a 70% da população (14 indivíduos) identificada de 20 peritos. Identificou-se que 100% dos respondentes possui graduação superior, variando entre o ensino superior completo (65%) e *lato* e *stricto sensu* (35%). Cercar de 57% da população pesquisada trabalha com método ágeis há mais de 5 anos, e o restante dos respondentes (43%) de 2 a 5 anos. Com relação a percepção do seu grau de conhecimento sobre Métodos Ágeis, 78% classifica entre regular e bom e, destes 50%, classifica seu conhecimento em Métodos Ágeis como bom.

4.1 Técnicas de elicitação e documentação – 1ª rodada

Foram elaborados dois questionários utilizando a ferramenta Google Forms com técnicas de elicitação e técnicas de documentação identificadas pela literatura pesquisada. As tabelas com as técnicas de elicitação e documentação foram ordenadas por ordem alfabética e com a respetiva descrição.

Foi realizada uma reunião com os peritos para explicar a metodologia e os questionários com as técnicas de elicitação e documentação, disponibilizados para preenchimento. A primeira rodada foi realizada em outubro de 2017. Obteve-se uma taxa de resposta 14 membros, correspondendo a 70%. Nessa primeira rodada, os respondentes poderiam acrescentar alguma técnica de elicitação ou documentação não citada no questionário e pontuá-la com o peso correspondente. Foi acrescentada somente uma técnica de elicitação por um dos respondentes: "Especificação das regras de negócio". Essa técnica foi inserida na segunda rodada do Delphi. A análise estatística da primeira rodada revelou um valor do coeficiente Kendall's W de 0,316 para as técnicas de elicitação e de 0,398 para as técnicas de documentação (Figura 2). O que significa uma concordância média dos membros do painel, não sendo estatisticamente significativa, pelo que se promoveu uma segunda rodada.

O coeficiente de concordância de Kendall [27] é um método não paramétrico que busca verificar qual o grau de associação ou correlação (concordância) entre um conjunto de 3 ou mais variáveis. Como todo método não paramétrico, não exige pré-especificações quanto ao tipo de distribuição da população ou qualquer outro parâmetro. Para utilizar o método, cada variável deve estar pelo menos no nível ordinal, para possibilitar a ordenação dos escores de cada variável em postos. O valor do coeficiente W está compreendido entre 0 e +1, sendo 0 um valor que significa falta de correlação entre as variáveis, enquanto que +1 significa uma correlação perfeita [27].

Com relação ao nível de significância assintótica, tipicamente, um valor menor do que 0,05 é considerado significante. A significância assintótica é baseada no pressuposto que o tamanho da amostra foi suficientemente grande. Ao contrário, se o tamanho da amostra é pequeno, poder-se-ia obter uma pobre indicação de significância. Nesse caso o nível de significância assintótica é 0, o que demonstra que o tamanho da amostra é significante.

Coeficiente de Concordância de Kendall

Coef	Qui-Quadrado	GL	P
0,398974	78,1988	14	0,0000

Coeficiente de Concordância de Kendall

Coef	Qui-Quadrado	GL	P
0,316275	79,7012	18	0,0000

Figura 2 – Testes estatísticos de concordância – 1a. Rodada do Delphi com Q-sort

4.2 Técnicas de elicitação e documentação – 2ª rodada

Nesta rodada, solicitou-se aos membros do painel que voltassem a ordenar os fatores constantes da lista de técnicas de elicitação e documentação seguindo os procedimentos do Q-Sort, utilizando-se a consolidação da lista de fatores ordenada da primeira rodada. Nesta segunda rodada, foi inserida a técnica citada na primeira rodada de "Especificação de regras de negócio". Ao todo, ficaram 20 técnicas de elicitação. Esta segunda rodada realizou-se em novembro 2017, tendo participado 13 peritos, o que corresponde a uma taxa de resposta de 65 %. A análise estatística revelou um valor do coeficiente Kendall's W de 0,579 para as técnicas de elicitação e de 0,437 para as técnicas de documentação (Figura 3), o que significa uma concordância mais alta dos membros do painel e sendo estatisticamente mais significativa para as técnicas de elicitação. Assim, decidiu-se aplicar uma terceira rodada para a técnica de documentação.

Coeficiente de Concordância de Kendall

Coef	Qui-Quadrado	GL	P
0,579725	143,192	19	0,0000

Coeficiente de Concordância de Kendall

Coef	Qui-Quadrado	GL	P
0,437784	68,2943	12	0,0000

Figura 3 – Testes estatísticos de concordância – 2ª. Rodada do Delphi com Q-sort

4.3 Técnicas de elicitação e documentação – 3ª rodada

Nesta terceira rodada, solicitou-se aos membros do painel que voltassem a ordenar os fatores constantes da lista de técnicas de documentação seguindo os procedimentos do Q-Sort, utilizando-se a consolidação da lista de fatores ordenada na segunda rodada. Esta terceira rodada realizou-se em dezembro 2017, tendo participado 13 peritos para a técnica de documentação (65%). Os resultados estão apresentados na Tabela 2 (Técnicas de elicitação – 2ª. rodada) e Tabela 3 (Técnicas de documentação – 3ª. rodada). A análise estatística revelou um valor do coeficiente Kendall's W de 0,691 para as técnicas de documentação (Figura 4). O que significa uma concordância alta dos membros do painel e sendo estatisticamente mais significativa.

Coeficiente de Concordância de Kendall

Coef	Qui-Quadrado	GL	P
0,691546	125,861	14	0,0000

Figura 4 – Testes estatísticos de concordância – 3ª. Rodada do Delphi com Q-sort

Os resultados estatísticos estão apresentados na Tabela 3 com as técnicas preferidas para a elicitação. Foi elaborada uma tabela similar para as técnicas de documentação.

Tabela 3. Aplicação das técnicas de elicitação

Técnicas	N	Média	Desvio-Padrão	Q1	Mediana	Q3
Entrevistas	13	1,92	2,50	1,00	1,00	1,50
Brainstorming	13	3,08	2,02	2,00	2,00	4,00
Reuniões	13	5,00	5,24	2,00	3,00	5,50
User story	13	4,15	1,21	3,50	4,00	5,00
Prototipação	13	6,00	4,81	4,00	5,00	6,00
Features	13	7,92	3,82	5,50	9,00	10,00
Grupo focal	13	8,15	4,43	6,00	7,00	9,50
Análise documental	13	9,00	4,49	6,00	8,00	11,50
Análise de domínio	13	9,31	4,50	6,50	8,00	12,00
Refining meetings	13	8,92	3,62	7,00	9,00	11,50
Brainwriting	13	11,38	3,97	9,50	12,00	15,00
Workshops	13	11,54	3,38	10,00	12,00	14,00
Observações	13	11,92	4,09	11,00	13,00	14,50
Cenários (*Scenários*)	13	12,08	4,70	8,00	14,00	15,50
Sessões de JAD	13	12,39	2,36	10,50	12,00	14,00
Mapa mental (*Mind Mapping*)	13	14,46	4,10	12,50	15,00	17,00
Personas	13	14,46	5,71	12,50	17,00	18,00
Especificação de Regras de Negócio	13	15,08	6,13	11,00	17,00	20,00
UI mockups	13	15,31	5,59	12,00	18,00	19,00
Questionários	13	15,46	4,37	14,50	17,00	18,00

A análise das médias, desvios padrões e variâncias obtidos pelas rodadas do Delphi com Q Sort, considerando as técnicas de elicitação e documentação, respectivamente, permitiu identificar que a dispersão do conjunto de valores em análise tendeu a diminuir. Ou seja, a classificação dada por cada perito na segunda e/ou terceira rodada, com relação a cada técnica, ficou relativamente mais próxima das outras classificações, que nas rodadas anteriores. Isso ratifica a concordância satisfatória encontrada.

A Figura 5 apresenta a evolução da média das técnicas de elicitação. É possível identificar a existência de técnicas com pouca ou nenhuma mudança significativa de médias considerando as duas rodadas do Delphi com Q-sort: Prototipação, Análise de Domínio, *Brainwriting, Workshops*, Observações, Cenários. A Figura 5 também permite identificar as técnicas de elicitação que obtiveram uma variação de médias mais significativas durante as rodadas do Delphi com Q-sort, tais como: Entrevistas, *Brainstorming, User story, Features, Refining meetings*.

A Figura 6 apresenta a evolução da média das técnicas de documentação na 1ª. e 3ª. rodadas. É possível identificar a existência de técnicas com pouca ou nenhuma mudança significativa de médias considerando as duas rodadas do Delphi com Q-sort: *Tasks, User stories, Story Card.* A Figura 6 também permite identificar as técnicas de elicitação que obtiveram uma variação de médias mais significativas durante as rodadas do Delphi com Q-sort, tais como: Protótipos, *Data Models, Structured Requirements List, Use Case Models* e Ontologias.

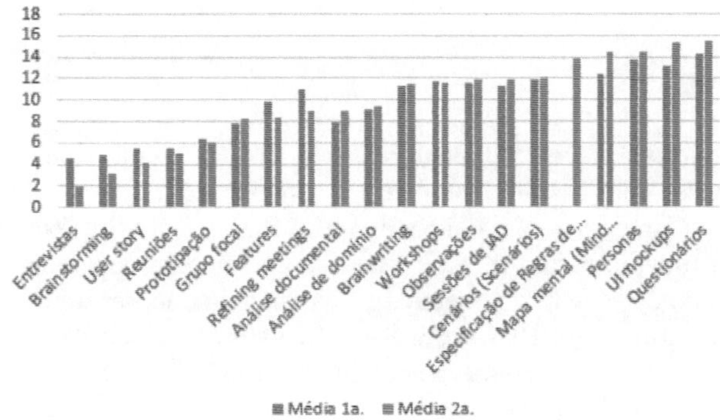

Figura 5 - Média por Técnica de elicitação e por rodada 1ª. e 2ª. do Delphi com Q-sort

Os resultados mostram que, no contexto do estudo de caso, as Técnicas de Elicitação utilizadas em Métodos Ágeis: Entrevistas (média na 2ª. rodada de 1,923), *Brainstorming* (média na 2ª. rodada de 3,07) e *User story* (média na 2ª. rodada de 4,15) foram as técnicas de elicitação consideradas de maior aplicabilidade.

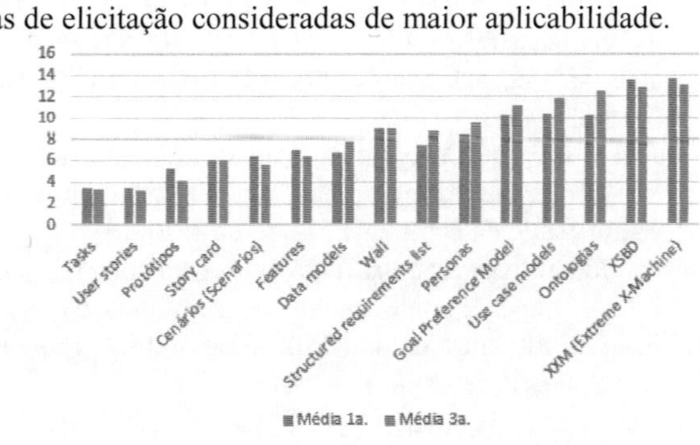

Figura 6 - Média por Técnica de documentação e por rodada 1ª. e 3ª. do Delphi com Q-sort

Foram consideradas as técnicas de elicitação com menor aplicabilidade, no contexto estudado: Questionários (média na 2ª. rodada de 15,46), *UI Mockups* (média na 2ª. rodada de 15,31) e Personas e Mapa mental (média na 2ª. rodada de 14,46). É interessante ressaltar a inclusão de uma técnica na 1ª. rodada: "Especificação de regras de negócio". Mas essa técnica não foi identificada por todos os participantes como importante, considerando o resultado da 2ª. rodada.

Os resultados mostram que, no contexto do estudo de caso, as Técnicas de Documentação utilizadas em Métodos Ágeis: Tasks (média na 3ª. rodada de 3,357), User Stories (média na 3ª. rodada de 3,286) e Protótipos (média na 3ª. rodada de 4,21) foram as técnicas de documentação consideradas de maior aplicabilidade.

Foram consideradas as técnicas de documentação com menor aplicabilidade, no contexto estudado: XXM (média na 3ª. rodada de 13), XSBD (média na 3ª. rodada de 12,85) e Ontologias (média na 3ª. rodada de 12,5).

5 Conclusões

O objetivo geral desta pesquisa foi identificar e analisar as técnicas de elicitação e documentação voltadas para os Métodos Ágeis e contextualizar sua atuação no processo ágil de desenvolvimento de uma indústria que utiliza o SCRUM. Para atingir os objetivos específicos identificaram-se as técnicas de elicitação e documentação mais citadas no contexto de um desenvolvimento ágil e realizou-se um estudo de caso em uma organização que utiliza o SCRUM para o desenvolvimento de software.

O instrumento elaborado para aplicação do método Delphi com Q-sort foi construído considerando a revisão de literatura elaborada e foram aplicadas 3 rodadas do Delphi com Q-sort e a segunda e terceira rodada apresentou um nível de concordância satisfatório. Para análise dos dados utilizou-se o software estatístico Minitab e o coeficiente Kendall's W .

Os resultados mostram que, no contexto do estudo de caso, as técnicas de elicitação utilizadas em Métodos Ágeis: Entrevistas, *Brainstorming* e *User Story* foram as técnicas de elicitação consideradas de maior aplicabilidade. Com relação a documentação, os resultados mostram que as Técnicas: *Tasks, User Stories* e Protótipos foram as técnicas de documentação consideradas de maior aplicabilidade. Esses resultados ratificam os estudos de [2,3, 4, 10, 16,23,24].

É interessante ressaltar que o Estudo de Caso é uma investigação empírica que pesquisa fenômenos dentro do seu contexto real e algumas características são essenciais para garantir a eficácia e a credibilidade da estratégia estudo de caso[16].

Validade do constructo – obtida através de constructos validados por revisão de literatura, utilização de múltiplas fontes, estabelecimento de caminhos de evidência. Nesse estudo fez-se uma revisão de literatura com utilização de múltiplas fontes, considerando que o Portal da CAPES acessa cerca de 134 bases;

Validade interna ou credibilidade – a validade e credibilidade são estabelecidas utilizando análises e análises cruzadas, assegurando a coerência interna dos achados e utilizando a triangulação como técnica para aumento da credibilidade. Essa triangulação foi possível através do levantamento bibliográfico e da coleta das percepções dos técnicos da área desenvolvimento;

Validade externa – garante que o escopo da pesquisa realizada pode ser replicado em casos de estudos aproximados. Envolve descrições sobre caso de estudo, protocolo de intenções dos questionários e procedimentos para codificação e análise. Os protocolos de pesquisa e instrumentos de coleta estão relacionados na pesquisa;

Confiabilidade – Habilidade para que outros pesquisadores possam aplicar este Estudo de Caso e encontrar resultados similares. A confiabilidade foi garantida através de registro dos dados coletados para que outros pesquisadores possam seguir o caminho da evidência e replicar em outros contextos. Infelizmente, o presente estudo foi aplicado em somente uma organização que utiliza somente o método ágil SCRUM.

Assim, como trabalhos futuros, sugere-se ampliar a pesquisa para outras organizações que utilizam SCRUM e/ou outros métodos ágeis para ratitificar ou retificar os resultados encontrados. Além disso, seria interessante realizar a pesquisa considerando outras áreas da Engenharia de Requisitos, tais como: análise e validação.

Referências

1. Lucassen, G., Dalpiaz, F., Van der Werf, J. M.: Forging high-quality User Stories: Towards a discipline for Agile Requirements. In: 23rd International Requirements Engineering Conference (RE), IEEE (2015)
2. Santos, K. B. C., Oliveira, S. R. B.: Um Estudo baseado em Evidências sobre Abordagens Ágeis de apoio ao Desenvolvimento de Requisitos de Software. In: XX Ibero-American Conference on Software Engineering (CIbSE), Buenos Aires, Argentina (2017)
3. Wagner, S., Fernández, D. M., Felderer, M., Kalinowski, M.: Requirements Engineering Practice and Problems in Agile Projects: Results from an International Survey. Cornell University Library (2017)
4. Wang, X., Zhao, L., Wang, Y., Sun, J.: The Role of Requirements Engineering Practices in Agile Development: An Empirical Study. Communications in Computer and Information Science, Requirements Engineering, v. 432, Springer (2014)
5. Vicente, A. A.: Definição e gerenciamento de métricas de teste no contexto de métodos ágeis. Dissertação. Instituto de ciências matemáticas e computação, Universidade São Paulo – USP (2010)
6. Williams, L. A.: Survey of Agile Development Methodologies. Arboricultural Journal, v. 38, Issue 2, UK (2006)
7. Kniberg, H.: Scrum and XP from the Trenchers. C4Media, USA (2007)
8. IEEE/Computer Science. Guide to the Software Engineering Body of Knowledge (SWEBOK). IEEE Institute of Electrical and Electronics Engineers, Los Alamitos, California (2004)
9. Inayat, I., Marczak, S., Salim, S.S., Daneva, M., Shahaboddin, S.: A systematic literature review on agile requirements engineering practices and challenges. Journal Computer in Human Behavior, v. 51 part B (2014)
10. Medeiros, J.D.R.V., Alves, D.C.P. : Engenharia de requisitos em projetos ágeis: uma revisão sistemática da literatura. Revista Principia. 26 ed., especial (2015)
11. Taniguchi, K., Correa, F. E.: Metodologias ágeis e a motivação de pessoas em projetos de desenvolvimento de software. Revista de Ciências exatas e tecnologia, v.4 (2009)
12. Fadel, A. C., Silveira, H. da M.: Metodologias ágeis no contexto de desenvolvimento de software_XP_SCRUM_Lean. Trabalho de conclusão. Pós Graduação da Faculdade Tecnologia da Universidade Estadual de Campinas, Campinas (2010)
13. Schawber, K.: Scrum development process. Business Object Design and Implementation, pp. 117-134, Springer London (1997)

14. Carvalho, B. V. , Mello, C. H. P.: Implementation of scrum agile methodology in software product project in a small technology-based company. Gestão & Produção. 3, 2012, v. 19, pp. 557-573 (2012)
15. Brasil. Portal de Periodicos CAPES/MEC. Missão e objetivos. Disponivel em https://www.periodicos.capes.gov.br/?option=com_pcontent&view=pcontent&alias=missao-objetivos&mn=69&smn=74, Acesso em 10 Jan 2018 (2017)
16. Yin, R. K.: Estudo de caso: Planejamento e métodos. 2a ed., Bookman, Porto Alegre : (2001)
17. Wright, J. T. C., Giovinazzo, R. A.: Delphi: uma ferramenta de apoio ao planejamento prospectivo. Cadernos de Pesquisa em Administração. 12, 2000, v. 1, pp. 54-65 (2000)
18. Soares, D.: Interoperabilidade entre Sistemas de Informação na Administração Pública. . Tese de Doutoramento. Universidade do Minho, Guimarães, Portugal (2009)
19. Samartinho, J.: MODoCOMPETE e-LÍDER: Estudo Delphi com Q-Sort sobre a compreensão de competências específicas e características em e-Liderança. In: 1º.Simpósio internacional - 7º EIN - Ciberespaço: liderança, segurança e defesa na sociedade em rede, Evora, Portugal (2013)
20. Castro, C. C., Andrade, A. M., Lagarto, J.: Identificação de fatores facilitadores da utilização de recursos educativos digitais pelos professores: a perspetiva de especialistas num estudo e-delphi . Revista Iberoamericana de Evaluación Educativa (2012)
21. Thomas, D. M., Watson, R. T.: Q-Sorting and MIS Research, a Primer. Communications of the Association for Information Systems. 8, pp. 141-156 (2001)
22. jarnason, E. , Unterkalmsteiner, M. , Borg, Markus , Engström , Emelie .A multi-case study of agile requirements engineering and the use of test cases as requirements . Information and Software Technology, 77, pp.61–79 (2016)
23. Schön, E.-M., Thomaschewski, Jörg , Escalona, María José. Agile Requirements Engineering:A systematic literature review. Computer Standards & Interfaces, 49, pp.79–91(2017)
24. Alves, D.C.P. Engenharia de requisitos em projetos ágeis: um mapeamento sistemático baseado em evidências da indústria. Dissertação. Universidade Federal da Pernambuco, Recife (2015).
25. Murman, C. Brainwriting: The Team Hack to Generating Better Ideas. Agile Aliance (2015).
26. Peroni, S.A Simplified Agile Methodology for Ontology Development . International Experiences and Directions Workshop on OWL, OWL: Reasoner Evaluation, International Workshop ORE, Stringer Link, pp 55-69 (2016)
27. Siegel, S.: Estatística não-paramétrica. McGraw-Hill, São Paulo (1975)

Mapeamento dos processos e artefatos da Engenharia de Requisitos para o eXtreme Programming

Ricardo Duarte Cardoso[1,3]; Renata Brasil Silva[2]; Fábio Levy Siqueira[1,2]

[1] PECE- Programa de Educação Continuada da Escola Politécnica da USP,
Av. Prof. Mello Moraes, nº 2373, 1º andar, 05508-900 São Paulo Brazil
[2] Escola Politécnica da Universidade de São Paulo,
Av. Prof. Luciano Gualberto, tr.3, no 158, 05508-900 São Paulo, Brazil
[3] Prosimulador Tecnologia de Transito,
Av. das Nações Unidas, no 14.261 04794-000 São Paulo, Brazil
ricardoduartecar@gmail.com, brasil.renata@usp.br,
levy.siqueira@usp.br

Resumo. Os métodos ágeis não seguem as abordagens tradicionais de Engenharia de Requisitos, que se baseiam em uma execução sequencial das atividades e em documentos formais. Contudo é importante que a Engenharia de Requisitos seja adequadamente executada nesses métodos, pois ela está diretamente ligada ao sucesso de um projeto. Este estudo analisa o atendimento das práticas de Engenharia de Requisitos por um método ágil, o eXtreme Programming (XP). São apresentados os processos e artefatos determinados pela norma ISO 29148 e o mapeamento deles para as práticas e artefatos do XP, seguindo a norma de avaliação de processos ISO 15504-2. Como conclusão da análise são expostas as lacunas encontradas nos processos e artefatos do XP.

Keywords: Engenharia de Requisitos, ISO 29148, métodos ágeis, eXtreme Programming, Mapeamento.

1 Introdução

As abordagens tradicionais de Engenharia de Requisitos consideram uma execução sequencial das atividades [4]. Em tais abordagens, a comunicação entre o processo de Engenharia de Requisitos e o processo de construção de software é baseada principalmente em documentos formais [4].

Os métodos ágeis têm crescido de popularidade nos últimos anos [19] e eles têm entre os valores definidos no Manifesto Ágil [1] que o software funcionando é mais importante do que uma documentação abrangente e que os indivíduos e iterações são mais importantes que processos e ferramentas. Esses valores podem causar a impressão de que a comunicação de informações importantes para a Engenharia de Requisitos pode não ocorrer corretamente nos métodos ágeis e que atividades fundamentais não são realizadas. Isso torna necessária a existência de estudos que auxiliam a aplicação da Engenharia de Requisitos nos métodos ágeis.

O objetivo deste trabalho é analisar como o eXtreme Programming (XP) atende aos processos e artefatos de Engenharia de Requisitos. Para isso analisou-se em qual parte do processo do XP são realizadas as atividades da Engenharia de Requisitos e onde estão as informações contidas nos documentos formalmente estipulados para essa disciplina. Para isso foi feito um mapeamento do XP aos processos e artefatos de Engenharia de Requisitos definidos pela norma ISO 29148 [11]. Essa norma foi escolhida pois ela é um padrão, compatível com outros padrões ISO para avaliação de processos, e porque descreve em detalhes tanto os processos quanto os artefatos (chamados de itens de informação) de Engenharia de Requisitos.

Existem alguns trabalhos que discutem a relação da Engenharia de Requisitos com métodos ágeis [5, 6, 7, 12, 13, 15, 16, 17, 20]. Porém nenhum deles analisa o atendimento de um método ágil às tarefas e aos artefatos esperados pelo processo de Engenharia de Requisitos. A maioria desses trabalhos é mais abrangente, falando sobre diversos métodos ágeis, o que difere deste trabalho, o qual mapeia o processo do XP aos processos e artefatos de Engenharia de Requisitos definidos por uma norma.

Este trabalho está estruturado da seguinte forma: a Seção 2 apresenta a ISO 29148, detalhando os processos e os artefatos definidos. Na Seção 3 é detalhada o método ágil analisado, o eXtreme Programming (XP). A Seção 4 apresenta os trabalhos relacionados com este estudo. A Seção 5 apresenta o mapeamento dos processos e artefatos da ISO 29148 para o eXtreme Programming. Por fim, na Seção 6 são apresentadas as considerações finais, expressando as conclusões e possíveis trabalhos futuros.

2 ISO 29148

A norma ISO 29148 [11] define os processos de Engenharia de Requisitos necessários para sistemas e software e provê guias para aplica-los. Além disso, a norma especifica os itens de informação (que chamaremos de artefatos) gerados pelos processos e o conteúdo de cada um deles.

Na Fig. 1 é apresentado um diagrama BPMN [14] com os processos e artefatos de Engenharia de Requisitos conforme definidos pela norma, evidenciando a relação entre eles. As atividades de Engenharia de Requisitos em um projeto se iniciam com a criação do *Conceito da Operação* (ConOps), apesar desse processo não ser formalmente descrito na norma. Este documento, que é opcional, apresenta "a forma pretendida pela liderança de operar a organização" [11, p.74], ou seja, descreve no nível organizacional como a organização imagina sua operação considerando os sistemas existentes e sistemas a serem construídos, incluindo o que será desenvolvido. Com isso o ConOps irá nortear todo o processo de desenvolvimento, pois ele contém as expectativas do cliente com o projeto.

Com base neste documento, o *Processo de definição dos requisitos de stakeholders* é executado. Este processo identifica os *stakeholders* e/ou classes de *stakeholders*, suas necessidades, expectativas e desejos. Essas informações são analisadas e transformadas em um conjunto de requisitos de *stakeholders* que expressam a intenção dos *stakeholders* com o sistema e como cada função será validada. Tais requisitos podem ser representados de diversas formas, como, por exemplo, um modelo de metas ou um modelo empresarial [18]. Como resultado do processo é gerado o *Documento de especificação de requisitos de* Stakeholder (StRS). O StRS contém a motivação da organização para alterar ou desenvolver o sistema. Ele define o processo, as políticas e as regras de como o sistema será utilizado no contexto da organização. Além disso, descreve como a organização busca novas oportunidades ou pretende mudar o negócio atual, e como utilizará o sistema como um meio de contribuir para esta mudança.

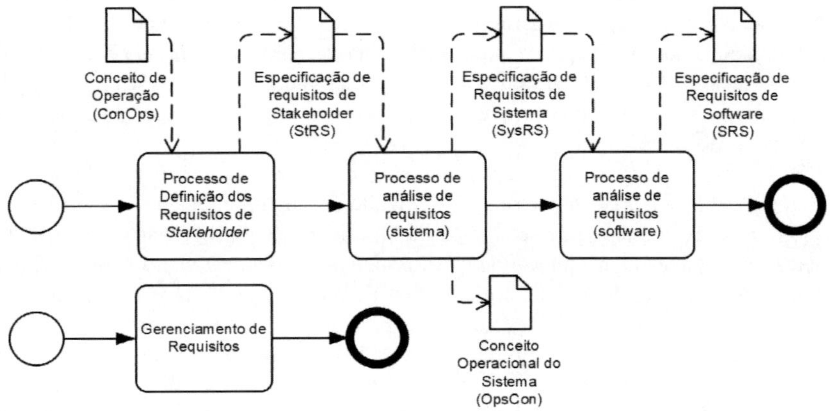

Fig. 1. - Sequência de processos e artefatos de requisitos (adaptado da ISO 29148 [11, p.18])

Neste momento são conhecidos os requisitos do projeto para atender aos *stakeholders*; esses requisitos serão analisados e transformados em requisitos de sistema pelo *Processo de análise de requisitos*. O processo irá converter os requisitos que estão em uma visão de negócio em requisitos em uma visão técnica - os requisitos de sistema -, determinando os serviços necessários que o produto deve atender. Este processo constrói uma representação do futuro sistema, resultando em requisitos mensuráveis que especificam, do ponto de vista do construtor do projeto, as características que o sistema deve possuir e o tamanho de cada característica com o fim de satisfazer as necessidades dos *stakeholders*. Como resultado, a análise de requisitos gera o *Documento de especificação de requisitos de sistema* (SyRS). Caso seja necessário, o processo deve ser executado para cada subsistema identificado, gerando um SyRS separado. Se o sistema possuir um ou mais softwares, este mesmo processo também é executado para cada deles (com os dados em nível de software) e gera um para o *Documento de especificação de requisitos de software* (SRS) para cada software. O SRS contém os mesmos elementos que o SyRS, porém são voltados apenas para a parte do software do sistema. Ou seja, são mais específicos, de menor abstração e abrange apenas informações referentes ao software e não do sistema como um todo.

O *Processo de análise de requisitos* é composto por duas atividades: *definir requisitos de sistema* e *analisar e manter os requisitos de sistema*. Na primeira atividade são definidas as fronteiras do sistema, as funções, as restrições, as medidas técnicas e de qualidade em uso (requisitos não funcionais) e a especificação dos requisitos. Na segunda atividade é analisada a integridade dos requisitos, atualizado o documento com a retroalimentação dos *stakeholders*, demonstrada a rastreabilidade dos requisitos e definido como manter esses requisitos junto com seu racional, decisões e fatos assumidos.

O *Conceito operacional do sistema* (OpsCon) é outro artefato gerado pelo processo de *Análise de requisitos*. É um documento que descreve o que sistema vai fazer pela perspectiva do usuário. Por ser um documento orientado ao usuário, ele não deve detalhar como fazer ou porque fazer, mas deve determinar as características que o sistema deve ter na visão do usuário. O OpsCon e o SyRS devem ser produzidos separadamente para que não haja nenhuma influência de elementos, incluindo requisitos do sistema no OpsCon. Para atingir um entendimento adequado, o OpsCon deve utilizar de ferramentas, vocabulários, ilustrações que são familiares os conhecimentos e experiências do usuário.

Em paralelo a todos esses processos é executado o *Gerenciamento de requisitos*, o qual que auxilia os demais processos. Os requisitos normalmente não são estáticos e o processo de gerenciamento de requisitos inclui atividades para gravar, manter os requisitos em evolução, manter o contexto associado a cada requisito e informações históricas do ocorrido durante os processos de Engenharia de Requisitos. Além disso, a gerência também estabelece procedimentos para definir, controlar e publicar a *baseline* de requisitos. A *baseline* de requisitos é o conjunto de requisitos que será atendido na nova versão do sistema. O *Gerenciamento de requisitos* é divido em duas tarefas: *a gestão de mudança*, que irá realizar um controle de cada mudança do requisito, e a *medição de requisitos*, que irá medir o processo de requisitos.

3 eXtreme Programming (XP)

O eXtreme Programming (XP) "é um conjunto coerente de valores, princípios e práticas para abordar problemas de desenvolvimento de software" [3, p.203]. Ele tem como base eliminar do desenvolvimento os comportamentos que afetam negativamente a produtividade do processo e dos indivíduos envolvidos [3]. O aumento da produtividade é alcançado por meio de ciclos de desenvolvimento curtos que resultam em *feedback* contínuo, flexibilidade para responder a mudanças, *design* que evolui durante o tempo de vida do software e através de boas práticas de desenvolvimento [2].

Doze práticas foram apresentadas na primeira versão do XP [2]: *jogo do planejamento, pequenos lançamentos, metáfora, design simples, testes, refatoração, programação em pares, autoria coletiva, integração contínua, semana de 40 horas, cliente no local* e *padrões de código*. Nenhuma delas foi criada pelo XP, mas segundo Beck [2], ao serem adotadas em conjunto, os pontos fortes de uma podem amenizar as deficiências da outra.

O processo de desenvolvimento do XP ocorre através de entregas sucessivas de incrementos de software, conhecida como *pequenos lançamentos*. Cada entrega deve ser tão pequena quanto possível, contendo as histórias mais importantes priorizadas pelo cliente no *jogo do planejamento*, para que assim, qualquer incremento possua valor para o negócio [2]. Cada ciclo de desenvolvimento é curto (em geral uma iteração pode durar até 4 semanas [2]) e conta com a execução de boas práticas de desenvolvimento no dia-a-dia. As histórias são implementadas por pares de desenvolvedores que escrevem os testes unitários e a implementação para cada teste criado. Os pares são trocados com frequência para que todos tenham oportunidade de trabalhar com trechos de código e funcionalidades diferentes e assim aumentem seu conhecimento sobre o sistema. Porém a integração de código deve ser feita tão breve quanto possível para que problemas sejam detectados e resolvidos o quanto antes e para que os desenvolvedores trabalhem sempre com código atualizado. Essa forma de trabalho permite que mudanças possam ser incorporadas mais facilmente e que o *design* possa evoluir durante as iterações de desenvolvimento, seja para acomodar novos requisitos, seja para simplificar as estruturas existentes através de *refatorações* que diminuem a complexidade das implementações.

No XP, os requisitos são representados por histórias. A história deve ser simples e deve permitir que o cliente utilize sua linguagem para comunicar o que precisa que o sistema tenha. Segundo Beck [2], uma história deve ter apenas um nome e um parágrafo curto contendo o seu propósito. Histórias também podem ser escritas por desenvolvedores se eles perceberem que precisam implementar algum benefício ao sistema ou ao processo que não é visível para o cliente. Uma outra responsabilidade do cliente é escrever os testes de aceitação. Os testes de aceitação devem conter o fluxo da funcionalidade e são usados para validar as histórias contidas no lançamento. As histórias são utilizadas no planejamento do lançamento para decidir o que a próxima versão a ser entregue deve conter em termos de funcionalidade. As atividades que são realizadas num planejamento de lançamento são a estimativa das histórias (desenvolvedores) e priorização (clientes).

Como as histórias contém apenas o básico sobre a funcionalidade, todas as demais informações devem ser extraídas através de comunicação verbal entre os *stakeholders*. Como o cliente está sempre disponível no local, seguindo a prática *cliente no local*, o XP defende que não é necessária a documentação abrangente de requisitos e nem processos formais de verificação e validação de documentos de requisitos. Além disso, o processo de Engenharia de Requisitos no XP acontece de forma iterativa.

4 Trabalhos relacionados

Foram analisados cinco estudos que também abordaram a relação da Engenharia de Requisitos nos processos ágeis. A seguir serão destacados os pontos centrais de cada estudo e as principais diferenças entre eles e este trabalho.

Medeiros et al. [13] realizam uma análise da qualidade do SRS (*Documento de especificação de requisitos de software*) no desenvolvimento ágil de software (ASD). O objetivo da pesquisa é auxiliar a escrever SRS mais eficazes em projetos ágeis, o que foi feito ao buscar respostas para a seguinte pergunta: "Como é afetada a qualidade da especificação de requisitos de software no desenvolvimento ágil de software?". A principal diferença entre a pesquisa de Medeiros et al. [13] e este trabalho é o foco da análise. Apesar de também realizar uma análise entre a norma ISO 29148 e métodos ágeis, Medeiros et al. analisam como atingir a qualidade necessária do SRS em um projeto de ASD. Os autores utilizam apenas um dos cinco artefatos citados pela norma e não analisam o processo de Engenharia de Requisitos em si. Além disso, não é apresentado o método usado para realizar essa análise.

No estudo de Heikkilä et al. [8] é feita uma revisão da literatura considerando a Engenharia de Requisitos no desenvolvimento ágil de software. A partir da análise de 28 artigos os autores concluíram que a definição de requisitos no ASD é vaga. Além da definição também foram pesquisados os benefícios e malefícios da Engenharia de Requisitos no ASD, apresentando propostas de soluções para os problemas identificados. Diferente deste trabalho, Heikkilä, et al. [8] busca as falhas de acordo com os estudos analisados, e não realiza uma comparação de processos. Com isso os resultados do estudo deles são mais abstratos e abrangentes.

Gebhart et al. [6] apresenta a análise de um projeto de construção de um sistema de decisões, o qual foi desenvolvido de forma ágil. Um dos fatores de sucesso do projeto, segundo os autores, foi o processo de Engenharia de Requisitos, o qual eles consideram as características de qualidade dos requisitos descritos na ISO 29148[11]. Diferente de Gebhart et al. [6], este trabalho é um mapeamento das práticas do XP ao processo da norma, enquanto Gebhart et al. [6] utiliza as características de qualidade da norma em um projeto de desenvolvimento de forma ágil.

Em um outro trabalho, Lucia e Qusef [12] abordam como os requisitos podem ser capturados e especificados no contexto ágil, identificando como as técnicas e processos de Engenharia de Requisitos podem ser combinados com as práticas ágeis e encontrar soluções para as dificuldades. Além disso, também é discutido como resolver o problema de rastreabilidade entre os artefatos no desenvolvimento de software ágil. Na comparação, os autores consideram apenas as atividades, não falando de tarefas e artefatos como se faz neste trabalho. Além disso, Lucia e Qusef citam diversos métodos ágeis para realizar a comparação e não apenas um.

Os pesquisadores Hess; Diebold; Seyff [20] buscam quatro objetivos em seu estudo, um deles é próximo ao objetivo do nosso estudo, buscando qual artefato utilizado em métodos ágeis contém os dados determinados em uma especificação de requisitos tradicional orientadas a tarefas, criada pelos autores, chamada TORE. Além disso eles também fazem entrevistas investigas as necessidades de times ágeis e suas especificações, propõem uma solução e analisam os resultados da solução. Com isso os estudos são diferentes pois nosso estudo utiliza o padrão de uma norma, ISO 29148 [11], para relacionar com os métodos ágeis.

Este estudo difere de todos pois é um mapeamento dos processos e artefatos da norma ISO 29148 [11] para os processos e artefatos do eXtreme Programming. Contudo é possível perceber que Medeiros et al. [13]; Lucia e Qusef [12] e este estudo contém resultados das análises similares, o que confirma a necessidade de criar soluções alternativas para os problemas encontrados e solidifica a conclusão dos estudos.

5 Avaliação do atendimento dos processos e artefatos da ISO 29148 pelo XP

O eXtreme Programming (XP) trata do processo de desenvolvimento como um todo, cobrindo desde atividades de requisitos a até atividades de teste e de gestão. Porém, a forma como essas atividades são executadas é bastante diferente da definida por abordagens tradicionais. Tratando especificamente da Engenharia de Requisitos, as atividades são abordadas por práticas como *cliente no local*, *jogo do planejamento* e *metáfora*; o único artefato criado especificamente para a Engenharia de Requisitos é a história.

Para analisar como as práticas de Engenharia de Requisitos são executadas pelo XP, mapeou-se os processos e artefatos definidos pela norma ISO 29148 [11] às práticas e artefatos do XP. Esse mapeamento foi analisado e revisado pelos três autores. Considerou-se como base as doze práticas do XP apresentadas pela primeira edição do livro de Beck [2]. Os critérios de avaliação foram definidos baseados na norma ISO 15504-2 [10], a qual trata da avaliação de processos:

- N (não atende): não há nenhuma evidência do processo ou do artefato da norma ISO 29148 no XP.
- P (parcialmente atendido): Há pouca evidência do atendimento. Para as atividades, há pouca descrição do que será feito no XP a respeito desta atividade da norma; para o artefato, a informação descrita pode ser obtida, mas não é de conhecimento de todos da equipe (e somente será obtida caso alguém da equipe pergunte essa informação).
- L (atendido em grande parte): há uma evidência clara do atendimento. Para as atividades, é possível identificar exatamente o que tem que ser feito, ainda que falte uma parte da atividade. Para os artefatos, a informação contida neles é de conhecimento de todos da equipe, mas isso não significa que está necessariamente documentada.
- F (Atendimento completo): Há evidência de que tudo que a norma define é coberto pelo XP; não existem pontos relevantes que o XP não atenda. Para os artefatos deve inclusive estar documentado.

Portanto, o "N" será usado para representar que a atividade ou o conteúdo do artefato é possivelmente tratado, mas é pouco provável que o seja; o "P" representa que *pode* ser tratado, mas não está explícito; o "L" representa que pode ser feito e está explícito; o "F" indica que *deve* ser feito e está explícito.

Para realizar a análise se examinou qual prática do XP cobre cada tarefa do processo definido pela norma. Na análise do atendimento aos artefatos determinados pela norma, foi considerado a disponibilidade da informação, não somente a documentação dela, seguindo a filosofia dos métodos ágeis que estabelece que se a informação não precisa estar necessariamente escrita: o importante é ser de conhecimento de todos. Porém conforme descrito na ISO 15504, mesmo com os critérios de julgamento definidos, a avaliação é subjetiva e baseia-se essencialmente no julgamento do avaliador de acordo com o entendimento das provas obtidas.

Essa análise não considerou o processo de Engenharia de Requisitos para requisitos de sistema. A norma define o mesmo processo para requisitos de software e para requisitos de sistema. Como o XP aborda apenas sistemas intensivos de software [9], o processo será analisado apenas sob o ponto de vista de requisitos de software. Pelo mesmo motivo o SyRS não será analisado, apesar de a norma ressaltar a importância da existência de ambos o SyRS e SRS.

A seguir serão apresentadas as análises de atendimento do XP, primeiro para os processos e posteriormente para os artefatos. Para cada processo ou artefato analisado será apresentada uma tabela que apresenta as tarefas (para os processos) e capítulos (para artefatos) da norma, quais práticas correspondem para o XP e o nível de atendimento. Além da tabela também são apresentados os pontos levados em consideração para qualificar o atendimento.

5.1 Processos

Foram analisados os processos de *definição dos requisitos de stakeholders* (Tabela 1), de *análise de requisitos* (Tabela 2) e de *gerenciamento de requisitos* (Tabela 3).

Tabela 1. – Avaliação do atendimento do processo de definição dos requisitos de *stakeholders* pelo XP

Atividades	Tarefas	XP	Nível
Elicitar requisitos de *stakeholder*	Identificar as classes de *stakeholders* e os *stakeholders*	Cliente no local	P
	Elicitar requisitos dos *stakeholders*	Cliente no local	L
Definir requisitos de *stakeholder*	Definir as restrições da solução sistêmica	Cliente no local	F
	Definir cenários de uso	-	N
	Identificar as interações entre usuários e o sistema	-	N
	Especificar qualidades críticas (saúde, segurança, meio ambiente)	Cliente no local	F
Analisar e manter os requisitos de *stakeholder*	Analisar o conjunto completo de requisitos elicitados	Jogo do Planejamento	F
	Resolver problemas nos requisitos	Jogo do Planejamento	F
	Realimentar os artefatos de requisitos com as alterações realizadas	Jogo do Planejamento	F
	Estabelecer com os *stakeholders* que seus requisitos são expressos corretamente	Cliente no local	F
	Gravar os requisitos adequadamente para o gerenciamento de requisitos	-	N
	Manter os requisitos rastreáveis até as necessidades	Cliente no local	P

A atividade *Elicitar requisitos de stakeholder* do processo de definição de requisitos de *stakeholders* é atendida pela prática de *cliente no local*. Apesar de a tarefa *Identificar as classes de stakeholders e os stakeholders* não estar prevista no XP, os *stakeholders* são identificados no decorrer do processo, porém nenhuma documentação é gerada a partir disso. Além disso, como não é conduzida de forma sistemática pode ser que alguns *stakeholders* não sejam identificados, por isso essa tarefa é atendida parcialmente pelo XP.

Na atividade de *Definir requisitos de stakeholder*, as tarefas *Definir as restrições da solução sistêmica* e *Especificar qualidades críticas (saúde, segurança, meio ambiente)* são atendidas completamente por práticas do XP. As demais tarefas são mais burocráticas sendo pouco provável seu atendimento pelas práticas do XP.

Em *Analisar e manter os requisitos de stakeholder*, as tarefas envolvidas implicam em analisar conjunto de requisitos, resolver conflitos e garantir que os requisitos foram expressos corretamente. No XP, isso pode ser atendido através das práticas de *cliente no local* e *jogo do planejamento*, nas quais se pode avaliar se os requisitos foram expressos corretamente a partir das dúvidas tiradas com o cliente e dos testes de aceitação escritos por ele.

No processo de análise de requisitos, na atividade *Definir requisitos de sistema*, apenas a tarefa *Definir restrições introduzidas por requisitos dos* stakeholders é atendida completamente pelo XP porque o conjunto de requisitos de *stakeholder* corresponde às histórias escritas, mas os requisitos de sistema não. Eles não são definidos em artefatos físicos, mas podem estar presentes na comunicação verbal.

Table 2. – Avaliação do atendimento do processo de análise de requisitos pelo XP

Atividades	Tarefas	XP	Nível
Definir requisitos de sistema	Definir a fronteira funcional do sistema	-	N
	Definir funções necessárias para o sistema funcionar	-	N
	Definir restrições introduzidas por requisitos dos *stakeholders*	Jogo do Planejamento	F
	Definir as medidas técnicas e medidas de qualidade	-	N
	Especificar requisitos e funções de riscos ou qualidades críticas	-	N
Analisar e manter os requisitos de sistema	Análise da integridade dos requisitos do sistema	Jogo do Planejamento	P
	Realimentar os requisitos de sistemas analisados	Jogo do Planejamento	P
	Demonstrar rastreabilidade entre os requisitos	-	N
	Manter o conjunto de requisitos e as razões associadas	-	N

No processo de gerenciamento de requisitos, a atividade *Gestão de Mudança* não é atendida por nenhuma prática do XP, pois não há evidências ou orientações que indiquem que no XP os requisitos podem ser armazenados para representar configurações que facilitam a identificação de mudanças específicas e suas motivações associadas. A atividade de *Medição dos requisitos* é atendida pelo jogo do planejamento, na qual a tarefa *Definir o plano de medição* é atendida apenas parcialmente porque a velocidade do projeto geralmente é a única medida utilizada para avaliar o processo no XP. Por sua vez, a tarefa *Executar a medição* é completamente atendida porque a única métrica definida, a velocidade do projeto, é medida ao final.

Table 3. – Avaliação do atendimento do processo de gerenciamento de requisitos pelo XP

Atividades	Tarefas	XP	Nível
Gestão de Mudança	Gerenciamento da configuração		N
	Gerenciamento da informação	-	N
Medição dos requisitos	Definir o plano de medição	Jogo do Planejamento	P
	Executar a medição	Jogo do Planejamento	F

5.2 Artefatos

Nos artefatos da norma existem elementos pré e pós-textuais que têm por objetivo facilitar a apresentação, entrega, identificar e fazer síntese do documento, dar acesso às fontes para produção do documento ou complementar o documento com elementos que apareceram durante a produção do documento. Esses elementos não são abordados pelos artefatos do XP, os quais contêm apenas os dados necessários para o desenvolvimento. Como esses elementos não apresentam conteúdos essenciais para o desenvolvimento do software não foram levados em consideração para avaliação do atendimento do documento, e serão classificados como "Pré ou pós-textual".

A Tabela 4 apresenta um resumo do mapeamento apresentando os artefatos determinados pela norma com seus respectivos capítulos e como o XP os contempla.

Dos artefatos, o *Conceito da Operação* (ConOps) não é atendido pelo XP. O XP trata do software partindo do princípio que o cliente já tem claramente definido a necessidade de um software. Como o ConOps é um documento que permite entender as intenções do cliente, ele é criado antes de iniciar o processo de desenvolvimento do software e, portanto, não é abordado.

O *Documento de especificação de requisitos de* Stakeholder (StRS) tem nove dos seus subcapítulos parcialmente atendidos pelo *cliente no local*; outros cinco foram atendidos pelas *histórias de usuários*. Os *testes* e *jogo planejamento* atenderam um subcapítulo cada e apenas dois subcapítulos não foram atendidos. O capítulo *Meta e objetivo* não foi atendido pois no XP os artefatos estão direcionados (em sua maioria) para construção do software e não para entendimento dos objetivos do cliente; o capítulo *Modos operacionais de negócios* também não é atendido pois nele deve conter descrição de como a operação deve reagir ao passar por situações inesperada como acidente ou desastre natural e o XP não prevê essa descrição.

No *Documento de especificação de requisitos de software* (SRS), o capítulo de *Requisitos específicos* – que descreve os requisitos de software – é tratado pelas *histórias de usuários*; apenas dois subcapítulos não são atendidos: *Interfaces externas* e *Informações de suporte*. No primeiro caso, no XP não existe artefato que descreva as interfaces pois elas serão construídas de forma dinâmica durante a codificação; no segundo, o XP não descrimina o detalhamento de informações complementares ao software tais como instruções de transporte e descrição dos problemas resolvidos. O capítulo de *Verificação* é atendido pelos *testes* do XP e o *Apêndice* pelas *Tarefas*.

O *Conceito operacional do sistema* (OpsCon) é o artefato com maior quantidade de subcapítulos atendidos pelo XP, sendo oito parcialmente atendidos com o *cliente no local*, quatro atendidos com as *histórias de usuários*. O *jogo de planejamento* atende a três subcapítulos, *testes* atende a dois subcapítulos, a *metáfora* atende a um subcapítulo e quatro subcapítulos não são atendidos *Justificativa para mudanças*; *Background, objetivos e escopo*; *Impactos organizacionais*; *Desvantagens e limitações*; *Alternativas consideradas*, esses subcapítulos não são atendidos pelo XP pois tratam de elementos adjacentes a construção do software e o XP tem foco apenas em sua construção.

Tabela 4. – Avaliação do atendimento dos artefatos pelo XP

Documento	Capítulo	Subcapítulos	Artefatos/Práticas	Nível
Conceito da Operação (ConOps)	1 Objetivo	-	Pré ou pós-textual	
	2 Escopo	-	Pré ou pós-textual	
	3 Plano estratégico	-	-	N
	4 Eficácia	-	-	N
	5 Operação global	5.1, 5.2, 5.3	-	N
	6 Governança	6.1, 6.2, 6.3, 6.4, 6.5, 6.6, 6.7	-	N
Documento de especificação de requisitos de Stakeholder (StRS)	1. Introdução	1.1, 1.2, 1.3, 1.5	Cliente no local	P
		1.4	Pré ou pós-textual	
	2. Referências	-	Pré ou pós-textual	
	3. Requisitos de gerenciamento do negócio	3.1	História de usuário	F
		3.3, 3.4	Cliente no local	P
		3.2	-	N
	4. Requisitos operacionais do negócioy	4.1, 4.2, 4.6	Cliente no local	P
		4.3, 4.5	História de usuário	F
		4.4	-	N
	5. Requisitos de usuários	-	História de usuário	F
	6. Conceito de sistema proposto	6.1	História de usuário	F
		6.2	Testes	F
	7 Limitações do Projeto	-	Jogo do Planejamento	P
	8. Apêndice	8.1	Pré ou pós-textual	
Documento de especificação de requisitos de software (SRS)	1. Introdução	1.1, 1.2, 1.3, 1.4	Pré ou pós-textual	
	2. Referencias	-	Pré ou pós-textual	
	3. Requisitos específicos	3.2, 3.3, 3.4, 3.5, 3.6, 3.7, 3.8	Histórias	P
		3.1, 3.9	-	N
	4. Verificação	-	Testes	L
	5. Apêndice	5.1	Tarefas	P
		5.2	Pré ou pós-textual	
Conceito operacional do sistema (OpsCon)	1 Escopo	1.1, 1.2, 1.3	Pré ou pós-textual	
	2 Documentos Referenciados	-	Pré ou pós-textual	
	3 Sistema/ situação atual	3.1, 3.2, 3.3, 3.4, 3.5, 3.6	Cliente no local	P
	4 Justificativa e natureza das mudanças	4.2, 4.5	História de usuário	P
		4.3	Jogo do Planejamento	F
		4.4	*Backlog*	L
		4.1	-	N
	5 Conceitos para o sistema proposto	5.2	História de usuário	P
		5.3	Metáfora	L
		5.4	Testes	L
		5.5, 5.6	Cliente no local	P
		5.1	-	N
	6 Cenários operacionais	-	História de usuário	L
	7 Resumo dos impactos	7.1	Testes	P
		7.3	Jogo do Planejamento	P
		7.2	-	N
	8 Análise do sistema proposto	8.1, 8.2, 8.3	-	N
	9 Apêndices	-	Pré ou pós-textual	
	10 Glossário	-	Pré ou pós-textual	

5.3 Conclusão da análise

A maioria dos processos definidos pela norma são de alguma forma executados pelo XP (apenas 11 tarefas de 25 não são atendidas por nenhuma prática do XP). Na sua maioria, as tarefas são atendidas por completo (8 tarefas atendidas completamente de um total de 25). O gráfico apresentado na Fig. 2 contém um resumo dos processos, suas atividades e do nível de atendimento delas pelo XP. Há uma predominância do "Completamente atendido" (F), embora o número de tarefas "Não atendidas" (N) também seja relevante, principalmente no processo de *Análise de requisitos de sistema*. Poucas são "Parcialmente atendidas" (P), e apenas uma é "Atendida em grande parte" (L).

Fig. 2. Gráfico do resumo da avaliação dos processos. Fonte: o autor.

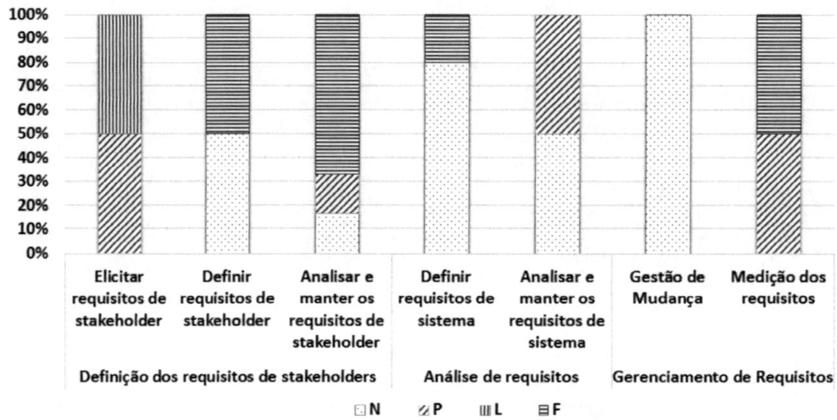

Fig. 3. Gráfico do resumo da avaliação dos artefatos.

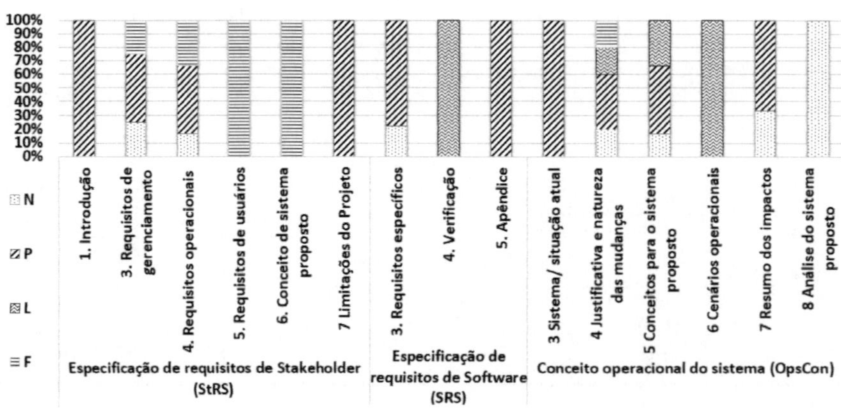

Dos artefatos propostos pela norma, o documento ConOps não é atendido pelo XP. O StRS é atendido completamente na maioria de seus subcapítulos; os documentos SRS e OpsCon têm a maioria dos subcapítulos atendidos parcialmente. Em todos os documentos, os subcapítulos que são atendidos parcialmente são, em sua maioria, a representação de como é a operação atual da empresa. Essa informação é passada pelo representante do cliente, que participa da equipe, porém a informação obtida não é formalmente documentada. A Fig. 3 apresenta um gráfico com o resumo da avaliação dos artefatos, sem levar em consideração o ConOps e os elementos textuais. No gráfico apesar de haver uma distribuição entre os níveis de atendimento do capítulo pelo XP, a maior parte está em P representando o "Parcialmente atendido".

6 Conclusão

Este trabalho analisou como o eXtreme Programming (XP) atende o processo de Engenharia de Requisitos. Para isso se usou como referência os processos e artefatos da norma ISO 29148 [11], usando como base os critérios definidos pela ISO 15504-2 [10]. A análise foi realizada no menor elemento do processo e do artefato, ou seja, nas tarefas e nos capítulos. As práticas do XP foram mapeadas a esses elementos, determinando o nível de atendimento deles.

Apesar de existirem outros estudos que discutem a relação entre a Engenharia de Requisitos e os métodos ágeis, eles possuem focos diferentes. Ainda assim, as conclusões deles são próximas, o que consolida a pesquisa aqui realizada.

Como resultado, foi possível concluir que o XP suporta os processos e artefatos da Engenharia de Requisitos definidos pela norma. As tarefas dos processos são quase todas atendidas e em grande parte por completo, com exceção das atividades relacionadas aos requisitos de sistema, na qual a maioria das tarefas não são atendidas pelas práticas do XP. Dos artefatos propostos pela norma, o documento ConOps não é atendido pelo XP. Os outros artefatos são quase todos atendidos, porém a maioria dos capítulos é atendido parcialmente. Em trabalhos futuros pode-se discutir como alterar o processo do XP para melhor atender a norma – sempre com a preocupação de manter os princípios e valores do XP e de métodos ágeis.

Agradecimento

Agradecimento a Prosimulador, que acredita e incentiva seus funcionários a evoluírem e ganharem mais conhecimento, apoiando pesquisas como esta.

Referências

1. Agile manifesto Homepage; Manifesto for Agile Software Development, http://www.agilemanifesto.org/, last accessed: 2017/02/15.
2. Beck, K.: Extreme Programming Explained: Embrace Change. EUA. Addison-Wesley Pro-fessional (1999).

3. Beck, K.; Andres, C. Extreme Programming Explained: Embrace Change (2nd Edition). 2. ed. Boston: Addison-Wesley Professional, 2004.
4. Bray, I.: An introduction to requirements engineering. Harlow, United Kingdom. Addison-Wesley (2002).
5. Eberlein, A., Leite, J.: Agile Requirements Definition: A View from Requirements Engineering. In: International Workshop on Time-Constrained Requirements Engineering on Proceedings, pp 4-8. Germany (2002).
6. Gebhart, M. et al. Quality-Oriented Requirements Engineering for Agile Development of RESTful Participation Service. In: ICSEA: The Ninth International Conference on Software Engineering Advances on Proceedings, pp. 69-74. France (2014).
7. Goetz, R. How Agile Processes Can Help in Time-Constrained Requirements Engineering. In: International Workshop on Time-Constrained Requirements Engineering on Proceedings. Rio de Janeiro (2002).
8. Heikkilä, V. et al. A Mapping Study on Requirements Engineering in Agile Software Development. In 41st Euromicro Conference on Software Engineering and Advanced Applica-tions (SEAA) on Proceedings, pp. 199-207. IEEE, Portugal (2015).
9. IEEE. IEEE Std 1471: recommended practice for architectural description of software-intensice systems. USA (2000).
10. ISO/IEC. ISO/IEC 15504-2: Software engineering — Process assessment. Switzerland (2003).
11. ISO/IEC/IEEE. ISO/IEC/IEEE 29148: Systems and software engineering — Life cycle pro-cesses — Requirements engineering. Switzerland (2011).
12. Lucia, A.; Qusef, A. Requirements engineering in agile software development. Journal of Emerging Technologies in Web Intelligence 3 (2), 212-220 (2010).
13. Medeiros et al. Towards a model about quality of software requirements specification in ag-ile projects. In 10th International Conference on the Quality of Information and Communica-tions Technology (QUATIC) on Proceedings, pp. 236 – 241. IEEE, Portugal (2016).
14. OMG, Business Process Model And Notation (BPMN) Version 2.0 http://www.omg.org/spec/BPMN/2.0/, last accessed 2017/07/20.
15. Paetsh, F.; Eberlein, A.; Maurer F. Requirements engineering and agile software development. In: WET ICE 2003 Twelfth IEEE International Workshops on Enabling Technologies: Infrastructure for Collaborative Enterprises on Proceedings, pp.309-313. IEEE, Austria (2003).
16. Ramesh, B.; Cao, L.; Baskerville, R. Agile requirements engineering practices and challeng-es: an empirical study. Information Systems Journal 5 (20), 449-480 (2010)
17. Sillitti, A.; Succi, G. Requirements Engineering for Agile methods. In: Aurum, A.; Wohlin, C. (eds). Engineering and Managing Software Requirements, pp. 309-326. Springer, Ger-many (2005).
18. Siqueira, F. L.; Muniz Silva, P. S. Analyzing the Use of an Enterprise Model as a Stakeholder Requirements Model: An Experiment. In: Workshop on Requirements Engineering, 2013, Montevideu, Uruguay. Anais do Workshop on Requirements Engineering, 2013.
19. VersionOne 10th Annual State of Agile Survey, http://info.versionone.com/state-of-agile-development-survey-ninth.html, last accessed 2017/02/07
20. Hess, A.; Diebold, P.; Seyff, N. Towards Requirements Communication and Documentation Guidelines for Agile Teams In IEEE 25th International Requirements Engineering Conference Workshops (REW) on Proceedings, pp.415-418. IEEE, Portugal (2017).

Hacía un marco de definición de requisitos para Big Data

Julio Moreno[1], Manuel A. Serrano[2], Eduardo Fernández-Medina[1]

[1] Grupo de investigación de Seguridad y Auditoría (GSyA), Universidad de Castilla-La Mancha, Ciudad Real, España
[2] Grupo de investigación Alarcos, Universidad de Castilla-la Mancha, Ciudad Real, España

{Julio.Moreno, Manuel.Serrano, Eduardo.FdezMedina}@uclm.es

Abstract. Big Data permite la toma de mejores decisiones por parte de las organizaciones y cada vez tiene una mayor importancia en el día a día de las compañías. Pero diseñar sistemas Big Data de forma que no haya conflicto con los objetivos de negocio y las diferentes regulaciones que lo afectan es un tema complejo. Como forma de abordar este problema, y debido a la falta de propuestas en este tema, proponemos un modelo de requisitos para Big Data, diferenciando el caso de requisitos de seguridad, por responder éstos a la existencia de amenazas y vulnerabilidades, además de ser obligatorio (o muy recomendado) cumplir con ciertas legislaciones o regulaciones en materia de seguridad.

Keywords: Modelado de requisitos, Big Data, Seguridad

1 Introducción

Organizaciones de cualquier ámbito son cada vez más conscientes de la importancia de Big Data [1]. Para todas, los datos son fundamentales para llevar a cabo sus actividades cotidianas, así como, ayudar a la gerencia en la toma de decisiones con la información extraída de dichos datos [2]. Big Data implica un cambio respecto a los sistemas tradicionales, fundamentalmente en tres aspectos: la cantidad de datos (volumen), el ratio de generación y transmisión de los datos (velocidad) y la heterogeneidad de los tipos de datos estructurados o no estructurados que puede manejar (variedad) [3]. Estas propiedades son conocidas como las tres Vs de Big Data [4]. Diversos autores han ido añadiendo nuevas Vs a este grupo inicial, como el valor o veracidad de los datos [5]. Con cada nueva tecnología surgen nuevos problemas, Big Data no es una excepción. Estos problemas no solo están relacionados con las Vs típicas de Big Data sino que también se encuentran en el ámbito de la privacidad y seguridad de los datos. Big Data no solo incrementa la escala de los problemas de privacidad y seguridad sino que también añade nuevos que deben ser gestionados mediante diferentes técnicas [6].

Aun con estas diferencias, un entorno Big Data no deja de ser un proyecto de Tecnologías de la Información (TI), cuyo desarrollo debe ser guiado por una serie de modelos o metodologías. Según una encuesta realizada a expertos del campo de las TI [7], uno de los principales retos que se encuentran a la hora de operar un entorno Big Data es su poca alineación con los objetivos de negocio de la compañía. Una forma de solucionar este problema es el uso de un marco de definición de requisitos cuyo primer paso sea tener como entrada el contexto en el que se va a encontrar el sistema Big Data, incluyendo los objetivos de negocio de la empresa y las diferentes regulaciones que lo afectan. Sin embargo, el conjunto de características y necesidades inherentes de un proyecto de creación de un entorno Big Data hace que sea complicado abarcar todos los aspectos posibles a considerar mediante el uso de metodologías tradicionales de definición de requisitos [8].

En la literatura, no existen muchos marcos o metodologías que traten el tema de la definición de requisitos en contextos Big Data. Diferentes autores proponen modelar requisitos utilizando un enfoque basado en *goals* del sistema. En [9], los autores exponen cómo usan los métodos GORE (Goal-Oriented Requirement Engineering), i* y KAOS (Knowledge Acquisition in autOmated Specification) para guiar la definición de requisitos. Si bien, toman en cuenta las características típicas de Big Data, no contemplan el contexto en el que se encuentra el entorno. Por otro lado la propuesta [10], también se encuentra basada en el método KAOS, sin embargo en este caso, los autores sí añaden una capa extra a su método que considera los objetivos de negocio de la compañía. El problema de esta propuesta es que se encuentra muy enfocada a la tecnología Apache Spark, por lo tanto, no es una solución genérica que pueda ser aplicada en cualquier proyecto Big Data. En cambio, en [11] los autores basan la definición de requisitos en los escenarios típicos de un entorno Big Data, es un enfoque interesante pero que se encuentra en un estado incompleto, ya que, solo contempla los requisitos relacionados con las fases de recogida y captura de datos. Finalmente en [12] se centran en cómo especificar requisitos de calidad en Big Data, para ello, se basan es las Vs básicas de Big Data en relación con características de calidad. Se trata de una propuesta interesante, pero que todavía se encuentra en una fase inmadura.

En nuestro caso, estamos trabajando en la creación de un marco de definición de requisitos que contemple por un lado las características básicas del Big Data (las diferentes Vs) y por otro el contexto en el que se va a encontrar el sistema (incluyendo los objetivos de negocio, sus políticas y las regulaciones legales que le pueden afectar). Para ello, nos basamos en los marcos básicos de ingeniería de requisitos, adaptándolos al nuevo escenario de esta tecnología. Por ello, este artículo se organiza en varias secciones: un apartado sobre el contexto que consideramos para nuestra propuesta, en el cual, se explica la arquitectura para Big Data que propone el National Institute of Standards and Technologies (NIST). A continuación, se define nuestra propuesta de marco para la definición en Big Data basada en sus dimensiones. Finalmente, se incluye una sección de conclusiones y trabajo futuro.

2 Contexto

En los últimos años, el NIST ha definido una arquitectura de referencia para Big Data que cuenta con el consenso general de la industria y la comunidad científica [13]. La última versión del manuscrito fue lanzada en agosto de 2017. La arquitectura aúna diferentes ideas y características sobre cómo crear un ecosistema Big Data, las cuales, han sido extraídas de diferentes propuestas realizadas por organizaciones del sector como Oracle o IBM. Como resultado, se ha obtenido la arquitectura que se muestra en la Figura 1. La arquitectura se divide en cinco componentes que interaccionan entre sí y tienen diferentes objetivos.

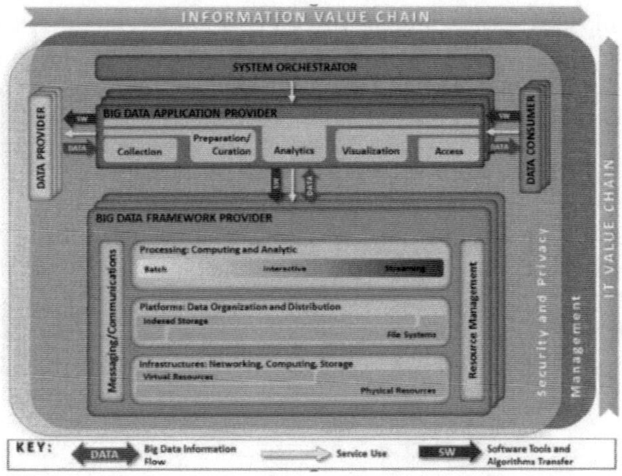

Figura 1. Arquitectura de referencia propuesta por el NIST

- **System Orchestrator (SO):** en relación con el tema de los requisitos, es el componente más importante, puesto que es el encargado de definir e integrar las actividades requeridas en el resto del ecosistema Big Data. Su principal objetivo es la configuración y gestión del resto de componentes.
- **Data Provider (DP):** este componente se encarga de alimentar al Big Data con nuevos datos. Para conseguirlo, dispone de una serie de interfaces que actúan como puerta entre el mundo exterior y el sistema Big Data.
- **Big Data Application Provider (BDAP):** el BDAP ejecuta una serie de servicios específicos siguiendo el ciclo de vida de los datos para cumplir con los requisitos establecidos en el SO. Su propósito principal es encapsular la lógica del negocio y las funcionalidades para ser ejecutados por la arquitectura.
- **Big Data Framework Provider (BDFP):** se puede considerar como la implementación de la lógica del sistema Big Data. Soporta las actividades definidas en el BDAP. En general, las implementaciones de Big Data son híbridos que combinan múltiples tecnologías.
- **Data Consumer (DC):** es similar al DP. Normalmente, el actor que interactúa con el componente es un usuario final y otro sistema. Similarmente al DP, está

compuesta por un conjunto de interfaces entre el usuario final y la información.

Tomando como base esta arquitectura de referencia, hemos realizado una ampliación sobre la misma, específicamente sobre el SO, para hacer un mayor hincapié en los requisitos. En la siguiente sección se define una primera aproximación a nuestra propuesta de marco de definición de requisitos para Big Data.

3 Marco de definición de requisitos para Big Data

Nuestra propuesta de marco de definición de requisitos para Big Data toma como primera consideración el marco típico de definición de requisitos definido en [14]. Este marco tiene tres componentes principales: el contexto del sistema, las actividades principales (documentación, elicitación y negociación) y los artefactos de requisito (*goals*, escenarios y requisitos orientados a la solución). Esta estructura general, la adaptaremos para que considere las características de Big Data.

Tal y como se comentó en la sección anterior, se ha realizado un ajuste del SO propuesto por NIST para que considere los requisitos como la parte central sobre la que gira la construcción del sistema Big Data. En la Figura 2 se muestra el diagrama de SO que proponemos [15]. Debido a las características de este componente, las actividades de seguridad se centran en los requisitos y cómo implementarlos y monitorizarlos. Dichos requisitos deben cumplir los *goals* del Big Data y estar alineados con los objetivos de negocio y las políticas de la compañía.

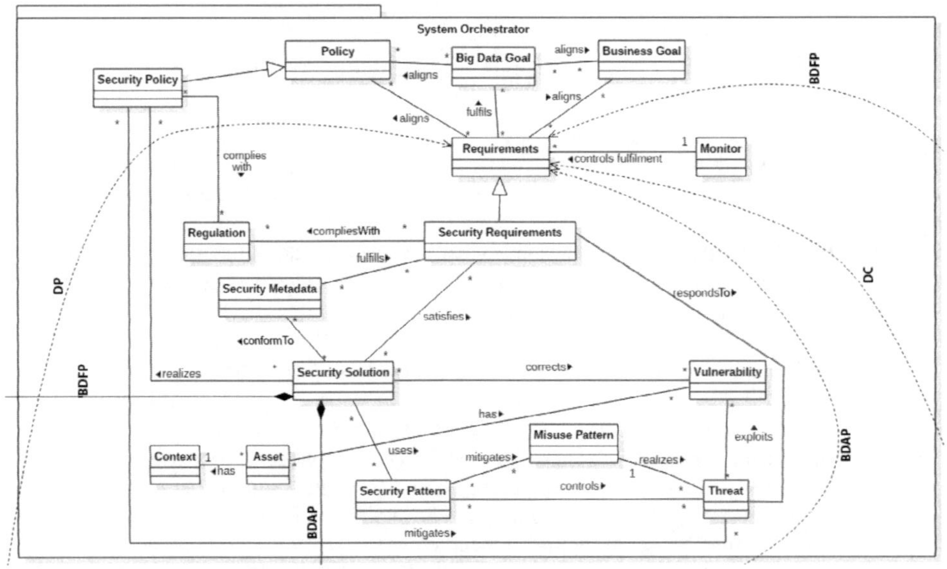

Figura 2. Diagrama de nuestra propuesta para el SO

Por otro lado, es necesario tener en cuenta el entorno ágil actual en el que se encuentran una gran cantidad de compañías relacionadas con Big Data. Para ello, definimos una iteración inicial en el que se define un escenario básico de alto nivel a partir del *goal* principal que se busca con el Big Data. Una vez creada dicha iteración inicial se procede a realizar una serie de iteraciones que siguen el mismo esquema. Del *goal* inicial se pasa a tener una serie de *subgoals* más específicos, los cuales, se pueden representar mediante un diagrama de grafos AND-OR de *goals* en el que se especifiquen las relaciones entre los mismos. Además, para la definición de requisitos en Big Data es necesario tomar en cuenta el contexto organizacional en el que se encuentre, incluyendo los objetivos de negocio y sus políticas. Por otro lado, también es importante tener en consideración las diferentes regulaciones legales que puede afectar a cómo son tratados los datos y la información que se genera. Al final de cada iteración se obtiene un conjunto de artefactos de requisitos que actuarán como entrada en la siguiente iteración. Cuando se considere que los requisitos se encuentran lo suficientemente detallados, se dará por finalizado el proceso. En la Figura 3 se muestra el esquema general nuestra propuesta.

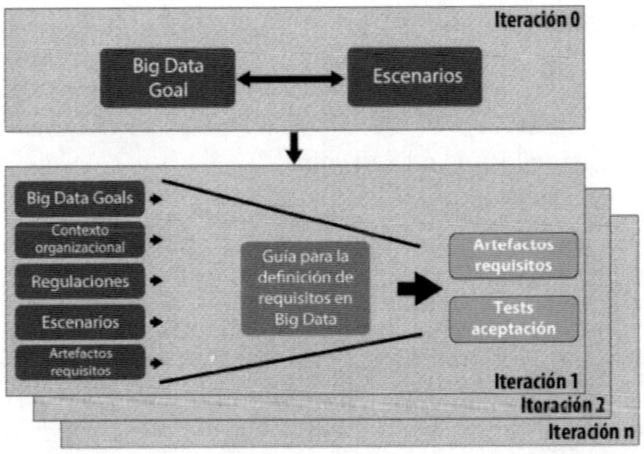

Figura 3. Esquema general de nuestra arquitectura

La guía de definición de requisitos se refiere a un artefacto que ayuda en el descubrimiento y clasificación de requisitos. Para ello, se tienen en cuenta las Vs básicas de Big Data: volumen, velocidad, variedad, valor y veracidad. Por otro lado, también se debe valorar una serie de características inherentes a los entornos Big Data, como son la analítica, seguridad y privacidad, funcionalidades o el hardware. Estas características deberán modificarse en función del contexto en el que vaya a desarrollar el sistema. La Figura 4 expresa una aproximación a cómo se realizaría esta guía con las diferentes dimensiones que considera. En las intersecciones que se producen es donde se deberán definir los diferentes artefactos de requisitos orientados a solución. Estos artefactos no tienen que ser definidos solo mediante lenguaje natural, sino que en iteraciones más avanzadas pueden ser diagramas o modelos.

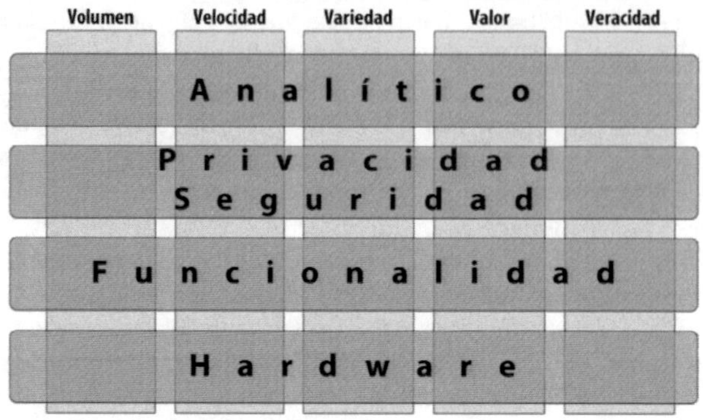

Figura 4. Guía para la definición de requisitos en Big Data

A modo de ejemplo, en la Tabla I se incluye un caso de uso de la guía, en el cual, se simula la necesidad de tener que definir los requisitos para un Big Data que tiene como *goal* principal "Predecir conflictos raciales en los distintos barrios de la ciudad". La tabla que se muestra pertenecería a una iteración intermedia, en la cual, ya se encuentran definidas las fuentes de datos que se van a utilizar y los diferentes *subgoals* del sistema. Como se puede observar, no es necesario completar todas las intersecciones; su objetivo no es ese, sino apoyar en la definición de requisitos sin olvidar aquellos relacionados con Big Data.

Tabla I. Ejemplo de uso de la guía de definición de requisitos

	Volumen	Velocidad	Variedad	Valor	Veracidad
Analítico	Tener una mínima cantidad de datos	Los datos se tienen que analizar en tiempo real	Integración de las diferentes fuentes de datos	Obtener porcentaje de probabilidad de ocurrencia de conflicto	
Privacidad y seguridad	Incapacidad de inferir datos personales		Proteger privacidad de datos personales en fuentes de datos	Control de acceso a los resultados obtenidos	Comprobar la autenticidad de las fuentes de datos
Funciona-lidad		Observar mapa interactivo con zonas con posible conflicto	Uso de diferentes fuentes de datos		
Hardware	Servidores suficientes para tratar con dicha cantidad de datos	Servidores suficientement e potentes para tratar el tiempo real			

Finalmente, como resultado final de las iteraciones se obtiene una serie de artefactos de requisitos orientados a la solución como modelos de las fuentes de datos, modelo de integración de las fuentes de datos, diferentes diagramas UML (como diagramas de escenarios y de comportamiento), el modelo de proceso ETL, y los tests de aceptación. El proceso de definición de requisitos no concluye aquí, sino que normalmente en contextos de Big Data y debido a la heterogeneidad de las fuentes de datos de que se dispone, es necesario abordar una fase en la que se integran los distintos modelos de las fuentes de datos.

3.1 Requisitos de seguridad

Tal y como se muestra en la Figura 2, en nuestro marco los requisitos de seguridad pueden ser satisfechos mediante el uso diferentes soluciones de seguridad que siguen las políticas de seguridad y tienen el principal objetivo de abordar las amenazas y reducir vulnerabilidades. Estas soluciones de seguridad serán implementadas en otros componentes del sistema Big Data como el BDAP o el BDFP. Sin embargo, estas soluciones de seguridad no son fáciles de implementar; por ello, nuestro modelo usa patrones de seguridad como guía. Un patrón de seguridad es una solución a un problema recurrente que indica cómo defenderse de una amenaza, o un conjunto de amenazas de un modo conciso y reusable [16]. Por ello, la definición de requisitos de seguridad en nuestra propuesta sigue un esquema similar al visto, pero debe tener un trato especial, ya que, se encuentra condicionado por una serie de legislaciones, normativas, amenazas y vulnerabilidades.

4 Conclusiones y trabajo futuro

En este artículo se presenta una primera aproximación a la creación de un marco de definición de requisitos para entornos Big Data. Nuestra propuesta se basa en metodologías y técnicas de definición de requisitos ampliamente aceptadas por la comunidad científica, además de la arquitectura Big Data propuesta por el NIST. Para ello, hemos tomado en cuenta nociones típicas de entornos ágiles como las iteraciones. Nuestro marco hace énfasis en el entorno que rodea al Big Data que se desea construir incluyendo las necesidades de la organización y las regulaciones legales que lo pueden afectar. Por otro lado, a la hora de definir requisitos es importante considerar las propiedades Vs típicas de Big Data además de las características inherentes del mismo como la seguridad y privacidad o la analítica. Para ayudar en el descubrimiento y definición de requisitos hemos generado una guía en la que estas propiedades se toman en consideración. Nuestra propuesta hace un especial hincapié en los requisitos de seguridad y privacidad debido a la importancia que tienen en un entorno de este tipo.

Este trabajo surge como respuesta a la necesidad sobre cómo definir de forma efectiva requisitos para el contexto Big Data. Aun así se encuentra todavía en una fase preliminar, con mucho trabajo futuro por delante incluyendo la definición formal y refinamiento tanto del proceso, como de los modelos que se obtienen como resultado de utilizar nuestro marco o la realización de casos de estudio para probar su eficacia.

Agradecimientos. Este trabajo ha sido financiado por el proyecto SEQUOIA (Ministerio de Economía y Competitividad y el Fondo Europeo de Desarrollo Regional FEDER, TIN2015-63502-C3-1-R).

Referencias

1. Akoka, J., Comyn-Wattiau, I., Laoufi, N.: Research on Big Data – A systematic mapping study. Computer Standards & Interfaces. 54, 105–115 (2017).
2. Mayer-Schönberger, V., Cukier, K.: Big Data: A Revolution that Will Transform how We Live, Work, and Think. Houghton Mifflin Harcourt (2013).
3. Chen, M., Mao, S., Liu, Y.: Big data: A survey. Mobile Networks and Applications. 19, 171–209 (2014).
4. S. Sagiroglu, D. Sinanc: Big data: A review. Collaboration Technologies and Systems (CTS), 2013 International Conference on. 42–47 (2013).
5. Ali-ud-din Khan, M., Uddin, M.F., Gupta, N.: Seven V's of Big Data understanding Big Data to extract value. In: American Society for Engineering Education (ASEE Zone 1), 2014 Zone 1 Conference of the. pp. 1–5. IEEE (2014).
6. Sharma, P.P., Navdeti, C.P.: Securing big data hadoop: a review of security issues, threats and solution. Int. J. Comput. Sci. Inf. Technol. 5, (2014).
7. Kelly, J., and J. Kaskade. "CIOS & BIG DATA what your IT team wants you to know." DOI= http://blog.infochimps.com/2013/01/24/cios-big-data (2013).
8. L. Liu: Security and Privacy Requirements Engineering Revisited in the Big Data Era. In: 2016 IEEE 24th International Requirements Engineering Conference Workshops (REW). pp. 55–55 (2016).
9. H. Eridaputra, B. Hendradjaya, W. Danar Sunindyo: Modeling the requirements for big data application using goal oriented approach. In: 2014 International Conference on Data and Software Engineering (ICODSE). pp. 1–6 (2014).
10. G. Park, L. Chung, L. Zhao, S. Supakkul: A Goal-Oriented Big Data Analytics Framework for Aligning with Business. In: 2017 IEEE Third International Conference on Big Data Computing Service and Applications (BigDataService). pp. 31–40 (2017).
11. Al-Najran, N., Dahanayake, A.: A Requirements Specification Framework for Big Data Collection and Capture. In: Morzy, T., Valduriez, P., and Bellatreche, L. (eds.) New Trends in Databases and Information Systems: ADBIS 2015 Short Papers and Workshops, BigDap, DCSA, GID, MEBIS, OAIS, SW4CH, WISARD, Poitiers, France, September 8-11, 2015. Proceedings. pp. 12–19. Springer International Publishing, Cham (2015).
12. Noorwali, I., Arruda, D., Madhavji, N.H.: Understanding quality requirements in the context of big data systems. In: Proceedings of the 2nd International Workshop on BIG Data Software Engineering. pp. 76–79. ACM, Austin, Texas (2016).
13. NBD-WG, NIST: NIST Big Data Reference Architecture, https://bigdatawg.nist.gov/_uploadfiles/M0639_v1_9796711131.docx.
14. Pohl, K.: Requirements Engineering: Fundamentals, Principles, and Techniques. Springer Publishing Company, Incorporated (2010).
15. Moreno, J., Serrano, M.A., Fernández-Medina, Fernandez, E.B.: Towards a Security Reference Architecture for Big Data. (2017). In: International Workshop on Design, Optimization, Languages and Analytical Processing of Big Data. Vienna, Austria (2018).
16. Fernandez, E.B.: Security patterns in practice: designing secure architectures using software patterns. John Wiley & Sons (2013).

La Elicitación de Requisitos No Funcionales en el Contexto de la Industria del Software: Un Reporte de Experiencias

Sandra L. Buitrón and Francisco J. Pino

[1] Universidad del Cauca, Calle 5 #4-70 Popayán, Colombia
{sandrabr,fjpino}@unicauca.edu.co

Resumen
La Ingeniería de Requisitos (IR) es una rama importante de la Ingeniería de software que permite, entre otras cosas, conocer y obtener los requisitos no funcionales para un producto software y es un punto de partida para lograr productos de calidad que satisfagan efectivamente las necesidades de los interesados. En la práctica de la Ingeniería de Requisitos, las empresas requieren adquirir y disponer, dentro de su estructura organizacional, de prácticas suficientes y adecuadas de IR que les permita determinar estos requisitos no funcionales y que a través de su posterior inclusión en el proceso de construcción del software posibilite alcanzar la calidad de una forma efectiva. En este artículo se presentan los resultados de prácticas empresariales llevadas a cabo para nueve proyectos reales, en cuatro empresas, cuyo objetivo era ejecutar actividades de IR en el contexto de requisitos no funcionales de manera que se logrará, con la información recolectada, establecer cómo estas pequeñas y medianas empresas desarrolladoras de software realizan las actividades relacionadas con el manejo de los requisitos no funcionales. La intervención en las empresas se hizo a través de la aplicación de artefactos para la especificación de RNF que propone MERliNN, el cual es un Marco de trabajo para la elicitación de requisitos no funcionales basado en gestion de conocimiento. Los resultados permiten concluir que sigue siendo relevante y necesario aumentar los esfuerzos organizados y sistemáticos, en las empresas desarrolladoras de software, para mejorar sus procesos de gestión de requisitos no funcionales, con apoyo de nuevas prácticas y procesos organizacionales requeridos para tal fin.

Palabra clave: Requisitos No Funcionales, Pequeñas y Medianas Empresas, Prácticas Empresariales, Experiencia.

1 Introducción

La Ingeniería de Requisitos (IR), como rama de la Ingeniería de Software, es considerada crucial para los proyectos de desarrollo software dado que comprende la definición de requisitos y elaboración del modelo conceptual del sistema [1]. Dentro de esta disciplina del software, la primera etapa para lograr obtener los requisitos del software es la Elicitación de requisitos (ER). En ésta etapa se deben tener en cuenta dos elementos principales, los requisitos funcionales y los no funcionales. Los requisitos funcionales se relacionan con lo que el sistema hace y su no funcionalidad se refiere a cómo se comporta el sistema frente a atributos observables como desempeño, reusabilidad, confiabilidad, mantenibilidad, entre otros. Con relación a los requisitos no funcionales (RNF), (i) las técnicas utilizadas para realizar el proceso de Elicitación de Requisitos sobre Requisitos No Funcionales (ERNF) no están aún claras [2], (ii) además en [3] se afirma que aunque existen técnicas bien desarrolladas para obtener requisitos funcionales, hay una falta de mecanismo de elicitación para requisitos no funcionales y no existe un consenso adecuado al respecto de los requisitos no funcionales. En este artículo se presenta los resultados de la aplicación del Marco de Trabajo MERLiNN, construido bajo el enfoque de la Gestión de Conocimiento [4], en procesos de elicitación de requisitos no funcionales de proyectos llevados a cabo en pequeñas y medianas empresas desarrolladoras de software. Los resultados muestran que la industria software, en pequeñas y medianas empresas, requieren realizar esfuerzos organizacionales y de ingeniería de requisitos desde varios enfoques para de ésta manera fortalecerse y ofrecer productos software de calidad.

A parte de la introducción, el documento se encuentra estructurado de la siguiente manera: en la sección 2 se presentan los trabajos relacionados con las formas prácticas reportadas para realizar el proceso de ERNF, en la sección 3 se describe el marco de trabajo MERLiNN aplicado en las organizaciones que participaron de la experiencia, en la sección 4 se presenta el reporte experiencias y por último en la sección 5 se exponen las conclusiones de la investigación.

2 Trabajos relacionados

Para conocer otras propuestas de investigación que presenten resultados prácticos acerca del proceso de Elicitación de requisitos no funcionales se realizó una revisión de la literatura de los últimos 4 años debido a que se pretendía encontrar las propuestas de investigación más recientes desarrolladas en esta temática, a partir de la cual se categorizan 31 propuestas publicadas entre el 2014 y el 2017 de la siguiente manera: el 54,8% de las propuestas han sido validadas a través de estudios de caso, seguidos de un 9,6% a través de entrevistas o encuestas a expertos, 9,6% a través de experimentos, 9,6% a través de experiencias, un 6,4% a través de prototipos, el mismo porcentaje usan validaciones empíricas, y finalmente un 3,1% de las propuestas a través de informes de campo (**Tabla 1**).

Tabla 1. Trabajos categorizados según formas de validación práctica

Categoría	Referencias
Estudio de caso	[5-21]
Experimento	[22-24]
Experiencias	[25-27]
Prototipo	[28, 29]
Validación empírica	[30, 31]
Informe de campo	[32]
Entrevistas	[3, 33, 34]

Esta revisión permite evidenciar esfuerzos de investigación permanentes por mejorar el proceso de Elicitación de Requisitos No Funcionales (ERNF) desde diferentes perspectivas y basadas en variados aspectos, sin embargo ninguna de ellas fundamenta su propuesta en la Gestión de Conocimiento (GC), como disciplina que involucra la creación, adquisición, uso y distribución del conocimiento frente a un concepto tanto individual como organizacional [4, 35, 36]; para este caso, es una gestión de conocimiento sobre el conocimiento generado a partir del proceso de ERNF. Dada la naturaleza de ésta disciplina (en la cual son relevantes los saberes sobre algún concepto, su entendimiento y la aplicación del mismo para toma de decisiones, así como, las experiencias individuales y en general el saber organizacional), propuestas basadas en GC podrían permitir experiencias de aplicación y aprovechamiento del conocimiento en contextos reales en empresas que pertenecen a la industria de software. En este sentido, el aporte de este trabajo es el descubrimiento del estado las actividades de elicitación de RNF en las pequeñas y medianas empresas en el escenario de la realización del proceso de elicitación de requisitos no funcionales a través de la aplicación del Marco de Trabajo MERliNN [37]. Este Marco de trabajo permite elicitar, bajo un enfoque de GC, los requisitos no funcionales que según la literatura suelen ser omitidos dentro del proceso de desarrollo de las empresas y por tanto el conocimiento y entendimiento de los mismos requiere mayor atención para poder ser gestionados en los proyectos tecnológicos de manera que impacten de forma directa en la calidad de los productos software.

3 Marco de trabajo para la elicitación de requisitos no funcionales basada en la gestión de conocimiento – MERliNN

MERliNN es construido conceptualmente basándose en la disciplina de la gestión del conocimiento para poder abordar los RNF en un proceso de Elicitación de Requisitos No Funcionales (ERNF). El Marco de trabajo está compuesto por elementos tales como: (i) un núcleo de transformación de conocimiento (denominado TCER), (ii) un método de ERNF, (iii) unas dimensiones y (iv) elementos de gestión de conocimiento que en conjunto pretenden apoyar el proceso de elicitación de requisitos no funcionales de manera sistemática en el contexto de la industria software (ver Fig. 1).

Una descripción general de los componentes de MERliNN se presenta a continuación, la descripción detallada se puede encontrar en [37, 38]. Como primer componente del marco de trabajo, se tienen 3 dimensiones a partir de las cuales se busca iniciar la estructuración de MERliNN. Estas dimensiones son 3: la dimensión organizacional, la técnica y la de conocimiento.

La dimensión organizacional incluye componentes que permiten consolidar la información relevante para los procesos de gestión de conocimiento en una organización, a partir de aspectos como: (i) las formas y grado de implementación de la GC de los RNF en los proyectos software, y (ii) las formas de comunicación organizacional que permitan apoyar la transferencia del conocimiento de los RNF. En la dimensión técnica del marco de trabajo se integran las actividades propias de ingeniería de requisitos, entre ellas: (i) identificar los RNF, (ii) elaborar especificación de RNF, y (iii) validar y negociar los RNF.

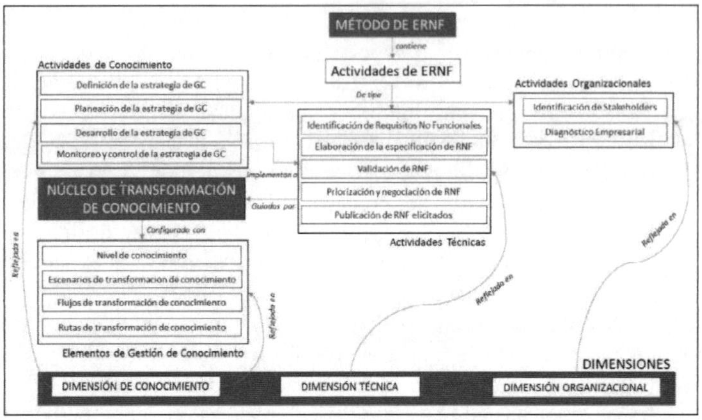

Fig. 1. Componentes del Marco de Trabajo para la Elicitación de Requisitos No Funcionales - MERliNN

La dimensión de conocimiento es el corazón del marco de trabajo puesto que permite implementar una GC de forma incremental en las organizaciones a través de cuatro actividades: (i) Definir una estrategia de GC, (ii) planear la estrategia de GC, (iii) ejecutar la estrategia de GC y (iv) monitorear y controlar la estrategia de GC. Un componente fundamental de MERliNN es su núcleo de transformación de conocimiento (TCER) el cual se configura con elementos exclusivos de GC y por tanto pretende describir las dinámicas del conocimiento al momento de la ejecución del proceso de Elicitación de RNF en un proyecto de desarrollo software. Entre los elementos de GC que constituyen el núcleo de transformación están: flujos, escenarios y rutas de transformación de conocimiento entre otros. Para poder integrar todos estos elementos, MERliNN cuenta con un Método de ERNF compuesto por tres tipos de actividades, cada una reflejando la naturaleza de las dimensiones y guiado por el núcleo TCER. Este método cuenta con artefactos específicos para cada uno de los procesos del método; el artefacto principal que permite la especificación de los RNF permite capturar y representar los procesos de negocio, sus relaciones dentro de un dominio de aplicación y las características de calidad a desarrollar para el producto software. A continuación presentamos un ejemplo aplicado de los artefactos para especificación de RNF propuestos por MERliNN (Fig. 2, Fig 3).

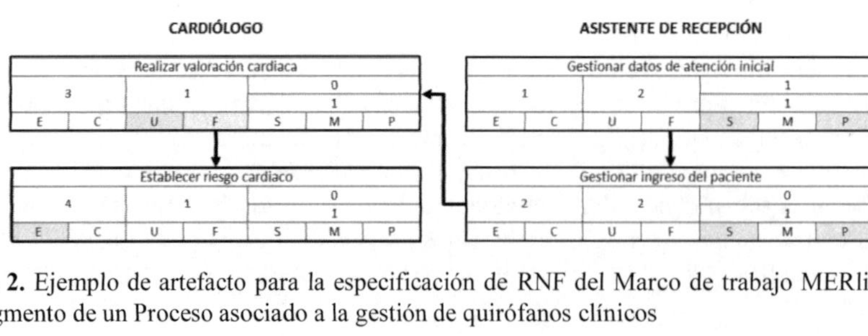

Fig. 2. Ejemplo de artefacto para la especificación de RNF del Marco de trabajo MERliNN – Fragmento de un Proceso asociado a la gestión de quirófanos clínicos

<table>
<tr><th colspan="3">Número del proceso</th><th>1</th><th colspan="2">Detalle de características de calidad</th></tr>
<tr><th colspan="3">Interfaces</th><th>Requisitos legales</th><th>Seguridad (S)</th><th>Portabilidad (P)</th></tr>
<tr><td>Interfaz 1</td><td>(Entradas)</td><td>(Salidas)</td><td rowspan="4">-Ley 1751 de 2015 - Articulo 8 sobre integralidad de la tecnología en el servicio de salud
-ley 1581 de 2012 - Ley de protección de datos personales
-Noma ISO/HL7 27932 para el intercambio de datos y archivos médicos (historia clínica electrónica global de un paciente basada en documentos clínicos)</td><td rowspan="2">Los datos recuperados del sistema de registro de pacientes deben ser fieles y pertenecer a cada paciente de manera inequivoca.</td><td rowspan="2">El intercambio de información se realiza en el momento que lo solicite el usuario, no es permanente.</td></tr>
<tr><td>Manual</td><td rowspan="3">La información básica del paciente como su nombre completo, edad, número de historia, entre otros se recupera del sistema de registro del paciente.</td><td rowspan="3">Se espera que toda esta información sea cargada en la parte inicial del formulario de ingreso del paciente.</td></tr>
<tr><td>Semi automática</td><td rowspan="2">Solamente el Asistente de Recepción puede tener acceso y diligenciar la información básica del paciente.</td><td rowspan="2"></td></tr>
<tr><td>Automática</td></tr>
</table>

Fig. 3. Ejemplo de artefacto para la especificación de RNF del Marco de trabajo MERliNN – Detalle de características de calidad requeridas para proceso de negocio número 1 (Fig 2)

Este artefacto permite además y de manera previa a la documentación de los RNF, en términos de características y atributos de calidad, representar y visualizar los procesos de negocio involucrados en el dominio de la aplicación así como las interrelaciones entre ellos, los perfiles necesarios para el software, las prioridades de desarrollo, el orden de estos procesos, las interfaces con otros sistemas externos y la reglamentación implicada en el alcance del producto software. Todos estos elementos aportan a la especificación de las necesidades y aspectos de calidad del producto.

4 Reporte de experiencias

La descripción de la experiencia sobre la aplicación de MERliNN ha sido organizada teniendo en cuenta la estructura para este tipo de informes de experiencia recomendados por [39]. A este respecto, la siguiente subsección describe este informe de experiencia en términos de: el contexto de aplicación, la descripción de las organizaciones participantes, el informe y el análisis del uso de marco de trabajo y una discusión sobre los resultados de la experiencia.

4.1 Contexto de aplicación

MERliNN ha sido aplicado en nueve proyectos de desarrollo de la industria del software, en 4 empresas mediante la ejecución del proceso de Elicitación de Requisitos No Funcionales de la dimensión técnica de MERliNN (ver Fig. 1). MERliNN se ha utilizado como herramienta para la especificación de RNF para dos contextos diferentes de la ingeniería: (i) un contexto donde el desarrollo del software inicia en la etapa de levantamiento de requisitos con el cliente, para el caso de 5 proyectos, y (ii) un contexto donde el producto software ya ha sido terminado en su primera versión y el proceso de ingeniería es la etapa de mantenimiento del mismo, en el caso de 4 proyectos. En el caso de los proyectos del primer contexto, el proceso de validación de los RNF identificados y especificados por los elicitadores se realizó contando con la participación directa del cliente o con quien hiciera sus veces (líder de producto), mientras que, para el caso de los proyectos del segundo contexto, este proceso de validación fue inexistente, lo que se realizó entonces fue un proceso de verificación entre el producto terminado y los RNF especificados, para lo cual se recibió el apoyo del líder del equipo de desarrollo asignado en cada organización.

Para llevar a cabo la experiencia se requirió determinar algunos roles que permitirían aclarar las responsabilidades de los participantes, para ellos se definió los siguientes roles: (i) un rol de elicitador, el cual tendría a cargo la ejecución como tal del proceso de ERNF a partir de las aplicaciones y/o de los proyectos de desarrollo que se estaban llevando a cabo en las empresas, y por tanto eran responsables de elaborar los artefactos respectivos de elicitación; cada proyecto contó, en promedio, con tres elicitadores, (ii) un rol de líder de proyecto, quien debía guiar al equipo de elicitadores bajo un plan de trabajo general del proyecto y atender las solicitudes de información que pudieran tener los elicitadores y en general el equipo del proyecto, y (iii) un rol de asesor del proceso de aplicación de MERliNN el cual fue desempeñado por el investigador principal del presente artículo, y es quien debía apoyar a los elicitadores de manera directa, y a través de consultorías, la ejecución del proceso de ERNF haciendo uso del artefacto de especificación correspondiente.

El objetivo de aplicar MERliNN en estos nueve proyectos de desarrollo de software fue aportar a las organizaciones participantes en el logro de la identificación y posterior representación de los RNF de sus productos software a partir de la aplicación de las actividades técnicas que MERliNN propone. Esta experiencia se llevó a cabo durante un periodo de 3 meses y fue apoyada por un grupo de 21 elicitadores conocedores de técnicas concretas de Elicitación de requisitos. El 100% de las empresas utilizan Scrum como metodología para gestionar el desarrollo software, sólo el 25% de ellas contaban con un proceso definido para la ERF más no para RNF. La elicitación de los RNF se logró ejecutar en los nueve proyectos y además permitió ver a las organizaciones la necesidad y aporte de identificar y representar estos requisitos para: (i) el desarrollo de sus productos nuevos o, (ii) incluirlos en versiones futuras de mantenimiento y mejoras de los productos ya terminados.

4.2 Características de las empresas

En este apartado, describiremos las características de las organizaciones participantes en la experiencia de aplicación de MERliNN junto con los proyectos que fueron seleccionados por cada una. MERliNN en un esfuerzo por respetar la necesidad de confidencialidad de las empresas llamará a estas empresas como: Empresa A, Empresa B, Empresa C y Empresa D. Sus principales características son (**Tabla 2**):

Tabla 2. Trabajos categorizados según formas de validación práctica

Empresa	Tiempo en el mercado	Núm. de empleados	Proyectos de la experiencia
Empresa A	18 años	45	Py1: Gestión de quirófanos e insumos para cirugía Py2: Gestión de historias clínicas
Empresa B	12 años	50	Py3: Gestión de procesos de visitas de campo

			Py4: Seguimiento y control de envíos Py5: Seguimiento de servicios de logística
Empresa C	5 años	4	Py6: Gestión de acueductos rurales Py7: Gestión de información educativa
Empresa D	1,5 años	3	Py8: Gestión de canchas sintéticas Py9: Gestión de jardines infantiles

4.3 Reporte y análisis del trabajo ejecutado en las empresas

El 100% de las empresas participantes, hoy en día no cuentan con un proceso definido y estandarizado para la elicitación de requisitos no funcionales, que pueda ser desplegado en cada uno de sus proyectos de desarrollo software. Este hallazgo permite evidenciar que los RNF no son considerados durante el proceso de construcción del software de manera que la calidad final que el cliente perteneciente a la industria del software requiere no es lograda. En la Tabla 3, se presentan algunos aspectos generales acerca del uso de MERliNN para la ERNF en las organizaciones.

Describimos a continuación cómo fue la práctica de la especificación de RNF en los proyectos, a través del uso del artefacto de especificación de RNF de MERliNN (ver Fig. 2 y Fig. 3):

Tabla 3. Aspectos acerca del uso general de MERliNN en las organizaciones

Empresa	Aspectos del uso de MERliNN en las organizaciones
Empresa A	Se utilizó el proceso definido de ERF estandarizado existente como línea base de adaptación para el proceso de ERNF.
Empresa B	Se requirió definir un proceso de ERNF desde cero dado que tampoco se contó con el proceso para ERF.
Empresa C	Dado que la organización venía teniendo acercamiento al proceso de ERNF la aplicación de MERliNN tuvo un uso adecuado dentro de los proyectos
Empresa D	El uso de MERliNN para sus procesos de ingeniería fue adecuado, suficiente y aportante dado el reciente nacimiento como empresa.

- A partir del Py1, se evidencia interés de las organizaciones en: (i) asignar el nivel de importancia a la característica no funcional, (ii) concretar la sub característica de calidad, (iii) definir esquemas para representar posibilidades de relación futuras entre procesos de negocio, (iv) optimizar la visualización de los RNF elicitados. De otro lado, los elicitadores expresan dificultades de uso al momento de la redacción de los atributos de calidad debido a la necesidad de mayor experiencia para lograr un nivel de abstracción software de estas características.
- A partir del Py2, se puede observar que: (i) los RNF pueden estar definidos por líderes técnicos de la organización que conocen de manera exhaustiva y crítica la necesidad del cliente y por tanto estos RNF pueden existir de manera predefinida a través de lineamientos de desarrollo, (ii) es viable, a nivel de la práctica, enlazar los procesos de negocio que se documentan a través de MERliNN con las historias épicas del proyecto.

- A partir de los proyectos Py3, Py4, Py5 y Py7 se demuestra que en la práctica de la ERNF: (i) se requieren estrategias propias de las organizaciones cuando se trata de recuperación de RNF, (ii) los procesos de ERNF para productos terminados se convierten en procesos de verificación de requisitos.
- A partir de los proyectos Py6 y P8, se observa que en la práctica: (i) los lideres técnicos de los proyectos visualizan la importancia de los RNF, (ii) un proceso de ERNF permite a las organizaciones analizar la columna vertebral de un producto software, permitiendo dar claridad al alcance del proyecto, (ii) el proceso de ERNF puede ser ejecutado de manera distribuida por un equipo de elicitadores, (iv) la elicitación de RNF permite especificar cualquier característica de calidad que sea de interés o prioritaria para el producto sin limitaciones.
- A partir de Py9, se puede constatar que: (i) un proceso de ERNF genera espacios de buen desempeño en los equipos de desarrollo de los proyectos, (ii) la ERNF apoya la tarea de definición del alcance del producto en situaciones en las que los clientes exponen muchas ideas o por el contrario cuando éstos no tienen claridad sobre su necesidad.

4.4 Discusión

Las cuatro empresas participantes en esta experiencia coinciden en que la elicitación de requisitos no funcionales permite incluir en el desarrollo comportamientos importantes de calidad, así mismo que los RNF apoyan a la gestión del alcance, el tiempo y los costos del proyecto, incluyendo la visualización de riesgos de diseño relevantes para el éxito del producto y del proyecto. Los elicitadores evidenciaron que un proceso de ERNF se requiere dominio del problema, un grado adecuado y suficiente de abstracción de ingeniería y de manera vital habilidades blandas como la comunicación y la capacidad de negociación con el equipo del proyecto, en el cual se incluyen los clientes, para poder entender y aportar en el establecimiento de estas características de calidad del software. Esta experiencia que contó con contextos de desarrollo tan variados permite observar que MERliNN es un mecanismo que aporta a la industria no sólo en la especificación de los RNF sino que permite a las organizaciones aumentar la visión de la calidad de sus procesos y sus productos software. Como investigadores, se logra percibir que MERliNN es un marco de trabajo que enriquece los procesos de gestión de requisitos en la industria software, no sólo porque permite visualizar y representar los requisitos no funcionales sino que aporta en el análisis de los requisitos funcionales y de los procesos de negocio de las organizaciones, tanto de las que actúan como clientes del desarrollo como de las mismas desarrolladoras del producto.

A continuación destacamos algunos aspectos de la aplicación de MERliNN en la industria del software, primero en términos de las lecciones aprendidas de los puntos de vista de las empresas, los elicitadores y los investigadores, luego en términos de las limitaciones de los resultados y finalmente las conclusiones de la experiencia.

4.4.1 Lecciones aprendidas desde la perspectiva de las empresas

Para el gerente de la Empresa A y los líderes de los proyectos, con quienes se tuvo un acercamiento directo luego de la finalización del periodo de la experiencia, fue fundamental contar con procesos organizacionales definidos dado que esto permitió una adaptación rápida y controlada de los nuevos elicitadores de requisitos no funcionales que se insertarían en los equipos de desarrollo. Frente a este aspecto, las otras empresas si debieron realizar esfuerzos adicionales de acoplamiento y planeación para insertar y asignar los nuevos elicitadores puesto que no contaban con estos procesos organizacionales definidos y estandarizados. Por otro lado, un aspecto importante durante el proceso de ERNF que se vió fuertemente marcado fue la necesidad de comunicación permanente de los elicitadores hacia los demás integrantes del equipo de desarrollo, dado que los elicitadores no hacían parte del equipo del proyecto desde el inicio del mismo. Esta comunicación hace que exista un esfuerzo diario y coordinado entre las tareas de los diferentes integrantes de los proyectos y así lograr un desempeño adecuado de todo el equipo. Desde la perspectiva técnica de la ingeniería, los líderes de los proyectos consideraron muy relevante el proceso para sus organizaciones y en especial por contar con recursos humanos fuertes en técnicas de elicitación de requisitos no funcionales lo cual facilitó la obtención de las especificaciones y generó una dinámica de grupo diferente en cada contexto. Como último elemento relevante para los gerentes y líderes de las organizaciones, el grado de compromiso de los elicitadores y en general del equipo de los proyectos fue primordial puesto que permitió lograr los productos de trabajo de elicitación específicos para cada proyecto incluso, para algunos casos, superando la cantidad de especificaciones planeadas.

4.4.2 Lecciones aprendidas desde la perspectiva de los elicitadores

Los participantes de la experiencia con el rol de elicitadores, contaban con conocimientos importantes acerca de técnicas especializadas de gestión de requisitos, por lo cual su participación en los proyectos permitió aplicar sus conocimientos a través de las dinámicas de los mismos. Algunas lecciones aprendidas relevantes para estos participantes son descritas a continuación:

- En procesos de ingeniería que no son establecidos de forma preliminar y estandarizada en las organizaciones implica que los elicitadores deben estar preparados para trabajar en escenarios de alta incertidumbre.
- En algunos casos, los recursos de elicitación se utilizaron para especificar versiones menores a la que actualmente se estaban trabajando en los proyectos; esto hace que los productos de trabajo se expongan a actualizaciones importantes o que incluso, queden obsoletos frente al estado real del producto.
- Como elicitadores es importante ahondar en los temas de normatividad del proyecto dado que en este tipo de información puede surgir la necesidad de ampliar el espectro de interesados y por tanto de RNF críticos.
- La realización de un proceso de ERNF de manera empírica no permite ejecutar un buen proceso y como punto más crítico no permite saber si los resultados son o no significativos para el objetivo del proyecto.

- Durante el proceso de ERNF se requiere la definición del alcance de manera previa a la ejecución del proceso para poder adelantar tareas concretas y que cumplan con las expectativas del proceso.
- Los procesos de ERNF que implique la definición de estrategias de recuperación de requisitos deben estar en el marco de un objetivo global a través de los planes de reingeniería de las organizaciones para sus productos comerciales.
- La elicitación de RNF implica asegurar la disponibilidad de los clientes, de los líderes del proyecto, de los recursos físicos y logísticos para poder ser llevada a cabo adecuadamente.
- Realizar un proceso de ERNF con los clientes permite darles a conocer que más allá de las funcionalidades del producto es vital reflexionar sobre aspectos de su futuro comportamiento y entorno de uso.

4.4.3 Lecciones aprendidas desde la perspectiva de investigación

Lograr tener una experiencia de uso de propuestas de investigación requiere un esfuerzo de gestión importante con todos los participantes, de manera que se deben definir planes generales de la experiencia, conseguir contextos viables de aplicación, negociar disponibilidades de los participantes y dejar claro cuáles serán las actividades a desarrollar por los elicitadores y por tanto los productos finales que se pueden esperar por las empresas. A partir de la experiencia como asesor de los procesos de ERNF se logró aprender que:

- Los procesos de ERNF requieren el manejo de técnicas tanto de ingeniería como habilidades de comunicación y negociación.
- Para los casos en que se dificulte la disponibilidad de los líderes de proyecto podría ser importante contar con un mecanismo intermedio que permita guiar a los elicitadores sobre cómo realizar el proceso de ERNF de manera fluida.
- Se evidencia que en proyectos donde el producto software ya está en etapas finales del ciclo de desarrollo, puede sesgarse la ejecución del proceso de ERNF por parte de los líderes y el proyecto, lo cual podría ser nocivo para el mantenimiento del producto y la toma de decisiones tecnológicas.
- MERliNN como herramienta que apoya los procesos de ERNF, aumenta la experticia de los ingenieros de sistemas que llevan a cabo roles de analistas o elicitadores en la industria del software.
- La experiencia permitió a cada participante reconocer y auto-evaluar sus habilidades de análisis y comunicación en contextos reales de desarrollo software.
- Es importante para el proceso de investigación, reconocer la importancia de aumentar las habilidades de diseño gráfico en los elicitadores de requisitos no funcionales de manera que desde los sketch instantáneos, que se realizan con el cliente, se puedan iniciar procesos recursivos de validación del producto, esto permitiría adelantar estas actividades de la ingeniería de requisitos desde estos primeros bosquejo del producto software.

4.4.4 Limitaciones

En el marco de la experiencia se identifican las siguientes limitaciones:

- Frente al contexto de los proyectos de desarrollo que participaron en la experiencia, el tiempo acordado con los gerentes de estas organizaciones, para un 77,7% de los proyectos, no fue finalmente suficiente debido a que en estos proyectos no se contaba con un proceso de elicitación previamente definido y esto limito el avance en los productos de trabajo referentes a los aspectos no funcionales del producto software.
- La disponibilidad de los participantes con roles de elicitador y de líder de proyecto, fue limitada, dado que estos participantes contaban con otros compromisos ajenos al proceso de la experiencia y esto afectó el desempeño del proceso de ERNF.
- El ejercicio de investigación fue soportado técnicamente por el investigador principal quien actúo como asesor de los elicitadores para la definición de las estrategias de ERNF, más no intervino de manera directa en los procesos de ERNF de los proyectos.

5 Conclusiones de la experiencia y trabajo futuro

En este documento, presentamos un reporte de la práctica de la especificación de RNF en un contexto de la industria del software a través de experiencias obtenidas del uso del marco de trabajo MERliNN.

A partir de la experiencia, las empresas que no contaban con procesos para la elicitación de requisitos, expresaron la intención de iniciar esfuerzos relacionados con la definición y documentación del proceso de ER para incluir los requisitos funcionales y los no funcionales. Por otro lado, la experiencia permitió concluir que es importante que las organizaciones cuenten con herramientas para la elicitación de los RNF, puesto que éstas permiten soportar las actividades relacionadas a este proceso para obtener la base principal y esencial del ciclo de desarrollo de software, como es la especificación de las características de calidad que debe cumplir el producto. Finalmente, frente a la Ingeniería de requisitos, MERliNN es una oportunidad práctica que en la relación cliente-proveedor, podría mejorar la forma de comunicación y entendimiento entre estos dos participantes. Estos resultados permiten ratificar que las pequeñas y medianas empresas desarrolladoras de software realizan aún las actividades relacionadas con la gestión de requisitos no funcionales de una manera empírica y que para ello no cuentan con herramientas adecuadas y suficientes que apoyen este proceso de ERNF para sus productos software. A partir del uso de este artefacto en los nueve proyectos de desarrollo de software, se pudo evidenciar que MERliNN a través de su elemento clave, puede aportar desde varias perspectivas tanto, a los procesos de desarrollo de las organizaciones como al producto software en sí mismo. Así mismo, MERliNN demuestra una vez más ser flexible y adaptable a los contextos del proyecto y a las restricciones que puedan llegar a tener.

Como trabajo futuro se realizarán mejoras a MERliNN de manera que se incluyan mecanismos para facilitar su uso, enriquecer la forma de visualización de los RNF elicitados y extender su alcance para incluir actividades de V&V. Por último se debe reflexionar acerca de que: independiente de si se realiza o no la especificación de los RNF, éstos siempre terminarán siendo implementados de alguna manera en los productos software, con la diferencia de que si los elicitamos desde las etapas tempranas del ciclo de desarrollo de software, podremos trabajar en asegurar, que en gran medida, cumplan las expectativas de calidad de los clientes y que la forma en que están implementados es el resultado de un proceso suficiente de ingeniería.

Agradecimientos

Los autores agradecen a la Universidad del Cauca, donde ellos trabajan como profesores, por el apoyo en el desarrollo de este trabajo.

Referencias

1. C. M. Zapata, G. L. Giraldo, and J. E. Mesa, "Una propuesta de metaontología para la educción de requisitos," *Ingeniare. Revista chilena de ingeniería,* vol. 18, pp. 26-37, 2010.
2. E. Serna-Montoya, "Current state of research on non-functional requirements," *Ingenieria y Universidad,* vol. 16, pp. 225-246, 2012.
3. L. Wu, N. C. Pa, R. Abdullah, W. N. A. Rahman, and M. Tee, "Exploring functional and non-functional requirements of social media on knowledge sharing," *Journal of Theoretical and Applied Information Technology,* vol. 93, pp. 595-605, 2016.
4. I. Nonaka and D. J. Teece, *Managing industrial knowledge: creation, transfer and utilization*: Sage, 2001.
5. S. Thew and A. Sutcliffe, "Value-based requirements engineering: method and experience," *Requirements Engineering,* pp. 1-22, 2017.
6. S. A. Mokhov, M. Song, S. Chilkaka, Z. Das, J. Zhang, J. Llewellyn, and S. P. Mudur, "Agile Forward-Reverse Requirements Elicitation as a Creative Design Process: A Case Study of Illimitable Space System v2," *Journal of Integrated Design and Process Science,* vol. 20, pp. 3-37, 2017.
7. M. Sadiq and Neha, "Elicitation of testing requirements from the selected set of software's functional requirements using fuzzy-based approach," in *Advances in Intelligent Systems and Computing* vol. 556, ed, 2017, pp. 429-437.
8. R. Jindal, R. Malhotra, and A. Jain, "Automated classification of security requirements," in *2016 International Conference on Advances in Computing, Communications and Informatics, ICACCI 2016*, 2016, pp. 2027-2033.
9. L. Barcelos and R. Penteado, "Especificação de requisitos no domínio de sistemas de informação com o uso de padróes," in *CIBSE 2016 - XIX Ibero-American Conference on Software Engineering*, 2016, pp. 338-351.
10. R. Djouab, A. Abran, and A. Seffah, "An ASPIRE-based method for quality requirements identification from business goals," *Requirements Engineering,* vol. 21, pp. 87-106, 2016.
11. V. Yadav, R. K. Joshi, and S. Ling, "Process Edification for traceability in evolving architectures," in *ACM International Conference Proceeding Series*, 2016, pp. 99-108.

12. M. Sarrab, Y. Baghdadi, H. Al-Shihi, and H. Bourdoucen, "A model for mobile learning non-functional requirement elicitation," *International Journal of Mobile Learning and Organisation,* vol. 10, pp. 129-158, 2016.
13. T. Shah and S. Patel, "A Novel Approach for Specifying Functional and Non-functional Requirements Using RDS (Requirement Description Schema)," in *Procedia Computer Science*, 2016, pp. 852-860.
14. J. Kamaroddin, "Requirements engineering for pervasive healthcare monitoring system," in *CEUR Workshop Proceedings*, 2016.
15. A. Gonçalves, A. Correia, and J. Fernandes, "Service elicitation of non-functional requirements: An approach using activity theory," in *2015 10th Iberian Conference on Information Systems and Technologies, CISTI 2015*, 2015.
16. S. Dragicevic, S. Celar, and L. Novak, "Use of method for elicitation, documentation, and validation of software user requirements (MEDoV) in agile software development projects," in *Proceedings - 6th International Conference on Computational Intelligence, Communication Systems and Networks, CICSyN 2014*, 2014, pp. 65-70.
17. S. Kopczyńska and J. Nawrocki, "Using non-functional requirements templates for elicitation: A case study," in *2014 IEEE 4th International Workshop on Requirements Patterns, RePa 2014 - Proceedings*, 2014, pp. 47-54.
18. "2014 IEEE 4th International Workshop on Requirements Patterns, RePa 2014 - Proceedings," in *2014 IEEE 4th International Workshop on Requirements Patterns, RePa 2014 - Proceedings*, 2014, p. 58.
19. P. Engiel, C. Cappelli, and J. C. S. Do Prado Leite, "Eliciting concepts from the brazilian access law using a combined approach," in *Proceedings of the ACM Symposium on Applied Computing*, 2014, pp. 1001-1006.
20. S. Chakraborty, C. Rosenkranz, and J. Dehlinger, "Getting to the shalls: Facilitating Sensemaking in Requirements Engineering," *ACM Transactions on Management Information Systems,* vol. 5, 2015.
21. H. T. Kanwal, F. Arif, and A. M. Zaidi, "'Software requirement engineering', a new leave towards the silver bullet," in *Proceedings of the 2015 Science and Information Conference, SAI 2015*, 2015, pp. 189-198.
22. A. Mahmoud, "An information theoretic approach for extracting and tracing non-functional requirements," in *2015 IEEE 23rd International Requirements Engineering Conference, RE 2015 - Proceedings*, 2015, pp. 36-45.
23. A. Filieri, H. Hoffmann, and M. Maggio, "Automated multi-objective control for self-adaptive software design," in *2015 10th Joint Meeting of the European Software Engineering Conference and the ACM SIGSOFT Symposium on the Foundations of Software Engineering, ESEC/FSE 2015 - Proceedings*, 2015, pp. 13-24.
24. A. Gregoriades, J. Hadjicosti, C. Florides, M. Pampaka, and H. Michail, "A driving simulator for discovering requirements in complex systems," presented at the Proceedings of the Conference on Summer Computer Simulation, Chicago, Illinois, 2015.
25. A. Silva, P. Pinheiro, A. Albuquerque, and J. Barroso, "Approach to define a non-functional requirements elicitation guide using a customer language," in *Proceedings of the International Conference on Software Engineering and Knowledge Engineering, SEKE*, 2016, pp. 575-578.

26. M. Feldgen and O. Clua, "Teaching effective requirements engineering for large-scale software development with scaffolding," in *Proceedings - Frontiers in Education Conference, FIE*, 2015.
27. I. Biscoglio and E. Marchetti, "Definition of software quality evaluation and measurement plans: A reported experience inside the audio-visual preservation context," in *Communications in Computer and Information Science* vol. 555, ed, 2015, pp. 63-80.
28. N. Kushiro, T. Shimizu, and T. Ehira, "Requirements Elicitation with Extended Goal Graph," in *Procedia Computer Science*, 2016, pp. 1691-1700.
29. A. Abdelatey, M. Elkawkagy, A. El-Sisi, and A. Keshk, "A multilateral agent-based service level agreement negotiation framework," in *Advances in Intelligent Systems and Computing* vol. 533, ed, 2017, pp. 576-586.
30. U. Franke, "Towards preference elicitation for trade-offs between non-functional properties," in *Proceedings - 2016 IEEE 20th International Enterprise Distributed Object Computing Conference, EDOC 2016*, 2016, pp. 89-98.
31. T. Ambreen, N. Ikram, M. Usman, and M. Niazi, "Empirical research in requirements engineering: trends and opportunities," *Requirements Engineering,* pp. 1-33, 2016.
32. A. Soska, I. Schroll-Decker, and J. Mottok, "Implementation of practical exercises in software engineering education to improve the acquirement of functional and non-functional competences: A field report about project-based learning in software engineering," 2015, pp. 338-345.
33. A. Silva, P. Pinheiro Adriano Albuquerque, and J. Barroso, "A survey about the situation of the elicitation of non-functional requirements," in *Iberian Conference on Information Systems and Technologies, CISTI*, 2016.
34. H. Hiisilä and M. Kujala, "Combining Process Modeling and Requirements Engineering: An Experience Report," in *Proceedings - 17th IEEE Conference on Business Informatics, CBI 2015*, 2015, pp. 242-249.
35. T. H. Davenport and L. Prusak, *Working knowledge: How organizations manage what they know*: Harvard Business Press, 1998.
36. D. O. C. D. Overton, "The Relationship Between Knowledge Transfer, Team Learning, and Project Success in the Information Technology Field," Capella University, 2017.
37. S. L. Buitrón, Pino, Francisco J. (in press), "Elicitación de requisitos no funcionales basada en la gestión de conocimiento de los stakeholders," *Revista Chilena Ingeniare,* vol. 26, No. 2, Abril - Junio 2018.
38. S. L. Buitrón, Pino, Francisco J. (in press), "Elicitación de requisitos no funcionales basada en la gestión de conocimiento: El marco de trabajo MERliNN," *Revista Ingenierias Universidad de Medellín,* vol. 17 No. 32, 2018.
39. M. Montesi and P. Lago, "Software engineering article types: An analysis of the literature," *Journal of Systems and Software,* vol. 81, pp. 1694-1714, 2008.

Ontología para la Especificación de Casos de Uso, Casos de Prueba y su Trazabilidad

Marcela Vegetti [1], M. Luciana Roldán [1], Marcelo Marciszack [2], Silvio Gonnet [1], Horacio Leone [1]

[1] Instituto de Desarrollo y Diseño (Conicet/UTN) Santa Fe, Argentina
{lroldan, mvegetti, sgonnet, hleone}@santafe-conicet.gov.ar

[2] Centro de Investigación, Desarrollo y Transferencia de Sistemas de Información (CIDS), Córdoba, Argentina
marciszack@gmail.com

Abstract. En este trabajo se propone una ontología que permite definir e integrar conceptos empleados en la especificación de casos de uso y casos de prueba. Estos conceptos son parte de los metamodelos de las diferentes herramientas de soporte a la Ingeniería de Requerimientos y su formalización en una ontología posibilita la interoperabilidad entre estas herramientas para lograr consistencia y trazabilidad de artefactos.

Keywords: Trazabilidad, Requerimientos, Ontología.

1 Introducción

Existe una estrecha relación, recíproca y positiva, entre las actividades de la ingeniería de requerimientos y las pruebas de sistemas intensivos en software. Por un lado, contar con una especificación completa, consistente, y legible de requerimientos es beneficioso para la definición de casos de prueba de alta calidad. Por otro lado, durante la realización de actividades de prueba, particularmente la definición de los casos de prueba, se obtienen resultados valiosos para la mejora de la especificación de los requerimientos. Dado que la mayoría de los procesos de desarrollo de software modernos tienen un enfoque iterativo, es posible comenzar a realizar pruebas lo antes posible. Siguiendo esta línea, el presente trabajo se alinea a las propuestas de iniciar las actividades de pruebas en forma temprana [1], utilizando los artefactos de requerimientos en forma de casos de uso para la generación de casos de prueba. Tales casos de pruebas pueden definirse con dos intenciones: como artefactos preliminares para validación de requerimientos, o como artefactos acabados que se emplearán para la realización de pruebas de sistemas y aceptación. Los casos de uso [2] son claves para el proceso de prueba, no solo porque de ellos se derivan otros artefactos, sino también porque identifican y establecen las condiciones que deberán tenerse en cuenta al implementar los casos de prueba, así como también son necesarios para verificar que se han implementados satisfactoriamente y con calidad todos los requisitos que debe cumplir el sistema resultante.

Las herramientas de soporte para la definición de casos de uso no siempre están integradas con las herramientas que se emplean en la generación y ejecución de casos de prueba. Sin embargo, dado que los casos de prueba pueden ser derivados a partir de la especificación de casos de uso, y que los casos de prueba, a su vez, requieren de trazabilidad hacia los requerimientos funcionales y casos de uso para conocer qué artefactos de requerimientos especificaron cierta funcionalidad, se requiere que exista integración o interoperabilidad entre dichas herramientas. A fin de lograr tal interoperabilidad semántica es necesaria la construcción de una ontología que defina todos los artefactos involucrados y las relaciones apropiadas entre éstos. Una ontología define formalmente un conjunto común de términos que se usan para describir y representar un dominio y proveen una compresión compartida y consensuada de un dominio del conocimiento, que puede ser comunicada entre personas y sistemas heterogéneos. En trabajos previos [3] se introdujo una ontología preliminar de requerimientos funcionales basados en casos de uso, con el objetivo de favorecer la interoperabilidad entre herramientas utilizadas en la especificación de casos de uso y herramientas de gestión de casos de pruebas.

El objetivo de este trabajo es dotar a la ontología propuesta en [3] de los elementos necesarios para representar la trazabilidad entre artefactos de requerimientos y pruebas que se emplean en las diferentes herramientas de especificación de casos de uso y gestión de casos de prueba. Esto significa la definición de un conjunto de conceptos, relaciones, y reglas adecuadas para para aprovechar las capacidades de recuperación de conocimiento e inferencia que las ontologías ofrecen. Asimismo, se introducen los principales aspectos metodológicos del desarrollo de dicha ontología.

El resto del trabajo se estructura de la siguiente manera. En la sección 2 se introducen los aspectos relevantes de la metodología aplicada para la definición de la ontología. En la sección 3, se define su propósito y alcance a través de preguntas de competencias. En la sección 4, se describe con mayor detalle el modelo conceptual que define la ontología. En la sección 5, se ilustra la propuesta mediante un caso de estudio y se muestra cómo se infieren algunas relaciones de trazabilidad en base a los conceptos definidos en la ontología. En la sección 6 se mencionan trabajos relacionados. Finalmente, en la sección 7 se presentan las conclusiones y trabajos a futuro.

2 Aspectos Metodológicos

En el contexto del desarrollo de software, existen numerosas propuestas en donde las ontologías juegan un rol prominente. Particularmente, en ingeniería de requerimientos, las ontologías se han empleado para minimizar o resolver diferentes tipos de problemas. Por ejemplo, contribuyen a la desambiguación del significado de los requerimientos, posibilitan el análisis de consistencia en requerimientos, obtener requerimientos completos, permiten modelar en forma explícita el conocimiento del dominio, y gestionar el conocimiento y el cambio de requerimientos [4].

Una ontología es una especificación de una conceptualización, donde tal conceptualización es entendida como una versión abstracta y simplificada del mundo que representa. Además, una ontología se refiere a un modelo de dominio formal que describe los conceptos y relaciones de ese dominio [5]. Las ontologías posibilitan la clasificación jerárquica de conceptos de dominio interrelacionados y pueden ser representadas empleando un esquema RDF[1] o el lenguaje OWL[2]. El uso de estos lenguajes permite que las ontologías sean legibles por los humanos e interpretable por las máquinas, permitiendo realizar consultas para obtener conocimiento, así como también inferir nuevo conocimiento. Además, los lenguajes de la Web Semántica, tales como RDF y OWL, facilitan la interoperabilidad en forma significativa. Éstos proveen una estructura social y un marco de trabajo técnico para reusar ontologías existentes, así como también mecanismos formales para expresar equivalencia lógica entre clases y propiedades en diferentes ontologías.

Para desarrollar la ontología se siguió una metodología ad-hoc basada en principios globalmente aceptados en el dominio de la ingeniería ontológica que involucra cuatro pasos, los cuales se encuentran presentes en las metodologías de desarrollo de ontologías más populares [5], [6], , [7], [8]:

- Especificación de requerimientos: identifica el propósito y alcance de la ontología.
- Conceptualización: organiza y convierte una vista informalmente percibida del dominio en una especificación semi-formal usando diagramas UML.
- Implementación/Formalización: implica la codificación de la ontología utilizando un lenguaje formal.
- Evaluación: permite hacer un juicio técnico de la calidad y utilidad de la ontología con respecto a la especificación de requisitos, preguntas de competencia y / o el mundo real.

Considerando la primera etapa de esta metodología, una manera de determinar el alcance de la ontología es bosquejando una lista de preguntas de competencia, según la metodología de Gruninger y Fox [6]. Las preguntas de competencia son preliminares y no necesitan ser exhaustivas. Además, servirán en la etapa de Evaluación para validar y controlar la calidad de la ontología definida, ya que permitirán verificar si ésta contiene suficiente información para responder a las preguntas, y analizar si las respuestas requieren que la ontología tenga mayor nivel de detalle o representación en un área en particular. Las preguntas de competencias generadas para definir el alcance de la ontología propuesta se detallan en la sección 3.

A partir de las preguntas de competencia que se definieron, se identificaron y enumeraron los términos que son importantes para la ontología (véase la segunda columna de la Tabla 1). Inicialmente, se generó una lista de términos sin tener en cuenta si existía solapamiento entre los conceptos que representan, las relaciones entre los términos, o las propiedades que caracterizan a dichos conceptos. En la etapa de Conceptualización, a partir de los términos identificados se deben definir cada una de las clases o conceptos que constituyen la jerarquía de clases de la ontología y sus propiedades [5]. Dado que las clases por sí solas no proveen suficiente información para responder las preguntas de competencia, es necesario describir la estructura interna de los conceptos que representan. Para ello, a partir de los términos identificados se ana-

[1] https://www.w3.org/TR/2004/REC-rdf-primer-20040210/
[2] https://www.w3.org/TR/owl2-overview/

lizó si éstos constituían propiedades intrínsecas, extrínsecas, partes (si el objeto que se está describiendo es estructurado) o relaciones con otros conceptos. Los modelos conceptuales que surgieron como resultado de esta etapa se describen en la sección 4.

Posteriormente, la etapa de Implementación de la ontología se llevó a cabo empleando la herramienta Protégé. Protégé incluye clasificadores deductivos para validar que los modelos sean consistentes y para inferir nueva información en base al análisis de una ontología. El modelo creado se representó en lenguaje OWL el cual es un lenguaje de etiquetado semántico para publicar y compartir ontologías en la Web. Se trata de una recomendación del W3C, y puede emplearse para representar ontologías de forma explícita, es decir, permite definir el significado de términos en vocabularios y las relaciones entre aquellos términos. OWL es una extensión del lenguaje RDF (Resource Description Framework) y emplea las tripletas de RDF, aunque es un lenguaje con más poder expresivo que éste. La ventaja de este lenguaje es que está diseñado para usarse cuando la información contenida en los documentos necesita ser procesada por programas o aplicaciones, en oposición a situaciones donde el contenido solamente necesita ser presentado a los seres humanos, lo cual lo hace adecuado para los objetivos de recuperación y reuso de conocimiento que tiene el enfoque del que forma parte la ontología.

La etapa de Evaluación se está llevando a cabo y se basa en la aplicación de la ontología en diversos casos de estudio, la formalización de las preguntas de competencia en lenguaje de consultas SPARQL[3] y la ejecución de las consultas en varios casos de estudio planteados para intentar responder las preguntas de competencia. Algunos de los resultados obtenidos en la ejecución de las últimas dos etapas mencionadas se introducen en la sección 5.

3 Ontología de Requerimientos. Definición del alcance

Durante la ejecución de la primera etapa de la metodología, se generaron diversas preguntas de competencia, algunas de las cuales se explicitan en la Tabla 1. Para guiar la definición de las mismas y no omitir aspectos de interés, se consideraron distintas dimensiones que permitieron agrupar preguntas de competencias relacionadas. Por ejemplo, preguntas relativas a requerimientos funcionales, casos de uso, casos de prueba, aspectos de trazabilidad, etc. La lista de preguntas de competencias se utiliza en la etapa siguiente para la identificación de los términos que son importantes para la ontología.

4 Ontología de Requerimientos. Modelo conceptual

4.1 Requerimientos funcionales y casos de uso

Los casos de uso describen una secuencia de interacciones que un actor puede llevar a cabo con un sistema para lograr algún resultado de valor [2, 9].

[3] https://www.w3.org/TR/rdf-sparql-query/

Tabla 1. Preguntas de competencia

Preguntas de Competencia	Términos identificados	Grupo
¿Cuáles son los requerimientos funcionales de un sistema? ¿Qué artefactos se emplean para su definición?	Requerimiento funcional, Sistema, Artefactos	Definición requerimientos funcionales
¿Cuáles son los casos de uso especificados para definir un requerimiento funcional dado?	Casos de uso, Requerimiento Funcional	Definición requerimientos funcionales
¿Cuál es el objetivo o meta de un caso de uso dado?	Objetivo, Caso de uso	Definición de caso de uso
¿Qué actores están involucrados en un caso de uso?	Actor, Caso de uso	Definición de caso de uso
¿Cuáles son las precondiciones de un caso de uso?	Precondiciones, Caso de Uso	Definición de caso de uso
¿Cuál es el escenario principal de un caso de uso? ¿Qué pasos abarca un escenario alternativo dado? ¿Existen alternativas o excepciones para el escenario principal?	Caso de Uso, Escenario principal, Paso de escenario	Definición de caso de uso
¿Cuáles son los escenarios alternativos de un caso de uso? ¿Qué pasos están involucrados en un escenario alternativo dado?	Caso de Uso, Escenario alternativo, Paso de escenario	Definición de caso de uso
¿Cuáles son los escenarios de excepción de caso de uso? ¿Qué pasos están involucrados en un escenario de excepción?	Caso de Uso, Escenario de excepción, Paso de escenario	Definición de caso de uso
¿Cuáles son las postcondiciones de un caso de uso dado?	Postcondiciones, Caso de Uso	Definición de caso de uso
¿Qué tipo de modelos se utiliza para transformar especificaciones de comportamiento de requerimientos funcionales a modelos de prueba?	Modelo de prueba	Definición de modelo de comportamiento/prueba
¿Cuáles son los escenarios de casos de prueba definidos para un cierto caso de uso?	Escenario de caso de prueba, Caso de uso	Definición de casos de prueba
¿Qué casos de prueba se derivaron a partir de un caso de uso? ¿Qué relaciones de trazabilidad se mantienen?	Caso de prueba, Caso de uso, Relación de Trazabilidad	Trazabilidad
¿Cuáles son los casos de prueba que se instancian a partir de cierto escenario de caso de prueba?	Caso de prueba, Escenario de caso de prueba	Definición de casos de prueba
¿Cuáles son los tipos de datos de entrada que se definen para un cierto escenario de caso de prueba?	Tipo de dato de entrada, Escenario de caso de prueba	Definición de casos de prueba
¿Cuáles son los tipos de resultados esperados que de definen para un cierto escenario de caso de prueba?	Tipo de resultado esperado, Escenario de caso de prueba	Definición de casos de prueba

Un caso de uso podría abarcar cierta cantidad de actividades relacionadas que tienen un objetivo común. Pohl define los casos de uso como la especificación de acciones, incluyendo secuencias, variantes, y secuencias de error, que el sistema, subsistema, o clase puede realizar interactuando con objetos externos para proveer un servicio de valor [10]. En otras palabras, un caso de uso es una colección de escenarios de uso relacionados, lo que implica además que un escenario es una instancia específica de un caso de uso en la cual se atraviesa, un curso de acción posible.

Para superar las limitaciones del lenguaje natural, para la especificación de los casos de uso se utilizan descripciones textuales basadas en plantillas estructuradas que incluyen una serie de atributos. En la Figura 1 se presenta un modelo que describe los principales conceptos que intervienen en una plantilla de caso de uso [10, 9]. Los objetivos (*Goal*) representan las intenciones de los "stakeholders". Los escenarios (*UseCaseScenario*) documentan las secuencias de interacciones por medio de las cuales se satisfacen o no tales objetivos. Los casos de uso (*UseCase*) agregan a múltiples escenarios que están asociados al mismo objetivo u objetivos. Según se indica en la Figura 1, se pueden tener diferentes tipos de escenarios en un caso de uso. Un escenario principal (*MainScenario*) documenta la secuencia de interacciones o pasos (*ScenarioStep*) que es normalmente ejecutada a fin de satisfacer un objetivo dado. Además, un caso de uso puede tener uno más escenarios alternativos (*AlternativeScenario*), los cuales documentan una secuencia de pasos que puede ser ejecutada en lugar del escenario principal y que resultan en la satisfacción de los objetivos asociados al escenario principal. En cuanto a los escenarios de excepción (*ExceptionScenario*), éstos documentan una secuencia de interacciones que se ejecuta en lugar de cualquier otro escenario (principal, alternativo, o excepción), a causa de la ocurrencia de un evento excepcional. Esto implica, que los objetivos asociados con el escenario principal no pueden ser satisfechos.

Dentro del proceso de desarrollo de un software, los casos de uso representan una primera definición de los requerimientos funcionales que los desarrolladores deben implementar. Además, éstos pueden ser utilizados para conducir la generación de los casos de prueba [11, 10] que se ejecutarán para verificar que el software cumple con los requerimientos planteados.

Un caso de prueba (*TestCase*) especifica la información requerida para la ejecución de una prueba. Comprende las precondiciones requeridas para la ejecución de la prueba (*TestPreconditions*), el conjunto de entradas y salidas esperadas (*TestInput* y *TestExpectedOutput*), las instrucciones para la prueba (cómo las entradas son pasadas al objeto de prueba y cómo las salidas son leídas desde el objeto de prueba) y las postcondiciones esperadas (TestExpectedPostconditions) [10]. Esta definición puede ser plasmada en el modelo conceptual presentado en la Figura 2.

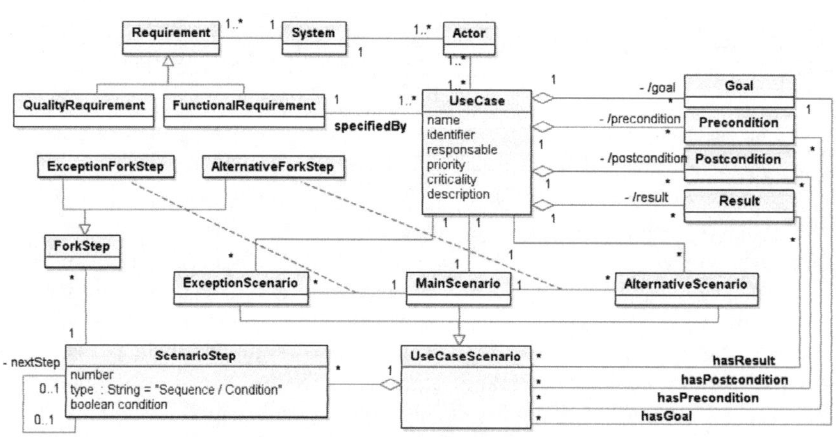

Fig. 1. Modelo conceptual de casos de usos y escenarios.

Un caso de prueba se ejecuta pasando la entrada especificada en el caso de prueba al objeto de prueba (*TestObject*). Por lo tanto, la ejecución de un caso de prueba comprende una secuencia de interacciones entre los elementos en el contexto de la prueba (por ejemplo, los testers o usuarios) y el objeto de la prueba. Al momento de definir un caso de prueba, las interacciones correspondientes pueden ser definidas por medio de escenarios a diferentes niveles de abstracción. Pohl define en [10] el concepto de escenario de caso de prueba (*TestCaseScenario*) para hacer referencia a "tipos de casos de prueba", los cuales describen a conjuntos de casos de prueba que tienen cierto tipo de entradas y ciertos tipos de salidas esperadas (*TestInputType* y *TestExpectedOutputType*, respectivamente).

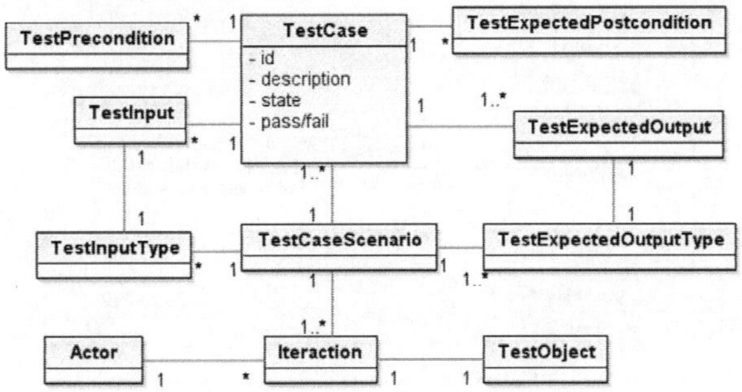

Fig. 2. Modelo conceptual de casos de pruebas.

4.2 Derivación de casos de prueba a partir de casos de uso

Diversos autores han propuesto estrategias para la derivación de casos de pruebas basadas en requerimientos [12, 11, 10]. Mientras que unos plantean la posibilidad de derivarlos directamente a partir de artefactos de requerimientos (como podrán ser una SRS, diagramas de casos de uso, o casos de usos textuales estructurados) [1], otros proponen su derivación a partir de los llamados "modelos de pruebas" (Model-based test-case derivation) [13, 14]. En este último caso, un modelo de prueba sirve como la base para derivar sistemáticamente casos de pruebas. Técnicas tales como las máquinas de estados (autómatas finitos, diagramas de estados UML, diagramas de actividades UML), y diagramas de flujos son adecuadas para crear los modelos de prueba. En este trabajo, se adaptó el enfoque de derivación de casos de prueba basado en requerimientos usando un modelo que propone Pohl [10] para la derivación de casos de prueba a partir de casos de uso según se presenta en la Figura 3. Dado que un caso de uso contiene uno o varios escenarios de caso de uso asociados (Figura 1), un modelo de prueba para este artefacto debe desarrollarse en base a los escenarios que posee el caso de uso. Luego, los escenarios de casos de prueba individuales se identifican en base al modelo de prueba generado. Finalmente, los casos de prueba se derivan a partir de los escenarios de casos de prueba, especificando valores concretos para las entradas y resultados esperados.

En trabajos previos [3], los autores han desarrollado un método para la generación de modelos de prueba, donde el comportamiento de un caso de uso se modela mediante un AFD (Autómata Finito Determinístico, *DFA*). Este tipo de modelo de prueba puede ser empleado en la derivación de casos de prueba de tipo de sistema y aceptación (de tipo caja negra), de manera que sea posible generar todos los flujos sobre el caso de uso que se desean probar. Para reflejar esta propuesta, se incorpora en el modelo conceptual de la Figura 3 una relación de generalización/especialización entre los conceptos *TestModel* y *DFA*.

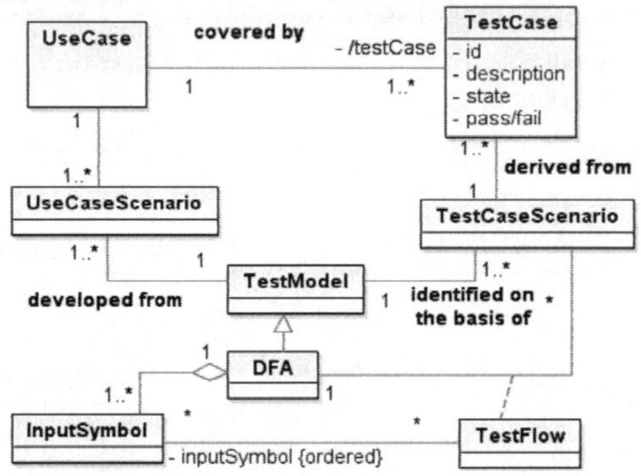

Fig. 3. Empleo de AFD como modelo de prueba.

Una ventaja importante que se logra con este enfoque para derivar casos de pruebas a partir de casos de uso son los enlaces de trazabilidad que se establecen entre los casos de uso y los casos de prueba. Esta trazabilidad entre artefactos permite determinar, por ejemplo, si un caso de uso es cubierto por los casos de pruebas definidos en base a qué criterio y en qué grado.

4.3 Trazabilidad

La trazabilidad de requerimientos refiere a la habilidad de describir y seguir la vida de un requerimiento tanto hacia delante como hacia atrás. Es decir, desde su origen, a través de su desarrollo y especificación, hasta su posterior despliegue y uso, durante todos los períodos de refinamiento e iteración en cualquiera de estas fases [15, 16]. La trazabilidad soporta, entre otras cosas, validar si un requerimiento ha sido considerado durante la implementación del sistema.

La información sobre la trazabilidad es usualmente capturada como relaciones o enlaces de trazabilidad. Entre los artefactos del proceso de diseño pueden establecerse diferentes tipos de relaciones de trazabilidad [10, 16]. Pohl sugiere que es conveniente contar con un modelo para definir y estructurar la información de la trazabilidad y los tipos de relaciones necesarias para un proyecto de desarrollo concreto [10]. Este modelo permite especificar entre qué artefactos se establecerán y qué tipo de relaciones de trazabilidad serán capturados. La Figura 4 introduce el modelo de trazabilidad que será implementado en la ontología propuesta. En dicha figura, los artefactos presentados en las secciones 3.1. y 3.2, cuya trazabilidad se desea representar, están definidos como especializaciones de la clase *TraceableArtifact*. Vale aclarar que una relación de trazabilidad tiene como origen y destino instancias de artefactos traceables.

Existen cinco categorías de tipos de relaciones de trazabilidad: *Condition*, *Content*, *Abstraction*, *Evolution* y *Miscellaneous* [8]. La ontología propuesta contempla estas cinco categorías. Sin embargo, por razones de espacio sólo algunas de ellas se muestran en la Figura 4. Los tipos de relaciones de trazabilidad que corresponden a la categoría *Evolution*, documentan relaciones temporales que se pueden establecer entre artefactos de requerimientos y/o entre éstos y otros artefactos del proceso de desarrollo. Dentro de esta categoría, en este trabajo se introducen los tipos *Formalizes* y *Refines*. *Formalizes* establece una relación de trazabilidad entre los artefactos *A* y *B* si *A* constituye una especificación formal del artefacto B. Por ejemplo, esta relación puede establecerse entre un escenario y una red de Petri, la cual formaliza su comportamiento, o entre un caso de uso y un diagrama de actividad UML. En tanto, el tipo de relación *Refines* se establece entre dos artefactos *A* y *B*, si *A* describe al artefacto *B* con mayor detalle. Por ejemplo, un escenario refina a un objetivo (ya que refleja un ejemplo de cómo alcanzarlo), o una plantilla de caso de uso refina un diagrama de caso de uso (ya que muestra las interacciones o pasos de un escenario de un elemento caso de uso presente en el diagrama).El tercer tipo de relación de trazabilidad que se presenta en este artículo es la relación *CoveredBy* (especialización de la relación *Miscelaneous*) que vincula un artefacto de prueba *A* con un artefacto de requerimiento *B* y que establece que *A* es utilizado para verificar *B*. Por ejemplo, cuando un caso de prueba se emplea para verificar un caso de uso, cubriendo cierto flujo o secuencia de pasos del mismo.

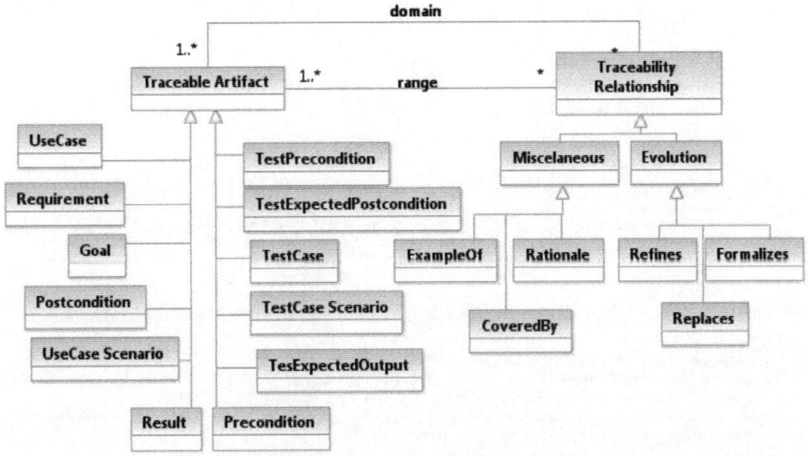

Fig. 4. Modelo de trazabilidad Propuesto

En la ontología propuesta, estas relaciones de trazabilidad mencionadas se computan mediante la definición de reglas de inferencia, las cuales se aplican a partir de las relaciones explícitas propuestas en los modelos conceptuales de las Figuras 1 a 3. Por cuestiones de espacio, sólo algunas de estas reglas serán ilustradas en la sección 5.

5 Ontología de Requerimientos. Formalización y Evaluación

La ontología se formalizó en OWL en términos de clases, individuos, y propiedades de estos individuos y clases, así como relaciones que existen entre ellas. En particular,

OWL permite expresar los siguientes diferentes tipos de propiedades: (i) propiedades de objeto, las cuales permiten definir relaciones entre individuos; (ii) propiedades de tipo de dato, las cuales definen relaciones entre individuos y literales (por ejemplo, strings, enteros, etc.); y propiedades de anotaciones (annotations), que pueden ser usadas para describir metadatos de individuos, clases y propiedades, tales como el idioma en que se encuentra, definiciones y comentarios de estos conceptos. Además, para las propiedades de objeto definidas se especificó su dominio y rango, mientras que para las propiedades de tipo de dato se indicó su tipo, valores admitidos y cardinalidad.

En particular, para los conceptos relacionados con la trazabilidad se ha implementado el concepto *TraceableArtifact* como una clase (constructor owl:Class). En cambio, los conceptos que representan los diferentes tipos de relaciones de trazabilidad se implementaron como propiedades de objetos (constructor owl:ObjectProperty). Es importante destacar que, a fin de lograr la navegabilidad por las relaciones de trazabilidad en ambos sentidos, se definieron también relaciones inversas de las asociaciones mostradas en la Figura 4 (*covers*, *isRefinedBy* e *isFormalizedBy*). Asimismo, las instancias de las relaciones de trazabilidad propuestas y de sus inversas no están explícitamente definidas en la ontología, sino que se infieren a través de reglas y la ejecución de un razonador. En la Figura 5 se presentan algunas vistas que se pueden observar en la especificación de la ontología en Protégé.

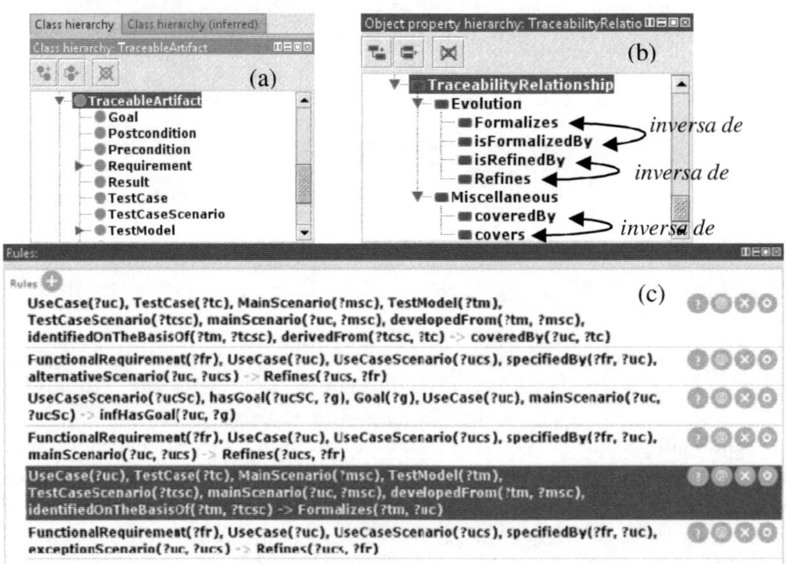

Fig. 5. Algunas vistas capturadas desde Protégé - Implementación de la ontología. (a) Jerarquía de Clases - (b) Jerarquía de Propiedades de Objetos - (c) Reglas

En particular allí, se muestra las jerarquías de clases (a) y relaciones de objetos (b) así como algunas de las reglas utilizadas para inferir las poblaciones de las relaciones *CoveredBy*, *Formalizes* y *Refines* (c). En los párrafos siguientes se explicará brevemente la definición de algunas de estas reglas por medio de un ejemplo.

La Figura 6 presenta un modelo de objetos que representa las diferentes instancias que componen al artefacto dado por un caso de uso *CU-01*, que modela las interacciones de un usuario que accede a un sistema. Las instancias que se muestran en ese modelo se definieron como individuos (*owl:NamedIndividual*) en la ontología.

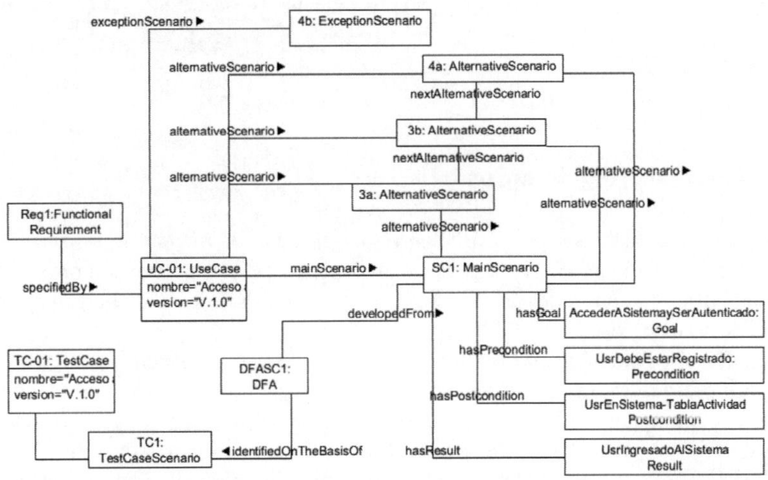

Fig. 6. Modelo de objetos del caso de uso CU-01 y su relación con otros artefactos.

La Figura 7 presenta las inferencias obtenidas correspondientes a las relaciones de trazabilidad propuestas, aplicadas a las instancias del ejemplo de la Figura 6. En ella se muestran dos vistas parciales del editor de ontologías de Protegé con los resultados de las inferencias computadas. En particular, la parte superior de la Figura 7 muestra que la instancia que representa al requerimiento *Req1* es refinado (*refinedBy*, inversa de la relación *Refines*) por los escenarios *4b*, *SC1*, *3b*, *4a*, *3a*. En la parte inferior, se muestra las relaciones de trazabilidad inferidas para el caso de uso CU-01. En particular, es posible inferir qué artefactos refinaron al requerimiento *Req1*. Asimismo, se infiere que el caso de uso *CU-01* se relaciona con TC-01 (instancia de *TestCase*) mediante la relación de trazabilidad *coveredBy* y con la instancia *DFASC1* (instancia de *DFA*) mediante la relación de trazabilidad *isFormalizedBy*. De esta manera, las reglas definidas permiten determinar los casos de prueba definidos para cubrir los flujos posibles de un caso de uso y, también mediante qué artefacto fue formalizado dicho caso de uso, el cual fue utilizado como modelo de prueba.

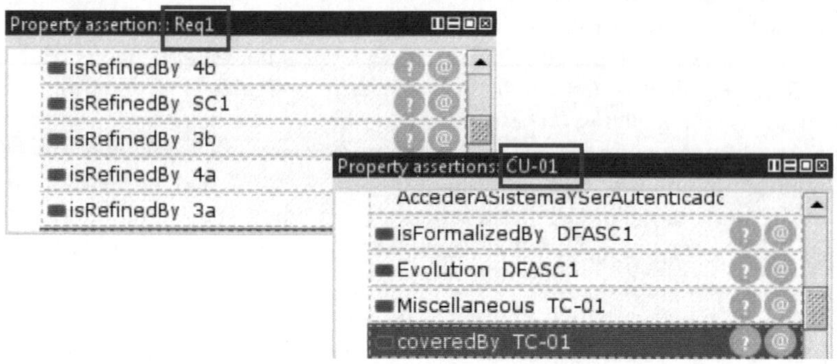

Fig. 7. Ejemplos de inferencias de relaciones de trazabilidad entre artefactos

6 Trabajos relacionados

Existen diversos trabajos que se basan en ontologías para la mejora de las actividades de Ingeniería de Requerimientos, pero pocos han aplicado éstas para lograr interoperabilidad entre herramientas para la especificación de casos de uso y herramientas de gestión de casos prueba.

Una revisión sistemática de literatura en el uso de ontologías en ingeniería de requerimientos, que abarca 66 publicaciones entre 2007 y 2013 [4], reporta que son escasas las ontologías desarrolladas que abarcan más de una fase del proceso de ingeniería de requerimientos. La mayoría se limita a la fase de especificación, seguidas por algunas que incluyen también análisis, gestión y elicitación. Finalmente, una pequeña minoría menor al 7% de los trabajos consideran las etapas de validación de requerimientos.

En relación a los tipos de artefactos de requerimientos que las propuestas con enfoques ontológicos han abordado, el mismo estudio [4] reporta que el 43% se basan en requerimientos textuales (utilizando lenguaje natural), representado alrededor del 24% los que definen a los escenarios y casos de uso como artefactos de requerimientos. En este estudio no se mencionan ontologías que se integren a otras fases del proceso de desarrollo, dentro de las cuales se incluye la presentada en este trabajo que mantiene relaciones de trazabilidad entre artefactos de requerimientos y testing.

Otro trabajo reciente [11] realiza un análisis del estado del arte en estrategias para la generación de casos de prueba basados en requerimientos, considerando varios criterios entre ellos qué tipo de artefacto de entrada toman, si emplean modelo de pruebas intermedio o no, las técnicas de transformación de modelos usadas entre otros, y el grado de cobertura, entre otros. Entre los resultados se reportan escasos trabajos que hagan énfasis en la trazabilidad entre artefactos y en cómo implementarla. Asimismo, no se mencionan propuestas que tengan un enfoque basado en ontologías, como el que aquí se propone. El uso de un enfoque ontológico permitiría: i) compartir un entendimiento común de la estructura de información entre las personas involucradas en la especificación de casos de uso y casos de prueba así como entre las aplicaciones que soportan estas actividades, ii) la reutilización del conocimiento en otros proyectos de desarrollo, y iii) explicitar las relaciones de trazabilidad que existen entre los artefactos resultantes de las actividades mencionadas (que se encuentran implícitas en el conocimiento representado).

7 Conclusiones y trabajos futuros

En este trabajo se presentó un enfoque basado en ontologías para la especificación de requerimientos funcionales basados en casos de uso estructurados y casos de prueba, que permite la representación de los enlaces de trazabilidad entre estos artefactos y los artefactos intermedios generados que dan soporte a la generación automática de casos de prueba. La propuesta conlleva las siguientes ventajas:

i) Posibilita que las características del sistema que son relevantes para los stakeholders clientes o usuarios sean documentadas como artefactos de tipo plantilla de casos de uso;

iii) provee el concepto de Modelo de prueba que permite utilizar diversos modelos formales para derivar un conjunto de casos de pruebas, especificando cierto criterio de cobertura. En particular, se ha aplicado un método de transformación de casos de uso en autómatas finitos deterministas que ha sido desarrollado en otro trabajo.

iv) propicia la interoperabilidad entre herramientas de soporte para la especificación de casos de uso y de gestión de casos de pruebas, ya que se basa en un modelo conceptual que soporta los metamodelos de esas herramientas.

v) permite inferir relaciones preestablecidas de trazabilidad entre artefactos de requerimientos y entre éstos y artefactos de casos de uso, y definir nuevas relaciones a través de la especificación de nuevas reglas.

Los resultados preliminares obtenidos con ejemplos de artefactos de requerimientos de diversos proyectos han permitido concluir que la propuesta es válida y de potencial aplicación en la industria del software, la cual se enfrenta todavía a desafíos y necesidades [12] en relación a la especificación de requerimientos bien estructurados y no ambiguos, a la generación de pruebas basadas en requerimientos, y la gestión de enlaces de trazabilidad entre requerimientos y casos de prueba.

Como trabajo a futuro, se continuará extendiendo la ontología con otros artefactos de requerimientos, como modelos UML (diagramas de clase, estado y actividad), y otros posibles tipos de enlaces de trazabilidad que involucren a otros artefactos del proceso de diseño.

8 Agradecimientos

Este trabajo ha sido financiado por la Universidad Tecnológica Nacional (Proyecto IPN4409 "Herramientas y Métodos de soporte a la Ingeniería de Software: requerimientos, estrategias ágiles, y calidad de procesos y productos") y el CONICET. Se agradece el apoyo brindado por estas instituciones.

References

1. Allmann, C., Denger, C., and Olsson, T, Analysis of Requirements-based Test Case Creation Techniques, IESE-Report No. 046.05/E, 2005.
2. Jacobson, I., Christerson, M., Jonsson, P., Övergad, G., Object Oriented Software Engineering. A Use Case Driven Approach. Addison Wesley, 1992.
3. Roldán, M.L., Vegetti, M., Gonnet, S., Marciszak, M., Leone, H. "Un Modelo Conceptual para la Especificación y Trazabilidad de Requerimientos Funcionales basados en Casos de Uso y Casos de Prueba," Congreso Nacional de Ingeniería en Informática/Sistemas de Información (CONAISII 2017), Santa Fe, 2017.
4. Dermeval, D., Vilela, J., Bittencourt, I. I., Castro, J., Isotani, S., Brito, P. , "A Systematic Review on the Use of Ontologies in Requirements Engineering", 2014 Brazilian Symposium on Software Engineering, Maceio, 2014, pp. 1-10.
5. Uschold, M., Gruninger M., "Ontologies: Principles, Methods and Applications", Knowledge Engineering Review, 1996.
6. Gruninger M., Fox M. S., "Methodology for the Design and Evaluation of Ontologies", IJCAI Workshop on Basic Ontological in Knowledge Sharing, Montreal, Canada, 1995.
7. Fernández-López, M., Gómez-Pérez, A., Sierra, J.P., Sierra, A.P..Building a chemical ontology using methontology and the ontology design environment. Intelligent Systems14,37–46, 1999.
8. Suárez-Figueroa, M.C., Gómez-Pérez, A., Motta, E., Gangeni, A. Ontology Engineering in a Networked World. Springer, Berlin, 2012.
9. Wiegers, K.E., Software Requirements. 3rd Edition, Microsoft Press, 2013
10. Pohl, K., Requirements Engineering: Fundamentals, Principles, and Techniques, Springer, 2010.
11. Mustafa, A., Wan-Kadir, W.M.N., Ibrahim, I., "Comparative Evaluation of the State-of-art Requirements-based Test Case Generation Approaches," International Journal on Advanced Science, Engineering and Information Technology, vol. 7, no. 4-2, pp. 1567-1573, 2017.
12. Hesari, S., Behjati, R., Yue, T. "Towards a systematic requirement-based test generation framework: Industrial challenges and needs," 2013 21st IEEE International Requirements Engineering Conference (RE), Rio de Janeiro, 2013, pp. 261-266.
13. Pretschner, A., Prenninger, W., Wagner, S., Kühnel, C., Baumgartner, M., Sostawa, B., Zölch, R., Stauner, T., "One evaluation of model-based testing and its automation." Proceedings of the 27th international conference on Software engineering (ICSE '05), ACM, NY, USA, 2005, pp. 392-401.
14. Reuys, A., Reis, S., Kamsties, E., Pohl, K., "The ScenTED Method for Testing Software Product Lines," Software Product Lines, 2006, Springer Berlin Heidelberg, pp. 479-520.
15. Gotel, O.C.Z., Finkelstein, A.C.W., 1993. An Analysis of the Requirements Traceability Problem, Technical Report TR-93- 41, Department of Computing, Imperial College.
16. Ramesh, B., Jarke, M. Toward Reference Models for Requirements Traceability, IEEE Transactions On Software Engineering, Vol. 27, No. 1, 2001.

Do users talk about the software in my product? Analyzing user reviews on IoT products

Kamonphop Srisopha, Pooyan Behnamghader, and Barry Boehm

University of Southern California, Los Angeles CA 90089, USA
{srisopha,pbehnamg,boehm}@usc.edu

Abstract. Consumer product reviews are an invaluable source of data because they contain a wide range of information that could help requirement engineers to meet user needs. Recent studies have shown that tweets about software applications and reviews on App Stores contain useful information, which enable a more responsive software requirements elicitation. However, all of these studies' subjects are merely software applications. Information on system software, such as embedded software, operating systems, and firmware, are overlooked, unless reviews of a product using them are investigated. Challenges in investigating these reviews could come from the fact that there is a huge volume of data available, as well as the fact that reviews of such products are diverse in nature, meaning that they may contain information mostly on hardware components or broadly on the product as a whole. Motivated by these observations, we conduct an exploratory study using a dataset of 7198 review sentences from 6 Internet of Things (IoT) products. Our qualitative analysis demonstrates that a sufficient quantity of software related information exists in these reviews. In addition, we investigate the performance of two supervised machine learning techniques (Support Vector Machines and Convolutional Neural Networks) for classification of information contained in the reviews. Our results suggest that, with a certain setup, these two techniques can be used to classify the information automatically with high precision and recall.

Keywords: Passive Crowdsourcing, Internet of Things, User Reviews, Text Classification, Software Evolution

1 Introduction

Online retail stores (*e.g.,* Amazon or eBay) provide a convenient platform for producers to compete and sell their products. They also provide consumers with the ability to compare a variety of options and purchase the one that best fits their budgets and needs. Consumers can share their experience of using a product through writing a review after purchase. This helps other consumers to have a better understanding of the quality of the products.

Not only do reviews help consumers make more informed decisions, but it also helps manufacturers get feedback on their products so that they can improve them over time. In fact, reviews contain a wealth of information that can be used to create new requirements. The idea of mining user reviews to improve the quality of the product is a form of "Passive Crowdsourcing." According to [8], Crowdsourcing "represents the act of a company or institution taking a function once performed by employees and outsourcing it to an undefined (and generally large) network of people in the form of an open call." Passive Crowdsourcing simply means harnessing the power of the crowd without their knowledge.

Mining app store reviews to improve the quality of software has already gained the attention of researchers [3]. In comparison with user reviews of a software application, user reviews of an IoT product are not all about software. They can be about different product elements, such as software, hardware, customer service, etc. In particular, they contain information such as subjective product evaluations, personal experiences, problems encountered, product descriptions, and users' visions on how the product should be. As a result, reviews of IoT products are more diverse. If such information in this huge volume of data is detected and classified correctly and efficiently, different stakeholders, such as software engineers, hardware engineers, etc. can better meet user expectations and needs, thus accelerating product or software evolution processes.

Motivated by these observations, we conducted an exploratory study by analyzing 1491 verified purchase reviews (7198 review sentences) of 6 IoT products to investigate how IoT product reviews can be categorized, whether enough software related information exists, and how much of this information is useful for software developers and requirement engineers. We also studied the extent to which two supervised machine learning techniques (SVM and CNN) can be used to classify information in the dataset automatically, and identified configurations that can effectively improve the classification performance. We believe that the work presented in this paper contributed to the growing knowledge in this area.

The rest of the paper is organized as follows. We formally define our research problems and describe data collection in Section 2. In Section 3, we describe the procedure to answer each research question and report the results. Thereafter in Section 4, we present factors that may affect the validity of our study. We discuss the related literature in Section 5. Finally, in Section 6, we conclude the paper and outline plans for future research.

2 Research Design

2.1 Research Questions

To guide our research, we formulate the following research questions:

RQ1: How can IoT product reviews be categorized?

- *Motivation.* As aforementioned, IoT product reviews can contain a wide range of information. This information includes, but is not limited to: subjective product evaluations (about hardware, software, or the product as a whole), personal experiences, problems encountered, product descriptions, and users' visions on how the product should be. In this question, we investigate what types of information are in the reviews.

RQ2: How much information in the studied product reviews is relevant to software engineers?

- *Motivation.* Once the taxonomy is defined in RQ1, the natural next step is to manually examine the reviews and to investigate the distribution of each category, *i.e.*, how often each category occurs. Specifically, we aim to find out how much of this data can help to enable a more responsive software requirements elicitation and software evolution process.

RQ3: How effective is a machine learning approach in classifying the reviews?

- *Motivation.* Sifting through each review manually to find the right information is a laborious task. Since SVM and CNN are often used for classification tasks, we investigate the extent to which they can be used to classify an unseen review based on the taxonomy previously defined in RQ1 automatically.

2.2 Data Collection

To conduct our analysis, we sampled 1491 verified purchase reviews from 6 IoT products from Amazon. The data was collected on September 22, 2017 through a web crawling tool we developed. Table 1 describes the characteristics of the 6 IoT products we considered.

Table 1. Details of the studied products

Product name	ASIN	Domain	Total Reviews
Amazon Echo Dot	B01DFKC2SO	Smart Home	54230
Fitbit Blaze	B019VM3F2M	Smart Watch	7349
GoPro Hero4 Silver	B00NIYJF6U	Action Camera	2327
PlayStation 4	B01LRLJV28	Gaming Console	3135
Pebble Time	B0106IS5XY	Smart Watch	1577
Amazon Echo Show	B01J24C0TI	Smart Home	2565

To mitigate some threats to the external validity, we selected products from various domains: smart home, smart watch, gaming console, and action camera. It is important to note that on Amazon, a user can subjectively give a star rating on a scale of 1 to 5. However, as far as we know, there is no clear cut definition to what each star in a five-star rating system means. Furthermore, there is no limit on how many characters a user can write for a review. Therefore, as to eliminate some bias in the dataset, we sampled 50 reviews per each star rating of each product (total of 250 per product) where each review consists of no more than 20 sentences. We used NLTK[1]'s sentence tokenizer to split a review into a list of sentences. However, at the time of our data collection, 2-star reviews of PlayStation 4 and of GoPro Hero4 Silver contain less than 50 reviews that meet the aforementioned criteria. In this case, we only fetched reviews that meet the criteria from them, 46 and 45 reviews respectively. Table 2 shows the number of

[1] http://www.nltk.org/

sentences for each star rating of each product. For replicability, our dataset is publicly available here[2].

Table 2. Number of sentences per star-rating of each product

#	Product	Star rating					Total
		1-star	2-star	3-star	4-star	5-star	
1	Amazon Echo Dot	155	282	280	385	354	1456
2	Fitbit Blaze	234	290	313	361	350	1548
3	GoPro Hero 4 Silver	228	196	165	278	357	1224
4	PlayStation 4	134	183	146	99	158	720
5	Pebble Watch	167	189	189	267	336	1148
6	Amazon Echo Show	235	254	149	204	260	1102
					Total sentences:		7198

3 Methodology and Results

3.1 RQ1

Procedure:

In this section, we discuss the procedure we used to answer **RQ1: How can IoT product reviews be categorized?**

We started by searching past literature for similar efforts on analyzing user reviews on IoT products. However, what we found was that most past literature limits its scope by focusing on analyzing user reviews of mobile applications on App Stores, such as Google Play or the Apple Store [9][13], and tweets on Twitter [4]. As a result, user reviews on firmware, operating systems, or embedded software are not explored, unless reviews of a product using them are investigated. In doing so, we cannot assume that the majority of review sentences are software related. Therefore, a taxonomy defined by most past literature would not work.

Top-level taxonomy We conducted three *content analysis* sessions [16] in order to see what information or pattern was contained in the reviews. Upon initial data inspection involving a few review samples, the first author came up with a rudimentary taxonomy which consists of 7 categories: *User Background, Usage Scenario, Software Feature Request, Software Complaint, Software Praise, Hardware Complaint*, and *Hardware Praise.* This resulted in our first draft taxonomy. In the next step, we assigned 52 Master's level CS students, who were taking a graduate level software engineering course at USC, to analyze and categorize IoT product review sentences based on the first draft taxonomy as the course's requirements elicitation activity[3]. Note that students could suggest a category if they felt that a review sentence cannot be classified into any categories in the first draft taxonomy. The responses were gathered and new categories suggested by students were noted. In the third step, a team of 4 Master's student, who

[2] https://goo.gl/M6BcB1
[3] https://goo.gl/wdAtUC

were not part of the students in the second step, and one PhD student, the first author, validated categories suggested in the second step by merging similar categories together and redefining them. The taxonomy resulting from this step consisted of 8 top-level categories, shown in Table 3. Additionally and initially, two of the top-level categories (Hardware and Software) had 5 additional sub-categories: *Praise, Complaint, Inquiry, Request*, and *Other*. However, through examining software categories that are relevant to software engineers from past literature discussed in detail in the next paragraph, we adopted its software taxonomy instead of our original 5 sub-categories. We adapted the sub-categories for Hardware category in the same way.

Software-level taxonomy In this level, we can assume that all review sentences are software related. Therefore, we could use the existing taxonomy from past literature. We used the *Taxonomy for Software Maintenance and Evolution* purposed by [18] as a starting point because they already evaluated the relevance of each category for developers performing software evolution and maintenance tasks. However, we modified the definitions to better reflect the nature of our data. In addition, upon inspecting the data, we found that sentences expressing dissatisfaction with the software of a product often contained information describing why the user was dissatisfied. We believe this is relevant to software developers and requirement engineers in order to better meet user needs or expectations. We added these sentences to the Problem Discovery category. On the other hand, sentences expressing satisfaction conveyed little value for software evolution process [18]. In this case, we combined these sentences with the Information Giving category. Table 4 shows the 4 sub-categories for Software category used in our study.

Table 3. 8 Top-level categories and their respective definitions

#	Category	Definition
1	Hardware	Sentences mentioning a hardware component, a physical characteristic, or a physical part of the product. ***Note:*** can be broken down into 4 sub-categories*****.
2	Software	Sentences mentioning a product's functionality, a set of capabilities, or GUI. ***Note:*** can be broken down. See Table 4.
3	General	Sentences describing the product as a whole, including persuading to and dissuading against buying or using the product.
4	User Background	Sentences discussing the background of the reviewer or the reviewer's character.
5	Other Product	Sentences referring to another product (*e.g.,* competitive products, accessories, products that should be used with this product, etc.).
6	Usage Scenario	Sentences mentioning a way to use the product, *i.e.,* a use case scenario.
7	Customer Service	Sentences recounting on the reviewer's experience with Amazon services (*e.g.,* package, return, shipment, etc).
8	Miscellaneous	Sentences that are not covered by or do not belong to another category.

*****the definition of each sub-category is similar to the definitions provided in Table 4, but with Hardware oriented terms.

Table 4. Categories and their respective definitions for software-related sentences

Category	Definition
Information Giving	Sentences expressing satisfaction or informing other users or the sellers about the functionality of the product
Inquiry	Sentences related to attempts to obtain information or help from other users or the seller about the software
Feature Request	Sentences expressing ideas, suggestions, or needs for improving or enhancing the software or functionality of the product
Problem Discovery	Sentences expressing dissatisfaction or describing issues or unexpected behaviors with the software of the product

Results:

The resulted taxonomy consisting of 8 top-level categories and their respective definitions is shown in Table 3. The second level of the Software category is shown in Table 4. This layer is also applicable to the Hardware category with hardware-oriented definitions.

3.2 RQ2

Procedure:

In this section, we discuss the procedure and applied the taxonomy defined in RQ1 to answer **RQ2: How much information in the studied product reviews is relevant to software engineers?**

Manual Classification To create the ground truth dataset for our experiment, we manually classified each sentence in the dataset. A team consists of 4 Master's level CS students and one PhD students, the first author, accomplished this task. To mitigate some threats to the internal validity, we performed the following procedures:

First, we created a category guide, which consists of the precise details of the category definitions and examples. Second, we conducted a pilot run by randomly selecting 80 reviews from the dataset and having each annotator annotate the selected reviews. We calculated the inter-rater reliability to assess validity and subjectivity of this pilot run using Fleiss's Kappa since we have more than two annotators [2]. The inter-rater reliability value was 0.65, which is in the *"Substantial Agreement"* range according to [11], one level below *"Almost Perfect Agreement"* range. Third, we held several meetings before actual classifying the data to make sure that all annotators had a mutual understanding of the concept regarding the definitions of the categories in the taxonomy and the descriptions of the products. Fourth, we instructed each annotator to annotate at most 100 sentences per day as to avoid errors due to fatigue. Fifth, the first author individually performed a quality check after the dataset was labeled by randomly selecting 50% of the entire dataset. Any inconsistencies detected, *i.e.,* assigned categories that did not adhere to the definitions in the taxonomy for that sentence, were reviewed and fixed. Sixth, categories of software-level categories were classified by only one annotator. This total process spanned 4 weeks.

Table 5 shows examples of sentences and their corresponding categories from the manual classification process.

Table 5. Examples of sentences classified by using the taxonomy in RQ1

Review Sentence	Top-level category	Second level
"I developed a Class IV allergic reaction to the wrist band."	Hardware	Hardware Problem Discovery
"The companion android app is crap though - very slow to start and not very functional."	Software	Software Problem Discovery
"Stay away from this product!"	General	
"Alexa does not answer general questions as Google Home seems to."	Software, Other Product	Software Information Giving
"I got the camera on time but the LCD screen is not working."	Customer Service, Hardware	Hardware Problem Discovery
"The software needs work: i am constantly having to uninstall reinstall the pebble time app for android."	Software	Software Problem Discovery
"If I could set my alarm to wake me up M-F @ 7 am that would be a 5 star moment."	Software	Software Feature Request
"Bought this as a birthday present for my daughter a month ago and gave it to her last night."	User Background	

Results:

The results of the manual classification process for the top-level categories is shown in Table 6. Only 26.72% of the review sentences were found to be software related which means that the majority of review sentences are not directly applicable to software engineers. Table 7 shows the manual classification results of only software related sentences by applying the taxonomy in Table 4. Only 8.79% (2.35% of all sentences) contain feedback on how to improve or enhance the software, 45.40% (12.12% of all sentences) contain information about problems users encountered or what made users dissatisfied with the software, and 1.09% (0.29% of all sentences) express an effort to acquire information about the software. This means that only 14.79% of all sentences are directly applicable to software engineers. These findings answer **RQ2**.

Table 6. Manual Classification Results for Top-level categories

Category	Count*	Frequency %
Hardware	1870	25.98%
Software	1923	26.72%
General	2290	31.81%
User Background	1711	23.77%
Other Product	549	7.63%
Usage Scenario	504	7.00%
Customer Service	199	2.76%
Miscellaneous	291	4.04%

*Each sentence can be classified into one or more top-level categories

Table 7. Manual Classification Results for software related sentences

Category	Count	Frequency % (software only)	Frequency % (all sentences)
Information Giving	860	44.72%	11.94%
Inquiry	21	1.09%	0.29%
Feature Request	169	8.79%	2.35%
Problem Discovery	873	45.40%	12.12%

3.3 RQ3

Procedure:

In this section, we discuss the background and procedure to answer **RQ3: How effective is a machine learning approach in classifying the reviews?** In particular, we can break this research question down into three sub-questions: first, what is the performance of each supervised machine learning technique (SVM vs CNN), second, what combination gives us the highest precision and recall, and third, how generalizable is the model.

In contrast with multi-class classification where each sentence is assigned to only one label, in our top-level categories, each sentence can be classified into one or more categories in the top-level. Such a problem is referred to as multi-label classification.

Text preprocessing We preprocessed the reviews in the following orders: (1) utilizing sentence tokenizer provided by NLTK, a widely used natural language processing toolkit in Python, to breakdown reviews into sentences, (2) lowercasing the resulted sentences, and (3) tokenizing the words on space and punctuation, removing any non-English character.

Vector Space Model:

Term frequency-inverse document frequency scheme (tf-idf) Tf-idf consists of two components: the term frequency and the inverse document frequency. The former considers the number of occurrences of a term in a document, while the latter takes into consideration the information on the frequency of a term in the entire corpus. In other words, the scheme reflects how important a term is to a document in a corpus [19]. This scheme has been widely used in information retrieval and text mining.

Word2Vec (W2V). This is based on the distributional hypothesis, which states that words that appear in a similar context tend to share similar meanings [6]. It learns to group similar words together in a vector space in an unsupervised manner. The algorithms to generate vector representations of words are described in detail in [15]. It has been widely found that, with enough data and context, word2vec model can improve the performance of a classifier [10]. To harness the power of this model, we trained our word2vec model on 2.4 million Amazon reviews (over 12 million sentences) based on the dataset made available by [14]. Note that we applied the aforementioned steps for text preprocessing before training a word2vec model. We only used reviews from Electronics and Apps for Androids category.

Implementation:

Support Vector Machines We used Scikit-learn[4], a widely used machine learning library for Python. We adopted the method based on combining SVM with tf-idf and SVM with W2V to classify the information presented in the reviews. With SVM + W2V, we selected certain features according to the part-of-speech of words, meaning that we considered only nouns, verbs, adjectives, and adverbs in a given sentence. We then combined vectors of these words and averaged them. In addition, we leveraged binary relevance method as a strategy to transform each label into an independent binary classification problem and train one classifier for each label [12].

Convolutional Neural Network We used TensorFlow[5], an open-source library for machine intelligence, to implement our CNN model based on Kim's CNN non-static model [10]. To make our CNN multi-label compatible, we made changes to the architecture as follows: first, we used sigmoid activation function instead of softmax at the output layer; second, we used *sigmoid cross entropy with logits* as our loss function; and third, since the predicted outputs are a set of probabilities, we used a simple rounding function to convert probabilities into one's and zero's in order to evaluate the accuracy against the ground truth.

Metrics Evaluating the performance of multi-label classification classifier is more complicated than that of multi-class classification. In multi-label classification, predictions can be fully correct (exact match), partially correct (partial match), or fully incorrect (none match) [20]. Therefore, several evaluation metrics should be reported. In this paper, we reported the performance of our classifier on 2 label-based metrics: Macro-average Precision and Macro-averaged Recall. However, the complete results for Example-based metrics (Hamming Loss, Jaccard Similarity, etc) can also be found in our project repository.

Label-based measures evaluate each label separately and then averages over all labels [20].

$$Precision_{MacroAvg} = \frac{1}{n}\sum_{k=1}^{n}\frac{TP_k}{TP_k + FP_k} \tag{1}$$

$$Recall_{MacroAvg} = \frac{1}{n}\sum_{k=1}^{n}\frac{TP_k}{TP_k + FN_k} \tag{2}$$

where n is the number of labels, TP_k is the total number of instances that are correctly identified by the approach for the label k, FP_k is the total number of instances incorrectly identified by the approach for the label k, and FN_k is the total number of true instances that are not identified by the approach for the label k.

[4] http://scikit-learn.org/stable/modules/svm.html

[5] https://www.tensorflow.org/

Results:

We decided to group category (3) User Background, (4) Other Product, (5) Usage Scenario, (6) Customer Service, and (7) Miscellaneous together because we believe that correctly identifying the information about the product (Hardware, Software, and General) itself matters the most. Another reason is that some of these categories occur much less frequently. A model that only returns predictions for categories that occur more frequently and never returns categories that occur less frequently will have high accuracy. However, this does not indicate that the model has a good predictive power as the model does not return any other label, except the most frequent one. This type of model is often used as a simple baseline model. For the sub-categories, we also decided to group category Inquiry with Problem Discovery because Inquiry occur much less frequently than any other category (Table 9). However, we decided not to group Feature Request category with any other category since this category is crucial for software engineers performing software evolution and maintenance tasks.

Furthermore, to prevent over-fitting and better test the generalizability of the model, we adopted two cross-validation measures. The results reported for the above metrics are based on these cross-validation measures.

10-fold cross validation We used the standard 10-fold cross validation to split the dataset in 10 folds and used 9 folds for training and 1 fold for evaluating. This process is repeated 10 times, rotating the training and testing folds.

6-fold product cross-validation Reviews of each product may contain words and jargon only applicable to the product. That means that term-features that work for one product may not work for others. We conducted a cross-product validation, a method previously proposed by [1]. In particular, we divided the dataset into 6 folds where each fold represents reviews of each product. We trained the classifier on 5 products reviews and tried to predict the classification of the reviews in the remaining product. The process is repeated 6 times, rotating the training and testing folds.

Table 8. Classification performance on the top level categories

Product#	**6-fold Product Cross Validation**																							
	SVM + tf-idf*								SVM + w2v‡								CNN + w2v‡							
	HW		SW		GN		OT		HW		SW		GN		OT		HW		SW		GN		OT	
	P	R	P	R	P	R	P	R	P	R	P	R	P	R	P	R	P	R	P	R	P	R	P	R
1	0.61	0.53	0.75	0.52	0.65	0.56	0.65	0.63	0.63	0.60	0.75	0.58	0.70	0.56	0.73	0.64	0.70	0.43	0.75	0.56	0.76	0.51	0.68	0.66
2	0.75	0.59	0.71	0.55	0.62	0.60	0.66	0.51	0.76	0.61	0.74	0.61	0.72	0.62	0.73	0.55	0.79	0.56	0.75	0.62	0.70	0.53	0.70	0.54
3	0.75	0.59	0.53	0.46	0.68	0.47	0.64	0.65	0.76	0.65	0.53	0.59	0.75	0.39	0.67	0.68	0.78	0.62	0.59	0.53	0.77	0.46	0.78	0.52
4	0.70	0.35	0.46	0.43	0.67	0.53	0.68	0.56	0.80	0.44	0.51	0.43	0.72	0.58	0.70	0.73	0.85	0.34	0.53	0.45	0.70	0.54	0.72	0.67
5	0.83	0.66	0.71	0.65	0.72	0.58	0.57	0.53	0.83	0.65	0.74	0.60	0.75	0.61	0.64	0.58	0.85	0.64	0.70	0.71	0.75	0.61	0.64	0.52
6	0.71	0.60	0.75	0.56	0.66	0.48	0.59	0.58	0.77	0.57	0.78	0.66	0.77	0.57	0.66	0.65	0.74	0.62	0.82	0.61	0.72	0.62	0.70	0.57
P(MA)	0.67								0.71								0.73							
R(MA)	0.55								0.59								0.56							
	10 fold Cross Validation																							
	0.77	0.63	0.72	0.60	0.69	0.59	0.65	0.60	0.77	0.65	0.74	0.64	0.75	0.59	0.71	0.64	0.80	0.62	0.77	0.61	0.73	0.61	0.72	0.60
P(MA)	0.71								0.74								0.76							
R(MA)	0.60								0.63								0.61							

HW = Hardware; SW = Software; GN = General; OT = Other; P = Precision; R = Recall; P(MA) = Macro Average Precision; R(MA) = Macro Average Recall; * included stop words; ‡ trained on the combination of 2.4 millions Amazon reviews with our dataset

Table 9. Classification performance on software related categories

Product#	6 fold Product Cross Validation																	
	SVM + tf-idf*						SVM + w2v‡						CNN + w2v‡					
	FR		IG		PD		FR		IG		PD		FR		IG		PD	
	P	R	P	R	P	R	P	R	P	R	P	R	P	R	P	R	P	R
1	0.73	0.41	0.71	0.58	0.64	0.81	0.74	0.49	0.77	0.60	0.68	0.87	0.87	0.22	0.75	0.53	0.62	0.90
2	0.55	0.35	0.73	0.75	0.72	0.72	0.58	0.41	0.78	0.87	0.83	0.74	1.00	0.24	0.73	0.88	0.83	0.70
3	0.62	0.56	0.78	0.65	0.72	0.83	0.75	0.33	0.84	0.75	0.78	0.90	0.00	0.00	0.79	0.62	0.68	0.88
4	0.33	0.33	0.59	0.61	0.79	0.78	0.33	0.33	0.79	0.67	0.81	0.88	0.00	0.00	0.82	0.70	0.82	0.91
5	0.55	0.60	0.82	0.65	0.58	0.78	0.40	0.40	0.87	0.64	0.57	0.83	1.00	0.20	0.88	0.65	0.56	0.86
6	0.81	0.41	0.59	0.79	0.72	0.64	0.84	0.38	0.61	0.85	0.80	0.71	0.90	0.13	0.50	0.84	0.74	0.58
P(MA)	0.67						0.71						0.70					
R(MA)	0.63						0.65						0.55					
	10-fold Cross Validation																	
	0.76	0.47	0.74	0.76	0.75	0.78	0.72	0.47	0.75	0.76	0.75	0.80	0.79	0.26	0.71	0.80	0.76	0.75
P(MA)	0.75						0.74						0.75					
R(MA)	0.67						0.68						0.60					

FR = Feature Request; IG = Information Giving; PD = Problem Discovery; P = Precision; R = Recall; P(MA) = Macro Average Precision; R(MA) = Macro Average Recall; * included stop words; ‡ trained on the combination of 2.4 millions Amazon reviews with our dataset

The performance results for classifying top-level categories in Table 8 show that incorporating Word2Vec improved precision and recall of SVM in both 6-fold and 10-fold. However, the performance of CNN + w2v and SVM + w2v are comparable. The 6-fold cross validation results show that the SVM + w2v and CNN + w2v generalized well, *i.e.,* their performances did not drop significantly as SVM + tf-idf. Table 9 shows the performance of different methods in classifying software sentences into different software categories. Since only a small quantity of Feature Request sentences are in the dataset, the performance of CNN dropped significantly. In fact, for product 3 (GoPro Hero4 Silver) and 4 (PlayStation 4), CNN did not classify any sentence in the Feature Request category. SVM + w2v's performance, on the other hand, did not drop as significantly as CNN + w2v from 10-fold to 6-fold product cross validation. This implies that the combination generalized well across different products. Surprisingly, SVM + tf-idf outperformed CNN + w2v on classifying software related sentence (R(MA) for 10-fold). However, with more software related sentences, we believe that CNN would perform as well as or slightly better than SVM. These findings answer **RQ3**.

4 Threats to Validity

The study presented in this paper has several factors that may affect the validity of the results. In the following, we discuss possible threats to the validity in our study.

Taxonomy This threat concerns the validity of our taxonomy. To mitigate this threat, we conducted both internal content analysis, involving a team of 5, and external content analysis, involving 52 master's level CS students, to analyze what information or pattern contained in the reviews (see Section 3.1). In addition, we also adapted taxonomy proposed by past literature in our work. However, other studies that use taxonomy with a different set of categories and definitions might lead to different results.

Subjectivity in manual classification This threat stems from the fact that our ground truth dataset is based on human judgment. However, it is not uncommon to involve humans to manually classify data in a text classification problem. To mitigate such a threat, we employ multiple measures as aforementioned in Section 3.2. Nevertheless, we cannot claim that our dataset is error-free as some bias may remain.

External Validity This threat concern how generalizable our results are. To mitigate such a threat, we selected products from different application domains: smart home, smart watch, action camera, and gaming console. Furthermore, to eliminate some bias in our dataset, we selected at most 50 reviews per star rating for each product, and each review contains less than 20 sentences. We also performed a project 6-fold cross validation (see Section 3.3) to test the generalizability of our machine learning models. Additionally, since all IoT products have the capability to transfer data or connect to its ecosystem or the Internet, this shared similarity should allow our results to generalize. Nevertheless, we encourage further research to investigate whether our results hold in other IoT domains.

5 Related Work

Analyzing user reviews for useful information has gained a lot of attention from researchers in recent years. We highlighted past literature that share similarities with our work.

Pagano and Maalej [17], Khalid et al. [9], Hoon et al. [7], and Harman et al. [5] conducted exploratory studies by investigating multiple aspects of user reviews from mobile application distribution platforms such as the Google Store, the Apple Store, or the BlackBerry Store. They found that user reviews contain information that is useful to the developers and the companies. Motivated by their findings, we investigated user reviews on IoT products to see whether enough software related information exists and how much of those information is directly applicable to software engineers.

Guzman et al. [4] conducted an exploratory study by analyzing the content in Twitter's tweets to find useful information for software engineers. They manually classified 1000 tweets and found that tweets contain relevant information for different stakeholders. They also investigated the automation potential by using several supervised machine learning techniques. Our work is similar to their work, however, our studies' subjects are not software applications.

Maalej and Nabil [13] compared multiple methods that can help with classifying user reviews on App stores automatically. Similarly, Panichella et al. [18] applied several machine learning techniques to classify information in user reviews from App stores. They applied Natural Language Processing (NLP), sentiment analysis, and text analysis to help with classification tasks. They found that combining NLP with sentiment analysis improves both precision and recall significantly. In contrast, we included a neural network approach (CNN) and investigated if vector space models such as Word2Vec and TF-IDF improve the performance of the classifiers.

6 Conclusions and Future Work

In this paper, we conducted an exploratory study by analyzing 1491 verified purchase reviews (7198 review sentences) of 6 IoT products obtained from Amazon. Our results demonstrate that only 26.72% of all sentences are software related, based on our taxonomy defined through external and internal content analysis sessions. We investigated how much information in those software related sentences is useful for software engineers performing software evolution and maintenance tasks. The results show that only 55.28% of software related sentences (14.79% of all sentences) are directly applicable to software engineers. Given that only a small quantity of sentences can help to accelerate software requirements elicitation or evolution process, we studied the extent to which two supervised machine learning techniques (SVM and CNN) can be used to differentiate information contained in the reviews automatically. The results show that utilizing Word2Vec improved the performance of SVM. In addition, Word2Vec also helped the model to generalize better, when classifying unseen reviews of a different product, than tf-idf.

This work can be extended to several directions. For instance, we plan to incorporate more product from several other IoT domains, to include software quality taxonomy to investigate different aspects of the product's software with regards to its software quality, to include feedback from the manufacturers on how useful the findings are, to incorporate sentiment analysis and other types of preprocessing approaches from past literature to further improve the performance of the classifier, to officially compare the performance of our classifier with that of past literature for software level sentences, and finally to investigate if we can capture and construct a formal requirement (*e.g.,* a user story) from these review sentences automatically.

Acknowledgement

This material is based upon work supported in part by the U.S. Department of Defense through the Systems Engineering Research Center (SERC) under Contract H98230-08-D-0171. SERC is a federally funded University Affiliated Research Center managed by Stevens Institute of Technology. It is also supported by the National Science Foundation grant CMMI-1408909, Developing a Constructive Logic-Based Theory of Value-Based Systems Engineering.

References

1. Bacchelli, A., Dal Sasso, T., D'Ambros, M., Lanza, M.: Content classification of development emails. In: Software Engineering (ICSE), 2012 34th International Conference on. pp. 375–385. IEEE (2012)

2. Fleiss, J.L.: Measuring nominal scale agreement among many raters. Psychological bulletin 76(5), 378 (1971)
3. Genc-Nayebi, N., Abran, A.: A systematic literature review: Opinion mining studies from mobile app store user reviews. Journal of Systems and Software 125, 207–219 (2017)
4. Guzman, E., Alkadhi, R., Seyff, N.: A needle in a haystack: What do twitter users say about software? In: Requirements Engineering Conference (RE), 2016 IEEE 24th International. pp. 96–105. IEEE (2016)
5. Harman, M., Jia, Y., Zhang, Y.: App store mining and analysis: Msr for app stores. In: Mining Software Repositories (MSR), 2012 9th IEEE Working Conference on. pp. 108–111. IEEE (2012)
6. Harris, Z.S.: Distributional structure. Word 10(2-3), 146–162 (1954)
7. Hoon, L., Vasa, R., Schneider, J.G., Grundy, J., et al.: An analysis of the mobile app review landscape: trends and implications. Faculty of Information and Communication Technologies, Swinburne University of Technology, Tech. Rep (2013)
8. Howe, J.: The rise of crowdsourcing. Wired magazine 14(6), 1–4 (2006)
9. Khalid, H., Shihab, E., Nagappan, M., Hassan, A.E.: What do mobile app users complain about? IEEE Software 32(3), 70–77 (2015)
10. Kim, Y.: Convolutional neural networks for sentence classification. arXiv preprint arXiv:1408.5882 (2014)
11. Landis, J.R., Koch, G.G.: The measurement of observer agreement for categorical data. biometrics pp. 159–174 (1977)
12. Luaces, O., Díez, J., Barranquero, J., del Coz, J.J., Bahamonde, A.: Binary relevance efficacy for multilabel classification. Progress in Artificial Intelligence 1(4), 303–313 (2012)
13. Maalej, W., Nabil, H.: Bug report, feature request, or simply praise? on automatically classifying app reviews. In: Requirements Engineering Conference (RE), 2015 IEEE 23rd International. pp. 116–125. IEEE (2015)
14. McAuley, J., Leskovec, J.: Hidden factors and hidden topics: understanding rating dimensions with review text. In: Proceedings of the 7th ACM conference on Recommender systems. pp. 165–172. ACM (2013)
15. Mikolov, T., Chen, K., Corrado, G., Dean, J.: Efficient estimation of word representations in vector space. arXiv preprint arXiv:1301.3781 (2013)
16. Morgan, D.L.: Qualitative content analysis: a guide to paths not taken. Qualitative health research 3(1), 112–121 (1993)
17. Pagano, D., Maalej, W.: User feedback in the appstore: An empirical study. In: Requirements Engineering Conference (RE), 2013 21st IEEE International. pp. 125–134. IEEE (2013)
18. Panichella, S., Di Sorbo, A., Guzman, E., Visaggio, C.A., Canfora, G., Gall, H.C.: How can i improve my app? classifying user reviews for software maintenance and evolution. In: Software maintenance and evolution (ICSME), 2015 IEEE international conference on. pp. 281–290. IEEE (2015)
19. Salton, G., McGill, M.J.: Introduction to modern information retrieval (1986)
20. Sorower, M.S.: A literature survey on algorithms for multi-label learning. Oregon State University, Corvallis 18 (2010)

Modelo De Proceso Para Proyectos De Ingeniería de Explotación De Información

Sebastian Martins

Programa de Doctorado en ciencias Informáticas. Universidad Nacional de La Plata
Grupo de Investigación en Sistemas de Información. Universidad Nacional de Lanús.
smartins089@gmail.com

Resumen. Antecedentes: Hace ya más de dos décadas, se registra un esfuerzo sostenido en el tiempo por definir un modelo de proceso que guíe el desarrollo de proyectos de Ingeniería de Explotación de Información, siendo las propuestas más utilizadas: CRISP-DM, KDD y SEMMA. **Definición del Problema**: Las propuestas existentes presentan una visión parcial e incompleta, conduciendo a una tasa de fracaso cercana al 60% [8; 9]. **Objetivo**: Definir un modelo de proceso que cubra las vacancias identificadas en la disciplina, integrando los procesos orientados al producto y a la gestión. **Método**: Se aborda el tema con un enfoque de investigación clásico mediante (i) revisiones sistemáticas para la captura de las necesidades y deficiencias existentes, y (ii) prototipado evolutivo experimental para el diseño de la propuesta. **Resultados Preliminares**: Se define un Modelo de Proceso para Proyectos de Explotación de Información (MoProPEI), el cual además de adaptar al tradicional proceso orientado al producto, incorpora un proceso orientado a la gestión del proyecto e integra una serie de métodos y técnicas ad hoc que guían de manera precisa el desarrollo de las actividades. **Trabajos Futuros**: validar el modelo de proceso, cuantificando las aportaciones con respecto a las propuestas más relevantes.

Palabras claves: Ingeniería de Explotación de Información, Extracción de Conocimiento / Minería de Datos, Modelo de Proceso, Metodología.

1 Introducción

En 1996, Fayyad, et al. [3] identifican la necesidad de establecer un proceso que permita sistematizar el desarrollo de proyectos de extracción de conocimiento, dentro del cual una de las actividades es la minería de datos. A partir de la existencia de múltiples tipos de minerías (de textos, imágenes, patrones en flujos de información, web, etc.), se conviene el término Ingeniería de Explotación de Información, a partir de la definición de Ingeniería de Software [6], como: la subdisciplina de los Sistemas de Información que aporta a la Inteligencia de Negocio de un enfoque sistemático, disciplinado y cuantificable para la transformación de información en conocimiento, con el propósito de extraer patrones interesantes y de regularidades importantes en grandes masas de información, que contribuya con la toma de decisiones y la generación de planes estratégicos en las organizaciones [1; 2]. Esto es, la aplicación al desarrollo de proyectos de explotación de información, y el estudio de este enfoque, es decir, la aplicación de la ingeniería a la explotación de información [7], la cual entiende en los procesos y las metodologías utilizadas para: ordenar, controlar y gestionar la tarea de encontrar patrones de conocimiento en masas de información.

En los últimos 15 años, numerosos autores han señalado dificultades y carencias identificadas a partir del desarrollo de distintos proyectos, afirmándose en [8; 9], que la tasa de proyectos que fracasan es aproximadamente del 60% (señalandose como la principal metodología utilizada CRISP-DM, la cual se mantiene como el estándar de facto [9]). Las principales carencias identificadas en las revisiones sistemáticas de la disciplina son: falta de procesos completos, detallados y estandarizados que incorporen un enfoque ingenieril, inexistente o inadecuado soporte al usuario (realizando un énfasis en las etapas de comprensión de las necesidades del cliente y definición de los alcances del proyecto, y en su vinculación con la solución propuesta), deficiencias en la estimación del proyecto (a causa de herramientas y guías inexistentes) y necesidades insatisfechas asociadas con la mala calidad de los resultados.

En adición, en [4] se señala que a partir del incremento en la complejidad de los proyectos, la necesidad de un enfoque riguroso se hace notable. La definición de un proceso que guíe el desarrollo de este tipo de proyectos es necesario para reducir los riesgos y problemas asociados con la gestión de proyectos y el aseguramiento de la calidad de los resultados, mejorando las prácticas y la productividad de los equipos de trabajo, evitándose obtener resultados indeseados que perjudiquen al proceso de toma de decisiones asociado e ingresar en periodos de crisis similares a las acontecidas en la ingeniería de software [9].

Como resultado de este trabajo de investigación, se busca definir un modelo de proceso que brinde una visión completa y detallada los pasos asociados al desarrollo de un proyecto de explotación de información, el cual incluya una visión ingenieril de la disciplina, esto es, no solo detallar la estructura y elementos del proceso, sino también incluir las técnicas y/o métodos que él mismo comprende, cubriendo las principales vacancias señaladas.

2 Estado de la Cuestión

A partir de 1993, se ha realizado un esfuerzo sostenido en el tiempo para definir una propuesta general que guíe el desarrollo de un proyecto de explotación de información. La figura 1, adaptada de do Nascimento y de Oliveira [10], resume la evolución en el tiempo de las propuestas, señalando los antecedentes sobre los cuales estas fueron definidas.

KDD es el primer abordaje en identificar la necesidad de un proceso que guíe el desarrollo de proyectos de explotación de información, siendo señalada como la piedra angular de las propuestas [11]. SEMMA, es otra propuesta ampliamente utilizada, gracias a su fuerte vinculación con las herramientas de explotación de información desarrolladas por la empresa SAS. Ambas propuestas son unas de las más utilizadas

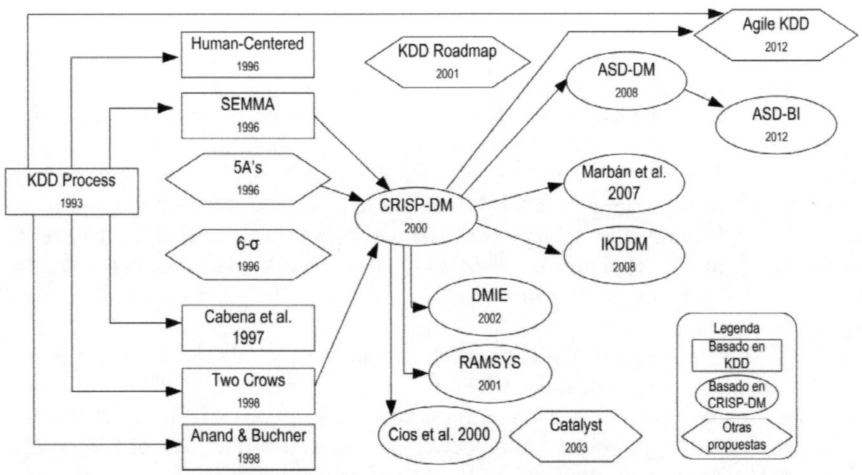

Fig. 1. Evolución de los Modelos de Procesos/Metodologías. Adaptada de [10]

en la disciplina y comparten sus principales críticas: falta de perspectiva del negocio [12], falta de integridad y detalle para llevar a cabo un proyecto [12; 13], carencia de la fase de implementación dificultando la evaluación de los resultados, restricciones en el ciclo de vida, no se almacena el conocimiento para mejorar procesos futuros e ignora la participación de los recursos humanos en el proceso [12].

CRISP-DM es la propuesta más utilizada en la disciplina, siendo el primer modelo de proceso en identificar las fases de entendimiento del negocio y de los datos, etapas relevantes en el desarrollo del proyecto [12]. Sin embargo, se han señalado varias deficiencias a la misma: el conocimiento extraído no es almacenado ni utilizado [12], ignora la participación de los recursos humanos en el proceso [12], falta de integridad y detalle para guiar el desarrollo de un proyecto [12; 9; 13], limitaciones y restricciones en el ciclo de vida integrado a la propuesta [14; 11] con respecto a la secuencialidad en la naturaleza del mismo, carencia en las iteraciones y que la última fase del proceso es un punto muerto, y falta de un método o proceso de selección de modelos [14; 15]. En adición, en [9] se señala que las tres propuestas previamente mencionadas, carecen de gestión del proyecto y presentan limitaciones con respecto a la posibilidad de adaptación del desarrollo del proyecto a las necesidades del mismo.

MPIMD [9], se destaca por ser el primer proceso en señalar la necesidad de una visión ingenieril, a partir de la creciente complejidad de los proyectos y los problemas asociados. Sin embargo, los autores señalan que el modelo no está completo, limitándose a señalar la necesidad de las actividades faltantes en CRISP-DM, por lo cual la propuesta puede ser identificada como bosquejo de proceso para proyectos de ingeniería de explotación de información. Adicionalmente, presenta dificultades en su comprensión e implementación a causa de contradicciones en su concepción: en [9], los autores señalan la diferencia en el objetivo de la disciplina (con respecto a la ingeniería de software) en que su resultado es la extracción de conocimiento de los datos y no el desarrollo de un producto software, sin embargo la propuesta incluye actividades como instalación, mantenimiento y retiro señalando que "puede necesitarse desarrollar algún software", pero no se incluye una paso de programación.Falta de claridad en la definición de los alcances de las actividades: dejando sin definir o sin describir como se adaptan aquellas actividades que se adoptan de la ingeniería de software (por ejemplo, del proceso de administración del proyecto: selección del ciclo de vida, planificación del proyecto y control y monitoreo del proyecto, del proceso Pre-Desarrollo: exploración de conceptos, Modelado del Negocio, entre otras), así como actividades cuyo alcance se sobreponen. Además, persisten las críticas realizadas al modelo de proceso de explotación de información base: falta de integridad y detalle para guiar el desarrollo de un proyecto, e ignora la participación de los recursos humanos en el proceso.

IKDDM [13], aborda la crítica realizada a la propuesta base (CRISP-DM) respecto a la dificultad en su implementación (falta de integridad y detalle para llevar a cabo un proyecto), proponiendo una metodología que describe los pasos a realizar, sin embargo, las demás críticas realizadas a la propuesta base aún persisten.ASD-BI [11], busca solucionar las críticas realizadas a CRISP-DM respecto a las limitaciones y restricciones en el ciclo de vida y su secuencialidad, proponiendo un modelo de proceso basado en los métodos agiles, sin embargo, las otras críticas realizadas a la propuesta base aún persisten.

De lo previamente expuesto, se observa que las propuestas vigentes presentan una visión general y parcial de las tareas involucradas en el desarrollo de proyectos, sin contemplar los aspectos de la gestión de proyectos (vitales para la ejecución exitosa de un proyecto), ni detallar el conjunto de métodos, técnicas y herramientas a utilizar, formalizando los alcances y entradas/salidas esperadas.

3 Investigación

A partir del contexto y carencias discutidas en las secciones previas, se define como problema abierto del proyecto de investigación: la necesidad de definir un modelo de proceso para proyectos de ingeniería de explotación de información [5; 25] el cual contemple los procesos orientado al producto y a la gestión de proyectos. El problema abierto identificado dividirse en dos sub objetivos, los cuales tienen asociados distintas preguntas de investigación:

I. Identificar mejoras a partir de las problemáticas identificadas en las propuestas existentes y definir un modelo de proceso cuya estructura cubra dichos aspectos.
   A. ¿Es posible desarrollar un modelo de proceso integral el cual defina las actividades y dependencias para proyectos de explotación de información desde una visión ingenieril que incorpore los conceptos de planificación, administración y control requeridos en todo proceso?
   B. De ser viable, ¿Es posible definir el modelo de acuerdo a las prácticas y propuestas vigentes?
   C. ¿Existen indicios que deriven en la necesidad de adaptar o redefinir las prácticas existentes?

II. Definir a partir de la estructura construida, una metodología (procedimientos, métodos y/o técnicas) que permita seleccionar las herramientas a utilizar de acuerdo a las características del proyecto.
   A. ¿Es posible articular técnicas o procedimientos de ingeniería de explotación de información desarrollados ad hoc en dicho modelo de proceso?
   B. En caso de poder articular las técnicas con el modelo de proceso propuesto: ¿Existen técnicas faltantes para las actividades? De existir, ¿pueden dichas técnicas ser adaptadas de otras disciplinas o desarrolladas ad hoc?

4 Metodología

Para construir el conocimiento asociado al presente proyecto de investigación, se sigue un enfoque de investigación clásico [16; 17] con énfasis en la producción de tecnologías [18]. La metodología de investigación está conformada por tres fases: Exploración, Desarrollo y Evaluación. En la primera fase, se utiliza el método revisiones sistemáticas [19] de artículos científicos siguiendo un método explícito para resumir la información sobre las propuestas de modelo de proceso / metodologías e identificar las carencias que las mismas poseen. De forma complementaria, se realiza un análisis de disciplinas afines (como la Ingeniería de Software) para evaluar los enfoques utilizados. A partir de las necesidades insatisfechas identificadas, en la segunda fase se utiliza el enfoque Prototipado Evolutivo Experimental [20], desarrollándose una solución inicial a las problemáticas identificadas. De manera posterior, se realiza el refinamiento de la propuesta de manera evolutiva por prueba de aplicación de dicha solución a casos de estudio de complejidad creciente. El proceso de refinamiento concluye al estabilizarse el prototipo en evolución. En la última fase, la viabilidad de la propuesta será verificada mediante tres casos de estudio de dominios diferentes y se validará sus aportes respecto a las propuestas existentes a partir de la metodología para la evaluación comparativa de modelo de procesos para explotación de información [24].

5 Realización de la Investigación

Se reportan como ***actividades realizadas***: la definición de un modelo de proceso para proyectos de explotación de información (MoProPEI), que surge a partir del análisis de las problemáticas identificadas en las propuestas existentes y las dificultades experimentadas en la implementación de las mismas. La propuesta se concibe desde la perspectiva de la compleja dinámica de los proyectos, a partir de la cual se define la incorporación de una capa transversal al tradicional proceso orientado al producto, que provee una visión de planificación, seguimiento, control y revisión de las tareas, así como la posibilidad de adaptar el flujo del proyecto a las necesidades del mismo. Adicionalmente, se introducen ajustes al proceso orientado al producto, identificados a partir de las dependencias entre las actividades.
MoProPEI se estructura de forma jerárquica mediante tres niveles (procesos, fases y actividades), cada uno de los cuales presenta un mayor grado de especificidad en los

objetivos de sus elementos. Cada actividad tiene asociado una o más técnicas, las cuales brindan un conjunto de pasos que permiten generar a partir de un conjunto de elementos de entrada, los elementos de salida deseados.
La propuesta está compuesta por dos subprocesos: Desarrollo (MoProPEI-D), presentado en detalle en [21], enfocado a las actividades del productoy Gestión (MoProPEI-G), presentado en detalle en [22], orientado a la planificación, control y administración de las tareas asociadas al proyecto. Por último, se especifican las aportaciones realizadas por la propuesta:

- Se introduce un modelo de proceso el cual presenta una visión integrada de los procesos necesarios para el desarrollo de un proyecto. Al proceso Desarrollo, se le incorpora una fase al proceso orientado al producto con el objetivo de vincular los conocimientos y necesidades del cliente con los modelos, reduciéndose iteraciones forzadas entre las fases de preparación de los datos e implementación.
- El subproceso Gestión, no solo presenta un mejor orden de las actividades existentes según sus objetivos y alcances, sino que incorpora un conjunto de tareas requeridas para el desarrollo de proyectos que no eran contempladas. Las tareas introducidas son: Definición de la comunicación, Estudio de viabilidad, Selección del ciclo de vida, Control de indicadores, Evaluación del cambio, Trazabilidad del proyecto y Contratación.
- La incorporación de las técnicas y formalismos para la ejecución de las actividades, precisan los alcances y resultados esperados de cada uno de los elementos de la propuesta, permitiendo al equipo unificar la visión del proceso y facilitar la comprensión del mismo.
- Se define al modelo de proceso propuesto de forma independiente al flujo de ejecución de las actividades. Presentándose tres modelos de ciclo de vida, que permiten al equipo de trabajo determinar a partir de las características del proyecto, el mejor flujo de trabajo.

Se identifica como ***trabajo futuro*** finalizar la última fase de la metodología de investigación (Evaluación), verificando la viabilidad del modelo de proceso y las técnicas en los casos de estudio seleccionados (pertenecientes a los dominios de educación, salud y análisis web), y realizar un estudio comparativo con las principales propuestas existentes, con el objetivo de evaluar y cuantificar las aportaciones realizadas, haciendo uso de la metodología para la evaluación comparativa de modelo de procesos para explotación de información [24]

6 Conclusiones

En respuesta al sub objetivo I y sus preguntas de investigación: se definió MoProPEI, un modelo de proceso el cual comprende los procesos orientados al producto y a la gestión. A partir de las carencias previamente señaladas en los procesos existentes, se utilizó CRISP-DM como elemento base para construir la solución propuesta. Dichos procesos proveen una visión integral requerida para el desarrollo de proyectos [22],

incorporando al tradicional subproceso Desarrollo, de un proceso transversal enfocado en la planificación, administración y control del proyecto (subproceso Gestión).
El proceso Desarrollo fue adaptado de acuerdo a las dependencias entre las actividades. Lafase "Modelado", fue separada en dos fases: "Modelado" e "Implementación". La primerade ellas, es una novación de la propuesta, en la cual se incorporan actividades que permitensistematizar el proceso de definición de las técnicas a utilizar para dar solución a losobjetivos identificados;mientras que la segunda cubre las actividades de explotación de información y optimizacióndel modelo y evaluación de la calidad y validez de los patrones obtenidos (consideradas enla fase original). La incorporación de dicha fase, surge a partir de las dependencias entre laconformación del set de datos y los algoritmos a utilizar, pudiéndose definir de maneraprevia, evitando iteraciones y esfuerzos innecesarios, previendo de manera temprana elenfoque a utilizar.
Adicionalmente, a partir del reordenamiento de actividades correspondientes a la gestión delproyecto y desestimación de actividades ajenas al alcance del modelo de proceso (revisióndel proyecto, plan de monitoreo y mantenimiento), se integran las fases de "Evaluación" y"Despliegue", modificando el segundo término a "Presentación", para enfatizar en lacorrecta transmisión los patrones y las piezas de conocimiento extraídas, como objetivo delproceso.
Como respuesta al sub objetivo II y sus preguntas de investigación: se utilizaron las siguientes técnicas desarrolladas ad hoc para utilizar en procesos de ingeniería de explotación de información, listadas según el área de interés: entendimiento del negocio [27], entendimiento de los datos [27], modelado [15], viabilidad del proyecto [29], estimación del esfuerzo del proyecto [29], selección de herramientas [28], métricas [30] y ciclos de vida [12; 31; 32]. Cuatro técnicas pertenecientes a otras disciplinas fueron adaptadas: Definición de la Comunicación, Designación de Responsabilidades, Reporte de Estado y Reporte de Cierre [22; 26].

Agradecimientos

Las investigaciones que se reportan en este artículo han sido financiadas parcialmente por beca PROMINF-UNLa-2015-2017 del Ministerio de Educación Argentina y por el Proyecto 80020160400001LA de la Secretaria de Ciencia y Tecnología de la Universidad Nacional de Lanús.
A la memoria del Dr. Ramón García-Martínez.

Referencias

1. Thomsen, E. (2003). BI's Promised Land. Intelligent Enterprise, 64: 21-25.
2. Negash, S., Gray, P. (2008). Business Intelligence. En Handbook on Decision Support Systems 2, ed. F. Burstein y C. Holsapple Heidelberg, Springer, Pág. 175-193.
3. Fayyad, U., Piatetsky-Shapiro, G., & Smyth, P. (1996). From data mining to knowledge discovery in databases. AI magazine, 17(3), 37.
4. Berry, M. J., & Gordon, L. (1997). Data mining techniques: For marketing, sales, and customer support. New York, NY: Wiley.
5. Mariscal, G., Marbán, Ó., & Fernández, C. (2010). A survey of data mining and knowledge discovery process models and methodologies. The Knowledge Engineering Review, 25(02), 137-166.

6. Abran, A., Moore, J. W., Bourque, P., Dupuis, R., Tripp, L. (2004). Guide to the Software Engineering Body of Knowledge. IEEE Computer Society Press. ISBN 0-7695-2330-7.
7. García-Martínez, R., Britos, P., Pesado, P., Bertone, R., Pollo-Cattaneo, F., Rodríguez, D., Pytel, P., Vanrell. J. (2011). Towards an Information Mining Engineering. ISBN 978-958-8692-32-6.
8. Gondar, J.E. (2005). Data Mining Methodology. Data Mining Institute. ISBN: 978-84-96272-21-7.
9. Marbán, O., Segovia, J., Menasalvas, E., & Fernández-Baizán, C. (2009). Toward data mining engineering: A software engineering approach. Information systems, 34(1), 87-107.
10. do Nascimento, G. S., & de Oliveira, A. A. (2013). Agilekdd: an agile process model to knowledge discovery in databases and business intelligence systematization.
11. Alnoukari, M., & El Sheikh, A. (2012). Knowledge Discovery Process Models: From Traditional to Agile Modeling. Business Intelligence and Agile Methodologies for Knowledge-Based Organization.
12. Hofmann, M. (2003). The development of a generic data mining life cycle (DMLC).
13. Sharma, S., Osei-Bryson, K. M., & Kasper, G. M. (2012). Evaluation of an integrated Knowledge Discovery and Data Mining process model. Expert Systems with Applications, 39(13), 11335-11348.
14. Rennolls, K., & AL-Shawabkeh, A. (2008). Formal structures for data mining, knowledge discovery and communication in a knowledge management environment. Intelligent Data Analysis, 12.147–163.
15. Martins, S., Rodríguez, D., García-Martínez, R. (2014). Deriving Processes of Information Mining Based on Semantic Nets and Frames. Lecture Notes on Artificial Intelligence, 8482: 150-159.
16. Riveros, H. y Rosas, L. (1985). El Método Científico Aplicado a las Ciencias Experimentales.
17. Creswell, J. (2002). Educational Research: Planning, Conducting, and Evaluating Quantitative and Qualitative Research. Prentice Hall. ISBN 10: 01-3613-550-1.
18. Sábato, J. y Mackenzie, M. (1982). La Producción de Tecnología. Editorial Nueva Imagen. México.
19. Argimón, J. (2004). Métodos de Investigación Clínica y Epidemiológica. Elsevier España.
20. Basili 1993. The Experimental Paradigm in Software Engineering. En Experimental Software Engineering Issues: Critical Assessment and Future Directions (Ed. Rombach, H., Basili, V., Selby, R.).
21. Martins, S., Pesado, P., García-Martínez, P. 2016. Information Mining Projects Management Process. Proceedings 28th International Conference on Software Engineering & Knowledge Engineering.
22. Martins, S., Pesado, P., García-Martínez, R., 2016. Intelligent Systems in Modeling Phase of Information Mining Development Process. Lecture Notes on Artifical Intelligence 9799: 3–15.
23. Project Management Institute, Inc. (2013). A guide to the project management body of knowledge (PMBOK® guide). Fifth edition. ISBN: 978-1-935589-67-9.
24. Moine, J. (2013). Metodologías para el descubrimiento de conocimiento en bases de datos: un estudio comparativo [Tesis de Maestría]. Argentina: Universidad Nacional de la Plata.
25. Kdnuggets. 2014. What main methodology are you using for your analytics, data mining, or data science projects? www.kdnuggets.com/polls/2014/analytics-data-mining-data-science-methodology.html
26. Verzuh, E. (2015). The fast forward MBA in project management. John Wiley & Sons.
27. Britos, P., Dieste, O., & García-Martínez, R. (2008). Requirements elicitation in data mining for business intelligence projects. In Advances in Information Systems Research, Education and Practice (pp. 139-150). Springer US.
28. Britos, P., Merlino, H., Fernández, E., Ochoa, M., Diez, E. y García Martínez, R. (2006). Tool Selection Methodology in Data Mining. Proceedings V Ibero-American Symposium on Software Engineering. Pág. 85-90.
29. Pytel, P., Hossian, A., Britos, P., García-Martínez, R. (2015). Feasibility and Effort Estimation Models for Medium and Small Size Information Mining Projects. Information Systems Journal, 47: 01-14.
30. Basso, D. 2014. Propuesta de métricas para proyectos de explotación de información. ReLaIS.
31. Alnoukari, M. (2010). ASD-BI: A Business Intelligence Modeling and Integration Framework based on Agile Methodologies (Doctoral dissertation, Arab Academy for Banking and Financial Sciences).
32. Arboleya, H.. 2013. Propuesta de Ciclo de Vida y Mapa de Actividades para Proyectos de Explotación de Información. ReLaIS, 1(3): 107-124, ISSN 2314-2642.

Un método colaborativo para determinar el alcance de líneas de productos software

Marta Cecilia Camacho Ojeda

Institución Universitaria Colegio Mayor del Cauca
Universidad del Cauca
Carrera 5 # 5 - 40 Claustro de la Encarnación, 69121 Popayán, Colombia
cecamacho@unimayor.edu.co

Abstract. Las compañías productoras de software buscan estrategias para competir en el mercado, una de ellas es la reutilización de software, como es el caso de las Líneas de Productos Software (SPL). Las SPLs son una estrategia de producción basada en la reutilización planificada. Una actividad esencial en el desarrollo de una SPL es la definición del alcance (SPL-S), el cual es una función de pertenencia a la SPL: identificar los productos del portafolio, especificar los dominios relevantes y la infraestructura de reutilización con la estrategia de producción. El SPL-S es una actividad crítica debido a la complejidad y la variedad de factores que deben considerarse, SPL-S es una actividad interdisciplinaria en el que se requiere asegurar que los participantes con diferentes intereses, preocupaciones y prioridades definan colectiva y correctamente el alcance de la línea. Pese a la importancia que los factores de comunicación y participación inciden en el éxito y fracaso del planteamiento y desarrollo de la línea de productos; La mayoría de los enfoques para SPL-S se enfocan en aspectos técnicos pero no en la interacción entre los roles participantes ni cómo lograr que esta interacción sea efectiva. Existe por lo tanto la necesidad de entender y proponer dinámicas que faciliten la participación efectiva de los roles para obtener de forma precisa y consistente este alcance durante la creación y evolución de la línea de productos. Esta propuesta doctoral busca proponer un método colaborativo para el SPL-S y verificar si esta propuesta aumenta la participación efectiva, facilita la toma de decisiones y permite determinar un alcance útil para el desarrollo de una SPL.

Keywords: Software Product Lines, Software Product Line Scoping, Collaboration engineering, Product line engineering.

1 Introducción

El enfoque SPL (Software Product Lines) es una estrategia de reutilización de software que busca incrementar la productividad de las empresas desarrolladoras de software. Una SPL es un conjunto de productos que comparten características comunes y satisfacen necesidades de un segmento del mercado [1]. Una SPL está basada en la reutili-

zación planificada mediante el desarrollo sinérgico de un conjunto de productos software [1]. Esta estrategia tiene beneficios como la reducción del tiempo de desarrollo, mejora de la calidad, reducción de costos y aumento de la productividad [2].
El ciclo de vida de SPL incluye las actividades Desarrollo de Activos Base y Desarrollo de Productos. El Desarrollo de Activos Base incluye el establecimiento de la capacidad de producción, la *determinación del alcance* de la línea y el desarrollo de los activos base. El desarrollo de productos son las actividades para construcción de cada producto de la línea a partir de los activos base [1] [3]. La *determinación del alcance* es una actividad donde se delimita la línea, se identifican los productos que pertenecen a la línea, se especifica el dominio, y se establece la infraestructura de reutilización [3] [4].

La *determinación del alcance* es una actividad crítica, si el alcance identificado es demasiado amplio amena la utilidad y reutilización de los activos base; Pero si el alcance es demasiado pequeño la empresa obtendrá un retorno a la inversión muy bajo; Además un alcance incorrecto puede orientar hacia productos incorrectos que no correspondan al mercado objetivo [1] [4]. La *determinación del alcance* no solo se refiere al tamaño correcto, sino que debe identificar los productos correctos de acuerdo a las oportunidades del mercado, la inversión necesaria y los objetivos comerciales [4].

1.1 Planteamiento del problema

El desarrollo de SPL es una actividad multidisciplinar e interdisciplinar que incluye las dimensiones de negocio, arquitectura, proceso y organización [1] [5] . Una actividad esencial en el desarrollo de una SPL es la *determinación del alcance* (SPL-S) [6].
SPL-S es una actividad difícil debido a la complejidad inherente para construir varios productos. Es necesario considerar diferentes factores, como los dominios relevantes, las metas de negocio, y las condiciones del mercado, que muchas veces son desconocidos por el equipo técnico [7]; Por lo tanto, SPL-S requiere la participación de expertos no técnicos que generalmente no son parte del equipo de desarrollo [7]. Los enfoques para SPL-S existentes proporcionan directrices desde la perspectiva técnica [8] [9], sin embargo la mayoría no tienen una definición detallada de los roles y el conocimiento requerido [8] [9] [10], ni indican cómo los participantes interactúan [11]. Esto pone en manifiesto que hay un mayor énfasis en aspectos técnicos que en los aspectos de interdisciplinariedad y trabajo en equipo. Sin embargo, Rommes [12] plantea que la participación de personas con conocimientos diferentes y parciales es un factor clave [13].

La diversidad de participantes es relevante en SPL-S, un equipo multidisciplinario es capaz de abordar la SPL-S desde diferentes puntos de vista. Menos diversidad reduce la capacidad análisis. De esta forma, Si se realiza SPL-S con solo participación técnica, esto puede crear productos incorrectos desde el punto de vista del mercado. Por otro lado, un SPL-S con una intervención mayor de expertos en ventas y marketing puede llevar a productos inviables y costosos de construir. Mientras que SPL-S sin participación administrativa llevaría a un conjunto de productos no alineados con los objetivos comerciales [12]. Por lo tanto, la SPL-S depende de una toma de decisiones equilibrada de los participantes [14]. La diversidad de participantes es importante, pero involucrar personas de diferentes áreas y con distintos intereses no es fácil [5] [15] [12] [15]. Bajo este escenario, existe la necesidad de mejorar la interacción entre los participantes, definir de una manera clara los roles necesarios, sus responsabilidades [12]. La pregunta de investigación es: ¿puede un método colaborativo para la determinación del alcance de una SPL, aumentar la participación efectiva de los interesados y facilitar la toma de decisiones para su correcta definición?

1.2 Hipótesis y Objetivo

Hipótesis: la aplicación del método colaborativo para determinar el alcance de una SPL, permite definir un alcance bien definido y útil mediante el aumento de la participación efectiva de los interesados y la facilitación de la toma de decisiones.

Hipótesis nula: la aplicación del método colaborativo para determinar el alcance de una SPL, aumenta la participación efectiva de los roles y facilita la toma de decisiones. Sin embargo, no es suficiente para lograr definir un alcance correcto y útil.

Objetivo general: Proponer un método colaborativo para establecer un alcance correcto y útil de las SPL, a través de un aumento de la participación efectiva de los interesados y facilitarles la toma de decisiones.

2 Trabajos relacionados

A pesar del impacto que tienen los factores humanos en el éxito de los procesos de desarrollo, la mayoría de las propuestas se enfocan en aspectos técnicos [16], el primer paso en este proyecto fue realizar una búsqueda y análisis de los diferentes enfoques de *determinación del alcance*, para saber si consideran elementos del trabajo de equipo, como los roles o algún elemento que describa como deben interrelacionarse.

Para realizar la búsqueda de enfoques se dividieron en dos grupos, para los enfoques anteriores al 2010 se tomó como base los hallazgos de dos revisiones del alcance [9] [8] y para enfoques del 2010 en adelante se realizó una revisión de la literatura, empleando como palabras claves: scoping o scope o planning en el título o abstract, combinadas con la frase "Software Product Line" en el abstract. La búsqueda se realizó en ACM digital library, IEEE xplorer y Springer, artículos publicados desde el año 2010 hasta el 2017. En total se identificaron 34 enfoques para SPL-S.

De acuerdo a los diferentes enfoques analizados, durante la SPL-S se requiere la intervención de diversos participantes [17] [5]. Rommes [12] reconoce la importancia de la diversidad de participantes en SPL-S, un grupo diverso es capaz de mirar el problema desde muchas perspectivas diferentes, sin embargo también advierte de los riesgos de la participación masiva, debates interminables, falta de acuerdos sobre detalles, ausencia de puntos claros para toma de decisiones, la burocracia y perdida de eficiencia.

De la revisión de los enfoques, puede observarse que las propuestas se han enfatizado en aspectos técnicos, relegando aspectos como los participantes y el trabajo en equipo. Si bien la mayoría de los enfoques considera que es necesario diversos conocimientos, falta detallar las responsabilidades e interdependencias de los participantes, para que cada integrante conozca el objetivo de su participación y con quien interactúa.

Dos de los enfoques analizados involucran aspectos colaborativos y de comunicación en la construcción de SPL. Noor et al. [18] [5] proponen un enfoque colaborativo para SPL-S basado en la reingeniería de producto, para que el equipo logre una visión común sobre el proyecto SPL. Sin embargo esta propuesta está enfocada a un solo escenario de producción de SPL cuando se deriva de sistemas exitosos y solo considera uno de los niveles del SPL-S el portafolio de productos, porque la empresa tiene experiencia en el dominio y parte de una infraestructura de sus productos.

Rommes propone un enfoque basado en escenarios, que se desarrolla conjuntamente por todos los participantes, utilizando un lenguaje común [12]. Sin embargo, la información de este enfoque es limitada, lo que dificulta que sea replicado por otra empresa. El trabajo de Rommes es una base para este proyecto y para la definición del problema.

Otras propuestas han combinado enfoques de SPL-S con metodologías agiles: RiPLE-SC [19] [20] es un proceso ágil para SPL-S. Este proceso reúne los beneficios de las metodologías ágiles y la estrategia de producción SPL. Sin embargo el proceso propuesto no describe de manera concreta prácticas colaborativas que describan la interacción entre los participantes. Esta propuesta fue evaluada en un estudio de caso industrial [21]. Los resultados obtenidos evidenciaron la ineficiencia de la comunicación y la colaboración entre los participantes. Los autores del estudio consideran que el uso de patrones de ingeniería colaborativa puede mejorar la participación en SPL-S.

RiPLE-ASC [22] [23] es un proceso que combina Scrum con SPL-S. El proceso detalla las características y responsabilidades de los interesados. El enfoque considera cinco actividades, tres de ellas sugieren el uso de patrones de colaboración, sin embargo no proporciona información detallada sobre las tareas de colaboración.

3 METODOLOGIA DE INVESTIGACION

Para lograr los objetivos del proyecto, la metodología global de este trabajo de investigación sigue el marco de Mario Bunge [24], en cada una de las fases se ha instanciado métodos específicos de investigación en el contexto de la ingeniería de software.

- Para el planteamiento del problema: plantear el problema requiere de establecer el estado del arte y extraer los problemas que la comunidad está resolviendo. Para ello el trabajo se apoya en el método de revisión del estado del arte [25], el cual tiene como objetivo brindar una imagen actual de desarrollo del área de investigación, en este caso, los métodos de *determinación del alcance* de una SPL, fue posible establecer el problema concreto a resolver por este trabajo doctoral.
  Para la construcción del método se sigue un proceso mixto. El Enfoque de ingeniería de colaboración para diseñar procesos de colaboración [26]. Algunos métodos del estado del arte son analizados en términos de tareas colaborativas tales como patrones y thinklets son seleccionados para diseñar el proceso colaborativo. Algunos métodos estudiados son modelados como procesos SPEM2.0, son analizados con co-AVISPA, que identifica puntos para incorporar aspectos colaborativos. [27] [28].
- El nuevo método integrará los fragmentos de proceso, desde el estado del arte en la determinación del alcance hasta los patrones de colaboración y thinklets. Todos estos elementos están siendo determinados e integrados siguiendo el enfoque de ingeniería

de método [29]. En este enfoque parte de los métodos existentes y de la ingeniería colaborativa. Los elementos candidatos son probados en la práctica usando ejemplos y experiencias piloto, se realiza iterativamente de manera incremental

- Deducción de consecuencias y validación: para validar se siguen las directrices de Yin para estudios de casos [30] [31]. El enfoque estudios de caso se usara para analizar y evaluar la colaboración durante la aplicación del método siguiendo el CSACE [32]. En el planteamiento se deben considerar las amenazas de validez.

4 PROPUESTA DE SOLUCION

4.1 Estudios empíricos preliminares

Para analizar los efectos de incluir elementos colaborativos en el SPLS-S se han realizado dos estudios exploratorios siguiendo las guías en [31] [33]. En uno de los estudios se planteó una aproximación colaborativa del enfoque PuLSE-Eco [13]. El objetivo fue evaluar la utilidad de prácticas colaborativas en SPL-S. La utilidad fue evaluada contrastando dos experiencias de desarrollo de SPL realizadas en contextos académicos. Un grupo incluyó los elementos colaborativos y otro grupo siguió el proceso original. Este estudio de caso permitió observar que los artefactos de alcance definidos de forma colaborativa, presentaron una mayor convergencia de las características del mercado.

4.2 Propuesta inicial

Para el diseño del método se seguirán las directrices propuestas por "Estrategia de construcción: ingeniería de método situacional" [29] en el cual se define un método por medio del ensamble de fragmentos reutilizados de enfoques ya probados. Y para integrar la ingeniería colaborativa se seguirá el enfoque de "Ingeniería de colaboración para diseñar procesos de colaboración" [26]. La propuesta inicial del Método Colaborativo para SPL-S se observa en la fig 1.

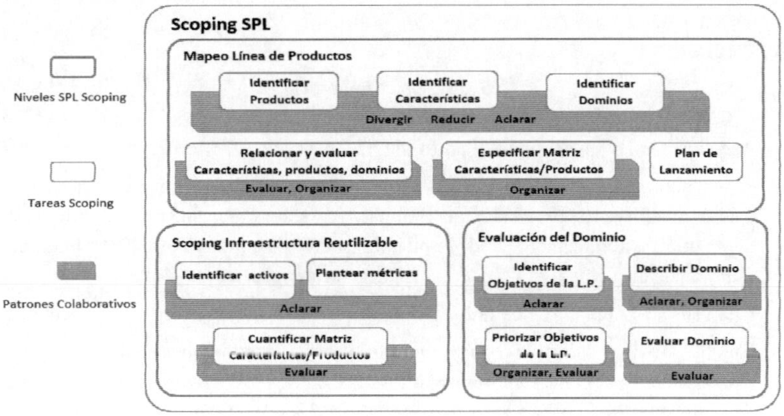

Fig. 1. Propuesta inicial Método colaborativo para SPL-S

5 Avances y trabajo futuro

Hasta el momento se ha definido la necesidad de facilitar la interacción efectiva entre los participantes del SPL-S, se ha revisado la literatura, se han seleccionado los enfoques base para la definición del método. Se han realizado dos estudios exploratorios donde se han analizado los efectos de incluir elementos colaborativos en SPL-S. Los estudios muestran que los equipos que trabajan con el enfoque colaborativo logran una mayor convergencia con las características del mercado. En este momento se descomponen los enfoques en sus elementos de proceso para evaluar la inclusión de patrones colaborativos y thinkLets.

Tabla 1. Proyección de actividades y artículos.

Actividad	Articulo	Estado
revisión de la literatura	Teamwork Importance in Software Product Lines Scoping	En revisión
Estudios exploratorios	Dislexpace un videojuego serio para niños con dislexia	I ENITED, 2017. Publicado.
	Diseñando videojuegos serios para niños con dislexia	Jornadas Iberoamericanas de HCI Abril 2018.
Planteamiento preliminar método colaborativo SPL-S	An Exploratory Study for Scoping Software Product Lines in a Collaborative Way	11th Workshop on Cooperative and Human Aspects of Software Engineering, (CHASE 2018)
Planteamiento de un método colaborativo SPL-S	Software Product Lines Scoping as a Collaborative Activity	22nd Software Product Line Conference. En revisión
	SPL Scoping since Reuse Infrastructure.	19th Conference on Product-Focused Software Process Improvement. En escritura.
Evaluación del método propuesto	A collaborative method for SPL Scoping.	IEEESoftware (proyectado)

Referencias

1. P. Clements y L. Northrop, Software Product Lines, Practices and Patterns, vol. 3 ed, Addison-Wesley Professional. Part of the SEI Series in Software Engineering, 2001.
2. P. Knauber y G. Succi, de Perspectives on Software Product Lines: report on first international worksho, First International Workshop on Software Product Lines: Economics, Architectures, and Implications, Workshop #15 at 22nd International Conference on Software Engineering (ICSE), Limerick, Ireland, 2000.
3. F. J. van der Linden, K. Schmid y E. Rommes, Software Product Lines in Action, The Best Industrial Practice in Product Line Engineering, Springer, 2007.
4. P. C. Clements, «On the Importance of Product Line Scope,» de International Workshop on Software Product-Family Engineering. PFE 2001. Lecture Notes in Computer Science, Berlin, Heidelberg, 2002.

5. M. A. Noor, R. Rabiser y P. Grünbacher, «A collaborative approach for product line scoping: a case study in collaboration engineering,» de *SE'07 Proceedings of the 25th conference on IASTED International Multi-Conference: Software Engineering*, 2007.
6. P. C. Clements, «On the Importance of Product Line Scope,» de *Software Product-Family Engineering, Lecture Notes in Computer Science*, vol. 2290, v. d. L. F, Ed., Berlin Heidelberg, Springer , 2002, pp. 70-78.
7. K. Schmid, «Scoping Software Product Lines, An Analysis of an Emerging Technology,» de *Software Product Lines: Experience and Research Directions*, P. Donohoe, Ed., kluwer academic publishers, 2000, pp. 513-532.
8. I. John y M. Eisenbarth, «A Decade of Scoping – A Survey,» *Proceedings of the 13th International Software Product Line Conference,* pp. 31-40, 2009.
9. M. Moraes, E. Almeida y S. Meira, «A Systematic Review on Software Product Lines Scoping,» *Proceedings of the 6th Experimental Software Engineering Latin American Workshop,* pp. 63-72, 2009.
10. M. B. S. Moraes, E. S. de Almeida y S. R. de Lemos Meira, «A Systematic Review on Software Product Lines Scoping,» de *ESELAW'09: Proceedings of the VI Experimental Software Engineering Latin American Workshop*, Sao Carlos-SP, Brazil, 2009.
11. M. Noor, P. Grünbacher y R. Briggs, «A collaborative approach for product line scoping: A case study in collaboration engineering,» de *IASTED International Conference on Software Engineering*, Innsbruck, Austria , 2007.
12. E. Rommes, «A People Oriented Approach to Product Line Scoping,» de PLEES 2003: International Workshop on Product Line Engineering: The Early Steps: Planning, Modeling and Managing, Kaiserslautern, Germany, 2003.
13. I. John, J. Knodel, T. Lehner y D. Muthig, «A Practical Guide to Product Line Scoping,» de 10th International Software Product Line Conference (SPLC'06), 2006.
14. A. Lanzen, A. Malucelli y S. Reinehr, «Scope definition in software product lines: A semi-automatic approach through linguistic annotation,» de *2012 XXXVIII Conferencia Latinoamericana En Informatica (CLEI)*, Medellin, 2012.
15. A. Helferich, K. Schmid y G. Herzwurm, «Reconciling Marketed and Engineered Software Product Lines,» de Software Product Line Conference, 2006 10th International, 2006.
16. M. John, F. Maurer y B. Tessem, «Human and Social Factors of Software Engineering – Workshop Summary,» de ACM SIGSOFT Software Engineering Notes, 2005.
17. G. Chastek, P. Donohoe y . K. Kang, «Digital Library Product Line Analysis: A Practical Introduction,» Abril 2001. [En línea]. Available: http://resources.sei.cmu.edu/library/asset-view.cfm?assetid=5589.
18. M. A. Noor y R. Rabiser, «A collaborative approach for reengineering-based product line scoping,» de *Workshop on Agile Product Line*, 2006.
19. M. Balbino Santos de Moraes, E. S. de Almeida y S. Meira, «An Agile Scoping Process for Software Product Lines,» de *Conference: Proceedings of the 23rd International Conference on Software Engineering & Knowledge Engineering (SEKE'2011)*, 2011.

20. M. B. S. de Moraes, «Riple-SC : An Agile Scoping Process for Software Product Lines,» Recife, 2010.

21. I. F. da Silva, P. A. da Mota Silveira Neto, P. O'Leary, E. Santana de Almeida y S. Romero de Lemos Meira, «Software product line scoping and requirements engineering in a small and medium-sized enterprise: An industrial case study,» *Journal of Systems and Software,* vol. 88, p. 189–206, 2014.

22. I. F. da Silva, «An agile approach for software product lines scoping,» de SPLC '12 Proceedings of the 16th International Software Product Line Conference, Salvador, Brazil, 2012.

23. I. F. da Silva, «A Scrum-inspired Process for Software Product Lines Scoping,» Recife, 2013.

24. M. Bunge, «Philosophy of Science,» *México: From Problem to Theory. New Brunswick, Transaction. Siglo Veintiuno Editores,* 2002.

25. M. Grant y A. Booth, «A typology of reviews: an analysis of 14 review types and associated methodologies,» *Health Information & Libraries Journal,* vol. 26, nº 2, pp. 91-108, 2009.

26. G. Kolfschoten y G.-J. de Vreede, «The Collaboration Engineering Approach for Designing Collaboration Processes,» *Groupware: Design, Implementation, and Use. CRIWG 2007. Lecture Notes in Computer Science,* vol. 4715, pp. 95-110, 2007.

27. M. C. Camacho Ojeda, J. A. Hurtado Alegría y P. H. Ruiz Melenje, «Un método incremental para el análisis visual de modelos de procesos software,» *Gerencia Tecnológica Informática,* vol. 15, nº 43, pp. 79-91, 2016.

28. J. A. Hurtado Alegría, M. C. Bastarrica y A. Bergel, «AVISPA: A Tool for Analyzing Software Process Models,» de Journal of software maintenance and evolution: Research and practice, 2013.

29. F. Harmsen, S. Brinkkemper y H. Oei, «Situational Method Engineering for Information System Project Approaches,» *Information Systems,* vol. 55, pp. 169-194, 1994.

30. R. K. Yin, Case Study Research: Design and Methods, vol. 5, SAGE, 2009.

31. P. Runeson y M. Höst, «Guidelines for conducting and reporting case study research in software engineering,» *(D. Sjoberg, Ed.) Empirical Software Engineering,* vol. , pp. 131-164, 2009.

32. J. A. Hurtado Alegría y C. A. Collazos, «Analyzing and Evaluating Collaborative Processes using Case Studies in the Software Development Context,» de *XV International Conference on Human Computer Interaction Interacción'14*, New York, NY, Usa, 2014.

33. C. Wohlin, M. Höst y K. Henningsson, «Empirical Research Methods in Software Engineering,» *Lecture Notes in Computer Science,* vol. 2765, pp. 7-23, 2003.

Formulación de Procesos para una Ingeniería de Explotación de Información Espacial

Giovanni Daián Rottoli

[1] Programa de Doctorado en Ciencias Informáticas. Facultad de Informática. Universidad Nacional de La Plata. Argentina
[2] Grupo de Investigación de Sistemas de Información (GISI). Universidad Nacional de Lanús. Argentina
rottolig@frcu.utn.edu.ar

Abstract. ***Antecedentes:*** El Proceso de Descubrimiento de Conocimiento en Base de datos (KDD, *Knowledge Discovery in Databases*) propuesto por Fayyad et al. (1996) proporciona una secuencia unificada de pasos para la obtención de patrones de conocimiento mediante la aplicación de algoritmos de minería de datos a partir de un conjunto de datos de entrada. Posteriormente fue propuesta una batería de procesos de explotación de información que concretan parcialmente al proceso KDD permitiendo combinar distintas familias de algoritmos de minería de datos para la obtención de patrones de conocimiento relevantes para la inteligencia de negocio. ***Definición del Problema:*** El arribo de nuevas tecnologías para la obtención de datos referenciados espacialmente, permitió adquirir nuevos tipos de patrones útiles para la toma de decisiones estratégicas. Sin embargo, debido a las particularidades de este nuevo tipo de información y a las diferencias semánticas asociadas a las mismas, los procesos de explotación de información tradicionales no resultan útiles para este objetivo. ***Objetivo.*** Se propone, entonces, un nuevo conjunto de procesos que combinen distintas técnicas de pre-procesamiento, minería, y pos-procesamiento de datos para satisfacer las necesidades de la inteligencia de negocio en relación con los datos espaciales. ***Método:*** Se aborda el tema con un enfoque de investigación clásico mediante (i) revisiones sistemáticas para la captura de las necesidades que se presentan en diferentes áreas, y (ii) prototipado evolutivo experimental para el diseño de los procesos. ***Resultados Preliminares:*** Se han diseñado hasta el momento procesos de explotación de información para (i) el descubrimiento de patrones de co-localización, (ii) el descubrimiento de agrupaciones espaciales, y (iii) el descubrimiento de anomalías locales y regionales. ***Trabajo Futuro:*** Un proceso de explotación de información para el descubrimiento de reglas de asociación espacial se encuentra en desarrollo. Posteriormente será efectuada una iteración para la mejora de los procesos propuestos y una prueba de aplicación integral de los mismos usando datos reales.

Keywords: Explotación de Información Espacial, Minería de Datos Espaciales, Patrones de Co Localización, Agrupamiento Espacial, Detección de Anomalías Espaciales

1 Introducción

La Explotación de Información es la disciplina encargada de obtener conocimiento implícito en grandes volúmenes de datos a fin de apoyar la toma de decisiones estratégicas de la Inteligencia de Negocio [1].

Esta disciplina se vale de los denominados "Procesos de Explotación de Información" para poder preparar, procesar y analizar grandes volúmenes de información haciendo uso de distintos algoritmos de minería de datos [2–4].

En los últimos años, debido a la llegada de nuevas tecnologías, una enorme cantidad de datos espacialmente referenciados han sido utilizados para múltiples propósitos tales como planificación urbana, logística, salud, ecología, entre otros [5, 6].

Los datos espaciales, a diferencia de los datos transaccionales tradicionales, poseen ciertas características tales como la dependencia espacial de sus atributos y los diferentes modelos de representación que hacen que los procesos de explotación de información utilizados hasta el momento [1] no se puedan aplicar de manera satisfactoria. Por otro lado, el hecho de que las entidades de datos se encuentren relacionadas con lugares determinados del espacio hace que existan relaciones más complejas que aquellas que se dan entre datos tradicionales, lo que producen variaciones semánticas en los patrones de conocimiento normalmente utilizados [7–9].

Debido a estas particularidades, resulta interesante proponer un nuevo conjunto de procesos de ingeniería para la explotación de información espacialmente referenciada que considere las particularidades inherentes a la naturaleza de los datos mencionadas anteriormente, y que especifique las transformaciones y actividades de procesamiento necesarias para la obtención de conocimiento útil para la toma de decisiones. Para esto, nos valemos de una metodología de trabajo clásica utilizando revisiones sistemáticas y prototipado evolutivo experimental para el diseño y prueba de los procesos [10, 11].

En las secciones siguientes se profundiza en los antecedentes que dan origen a esta investigación (sección 2), se enumeran los objetivos de investigación planteados (sección 3) y la metodología utilizada (sección 4), se detalla el grado de avance del trabajo realizado y las actividades pendientes de ser ejecutadas (sección 5), para finalmente presentar conclusiones (sección 6).

2 Antecedentes

En la presente sección se menciona y analiza el marco teórico y las necesidades que dan origen al trabajo de investigación presentado en este artículo. Cuestiones sobre la explotación de información y la minería de datos son abordadas en la sección 2.1, mientras que en la sección 2.2 se analizan las particularidades de los datos espacialmente referenciados en contraste con los datos transaccionales tradicionales.

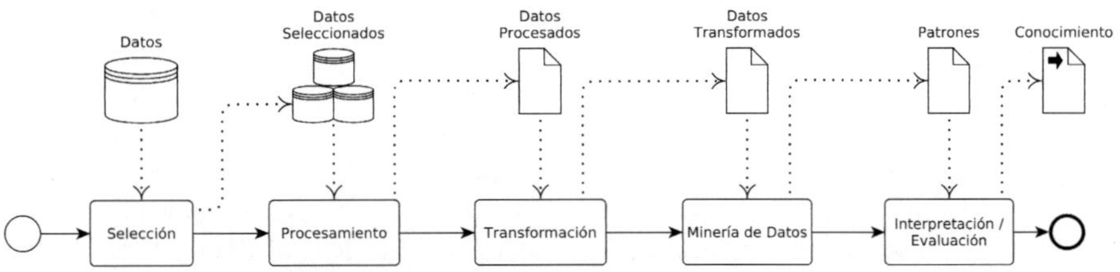

Fig. 1: Proceso de Descubrimiento de Conocimiento en Base de Datos (*KDD Process*).

2.1 Explotación de Información y Minería de Datos

La Explotación de Información es la disciplina que da a la Inteligencia de Negocio herramientas para la transformación de información en conocimiento mediante la búsqueda de patrones interesantes y de regularidades importantes en grandes masas de información [1].

Dentro de esta disciplina, se define *proceso de explotación de información* como un conjunto de tareas lógicamente relacionadas que permiten agregar valor a un conjunto de datos provistos como entrada [3, 4].

Fayyad et al. (1996) [2] propone por primera vez un proceso de explotación de información denominado proceso KDD –*Knowledge Discovery in Databases* que unifica de una manera abstracta la secuencia de pasos utilizada para la extracción de conocimiento de los datos de entrada (Fig. 1). Dentro de este proceso distintos algoritmos de minería de datos, provenientes en su mayoría del campo del Aprendizaje Automático, son susceptibles de ser utilizados de forma independiente o combinados a fin de obtener distintas clases de patrones.

Posteriormente, Britos (2008) [1] diseña un conjunto de procesos de explotación de información que se basan en el abstracto proceso KDD y que en contraste con el mismo proponen distintas combinaciones de algoritmos y técnicas de pre-procesamiento y transformación de los datos de entrada en función de los patrones que se desean obtener. Estos patrones no son arbitrarios, sino que se fundamentan en los intereses de la inteligencia de negocio [12, 13]. Entre ellos se pueden mencionar tres procesos básicos y dos procesos adicionales que surgen de la combinación de los primeros:

- Proceso para el Descubrimiento de Reglas de Comportamiento
- Proceso para el Descubrimiento de Grupos
- Proceso para la Ponderación de Interdependencia de Atributos
- Proceso para el Descubrimiento de Reglas de Pertenencia a Grupos
- Proceso para la Ponderación de Reglas de Pertenencia a Grupos

2.2 Particularidades de la Información Espacial

Los datos que se asocian con un lugar de un espacio determinado se denominan datos espacialmente referenciados o datos espaciales. Estos se encuentran compuestos por dos clases de atributos: (i) *Atributos No-Espaciales*, que brindan información sobre el dominio del problema que se está analizando, y (ii), *Atributos Espaciales*, que asocian los valores de los atributos no-espaciales con una ubicación espacial determinada. Por ejemplo, para estudiar el comportamiento del clima de un país contamos con datos de centrales meteorológicas o puntos de control: atributos como temperatura, humedad, dirección y velocidad del viento, entre otros, corresponderían a atributos no-espaciales, mientras que la latitud, longitud y altura sobre el nivel del mar de la fuente de información corresponderían a atributos espaciales [14].

Por otro lado, existen diferentes tipos de datos para representar objetos en el espacio, dependiendo de su naturaleza. Los más básicos son: (i) los *Puntos*, que permiten representar objetos o hechos en un lugar determinado del espacio, como en el caso de las centrales meteorológicas mencionadas en el punto anterior, (ii) las *Líneas*, utilizadas para representar elementos que se extienden de manera lineal en el espacio, tales como ríos, carreteras o trayectorias de vehículos o animales, y (iii) las *Superficies*, usadas para representar áreas como parcelas de terreno, extensiones de bosques, entre otros [15].

Por último, los patrones de conocimiento obtenidos de la información espacial poseen diferencias semánticas en contraste con aquellos obtenidos a partir de información tradicional o relacional. Estas diferencias surgen a partir de relaciones más complejas entre los datos, tales como distancia y conexión entre objetos espaciales o relaciones topológicas entre los mismos. De esta forma, por ejemplo, los grupos espaciales no solo deben poseer elementos similares sino que sus elementos deben ser vecinos o conexos en el espacio, o bien las reglas de asociación no solo deben relacionar valores de atributos no-espaciales, sino que deben considerar cuestiones de posición como "A se encuentra arriba de B" o "X interseca a Y" [7, 8, 15–17]

Esta variedad de modelos de representación de los datos, la dependencia espacial de los atributos y las consecuentes variaciones semánticas en los tipos de patrones buscados, hacen que los procesos de explotación de información tradicionales y los algoritmos de minería de datos utilizados no puedan ser aplicados con resultados satisfactorios para la inteligencia de negocio [9, 18].

3 Objetivos de Investigación

Debido a las particularidades de la información espacial que hacen que los procesos de explotación de información y algoritmos de minería de datos tradicionales no puedan ser aplicados, tal como se mencionó en el apartado anterior, resulta de interés proponer un conjunto de procesos de explotación de información espacialmente referenciada útiles para la Inteligencia de Negocio.

Para esto, es necesario la identificación de los patrones de conocimiento interesantes para definir por cada uno de ellos un proceso que incluya las técnicas de preparación de datos necesarias, los algoritmos de minería de datos intervinientes y la secuencialidad de la aplicación de los mismos.

En consecuencia, se define como objetivos del trabajo de investigación:

1. Identificar patrones de conocimiento útiles para la inteligencia de negocio, a ser obtenidos a partir de datos espacialmente referenciados.
2. Diseñar un conjunto de procesos de explotación de información espacialmente referenciada, definiendo:
   - El formato de los datos de entrada, de los datos en estancias intermedias del proceso, y de los resultados del proceso.
   - La secuencia de actividades a realizar, incluyendo la preparación de los datos, el modelado y la interpretación de los resultados.
   - Los algoritmos o familia de algoritmos de minería de datos susceptibles a ser utilizados en cada actividad.
3. Validar las propuestas realizadas mediante su aplicación a datos espaciales de escenarios reales y mediante el juicio de expertos.

4 Metodología

Para construir el conocimiento necesario para el cumplimiento de los objetivos de investigación propuestos en la sección 3.1 del presente artículo, se utiliza un enfoque de investigación clásico [10] haciendo énfasis en la producción de tecnologías [11].

Se realiza una exploración documental mediante el método de revisiones sistemáticas [19, 20] para la determinación de las necesidades de la inteligencia de negocio, esto es, cuáles son los patrones de conocimiento de interés asociados a los datos espaciales. Por cada uno de dichos patrones identificados, se realiza un relevamiento de los algoritmos y técnicas utilizadas comúnmente para la preparación, el pre-procesado y el minado de los datos espaciales.

Posteriormente, por cada necesidad planteada, se utiliza el método de prototipado evolutivo experimental [21] para el diseño de los procesos de explotación de información. En este paso se seleccionan del relevamiento llevado a cabo en el paso anterior los algoritmos y técnicas mencionados en el estado del arte factibles de ser utilizados, se realizan modificaciones a los mismos en caso de ser necesarios, se especifica la secuencialidad de las actividades, se definen cuáles son los atributos de los datos que intervienen en el proceso y de qué forma lo hacen, y se realizan pruebas de funcionamiento mediante el uso de datos tanto simulados como reales.

Al finalizar cada una de las etapas, se realizará una prueba integral de todos los procesos frente a escenarios reales, contrastando los resultados obtenidos con la opinión de expertos.

5 Realización de la Investigación

En esta sección se detallan las distintas actividades llevadas a cabo (sección 5.1) y las actividades pendientes de ejecución (sección 5.2) para el cumplimiento de los objetivos especificados anteriormente siguiendo las formas metodológicas mencionadas.

5.1 Actividades Realizadas

La investigación comenzó formalmente en el mes de febrero del año 2016. Desde ese momento hasta la actualidad se han diseñado tres procesos de explotación de información en el marco de este trabajo académico y mediante la metodología mencionada anteriormente: (i) Un proceso para el descubrimiento de patrones de co-localización, (ii) un proceso para la caracterización de regiones espaciales, y (iii) un proceso para el descubrimiento de anomalías espaciales.

De esta forma, el primer proceso mencionado utiliza reglas de clasificación para poder detectar patrones de co-localización dada una clase de objeto espacial de referencia tras la generación de datos transaccionales usando cliques máximos; el segundo proceso diseñado permite la generación de regiones espaciales utilizando algoritmos de agrupamiento espacial y una descripción de cada región detectada utilizando árboles de decisión sobre los atributos no espaciales de los datos; por último, el tercer proceso desarrollado permite una regionalización automática del conjunto de datos mediante algoritmos de agrupamiento espacial para una posterior búsqueda de anomalías en cada uno de los grupos generados y una posterior detección del grado de anormalidad de cada uno de las regiones halladas a fin de determinar si son anormales en su vecindario.

Estos diseños han dado lugar a dos publicaciones en el Congreso Argentino de Ciencias de la Computación (CACIC) [22, 23], dos publicaciones en *International Conference on Industrial, Engineering & Other Applications of Applied Intelligent Systems* (IEA-AIE) [24] (uno pendiente de publicación), y una publicación en *International Conference on Software Engineering and Knowledge Engineering* (SEKE) [25].

5.2 Actividades Futuras

En la actualidad, un proceso de explotación de información para la detección de asociaciones espaciales se encuentra en proceso de ser diseñado.

Posteriormente se planea la realización y publicación de un artículo en un congreso de alcance internacional para la comunicación de los resultados que se obtendrán tras el diseño del proceso mencionado y un artículo para una revista indizada de alcance internacional que integre toda la producción científica de este trabajo de investigación.

Por último, para finalizar el trabajo relacionado con la tesis doctoral, se planea validar los procesos producto de este trabajo de investigación utilizando datos de escenarios reales variados contrastando los resultados con la opinión de expertos en dichos campos.

Continuamente y en función de los nuevos avances en materia de algoritmia para minería de datos espaciales, se evalúa la mejora de los procesos diseñados hasta el momento.

6 Conclusiones

El trabajo de investigación detallado en el presente artículo contribuye aportando un conjunto de procesos de ingeniería para la explotación de información espacialmente referenciada. Estos procesos detallan la forma en la cual esta información particular debe ser tratada y procesada a fin de poder descubrir, hasta el momento, (i) reglas de asociación espaciales, (ii) patrones de co-localización, (iii) regiones espaciales, y (iv) anomalías espaciales, útiles para la Inteligencia de Negocio para la toma de decisiones estratégicas.

Para esto, por cada uno de ellos se especifican: (i) las fuentes y formatos de los datos de entrada y la forma de integrarlos, (ii) las transformaciones de los mismos, (iii) los algoritmos de minería de datos a ser aplicados, (iv) las salidas del proceso, (v) la forma en la cual los resultados deben ser interpretados, y (vi) el orden de ejecución de las tareas.

Cada uno de estos procesos estarán validados mediante su aplicación ante escenarios tanto simulados como reales y mediante el juicio de expertos.

Agradecimientos

Esta investigación ha sido parcialmente financiada por el Programa de Becas Doctorales para el Fortalecimiento de Áreas I+D+i (2016-2020) de la Universidad Tecnológica Nacional, por el Proyecto de Investigación 80020160400001LA de la Universidad Nacional de Lanús, y por PIO CONICET-UNLa 22420160100032CO del Consejo Nacional de Investigaciones Científicas y Técnicas (CONICET), Argentina. Se agradece además a los atentos revisores de este trabajo por su mirada crítica y por sus valiosos comentarios. En memoria del Prof. Dr. Ramón García-Martínez.

Referencias

1. Britos, P. V. (2008). Procesos de explotación de información basados en sistemas inteligentes (Doctoral dissertation, Facultad de Informática).
2. Fayyad, U. M., Piatetsky-Shapiro, G., & Smyth, P. (1996, August). Knowledge Discovery and Data Mining: Towards a Unifying Framework. In KDD (Vol. 96, pp. 82-88).
3. García Martínez, R. (1997). Sistemas Autónomos. Aprendizaje Automático. Editorial Nueva Librería (p. 2004). ISBN 950-9088-84-6. García Martínez, R. y Britos.
4. García Martínez, R., Servente, M., & Pasquini, D. (2003). Sistemas Inteligentes. Editorial Nueva Librería. Buenos Aires. ISBN 987-1104-05-7.
5. Mennis, J., & Guo, D. (2009). Spatial data mining and geographic knowledge discovery—An introduction. Computers, Environment and Urban Systems, 33(6), 403-408.
6. Mazimpaka, J. D., & Timpf, S. (2016). Trajectory data mining: A review of methods and applications. Journal of Spatial Information Science, 2016(13), 61-99.
7. Yang, H., & Parthasarathy, S. (2006). Mining spatial and spatio-temporal patterns in scientific data. In Data Engineering Workshops, 2006. Proceedings. 22nd International Conference on (pp. x146-x146). IEEE.
8. Leung Y. (2010) Introduction. In: Knowledge Discovery in Spatial Data. Advances in Spatial Science (The Regional Science Series). Springer, Berlin, Heidelberg. Online ISBN: 978-3-642-02664-5. DOI: 10.1007/978-3-642-02664-5

9. Goudarzi, A. H., & Ghadiri, N. (2017). A hybrid spatial data mining approach based on fuzzy topological relations and MOSES evolutionary algorithm. arXiv:1704.06621.
10. Creswell, J. W. (2002). Educational research: Planning, conducting, and evaluating quantitative (pp. 146-166). Upper Saddle River, NJ: Prentice Hall.
11. Sabato, J. A., & McKenzie, M. (1982). La producción de tecnología: autonoma o transnacional. Medellín: Nueva Imagen.
12. García-Martínez, R., Britos, P., Pesado, P., Bertone, R., Pollo-Cattaneo, F., Rodríguez, D., ... & Vanrell, J. (2011). Towards an information mining engineering. Software Engineering, Methods, Modeling and Teaching, 83-99.
13. García-Martínez, R., Britos, P., & Rodríguez, D. (2013, June). Information mining processes based on intelligent systems. In International Conference on Industrial, Engineering and Other Applications of Applied Intelligent Systems (pp. 402-410). Springer, Berlin, Heidelberg.
14. Koperski, K., Adhikary, J., & Han, J. (1996, June). Spatial data mining: progress and challenges survey paper. In Proc. ACM SIGMOD Workshop on Research Issues on Data Mining and Knowledge Discovery, Montreal, Canada (pp. 1-10).
15. Malerba, D. (2008). A relational perspective on spatial data mining. International Journal of Data Mining, Modelling and Management, 1(1), 103-118.
16. Malerba, D., & Lisi, F. (2001). Discovering associations between spatial objects: An ILP application. Inductive logic programming, 156-163.
17. Liu, Q., Deng, M., Shi, Y., & Wang, J. (2012). A density-based spatial clustering algorithm considering both spatial proximity and attribute similarity. Computers & Geosciences, 46, 296-309.
18. Kataria, P., & Rupal, N. (2012). Mining Spatial Data & Enhancing Classification Using Bio-Inspired Approaches. International Journal of Science and Research (IJSR), 3(2), 1473-1479.
19. Kitchenham, B. (2004). Procedures for performing systematic reviews. Keele, UK, Keele University, 33(2004), 1-26.
20. Kitchenham, B., Brereton, O. P., Budgen, D., Turner, M., Bailey, J., & Linkman, S. (2009). Systematic literature reviews in software engineering–a systematic literature review. Information and software technology, 51(1), 7-15.
21. Basili, V. R. (1993). The experimental paradigm in software engineering. In Experimental Software Engineering Issues: Critical Assessment and Future Directions (pp. 1-12). Springer, Berlin, Heidelberg.
22. Rottoli, G., Merlino, H., & García Martínez, R. (2016a). Proceso de descubrimiento de patrones de co-localización alrededor de tipos de eventos de referencia. In XXII Congreso Argentino de Ciencias de la Computación (CACIC 2016).
23. Rottoli, G., Merlino, H., & García Martínez, R. (2016b). Proceso de descubrimiento de reglas de caracterización de grupos espacialmente referenciados. In XXII Congreso Argentino de Ciencias de la Computación (CACIC 2016)..
24. Rottoli, G. D., Merlino, H., & García-Martinez, R. (2017a). Co-location Rules Discovery Process Focused on Reference Spatial Features Using Decision Tree Learning. In International Conference on Industrial, Engineering and Other Applications of Applied Intelligent Systems (pp. 221-226). Springer, Cham. DOI: 10.1007/978-3-319-60042-0_25
25. Rottoli, G. D., Merlino, H., & García-Martinez, R. (2017b). Knowledge Discovery Process for Description of Spatially Referenced Clusters. In International Conference on Software Engineering & Knowledge Engineering. (pp.410–415) Ed. USA KSI Research Inc. and Knowledge Systems Institute. DOI: 10.18293/SEKE2017-013

An Extension to Pre-conceptual Schemas for Refining Event Representation and Mathematical Notation

Paola Andrea Noreña Cardona[1]

[1] Universidad Nacional de Colombia, Medellín, Colombia
panorenac@unal.edu.co

Abstract. An event is something that happens and produces changes in the system behavior. Events are used for representing the beginning or the end of automatic and human processes in scientific software domains. Such domains comprise software systems with a high scientific knowledge content. Computational and scientific modeling tools are used for representing events in a domain by using linguistic, mathematical, and graphical structures. Pre-conceptual Schemas (PSs) are computational modeling tools used for recognizing knowledge domain. PSs integrate some structures for representing events in a domain. However, PSs lack linguistic, mathematical, and graphical structures for representing events in scientific software domains. In this paper, we present Ph.D. Thesis advances for refining event representation and mathematical notation by using PSs. Such extension includes linguistic, mathematical, and graphical structures for improving the event representation in scientific software domains. So, the PSs can be used as tools for recognizing the knowledge of such domains.

Keywords: Computational Modeling, Events, Pre-conceptual Schema, Scientific Software Domain.

1 Introduction

An event is defined as something that happens in a certain time and of a software system [1–2]. Events contain conditions and constraints, which are executed for triggering processes and affecting state change in system behavior [3]. Events can be classified by *trigger* and *result* [4]. *Trigger event* is used for representing the beginning of automatic and human processes [5]. Also trigger event can generate other trigger events, *i.e., none or statement (*an instruction causing a trigger for generating a process)*; conditional* (a constraint specifying a condition), and *timer* (specific time or a specific cycle can trigger the start of processes). *Result* event is represented for indicating the end of a sequence processes flow of the process [5–6].

Event are used in scientific software domains, which focus on addressing the needs of scientific processes, specific research, and science students. Usually, in such domain are developed software system for solving a real-life problem by using mathematical structures from scientific modeling. Such specific domains can be mathematics, engineering (*i.e.,* electronic, electric, mechanic, control, petroleum), medicine, and sciences (*i.e.,* geography, biology, meteorology, geology) [7].

Usually, analyst use linguistic, mathematical and graphical for representing events. Linguistic structures are linguistic elements interrelated for giving a meaning to a sentence *i.e.,* a verb, a noun [8]. Mathematical structures are mathematical elements (numbers, concepts, and operations) related, which are expressed by using axioms (formulas). Operations are represented by using logical operators (which are used in conditions for jointing relational operators *i.e.,* and, or, xor); relational operators (which are used in conditions *i.e.,* <, >, =, !=), basic operators (which are used in basic math formulas, *i.e.,* +, -, *, /), and complex (which are used in complex formulas i.e., trigonometric functions) [9–10]. Graphical structures are symbols set allowing a visual and organized result *i.e.,* a circle, a triangle.

Computational modeling comprises tools for representing a business domain in software development *i.e.,* organizational domain; such tools can be classified by structural and behavioral views [11]. Some of such tools are used for representing events by using linguistic and graphical structures [5, 11–18]. Scientific modeling comprises tools for representing a scientific domain *i.e.,* engineering, sciences, and math. Generally, some of such tools are used for representing events by using mathematical structures [19–24].

Pre-conceptual Schemas (PSs) are computational modeling tools (conceptual model) for recognizing main elements of a domain in software engineering processes. PSs link structural and dynamic features of such domain in opposed of the other computational modeling tools [6]. Also, in the PSs notation (see Fig. 1.) are included elements with linguistic, mathematical, and graphical structures for modeling trigger and result events [3–4]. The suffix "pre" was determined by Zapata [25] based in pre-concepts defined by Heidegger related with "schema" about pre-knowledge defined by Piaget. However, PSs lack linguistic, mathematical, and graphical structures for representing elements, vocabulary, and complex mathematical equations, which are used in event representation from scientific software domains.

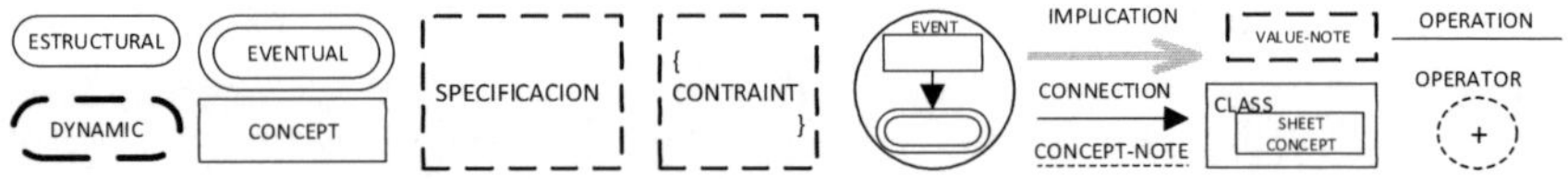

Fig. 1. EP Notation.

Consequently, in this paper we present Ph.D. Thesis advances; thus, we propose an extension to the pre-conceptual schema for representing events and refining mathematical notation from scientific software domains. Such extension contains elements with new linguistic, mathematical, and graphical structures, which are used in scientific software domains for representing events. Scientific (engineering, science, math) and business (software, administration, economy) analysts can use the PSs refined for recognizing and solving the problem knowledge from a scientific software domain.

This paper is structured as follows: in Section 2, we present the methodology; in Section 3, we include the state of the art; in Section 4, we state of the problem; in Section 5, we propose a solution; in Section 6, we describe the results. Finally, we establish conclusions and future work in Section 7.

2 Methodology

We use *empirically-based technology transfer* methodology defined by Wohlin *et al.* [26]; such methodology is applicated for observing problems in industry and proposing solutions. Phases are: i) *Exploration* (planning and executing systematic literature review); ii) *Problem formulation* (problem statement, the research question, and the hypothesis); iii) *Solution* (characterizing events, analyzing event types, defining linguistic, mathematical, and graphical structures, and including the extension to PSs; and iv) V*alidation* (planning, executing and analyzing experiment by measuring learnability from usability, software quality feature); Our research is in the *solution* phase.

3 State of the Art

Computational modeling tools are conceptual and graphical models, which can be *behavioral views* used for representing events by using linguistic (verbs and objects) and graphical structures as process information model metamodel [1], SysML state machine diagram [12], and event interaction graph adapted to PSs [3]. In addition, Business Process Model Notation (BPMN) [13], Unified Modeling Language (UML) state machine and activity diagrams [11], and event-driven process chain [14] include mathematical (logical and relational) structures. However, they lack complex mathematical structures and structural views. *Structural views* are used for representing events by using linguistic and graphical structures as event-driven architecture [5], complex event process [15], basic event model [16], event ontology description framework [17], and ontology pattern for emergency event modeling [2], However, they lack mathematical structures and behavioral views. Sowa conceptual graph [18] include structural and behavioral views, but it lacks element for representing events.

Some scientific modeling tools are used for representing events by using mathematical structures (math formulas) as Event-Triggered Control (ETC) [19], Model-based ETC scheme [20], Markov model [21], and Event-triggered output feedback control [22]. In addition, finite state automaton [23] and Petri net [24] include linguistic, mathematical, and graphical structures. However, they lack notation from computational modeling for developing software systems.

PSs integrate structural and dynamic views in a single tool, include linguistic structures for representing events as verbs (*eventual relationships*) for representing *statement* trigger event *i.e.,* arrive, come, emerge and result events, which are preceding dynamic relationship, in past participle form *i.e.,* updated. Such events are represented by using graphical structures as circle (event), rectangle (concept), implication (cause-effect arc), and eventual relationship (double-line oval) [6]. Also, PSs include elements of mathematical structures for representing conditional (trigger) events as: logical and relational operators [6, 4], and basic operators in dynamic relationship specifications for representing basic math formulas [27]. Such operators are integrated in a circle dotted line (graphical structure).

4 Problem Statement

Scientific analysts and developers produce scientific software themselves, but lack software engineering practices affecting software quality [28]. Also, business analysts require knowing from scientific domains. Accordingly, scientific and business analysts lack a modeling tool, which integrates software and scientific components. We select the PS as the modeling tool for solving the problem. However, PSs lack linguistic, mathematical, and graphical structures for representing events in scientific software domains. Since, PSs lack verbs, objects, and actors related to events in such domain; dynamic relationships only are used for representing human processes, then PSs lack elements for representing events in automatic processes; one single value can be represented with sheet concepts (attributes), so, PSs lack mathematical structures for complex math formulas, and elements for tracking process time by using events, such tracking is used for controlling process in scientific software domains. PSs lack the graphical structures for representing other type events and new linguistic and mathematical structures from scientific software domain. So, we formulate the *research question*: how we can refine event representation and mathematical notation in scientific software domain by using pre-conceptual schemas? and the *hypothesis*: an extension to pre-conceptual schemas by using linguistic, mathematical and graphical structures refine event representation and mathematical notation from scientific software domain. PSs with such extension can be used as a tool for representing events in scientific software domains.

5 Solution Proposal

We propose an extension to the pre-conceptual schema for representing events in scientific software domains by using linguistic, mathematical, and graphical structures used from such domain. So, we propose the *general objective*: refining event representation and mathematical notation by using an extension to PSs and the *objective specifics*: i) characterizing events emerging from scientific software domains; ii) defining linguistic, mathematical, and graphical structures for event representation in PSs; iii) proposing an extension to PSs for the sake of event representation and mathematical notation refinement by using linguistic, mathematical, and graphical structures for representing events in scientific software domains; and iv) validating the PSs extension in an experiment in order to analyze the proposed structures understanding level.

Characterizing events. We researched the event and the representation used in scientific software domain: linguistic (verbs, objects and concepts), mathematical (math formulas) and graphical structures for event representation (see next analyzing and defining).

Analyzing event types. Some events usually used in scientific software domains are signal (communication between two devices *i.e.,* call arrives), message *i.e.,* alert emerges), and time event (see definition in section 2.2. and representation in Fig. 2. and 3.). Some events in specific domains are (see Fig. 2.) meteorology (it thunders), geology (volcano erupts) medicine (patient suffers hemorrhage, cholesterol increases), statistic (dolar price decreases), electronic and electrical (voltage rises, electric wave appears).

Defining linguistic structures. We propose linguistic structures based in semantic roles (relationship among verb in other elements from a sentence) among zero to two actants (arguments of a verb), which are *experiencer* and *patient* (object or actor experimenting an event, *i.e., patient* in Fig. 2.) and a circumstant (circumstantial complements of a verb) *cause (*situation generated by an event), (see Fig. 2.) [29].

Defining mathematical structures. We use the binary expression tree (commonly used for representing algebraic and Boolean expressions [30]). Some elements integrated (see Fig. 2.) are the operations with multiple values of independent and dependent variables *i.e.,* the independent vector (*term* is the vector position); parameter (constant); and complex operators *i.e., sin* operator. Also, we propose include every concept from complex math formulas for a better understanding, *i.e.,* differential equation (1) is translated and used in equation (2) from the PS in Fig. 1. So, *PatientNumber[term]* is related as a vector, which changes in function of the independent variable *time.*

$$f(t)=P / 1+B * e^{-ct} \tag{1}$$

$$PatientNumber\ [term]=Population\ /\ 1 + Constant\ of\ integration\ *\ e^{-growth\ rate\ *\ time[term]} \tag{2}$$

Defining graphical structures. We use PS notation and new elements for representing linguistic and mathematical structures proposed (see Fig.2.). *i.e., initial conditions* are new specifications for initialing values of variables and parameters (constants); *parameters* with hexagons form; *independent variable* with a parallelogram, vector as concept (term is vector position). operator for every operation *i.e,* sin (sine), sqr (square root). Events should a specification a constraint and they are represented by using linguistic structures defined.

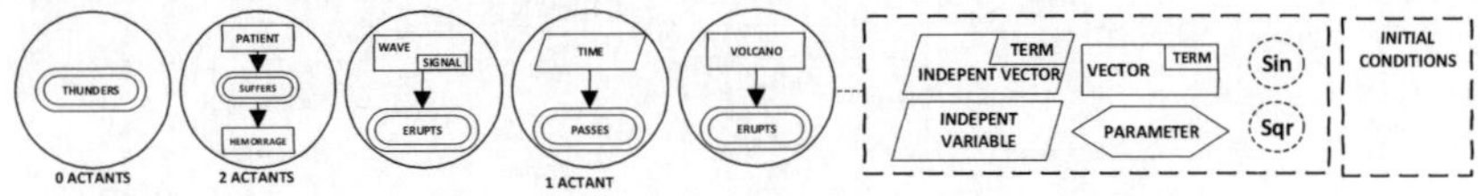

Fig. 2. New graphical structures for events and mathematical structures.

6 Results

We present an epidemical model of a city infected with influenza from the specific scientific software domain *medicine* by using a PS (see Fig. 3.) for applying the structures proposed in event representation. We use *initial conditions* specification for including parameters and variables. The parameters are *population* = *'500.000 per-*

sons'; constant of integration = '2499 persons', which is represented from the equation (3); and *growth rate = '0.916891 persons/week',* which is represented from the equation (4). The independent variable is *time,* so is represented with a vector *time[0] = '0 weeks'* and *time [1]= '1 week'.*

$$\text{Constant of integration} = (e^{\text{growth rate} * \text{time}[0]} * \text{Population-NumberPatient}[0]) / \text{NumberPatient}[0] \quad (3)$$

$$\text{Growth rate} = -\ln((\text{Population-NumberPatient}[1]) / (\text{NumberPatient}[1] * \text{Constant of integration})) / \text{time}[1] \quad (4)$$

The *behavioral view* is represented for analyzing events flow. The timer-trigger event type *time passes* contains a specification, where is included the dynamic relationship *update term* (vector position) incrementing in the value *'1'.* Such relationship is implicated with dynamic relationship *updates time[term]* incrementing in the value *'1 week'.* The event *time passes* triggers other event *PatientNumber[term] grows,* which is specificated by using the differential equation (2) for obtaining the incremental value of the *PatientNumber* in six weeks. The class *patient* is related with *number* vector by using structural relationship *has*, such elements are used for representing the *structural view* of the model. Such view is used for observing the concepts relationships and the data registered (*term, time, number*) in the array table *Patient* class, where for *time[6]='6 weeks'* the *PatientNumber[6] = '44624 persons'* with influenza.

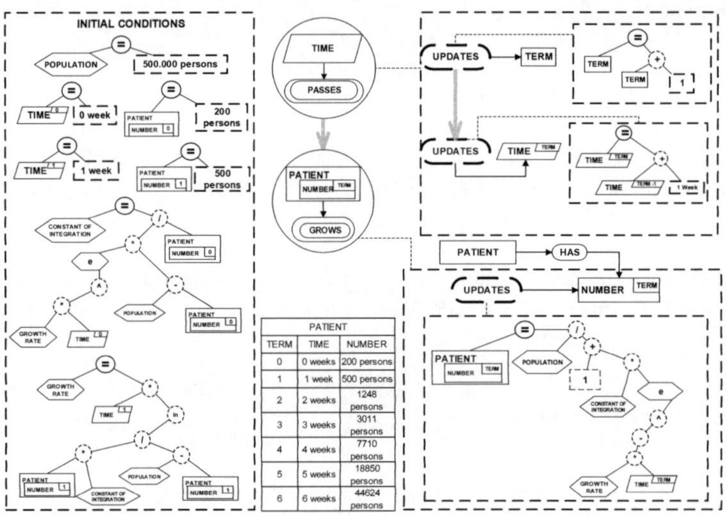

Fig. 3. PSs of an epidemiological model from the scientific software domain *medicine*.

7 Conclusions and future work

New linguistic, mathematical, and graphical structures for representing events from scientific software domain are proposed by using pre-conceptual schemas. PSs are tools used in academy and industry for easing understand a domain and producing software. Scientific and business analysts may be model their scientific software domains by using PSs with the extension proposed. So, our proposal is a new approach for relating scientific domain to software development, by using behavioral and structural views in a same tool.

We suggest as future work exploring and representing other domains, considering other elements, and validating the new structures with experts and students. Also, PSs may be considered for learning mathematics in other areas.

Acknowledgments. This paper is a product of the Ph.D. project *an extension to pre-conceptual schemas for refining event representation and mathematical notation* with Hermes code 39886 at Universidad Nacional de Colombia. This work is sponsored by Colciencias from Colombia, in the program doctoral students, bid 727 of 2015.

References

1. Ravikumar, G., Khaparde, S. A., Joshi, R. K.: Integration of Process Model and CIM to Represent Events and Chronology in Power System Processes. IEEE Systems Journal, vol. 99, pp. 1–12 (2016).
2. Liu, W. Tan, Y. Ding, N. Zhang, Y., Liu, Z.: An Ontology Pattern for Emergency Event Modeling. IEEE 14th Intl Conf on Dependable, Autonomic and Secure Computing, 14th Intl Conf on Pervasive Intelligence and Computing, 2nd Intl Conf on Big Data Intelligence and Computing and Cyber Science and Technology Congress, pp. 151-156. Auckland, New Zeland, (2016).
3. Zapata, C.M., Noreña, P.A., Gonzales, N.: Representación de eventos disparadores y de resultado en el grafo de interacción de eventos. Ing. UsbMed, vol. 4 no. 2, pp. 23–32 (2013).
4. Noreña, P.A.: Un mecanismo de consistencia en los eventos disparador y de resultado para los artefactos de UNC-Method. Tesis de maestría. Universidad Nacional de Colombia, Medellín, Colombia (2013).
5. Klusman, M., Plasmeijer, R., Wolter, R.: Event-Driven Architecture in software development projects. Master Thesis Computing Science, Radboud University, Nijmegen (2016).
6. Zapata, C.M.: The UNC-Method revisited: elements of the new approach. Saarbrucken: Lambert (2012).
7. Kelly, D.: Scientific software development viewed as knowledge acquisition: Towards understanding the development of risk-averse scientific software. Journal of Systems and Software, vol. 109, pp. 50-61 (2015).
8. Matthews, Peter. (2001). A Short History of Structural Linguistics. England: Cambridge Univ. Press.
9. Jaramillo, C. M., Duarte, P. V.: Enseñanza y aprendizaje de las estructuras matemáticas a partir del modelo de Van Hiele. Revista Educación y pedagogía, vol. 18, no. 45, pp. 109-118 (2009).
10. Vélez, C.C.: La matemática como teoría de estructuras. Revista Colombiana de Filosofía de la Ciencia, vol. 13, no. 26, pp. 7-30 (2013).
11. OMG, Object Management Group.: Superstructure 2.5. Standard Document (2015), http://www.omg.org/spec/UML/2.5/

12. Baouya, A. Bennouar, D., Mohamed O. A., Ouchani S.: A probabilistic and timed verification approach of SysML state machine diagram. Programming and Systems (ISPS), 12th International Symposium, pp. 1-9. Algiers, Algeria. (2015).
13. Haisjackl, C., Soffer, P., Lim, S., Weber, B.: How do humans inspect BPMN models: an exploratory study? Software and Systems Modeling, vol. 15, no. 58, pp. 1-19 (2016).
14. Xia, W., Junpeng, M.: Research on Flexible Business Process of Bank Modeling Based on EPC. Management of e-Commerce and e-Government (ICMeCG), 2014 International Conference, pp. 54-60. Shanghai, China (2014).
15. Dávid, I., Ráth, I., Varró, D.: Foundations for Streaming Model Transformations by Complex Event Processing. Software and Systems Modeling, vol. 15, no. 58, pp. 1-28 (2016).
16. Wang, Y., Zhou, X., Shan, L., Miao, K.: Study on complex event processing for CPS: An event model perspective. In Ubiquitous Intelligence and Computing. IEEE 11th Intl Conf on and Autonomic and Trusted Computing, pp. 305-310. Bali, Indonesia (2014).
17. Zhang, Y., Liu, W., Ding, N., Wang, X., Tan, Y.: An Event Ontology Description Framework Based on SKOS. In Ubiquitous Intelligence and Computing. IEEE 12th Intl Conf on Autonomic and Trusted Computing, pp. 1774-1779. Bali, Indonesia (2015).
18. Miranda, S., Gelbukh, A., Sidorov, G. Generación de resúmenes por medio de síntesis de grafos conceptuales, Revista signos, vol. 47, no. 86, pp. 463-485 (2014).
19. Borgers D.P., Heemels., W.P.: On minimum inter-event times in event-triggered control. 52nd IEEE Conference on Decision and Control, pp. 7370-7375. Florence, Italy. (2013).
20. Sahoo, A., Xu, H., Jagannathan, S.: Adaptive neural network-based event-triggered control of single-input single-output nonlinear discrete-time systems. IEEE transactions on neural networks and learning systems, vol. 27, no. 1, pp. 151-164 (2016).
21. Chen, W., Wang, J., Shi, D., Shi, L.: Event-based State Estimation of Hidden Markov Models through a Gilbert-Elliott Channel. IEEE Transactions on Automatic Control, vol. 99, pp. 1-8 (2017).
22. Xue, D., El-Farra, N.: Output feedback-based event-triggered control of distributed processes with communication constraints. Decision and Control (CDC), IEEE 55th Conference, pp. 4296-4301. Las Vegas, USA (2016).
23. Zhang, K. Zhang, L.: Observability of Boolean Control Networks: A Unified Approach Based on Finite Automata. IEEE Transactions on Automatic Control, vol. 61, no. 9, pp. 2733-2738 (2016).
24. Sarno, R., Kartini, Wibowo, W. A., Solichah, A.: Time based Discovery of parallel business processes. Computer, Control, Informatics and its Applications (IC3INA), 2015 International Conference, pp. 28-33. Bandung, Indonesia (2015).
25. Zapata, C.: Definición de un esquema preconceptual para la obtención automática de esquemas conceptuales de UML, Ph.D. Thesis, Universidad Nacional de Colombia, sede Medellín (2007).
26. Wohlin, C., Runeson, P., Höst, M., Ohlsson, M. C., Regnell, B., Wesslén, A.: Experimentation in software engineering. New York: Springer Science & Business Media (2012).
27. Chaverra, J.: Generación automática de prototipos funcionales a partir de esquemas preconceptuales. Tesis de maestría. Universidad Nacional de Colombia, Medellín, Colombia (2011).
28. Wilson G., Aruliah, D., Brown C., Chue, N.P., Davis, M., Guy, R.T., Steven, H.D. Huff, K., Mitchell, I.M., Plumbley, M., Waugh, B., White E.P., Wilson, P.: Best Practices for Scientific Computing, PLOS Biology, vol. 12, no.1 e1001745, (2014).
29. Tesnière, L.: Éléments de syntaxe structural. Paris: Klincksieck (1966).
30. Kuipers, J., Ueda, T., Vermaseren, J.A.M.: Code optimization in FORM, Computer Physics Communications, vol. 189, pp. 1-19 (2015).

Método de automatización del despliegue continuo en la nube para la implementación de microservicios

Fredy H. Vera-Rivera [1]

[1] Universidad del Valle, Cali, Colombia
[1] Universidad Francisco de Paula Santander, Cúcuta, Colombia
fredyhumbertovera@ufps.edu.co
fredy.vera@correounivalle.edu.co

Abstract. La tendencia actual en el desarrollo de aplicaciones orientadas a servicios se centra en los microservicios, como una alternativa para construir las aplicaciones uniendo o componiendo una serie de servicios independientes, autónomos, que pueden ser individualmente desarrollados, probados, configurados, desplegados y escalados. En el presente trabajo de investigación doctoral se pretende crear un modelo de especificación de la arquitectura de aplicaciones basadas en microservicios con el fin de modelar, orquestar, adaptar, componer y evaluar los microservicios que hacen parte de una aplicación. Como resultados preliminares se presenta la caracterización del proceso de desarrollo de la arquitectura de microservicios, se propone un método de automatización del despliegue continuo de microservicios; este método se probó usando el deployment pipeline de Bitbucked, obteniendo la posibilidad de realizar pruebas estáticas, unitarias y funcionales automatizadas y desplegar a un servidor de pruebas y de producción automáticamente, sin intervención humana, el despliegue se hace a una instancia EC2 de AWS. También se presenta la identificación de los desafíos y problemas de investigación existentes en el área de los microservicios.

Keywords: Microservicios, especificación, DevOps, automatización del despliegue continuo, deployment pipeline.

1 Introducción

Cada vez es más el enfoque histórico de la arquitectura de aplicaciones monolíticas (en la que se crea una sola aplicación integrada que contiene la mayoría de sus funcionalidades y componentes están muy acoplados), comienza a ser reemplazado por diseños basados en Microservicios. Los microservicios son una nueva tendencia de arquitectura de software que está fuertemente influenciada por la computación distribuida, la idea principal es dividir una aplicación en pequeños servicios; cada servicio debe ser lo más independiente posible de los demás. Cada uno se ejecuta en procesos separados, en un contenedor aislado y único, es posible asignar más recursos computacionales al microservicio que más lo necesite, a diferencia de las aplicaciones monolíticas que asignan recursos a toda la aplicación, que en ocasiones son recursos que posiblemente no serán utilizados y aprovechados en su totalidad [1].

Según Lewis y Fowler un microservicio es: "Un enfoque arquitectónico que consiste en construir sistemas para servicios de escala reducida, cada uno en su propio proceso, que se comunican a través de protocolos ligeros" [2]. Los microservicios se presentan como un enfoque de implementación de la Arquitectura Orientada a Servicios (SOA), que pretende mejorar las desventajas y problemas presentados en SOA. La resiliencia, la escalabilidad, la entrega rápida de software y el uso de menos recursos son características esenciales en los sistemas empresariales actuales. La arquitectura de microservicios llegó a cumplir esas expectativas [3], sin embargo, aún se presentan muchos desafíos como la complejidad de tener que gestionar pequeños sistemas distribuidos, la latencia de la red y la falta de fiabilidad, la tolerancia a fallas, la coherencia e integración de datos, la gestión de transacciones distribuidas, las capas de comunicación, el balanceo de carga, la orquestación, el monitoreo y la seguridad [4].

La automatización de la infraestructura usando prácticas de DevOps reducen el esfuerzo manual involucrado en la construcción, implementación y operación de microservicios, lo que facilita la entrega y despliegue continuo. El gobierno descentralizado y la gestión de datos permiten que los servicios sean independientes y evitan que una aplicación estandarice una sola tecnología. Las arquitecturas de microservicio son especialmente adecuadas para las infraestructuras en la nube, ya que se benefician enormemente de la elasticidad y el rápido aprovisionamiento de recursos [5].

DevOps es un paradigma emergente que permite integrar al equipo de desarrollado con el personal de operaciones, de ahí su sigla Dev (Developers) – Ops (Operations). Sus prácticas permiten liberaciones rápidas y frecuentes [6]. DevOps es un nuevo término que surge con la colisión de dos nuevas tendencias, infraestructura ágil u operaciones ágiles, y colaboración entre el personal de desarrollo y de operaciones a lo largo de todas las etapas del ciclo de vida del desarrollo desde la codificación hasta despliegue a producción [7].

En este trabajo de investigación doctoral se presenta en la sección 2 el estado del arte, en la sección 3 las preguntas de investigación, posteriormente en la sección 4 se plantea la metodología, en la sección 5 se detallan los resultados obtenidos, se caracteriza el procesos de desarrollo de microservicios y se propone un método de automatización del despliegue continuo para la implementación de microservicios.

2 Estado del arte

Di Francesco, P. Malavolta y P. Lago (2017), evalúan el estado del arte de los microservicios desde las siguientes tres perspectivas: tendencias de publicación, foco de investigación y potencial para la adopción industrial. Afirman que existen pocos trabajos que investigan patrones de diseño y lenguajes arquitectónicos para microservicios. Proponer un lenguaje arquitectónico para microservicios podría ayudar a los arquitectos en muchas actividades. Existen vacíos de investigación en las áreas relacionadas con atributos de calidad [5].

Hulya V, Murat K y Sinem G (2017) realizan una revisión de literatura para conocer las tendencias de los microservicios, los estándares emergentes y las posibles lagunas de investigación. Concluyen que "los microservicios son un tema de tendencia y la predicción es que veremos una tendencia creciente en el futuro cercano. No hay investigación específicamente dirigida a los puntos débiles de los microservicios, como las transacciones distribuidas" [8]. Las principales tendencias o motivaciones de investigación están relacionadas con el diseño y la funcionalidad seguida de las técnicas de rendimiento y de prueba [8].

N. Alshuqayran, N. Ali y R. Evans (2016), realizan otro estudio, enfocándose en la identificación de desafíos arquitectónicos, los diagramas / vistas arquitectónicos y los atributos de calidad de los microservicios. Observan que el rastreo es uno de los problemas más comunes que enfrentan este tipo de aplicaciones. Los gráficos de dependencia ayudan a los arquitectos a refaccionar y tomar decisiones con confianza. Plantean la necesidad de futuras investigaciones en temas como la seguridad, distribución de carga en la nube, integración continua, gestión organizacional y DevOps, así como la automatización de la gestión de contenedores y su despliegue [9].

Claus Pahl y Pooyan Jamshidi (2016), evidencian la falta de tecnologías comprobadas para realizar una arquitectura de microservicios, falta de soporte de herramientas para automatizar y facilitar el uso de microservicios en la nube. Ausencia de herramientas de monitoreo, patrones arquitectónicos, enfoques experimentales para comparar microservicios empíricamente con otros estilos, herramientas para habilitar DevOps, métodos de creación de software (metodologías, patrones de diseño, mejores prácticas, garantía de calidad, revisión de sistemas, gestión de cambios) para el desarrollo de arquitectura de microservicios [10].

Olaf Zimmermann (2017) resalta los puntos críticos en la literatura de microservicios en forma de preguntas prácticas, como resultado de la revisión de la literatura SOA / microservicios y de discusiones con líderes de opinión industrial, desarrolladores y miembros de la comunidad de informática orientada a servicios. Enuncia estos temas de investigación: (1) Diseño de interfaz de servicio (contratación y control de versiones), (2) Ensamblaje y alojamiento de microservicio. (3) Integración y descubrimiento de microservicios, (4) Gestión de dependencias del servicio. (5) Prueba del servicio y de la aplicación de usuario final / cliente [11].

Como trabajos relacionados se encuentran Balalaie, Heydarnoori y Jamshidi (2016) presentan las lecciones aprendidas y buenas prácticas de la migración de una aplicación móvil comercial a microservicios, adoptando DevOps y despliegue en la nube [12]. Villamizar y otros realizan una evaluación del rendimiento de una aplicación monolítica en contraste a una aplicación basada en microservicios desplegadas en la nube [13]. Di Francesco, identifica las propiedades clave en la arquitectura de microservicios, propone MicroArt una herramienta ágil para el diseño de arquitecturas basadas en microservicios [14]. Oberhauser propone Microflows un enfoque para automatizar el modelado y la implementación del flujo de trabajo en un entorno de microservicio dinámico [15]. Xu, Chengzhi y otros presentan CAOPLE un lenguaje de programación para microservicios SaaS [16] y CIDE un ambiente integrado de desarrollo para microservicios usando el lenguaje CAOPLE [17].

3 Preguntas de investigación

Al usar microservicios se puede desplegar una aplicación grande como un conjunto de aplicaciones pequeñas que pueden ser desarrolladas, implementadas, ampliadas, manejadas y monitoreadas de manera independiente. La agilidad, la reducción de costos y la escalabilidad granular, trae algunos desafíos y la complejidad de manejar sistemas distribuidos [13]. En el presente trabajo de investigación doctoral se plantean las siguientes preguntas de investigación: **PI-1:** ¿Qué desafíos y problemas de investigación presenta el desarrollo de aplicaciones que usan microservicios? **PI-2:** ¿Cómo es el proceso de desarrollo de aplicaciones que usan microservicios? **PI-3:** ¿Cómo especificar las relaciones existentes entre los microservicios que hacen parte de una aplicación y qué características debe incluir esa especificación? **PI-4:** ¿Cómo demostrar que el modelo de especificación propuesto proporciona una mejora al proceso de desarrollo de aplicaciones que usan microservicios?

Se han resuelto las dos primeras preguntas de investigación: Para resolver la pregunta PI-1, se hizo una búsqueda en las bases de datos científicas más importantes en el área de la computación como son IEEE y Scopus, se seleccionaron y revisaron un total de 95 artículos. Como resultado se refleja una inmadurez en este campo y una continua evolución, los retos de investigación se centran en la definición del nivel de granularidad del microservicio, en la seguridad, en la orquestación, el monitoreo, en la definición de técnicas, procesos, modelos, herramientas y buenas prácticas a nivel de diseño, implementación y mantenimiento de los microservicios. Para resolver la PI-2 se caracterizó el proceso de desarrollo de aplicaciones basadas en microservicios en el cual las prácticas de DevOps juegan un papel fundamental, resaltando la automatización de pruebas, la entrega continua y el "pipeline" de despliegue continuo como esenciales. Se propone un método de automatización del despliegue continuo que fue probado usando el Bitbucked pipeline, el cual permite realizar pruebas automáticas y despliegue a un contenedor de pruebas y otro de desarrollo en una instancia EC2 de Amazón Web Services.

4 Metodología

A continuación se detalla la metodología que se está llevando a cabo, identificando las fases, métodos, actividades y resultados esperados, se puede apreciar en la fig. 1. Los métodos que se van a usar en cada fase son: revisión sistemática de literatura, análisis de casos de estudio, experimentación práctica, realizar estudio de caso y validación experimental en la cual se busca comparar el modelo propuesto con otros similares. También se resaltan los resultados a obtener en cada fase y al realizar cada fase se resuelven las preguntas de investigación propuestas.

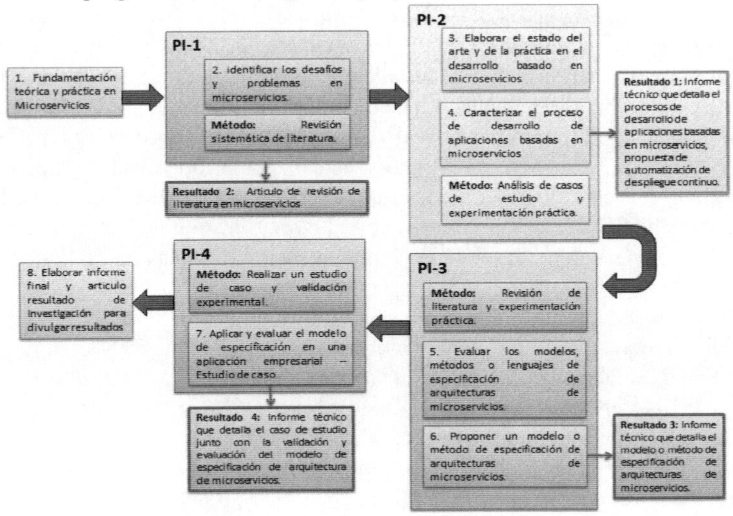

Fig. 1. Metodología de la investigación

5 Resultados

Con este trabajo de investigación doctoral se pretende proponer un modelo para especificar la arquitectura de microservicios, luego a partir de este modelo se podría probar diferentes características como son la calidad del servicio, el rendimiento, las fallas y los costos; de tal forma que el arquitecto o desarrollador pueda encontrar una solución óptima para su implementación. En la fig. 2 se presenta la solución propuesta y la caracterización del proceso de desarrollo de aplicaciones basadas en microservicios.

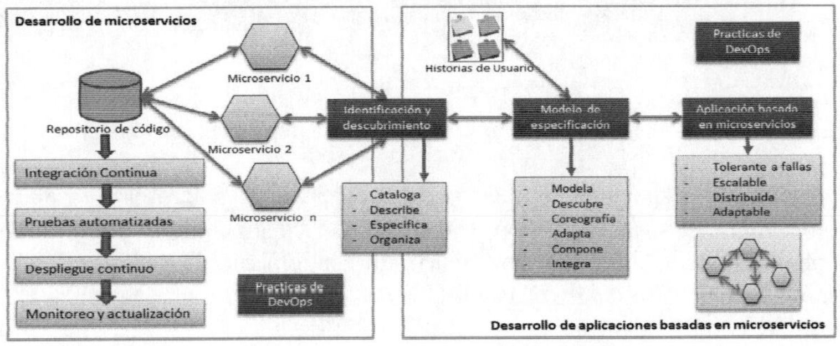

Fig. 2. Solución propuesta – Caracterización del proceso de desarrollo de microservicios

El proceso de desarrollo de aplicaciones basadas en microservicios se divide en dos partes fundamentales, primero el desarrollo de cada microservicio y segundo en el desarrollo de aplicaciones que usan esos microservicios. En la fig. 2 se pueden apreciar las partes fundamentales de ese proceso de desarrollo. El desarrollo de cada microservicio lo realiza un equipo de desarrollo separado de los demás de forma autónoma e independiente, inclusive usando lenguajes de programación diferentes, gestores de bases de datos diferentes y posiblemente ubicados en diferentes partes del mundo. Para cada microservicio se realiza una integración continua, pruebas automatizadas, despliegue continuo, monitoreo y actualización individual. Las prácticas de DevOps son esenciales para el proceso de desarrollo de los microservicios, DevOps tiene como objetivo reducir el tiempo entre el compromiso de un cambio del sistema y colocar el cambio en producción, al tiempo que garantiza una alta calidad [18].

En la fig. 3 se presenta la automatización del "deployment pipeline" propuesta, garantizando integración y despliegue continuo; una vez se confirma (commit) un cambio en el código fuente del microservicio se ejecutan las siguientes acciones automáticas: (1) Análisis estático: se revisa el código fuente para asegurar que cumplen con un estándar, (2) pruebas de predespliegue: se realzan pruebas unitarias, (3) Empaquetar código, (4) Desplegar al contenedor de pruebas (Instancia EC2 de AWS), (5) Aseguramiento de la calidad: se realizan pruebas funcionales, pruebas de carga y rendimiento, todo con el fin de asegurar la calidad del microservicio desarrollado, (6) Desplegar a producción, si pasa todas las pruebas se despliega al contenedor de producción (Instancia EC2 de AWS), (7) Pruebas de post – producción, se ejecutan prueba adicionales para garantizar que la nueva versión funciona adecuadamente en el contender de producción . En caso que se encuentre una falla se cancela el despliegue y se envía una notificación. Este método se basa en lo propuesto por Viktor Farcic en [19]

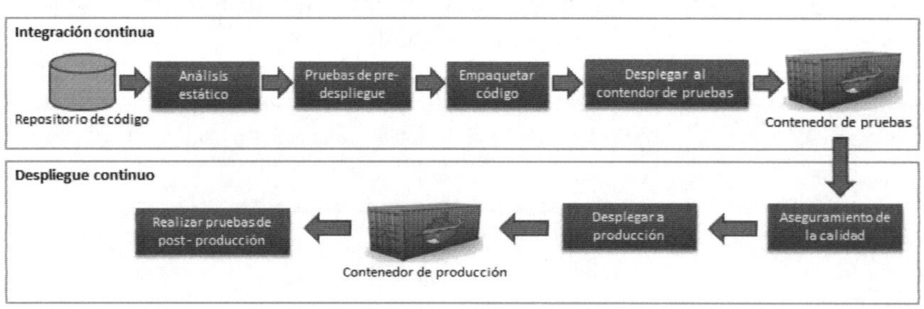

Fig. 3. Automatización del despliegue continúo para la implementación de microservicios

Este proceso de despliegue continuo se realiza para cada microservicio que se esté implementando, se evaluó y probó usando Bitbucked pipeline, se pudo automatizar las pruebas estáticas, funcionales y unitarias de un conjunto de microservicios implementados para un caso de estudio y despliegue automático a una instancia EC2. Los contenedores son fundamentales en el desarrollo de aplicaciones basadas en microservicios. Los contenedores son paquetes autosuficientes que contienen todo lo que necesitamos (con la excepción del kernel), se ejecutan en un proceso aislado y son inmutables. Ser autosuficiente significa que un contenedor comúnmente tiene los siguientes componentes. (1) Bibliotecas de tiempo de ejecución (JDK, Python o cualquier otra biblioteca necesaria para que la aplicación se ejecute), (2) Servidor de aplicaciones (Tomcat, nginx, otro), (3) Base de datos, (4) Artefacto (JAR, WAR, archivos estáticos, etc.) [19].

La gestión de la configuración y su automatización ahorran tiempo y problemas que surgen a la hora de subir la aplicación a producción. Cualquier persona que administre más de unos pocos servidores puede confirmar que realizar dicha tarea manualmente es una pérdida de tiempo y riesgosa. La gestión de la configuración (CM) existe desde hace mucho tiempo [20]. Ahora con el uso de contenedores y microservicios el número de instancias de desarrollo, prueba y producción se pueden incrementar considerablemente y su administración va ser mucho más tediosa. Herramientas que ayudan a automatizar esta gestión son: CFEngine, Chef y Ansible. La identificación y descubrimiento de servicios son parte fundamental en el desarrollo de aplicaciones que usen los microservicios que fueron creados y desplegados con anterioridad. Este mecanismo permite catalogar, describir, especificar y organizar los microservicios para que puedan ser utilizados. El problema del descubrimiento de servicios es permitir que los consumidores del servicio localicen proveedores de servicios en tiempo real para facilitar la comunicación [20]

6 Conclusiones

El área de investigación en microservicios es relativamente nueva se encuentra en proceso de maduración y evolución. Existen muchos desafíos de investigación por trabajar y resolver. El manejo de seguridad, el nivel de granularidad del microservicio, la orquestación, el monitoreo, la definición de técnicas, procesos modelos, herramientas y buenas prácticas a nivel de diseño, implementación y mantenimiento, son los principales temas y retos de investigación.

El proceso de desarrollo de microservicios se divide en dos partes fundamentales, la primera el desarrollo de los microservicios y la segunda el desarrollo de aplicaciones que usan esos microservicios, siendo las prácticas de DevOps muy importantes. La automatización del despliegue continúo, facilitan las tareas de prueba y despliegue, el uso de contenedores inmutables garantiza tener las mismas características tanto en el servidor de prueba como en el servidor de producción, por lo tanto se reducen considerablemente los errores de las aplicaciones al subirlas a producción. El proceso de despliegue continuo agiliza la puesta en producción de una nueva versión realizando procesos automatizados para probar y garantizar la calidad del software desarrollado.

Referencias

1. J. Thönes, "Microservices," IEEE Softw., vol. 32, no. 1, 2015.

2. J. Lewis and M. Fowler, "Microservices," 2014. [Online]. Available: https://martinfowler.com/articles/microservices.html. [Accessed: 13-Sep-2017].
3. T. Salah, M. Jamal Zemerly, Chan Yeob Yeun, M. Al-Qutayri, and Y. Al-Hammadi, "The evolution of distributed systems towards microservices architecture," in 2016 11th International Conference for Internet Technology and Secured Transactions (ICITST), 2016, pp. 318–325.
4. C. Pautasso, O. Zimmermann, M. Amundsen, J. Lewis, and N. Josuttis, "Microservices in Practice, Part 1: Reality Check and Service Design," IEEE Softw., vol. 34, no. 1, pp. 91–98, 2017.
5. P. Di Francesco, I. Malavolta, and P. Lago, "Research on Architecting Microservices: Trends, Focus, and Potential for Industrial Adoption," in 2017 IEEE International Conference on Software Architecture (ICSA), 2017, pp. 21–30.
6. J. Wettinger, U. Breitenbucher, and F. Leymann, "Standards-based DevOps automation and integration using TOSCA," Proc. - 2014 IEEE/ACM 7th Int. Conf. Util. Cloud Comput. UCC 2014, pp. 59–68, 2014.
7. E. Mueller, J. Wickett, K. Gaekwad, and P. Karayanev, "What Is DevOps? | the agile admin," 2017. [Online]. Available: https://theagileadmin.com/what-is-devops/. [Accessed: 12-Mar-2018].
8. H. Vural, M. Koyuncu, and S. Guney, "A Systematic Literature Review on Microservices," Springer, Cham, 2017, pp. 203–217.
9. N. Alshuqayran, N. Ali, and R. Evans, "A Systematic Mapping Study in Microservice Architecture."
10. C. Pahl and P. Jamshidi, "Microservices: A Systematic Mapping Study," Proc. 6th Int. Conf. Cloud Comput. Serv. Sci., no. May, pp. 137–146, 2016.
11. O. Zimmermann, "Microservices tenets: Agile approach to service development and deployment," Comput. Sci. - Res. Dev., vol. 32, no. 3–4, pp. 301–310, 2017.
12. A. Balalaie, A. Heydarnoori, and P. Jamshidi, "Microservices Architecture Enables DevOps: Migration to a Cloud-Native Architecture," IEEE Softw., vol. 33, no. 3, pp. 42–52, 2016.
13. M. Villamizar, O. Garcés, H. Castro, M. Verano, L. Salamanca, and S. Gil, "Evaluating the Monolithic and the Microservice Architecture Pattern to Deploy Web Applications in the Cloud Evaluando el Patrón de Arquitectura Monolítica y de Micro Servicios Para Desplegar Aplicaciones en la Nube," 10th Comput. Colomb. Conf., pp. 583–590, 2015.
14. P. Di Francesco, "Architecting microservices," Proc. - 2017 IEEE Int. Conf. Softw. Archit. Work. ICSAW 2017 Side Track Proc., pp. 224–229, 2017.
15. R. Oberhauser, "Microflows: Automated Planning and Enactment of Dynamic Workflows Comprising Semantically-Annotated Microservices," Springer, Cham, 2017, pp. 183–199.
16. C. Xu, H. Zhu, I. Bayley, D. Lightfoot, M. Green, and P. Marshall, "CAOPLE: A programming language for microservices SaaS," Proc. - 2016 IEEE Symp. Serv. Syst. Eng. SOSE 2016, no. 1, pp. 42–52, 2016.
17. D. Liu et al., "CIDE: An integrated development environment for microservices," Proc. - 2016 IEEE Int. Conf. Serv. Comput. SCC 2016, no. 0, pp. 808–812, 2016.
18. L. Zhu, L. Bass, and G. Champlin-Scharff, "DevOps and Its Practices," IEEE Softw., vol. 33, no. 3, pp. 32–34, 2016.
19. V. Farcic, The DevOps 2.0 Toolkit: Automating the Continuous Deployment Pipeline with Containerized Microservices. leanpub.com., 2016.
20. J. Stubbs, W. Moreira, and R. Dooley, "Distributed Systems of Microservices Using Docker and Serfnode," in 2015 7th International Workshop on Science Gateways, 2015, pp. 34–39.

Coordinación de dispositivos en ambientes ubicuos mediante coreografías

Oscar A. Testa

Universidad Nacional de San Luis
Facultad de Ciencias Físico-Matemáticas y Naturales
San Luis - Argentina
Universidad Nacional de La Pampa
Facultad de Ciencias Exactas y Naturales
La Pampa - Argentina
otesta@exactas.unlpam.edu.ar

Resumen: ***Contexto:*** Actualmente nos encontramos inmersos en ambientes donde los dispositivos ubicuos forman parte de nuestra vida cotidiana y de nuestras tareas diarias. De forma permanente estamos interactuando con dichos dispositivos, y más aún, con los servicios que ellos nos brindan. ***Problema:*** Los dispositivos ubicuos no proporcionan servicios de forma aislada, sino que deben cooperar con otros dispositivos. Los mecanismos de cooperación disponibles son fundamentalmente de tipo propietario, y las pocas propuestas provenientes de la academia no han tenido apenas impacto en la práctica. Esto contrasta con los servicios web en ambiente de internet, los cuales proporcionan mecanismos para la composición de servicios. Las orquestaciones y coreografías permiten construir sistemas complejos a partir de una gran cantidad de servicios heterogéneos, simples y distribuídos. ***Objetivos:*** Si pensamos que cada dispositivo ubicuo en un ambiente pervasivo es proveedor, o consumidor de un servicio, la coordinación de dispositivos se ajusta perfectamente con la composición de servicios en ambientes distribuídos. Nuestra propuesta es adaptar y aplicar las especificaciones de coreografías actualmente existentes en SOA para la coordinación de servicios proporcionados por dispositivos ubicuos. ***Método:*** Se utilizará como metodología de investigación design science. Los artefactos a construir serán: 1) una especificación de coreografías adaptada a los dispositivos ubicuos y 2) un framework que implementa dicha especificación al nivel de prueba de concepto. ***Resultados preliminares:*** Hasta el momento se obtuvo una primera versión del framework de ejecución de coreografías en ambientes ubicuos. Se ha podido incorporar dicho framework a dispositivos de pequeño tamaño y limitado poder de procesamiento. ***Trabajos futuros:*** Se espera poder adaptar el framework para que pueda ser ejecutado en dispositivos con escasa memoria, así como también realizar adaptaciones del lenguaje de coreografías para dar soporte a otras características de los dispositivos ubicuos.

Palabras Claves: Ingeniería de Software; SOA; Dispositivos ubicuos; Servicios; Coreografías de servicios

1. Introducción

La tendencia actual es hacia los ambientes ubicuos, los cuales se caracterizan por estar poblados de numerosos dispositivos que, gracias a la integración extrema de los elementos electrónicos, son invisibles al usuario y están en permanente rastreo de la actividad humana [0].

Dispositivos ubicuos son todos aquellos dispositivos que pueden existir en todas partes, es decir, son dispositivos electrónicos que tienen capacidad de procesamiento y comunicación y pueden ser encontrados en cualquier lugar: la oficina, el auto, o la misma ropa con la que vestimos.

Los avances del hardware y las comunicaciones han permitido que los dispositivos ubicuos sean al mismo tiempo generadores y consumidores de servicios, es decir, de acuerdo a las capacidades del dispositivo éste puede no solo obtener, sino también ofrecer, sus funciones, y así cooperar entre ellos. Por composición, entendemos la forma en que los dispositivos ubicuos se pueden combinar para llevar adelante una tarea determinada. La composición en este tipo de ambientes implica que los dispositivos deben dialogar entre ellos con la finalidad de obtener un servicio con valor agregado, lo que puede incluír afrontar desafíos tales como la tolerancia a fallas, escaso nivel de procesamiento, problemas de conectividad, por mencionar algunos ejemplos.

Si bien hoy en día podemos decir que distintos sensores o dispositivos se pueden comunicar entre ellos, compartiendo de alguna manera sus servicios, generalmente lo realizan a partir de protocolos propietarios y sin seguir definiciones estándar, provocando que otros dispositivos de otros proveedores (o incluso de los mismos) no puedan ser utilizados. Esto representa una importante limitación en la composición de dispositivos ubicuos. La composición de dispositivos presenta desafíos adicionales tales como: la heterogeneidad (ya sea por la diversidad de dispositivos involucrados, como por la presencia de dispositivos de varios fabricantes), las contingencias de los dispositivos, y la personalización de los mismos (ej: provisión de servicios de acuerdo a las preferencias del usuario). Dado que los dispositivos ubicuos poseen limitaciones de recursos (ej. poca memoria y batería), se deben hacer consideraciones especiales respecto a la eficiencia y rendimiento de la composición de dispositivos. Todas estas dificultades hacen que la composición de dispositivos constituya un área de investigación muy importante donde los avances no han sido claros al día de hoy [0].

2. Antecedentes

2.1. Trabajos relacionados

Existen actualmente diversos trabajos de investigación relacionados con la temática de la coordinación y composición de dispositivos en ambientes ubicuos. Sin embargo en dichos trabajos apenas se aborda el protocolo de composición.

Mirko Viroli [0] propone un framework para la composición de dispositivos en ambientes pervasivos, específicamente en ambientes con dispositivos móviles, inspirado en las reacciones químicas de los elementos. Si bien el trabajo se orienta en la forma de coordinar los dispositivos, solamente toma en cuenta los dispositivos móviles, dejando de lado sensores, dispositivos biométricos, etc.

Otros trabajos como el de Loke [0] enfocan la problemática de coordinación de sensores, móviles y demás dispositivos en ambientes sensibles al contexto, combinados para que éstos brinden información en la nube. A partir de este nuevo modelo de aplicaciones, se pueden utilizar dispositivos sensibles al contexto a demanda, y con un pago por la utilización de esa información.

Existen otros trabajos como los de Francesco Palmieri [0] y el de Salma Najar et. al. [0] donde se aborda la problemática de la composición de dispositivos desde un punto de vista del descubrimiento de los mismos en forma dinámica. En el primero de dichos trabajos [0], el autor propone una nueva manera de descubrimiento basada en un modelo de búsqueda totalmente distribuida y paralela. En el segundo trabajo [0], los autores plantean un nuevo modelo de predicción y descubrimiento de dispositivos centrados en el usuario, basados en el contexto que se encuentra y en sus intenciones.

2.2. Computación orientada a servicios

La computación orientada a servicios (SOA), y en particular los servicios web en ambiente de internet, proporcionan mecanismos para la composición de servicios. Dichos mecanismos, como las orquestaciones y coreografías, son aspectos bien conocidos en SOA que permiten construir sistemas de negocio complejos y aplicaciones a partir de una gran cantidad de servicios heterogéneos, simples y distribuídos. Podría pensarse que dichos conceptos son aplicables a ambientes ubicuos, en especial las coreografías, las cuales pueden fácilmente interpretarse en términos de dispositivos y ambientes ubicuos. Sin embargo, en contextos como la Internet de las Cosas (IoT), donde los servicios son dinámicos, móviles, menos fiables y dependientes del dispositivo, los mecanismos de composición establecidos para servicios web no son directamente aplicables [0].

Adicionalmente, la composición de múltiples dispositivos ubicuos presenta nuevos desafíos que no son compatibles con la composición de servicios web. En particular, los mecanismos de composición en ambientes masivos como son los de dispositivos móviles necesitan hacer frente a distintas contingencias que pueden ocurrir con estos elementos, así como también contemplar la heterogeneidad de los mismos. Estos dispositivos tienen distintas limitantes como son la cantidad de memoria disponible, la durabilidad de la batería, la disponibilidad de acuerdo a la red del lugar donde se encuentre en un momento determinado, etc. En ambientes ubicuos, la disponibilidad y confiabilidad de los dispositivos no puede ser garantizada. No obstante, a pesar de todas las dificultades, existen ventajas que la adaptación de los conceptos de SOA puede tener para la composición de dispositivos ubicuos, como son la estandarización tanto de los protocolos como de los mecanismos de comunicación entre los dispositivos, y la compatibilidad con otras plataformas de servicios ya existentes.

2.3. Importancia de la composición de dispositivos ubicuos

Existen distintas situaciones en la actualidad donde se intenta integrar sensores y dispositivos ubicuos en la vida cotidiana. Como un ejemplo próximo podemos mencionar la domótica, donde varios dispositivos y sensores deben actuar en coordinación para prevenir un incidente de seguridad en nuestros hogares. Sin embargo, existen áreas de aplicación más relevantes. En la industria, existe lo que se llama Industria 4.0 [0], donde lo que se intenta es conseguir dentro de una planta fabril la intercomunicación de todos los dispositivos que componen la cadena de producción con el fin de que coordinen entre ellos las tareas a realizar en base a los tiempos a cumplir, stocks disponibles, demanda en línea de los productos, etc. Otra área donde los dipositivos ubicuos están ganando importancia es la automotriz, donde los esfuerzos se enfocan en que distintos sensores monitoreen funciones vitales del conductor, y en caso de que detecten anomalías, actúen en conjunto con otros dispositivos del vehículo para evitar accidentes.

3. Objetivos de la investigación

El presente trabajo de tesis se encuadra en la línea de investigación relacionada con la composición de dispositivos ubicuos, planteando una estrategia de solución basada en la transposición de los conceptos de SOA. La propuesta consiste en adaptar y aplicar las especificaciones actualmente existentes en SOA para la coordinación de servicios disponibles en ambientes ubicuos. Más concretamente, el objetivo de esta Tesis es:

- Definir un mecanismo de coordinación de dispositivos ubicuos que garantice su interoperabilidad independientemente del modelo y fabricante del mismo; utilizando los estándares de SOA y de coreografías para la composición de servicios.

Debemos destacar que la aplicación de los conceptos de SOA a dispositivos ubicuos no consiste en una mera traslación de los conceptos de un ambiente a otro, sino que será necesario para ello extender las especificaciones de SOA existentes de modo que se adapten a las circunstancias particulares de los sistemas ubicuos. Asimismo, se deberá mantener total compatibilidad con las especificaciones relacionadas con SOA y coreografías.

4. Método de Investigación

De acuerdo a la naturaleza del problema y en base al objetivo planteado en el presente trabajo de investigación, la metodología seleccionada para llevar adelante el proyecto es "design science".

El paradigma de design-science tiene sus raíces en la ingeniería. Esta metodología, como bien expresan March y Smith [0], tiene como bloque fundamental la creación o construcción de un artefacto y su posterior evaluación para evaluar tanto su impacto como las características de su diseño. Estos artefactos están representados de forma estructurada y van desde software, lógica formal y matemática rigurosa, hasta descripciones informales en lenguaje natural.

Analizado de forma general el paradigma de design-science como metodología de investigación, vemos que el mismo se adapta de manera natural al problema y objetivo planteado en este trabajo de tesis. De acuerdo a los 3 ciclos de "design science"según Hevner [0], podemos decir que esta investigación se relaciona principalmente con el ciclo de diseño. Al finalizar la investigación, el conocimiento científico obtenido aportará mejoras a las especificaciones relacionadas con la coordinación de dispositivos, lo cual está relacionado con el ciclo de rigor de "design science". El ciclo de relevancia no será abordado durante la realización de la tesis doctoral.

Los pasos de investigación son los siguientes:

- **Estudio inicial**: estudio profundo y en detalle de las especificaciones existentes acerca de composición de servicios y coreografías, específicamente Web Service Choreography Description Language (WS-Choreography) y Web Service Choreography Interface (WSCI).
- **Selección de escenario**: selección de uno o varios escenario(s) de trabajo, que sea(n) posible(s) simular e implementar en laboratorio.
- **Contrucción de Prototipos**: elaboración de un prototipo inicial, el cual es el motor para los siguientes refinamientos hasta alcanzar el mecanismo de coordinación final que se espera obtener. La complejidad en este paso se centra fundamentalmente en adaptar los conceptos de SOA y coreografías a las características de los dispositivos/sistemas ubicuos, antes citados: heterogeneidad, contingencias de los dispositivos, la personalización de los mismos así como la limitación de recursos que poseen.
- **Análisis de resultados**: al ser un proyecto donde se espera producir un artefacto o entregable, el análisis de los resultados de la implementación práctica de los prototipos haciendo funcionar el escenario planteado es de fundamental importancia. Los resultados brindarán una proyección de los cambios y ajustes que se deben hacer tanto al prototipo, así como al mecanismo de coordinación que se espera plantear. Se analizarán los problemas encontrados en los distintos protocolos de comunicación existentes, así como los problemas de transporte de datos, memoria, batería, etc., y la adecuación a distintos estándares como puede ser el manejo de transacciones en ambientes ubicuos.
- **Aplicación de mejoras**: una vez analizados los resultados y realizadas las evaluaciones del prototipo, se realizarán los ajustes y mejoras que den lugar a resolver los problemas detectados en el análisis previo. Este proceso de análisis/evaluación y aplicación de mejoras se realiza de manera incremental hasta lograr los resultados esperados.
- **Especificación del mecanismo de coordinación**: finalmente se formalizará el mecanismo de coordinación por el cual se puedan llevar adelante coreografías

en ambientes ubicuos, manteniendo la compatibilidad con los estándares de coreografías actualmente existentes.

Para poder llevar adelante el prototipo que simule el escenario seleccionado se trabajará con dispositivos móviles con sistema operativo Android, con plataformas de bajo costo Raspberry Pi y con placas Arduino. En el futuro se adicionarán dispositivos del estilo tarjetas y etiquetas RFID, de manera que abordemos una amplia tipología de dispositivos ubicuos.

5. Realización de la Investigación

5.1. Resultados preliminares

La investigación comenzó en Octubre del 2015, a tiempo parcial. Durante 1 año, el doctorando se familiarizó con el área de trabajo y posteriormente llevó a término el *Estudio inicial*. Los distintos trabajos encontrados mostraban la importancia del problema. Una vez determinada la importancia del problema, se abordó la *Selección del escenario y construcción de Prototipos*, donde se ha seleccionado el escenario de trabajo y se ha desarrollado tanto el prototipo de ejecución de coreografías así como la primera y segunda prueba de concepto.

El escenario de trabajo que se plantea es específico. Sin embargo, no deja de dar solución a un problema que se puede generalizar hacia prácticamente cualquier ambiente de trabajo. Este escenario se relaciona con los problemas de tránsito y vehicular a lo largo de carreteras, haciendo de ellas un entorno inteligente. Se plantea un ambiente donde los ómnibus que transportan personas posean ciertos elementos de comunicación y sensores (los cuales podrían ser aquellos que monitorean la salud del conductor en tiempo real, las funciones de seguridad del rodado, etc.) que permitan convertirlo en un vehículo con seguridad y que pueda prevenir accidentes. A su vez, la carretera deberá disponer de balizas de contacto con los vehículos que transitan por ella. Estas balizas deberán poder tener posibilidad de conectividad hacia los automóviles que transitan, así como contactarse a centros de asistencia y de ayuda. Los vehículos también podrán tener elementos de conectividad, que permitan comunicarse con otros vehículos que estén transitando la ruta/carretera, con las balizas dispuestas a lo largo del camino, con centros de atención, etc.

Como resultados de la ejecución de la primera prueba de concepto, hemos comprobado que el prototipo ha funcionado correctamente. Dentro de los dispositivos utilizados en esta primera prueba se encuentran computadoras personales y un equipo Raspberry Pi B+. En cada uno de ellos se ha implementado la arquitectura de servicios web REST. Cada dispositivo ha simulado ser uno de los roles de la coreografía especificada en el lenguaje de descripción de coreografías WS-CDL.

Durante la segunda prueba de concepto, se han incorporado dispositivos de menor capacidad (tanto de procesamiento como de almacenamiento), como es el caso de una placa Arduino Mega 2560, con conectividad realizada a través de un módulo wifi ESP8266-01. Para este caso en particular, se ha necesitado implementar un servidor web *ad-hoc* con capacidad de procesamiento de peticiones REST. En esta segunda prueba de concepto hemos realizado adaptaciones al lenguaje de coreografías WS-CDL para que las ejecuciones en paralelo se lleven a cabo de una manera secuencial debido a las limitaciones de la placa Arduino, la cual no posee la capacidad de manejar hilos de ejecución en forma paralela. Hubo también que realizar adaptaciones al prototipo de ejecución de la coreografía, debido a que no se puede incluir la descripción de la misma en este tipo de placas, ya que su escasa capacidad de memoria no lo permite. Para ello se han generado fragmentos de la especificación que son inherentes al rol que cumple dentro de la coreografía la placa Arduino Mega.

Dichos resultados preliminares se han presentado en el Congreso Nacional de Ingeniería Informátcia (CONAIISI) [0], así como también en un Workshop de Investigadores en Ciencias de la Computación (WICC) [0].

5.2. Trabajos futuros

Actualmente, se está realizando la escritura del *Escenario seleccionado y del Prototipo*, y finalizando la escritura del *Estudio inicial*. Se espera que para mediados de 2018 se comience con los pasos finales de la escritura de la tesis doctoral, para ser presentada sobre final del presente año o a comienzos del año 2019.

Se está trabajando en una tercera prueba de concepto, donde se incorporan placas Arduino con muy pocas capacidades, como es el caso de una placa Arduino Nano o Gema, donde será necesario hacer adaptaciones al código del framework de ejecución, ya que el código objeto es demasiado voluminoso para poder ser soportados en dichas placas.

Como resultado de estas investigaciones, pretendemos obtener publicaciones en congresos iberoamericanos, congresos internacionales (como ASE, ICSOFT o SEKE), además de un artículo en una revista como puede ser el Journal of Systems and Software.

6. Conclusiones

Son varios los aportes que se han necesitado realizar al lenguaje de especificación de coreografías WS-CDL para ser adaptado para la ejecución de coreografías en ambientes ubicuos, en línea con el objetivo de tesis planteado. Hasta el momento podemos mencionar: la adaptación del concepto de paralelismo en coreografías a través de llamadas secuenciales debido a la falta de un sistema operativo que brinde la capacidad de multiprocesamiento en placas Arduino; la transformación de la descripción de la coreografía en lenguaje XML a un conjunto de vectores en memoria con la información necesaria para que se ejecute la coreografía desde los dispositivos con menor capacidad de memoria; la codificación de un motor de ejecución de coreografías para distintos dispositivos (con adaptaciones diversas para los que tienen menores capacidades), etc.

Será necesario realizar durante esta investigación otros aportes para adaptar WS-CDL a algunas de las características de los sistemas ubicuos como pueden ser desapariciones por problemas de red, falta de batería u otros.

Agradecimientos: Esta investigación ha sido parcialmente financiada por la Universidad Nacional de La Pampa, con una beca de Iniciación de Doctorados.

Referencias

1. M. Weiser, "Hot topics-ubiquitous computing," *Computer*, vol. 26, pp. 71–72, Oct 1993.
2. Q. Z. Sheng, X. Qiao, A. V. Vasilakos, C. Szabo, S. Bourne, and X. Xu, "Web services composition: A decade's overview," *Information Sciences*, vol. 280, no. 0, pp. 218–238, 2014.
3. M. Viroli, "On competitive self-composition in pervasive services," *Science of Computer Programming*, vol. 78, no. 5, pp. 556–568, 2013. Special section: Principles and Practice of Programming in Java 2009/2010 & Special section: Self-Organizing Coordination.
4. S. W. Loke, "Supporting ubiquitous sensor-cloudlets and context-cloudlets: Programming compositions of context-aware systems for mobile users," *Future Generation Computer Systems*, vol. 28, no. 4, pp. 619–632, 2012.
5. F. Palmieri, "Scalable service discovery in ubiquitous and pervasive computing architectures: A percolation-driven approach," *Future Generation Computer Systems*, vol. 29, no. 3, pp. 693–703, 2013. Special Section: Recent Developments in High Performance Computing and Security.
6. S. Najar, M. K. Pinheiro, and C. Souveyet, "A New Approach for Service Discovery and Prediction on Pervasive Information System," *Procedia Computer Science*, vol. 32, pp. 421–428, 2014. The 5th International Conference on Ambient Systems, Networks and Technologies (ANT-2014), the 4th International Conference on Sustainable Energy Information Technology (SEIT-2014).
7. G. Cassar, P. Barnaghi, W. Wang, S. De, and K. Moessner, "Composition of services in pervasive environments: A Divide and Conquer approach," in *Computers and Communications (ISCC), 2013 IEEE Symposium on*, pp. 000226–000232, July 2013.
8. Wikipedia, "Industria 4.0 — Wikipedia, La enciclopedia libre," 2016. [Internet; descargado 4-noviembre-2016].
9. S. T. March and G. F. Smith, "Design and Natural Science Research on Information Technology," *Decis. Support Syst.*, vol. 15, pp. 251–266, Dec. 1995.
10. A. R. Hevner, "A Three Cycle View of Design Science Research," *Scandinavian Journal of Information Systems*, pp. 87–92.
11. O. Dieste, E. R. F. C., G. Montejano, and O. Testa, "Desafíos en el desarrollo de sistemas ubicuos: Una propuesta de solucio´n basada en SOA," in *Memorias 3er Congreso Nacional de Ingeniería Informática / Sistemas de Información*, Nov. 2015.
12. G. Montejano, O. Testa, R. Pizarro, D. Segovia, O. Dieste, and E. R. F. C., "Coordinación de Dispositivos en Ambientes Ubicuos Mediante Coreografías," in *Memorias XIX Workshop de Investigadores en Ciencias de la Computación*, Apr. 2017.

Marco de Trabajo para la Elicitación y Evolución de Requisitos No Funcionales Basadas en la Gestión de Conocimiento

Sandra L. Buitrón

Universidad del Cauca, Calle 5 #4-70 Popayán, Colombia
sandrabr@unicauca.edu.co

Resumen
Frente a la calidad de los productos software, es importe gestionar el ciclo de vida de los requisitos no funcionales, los cuales deben ser especificados durante la etapa de elicitación de requisitos del producto. Dentro del ciclo de vida del requisito no funcional, la gestión de la evolución de dicho requisito apoya a las organizaciones en la toma de decisiones a lo largo ciclo de vida del producto software (desarrollo, operación, mantenimiento y retirada). En este artículo se presenta el avance de una tesis doctoral que pretende construir un marco de trabajo para la elicitación y evolución de requisitos no funcionales basadas en la gestión de conocimiento. Dentro del avance del proyecto de doctorado ha sido definido un método de elicitación de requisitos no funcionales y éste se ha validado preliminarmente a través de un Focus Group y su aplicación en organizaciones desarrolladoras de software mediante estudios de caso. Los resultados iniciales indican que el método es adaptable y útil para las empresas desarrolladoras que están interesadas en hacer énfasis en mejorar la calidad de los productos a través de identificar los requisitos no funcionales del producto.

Palabra clave: Requisitos No Funcionales, Elicitación de Requisitos no funcionales, Gestión de Conocimiento, Evolución de Requisitos

1 Introducción

La disciplina de Elicitación de requisitos (ER) es considerada fundamental para la Ingeniería del software, y en ésta se deben tener en cuenta dos elementos principales, los requisitos funcionales y los no funcionales. Sin embargo con relación a los requisitos no funcionales (RNF), (i) las técnicas utilizadas para realizar el proceso de Elicitación de Requisitos sobre Requisitos No Funcionales no están aún claras [1], (ii) además en [2] se afirma que "aunque existen técnicas bien desarrolladas para obtener requisitos funcionales, hay una falta de mecanismo de elicitación para requisitos no funcionales y no existe un consenso adecuado al respecto de los requisitos no funcionales" y (iii) según [3] para que el equipo de ER sea exitoso requiere un profundo conocimiento del dominio de aplicación, las tecnologías de la información y del proceso de Elicitación.

Por su parte, la evolución de los requerimientos se define como un proceso de cambio continuo de requisitos en una cierta dirección y ocurre durante todo el ciclo de vida del software (excluyendo la fase de elicitación de requisitos, hasta la etapa de mantenimiento del software) [4]. Esta evolución ocurre frecuentemente y es difícil predecirla;

involucra la volatilidad de los requerimientos que puede causar sobrecostos e incumplimiento en los objetivos del proyecto [5]. Muchos de los estudios existentes sobre evolución de requerimientos se centran en cómo tratar dicha evolución después de que éstos cambios han ocurrido, es decir, con un sentido correctivo [5]. Por tanto es importante considerar gestionar los cambios en los requisitos definidos, desde la etapa de elicitación, como una estrategia para tener bajo control la evolución de los mismos [6] de manera preventiva.

Considerando los aspectos descritos anteriormente, los productos software deben tener en cuenta como aspecto fundamental para su diseño e implementación una adecuada especificación de requisitos no funcionales [9], la cual debe soportar y dar paso a gestionar la evolución de éstos requisitos durante su ciclo de vida. Durante este ciclo, las organizaciones aplican principios de gestión de conocimiento con el objetivo de lograr una adaptación al cambio y logran identificar y capturar conocimientos para su posterior transferencia y reutilización [7]. Las organizaciones dedicadas al desarrollo de software son entidades altamente intensivas en el uso de conocimiento [8], además el proceso software involucra adiestramiento intensivo de conocimiento organizacional y necesita apoyarse en técnicas de gestión de conocimiento [9]. Así, utilizar la gestión de conocimiento en el campo de desarrollo de software permite explotar las experiencias de desarrollos previos con el fin de reducir costos y defectos, mejorar la calidad del producto y apoyar el proceso de desarrollo de software [10].

Considerando lo descrito anteriormente, este paper presenta el avance del proyecto de doctorado denominado "Marco de trabajo para la elicitación y evolución de requisitos no funcionales basadas en gestión de conocimiento" el cual pretende aportar para que las organizaciones desarrolladoras de software eliciten los requerimientos no funcionales de manera adecuada y gestionen su evolución. Una estrategia, para lograr estos aspectos en el desarrollo del producto software es considerar e incorporar en la investigación el uso de la gestión del conocimiento (KM), la cual podría impactar positivamente a los proyectos de desarrollo software.

Además de esta introducción, en la sección 2 se presentan los objetivos e hipótesis de la investigación, en la sección 3 se describe el estado de los trabajos existentes sobre los procesos de elicitación y evolución de requisitos no funcionales, en la sección 4 se describe el marco de trabajo MERliNN aplicado en las organizaciones que participaron de la experiencia, en la sección 5 se presenta el reporte experiencias y por último en la sección 6 se exponen las conclusiones de la investigación.

2 Objetivos y pregunta de investigación

La propuesta pretende ofrecer un marco de trabajo para la elicitación y evolución de requisitos no funcionales siguiendo un enfoque de KM, que permita apoyar a las organizaciones de software en mejorar la calidad de sus productos software a partir de la identificación y gestión de sus requisitos no funciones. Para el cumplimiento de este objetivo general se realizarán las siguientes objetivos específicos: (i) identificar, desde la literatura, los elementos para la elicitación y evolución de los requisitos no funcionales de un producto software, (ii) identificar, desde la literatura, elementos pertenecientes a la representación de requisitos no funcionales que permitan apoyar su especificación y evolución, (iii) proponer un marco de trabajo para la elicitación y evolución de requisitos no funcionales basado en KM, y (iv) determinar la validez del marco de trabajo propuesto usando un método de investigación idóneo (estudios de caso, experimentos y/o estudios focales). La pregunta de investigación para esta propuesta es ¿Cómo, mediante un enfoque de KM, apoyar a las organizaciones en sus procesos de elicitación y evolución de requisitos no funcionales?

3 Estado de las soluciones existentes

La propuesta de investigación involucra conceptos relacionados con: (i) el proceso de elicitación de requisitos no funcionales, (ii) evolución de requisitos no funcionales, y (iii) KM, a partir de los cuales se estructura una solución metodológica para aportar a mejorar la calidad de los productos software. Sobre estos temas, a continuación se describen los siguientes trabajos relacionados.

Frente a la elicitación de requisitos no funcionales basada en KM (ERNF), en la Tabla 1, se muestra una síntesis de algunos trabajos en términos del aporte, la forma de abordar el conocimiento y el fundamento de cada propuesta.

Tabla 1. Trabajos categorizados según formas de validación práctica

Ref	Aporte	Forma que aborda el conocimiento	Fundamento
[11]	Soportar el proceso de elicitación de requisitos desde la práctica, incluyendo el proceso de priorización de requisitos	Definición de ontología de requisitos No Funcionales a partir de la norma 9126 y combinándola con técnicas de KM.	Ontología y conocimiento en la norma 9126
[12]	Orientación a producto y al proceso de elicitación de RNF, apoyaando la definición y análisis de los RNF usando catálogos de conocimiento	Reutilización del conocimiento de RNF definidos anteriormente para aumentar las alternativas de requisitos a implementar.	Ontología y Reutilización del conoci miento (web semántica)
[13]	Relacionar funcional y no funcionalmente, a través de capas, las variables y contextos tecnológicos con variables y abstracciones clínicas	Las variables son dimensiones de calidad que se relacionan y descomponen de manera jerárquica para afinar los RNF.	Jerarquía y Capas relacionadas y afinamiento del conocimiento
[14]	Asegurar los requisitos de calidad a partir del documento de especificación a través de text-mining y diccionario de conceptos	Definición de requisitos de calidad (RNF) basado en la norma 9126.	Documento de especificación y conocimiento en la norma 9126
[15]	Soportar el proceso de ingeniería de requerimientos para colaboración, participación y negociación de los requerimientos usando prototipado.	Niveles de conocimiento, que se combina, disemina e intercambia entre los stakeholders, el cual debe ser entendido por los elicitadores.	Prototipado e intercambio de conocimiento
[16]	Clasificación de los enfoques de RNF haciendo un análisis multi-dimensional	Analizar los enfoques del proceso de elicitación de RNF desde el contexto, proceso y aplicación.	Análisis multi-dimensional de enfoques existentes
[17]	Conocer desde la perspectiva de los arquitectos de software, cómo se obtienen los RNF	Cualidades externas e internas del software. ¿Quién decide y qué tipo de RNF importan a arquitectos?	Perspectiva de los arquitectos y cualidades del software
[18]	Soportar la obtención de requisitos tempranos, apoyando en su trazabilidad desde diferentes dominios	Tiene en cuenta el conocimiento de los stakeholders para iniciar el proceso de modelado visual.	Trazabilidad de requisitos tempranos y modelado visual
[19]	Soportar un enfoque lógico para los RNF usando concepto de soft-goal.	Uso de formalización para representar los RNF.	Soft goal y representación de requisitos.
[20]	Identificar los RNF, elicitarlos y analizarlos. Metodología orientada a objetos UML, usando casos de uso	El conocimiento sobre los RNF está dentro del documento de especificación.	Metodología UML y documento de especificación

Frente a la evolución de requisitos no funcionales, la Tabla 2 sintetiza de algunos trabajos con información sobre el aspecto de evolución que plantea cada propuesta.

Tabla 2. Trabajos categorizados según formas de validación práctica

Aspectos de evolución	Referencia	Criterio en el que se fundamenta la propuesta
Trazabilidad del requisito	[21]	Requisitos comunes, variables y específicos
	[22]	Trazabilidad de los requisites
	[23]	Rastreadores para identificar duplicidad de requisitos
	[24]	Negligencia en los requisites no funcionales
Cambios del requisito	[25]	Complejidad y cambios contínuos
	[26]	Propiedades emergentes del software
	[27]	Conflictos en el proceso de evolución de RNF
	[28]	Cambios en las intenciones de los stakeholders
	[29]	Resistencia a los cambios de los requisitos
	[30]	Nuevas funcionalidades del sistema
	[31]	Evolución en los documentos de requisitos

Tomando como base el estado del arte y los resultados se puede observar que no se evidencian trabajos de investigación que integren elementos de KM concretos en el proceso de elicitación de requisitos no funcionales. Del mismo modo, se observa que el concepto de evolución de requisitos se mantiene mayoritariamente restringido a aspectos como: trazabilidad del requisito y cambios del requisito, sin embargo, estos dos aspectos no usan elementos de KM que puedan aportar a la gestión y adecuado manejo de la evolución del requisito desde una perspectiva más amplia.

De esta manera, el presente trabajo pretende aportar a las organizaciones un marco de trabajo para la realización del proceso de elicitación de requisitos no funcionales usando el enfoque de KM desde las etapas tempranas del proceso evitando así la generación de problemas derivados de la falta de participación activa y dinámica de los usuarios, así como proponer una estrategia para gestionar la evolución de los requisitos no funcionales durante el ciclo de vida del software (desarrollo, operación, mantenimiento y retirada). Dentro del contexto específico de KM, el marco de trabajo define elementos como las dimensiones, escenarios, rutas, flujos de transformación de conocimiento, entre otros, adicionales a los aspectos de representación del requisito no funcional, de manera que soporten la elicitación y evolución del mismo.

4 Esquema de metodología de investigación

La propuesta de doctorado utilizará la metodología investigación-acción multi-ciclo con bifurcación [32] para la aplicación y construcción del marco de trabajo. Esta metodología permite gestionar y desarrollar proyectos de investigación en el campo de Ingeniería de software a partir de diversos ciclos de investigación que abordan diferentes problemas que se presentan a lo largo del desarrollo del proyecto. La estrategia de investigación consta de los siguientes ciclos: (i) Ciclo conceptual: análisis conceptual del problema y estudio de la literatura, (ii) Ciclo metodológico: identificación de componentes del marco y construcción del marco a partir de los componentes, (iii) Ciclo de Evaluación: Diseño y ejecución del protocolo de evaluación y Análisis y conclusiones.

5 Solución propuesta y aspectos diferenciadores

El "Marco de trabajo para la elicitación y evolución de requisitos no funcionales basadas en KM" es construido conceptualmente basándose en la disciplina de KM para poder abordar los RNF en un proceso de elicitación de requisitos no funcionales. El modelo conceptual del marco de trabajo permite integrar de manera correlativa el conocimiento de los requisitos no funcionales con los stakeholders involucrados dentro del proceso de elicitación de requisitos (ver Figura 1).

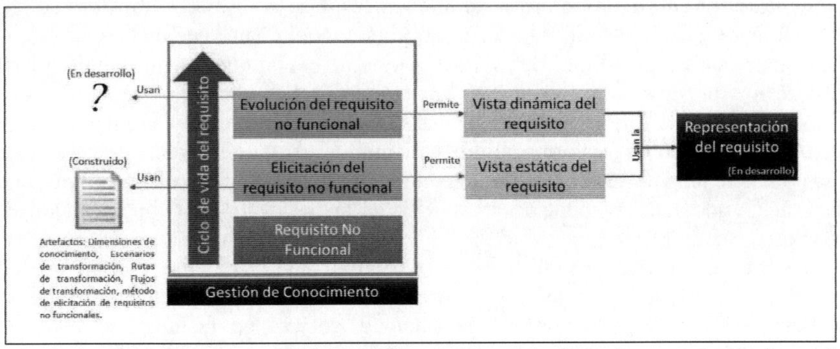

Figura 1. Modelo conceptual del Marco de trabajo para la elicitación y evolución de requisitos no funcionales basadas en KM

En la propuesta el requisito no funcional es inicialmente elicitado generando una vista estática del mismo, a partir de la cual, durante el ciclo de desarrollo de software puede ir evolucionando. Esta evolución puede ser entendida como la vista dinámica del requisito y utiliza, al igual que la vista estática, la representación del requisito para poder ser entendido y gestionado dentro del ciclo de vida del producto software, el cual incluye etapas de desarrollo, operación, mantenimiento y retirada del software.

Se tiene una propuesta inicial del marco de trabajo que aborda sólo el aspecto de elicitación de RNF basada en KM, el cual está construido por componentes relacionados con ésta última disciplina. Como fundamento de KM se ha considerado la propuesta de flujos de transformación de conocimiento según Modelo SECI [33]; del cual se ha usado los tipos de conocimiento tácito y explícito a considerar en la Elicitación de RNF.

Actualmente, se ésta trabajando en el aspecto de la evolución del requisitos y su representación como elementos fundamentales del marco.

El análisis de información de propuestas existentes de investigación, relacionadas con la temática del proyecto doctoral, permite identificar las siguientes diferencias con esta propuesta: (i) no existen técnicas específicas para la elicitación de requisitos no funcionales, (ii) usa conceptos concretos de la disciplina de KM para nutrir el proceso de elicitación de requisitos no funcionales con elementos que pueden ser identificados y gestionados en cualquier proyecto de desarrollo software como lo es: escenarios de transformación de conocimiento flujos de transformación de conocimiento entre otros, (iii) involucra de manera participativa a los stakeholders del proyecto, y (iv) aumenta el conocimiento del elicitador tanto en los procesos de negocio involucrados en el proyecto como en las características de calidad que los productos software a desarrollar.

6 Resultados logrados hasta el momento y trabajo futuro

Hasta el momento, la propuesta doctoral ha logrado desarrollar componentes que apoyan la elicitación de requisitos no funcionales, tomando como base KM, tales como: (i) tres dimensiones de conocimiento, que permiten integrar elementos de KM e información organizacional, en éste contexto de KM, con los procesos técnicos de elicitación de requisitos, (ii) cuatro escenarios de transformación del conocimiento a través de los cuales ocurre la instauración, configuración, afianzamiento e institucionalización del conocimiento frente a los requisitos no funcionales, (iii) tres rutas de transformación de conocimiento que apoyan la transformación del conocimiento acerca de requisitos no funcionales, (iv) cuatro flujos de transformación de conocimiento que soportan las tareas de KM del marco de trabajo, (v) un método para la elicitación de requisitos no funcionales, que define las actividades para la elicitación de estos requisitos, el cual incluye un "núcleo de trasformación de conocimiento" que representa cómo en la elicitación de requisitos no funcionales el conocimiento se transforma hasta lograr un conocimiento adoptado, reconocido y explícito de los requisitos nos funcionales dentro de la organización.

Desde la perspectiva de publicaciones, se han publicado 4 artículos científicos y además se han realizado aplicaciones del marco de trabajo para la elicitación de requisitos no funcionales en 10 proyectos de organizaciones desarrolladoras de software.

Adicional a estos resultados, actualmente ya se cuenta con información que permite ampliar el concepto de evolución, a partir de la realización de un Focus Group con expertos en: antropología, biología y comunicación social, dado que se pretende aportar el concepto de evolución de requisitos con aspectos de otras ciencias del saber.

Finalmente, la propuesta de doctorado espera resultados como: (i) generar la propuesta para gestionar la evolución de éste tipo de requisitos basada en KM (Fig. 1), (ii) identificar y posteriormente definir la representación de los requisitos no funcionales, tanto para la vista estática como la dinámica del requisito, (iii) afinar el estado del arte relacionado con elicitación de requisitos no funcionales y evolución de los mismos, usando KM para la ingeniería de software, (iv) obtener información acerca de la valoración de la propuesta, y (iii) fortalecer el intercambio y la apropiación del conocimiento dentro de la comunidad científica, universitaria y empresarial.

7 Conclusiones

El presente paper pretende presentar una alternativa de solución dentro del contexto de la ingeniería del software que aporte a resolver problemas relacionados con la calidad de los productos software debido a la no inclusión de los RNF y a la baja participación de los stakeholders en el proceso de elicitación de requisitos. Considerando este problema se establece como objetivo general de la investigación construir un marco de trabajo para la elicitación y evolución de requisitos no funcionales basadas en KM. Dentro de la metodología de investigación seleccionada, se cuenta con un ciclo de conceptualización a partir del cual se obtuvo una vista organizada del estado del arte acerca de la elicitación de requisitos no funcionales y su evolución basadas en KM. Esta vista permitió concluir que podría haber lugar para proponer un marco de trabajo para este proceso de ingeniería software.

A partir de esta idea se vienen realizando tres actividades fundamentales para la construcción del marco de trabajo: (i) identificar elementos desde las perspectivas del proceso de elicitación y evolución de RNF, (ii) identificar elementos desde la perspectiva de KM, e (iii) identificar aspectos de representación de requisitos no funcionales. A partir de esta conceptualización se define un marco de trabajo para la elicitación de requisitos no funcionales basada en KM, el cual fue expuesto a un proceso de validación preliminar a través del método de Focus Group y posteriormente a través del método de estudio de caso. A través de estas validaciones se evidencia la necesidad y aplicabilidad del marco de trabajo para elicitación de requisitos no funcionales como herramienta para favorecer éste proceso en las organizaciones desarrolladoras de software.

El marco de trabajo para la elicitación de requisitos no funcionales logrado está siendo extendido hacia el concepto de evolución de éstos requisitos dentro del ciclo de vida de un producto software, lo que capacita a la propuesta de investigación en permitir visualizar los requisitos no funcionales desde una vista estática (especificación de requisitos no funcionales) y una vista dinámica del requisito (modificaciones futuras de un requisito especificado). Los primeros resultados de validación, para el aspecto de evolución, a través de un Focus Group con antropólogos, biólogos y comunicadores sociales, ha permitido obtener información relevante que está siendo analizada para continuar con la construcción del marco de trabajo propuesto.

Referencias

1. Serna-Montoya, É., *Estado actual de la investigación en requisitos no funcionales.* Ingeniería y Universidad, 2012. **16**(1): p. 225-246.
2. Mijanur Rahman, M. and S. Ripon, *Elicitation and Modeling Non-Functional Requirements – A POS Case Study.* International Journal of Future Computer and Communication, 2013: p. 485-489.
3. Hofmann, H.F. and F. Lehner, *Requirements engineering as a success factor in software projects.* IEEE software, 2001. **18**(4): p. 58.
4. Li, J., et al., *Preliminary results of a systematic review on requirements evolution.* 2012.
5. Chen, J.-C. and S.-J. Huang, *An empirical analysis of the impact of software development problem factors on software maintainability.* Journal of Systems and Software, 2009. **82**(6): p. 981-992.
6. Chang, C. and L. Cai. *Agent based requirements evolution over the Internet.* in *Applications and the Internet Workshops, 2001. Proceedings. 2001 Symposium on.* 2001. IEEE.
7. Foguem, B.K., et al., *Knowledge formalization in experience feedback processes: An ontology-based approach.* Computers in Industry, 2008. **59**(7): p. 694-710.
8. Dingsøyr, T., F.O. Bjørnson, and F. Shull, *What do we know about knowledge management? Practical implications for software engineering.* IEEE software, 2009. **26**(3): p. 100-103.
9. Wan, J., et al., *Research on explicit and tacit knowledge interaction in software process improvement project.* Journal of Software Engineering and Applications, 2011. **4**(06): p. 335.
10. Dingsøyr, T. and R. Conradi, *A survey of case studies of the use of knowledge management in software engineering.* International journal of software engineering and knowledge engineering, 2002. **12**(04): p. 391-414.
11. Al Balushi, T.H., P.R.F. Sampaio, and P. Loucopoulos, *Eliciting and prioritizing quality requirements supported by ontologies: A case study using the ElicitO framework and tool.* Expert Systems, 2013. **30**(2): p. 129-151.
12. de Araújo, A.L., L.M. Cysneiros, and V.M.B. Werneck. *NDR-Tool: A Tool to Support Knowledge Reuse in Non-Functional Requirements.* in *CIBSE 2014: Proceedings of the 17th Ibero-American Conference Software Engineering.* 2014.

13. Larburu, N., R.G. Bults, and H.J. Hermens. *Making medical treatments resilient to technological disruptions in telemedicine systems*. in *Biomedical and Health Informatics (BHI), 2014 IEEE-EMBS International Conference on*. 2014. IEEE.
14. Terawaki, Y., *Supporting of requirements elicitation for ensuring services of information systems used for education*, 2011. p. 58-65.
15. Terawaki, Y. *Supporting of requirements elicitation for ensuring services of information systems used for education*. in *Symposium on Human Interface*. 2011. Springer.
16. Loucopoulos, P., et al., *A systematic classification and analysis of NFRs*. 2013.
17. Ameller, D., et al. *How do software architects consider non-functional requirements: An exploratory study*. 2012.
18. Helming, J., et al. *Towards a unified requirements modeling language*. in *Requirements Engineering Visualization (REV), 2010 Fifth International Workshop on*. 2010. IEEE.
19. Wei, B., Z. Jin, and L. Liu. *A formalism for extending the NFR Framework to support the composition of the goal trees*. in *Software Engineering Conference (APSEC), 2010 17th Asia Pacific*. 2010. IEEE.
20. Song, X., Z. Duan, and C. Tian. *Non-functional requirements elicitation and incorporation into class diagrams*. in *International Conference on Intelligent Information Processing*. 2010. Springer.
21. de Oliveira, R.P. and E.S. de Almeida. *Requirements Evolution in Software Product Lines: An Empirical Study*. in *Components, Architectures and Reuse Software (SBCARS), 2015 IX Brazilian Symposium on*. 2015. IEEE.
22. Jayaraman, S.C. and M. Anand, *The Impact of Visualizing Traceability Links for Evolving Requirements in Software Maintenance–A Controlled Experiment.*
23. Heck, P. and A. Zaidman. *An analysis of requirements evolution in open source projects: Recommendations for issue trackers*. in *Proceedings of the 2013 International Workshop on Principles of Software Evolution*. 2013. ACM.
24. Khatter, K. and A. Kalia. *Impact of Non-functional Requirements on Requirements Evolution*. in *Emerging Trends in Engineering and Technology (ICETET), 2013 6th International Conference on*. 2013. IEEE.
25. Robinson, W. and R. Vlas, *Requirements evolution and project success: an analysis of SourceForge projects*. 2015.
26. Luo, J. and A.G. Hessami. *Emergent properties and requirements evolution in engineering systems and a roadmap*. in *Complex Systems (WCCS), 2015 Third World Conference on*. 2015. IEEE.
27. Liu, C.-L., *CDNFRE: Conflict detector in non-functional requirement evolution based on ontologies*. Computer Standards & Interfaces, 2016. **47**: p. 62-76.
28. Grubb, A.M. and M. Chechik. *Looking into the crystal ball: requirements evolution over time*. in *Requirements Engineering Conference (RE), 2016 IEEE 24th International*. 2016. IEEE.
29. Massacci, F., F. Paci, and A. Tedeschi, *Assessing a requirements evolution approach: Empirical studies in the air traffic management domain*. Journal of Systems and Software, 2014. **95**: p. 70-88.
30. Nguyen, C.M., et al. *Requirements evolution and evolution requirements with constrained goal models*. in *International Conference on Conceptual Modeling*. 2016. Springer.
31. Joshi, S. and J.D. Summers, *Requirements evolution: Understanding the type of changes in the requirement document of novice designers*, in *ICoRD'15–Research into Design Across Boundaries Volume 2*2015, Springer. p. 471-481.
32. Pino, F.J., M. Piattini, and G. Horta Travassos, *Managing and developing distributed research projects in software engineering by means of action-research*. Revista Facultad de Ingeniería Universidad de Antioquia, 2013(68): p. 61-74.
33. Nonaka, I. and D.J. Teece, *Managing industrial knowledge: creation, transfer and utilization*2001: Sage.

CIbSE - IberoAmerican Conference on Software Engineering
c/o Luca Cernuzzi
Universidad Católica "Nuestra Seóra de la Asunción",
Campus Universitario, Asunción
Barrio Santa Ana, C.C.1683, C.P. 1364
Asunción - Paraguay

ISBN 978-1-5108-6937-0

9 781510 869370

CURRAN ASSOCIATES INC.
proceedings.com